Learning Companion for Counselors About *DSM-5-TR®*

Authors:
Carman S. Gill, Stephanie F. Dailey, Shannon L. Karl, and Casey A. Barrio Minton.

American Counseling Association
2461 Eisenhower Avenue, Suite 300
Alexandria, VA 22314
www.counseling.org

Learning Companion for Counselors About *DSM-5-TR®*

American Counseling Association
2461 Eisenhower Avenue, Suite 300
Alexandria, VA 22314

Library of Congress Cataloging-in-Publication Data

Names: Gill, Carman S., author.
Title: Learning Companion for Counselors About DSM-5-TR® / Carman S. Gill, Stephanie F. Dailey, Shannon L. Karl, and Casey A. Barrio Minton.
Description: Alexandria, VA : American Counseling Association, [2024] | Includes bibliographical references and index.
Identifiers: LCCN 2023031257 | ISBN 9781556200267 (paperback)
Subjects: LCSH: Diagnostic and statistical manual of mental disorders. | Mental illness—Diagnosis. | Mental illness—Classification.
Classification: LCC RC469 .G45 2024 | DDC 616.89/075—dc23/eng/20230925
LC record available at https://lccn.loc.gov/2023031257

This was previously published as "DSM-5-TR Learning Companion for Counselors," ISBN 9781556204166. The title has been changed but the original text remains unchanged.

Dedication

This book is dedicated to professional counselors who draw upon the art and science of counseling in courageous attempts to foster growth in those seeking relief, wellness, and personal empowerment.

Table of Contents

Part One

Clinical Utility and Practice Implications for Counselors

Part Two

Changes and Implications Involving
Mood, Anxiety, and Stressor-Related Concerns

Part Four

Changes and Implications Involving Diagnoses Commonly Made by Other Professionals

Chapter 19

Foreword

The *Diagnostic and Statistical Manual of Mental Disorders, Fifth Edition, Text Revision* (*DSM-5-TR*), published in 2022 by the American Psychiatric Association, is a dense book that spans 1,048 pages and describes hundreds of mental disorders. Keeping abreast of the manual's evolving changes is a tedious but necessary task for counselors. In their text, *Learning Companion for Counselors About DSM-5-TR®*, the authors Gill, Dailey, Karl, and Barrio Minton provide readers with an exceptionally practical, straightforward, and, most importantly, readable summary of the *DSM-5-TR*.

One of the many highlights of the text is its focus on clinical utility and counselor practice implications. Care is taken to ensure readers understand what the changes from the *DSM-IV-TR* to *DSM-5*, and the *DSM-5* to *DSM-5-TR*, mean to them and how these changes can be applied in their day-to-day practice.

Structural changes to the *DSM-5-TR*, diagnostic changes, and newly added disorders are discussed, and Gill and colleagues take care to avoid distracting readers with diagnostic material that has not changed. It is easy to feel overwhelmed by the sheer volume of diagnostic changes presented in the updated iteration of the *DSM*, yet the authors ease this transition by highlighting the changes that relate to disorders counselors more commonly address (e.g., depressive, anxiety, obsessive-compulsive disorders). Consistent with the new text revision, attention is also paid to the risk factors associated with systematic racism and discrimination and to the intentional removal of stigmatizing language from the manual. The authors' understanding of the manual's evolutions is obvious, and their discussion of this in Chapter 2 is a must-read for all practicing counselors.

The fifth chapter is a gem and explains practical *DSM-5* resources that will inform practitioners' counseling practice. In terms of assessment, the authors discuss updated diagnostic coding processes, the diagnostic interview, culturally informed assessments (specifically the Cultural Formulation Interview), and the World Health Organization Disability Assessment Schedule; these are excellent counselor resources and can serve to enrich diagnostic practices. Essential information regarding the upcoming changes to the

Health Insurance Portability and Accountability Act to require *International Statistical Classification of Diseases and Related Health Problems, 10th Revision* (*ICD-10*) diagnoses is also provided and deepens readers' understanding of the emerging, broader landscape of diagnosis beyond just the *DSM* system.

The material in this *Learning Companion* is presented in a highly engaging format. The authors address and clearly explain the changes from the *DSM-IV-TR* to *DSM-5*/*DSM-5-TR*. They apply lively case studies to illustrate the diagnostic features of the newest *DSM-5-TR* disorders. The authors also provide "notes" that highlight the information to which readers should pay special attention. These features help readers connect with the essential information they need to successfully use the newest edition of the *DSM*. The case examples are thought provoking and serve to bring the *DSM* disorders to life.

In addition, and consistent with counselors' values and practices, the authors pay close attention to the developmental considerations that have been integrated into the *DSM-5-TR*, as well as the situational and environmental contexts that relate to the changes. Paralleling the increased emphasis placed on culture in the *DSM-5-TR* and within our broader society, cultural considerations relating to the diagnoses are also addressed.

The authors are to be commended for providing a resource that is thorough and comprehensive, yet engaging and highly readable—a tall order for a topic as detailed and complex as the *DSM* system of diagnosis. This book is an essential read for all practicing counselors who wish to stay contemporary in their practices and stay connected with the current edition of the *DSM*.

—Victoria E. Kress, PhD

Acknowledgments

We wish to acknowledge the following individuals for making this book possible:
Clara Bossie, Nubah Anan, and Xander Price

We also wish to acknowledge those who touch not only our lives but also our hearts:

Carman S. Gill
To Rob for your patience and love. To my family and friends,
Dean, Mark, Ashley, Patti, and Tara.
Thank you for your listening ears!

Stephanie F. Dailey
To my son, Michael, for your love of life, equality, and friendship.

Shannon L. Karl
To my amazing Mom for her vast love and support.

Casey A. Barrio Minton
To my daughter, Leah, for her joy, quick wit,
and constant reminder of what it means to live fully.

About the Authors

Carman S. Gill, PhD, LPC, NCC, ACS, is a professor and department chair at Florida Atlantic University. She has worked with client populations including individuals who are dually diagnosed, individuals with chronic mental illness, children, and individuals experiencing acute mental health crises. Her research focus includes wellness and women's issues, as well as spirituality and religion in counseling. Dr. Gill is a past-president of ASERVIC and has served that organization as conference cochair twice, as well as newsletter editor, member of the board of directors, and secretary. Dr. Gill has coauthored multiple peer-reviewed journal articles on spiritual topics. She has coedited a book on spirituality and religion in counseling, in addition to the previous version of this *Learning Companion*. Dr. Gill lives in Delray Beach, Florida, and enjoys going to the beach and watching Manchester United matches.

Stephanie F. Dailey, EdD, LPC, NCC, is a licensed professional counselor and assistant professor of counseling at George Mason University. Dr. Dailey's research and clinical work is directed at better understanding trauma-informed response protocols for mass casualty events, increasing resilience in first responders, and working with individuals diagnosed with severe mental illness and complex trauma. Her work at the federal level has included trauma-informed mitigation protocols for public schools during active shooter events, officer wellness programs aimed at improving use-of-force decision-making, and stress inoculation training to increase resilience in military medical providers. Dr. Dailey also coleads a national school-based program to address current K–12 school shooter vulnerabilities. She has published and presented extensively on the *Diagnostic and Statistical Manual of Mental Disorders*, counseling assessment, and case conceptualization. Dr. Dailey is a former cochair of the American Counseling Association Ethics Committee (2013–2015); a past-president of the Association for Spiritual, Ethical, and Religious Values in Counseling (ASERVIC, 2016–2017); and former chair of the American Counseling Association Foundation (2020–2023). Dr. Dailey lives in Arlington, Virginia, with her partner, their two sons (ages 8 and 10), and a loyal, yet cantankerous rescue dog. When she is not teaching, working with clients, or engaging in research, she loves spending time with her family and friends.

Shannon L. Karl, PhD, LMHC, NCC, CCMHC, ACS, is a professor in the College of Psychology at Nova Southeastern University. She has extensive clinical mental health experience and is a licensed mental health counselor and qualified clinical supervisor in the state of Florida. Dr. Karl has published in the areas of eating disorders, domestic violence, counseling student performance, spirituality, addictions, and the *Diagnostic and Statistical Manual of Mental Disorders*. She is a past-president of ASERVIC and past-secretary of the Association for Counselor Education and Supervision. She frequently presents at regional, national, and international conferences and serves as a longtime team lead at the Council for Accreditation of Counseling and Related Educational Programs. Dr. Karl enjoys travel, running, and spending time with family and friends.

Casey A. Barrio Minton, PhD, NCC, is a professor of counselor education and interim head of the Department of Educational Psychology and Counseling at the University of Tennessee, Knoxville. Her scholarly work focuses on crisis intervention, clinical mental health issues, and professionalization through teaching and leadership. Founding editor of the *Journal of Counselor Leadership and Advocacy*, Dr. Barrio Minton is a past-president of Chi Sigma Iota International, the Association for Assessment and Research in Counseling, the Southern Association for Counselor Education and Supervision, and the Association for Counselor Education and Supervision. She continues to actively serve these organizations through their mentorship programs and committees. She is a fellow of the American Counseling Association. Dr. Barrio Minton enjoys spending time outdoors, exploring new food and drink, and setting running goals just out of reach.

Chapter 1

Introduction and Overview

Regardless of background, training, or theoretical orientation, professional counselors need to have a thorough understanding of the *Diagnostic and Statistical Manual of Mental Disorders, Fifth Edition, Text Revision* (*DSM-5-TR*), published by the American Psychiatric Association (APA, 2022a). The *DSM-5* (APA, 2013) and its earlier editions have become the world's standard reference for client evaluation and diagnosis (Eriksen & Kress, 2006; Hinkle, 1999; Zalaquett et al., 2008). Most important, the manual allows professional counselors to break down the complexity of clients' presenting problems into practical language for practitioners and clients alike (Dailey et al., 2014b). Sometimes controversially referred to as the "the psychiatric bible" (see Caplan, 2012; Kutchins & Kirk, 1997), the *DSM* is intended to be applicable in various settings and used by mental health practitioners and researchers of differing backgrounds and orientations (Dailey et al., 2014b).

Because of the prevalent use of the *DSM*, professional counselors who provide services in mental health centers, psychiatric hospitals, employee assistance programs, detention centers, private practice, or other community settings must be well versed in client conceptualization and diagnostic assessment using the manual. For those in private practice, agencies, and hospitals, a diagnosis using *DSM* criteria is necessary for third-party payments and for certain types of record keeping and reporting (Dailey et al., 2014b; Kress et al., 2013). Of the 50 states and U.S. territories, including the District of Columbia, that have passed laws to regulate professional counselors, 36 include diagnosis within the scope of practice for professional counselors and 19 do not directly restrict or address diagnosis (Norton, 2022). Even professionals who are not traditionally responsible for diagnosis as a part of their counseling services, such as school or career counselors, should understand the *DSM* so they can recognize diagnostic problems or complaints and participate in discussions and treatment regarding these issues (Norton, 2022). Although other diagnostic nomenclature systems such as the World Health Organization's (WHO, 2022) *International Statistical Classification of Diseases and Related Health Problems, 11th Revision* (*ICD-11*) are available to professional counselors, the *DSM* is and will continue to be the most widely used manual within the field. For these reasons, the ability to navigate and use the *DSM* responsibly has become an important part of a professional counselor's identity.

Counseling Identity and Diagnosis

Counseling is defined as a "professional relationship that empowers diverse individuals, families, and groups to accomplish mental health, wellness, education, and career goals" (American Counseling Association [ACA], 2013, para. 2). To accomplish this role, practitioners often incorporate diagnosis as one component of the counseling process (Norton, 2022). Therefore, it is not surprising that ethical guidelines for the profession and accreditation standards for counselor education programs encourage counselors to understand diagnostic nomenclature. For example, the *ACA Code of Ethics* (ACA, 2014) Section E.5.a., Proper Diagnosis, requires counselors to "take special care to provide proper diagnosis of mental disorders" (p. 11). The Council for Accreditation of Counseling and Related Educational Programs (CACREP, 2024) requires that counselors learn strategies for collaborating and communicating with other human service providers as part of their common core curricular experiences. Thus, learning outcomes for specialty areas, including addictions counseling; clinical mental health counseling; clinical rehabilitation counseling; and marriage, couple, and family counseling, require demonstrated knowledge regarding the most recent edition of the *DSM*. Any professional counselor is likely to agree that a thorough understanding of the *DSM* is an essential aspect of interdisciplinary communication.

Despite widespread guidance encouraging counselors to be familiar with the *DSM*, utilization of the manual is not without challenges and controversy (Bonino & Hanna, 2018). Many professional counselors feel unprepared or uncomfortable when faced with the task of assigning clients a diagnosis (Mannarino et al., 2007). Other professionals are conflicted about the *DSM*'s focus on psychopathology and feel the mechanistic approach reduces "complex information about people into a few words . . . describing a person's parts (symptoms) as static" (Mannarino et al., 2007). As counselors are only too aware, clients cannot be encapsulated into fixed categories. Each client comes to counseling with numerous sociocultural issues that the counselor must consider before making a diagnosis and putting together an approach for treatment. This is particularly important given a large body of research that provides support for the far-reaching impact of poverty and social class on psychological and emotional well-being (e.g., American Psychological Association, 2017; Hodgkinson et al., 2017; Marbin et al., 2022). For example, studies of children and adolescents from lower socioeconomic families report higher instances of emotional and conduct problems, including chronic delinquency and early onset of antisocial behavior (Shaw & Shelleby, 2014). Low income has also been correlated to higher levels of family distress and discord as well as higher rates of parental mental illness.

Finally, many counselors believe the "medicalization" of clients ignores the strengths-based, developmental, wellness approach that is the hallmark of the counseling profession (Frances, 2013). Others posit methods for integrating this system into a multicultural, wellness-based approach to clients (Tomlinson-Clarke & Georges, 2014). The change from the *DSM-5* to the *DSM-5-TR* renews this controversy, presenting counselors with a new challenge—the application of an updated nomenclature system.

Why We Updated This *Learning Companion*

The *DSM-5* (APA, 2013) represented the most radical revision of the *DSM*, as well as the most controversial (Dailey et al., 2014b). We originally designed the *DSM-5 Learning Companion for Counselors* (Dailey et al., 2014a) to assist counselors with transitioning from the *DSM-IV-TR* (APA, 2000) to the *DSM-5* (APA, 2013). The original *Learning Companion* was widely distributed and was a bestseller for years. During that time frame, research and clinical use of the *DSM-5* increased significantly, with over 98% of counselors stating they intend to use the nosology (Gayle & Raskin, 2017). Given this, we are compelled to provide counselors with an updated version of the *Learning Companion* based on the changes presented in the *DSM-5-TR*, alongside updated research regarding etiology of disorders, impact of systemic injustice on mental health, and evidence-based practice.

The purpose of this book remains relatively consistent with our original text, but there are noteworthy changes corresponding with the new *DSM*. In an effort to emphasize the distinct foci of counseling as prevention, development, and wellness-based modality that operates within the umbrella of social justice, we begin by addressing sociocultural issues in diagnosis and the *DSM-5-TR*, culturally responsive case conceptualization, and practice implications for counselors. We highlight culturally responsive practice, which includes using language designed to avoid perpetuating systematic racism and oppression, promoting gender-inclusive terminology, and expanding counselor understanding regarding how social determinants of health play a role in health outcomes. For example, we incorporate the impact of adverse childhood and community experiences to include systemic racism and oppression, which can affect health and mental health. Because diagnosis is fundamental to case conceptualization and evidence-based treatment, we focus on the integration of case conceptualization and culture and cover sociocultural issues and social determinants of mental health, diagnostic bias, and strategies for buffering diagnostic bias. Toward that purpose, we provide two new chapters, including Sociocultural Issues in Diagnosis in the *DSM-5-TR* (Chapter 3) and Culturally Responsive Case Conceptualization and Treatment Planning: Cultural Formulation (Chapter 4).

The *DSM-5-TR* includes diagnostic changes and additions that will impact the work of counselors. For example, the revised manual contains changes to depressive disorder, including the addition of prolonged grief disorder, changes to the wording of Criterion D for major depressive disorder, changes to the wording for persistent depressive disorder, the restoration of unspecified mood disorder, the addition of major depressive episode superimposed to other specified depressive disorder, and updated language for depressive disorder due to another medical condition. Likewise, there are several changes in the bipolar and related disorders chapters (APA, 2022a). Throughout this book, we address major changes to the nosology, as well as additional changes, such as the addition of a section on "association with suicidal thoughts or behavior" to applicable diagnoses and the acknowledgment of new *ICD-10–Clinical Modification* (*ICD-10-CM*; National Center for Health Statistics, 2023) codes for suicidal behavior and nonsuicidal self-injury. Minor changes, including updates to descriptive text and updated codes for all disorders, are highlighted in each chapter where applicable. In alignment with advances in clinical knowledge and research, we update all chapters with recent data on prevalence, risk, prognosis, differential diagnosis, and comorbidity. For each diagnosis, we highlight culture-related diagnostic considerations, functional barriers for clients, and other relevant features of particular concern for professional counselors. Furthermore, we incorporate updated research regarding etiology, intersections with sociocultural context, and evidence-based practice. Holistically, this edition reflects the *DSM-5-TR*'s focus on ethnoracial equity and inclusion, highlighting intersections between culture, racism, discrimination, oppression, and misdiagnosis.

The Revision Process

APA began revising the *DSM-5* in Spring 2019, a process that included 200 mental health professionals. Most of these professionals worked on the original *DSM-5* and were either psychiatrists or psychologists (APA, 2022d). Counselors were not well represented in this process, with just 6% of other professionals who fell into the "other health professionals" category (Norton, 2022). A DSM-5 Task Force, a DSM Steering Committee, and a Revision Subcommittee became the original working groups. However, APA created 20 expert disorder review groups and four cross-cutting review groups, whose purpose was to focus on the areas in which they were experts (APA, 2022a, 2022d). Any recommended revisions that were included in the *DSM-5-TR* were reviewed and accepted by the Steering Committee and the APA Board of Trustees.

In September 2022, APA published the *DSM-5-TR* Update: Supplement to the Diagnostic and Statistical Manual of Mental Disorders, Text Revision (APA, 2022c). This document introduced changes to the *DSM-5-TR*. Many of these changes were noteworthy, such as the removal of suicidal behavior disorder from the Conditions for Further Study chapter. Although suicidal behavior disorder was removed from that section, the diagnostic codes in "other conditions that may be a focus of clinical attention" related to suicidal behavior were not removed and are still available for clinical use (APA, 2022c). Within the diagnostic criteria of certain disorders, the *DSM-5-TR* authors changed language regarding suicide, intending to be more accurate while reducing stigma surrounding the act. For example, both bipolar I and II disorders, as well as major depressive disorder, should state "a specific suicide plan, or a suicide attempt," replacing "or a suicide attempt or specific plan for committing suicide." A differential of prolonged grief disorder was added to major depressive disorder, and the codes for prolonged grief disorder, other specified trauma- and stressor-related disorder, and hepatic encephalopathy, listed under catatonic disorder due to another medical condition, were updated in keeping with the *ICD*-10-CM. Codes for opioid-induced anxiety disorder, mild, moderate, and severe were also updated, and additions as well as coding updates were made throughout for neurocognitive disorders. Additional coding updates were made to the "conditions for further study," and a new condition, "impairing emotional outbursts," was added. Language changes were made within the assessment measures and to the criteria of depressive episodes with short-duration hypomania in Section III of the manual (APA, 2022c).

We purchased physical copies of the *DSM-5-TR* published before these changes and again in January 2023. We found that the changes in the *DSM-5-TR* supplement (APA, 2022c) were applied inconsistently. For example, suicidal behavior disorder is not included in the December manual, but prolonged grief disorder is not included in the differential diagnosis for major depressive disorder, nor is the language regarding suicide updated for major depressive disorder, depressive episodes with short-duration hypomania, and bipolar disorders. We recommend that counselors become familiar with the September 2022 supplement (see APA, 2022c), and we describe the changes related to this supplement in this *Learning Companion*. Counselors are encouraged to use the information provided here when diagnosing. Although removed from the *DSM-5-TR* with the supplement, the description of suicidal behavior disorder is included here because the codes are available for clinical use, and we believe that understanding the basis for these codes is important for counselors. In October 2022, APA published the *DSM-5-TR* Neurocognitive Disorders Supplement: Updated Excerpts for Delirium Codes Major and Mild Neurocognitive Disorders, further updating these codes; this document was updated again in November 2022 (APA, 2022b).

Another supplement was released in September 2023. This document addressed coding changes for Parkinson's disease and inadequate housing (in the Other Conditions That May Be a Focus of Clinical Attention chapter), as well as a listing of *ICD*-10 coding updates. Further text updates included for differential diagnosis for three disorders. For delusional disorder and schizophrenia, the differential diagnosis regarding obsessive-compulsive and related disorders was elucidated. The language regarding differential diagnosis for conduct disorder was clarified, aligning this with Criterion E of adjustment disorders. The authors also included warning regarding the use of clinical judgment and not to use the manual in a "rigid cookbook fashion" (APA, 2023, p. 3). More information is located on the American Psychiatric Association website.

Organization of the *Learning Companion for Counselors About DSM-5-TR*®

In Chapter 2 of this *Learning Companion*, we describe the history of the *DSM* and some major modifications in the *DSM-5*. We provide an overview of the creation of the manual and an in-depth look at the revisions process for this new text revision. We offer an overview of the changes made in the *DSM-5-TR*, along with implications for clients and counselors, and the speculation regarding the future of the nosology.

Chapter 2 also addresses issues such as the nonaxial system, neurobiological foundations, other and unspecified diagnoses, and assessment instruments such as the WHO Disability Assessment Schedule 2.0 (WHODAS 2.0; WHO, 2010). In addition, Chapter 2 contains information regarding diagnostic coding and changes counselors can expect consistent with the *ICD-10-CM* (National Center for Health Statistics, 2023) coding required for Health Insurance Portability and Accountability Act of 1996 (HIPAA) purposes. We also explore ways in which counselors can continue to be an active part of future revisions of diagnostic nomenclature systems.

Following Chapter 2, this *Learning Companion* includes four separate parts, with each of the chapters grouped first by clinical utility and practice implication for counseling. The next three portions are grouped by diagnostic similarity and relevance to the counseling profession. In each of the final three parts, we provide a basic description of the diagnostic classification and an overview of the specific disorders covered, highlighting essential features as they relate to the counseling profession. We also provide a comprehensive review of specific changes, when applicable, from the *DSM-5* to the *DSM-5-TR*. When there are no specific or significant changes made to a diagnostic category or diagnosis, we provide a general review of either the category or the diagnosis, but we refrain from providing the reader with too much detail because the purpose of this *Learning Companion* is to focus on changes from the *DSM-5* to the *DSM-5-TR*. For example, we do not go into detail about personality disorders, found in Part Three, because the diagnostic criteria for these disorders have not changed.

Within each part of the book, readers will find individual chapters highlighting key concepts of each disorder (including differential diagnoses), new or revised diagnostic criteria, and implications for professional counseling practice. We provide "Notes" to highlight significant information and include case studies to assist counselors in further understanding and applying the new or revised diagnostic categories. All case studies are fictitious composites and do not depict real clients. Any similarity to any person or case is simply coincidental.

Readers should also note that we provide more detail for disorders that counselors are more likely to see in their clients. Therefore, this *Learning Companion* is organized in order of diagnoses counselors are most likely to diagnose, and each consecutive part of the book provides the reader with less specific detail about each diagnostic grouping. For example, Part Two includes a detailed synthesis for key disorders, including cultural considerations, differential diagnosis, and special considerations for counselors. We have also included a description of other specified and unspecified diagnoses for each diagnostic class. Conversely, Part Four provides less detail about neurodevelopmental disorders because these diagnoses are typically made by other professionals.

Part One, Clinical Utility and Practice Implications for Counselors, starts with Chapter 3 covering sociocultural issues in diagnosis in the *DSM-5-TR*, including ethics, health disparities, ecological models and differences in expressing distress, as well as the impact of adverse childhood experiences. Here, we discuss the crucial nature of counselor self-awareness, addressing personal bias and systemic influences on diagnosis. In Chapter 4, culturally responsive case conceptualization is covered, and a model for integrating the impact of culture into effective case conceptualization is provided. Although all parts of the book focus on professional counselors, these chapters highlight the clinical utility of the *DSM-5* as well as future changes that may affect the counseling profession. For example, Chapter 14 addresses the personality disorders section of the *DSM-5*. Although personality disorders did not change from the *DSM-IV-TR* to the *DSM-5*, proposed changes were included in Section III of the *DSM-5*. If these changes were implemented, they would significantly alter the way counselors diagnose and treat clients with these disorders.

Part Two, Changes and Implications Involving Mood, Anxiety, and Stressor-Related Concerns, includes chapters on depressive disorders, bipolar and related disorders, anxiety disorders, obsessive-compulsive and related disorders, trauma- and stressor-related disorders, and gender dysphoria. In terms of presenting diagnoses, we list this section first because these disorders, both within and outside of the counseling profession, are some of the highest reported mental disturbances within the United States (Centers for Disease Control and Prevention, 2011). Readers will note that this is the only section in which other specified and unspecified diagnoses are listed.

Part Three, Changes and Implications Involving Addictive, Impulse-Control, and Specific Behavior-Related Concerns, includes chapters focused on behavioral diagnoses such as substance-related and addictive disorders; disruptive, impulse-control, and conduct disorders; personality disorders; and specific behavioral disruptions consisting of feeding and eating, specific eating disorders, elimination, sleep-wake, sexual dysfunction, and paraphilic disorders. Similar to the disorders found in Part Two, counselors are often exposed to the disorders listed in Part Three in their clinical practice, but these disorders frequently manifest through more visible, external behavioral concerns rather than less visible, internal experiences (i.e., depression vs. sexual dysfunction). Moreover, counselors may or may not diagnose these disorders. This is not to say that counselors do not frequently diagnose substance use disorders. However, compared with depression and anxiety disorders, substance use disorders are more often diagnosed by a combination of counselors and other health professionals.

Part Four, Changes and Implications Involving Diagnoses Commonly Made by Other Professionals, includes chapters focused on neurodevelopmental and neurocognitive, schizophrenia spectrum and other psychotic, dissociative, and somatic and related disorders. Many of these disorders, specifically neurodevelopmental and somatic issues, require highly specialized assessment or extensive medical examination by physicians or other qualified medical professionals. These chapters focus on helping professional counselors understand major changes and the potential impact of these changes on the clients they serve. We do not provide a detailed description of each disorder in this chapter; rather, we address major changes, if applicable, and considerations for counselors.

In addition to this *Learning Companion*, ACA and APA provide resources for understanding and using the *DSM-5-TR*. These resources include *Counseling Today's* online's article "What's New With the *DSM-5-TR*?" (Norton, 2022). Although APA resources focus more on the medical model and are less wellness oriented than those provided by counseling organizations, counselors may find the *DSM-5-TR Clinical Cases* (Barnhill, 2023) useful, as well as the *DSM-5 Handbook of Differential Diagnosis* (First, 2022). APA (n.d.) also provides fact sheets and online assessment measures specifically for the *DSM-5* and *DSM-5-TR*.

Questions for Consideration

1. Why do counselors care about diagnosis?
2. What are the major differences between counseling and psychiatry?
3. What do you want to know about the *DSM-5-TR*?

References

American Counseling Association. (2013). *What is professional counseling?* http://www.counseling.org/learn-about-counseling/what-is-counseling

American Counseling Association. (2014). *ACA code of ethics.* https://www.counseling.org/resources/aca-code-of-ethics.pdf

American Psychiatric Association. (n.d.). *Educational resources.* https://www.psychiatry.org/psychiatrists/practice/dsm/educational-resources

American Psychiatric Association. (2000). *Diagnostic and statistical manual of mental disorders* (4th ed., text rev.). https://doi.org/10.1176/appi.books.9780890423349

American Psychiatric Association. (2013). *Diagnostic and statistical manual of mental disorders* (5th ed.). https://doi.org/10.1176/appi.books.9780890425596

American Psychiatric Association. (2022a). *Diagnostic and statistical manual of mental disorders* (5th ed., text rev.) https://doi.org/10.1176/appi.books.9780890425787

American Psychiatric Association. (2022b). *DSM-5-TR neurocognitive disorders supplement: Updated excerpts for delirium codes major and mild neurocognitive disorders.* https://psychiatryonline.org/pb-assets/dsm/update/*DSM-5-TR*_Neurocognitive-Disorders-Supplement_2022_APA_Publishing.pdf

American Psychiatric Association. (2022c). *DSM-5-TR update: Supplement to the Diagnostic and statistical manual of mental disorders, fifth edition, text revision.* https://www.psychiatry.org/getmedia/34c43e15-2618-4d2b-9f67-6bef5c40f75a/APA-DSM5TR-Update-September-2022.pdf

American Psychiatric Association (2022d). *The people behind DSM-5-TR.* https://www.psychiatry.org/getmedia/5635958b-ee71-4352-b02a-fb24ecab86c6/APA-DSM5TR-ThePeopleBehindDSM.pdf

American Psychiatric Association. (2023). *DSM-5-TR update: Supplement to the Diagnostic and statistical manual of mental disorders, fifth edition, text revision.* https://www.psychiatry.org/getmedia/eecccfbe-91de-4171-b7ba-8d6c1aae3d11/APA-DSM5TR-Update-September-2023.pdf

American Psychological Association. (2017). *Education and socioeconomic status.* https://www.apa.org/pi/ses/resources/publications/education

Barnhill, J. W. (2023). *DSM-5-TR clinical cases.* American Psychiatric Association.

Bonino, J. L., & Hanna, F. J. (2018). Who owns psychopathology? The *DSM*: Its flaws, its future, and the professional counselor. *The Journal of Humanistic Counseling, 57*(2), 118–137. https://doi.org/10.1002/johc.12071

Caplan, P. J. (2012, April 27). Psychiatry's bible, the *DSM*, is doing more harm than good. *Washington Post.* http://www.washingtonpost.com/opinions/psychiatrys-bible-the-DSM-Is-doing-more-harm-than-good/2012/04/27/gIQAqy0WlT_story.html

Centers for Disease Control and Prevention. (2011). *Burden of mental illness.* http://www.cdc.gov/mentalhealth/basics/mental-illness/depression.htm

Council for Accreditation of Counseling and Related Educational Programs. (2024). *2024 CACREP standards.* https://www.cacrep.org/wp-content/uploads/2023/06/Combined-version-6.21.23.pdf

Dailey, S. F., Gill, C. S., Karl, S. L., & Barrio Minton, C. A. (2014a). *DSM-5 learning companion for counselors.* American Counseling Association.

Dailey, S. F., Gill, C. S., Karl, S. L., & Barrio Minton, C. A. (2014b). Historical underpinnings, structural alterations and philosophical changes: Counseling practice implications of the *DSM-5*. *The Professional Counselor, 4*(3), 166–178. https://doi.org/10.15241/sfd.4.3.166

Eriksen, K., & Kress, V. E. (2006). The *DSM* and the professional counseling identity: Bridging the gap. *Journal of Mental Health Counseling, 28*(3), 202–216. https://doi.org/10.17744/mehc.28.3.4f39a6wr1n3fceh2

First, M. B. (2022). *DSM-5 handbook of differential diagnosis.* American Psychiatric Association.

Frances, A. (2013). *Essentials of psychiatric diagnosis: Responding to the challenge of DSM-5.* Guilford Press.

Gayle, M. C., & Raskin, J. D. (2017). *DSM-5*: Do counselors really want an alternative? *Journal of Humanistic Psychology, 57*(6), 650–666. https://doi.org/10.1177/0022167817696839

Health Insurance Portability and Accountability Act of 1996, Pub. L. 104–191, 110 Stat. 1936.

Hinkle, J. S. (1999). A voice from the trenches: A reaction to Ivey and Ivey (1998). *Journal of Counseling & Development, 77*(4), 474–483. https://doi.org/10.1002/j.1556-6676.1999.tb02475.x

Hodgkinson, S., Godoy, L., Beers, L. S., & Lewin, A. (2017). Improving mental health access for low-income children and families in the primary care setting. *Pediatrics, 139*(1), e20151175. https://doi.org/10.1542/peds.2015-1175

Kress, V. E., Hoffman, R. M., Adamson, N., & Eriksen, K. (2013). Informed consent, confidentiality, and diagnosing: Ethical guidelines for counselor practice. *Journal of Mental Health Counseling, 35*(1), 15–28. https://doi.org/10.17744/mehc.35.1.5q82020u18r46007

Kutchins, H., & Kirk, S. A. (1997). *Making us crazy—DSM: The psychiatric bible and the creation of mental disorders.* Free Press.

Mannarino, M. B., Loughran, M. J., & Hamilton, D. (2007, October). *The professional counselor and the diagnostic process: Challenges and opportunities for education and training* [Paper presentation]. Association for Counselor Education and Supervision Conference, Columbus, OH, United States.

Marbin, D., Gutwinski, S, Schreiter, S., & Heinz, A. (2022). Perspectives in poverty and mental health. *Frontiers in Public Health, 10,* Article 975482. https://doi.org/10.3389/fpubh.2022.975482

National Center for Health Statistics. (2023). *The international classification of diseases, 10th revision, clinical modification (ICD-10-CM).* Centers for Disease Control and Prevention. https://www.cdc.gov/nchs/icd/icd-10-cm.htm

Norton, A. L. (2022, September 29). What's new with the *DSM-5-TR*? *Counseling Today.* https://ct.counseling.org/2022/09/whats-new-with-the-dsm-5-tr/

Shaw, D. S., & Shelleby, E. C. (2014). Early-starting conduct problems: Intersection of conduct problems and poverty. *Annual Review of Clinical Psychology, 10,* 503–528. https://doi.org/10.1146/annurev-clinpsy-032813-153650

Tomlinson-Clarke, S. M., & Georges, C. M. (2014). *DSM-5*: A commentary on integrating multicultural and strength-based considerations into counseling training and practice. *The Professional Counselor, 4*(3), 272–281. https://doi.org/10.15241/stc.4.3.272

World Health Organization. (2010). *WHO Disability Assessment Schedule 2.0–WHODAS 2.0.*

World Health Organization. (2022). *International statistical classification of diseases and related health problems, 11th revision.* https://icd.who.int/en

Zalaquett, C. P., Fuerth, K. M., Stein, C., Ivey, A. E., & Ivey, M. N. (2008). Reframing the *DSM-IV-TR* from a multicultural/social justice perspective. *Journal of Counseling & Development, 86*(3), 364–371. https://doi.org/10.1002/j.1556-6678.2008.tb00521.x

Chapter 2

Structural and Philosophical Changes to the *DSM:* A Historical Overview

The *DSM-5-TR* (APA, 2022b) is intended to provide additional clarity and guidance for the diagnosis and treatment of mental disorders but does not represent a major revision of the *DSM-5* (APA, 2013a). As outlined in the previous chapter, the *DSM-5-TR* includes some minor changes, corrections, and updates but, with few exceptions, these changes do not represent a significant departure from what was published previously. However, publication of the *DSM-5* marked considerable structural and philosophical changes to diagnostic nosology. These changes are both evident in the current text revision and will continue to be evident in future iterations of the manual. As such, in this chapter, we provide counselors with a general history of the *DSM* and highlight major structural and philosophical modifications first introduced with the release of the *DSM-5*. We present these changes, both in this chapter and throughout the *Learning Companion*, because these modifications represent a major shift in the way in which the manual was organized, including grouping disorders into different chapters based on their common features or etiology, as well as significant philosophical changes that present a more dimensional and contextual approach to diagnostic assessment. To help readers better understand the impact of these changes and the philosophy behind these revisions, we begin with a brief description of the historical background and evolution of the *DSM*. We then provide a deeper look at changes from the *DSM-IV-TR* (APA, 2000) to the *DSM-5* (APA, 2013a) and conclude with information regarding how these changes may influence future iterations.

History of the *DSM*

The original *DSM*, published by APA in 1952, was psychiatry's first attempt to standardize the classification of mental disorders. Developed by the APA Committee on Nomenclature and Statistics, the *DSM-I* (APA, 1952) served as an alternative to the sixth edition of the *ICD* (WHO, 1949), which, for the first time, included a section for mental disorders (APA, 2000). Differing slightly from the *ICD*, which primarily served as an international system to collect health statistics, the *DSM-I* focused on clinical utility and was grounded in psychodynamic formulations of mental disorders (Sanders, 2011). This version highlighted prominent psychiatrist Adolf Meyer's (1866–1950) psychobiological view, which posited that mental disorders denoted "reactions" of the personality to biological, psychological, or social aspects of client functioning (APA, 2000). The *DSM-I* included three categories of psychopathology (organic brain syndromes, functional disorders, and mental deficiency) and 106 narrative descriptions of disorders in about as many pages. Only one diagnosis, adjustment reaction of childhood/adolescence, was applicable to children (Sanders, 2011).

Meyer's influence was abandoned in the initial revision of the *DSM-II* published in 1968. This version contained 11 categories and 182 disorders (APA, 1968). Similar to the previous version, the development of the *DSM-II* coincided with the development of the WHO's (1968) revised *ICD-8*. Although only incremental changes were evident, the focus of the manual shifted from causality to psychoanalysis, as evidenced by the removal of the word *reactions* and retention of terms such as *neuroses* and *psychophysiological disorders* (Sanders, 2011). With the intent on reform, this shift was significant because separation meant removing unverified or speculative diagnoses from the manual. Critics, however, argued that actual separation of diagnostic labels from etiological origins would not actually occur until the next revision (Rogler, 1997).

Work on the third version, *DSM-III*, began in 1974 and continued until the edition was published in 1980. A considerable divergence from previous editions, the *DSM-III* represented a dramatic shift with inclusion of descriptive diagnoses and emphasized a medical, rather than psychosocial, model for mental health treatment (APA, 1980; Wilson, 1993). Unlike psychosocial models, which recognize the interplay of psychological and social factors in the development and experience of physical and mental health problems, medical models view illness and disease as physical problems that can be diagnosed and treated through biomedical interventions. Psychosocial models take into account an individual's personal experiences, relationships, social circumstances, and cultural context in addition to biological factors. This model views health and illness as being shaped by a complex array of biological, psychological, and social factors, and that effective treatment should address all these factors. Clearly a profound reframing of diagnostic assessment, adoption of a medical model to classify mental illness represented a clear follow-through on previous attempts to separate the *DSM* from psychoanalytic origins. Supporters claimed "theoretical neutrality" (Maser et al., 1991, p. 271) of the *DSM-III*. As Rogler (1997) argued, "The *DSM-III* was an official attempt to abruptly, not gradually, reduce reliance on the vagaries of the diagnosticians' subjective understandings by specifying sets of diagnostic criteria" (p. 9).

Fueled by the emergence of managed care and the rise of psychopharmacology, publication of the *DSM-III* resulted in widespread acceptance of the medical model (Hansen, 2014). Mental health professionals repositioned themselves toward positivistic, operationally defined symptomatology based on specific descriptive measures (Wilson, 1993). This modification included the introduction of explicit diagnostic criteria (i.e., a checklist) as opposed to narrative descriptions. The *DSM-III* also introduced the multiaxial system and diagnostic classifications free from specific theoretical confines or etiological assumptions. This version integrated demographic information such as gender, familial patterns, and cultural features into diagnostic classifications (Sanders, 2011). On the basis of these philosophical changes, mental health professionals began to emphasize the structured interview and insisted on empirically validating *DSM-III* diagnostic criteria. The age of empirically based treatments had arrived, and widespread use of the *DSM-III*, as opposed to the *ICD-9* (WHO, 1975), became commonplace. Wilson (1993) wrote,

> The biopsychosocial model [alone] did not clearly demarcate the mentally well from the mentally ill, and this failure led to a crisis in the legitimacy of psychiatry by the 1970s. The publication of *DSM-III* in 1980 represented an answer to this crisis, as the essential focus of psychiatric knowledge shifted from the clinically-based biopsychosocial model to a research-based medical model. (p. 399)

While history may suggest that the medical model was widely accepted, it was and remains highly criticized for neglecting social, psychological, and cultural factors that contribute to mental illness (Hansen, 2013). A purely biological approach to human concerns oversimplifies complex human experiences by reducing mental illness to a series of symptoms and biological factors, neglecting the influence of psychological and social factors (Sedler, 2016). A purely medical approach, particularly when psychopharmacological treatments are deemed ineffective, serves to reinforce the idea that mental illness is a personal weakness or moral failing rather than a legitimate mental health condition. Finally, overreliance on psychopharmacology and other biomedical treatments is not always effective or appropriate for some individuals or conditions.

For professional counselors, the release of the *DSM-III* was more than just a shift in diagnostic nosology. Release of the *DSM-III* represented a critically important, and diametrically different, shift in the way in which mental health concerns were understood and treated (Hansen, 2013). Claims that diagnostic nosology in the *DSM-III* was intentionally atheoretical, clustered only by symptoms rather than etiological origins, were in direct conflict with the humanistic, relational, and strength-based tenets of professional counseling. Counseling, with a distinct focus on prevention, human growth and development, wellness, and social justice (e.g., Myers, 1992), was and remains philosophically in opposition to medical models of treatment.

Intended only to be a minor change to the third version, the revised *DSM-III-R* (APA, 1987) renamed, added, and deleted categories; made changes to diagnostic criteria; and increased reliability by incorporating data from field trials and diagnostic interviews (APA, 2000; Blashfield, 1998; Scotti & Morris, 2000). Despite these innovations, the *DSM-III* and *DSM-III-R* were profoundly criticized. The manual had increased from 106 to 297 diagnoses (APA, 1987). Descriptions of Axis I disorders topped at 300 pages whereas explanations of Axis IV and V disorders totaled only two pages, leading many to question the multiaxial system (Rogler, 1997). Additionally, critics questioned field trials and claimed lack of objectivity among researchers, further contributing to strong criticism of the *DSM-III* and *DSM-III-R*.

Heavy critique of the *DSM-III* and its revision led to relatively mild changes to the *DSM-IV*, published in 1994. Despite few changes, the revision process was considerable and involved a steering committee, 13 work groups, work group advisers, extensive literature reviews, and numerous field trials to ensure clinical utility. The *DSM-IV* (APA, 1994) included 365 diagnoses; and at 886 pages, it was almost seven times the length of the *DSM-I*. A "text revision" (*DSM-IV-TR*) was published in 2000 and included additional empirically based information for each diagnosis as well as changes to diagnostic codes for the purpose of maintaining consistency with the *ICD* (APA, 2000). In the *DSM-IV-TR* (APA, 2000), wording of the manual was modified in an attempt to differentiate people from their diagnoses; for example, "a schizophrenic" was modified to read "an individual with schizophrenia" (Scotti & Morris, 2000).

Like their predecessors, the *DSM-IV* and *DSM-IV-TR* were heavily critiqued by helping professionals (Eriksen & Kress, 2006). Many felt the manual leaned too heavily on the medical model with its rigid classification system, despite claims of diagnostic neutrality (Eriksen & Kress, 2006; Ivey & Ivey, 1998; Scotti & Morris, 2000). Issues of comorbidity, questionable reliability, and controversial diagnoses were hot topics among critics, and the multiaxial system continued to be controversial (Houts, 2002; Malik & Beutler, 2002). Because of the changing nature of how the *DSM* was being used and by whom, many practitioners began demanding that a more holistic or dimensional approach be used and that psychometrically sound assessments be included (Kraemer, 2007). Other critics, specifically those directly involved in writing the *DSM-5*, advocated for incorporating scientific advances from psychiatric research, genetics, neuroimaging, cognitive science, and pathophysiology (functional changes associated with or resulting from disease or injury) into diagnostic nosology (Kupfer & Regier, 2011).

Counselors expressed concerns that overreliance on *DSM* diagnoses can "narrow a counselor's focus by encouraging the counselor to only look for behaviors that fit within a medical-model understanding of the person's situation" (Eriksen & Kress, 2006, p. 204). In contrast to those who support the medical model, many counselors use diagnosis as only one aspect of understanding the client. Fundamentally, the counseling profession views individuals as having strengths and difficulties across myriad emotional, cognitive, physiological, social, occupational, cultural, and spiritual areas. Counselors recognize the whole person and nurture a strength-based approach to achieve wellness, not a process aimed solely at symptom reduction. Myers et al. (2000) defined wellness as

> a way of life oriented toward optimal health and well-being, in which body, mind, and spirit are integrated by the individual to live life more fully within the human and natural community. Ideally, it is the optimum state of health and well-being that each individual is capable of achieving. (p. 252)

The controversial issues of rigid classification, comorbidity, questionable reliability, and controversial diagnoses were the driving force for numerous structural and philosophical changes included in the *DSM-5*. While these changes in no way represent a return to psychosocial models of mental health, changes from the *DSM-IV-TR* to *DSM-5-TR* do signal an attempt to consider the roles that social and cultural factors play in the development and maintenance of mental health conditions. Information regarding these major changes is provided in the next section.

Emergence of the *DSM-5* and *DSM-5-TR*

The *DSM-5*, after 14 years of debate and deliberation, was intended to be the most radical revision to date (Frances & First, 2011; Jones, 2012b; Miller & Levy, 2011). Beginning in 1999, a year before the *DSM-IV-TR* was published, APA began collaboration with the National Institute of Mental Health (NIMH) on a new edition. The intent of these meetings was to develop a more scientifically based manual that would increase clinical utility while maintaining continuity with previous editions (APA, n.d.-a). The process began with an initial *DSM-5* Research Planning Committee Conference, held in 1999, in which APA and NIMH deliberated on a research agenda and priorities for the new manual. Additional conferences, sponsored by APA, NIMH, and WHO, took place in 2000 and resulted in the formation of six work groups. These initial work groups focused on nomenclature, neuroscience and genetics, developmental issues and diagnosis, personality and relational disorders, mental disorders and disability, and cross-cultural issues. In 2002, a series of six white papers were published with the intent of "providing direction and potential incentives for research that could improve the scientific basis of future classifications" (Kupfer et al., 2002, p. xv). Two final manuscripts were published in 2007. One focused on mental disorders in infants, young children, and older persons and the other on gender, cultural, and spiritual issues.

After the release of the initial research agenda for the *DSM-5*, it became clear that further deliberation was needed regarding nomenclature, neuroscience, developmental science, personality disorders, and the relationship between culture and psychiatric diagnoses (APA, 2000; Kupfer et al., 2002). Steered by APA, NIMH, and WHO, 13 conferences were held between 2004 and 2008 in which participants discussed relevant diagnostic questions and solicited feedback from colleagues and other professionals regarding potential changes. Findings from these conferences facilitated the research base for proposed revisions of the *DSM-5* and fueled the agenda of the *DSM-5* work groups (see Kupfer et al., 2002, for the full *DSM-5* research agenda).

In 2007, APA officially commissioned the DSM-5 Task Force, made up of 29 members, including David J. Kupfer, chair, and Darrel A. Regier, vice-chair (APA, n.d.-a, 2022b). The DSM-5 Task Force expanded the work groups from six to 13. These included attention-deficit/hyperactivity disorder (ADHD) and disruptive behavior disorders; anxiety, obsessive-compulsive spectrum, posttraumatic, and dissociative disorders; childhood and adolescent disorders; eating disorders; mood disorders; neurocognitive disorders; neurodevelopmental disorders; personality disorders; psychotic disorders; sexual and gender identity disorders; sleep-wake disorders; somatic symptoms disorders; and substance-related disorders. Although each of these work groups investigated specific disorders, cross-collaboration was common. Kupfer and Regier provided clear direction to the work groups to, among other things, eradicate the use of "not otherwise specified" (NOS) diagnoses within categories, do away with functional impairments as necessary components of diagnostic criteria, and use empirically based evidence to justify diagnostic classes and specifiers (Gever, 2012; Regier et al., 2009). With these marching orders, each work group proposed draft criteria and changes for the revised manual.

Three rounds of public comment regarding proposed changes took place between April 2010 and June 2012. An estimated 13,000 mental health professionals commented on the proposed criteria (APA, 2013b; Dailey et al., 2014). Furthermore, mental health experts conducted field trials with the aim of evaluating the practicability, clinical effectiveness, consistency, and, whenever feasible, the accuracy of the preliminary criteria and the diagnostic-specific and cross-cutting dimensional assessments proposed for inclusion in *DSM-5* (APA, 2013a). The first trial, held between April 2010 and December 2011, took place in 11 large academic or medical centers and involved a total of 279 clinicians. The second trial, which included solo or small group practices, took place between October 2010 and February 2012. APA recruited a volunteer sample of psychiatrists, psychologists, licensed clinical social workers, licensed counselors, licensed marriage and family therapists, and licensed psychiatric mental health nurses to participate in the second field trial. Feedback from public comment periods and field trials was shared with work group members, who edited proposed criteria as indicated. The final version of the *DSM-5* went before the APA Board of Trustees in December 2012 and was released in May 2013. The following outlines the complete timeline of the development of the *DSM-5*.

1999–2001	Development of the *DSM-5* research agenda
2002–2007	APA/WHO/NIMH *DSM-5/ICD-11* research planning conferences
2006	Appointment of DSM-5 Task Force
2007	Appointment of *DSM-5* work groups
2007–2011	Literature review and data reanalysis
2010–2011	First-phase field trials
2010–2012	Second-phase field trials
July 2012	Final draft of *DSM-5* for APA review
May 2013	*DSM-5* released to the public

Revision Feedback

Although no professional counselor was invited to serve on the DSM-5 Task Force, ACA served as an important advocate for professional counselors during the revision process. Through advocacy efforts of the ACA Professional Affairs Office and the ACA *DSM-5* Revisions Task Force, two ACA presidents sent letters to APA indicating concern over proposed changes. The first was sent by Lynn E. Linde, ACA 2009–2010 president, to David J. Kupfer, DSM-5 Task Force chair. The letter indicated that ACA members had concerns regarding five areas of particular importance to professional counselors: (a) applicability across all mental health professions, (b) gender and culture, (c) organization of the *DSM-5* multiaxial system, (d) lowering of diagnostic thresholds and combining diagnoses, and (e) use of dimensional assessments. The second letter was sent by Don W. Locke, ACA 2011–2012 president, informing John Oldham, APA president, that licensed professional counselors were the second largest group to routinely use the *DSM-IV-TR*. He noted uncertainty among professional counselors about the quality and credibility of the *DSM-5* and included a prioritized list of concerns APA should consider before publishing the *DSM-5*. APA responded to this letter on November 21, 2011 (APA, 2011).

In addition to feedback provided by ACA, several divisions of the American Psychological Association voiced concern about the writing process of the *DSM-5* (Jones, 2012a). As a result, the Society for Humanistic Psychology, Division 32 of the American Psychological Association, sponsored a petition outlining its concerns and inviting other mental health professionals, including counselors, to sign the petition (for a review of these concerns, see British Psychological Society, 2011). It is important to note that nine out of 19 ACA divisions endorsed this petition, including the Association for Adult Development and Aging; Association for Creativity in Counseling; American College Counseling Association; Association for Counselor Education and Supervision; Association for Humanistic Counseling; Association for Lesbian, Gay, Bisexual, and Transgender Issues in Counseling (now called the Society of Sexual, Affectional, Intersex, and Gender Expansive Identities); American Rehabilitation Counseling Association; Association for Specialists in Group Work; and Counselors for Social Justice.

DSM-5-TR

The text revision process for the *DSM-5-TR* followed a similar revision process as the *DSM-5*. Twenty disorder work groups and four overarching work groups reviewed diagnostic criteria and descriptive text. Feedback incorporated the latest empirical evidence and literature as well as special attention to issues associated with diagnostic prevalence, risk factors, culture- and gender-related diagnostic features, comorbidity, and associations with suicidal ideation or suicide attempts (APA, 2022b). Unique to the DSM-5-TR Task Force, an Ethnoracial Equity and Inclusion Work Group reviewed the entire text to ensure that "appropriate attention" (APA, 2022b, p. xxi) was given to risk factors associated with systematic racism and discrimination and to remove stigmatizing language from the manual.

Like many text revisions of the *DSM*, changes found within the *DSM-5-TR* are predominantly limited to minor modifications of diagnostic criteria or descriptive text to enhance clarity and reflect current literature and research. Although the *DSM-5-TR* did introduce one new disorder—prolonged grief disorder—and introduced symptom codes for reporting suicidal and nonsuicidal self-injury, specific changes to diagnostic criteria were limited. The most notable change, atypical for a text revision, was review and modifications based on the work of the Ethnoracial Equity and Inclusion Work Group. This work group represented a key differentiator for *DSM-5-TR* and was composed of 10 psychiatric and mental health clinicians from diverse racial and ethnic backgrounds (APA, 2022a). Each member was skilled in disparity-reduction treatment methods. The work group was tasked with reviewing the totality of the *DSM-5-TR* text to ensure that as diagnosis and symptomatology were described in terms of cultural and ethnoracial impact, the influences of racism, discrimination, and stigma were also a part of the narrative and stigmatizing language was removed and avoided throughout the manual (APA, 2022c). Changes made in the *DSM-5-TR* by this work group challenge the idea of races as discrete and natural entities. Described in more detail in the next chapter, discussions on variations in symptom expression, disorder causes, and factors associated with differential prevalence across demographic groups have been expanded; cultural norms affecting perceived pathology are reported; and the risk of misdiagnosis in socially oppressed ethnoracial groups is addressed more throughout the manual.

Overall, the changes made by the Ethnoracial Equity and Inclusion Work Group represent the first effort of the *DSM* to address concerns about cultural sensitivity and health disparities in the diagnosis and treatment of mental health conditions. Changes included a new section on cultural considerations that provides additional guidance in Section III (pp. 859–880) on considerations relevant to cultural context. The work group influenced greater recognition and expansion of cultural expressions of distress, also found in Section III, noting that symptoms of mental illness may be expressed differently across cultures. Throughout the manual, additional information on how to assess symptoms in a more culturally sensitive manner is provided. The work group also oversaw the addition of new cultural concepts of distress, recognizing that certain mental health conditions may have unique presentations in different cultural contexts. While the *DSM-5-TR* still adheres to a medical model of classification, the work of the Ethnoracial Equity and Inclusion Work Group was a notable attempt to address concerns about cultural sensitivity and the potential for disparities in diagnosis and treatment, including acknowledgment that health disparities such as access to care are significant in the development, course, and treatment of mental health concerns. An expanded discussion of sociocultural issues and the *DSM-5-TR* is provided in the next chapter of this *Learning Companion.*

Major Changes From *DSM-IV-TR* to *DSM-5-TR*

Release of the *DSM-5* marked a significant structural and philosophical shift in diagnostic classification and included major revision to organization of the manual and added new diagnostic categories, cross-cutting and dimensional approaches to assessment, a nonaxial system for recording, and numerous changes to diagnostic criteria. In this section, we highlight major structural and philosophical changes from the *DSM-IV-TR* to the *DSM-5-TR*. Unless otherwise noted, these changes were first introduced with the release of the *DSM-5* and mark significant historical changes from the *DSM-IV-TR* to the latest manual.

Structural Changes

The *DSM-5-TR* includes approximately the same number of disorders as the *DSM-IV-TR*. This goes against a popular trend within health care to increase, rather than decrease, the number of diagnoses available to practitioners (APA, 2013a, 2022b). Despite being similar in number, several major changes affected the manual. Unlike the *DSM-IV-TR*, which was organized by 16 diagnostic classes, one general section, and 11 appendixes, the *DSM-5-TR* is divided into three sections, 20 diagnostic classes, two general sections for medication-induced problems and other conditions that may be a focus of clinical attention, and seven appendixes. The *DSM-5-TR* also includes the latest *ICD-10-CM* codes (National Center for Health Statistics, 2023). This is an update from the *DSM-5*, which listed two sets of *ICD* codes, using *ICD-9-CM* (National Center for Health Statistics, 1998) codes as the standard coding system with *ICD-10-CM* (National Center for Health Statistics, 2014) codes in parentheses. *ICD-10-CM* codes were included in the *DSM-5* because as of October 1,

2014, approximately 1 year after publication of the *DSM-5*, all practitioners were required to be in alignment with HIPAA, which required the use of *ICD-10-CM* codes. For more information about coding systems, Part Four of this *Learning Companion* comprehensively reviews diagnostic coding in counseling practice.

Section Overview

Section I of the *DSM-5-TR* provides a summary of revisions and changes as well as information regarding utilization of the revised manual. Section II includes all diagnoses broken into 20 separate chapters ordered by similarity to one another. Because comorbid symptoms are clustered together, counselors can now better differentiate between disorders that are distinctively different but have similar symptom characteristics or etiology (e.g., body dysmorphic disorder vs. obsessive-compulsive disorder; acute stress disorder vs. adjustment disorder). Section III of the *DSM-5-TR* includes conditions that require further research before they can be considered for adoption in an upcoming version of the *DSM*, dimensional assessment measures, an expanded look at how practitioners can better understand clients from a multicultural perspective, and a proposed alternative model for diagnosing personality disorders.

Cultural Inclusion in the DSM-5-TR

New to the *DSM-5* and carried over into the *DSM-5-TR*, Section III (see pp. 859–926 of the *DSM-5-TR*) includes special attention to diverse ways in which individuals in different cultural groups can experience and describe distress. One change from the *DSM-5* to the *DSM-5-TR* is additional information within Section III regarding cultural considerations related to diagnosis, inclusive of defining culture, race, and ethnicity, and illustrative examples selected for inclusion because "they have been well studied and their lack of familiarity to many U.S. clinicians" (p. 859 of the *DSM-5-TR*). The *DSM-5-TR* also further expanded on the Outline for Cultural Formulation (pp. 860–862 of the *DSM-5-TR*) found in the *DSM-5*. This section also includes a Cultural Formulation Interview (pp. 864–861 of the *DSM-5-TR*) to help clinicians gather relevant cultural information. Expanding on information provided in the *DSM-IV-TR*, the Cultural Formulation Interview calls for clinicians to outline and systematically assess cultural identity, the cultural conceptualization of distress, psychosocial stressors related to cultural features of vulnerability and resilience, cultural differences between the counselor and client, and cultural factors relevant to help seeking.

In addition to being highlighted in Section III of the *DSM-5-TR*, specific attention was given by the DSM-5-TR Task Force to the impact of racism and discrimination on diagnostic assessment, cultural and social structural issues that impact diagnosis, and the use of nonstigmatizing language throughout the manual. These changes, and the others noted above as being new to the *DSM-5-TR*, are a result of two newly formed revision work groups—the Ethnoracial Equity and Inclusion Work Group and the Cross-Cutting Culture Review Group—which aimed to better address the impact of culture, race, ethnicity, and sociocultural determinants on diagnosis. Both groups made overarching changes to the text descriptions for over 70 disorders found within Section II as well as numerous modifications to the Culture and Psychiatric Diagnosis chapter in Section III. Overall, the changes made by the Ethnoracial Equity and Inclusion Work Group represent a significant effort to address concerns about cultural sensitivity and health disparities in the diagnosis and treatment of mental health conditions.

As a result, the *DSM-5-TR* includes text modifications to replace *race/racial* with the term *racialized*. This change serves to emphasize that race is a socially constructed concept. The term *Latinx*, instead of Latino/Latina, is now used to reflect more gender-inclusive terminology. The *DSM-5-TR* now utilizes the term *ethnoracial* to address U.S. Census categories (e.g., Hispanic, White, or African American) that fail to recognize that race and ethnicity are distinctly different concepts. The *DSM-5-TR* also avoids references to "minority" and "non-White" populations, which infer deference to a dominant group. References to "Caucasian" were removed, because this term is deemed an erroneous reference to an overly generalized geographic origin that implies pan-European ethnicity. The work groups also attempted to update data throughout the manual associated with diagnostic prevalence, to ensure that better representation and more reliable estimates based on representative samples were provided. Information about cross-cultural variations in symptom presentation and key aspects of sociocultural context relevant to diagnostic classifications are included in each chapter of this *Learning Companion*, and information on sociocultural issues related to diagnosis and assessment as well as cultural considerations in treatment planning and practice can be found in Chapter 3 of this *Learning Companion*. Information on using the Cultural Formulation Interview and approaches for culturally informed case conceptualization can be found in Chapter 4.

Personality Disorders

Section III of the *DSM-5-TR* also provides an alternative model for diagnosing personality disorders. This proposed model, first introduced in the *DSM-5*, is a radical change from the current diagnostic structure, introducing a hybrid dimensional-categorical model that evaluates symptomatology and characterizes five broad areas of personality pathology. As opposed to separate diagnostic criteria, this proposed model identifies six personality types with a specific pattern of impairments and traits. We review this model and the Cultural Formulation section in Chapter 4 of this *Learning Companion*.

Adoption of a Nonaxial System

One of the most far-sweeping structural modifications, first introduced in the *DSM-5*, is the removal of the multiaxial system and discontinuation of the Global Assessment of Functioning (GAF) scale. Table 2.1 compares the traditional multiaxial system and the new nonaxial system. Axes I, II, and III are combined with the assumption that there is no differentiation between medical and mental health conditions. Rather than list psychosocial and contextual factors affecting clients on Axis IV, counselors list F codes, Z codes (conditions in which symptoms do not indicate a specific disorder but treatment is still needed), or T codes (instances of adult physical, sexual, or psychological abuse) as stand-alone diagnoses or alongside another diagnosis as long as the stressors are relevant to the client's mental disorder(s).

F codes are the most common *ICD-10-CM* mental health codes and relate to mental, behavioral, and neurodevelopmental disorders for which a specific diagnosis within the *DSM-5-TR* is not listed. In addition to the aforementioned Z and T codes, counselors will also find G codes to describe conditions relevant to the nervous system, but these are limited to instances of parkinsonism, sleep disorders, medication-induced disorders, and neurocognitive conditions. An expanded listing of *ICD-10-CM* codes are included in the *DSM-5*. Although the *DSM-5* does not include direction for formatting, counselors may also use special notations for psychosocial and environmental considerations relevant to the diagnosis. Similarly, counselors will no longer note a GAF score on Axis V. Rather, the *DSM-5* advises that clinicians find ways to note distress and/or disability in functioning, perhaps using the WHO's (2010) WHODAS 2.0 as a dimensional assessment of functioning. Again, the manual does not include directions for formatting or presenting this assessment.

Note: Counselors are not qualified to diagnose medical conditions. However, it is important to record all historical medical information. Counselors must work closely with medical professionals to identify any medical conditions.

Once the *ICD-10-CM* was implemented (October 2014), all codes in the Other Conditions That May Be a Focus of Clinical Attention chapter of the *DSM-5* changed. Z codes replaced V codes, and T codes replaced 900 codes. There were exceptions, as some R codes (R45.88 nonsuicidal self-injury, current) remain. Counselors are strongly encouraged to utilize the most recent iteration of the *DSM-5-TR* for the latest code updates or check the National Center for Health Statistics website for *ICD-10-CM* updates.

While dropping the multiaxial system is a significant change to recording diagnostic information, it confirms what counselors from a wellness perspective have been claiming for decades—that differentiation among emotional, behavioral, physiological, psychosocial, and contextual factors is misleading and conveys a message that mental illness is unrelated to physical, biological, and medical problems. Combining these axes has the potential to be more inclusive, embracing more aspects of client functioning. However, practitioners will need to be intentional and systematic when incorporating more holistic assessments and notations into the diagnostic process so that their diagnoses do not become a simple listing of primary *DSM-5-TR* disorders.

Note: The *DSM-5* dropped the GAF scale because of a lack of clinical utility and reliability. The WHODAS 2.0 (WHO, 2010) has been included in Section III of the manual. This scale is used in the *ICD* as a standardized assessment of functioning for individuals diagnosed with mental disorders. The *DSM-5-TR* notes, however, that "it has not been possible to completely separate normal and pathological symptom expressions contained in diagnostic criteria" (APA, 2022b, p. 23). Counselors who use the WHODAS 2.0 are responsible for ensuring they do so in accordance with the *ACA Code of Ethics* (ACA, 2014); this includes ensuring appropriateness of instruments through review of psychometric properties, appropriateness for client population, and appropriate use of interpretation. This is particularly important because the *DSM-5-TR* does not include information regarding the validity or reliability of the WHODAS 2.0.

Critics of the multiaxial system argued that the system was cumbersome and ambiguous, thus providing poor clinical utility (Bassett & Beiser, 1991; Jampala et al., 1986; Paris, 2013). Furthermore, many clinicians will agree that although the multiaxial system was well intentioned, client reports typically stopped at Axis I. In cases where Axis II was listed, some clients would feel stigmatized by their diagnostic label (Aviram et al., 2006; Fritz, 2012). Enhanced attention to F and Z codes within the nonaxial system may help counselors emphasize a client's entire worldview and systemic context in a way that informs the therapeutic process. If used intentionally, movement to a nonaxial system is intended to increase client understanding, remind counselors that medical and psychosocial issues are just as important as mental health diagnoses, and reduce stigma.

Accurate reporting in a nonaxial format cites the client's primary diagnosis first, followed by all psychosocial, contextual, and disability factors. For example, a client presents with depressive symptoms during withdrawal of a severe cocaine use disorder. She has just revealed that she is being sexually abused by her husband, who just kicked her out of her home. This client would receive a diagnosis of F14.24 cocaine-induced depressive disorder, with onset during withdrawal. An additional diagnosis of F14.20 severe cocaine use disorder would also be recorded, as well as T76.21XA spouse violence, sexual, suspected, initial encounter and Z59.1 inadequate housing. Any subsequent notations related to a mental health diagnosis would follow. More information regarding recording diagnoses can be found in Chapter 5 of this *Learning Companion*.

While the multiaxial system was dropped upon release of the *DSM-5* in 2013, counselors should remain aware of the challenges that remain related to nonaxial assessment. Moving to a nonaxial system added a conceptual lack of clarity regarding how clinicians document and report diagnostic classifications. If clinicians struggled to use holistic assessment within a multiaxial system that essentially required some attention to psychosocial and environmental issues and overall distress and disability, questions remain as to whether clinicians are taking the time to incorporate these elements into a nonaxial format. Although counselors can include subjective descriptors next to the client's diagnosis, there is no telling whether these are being carried over to the next clinician or if information is clear when transferred to a different party. Because there were significant delays as insurance companies and governmental agencies updated their claim forms and reporting procedures to accommodate *DSM-5* changes, research on the impact of a nonaxial system is limited. What counselors can do is ensure their nonaxial documentation of diagnosis follows a clear format and incorporates psychosocial and environmental issues relevant to the client's presenting problem(s).

Chapter Organization

Overall organization of chapters changed significantly from the *DSM-IV-TR* to the *DSM-5* to reflect a developmental approach to listing diagnoses. Diagnoses are now ordered by similar symptomatology with presumed underlying vulnerabilities grouped together. This organization is indicative of the life span (i.e., developmental) approach taken by the DSM-5 Task Force. Disorders more frequently diagnosed in childhood, such as intellectual and learning disabilities, were renamed as neurodevelopmental disorders and appear at the beginning of the manual. Diagnoses more commonly seen in older adults, such as neurocognitive disorders, appear at the end. This modification more closely follows the *ICD* and was intended to increase practitioners' use of the manual for differential diagnosis.

Other structural changes include significant modifications to overall classification of disorders. The mood disorders are now separated into two distinct classes: bipolar and related disorders and depressive disorders. Anxiety disorders are broken out into three separate diagnostic chapters: anxiety disorders, obsessive-compulsive and related disorders, and trauma- and stressor-related disorders. In another large structural and philosophical change, the *DSM-5* eliminated disorders usually diagnosed in infancy, childhood, or adolescence. Disorders within this section are incorporated into the chapter on neurodevelopmental disorders or, if not presumed to be neurodevelopmental in nature, relocated to other specific sections of the manual. The DSM-5 Task Force justified this change because many of the disorders in this section are also seen in adulthood (e.g., ADHD; Dailey et al., 2014), and many disorders seen in childhood may be precursors to concerns in adulthood. This section, originally created for convenience, led clinicians to erroneously believe there was a clear distinction between "adult" and "childhood" disorders. Critics felt this division was confusing and prevented clinicians from diagnosing children with "adult" disorders such as major depression or posttraumatic stress disorder (PTSD). Likewise, adults diagnosed with disorders such as ADHD have reported feeling stigmatized with limited treatment options (Katragadda & Schubiner, 2007). In terms of structure, diagnoses that were removed from this section, such as childhood feeding and eating disorders, can now be found within their associated sections, just later in the manual. For example, the feeding and eating disorders section of the *DSM-5-TR* includes pica and rumination.

Other comprehensive structural changes included the removal of labeling disorders as *not otherwise specified* (NOS) so practitioners can be more specific and accurate in their diagnosis. As a replacement, the *DSM-5-TR* has two options for cases in which the client's presenting condition does not meet the criteria for a specific category: other specified disorder and unspecified disorder. The use of *other specified disorder* allows counselors to identify the specific reason why the client does not meet the criteria for a disorder. *Unspecified disorder* is used when a clinician chooses not to specify a reason for not diagnosing a more specific disorder or determines there is not enough information to be more specific.

This is also supportive of dimensional, rather than categorical, classification (this idea is expanded on in the next section, "*DSM-5* Philosophical Changes"). Finally, language throughout the *DSM-5-TR* has changed so that medical conditions that were previously referred to as general medical conditions are renamed *another medical condition*. This change reflects the philosophical assumption that mental health disorders *are* medical conditions.

Table 2.1
Comparison of Multiaxial Versus Nonaxial Systems

DSM-III *and* DSM-IV *Multiaxial System*	DSM-5 *Nonaxial System*
Axis I: Clinical disorders and other conditions that are the focus of treatment *Axis II:* Personality disorders and intellectual disability (i.e., mental retardation) *Axis III:* General medical conditions	Combined attention to clinical disorders, including personality disorders and intellectual disability (i.e., mental retardation); other conditions that are the focus of treatment; and medical conditions continue to be listed as a part of the diagnosis.
Axis IV: Psychosocial and environmental stressors	Special notations for psychosocial and contextual factors are now listed by using V codes or *ICD-10-CM* Z codes. An expanded list of V codes has been provided in the *DSM-5*. In rare cases where psychosocial and contextual factors are not listed, counselors can include the specific factor as it is related to the client's diagnosis.
Axis V: Global Assessment of Functioning (GAF)	Special notations for disability are listed by using V codes or *ICD-10-CM* Z codes. The World Health Organization Disability Assessment Schedule 2.0 (WHODAS 2.0) has been included in Section III and is listed on APA's website (www.psychiatry.org) within the online assessment measures section.

Note: Clinical judgment is the driving force for whether the client's presenting condition should be "other specified" or "unspecified." APA is very clear in that the use of either is the decision of the clinician.

Readers will also note that, unlike the *DSM-5*, the *DSM-5-TR* includes only *ICD-10-CM* codes. The *DSM-5* included both *ICD-9-CM* and *ICD-10-CM* codes. The decision to print both sets of codes in the *DSM-5* was in response to a mandate from the U.S. Department of Health and Human Services that required all health care providers to transition to *ICD-10-CM* codes by October 2014 (which was later moved to October 2015). To ease this transition, the *DSM-5* listed both code numbers alongside diagnoses and in the Appendix section. The purpose was to aid in standardization among mental health care providers and to allow for easier transition to the new *ICD-10-CM* codes and revised billing processes. Upon publication in 2022, the *DSM-5-TR* removed references to *ICD-9-CM* codes.

To summarize, the following list outlines major structural changes from the *DSM-IV-TR* to the *DSM-5-TR*:

- Removal of the multiaxial system
- Modified chapter order to reflect a developmental approach
- Division into three sections: Section I: *DSM-5-TR* Basics; Section II: Diagnostic Criteria and Codes; and Section III: Emerging Measures and Models

- Replacement of the first diagnostic chapter of the *DSM-IV-TR*, Disorders Usually First Diagnosed in Infancy, Childhood, or Adolescence, with a new Neurodevelopmental Disorders chapter
- Inclusion of *ICD-10-CM* codes
- Modifications to the classification of disorders: Bipolar and related disorders and depressive disorders are now stand-alone chapters; anxiety disorders are separated into three distinct categories (anxiety disorders, obsessive-compulsive and related disorders, and trauma- and stressor-related disorders)
- Removal of NOS and inclusion of other specified and unspecified disorders

Note: Whereas *ICD* code numbers were originally created for statistical tracking of diseases, not reimbursement, most medical systems within the United States use these codes for billing purposes. The *DSM-III* was coordinated with the development of the *ICD-9*. Other versions of the *DSM* continued to use the *ICD-9* codes, despite the fact that the *ICD-10* was first published in 1992.

DSM-5 Philosophical Changes

Two philosophical changes, spearheaded by the DSM-5 Task Force, have modified the way in which counselors will approach diagnosis when using the *DSM-5*. The first philosophical change involves a shift in focus from phenomenological interpretations (i.e., symptom identification and behavioral observations—a medical model) to identifiable pathophysiological origins (i.e., functional changes associated with or resulting from disease or injury—a biological model). The second philosophical change involves the use of dimensions as opposed to diagnostic categories. Although these two changes are theoretically similar, each philosophy has a unique impact on the way in which counselors approach diagnosis, treatment planning, and interdisciplinary communication.

Regarding the first shift, the DSM-5 Task Force decided that using a bioecological perspective, as opposed to identifying symptomatology, was a more empirically sound way to approach diagnostic classifications (Kupfer & Regier, 2011). Neurobiologists believe that problems with growth and development of the brain or central nervous system adversely affect behavioral patterns, learning, and social interactions. Officially included in the *DSM-5 Research Agenda* (Kupfer et al., 2002), the idea that disorders should be grouped by underlying neurobiological similarities rather than phenomenological observations (i.e., criteria) is not a new one (Kupfer & Regier, 2011). Supporters of a pathophysiologic (i.e., biological) approach to mental illness emphasize that findings from genetics, neuroimaging, cognitive science, and pathophysiology need to drive psychiatric diagnosis. Followers claim the overuse of NOS diagnoses and problems with comorbidity as key indicators that previous versions of the *DSM* relied too heavily on "psychodynamic, a priori hypotheses" rather than "external, empirical indicators" (Kupfer & Regier, 2011, p. 672). Kupfer and Regier (2011) even proposed "keeping the *DSM* as a 'living document' that can be readily updated to reflect changes in our understanding of neuroscience and pathophysiology in a world of (sometimes) rapid and dramatic neuroscience discovery" (p. 674).

The impact of this philosophical shift on the current *DSM* is not as significant as proponents would have hoped. With regard to grouping disorders by underlying pathophysiological similarities, Kupfer and Regier (2011) stated,

> We realized from our Research Agenda conference series that we would not be able to accomplish by the DSM-5's deadline all of the things we set out to and, in fact, that portions of that agenda related to advances in neurosciences were already being addressed in other arenas . . . [which] will be very informative for subsequent versions: DSM-5.1, DSM-5.2, and beyond. (p. 673)

Although not as significant as some would have liked, this movement has affected the *DSM-5-TR* and will most certainly have an impact on future iterations of the manual. First, the way in which disorders are grouped, as previously mentioned, has changed. By listing diagnoses in terms of clinical expressions across the life span, the DSM-5 Task Force highlighted neurodevelopmental disorders such as autism and ADHD as having biological origins. This movement led the task force to eliminate the first section because they felt using a bioecological perspective to focus on the first 2 decades of life, when rapid changes in behavior, emotion, and cognition occur, was more empirically sound. Although critics claim that removal of disorders usually diagnosed in infancy, childhood, or adolescence points too heavily to a biological basis of behavior and deemphasizes sociocultural variations, this position is in alignment with the pathophysiologic movement adopted by the DSM-5 Task Force.

Within the narrative sections of the *DSM-5*, readers will notice inclusion of neurobiological findings, such as genetic and physiologic risk factors, and life span development and course alongside diagnostic criteria. Proponents claim this biological and life-span information, in conjunction with current criteria, will allow practitioners to better understand the role of genetic and physiologic risk factors, prognostic indicators, and biologic markers in shaping client risk and prognosis.

The DSM-5 Task Force did not fully accept or wholly incorporate classification of all mental illness from a neurodevelopmental and biological perspective. However, even the slightest movement toward adoption of this philosophy has had a significant impact on the current manual, as evidenced by the changes just described. Moreover, this movement has fueled another philosophical shift: recognition that categorical systems found within the *DSM-IV-TR* should be supplemented with dimensional models of assessment.

Although professional counselors may find themselves flipping through the *DSM-5-TR* in search of reorganized diagnoses, we suspect they may be most affected by the shift from categorical to dimensional assessment. The philosophical change and resulting implications are addressed throughout the remainder of this chapter. We begin the discussion with a historical overview of categorical and dimensional assessment along with explanation of philosophical challenges of dimensional assessment; we conclude by explaining dimensional assessments within the *DSM-5-TR*.

From Categorical to Dimensional Assessment

In the 1960s and 1970s, scholars criticized psychiatric diagnosis for lack of diagnostic reliability, meaning there was little diagnostic agreement among helping professionals who evaluated the same individual (Spitzer & Fleiss, 1974). Revisions to the *DSM*, beginning with the *DSM-III*, provided practitioners and researchers with a more reliable common language for diagnostic criteria (Scotti & Morris, 2000). Rather than providing only narrative descriptions regarding manifestation of disorders, the *DSM-III* and *DSM-IV* included discrete clinical criteria that, when considered together, allowed professionals to identify the presence or absence of a disorder (APA, 2000; Jones, 2012a; Scotti & Morris, 2000). This system was intended to help users better understand complex and obscure phenomena of mental illness. In turn, creators of the system assumed a categorical approach would help mental health professionals find a common language for treatment, select empirically based interventions, calculate course and prognosis, and differentiate between clients who present with a mental health disorder and those who do not (First, 2010; Jones, 2012b). This philosophical shift resulted in etiologically based treatment options that integrated seemingly varied symptoms into a particular diagnosis (Millon, 1991). Even researchers were affected, as the *DSM* now serves as an important foundation for research conceptualization.

Several professionals have applauded modifications to this categorical classification system for allowing clinicians to plan treatments tailored to the special needs of the client

(Bedell et al., 1997; Millon, 1991; Widiger & Frances, 1985). Categorical diagnoses have also assisted with accountability and record keeping, treatment planning, communication between helping professionals, and identification of clients with issues beyond one's areas of expertise (Hinkle, 1999). These revisions have been praised for including more empirically based criteria, thus allowing for what was assumed to be a more scientifically sound classification system (Maser et al., 1991). Although the categorical system was a vast improvement over the descriptive categories of *DSM-I* and *DSM-II*, the categorical approach poses several important limitations that DSM-5 Task Force members attempted to address.

Challenges to the Categorical Philosophy

Categorical diagnosis assumes that all individuals diagnosed with a given disorder have similar symptoms and attributes (First, 2010; Jones, 2012a). This system also presumes that mental disorders have little variation, that populations are relatively homogeneous, and that diagnoses are objective, discrete phenomena. However, the absoluteness of this yes/no approach has caused significant problems in terms of clinical utility among researchers and clinicians (Brown & Barlow, 2005; Demjaha et al., 2009; First, 2010). Critics of the categorical system point to significant limitations in terms of diagnostic agreement and dispute the assumption that there is a clear-cut line between having and not having a mental disorder (Kraemer et al., 2004). Overuse of NOS diagnoses is sufficient evidence that the line between diagnosis and no diagnosis is not as clear as practitioners would like it to be. Specifically, among counselors, there is excessive use of the NOS specifier when clients face significant distress or impairment but do not meet all criteria for a given disorder (Jones, 2012a).

Other problems with categorical diagnosis include disproportionate comorbidity among disorders and disputes regarding psychological constructs. For example, epidemiologic researchers argue that comorbidity between depressive and anxiety disorders is aberrantly high (Kessler et al., 1997; Mineka et al., 1998). Magee et al. (1996) reported that agoraphobia, simple phobia, and social phobia are highly comorbid. Researchers also found that individuals with coexisting disorders experience more severe symptomatology. Diagnostic concurrence has also been identified between substance abuse and mood, anxiety, somatoform, personality, and eating disorders (Andrews et al., 2002; Mineka et al., 1998; Subica et al., 2012; Widiger & Coker, 2003). In response to these findings, Jones (2012b) claimed, "It seems that diagnostic comorbidity is more the norm rather than the exception" (p. 482). Because the limitations of a purely categorical approach are widely documented, APA introduced dimensional assessments within the *DSM-5*.

Dimensional Assessments in the DSM-5-TR

The *DSM-5* proposed specific assessment tools to help mental health professionals diagnose disorders. This philosophy, seen throughout the manual, moves beyond categorical description and considers etiological, biological, and behavioral dimensions of psychopathology. Dimensional assessments are a significant change to the philosophy of previous versions of the *DSM* in that the *DSM-5* attempts to capture characteristics such as frequency, duration, and severity of individuals' experiences with disorders.

Although the categorical model has not been abandoned, dimensional assessments have been included in some areas to allow clinicians to evaluate clients on a full range of symptoms. This approach also allows clinicians to gather additional information to diagnose, create individualized treatment plans, and—as opposed to categorical models—evaluate client outcomes more effectively. Severity ratings for anxiety and depression as well as guidance for assessing suicide risk can now be found within the new manual. Beginning in Chapter 6, Depressive Disorders, of this *Learning Companion*, we provide several examples of assessments that measure severity (i.e., dimensional assessments). These can also be found on APA's website under *DSM-5-TR* Online Assessment Measures (APA, n.d.-b).

Readers should note that the use of dimensional assessments is in its infancy. A dimensional approach to rating severity for the core symptoms of schizophrenia spectrum and other psychotic disorders, for example, is included in the *DSM-5-TR*'s Section III, Emerging Measures and Models. Under the previous categorical model followed in *DSM-III* and *DSM-IV*, a client diagnosed with schizophrenia who was experiencing severe positive symptoms such as persecutory hallucinations would have no way for this to be included as a part of their diagnostic classification. With the proposed rating system, counselors can indicate levels of severity on various criteria so that they can document concerns more effectively and determine the degree to which the client is experiencing decreases in symptomatology as a result of treatment (APA, 2022b). Because disorders present with different degrees of severity and in the company of comorbid symptoms, the *DSM-5-TR* includes several standardized dimensional assessments proposed for future iterations of the manual. Similar to the idea of incorporating pathophysiological etiologies, these ideas need to evolve through research and continued advancements within psychiatry and counseling. To date, only one-dimensional assessment is included in the *DSM-5-TR*.

Critics of Dimensional Assessment

Some counselors speculate that introduction of dimensional assessments will bring about considerable potential for diagnostic inflation, claiming that APA-approved dimensional assessments are cumbersome, are difficult to administer, and lack rigorous psychometric validation (First, 2010; Jones, 2012a). Data from more than 300 psychiatrists revealed that, despite the wide availability of assessments, fewer than 20% of providers use assessment measures to evaluate depression (Hong et al., 2021). Zimmerman and McGlinchey (2008) found that clinicians identified three reasons why they did not administer a scale: (a) lack of confidence in scale utility, (b) lack of training, and (c) lack of time to administer an assessment. Although some studies have documented improvements in clinical care as a result of assessment (Trivedi et al., 2006), First (2010) expressed concerns that "clinicians are likely to view dimensional measures more as an administrative burden than as a clinically useful tool" (p. 471). While research is limited on the number of clinicians using dimensional assessments, the debate around clinical utility remains (Phillips, 2016).

Critics also warn that severity specifiers already included in some *DSM* diagnoses lack clinical utility (First, 2010). For example, the *DSM-III-R* introduced severity and course specifiers for all but eight diagnoses. These specifiers were ignored by clinicians and, with the exception of specifiers for major depressive and manic episodes, were removed from the *DSM-IV-TR*. Research has provided little insight into why clinicians continue to ignore these specifiers (First, 2010; First et al., 2004). Given these criticisms and potential shortcomings of the *DSM-5*, we are intentional about highlighting dimensional components of diagnoses and incorporating implications in case studies and associated learning activities throughout this *Learning Companion*.

Cross-Cutting Assessments in the *DSM-5-TR*

In addition to incorporating dimensional assessments for specific diagnoses, the *DSM-5-TR* also includes several cross-cutting assessment measures in Section III of the manual (APA, 2022b). Although they are not required for use at this time, the measures are included for research and exploration purposes. Cross-cutting measures are not specific to any individual disorder, taking into consideration symptoms characteristic of clients in nearly all clinical settings (APA, 2022b; Jones, 2012a). These assessments evaluate symptoms that are of high importance to all clinicians, such as suicidal ideation, depressed mood, sleep disturbance, and substance abuse. Cross-cutting assessment scales included in the *DSM-5-TR* were developed by the National Institutes of Health's Patient-Reported Outcomes Measurement Information System and consist of two levels. The first level includes self-report measures that evaluate major clinical domains. Clients rate items on a Likert-type scale ranging from 0 (*none–not at all*) to 4 (*severe–nearly every day*). If any Level 1 area is considered clinically significant, counselors will follow up with a Level 2 measure. Level 2 measures provide a more detailed assessment of specific symptoms identified by the Level 1 measure. Like dimensional assessments, these measures are in their infancy; researchers do not yet know how use of the measures will influence diagnostic process and clinical utility. Still, it is likely that future editions of the *DSM* will include enhanced attention to cross-cutting assessments.

Critics of cross-cutting assessments claim there is a lack of psychometric data backing up some of these measures (Widiger & Samuel, 2005). A hot topic of debate during the development of the *DSM-5*, concerns over the utilization of cross-cutting assessments include lack of clinical utility due to the complexity and time-consuming nature of the assessments, need for extensive training for counseling professionals, and variance in validity and reliability of specific instruments (First, 2010; Jones, 2012a). These constraints, as well as the potential cost for procuring the assessments, fuel skepticism regarding the cross-cutting assessment approach.

We realize these structural and philosophical changes are significant. Readers will note that we include focused commentary regarding how philosophical shifts, structural changes, and specific diagnostic changes affect the counseling profession. In the next section, we highlight major diagnostic changes found within the *DSM-5* and carried over to the *DSM-5-TR*. Each of these changes will be explored in greater depth throughout this *Learning Companion*.

Major Diagnostic Changes From *DSM-IV-TR* to *DSM-5*

Although the following changes will be addressed comprehensively in subsequent chapters, we provide a general idea of the major changes from the *DSM-IV-TR* to *DSM-5* covered in this *Learning Companion*.

1. Mental retardation is now referred to as intellectual disability (intellectual developmental disorder). Severity of disability is now determined by adaptive functioning rather than IQ score. New criteria include severity measures for mild, moderate, severe, and profound intellectual disability. Intellectual developmental disorder is placed in parentheses to reflect the term used in the *ICD*.
2. Communication disorders have been restructured to include social communication disorder (SCD). SCD is intended to identify persistent difficulties in the social use of verbal and nonverbal communication. Individuals diagnosed under the *DSM-IV-TR* with pervasive developmental disorder NOS may meet criteria for SCD.
3. Two diagnostic categories have been added to communication disorders: language disorder and speech disorder. Language disorder combines *DSM-IV-TR* expressive and mixed receptive-expressive language disorders.
4. Phonological disorder is now referred to as speech sound disorder.
5. Stuttering is now referred to as childhood-onset fluency disorder.
6. Autism, Asperger's disorder, childhood disintegrative disorder, and pervasive developmental disorder have been replaced with one umbrella diagnosis: autism spectrum disorder. The purpose of this change is to improve diagnostic efficacy, accuracy, and consistency.
7. Specific learning disorders have been expanded to represent distinct disorders that involve problems with the acquisition and/or use of one or more of the following skills: oral language, reading, written, and/or mathematical operations. Now referred to as a specific learning disorder, this diagnosis is intended to combine reading disorder, mathematics disorder, disorder of written expression, and learning disorder NOS.

8. Schizophrenia spectrum and other psychotic disorders remove special treatment of bizarre delusions and hallucinations involving conversations or commentary. Schizophrenia no longer includes attention to five subtypes.
9. Disruptive mood dysregulation disorder is added with the intent of addressing overdiagnosis of bipolar disorder in children. Symptoms include persistent irritability and persistent outbursts three or more times a week for a year.
10. Premenstrual dysphoric disorder is added to depressive disorders.
11. The *DSM-5* eliminates Criterion E, also known as the "grief exclusion," for a major depressive episode. Individuals who have experienced the loss of a loved one can now be diagnosed with depression if they meet other criteria for a major depressive episode.
12. Depressive and bipolar disorders include new specifiers such as with catatonia, with anxious distress, and with mixed features. These specifiers are intended to account for experiences often comorbid with mood disorders yet not part of standard criteria.
13. Anxiety disorders include separate diagnostic categories for agoraphobia and panic disorder. Clients no longer need to experience panic to be diagnosed with agoraphobia.
14. The anxiety disorders section includes diagnostic criteria for panic attacks. The specifier with panic attack may now be used across all diagnostic categories of anxiety and within other sections of the *DSM-5*.
15. A new chapter on obsessive-compulsive and related disorders groups together disorders such as obsessive-compulsive disorder, body dysmorphic disorder, and trichotillomania as opposed to having them scattered throughout the manual. It also includes several new disorders including excoriation (skin-picking) disorder and hoarding disorder. Hoarding disorder is characterized by persistent difficulty disposing of possessions, regardless of monetary or personal value.
16. A new chapter on trauma- and stressor-related disorders groups disorders related to trauma and/or situational stress factors such as reactive attachment disorder, disinhibited social engagement disorder, PTSD, acute stress disorder, and adjustment disorder.
17. PTSD was revised to include four distinct diagnostic clusters (as opposed to three in the *DSM-IV-TR*); the section pays considerable attention to developmentally appropriate criteria for children and adolescents.
18. The feeding and eating disorders section includes a new disorder, binge eating disorder.
19. The personality disorders section has not changed and will maintain the same 10 categories as the *DSM-IV-TR*. However, Section III on emerging measures and models includes a framework for diagnosing personality disorders using trait-specific methodology.
20. The previous sexual and gender identity disorders section is now divided into three separate sections: sexual dysfunctions, gender dysphoria, and paraphilic disorders. Pedophilia disorder is now referred to as pedophilic disorder.
21. The sleep-wake disorders section includes revisions with enhanced attention to biological indicators for diagnosis of many disorders.
22. The substance-related and addictive disorders section is expanded to include addictive disorders; however, only gambling disorder falls in this category. Previous substance dependence and substance abuse criteria are combined into one overarching disorder: substance use disorders. Significant changes have been made to coding, recording, and specifiers for these disorders.
23. The chapter on neurocognitive disorders (previously cognitive disorders) removes language regarding dementia, includes enhanced attention to a range of impairment as evidenced by incorporation of major and mild neurocognitive disorders, and includes additional attention to neurological assessment and basis of the condition.

24. Section III includes several new disorders for study, such as attenuated psychosis syndrome (which describes individuals at high risk for psychosis but do not meet the criteria for a psychotic disorder), internet gaming disorder, nonsuicidal self-injury, and suicidal-behavioral disorder.
25. Section III also contains a detailed discussion of culture and diagnosis, including tools for in-depth cultural assessment and a description of some common cultural syndromes, idioms of distress, and causal explanations relevant to clinical practice.
26. Within each diagnostic category, the NOS diagnosis has been replaced with other specified and unspecified diagnoses. The other specified category is used in situations in which the clinician chooses to communicate the specific reason that the presentation does not meet the criteria for the specific disorder.

Note: Readers will notice that only in Part One of this *Learning Companion* are other specified and unspecified diagnoses included. With the exception of Part One, readers can find more information on other specified and unspecified diagnoses in Chapter 17.

Implications of the *DSM-5-TR*

Implications for Clients

The *DSM-5-TR* changes outlined in this chapter and in the remainder of this *Learning Companion* are likely to have significant implications for clients who experience mental health concerns. Some believe the shift toward viewing mental illness as organic, with less focus on environmental precipitants of symptoms, could potentially reduce the stigma associated with mental disorders (Yang et al., 2010), whereas others wonder whether this philosophy will lead individuals to be viewed as fundamentally flawed rather than as human beings who are struggling with developmental and environmental life tasks (Ben-Zeev et al., 2010; Frances, 2012b). In addition, the potential for dimensional criteria to lower diagnostic thresholds may increase the number of individuals diagnosed and boost false positives, increase labeling and associated stigma, and raise health care costs within the general population (Ben-Zeev et al., 2010; Frances, 2010; Jones, 2012a). Loosening criteria for diagnosis also raises the potential for an increase in unnecessary pharmaceutical treatment among those who seek first-line treatment from medical providers (First, 2011; Frances, 2010, 2012b). Thus, counselors need to be especially careful not to overpathologize symptoms that could be better explained by factors external to individuals (Dailey et al., 2014). Conversely, some proponents of the *DSM-5* believe a more dimensional system could normalize mental health concerns and facilitate help seeking and access to care among consumers (Andrews et al., 2007; Rosenbaum & Pollock, 2002).

Initial research on new diagnostic thresholds seems to indicate an increase in the rates of diagnosis for the general population, particularly in the areas of behavioral addictions and psychosis, as well as depressive, anxiety, eating, and neurocognitive disorders (Frances, 2010; Jones et al., 2012; Mewton et al., 2011). For example, under the new combined substance use disorders, prevalence rates may increase to a staggering 12.4% (Jones et al., 2012). Similarly, lower diagnostic thresholds for ADHD have been noted as areas of concern among mental health professionals (British Psychological Society, 2011). Although these are all legitimate concerns, the reality of lower diagnostic thresholds remains to be seen.

In response to worries regarding loosened criteria, APA published documentation regarding reliability and prevalence of some diagnoses based on the field trials. However, this attempt at clarifying the anticipated increase in diagnoses has been met with strong criticism from scholars who believe the research is not adequate (Frances, 2011, 2012a; Jones, 2012a). It was hoped implementation of the *DSM-5* would result in data that help mental health professionals clarify usefulness of diagnostic thresholds for reaching consumers without artificially inflating diagnostic prevalence rates.

Concerns regarding potential increases in medications accompany concerns around the shift toward viewing mental illness as organic. Many mental health professionals fear that lowering diagnostic thresholds and viewing symptoms as biological will end in more medications prescribed to newly diagnosed clients (Frances, 2010, 2012b; Jones, 2012b). This is of particular concern, given questions about financial relationships between task force members and pharmaceutical companies (Moisse, 2012). Although essential for some clients, the long- and short-term effects of medications are often unknown. For clients, the outcome could be an increase in the recommendation to take medications with less focus on other types of empirically supported treatments that are, by nature, less invasive. Finally, some frequently assigned disorders such as substance abuse, substance dependence, and disorders within NOS categories are no longer included in the *DSM-5*, resulting in reevaluation and perhaps reassignment of long-standing diagnoses.

Implications for Counselors

The *DSM-5* represented the first major structural change to the diagnostic classifications (including the layout, biopsychological model, and collapsing of the multiaxial system) since publication of the *DSM-III* in 1980. As a result, there will always be a need for comprehensive training for counselors to understand diagnostic nomenclature across a wide variety of settings. Radical changes from *DSM-IV-TR* to the *DSM-5* affected seasoned counselors as well as new professionals, counselor educators, and counseling students (Dailey et al., 2014). As such, even subtle changes such as those found within the *DSM-5-TR* must be understood. Without competence in current diagnostic nomenclature, counselors will have trouble with reimbursement and thus suffer reduced credibility and potentially lose the opportunity to help clients. Whether counselors agree or disagree with the philosophy and current classification system, there is no disputing the *DSM* "is the key to millions of dollars in insurance coverage for psychotherapy, hospitalization, and medications" (Kutchins & Kirk, 1997, p. 12).

Because of the pathophysiological model purported in the *DSM-5-TR*, there are extant concerns regarding potential increases in psychopharmacological treatment (Mewton et al., 2011). The potential for a concomitant reduction in psychotherapeutic treatments may significantly affect provision of counseling services and holistic client care (First, 2011; Frances, 2010, 2012b). Because the psychiatric profession is trained in the medical model, the importance of retaining the efficacy of psychotherapy is critical. Counselors can and should advocate on community, state, and national levels in addition to actively engaging in research on evidenced-based practices.

A primary concern for counseling professionals is the lowering of diagnostic thresholds. The criteria for PTSD, acute stress disorder, ADHD, and substance use disorders have all been lowered (Frances, 2010; Jones et al., 2012; Mewton et al., 2011), leading to concerns about vast overdiagnosis (Jones et al., 2012). According to Mewton et al. (2011), reducing the number of criteria for diagnosis in the *DSM-5* could increase prevalence rates of alcohol use disorders by 61.7%. As previously stated, however, the credibility of these studies remains to be seen as others have found low or no impact on prevalence rates (Beesdo-Baum et al., 2011; Pardini et al., 2010). In response to these critiques, David Kupfer, chair of the DSM-5 Task Force, stated,

> Charges that *DSM-5* will lower diagnostic thresholds and lead to a higher prevalence of mental disorders are patently wrong. Results from our field trials, secondary data analyses, and other studies indicate that there will be essentially no change in the overall rates of disorders once *DSM-5* is in use. For most disorders, including the addictive disorders that recently drew

> headlines, thresholds will remain the same or will increase. With other disorders, diagnostic criteria are being refined to hone specificity. The challenge is to balance specificity and sensitivity, to make sure that the language characterizes a disorder as accurately as possible. (Kupfer, 2012, p. 1)

There is also a concern of pathologizing normal behavioral patterns that lead to potential deleterious effects. The extant stigma of incurring a mental health diagnosis, including the cultural and spiritual impact it holds, should be carefully addressed across helping professions. The cost of treatment and ensuing medications can be burdensome as well. Because evidence-based practices support the efficacy of psychotherapeutic treatment, medication can potentially be unnecessary and even dangerous (Olfson & Marcus, 2010). All these factors hold specific implications for counselors across all levels of training.

Future of the *DSM-5-TR*: Where Will It Go From Here?

Even as we work to understand implications of the *DSM-5-TR*, others are already speculating on changes to upcoming iterations of the *DSM*. Research on the utility and efficacy of new diagnostic categories and modifications to disorder descriptions, including greater recognition of cultural expressions of distress and inclusion of risks associated with experiencing racism and discrimination, will affect the future direction of the manual. The ramifications of this, positive and negative, will not be completely understood until the *DSM-5-TR* is fully implemented across a multitude of settings. Ultimately, professional counselors are responsible for using the *DSM* in a manner consistent with the mission of our profession and the *ACA Code of Ethics* (ACA, 2014). A thorough understanding of the revision process, including text revisions, associated changes, the rationale for changes, and the impact of any changes to diagnostic nosology, will undoubtedly help professional counselors decide how they would like to use the *DSM* in practice. We also believe this information will allow counselors to consider possibilities for future revisions and advocacy efforts, giving them a greater voice in the next revision of the *DSM*. As such, in Chapter 5 of this *Learning Companion*, we conclude our discussion of clinical utility and practice implications by including a summary of research and practice implications for counselors. We hope to provide avenues for counseling professionals to have an active and informed voice in upcoming revisions to the *DSM* to advocate for both the profession and our clients.

Questions for Consideration

1. How does the medical model impact diagnosis in an ongoing way?
2. Having read this overview, what do you believe is the most important change to the manual?
3. What are the pros and cons of dimensional assessment, and which one do you endorse?
4. What effect does the new focus and language on discrimination and stigma have on the manual?

References

American Counseling Association. (2014). *ACA code of ethics.* https://www.counseling.org/resources/aca-code-of-ethics.pdf

American Psychiatric Association. (n.d.-a). *DSM history.* https://www.psychiatry.org/psychiatrists/practice/dsm/about-dsm/history-of-the-dsm

American Psychiatric Association. (n.d.-b). *DSM-5-TR online assessment measures.* https://www.psychiatry.org/psychiatrists/practice/dsm/educational-resources/assessment-measures

American Psychiatric Association. (1952). *Diagnostic and statistical manual of mental disorders.*

American Psychiatric Association. (1968). *Diagnostic and statistical manual of mental disorders* (2nd ed.).

American Psychiatric Association. (1980). *Diagnostic and statistical manual of mental disorders* (3rd ed.).

American Psychiatric Association. (1987). *Diagnostic and statistical manual of mental disorders* (3rd ed., rev.).

American Psychiatric Association. (1994). *Diagnostic and statistical manual of mental disorders* (4th ed.).

American Psychiatric Association. (2000). *Diagnostic and statistical manual of mental disorders* (4th ed., text rev.).

American Psychiatric Association. (2011). *DSM-5: APA responds to American Counseling Association concerns.* https://www.psychiatrictimes.com/view/dsm-5-apa-responds-american-counseling-association-concerns

American Psychiatric Association. (2013a). *Diagnostic and statistical manual of mental disorders* (5th ed.). https://doi.org/10.1176/appi.books.9780890425596

American Psychiatric Association. (2013b). *From planning to publication: Developing DSM-5.* https://www.psychiatry.org/File%20Library/Psychiatrists/Practice/DSM/APA_DSM-Development-of-*DSM-5*.pdf

American Psychiatric Association. (2022a). *Attention to culture, racism, and discrimination in the DSM-5-TR.* https://www.psychiatry.org/File%20Library/Psychiatrists/Practice/DSM/*DSM-5-TR*/APA-DSM5TR-AttentiontoCultureRacismandDiscrimination.pdf

American Psychiatric Association. (2022b). *Diagnostic and statistical manual of mental disorders* (5th ed., text rev.). https://doi.org/10.1176/appi.books.9780890425787

American Psychiatric Association. (2022c). *The people behind DSM-5-TR.* https://www.psychiatry.org/File%20Library/Psychiatrists/Practice/DSM/*DSM-5-TR*/APA-DSM5TR-ThePeopleBehindDSM.pdf

Andrews, G., Brugha, T. S., Thase, M. E., Duffy, F. F., Rucci, P., & Slade, T. S. (2007). Dimensionality and the category of major depressive episode. *International Journal of Methods in Psychiatric Research, 16*(S1), S41–S51. https://doi.org/10.1002/mpr.216

Andrews, G., Slade, T., & Issakidis, C. (2002). Deconstructing current comorbidity: Data from the Australian National Survey of Mental Health and Well-Being. *British Journal of Psychiatry, 181*(4), 306–314. https://doi.org/10.1192/bjp.181.4.306

Aviram, R. B., Brodsky, B. S., & Stanley, B. (2006). Borderline personality disorder, stigma, and treatment implications. *Harvard Review of Psychiatry, 14*(5), 249–256. https://doi.org/10.1080/10673220600975121

Bassett, A. S., & Beiser, M. (1991). *DSM-III*: Use of the multiaxial diagnostic system in clinical practice. *The Canadian Journal of Psychiatry, 36*(4), 270–274. https://doi.org/10.1177/070674379103600406

Bedell, J. R., Hunter, R., & Corrigan, P. W. (1997). Current approaches to assessment and treatment of persons with serious mental illness. *Professional Psychology: Research and Practice, 28*(3), 217–228. https://doi.org/10.1037/0735-7028.28.3.217

Beesdo-Baum, K., Winkel, S., Pine, D. S., Hoyer, J., Höfler, M., Lieb, R., & Wittchen, H. (2011). The diagnostic threshold of generalized anxiety disorder in the community: A developmental perspective. *Journal of Psychiatric Research, 45*(7), 962–972. https://doi.org/10.1016/j.jpsychires.2010.12.007

Ben-Zeev, D., Young, M., & Corrigan, P. W. (2010). *DSM-V* and the stigma of mental illness. *Journal of Mental Health, 19*(4), 318–327. https://doi.org/10.3109/09638237.2010.492484

Blashfield, R. K. (1998). Diagnostic models and systems. In A. S. Bellack, M. Herson, & C. R. Reynolds (Eds.), *Clinical psychology: Assessment* (Vol. 4, pp. 57–79). Elsevier Science.

British Psychological Society. (2011). *Response to the American Psychiatric Association: DSM-5 development.* https://dxrevisionwatch.files.wordpress.com/2012/02/dsm-5-2011-bps-response.pdf

Brown, T. M., & Barlow, D. H. (2005). Dimensional versus categorical classification of mental disorders in the fifth edition of the *Diagnostic and statistical manual of mental disorders* and beyond: Comment on the special section. *Journal of Abnormal Psychology, 114*(4), 551–556. https://doi.org/10.1037/0021-843x.114.4.551

Dailey, S. F., Gill, C. S., Karl, S. L., & Barrio Minton, C. A. (2014). *DSM-5 learning companion for counselors.* American Counseling Association.

Demjaha, A., Morgan, K., Morgan, C., Landau, S., Dean, K., Reichenberg, A., Sham, P. C., Fearon, P., Hutchinson, G., Jones, P. B., Murray, R. M., & Dazzan, P. (2009). Combining dimensional and categorical representation of psychosis: The way forward for *DSM-V* and *ICD-11*? *Psychological Medicine, 39*(12), 1943–1955. https://doi.org/10.1017/s0033291709990651

Eriksen, K., & Kress, V. E. (2006). The *DSM* and the professional counseling identity: Bridging the gap. *Journal of Mental Health Counseling, 28*(3), 202–217. https://doi.org/10.17744/mehc.28.3.4f39a6wr1n3fceh2

First, M. B. (2010). Clinical utility in the revision of the *Diagnostic and statistical manual of mental disorders (DSM). Professional Psychology: Research and Practice, 41*(6), 465–473. https://doi.org/10.1037/a0021511

First, M. B. (2011). *DSM-5* proposals for mood disorders: A cost-benefit analysis. *Current Opinion in Psychiatry, 24*(1), 1–9. https://doi.org/10.1097/yco.0b013e328340b594

First, M. B., Pincus, H. A., Levine, J. B., Williams, J. B. W., Üstün, B., & Peele, R. (2004). Clinical utility as a criterion for revising psychiatric diagnoses. *American Journal of Psychiatry, 161*(6), 946–954. https://doi.org/10.1176/appi.ajp.161.6.946

Frances, A. (2010, March). Opening Pandora's box: The 19 worst suggestions for *DSM-5. Psychiatric Times,* 27(3), 1–3.

Frances, A. (2011, June 3). Who needs *DSM-5*? A strong warning comes from professional counselors. *Psychology Today.* http://www.psychologytoday.com/blog/dsm5-in-distress/201106/who-needs-dsm-5

Frances, A. (2012a, October 30). *DSM 5* field trials discredit APA. *Psychology Today.* http://www.psychologytoday.com/blog/dsm5-in-distress/201210/dsm-5-field-trials-discredit-apa

Frances, A. (2012b, December 2). *DSM 5* is guide not bible—Ignore its ten worst changes. *Psychology Today.* http://www.psychologytoday.com/blog/dsm5-in-distress/201212/dsm-5-is-guide-not-bible-ignore-its-ten-worst-changes

Frances, A., & First, M. B. (2011). Hebephilia is not a mental disorder in *DSM-IV-TR* and should not become one in *DSM-5. Journal of the American Academy of Psychiatry and the Law Online, 39*(1), 78–85.

Fritz, J. C. (2012). *"She's such a borderline": Exploring the stigma of borderline personality disorder through the eyes of the clinician* [Unpublished doctoral dissertation]. Smith College School for Social Work.

Gever, J. (2012, May 10). *DSM-5: What's in, what's out.* http://www.medpagetoday.com/Meeting-Coverage/APA/32619

Hansen, J. T. (2013). *Philosophical issues in counseling and psychotherapy: Encounters with four questions about knowing, effectiveness, and truth.* Rowman & Littlefield.

Hansen, J. T. (2014). Talking about counseling: A plea to return to humanistic language. *The Journal of Humanistic Counseling, 53*(1), 22–33. https://doi.org//10.1002/j.2161-1939.2014.00047.x

Health Insurance Portability and Accountability Act of 1996, Pub. L. 104–191, 110 Stat. 1936.

Hinkle, J. S. (1999). A voice from the trenches: A reaction to Ivey and Ivey (1998). *Journal of Counseling & Development, 77*(4), 474–483. https://doi.org/10.1002/j.1556-6676.1999.tb02475.x

Hong, R., Murphy, J., Michalak, E. E., Chakrabarty, T., Wang, Z., Parikh, S. V., Culpepper, L., Yatham, L. N., Lam, R. W., & Chen, J. (2021). Implementing measurement-based care for depression: Practical solutions for psychiatrists and primary care physicians. *Neuropsychiatric Disease and Treatment, 17,* 79–90. https://doi.org/10.2147/ndt.s283731

Houts, A. C. (2002). Discovery, invention, and the expansion of the modern diagnostic and statistical manuals of mental disorders. In M. L. Malik & L. E. Beutler (Eds.), *Rethinking the DSM: A psychological perspective* (pp. 17–65). American Psychological Association.

Ivey, A. E., & Ivey, M. B. (1998). Reframing *DSM-IV*: Positive strategies from developmental counseling and therapy. *Journal of Counseling & Development, 76*(3), 334–350. https://doi.org/10.1002/j.1556-6676.1998.tb02550.x

Jampala, V. C., Sierles, F. S., & Taylor, M. J. (1986). Consumers' views of *DSM-III*: Attitudes and practices of U.S. psychiatrists and 1984 graduating psychiatric residents. *American Journal of Psychiatry, 143*(2), 148–153. https://doi.org/10.1176/ajp.143.2.148

Jones, K. D. (2012a). A critique of the *DSM-5* field trials. *Journal of Nervous and Mental Disease, 200*(6), 517–519. https://doi.org/10.1097/nmd.0b013e318257c699

Jones, K. D. (2012b). Dimensional and cross-cutting assessment in the *DSM-5*. *Journal of Counseling & Development, 90*(4), 481–487. https://doi.org/10.1002/j.1556-6676.2012.00059.x

Jones, K. D., Gill, C. S., & Ray, S. (2012). Review of the proposed *DSM-5* substance use disorder. *Journal of Addictions & Offender Counseling, 33*(2), 115–123. https://doi.org/10.1002/j.2161-1874.2012.00009.x

Katragadda, S., & Schubiner, H. (2007). ADHD in children, adolescents, and adults. *Primary Care, 34*(2), 317–341. https://doi.org/10.1016/j.pop.2007.04.012

Kessler, R. C., Zhao, S., Blazer, D. G., & Swartz, M. S. (1997). Prevalence, correlates, and course of minor depression and major depression in the National Comorbidity Survey. *Journal of Affective Disorders, 45*(1–2), 19–30. https://doi.org/10.1016/s0165-0327(97)00056-6

Kraemer, H. C. (2007). *DSM* categories and dimensions in clinical and research contexts. *International Journal of Methods in Psychiatric Research, 16*(S1), S8–S15. https://doi.org/10.1002/mpr.211

Kraemer, H. C., Noda, A., & O'Hara, R. (2004). Categorical versus dimensional approaches to diagnosis: Methodological challenges. *Journal of Psychiatric Research, 38*(1), 17–25. https://doi.org/10.1016/s0022-3956(03)00097-9

Kupfer, D. J. (2012, June 1). Dr. Kupfer defends *DSM-5*. *Medscape*. https://www.medscape.com/viewarticle/764735

Kupfer, D. J., First, M. B., & Regier, D. A. (Eds.). (2002). *A research agenda for DSM-V.* American Psychiatric Association.

Kupfer, D. J., & Regier, D. A. (2011). Neuroscience, clinical evidence, and the future of psychiatric classification in *DSM-5*. *American Journal of Psychiatry, 168*(7), 672–674. https://doi.org/10.1176/appi.ajp.2011.11020219

Kutchins, H., & Kirk, S. A. (1997). *Making us crazy: DSM—The psychiatric bible and the creation of mental disorders.* Free Press.

Magee, W. P., Eaton, W. W., Wittchen, H., McGonagle, K. A., & Kessler, R. C. (1996). Agoraphobia, simple phobia, and social phobia in the National Comorbidity Survey. *Archives of General Psychiatry, 53*(2), 159–168. https://doi.org/10.1001/archpsyc.1996.01830020077009

Malik, M. L., & Beutler, L. E. (2002). *Rethinking the DSM: A psychological perspective.* American Psychological Association.

Maser, J. D., Kaelber, C. T., & Weise, R. E. (1991). International use and attitudes toward *DSM-III* and *DSM-III-R*: Growing consensus in psychiatric classification. *Journal of Abnormal Psychology, 100*(3), 271–279. https://doi.org/10.1037/0021-843x.100.3.271

Mewton, L., Slade, T., McBride, O., Grove, R., & Teesson, M. (2011). An evaluation of the proposed *DSM-5* alcohol use disorder criteria using Australian national data. *Addiction, 106*(5), 941–950. https://doi.org/10.1111/j.1360-0443.2010.03340.x

Miller, J. D., & Levy, K. N. (2011). Personality and personality disorders in the *DSM-5*: Introduction to the special issue. *Personality Disorders: Theory, Research, and Treatment, 2*(1), 1–3. https://doi.org/10.1037/a0022509

Millon, T. (1991). Classification in psychopathology: Rationale, alternatives, and standards. *Journal of Abnormal Psychology, 100*(3), 245–261. https://doi.org/10.1037/0021-843X.100.3.245

Mineka, S., Watson, D. I., & Clark, L. A. (1998). Comorbidity of anxiety and unipolar mood disorders. *Annual Review of Psychology, 49*(1), 377–412. https://doi.org/10.1146/annurev.psych.49.1.377

Moisse, K. (2012, March 13). *DSM-5* criticized for financial conflicts of interest. *ABC News*. http://abcnews.go.com/Health/MindMoodNews/dsm-fire-financial-conflicts/story?id=15909673

Myers, J. E. (1992). Wellness, prevention, development: The cornerstone of the profession. *Journal of Counseling & Development, 71*(2), 136–139. https://doi.org/10.1002/j.1556-6676.1992.tb02188.x

Myers, J. E., Sweeney, T. J., & Witmer, J. M. (2000). The wheel of wellness counseling for wellness: A holistic model for treatment planning. *Journal of Counseling & Development, 78*(3), 251–266. https://doi.org/10.1002/j.1556-6676.2000.tb01906.x
National Center for Health Statistics. (1998). *The international classification of diseases, ninth revision, clinical modification (ICD-9-CM).* Centers for Disease Control and Prevention. https://www.cdc.gov/nchs/icd/icd9cm.htm
National Center for Health Statistics. (2014). *The international classification of diseases, 10th revision, clinical modification (ICD-10-CM).* Centers for Disease Control and Prevention. https://www.cdc.gov/nchs/icd/icd-10-cm.htm
National Center for Health Statistics. (2023). *The international classification of diseases, 10th revision, clinical modification (ICD-10-CM).* Centers for Disease Control and Prevention. https://www.cdc.gov/nchs/icd/icd-10-cm.htm
Olfson, M., & Marcus, S. C. (2010). National trends in outpatient psychotherapy. *American Journal of Psychiatry, 167*(12), 1456–1463. https://doi.org/10.1176/appi.ajp.2010.10040570
Pardini, D. A., Frick, P. J., & Moffitt, T. E. (2010). Building an evidence base for *DSM-5* conceptualizations of oppositional defiant disorder and conduct disorder: Introduction to the special section. *Journal of Abnormal Psychology, 119*(4), 683–688. https://doi.org/10.1037/a0021441
Paris, J. (2013). *The intelligent clinician's guide to the DSM-5.* Oxford University Press.
Phillips, M. R. (2016). Would the use of dimensional measures improve the utility of psychiatric diagnoses? *World Psychiatry, 15*(1), 38. https://doi.org/10.1002/wps.20289
Regier, D. A., Narrow, W. E., Kuhl, E. A., & Kupfer, D. J. (2009). The conceptual development of *DSM-5*. *American Journal of Psychiatry, 166*(6), 645–650. https://doi.org/10.1176/appi.ajp.2009.09020279
Rogler, L. H. (1997). Making sense of historical changes in the *Diagnostic and statistical manual of mental disorders*: Five propositions. *Journal of Health and Social Behavior, 38*(1), 9–20. https://doi.org/10.2307/2955358
Rosenbaum, J. F., & Pollock, R. (2002, June 20). *DSM V*: Plans and perspectives. *Medscape Psychiatry.* http://www.medscape.org/viewarticle/436403
Sanders, J. O. (2011). A distinct language and a historic pendulum: The evolution of the *Diagnostic and statistical manual of mental disorders. Archives of Psychiatric Nursing, 25*(6), 394–403. https://doi.org/10.1016/j.apnu.2010.10.002
Scotti, J. R., & Morris, T. L. (2000). Diagnosis and classification. In M. Hersen & R. T. Ammerman (Eds.), *Advanced abnormal child psychology* (pp. 15–32). Erlbaum.
Sedler, M. J. (2016). Medicalization in psychiatry: The medical model, descriptive diagnosis, and lost knowledge. *Medicine Health Care and Philosophy, 19*(2), 247–252. https://doi.org/10.1007/s11019-015-9670-5
Spitzer, R., & Fleiss, J. L. (1974). A re-analysis of the reliability of psychiatric diagnosis. *British Journal of Psychiatry, 125,* 341–347. https://doi.org/10.1192/bjp.125.4.341
Subica, A. M., Claypoole, K. H., & Wylie, A. M. (2012). PTSD's mediation of the relationships between trauma, depression, substance abuse, mental health, and physical health in individuals with severe mental illness: Evaluating a comprehensive model. *Schizophrenia Research, 136*(1–3), 104–109. https://doi.org/10.1016/j.schres.2011.10.018
Trivedi, M. H., Rush, A. J., Wisniewski, S. R., Nierenberg, A. A., Warden, D., Ritz, L., Norquist, G., Howland, R. H., Lebowitz, B. D., McGrath, P. J., Shores-Wilson, K., Biggs, M. M., Balasubramani, G. K., & Fava, M. (2006). Evaluation of outcomes with citalopram for depression using measurement-based care in STARD: Implications for clinical practice. *American Journal of Psychiatry, 163*(1), 28–40. https://doi.org/10.1176/appi.ajp.163.1.28
Widiger, T. A., & Coker, L. A. (2003). Mental disorders as discrete clinical conditions: Dimensional versus categorical classification. In M. Hersen & S. M. Turner (Eds.), *Adult psychopathology and diagnosis* (4th ed., pp. 3–35). Wiley.
Widiger, T. A., & Frances, A. (1985). The *DSM-III* personality disorders: Perspective from psychology. *Archives of General Psychiatry, 42*(6), 615–623. https://doi.org/10.1001/archpsyc.1985.01790290097011
Widiger, T. A., & Samuel, D. B. (2005). Diagnostic categories or dimensions? A question for the *Diagnostic and statistical manual of mental disorders–fifth edition. Journal of Abnormal Psychology, 114*(4), 494–504. https://doi.org/10.1037/0021-843x.114.4.494

Wilson, M. P. (1993). *DSM-III* and the transformation of American psychiatry: A history. *American Journal of Psychiatry, 150*(3), 399–410. https://doi.org/10.1176/ajp.150.3.399
World Health Organization. (1949). *International statistical classification of diseases, 6th revision.*
World Health Organization. (1968). *International statistical classification of diseases, 8th revision.*
World Health Organization. (1975). *International statistical classification of diseases, 9th revision.*
World Health Organization. (2010). *World Health Organization Disability Assessment Schedule 2.0–WHODAS 2.0.*
Yang, L. H., Wonpat-Borja, A. J., Opler, M. G., & Corcoran, C. M. (2010). Potential stigma associated with inclusion of the psychosis risk syndrome in the *DSM-V*: An empirical question. *Schizophrenia Research, 120*(1–3), 42–48. https://doi.org/10.1016/j.schres.2010.03.012
Zimmerman, M., & McGlinchey, J. (2008). Why don't psychiatrists use scales to measure outcome when treating depressed patients? *Journal of Clinical Psychiatry, 69*(12), 1916–1919. https://doi.org/10.4088/jcp.v69n1209

Introduction
to Diagnostic Changes

Part One to Part Four Overview

In the remaining chapters, we provide an overview of changes to the diagnostic criteria from the *DSM-5* to the *DSM-5-TR*, as well as render comprehensive information for all new diagnoses. We help readers understand these changes and additions by highlighting similarities and differences among diagnostic clusters, explaining common differential diagnoses, and providing case studies and questions to enhance clinical utility. Because we are licensed professional counselors with unique areas of expertise in addictions, rehabilitation, career, and school counseling, we present this information in a way that closely relates to the work that our readers, as counselors, typically perform.

In terms of organization of this *Learning Companion*, the reader will find diagnostic classifications presented in a sequence of what counselors or counselors-in-training typically encounter. For example, mood and anxiety disturbances are addressed before diagnoses commonly made by other professionals, such as neurodevelopmental disorders. Our intent is to target areas that will most significantly affect counselors. While no guidebook can speak to the myriad tasks that counselors perform or the wide range of settings in which counselors work, we did organize this *Learning Companion* in such a way that it is useful and relevant to work typically performed by counselors. Rather than adhering to the developmental format of the *DSM-5-TR* or ordering our chapters by prevalence within the general population, we have organized this book by what counselors most frequently diagnose. With the role of a counselor in mind, the *Learning Companion* is divided, by relevance, into four sections:

Part One:	Clinical Utility and Practice Implications for Counselors
Part Two:	Changes and Implications Involving Mood, Anxiety, and Stressor-Related Concerns

Part Three:	Changes and Implications Involving Addictive, Impulse-Control, and Specific Behavior-Related Concerns
Part Four:	Changes and Implications Involving Diagnoses Commonly Made by Other Professionals

The goal of this organizational structure is to assist counselors in their everyday work. For example, following a foundational discussion of clinical utility and practice implications of the *DSM-5-TR* in Part One, the first chapter in Part Two addresses depressive disorders because depression is one of the most prevalent mental illnesses worldwide. The third chapter in Part Two addresses anxiety disorders, which is, to date, the most common class of mental illness present in the general population. Aside from being relevant to the work that most counselors perform, this layout parallels the *DSM-5-TR* by grouping together diagnoses that have higher rates of co-occurrence. Although all diagnoses have clinical utility within a counseling setting, we organized this *Learning Companion* in a way that is most relevant to the actual work that counselors do. In keeping with our aim of making this *Learning Companion* an accessible and handy guidebook for readers, we have grouped the references of related chapters at the end of each part of the book.

Part One

Clinical Utility and Practice Implications for Counselors

Introduction

In Part One, we cover sociocultural issues in diagnosis, provide an overview of culturally responsive case conceptualization, and describe practice implications for counselors using the *DSM-5-TR*. In Chapter 3, Sociocultural Issues in Diagnosis in the *DSM-5-TR*, we provide a brief description of sociocultural considerations and context in the *DSM-5-TR* and focus the rest of the chapter on systemic issues with diagnosis and reducing biases. We placed this chapter at the beginning of Part One because of the renewed focus on the impact of culture, race, racism, and discrimination on mental health and diagnostic practice. We focus on systemic impact in terms of oppression and resulting mental health consequences, factors that should influence how professional counselors conceptualize and diagnose their clients. Chapter 4, Culturally Responsive Case Conceptualization and Treatment Planning: Cultural Formulation, includes issues surrounding case conceptualization, offers a model toward integrating cultural formulation into conceptualization, and reviews the Cultural Formulation Interview in the *DSM-5-TR*. In Chapter 5, Practice Implications for Counselors, we continue looking ahead with a focus on clinical practice. This chapter includes a reflection on diagnosis and the counseling profession, coding and recording issues, and diagnostic assessments and other screening instruments.

Throughout Part One, we urge counselors to become advocates for appropriate and empirically based uses of diagnostic nomenclature, holding these processes alongside our developmental and strength-based professional identities. We encourage counseling professionals to become stewards of diagnostic research. Regardless of the platform, counselors need to find their voice within the future of diagnostic nomenclature so our profession can have a stronger foothold in these discussions.

Chapter 3

Sociocultural Issues in Diagnosis in the *DSM-5-TR*

Individuals' social and cultural identities encompass a wide variety of beliefs, values, norms, and expectations for behavior. Although the complex interplay of cultural and social identities makes every person so beautifully unique, it may affect how counselors recognize and diagnose. The purpose of this chapter is to help professional counselors understand sociocultural issues associated with the *DSM* and understand how sociocultural factors influence clinical assessment, presentation, and treatment of mental health concerns in their own counseling practice. We also aim to help counselors consider how the *DSM* may contribute to pathologizing cultural norms and perpetuate or exacerbate health disparities. By facilitating this understanding, counselors can take a more holistic and culturally sustaining approach to diagnostic assessment.

We begin this chapter by discussing how culture is defined in the *DSM-5-TR*, including recent updates intended to better reflect the impact of culture, race, and social determinants on health. We continue with an explanation of sociocultural considerations in diagnosis and treatment planning, as well as common critiques of the *DSM*. We introduce an ecosystemic framework that can guide counselors in understanding limitations of the *DSM-5-TR* classification system and opportunities to approach diagnosis and treatment planning more holistically. We highlight the importance of understanding diagnostic bias and how this influences what counselors "see" and don't "see." We continue with a discussion of adverse childhood experiences, how the *DSM-5-TR* may perpetuate systemic issues of racism and discrimination, and how the *DSM* has been criticized for pathologizing systemic barriers to equitable health outcomes for many individuals. In all of this, we emphasize that embracing a culturally responsive understanding of the *DSM-5-TR* is vital for accurate diagnostic assessment and treatment.

Sociocultural Considerations and the *DSM-5-TR*

Sociocultural considerations refer to the influence of social and cultural factors on individuals' behavior, attitudes, beliefs, and experiences. In the context of mental health diagnosis, attention to sociocultural considerations is vital. Without fully understanding the cultural context in which clients experience and express concerns, counselors are unable to diagnose effectively and accurately. Within Section II of the *DSM-5-TR*, social and cultural factors pertinent to each disorder are found in text descriptions under culture-, sex-, and gender-related diagnostic issues; if sufficient empirical evidence is available, these are also addressed under prevalence. Section III of the manual addresses considerations relevant to cultural context, including definitions of culture, race, and ethnicity; guidelines for cultural assessment; and culturally specific concepts of distress with which many clinicians are unfamiliar. These factors can include clients' and counselors' racial, ethnic, gender, and affectional identity; practices related to mental health and wellness; structural factors associated with health disparities; and other aspects of identity.

Defining Culture in the *DSM-5-TR*

The range of possible interactions between sociocultural identities and clinical diagnoses is broad and multifaceted. Understanding how the *DSM-5-TR* defines culture, race, and ethnicity is important. In Section III of the *DSM-5-TR*, culture is explicitly defined as

> systems of knowledge, concepts, rules, and practices that are learned and transmitted across generations. Culture includes language, religion, and spirituality, family structures, life-cycle stages, ceremonial rituals, customs, and ways of understanding health and illness, as well as moral, political, economic, and legal systems. Cultures are open, dynamic systems that undergo continuous change over time. . . . [C]ulture involves background knowledge, values, and assumptions that remain implicit or presumed and so may be difficult for individuals to describe. (APA, 2022, p. 860)

Clients' cultural contexts strongly influence how they present and report mental health concerns. For example, in Western cultures, major depressive disorder is often characterized by sadness, tearfulness, hopelessness, and guilt, whereas in some Eastern cultures, somatic complaints (e.g., fatigue, headaches, back pain), irritability, and decreased appetite are more commonly reported. Indigenous cultures may present with spiritual or cultural distress, including disconnection from community, spiritual loss, and sense of powerlessness. Counselors would expect to see more nuanced variations based on clients' ethnic and racial identity, age, gender identity, and other cultural identities relevant to the client. This example demonstrates the wide range of symptom expressions that can be associated with even a highly generalized comparison of Western, Eastern, and Indigenous expressions of major depressive disorder. These variations, if not fully understood, can lead to misdiagnosis, underdiagnosis, or pathologizing of cultural norms. The *DSM-5-TR*'s definition of culture clearly emphasizes the importance of understanding cross-cultural variations:

> It [is] crucial not to overgeneralize cultural information or stereotype groups in terms of fixed cultural traits. In relation to diagnosis, it is essential to recognize that all forms of illness and distress, including the *DSM* disorders, are shaped by cultural contexts. Culture influences how individuals fashion their identities, as well as how they interpret and respond to symptoms and illness. (APA, 2022, p. 860)

Contextual Clarity

Before diving deeper into sociocultural considerations and diagnosis, we should clarify that our discussion of social and cultural factors is not exclusive to clients or limited within the context of historically marginalized groups. First, counselors bring their own biases, stereotypes, and prejudices to diagnostic practice. Counselors are responsible for engaging in a thorough, continuous understanding of how their social and cultural experiences may enhance, impede, or bias the counseling process. Failure to do so can lead counselors to overlook important cultural factors and misinterpret symptoms and experiences that impact mental health. Next, information presented in this chapter is relevant to all populations and communities. Reducing discussion to one that narrowly addresses specific cultural groups only perpetuates the idea that there are (or should be) dominant cultural norms and values. Within the context of clinical assessment, this negates differences based on symptom expression and etiology (including systemic oppression and racism) and supports the position that sociocultural factors are more relevant to prevention and treatment but not necessarily relevant to diagnostic classification systems.

Discussion of sociocultural disparities relevant to racialized communities, immigrants, refugees, and other historically marginalized populations is useful, and we work to do so throughout this *Learning Companion*. Still, it would be a great disservice to our readers and clients to infer cultural conditions are monolithic. A monolithic lens assumes that all members of a particular cultural group (e.g., Black Americans, Latinx adolescents, cisgender Asian Americans) have the same beliefs, values, experiences, and behaviors and that these cultural characteristics remain static over time (O'Hara et al., 2021). Widely problematic for a variety of reasons, this perspective ignores the diversity and complexity of cultural experiences and perspectives within a given cultural group. This view can lead to stereotypes and oversimplification of cultural experiences. People from the same cultural background have unique and varied experiences and may hold different beliefs, values, and behaviors—in addition to shared group membership.

It is more helpful to adopt a dynamic view of sociocultural identity that recognizes the diversity and complexity of cultural experiences and perspectives. Embracing the multiple identities and group memberships of individuals allows counselors to have greater understanding of clients and their experiences. Diagnostic classification is philosophically flawed and often in direct opposition to the profession of counseling. Counselors, with a professional identity that is firmly rooted in prevention and wellness, can dually understand and use diagnostic classification systems to enhance access to systems of care while also rejecting monolithic, medical models. To embrace a culturally sustaining and socially just approach to diagnostic assessment, counselors must have a working knowledge of how to use the *DSM-5-TR*, including how the manual may perpetuate or exacerbate health disparities, stereotypes, and biases. In the next section, we discuss how social and cultural factors have, and have not, been included in the *DSM-5-TR*.

Sociocultural Inclusion Within the *DSM-5-TR*

As discussed in the previous chapter, the Ethnoracial Equity and Inclusion Work Group and the Cross-Cutting Culture Review Group made several changes to the *DSM-5-TR* to address concerns about cultural sensitivity and the potential for disparities in diagnosis and treatment. In addition to reviewing and updating all diagnostic chapters in Section II to reflect more culturally inclusive and nonstigmatizing language, these work groups attempted to better recognize the role health disparities, such as access to care, play in the development and experience of mental health conditions. Additional information on how these disparities may impact diagnosis and treatment has been included throughout the *DSM-5-TR*.

Altha Stewart, member of the *DSM-5-TR* Ethnoracial Equity and Inclusion Work Group, noted,

> We were highly committed to use of language that challenged the view that race and genetics are the same thing. . . . We offered disclaimers and clarifications whenever needed to provide the reader with background information such as when higher prevalence rates of disorders are reported in the Black or Indigenous communities. (Moran, 2022, paras. 7, 8)

For example, earlier editions of the manual indicated that alcohol use disorder "is clearly greater among Native Americans and Alaska Natives (12.1%) than among whites (8.9%)" (APA, 2013b, p. 493). Roberto Lewis-Fernández, cochair of the Ethnoracial Equity and Inclusion Work Group and the Cross-Cutting Culture Review Group, acknowledged that this information was erroneously based on limited samples sizes that could not be generalized to all tribal nations, also noting that not all tribal nations have high rates of substance use (Moran, 2022). In addition to erroneous overgeneralizations for substance use among tribal nations, APA also noted that "the studies and resulting language did not reflect the social determinants of health and mental health—including a history of collective trauma—that may impact rates of substance use disorders" (see Moran, 2022, para. 10).

In addition to making several updates to reflect more rigorous examination of terminology and content within diagnostic criteria, the *DSM-5-TR* includes an expanded Section III to provide additional information about cultural context and diagnostic assessment. There is greater recognition of cultural expressions of distress and additional guidance on how to assess symptoms in a culturally sensitive manner (see APA, 2022, pp. 859–880). A slightly expanded discussion on cultural concepts of distress, found in Section III, provides context and examples of mental health conditions that may have unique meanings or presentations in different cultural contexts.

Cross-Cultural Variations in Diagnostic Assessment

Cross-cultural variations in diagnostic assessment refer to differences in how disorders are understood and diagnosed across different cultures and societies (La Roche et al., 2015). These variations may arise because of differences in attitudes toward mental health based on cultural beliefs, values, and social norms, as well as differences in the prevalence of certain traits and disorders. Some common cross-cultural variations include differences in the prevalence of specific disorders, differences in interpreting criteria used to diagnose disorders, and differences in perception of disorders (Bredström, 2019; Eap et al., 2010). For example, some cultures may have a greater emphasis on collectivism and interdependence, which may lead to a different understanding of symptoms associated with dependent personality disorder. As an extension to understanding cultural concepts of distress, it is important for counselors to be aware of differences in help seeking and utilize strategies to provide accurate and culturally informed diagnosis and treatment.

Symptom Expression and Experience

Different cultures have different norms and expectations for behavior, which can affect how symptoms are expressed and experienced by clients. People from some cultures may view certain beliefs or behaviors as appropriate or acceptable, whereas those from other cultures may consider these same beliefs or behaviors as problematic. Known as "cultural concepts of distress" in the *DSM*, these references apply to current knowledge associated with how cultural beliefs, values, and experiences shape perception of symptoms (APA, 2022). Cultural context can strongly influence the manifestation, severity, and interpretation of mental health symptoms. Three concepts—cultural idioms, cultural explanations, and cultural syndromes—are described in the *DSM-5-TR* to help define culture-related suffering and concerns that are not directly captured with current nosology. *Cultural idioms* are "behaviors or linguistic terms, metaphors, phrases, or ways of talking about symptoms, problems, or suffering that are commonly used by individuals with similar cultural backgrounds to convey a wide range of concerns" (APA, 2022, p. 871). *Cultural explanations* are contextually relevant etiological origins of disease or distress which, like cultural idioms, are not specifically noted in the *DSM*. *Cultural syndromes* are specific sets of symptoms and behaviors that have been reported and are widely recognized within cultural contexts.

The *DSM-5-TR* provides examples of symptoms and behaviors that are strongly influenced by cultural beliefs, values, and practices. To encourage culturally sensitive assessment and treatment, these examples are meant to be illustrative, considering cultural differences in how distress is perceived and experienced (APA, 2022). Counselors need to understand that these are *examples* and serve to demonstrate how culture can influence symptom expression. Examples within the manual include:

- *Ataque de nervios*: A syndrome reported in Latinx cultures characterized by sudden and intense episodes of emotional distress, dissociation, and feelings of being out of control, ataque de nervios is often acute and triggered by a stressful or traumatic event.
- *Khyâl cap*: Also referred to as "khyâl attacks," this syndrome within a Cambodian cultural context has symptoms similar to panic attacks (e.g., dizziness, shortness of breath) associated with concerns that khyâl (wind) will rise in the body and blood.
- *Hikikomori*: A syndrome based on Japanese terminology of hiku (meaning to pull back) and moru (seclude oneself), hikikomori is reported within Japanese, South Korean, and Japanese American cultural contexts marked by severe social withdrawal.

These examples, and others presented in the *DSM-5-TR* (see pp. 873–879), are not exhaustive. They are meant to provide illustrative context for how distress can be expressed, experienced, and reported. The larger point is that careful understanding, consideration, and consultation must be conducted before mental health professionals can truly understand cultural idioms, explanations, and syndromes. The stark difference between professional counselors, whose identity "empowers diverse individuals, families, and groups to accomplish mental health, wellness, education, and career goals" (Kaplan et al., 2014, p. 366), and other mental health providers is that the *DSM* is not our first introduction to the centrality of culture in experiences of mental health and well-being. Constance Dunlap, member of the Ethnoracial Equity and Inclusion Work Group, noted that the *DSM-5* "might be the first place our trainees [psychiatry residents and fellow] are exposed to the effects of race on mental health and on diagnosis" (see Moran, 2022, para. 15). The depth with which professional counselors are prepared in multicultural and social justice competencies is dramatically different from the training experiences of other mental health professionals.

Approaches to Help Seeking and Coping

In addition to influencing how symptoms are reported and experienced, clients' cultural values and beliefs can influence their help seeking. Some communities have traditional healers, faith leaders, or ways of coping with mental health issues that may not be recognized or respected by Western mental health professionals (Gill et al., 2020). Counselors need to recognize that many individuals tend to seek help from others within their community or family rather than from the broader medical or psychiatric community (Dailey, 2018). These systems often serve as a huge resource for coping. Even after accessing counseling, a person's cultural beliefs, values, and experiences impact the counseling process. It is important for counselors to consider a client's cultural context when assessing and treating the client. Failing to consider these factors can perpetuate health disparities and bias in the mental health system.

Individuals use a variety of coping strategies and techniques to manage stress and distress. Coping can be influenced by various factors, which are often direct manifestations of cultural beliefs, values, traditions, and practices. For example, relying on family, friends, and community members for emotional support and practical assistance may be common or expected within some clients' cultural context but considered unacceptable by others. Many individuals turn to religious or spiritual beliefs and practices for comfort and guidance in times of stress, but clients who feel abandoned by their divine power or who have been injured in faith communities may have trouble seeking comfort in this way (Gill et al., 2020). Turning to traditional healing practices to manage physical and mental health symptoms is not uncommon, but counselors must understand that these practices may directly challenge or conflict with the assumptions of contemporary treatment. Kirmayer (2013) stated,

> The understanding of illness and healing within biomedicine tends to be narrowly conceived in terms of physiological processes and does not always attend to powerful psychological, social, moral, and political dimensions of medical interventions. These wider dimensions have demonstrable physiological effects as well as involving psychological and social processes, which are important in their own right for individual well-being and recovery from illness. (p. 40)

Counselors need to uncover, seek to understand, and respect these culturally sustaining strategies that can be an important lifeline for clients seeking relief from mental disorder.

Cultural Mistrust

Counselors should be cognizant of how cultural norms, stigmatization, medical trauma, and cultural mistrust can affect access to care (Mukhtar, 2023). Cultural mistrust originally referred to African Americans' distrust of White-controlled institutions stemming from race-based experimentation (e.g., Tuskegee Syphilis Study, forced sterilization; see Jaiswal & Halkitis, 2019; Lawrence, 2000; Whaley, 2001). Cultural mistrust is a critical factor in understanding underutilization of health services among minoritized populations and is related to stigmatization and treatment satisfaction (Alvarez et al., 2022; Brooks & Hopkins, 2017). Understandably, cultural mistrust has also resulted in considerable deficits in biomedical research participation. While scholars may blame historically minoritized groups as subscribing to conspiracy theories (Earnshaw et al., 2019), Jaiswal and Halkitis (2019) noted,

> It is also too common that researchers and clinicians impose their will, research and clinical programs on populations without necessarily understanding the group's particular needs or desires. In this sense, researchers' prioritization of their own agenda can also fuel mistrust. (p. 81)

Critiques of the *DSM-5-TR*

Eurocentrism

One of the major sociocultural critiques of the *DSM-5-TR* is that the way in which mental disorders are conceptualized is based on Western cultural values, which may not always be applicable or relevant to individuals seeking mental health services. This bias can lead to a lack of recognition of cultural differences in symptoms and experiences, which can result in misdiagnosis. Understanding the narrative descriptions of each disorder is imperative to making an accurate diagnosis, but it should be done with caution. The *DSM-5-TR* does not explicitly discuss or use criteria that are based on Eastern or Indigenous cultural experiences. As such, it is not uncommon to see disorders diagnosed more or less frequently across racial or cultural groups, making it very difficult to differentiate whether prevalence data are related to the Eurocentric views of mental health or whether a particular disorder is actually more common in specific cultural groups. As with the earlier substance use example with Native American tribal nations, disparities in rates of schizophrenia among African American are well documented (Perry et al., 2013; Schwartz & Blankenship, 2014).

A deeper look may reveal that prevalence rates among the general population are more closely tied to how symptoms are interpreted based on societal norms and values. While there is no conclusive evidence as to *why* African Americans are disproportionately diagnosed with schizophrenia, clinician bias, underdiagnosis of mood disorders, and clinician race are most common (Schwartz & Blankenship, 2014; Schwartz & Feisthamel, 2009). Constance Dunlap, a member of the Ethnoracial Inclusion and Diversity Work Group, noted, "One of the reasons Blacks are misdiagnosed with schizophrenia is because people don't follow [*DSM-5*] but let their biases and projections influence diagnosis" (see Moran, 2022, para. 14).

Lack of Cultural Sensitivity

Another related concern is an overall lack of cultural inclusivity, with critics arguing that the *DSM* is not representative of the experiences of people from diverse backgrounds and does not adequately consider the ways in which social and cultural factors affect mental health and, instead, perpetuate stereotypes and biases. Arguments supporting this perspective point to limited cultural representation and cultural insensitivity, noting that some mental health conditions and symptoms may be misunderstood or stigmatized because of cultural differences in attitudes and beliefs (Schwartz & Blankenship, 2014). Furthermore, individuals from minoritized cultural groups may not receive appropriate diagnosis or treatment because of a lack of cultural understanding on the part of the provider or broader mental health profession. These accounts widely criticize the *DSM* for reflecting the biases and cultural values of its creators, lacking cultural representation that contributes to misdiagnosis or underdiagnosis of mental health conditions (Bredström, 2019). Moreover, many disorders require that symptoms cause significant distress or impairment in social, occupational, or other important areas of functioning, which prompts debates among scholars about whether client or societal norms dictate what constitutes significant distress (Ecks, 2015).

Relatedly, critics cite the *DSM-5-TR* as overly reliant on labels and categories, which can be stigmatizing to individuals seeking help for their mental health concerns (Gaete et al., 2017). People may feel as if they are defined by their diagnosis rather than seen as individuals with unique experiences and needs. While this may be a common critique for all persons, for historically minoritized communities, diagnostic labels may perpetuate stereotypes and biases (Tomlinson-Clarke & Georges, 2014).

Finally, critics also argue that the *DSM-5-TR* does not provide adequate guidance for culturally sustaining practice, leading to inadequate services for minoritized people. This is centered around the *DSM-5-TR*'s narrow focus on psychopathology *within the individual*, which may overlook the impact of social and cultural factors, including oppression and marginalization, on mental health and the importance of considering context, strengths, and resources.

Sex and Gender Bias

Throughout the *DSM*, counselors will find prevalence rates associated with gender. For example, borderline personality disorder (BPD) is reported as more common in women, whereas conduct disorders are more prevalent in men. Studies have shown that women with a history of childhood trauma, such as physical or sexual abuse, are more likely to develop BPD than women without such trauma (Porter et al., 2020). This suggests that trauma, as opposed to personality disturbances (e.g., affect instability, interpersonal difficulties, harmful behaviors), may be a contributing factor to the development of symptoms associated with BPD. Likewise, ADHD is often overdiagnosed in boys (Kazda et al., 2021; Merten et al., 2017; Morgan et al., 2023); thus, girls with ADHD symptoms may not receive the same level of attention or have their symptoms treated as effectively as boys.

Moreover, across the large breadth of research related to diagnosis, there is virtually no research on diagnostic classifications and considerations for transgender and nonbinary individuals. This exclusion implies that there is no differentiation in diagnostic presentation among cisgender, nonbinary, and transgender individuals. Just one of the potential issues with this assumption is that clients' accounts of symptom history may be largely influenced by social conditioning and cultural expectations associated with gender roles and norms (Riggs et al., 2019). As such, client expressions of symptoms and behaviors may be inherently misaligned with social norms and expectations based on the client's sex assigned at birth and their experienced gender. While not associated with dissonance, clinicians might erroneously account for these concerns as gender dysphoria. Moreover, there are high levels of trauma experienced within the lesbian, gay, bisexual, transgender, queer, plus (LGBTQ+) community that, similar to gender bias, may heavily influence symptom expression.

Adverse Childhood Experiences

Adverse childhood experiences (ACEs) are potentially traumatic events that occur in a person's early life (between birth and 17 years of age), including physical, emotional, and sexual abuse; neglect; household dysfunction; and exposure to violence (Karatekin & Hill, 2019). The Centers for Disease Control and Kaiser Permanente launched the ACE Study from 1995 to 1997 to investigate the impact of childhood trauma on later-life health and well-being, and the study found that ACEs were associated with a wide range of health and mental health consequences (see Felitti et al., 1998). The study, with a U.S. sample of more than 17,000 adults, revealed that nearly one in six Americans experienced at least one ACE. Findings also confirmed that the more ACEs individuals experienced, the higher their risk for developing mental health problems. A subsequent study by Merrick et al. (2019), with a sample of 144,017 adults from 25 states, revealed that nearly one in six Americans experienced at least one ACE. Findings also confirmed that the more ACEs individuals experienced, the higher their risk for developing mental health problems. Other studies have also replicated the original ACE Study and highlighted how childhood trauma not only affects physical and mental health but also growth and connectivity of the brain, leading to long-lasting changes in cognitive, emotional, and behavioral functioning (Anda et al., 2006).

Neurological changes attributed to childhood trauma occur through a process known as neuroplasticity, in which experiences and environmental factors can alter the structure and function of the brain (Cross et al., 2017). Traumatic experiences can lead to changes in the stress response system and affect the development of brain regions that are involved in regulation of emotions, memory, and executive functions (Assogna et al., 2020). These changes can persist into adulthood and increase the risk for anxiety, depression, and PTSD. For example, chronic childhood physical abuse can alter the functioning of serotonin, a neurotransmitter involved in regulating mood and behavior. Serotonin is produced and released by nerve cells and acts on other neurons to regulate their activity (Assogna et al., 2020). It acts as an inhibitory neurotransmitter, meaning that it dampens the activity of neurons that release it. When it comes to regulating mood and behavior, serotonin helps reduce feelings of anxiety, worry, and irritability. Serotonin is also involved in regulating appetite, sleep, and digestion. By moderating (or inhibiting) the activity of these neurons, serotonin can have an overall calming effect on the brain and improve mood and behavior regulation. In addition to regulating mood, serotonin also regulates appetite, sleep, and digestion. For example, low levels of serotonin have been linked to depression, anxiety, and sleep disorders, whereas elevated levels of serotonin can lead to increased appetite and weight gain.

Although the *DSM-5-TR* includes diagnoses related to the effects of trauma (e.g., PTSD), it does not specifically mention ACEs as a risk factor for these conditions, nor is there attention to the broader concept of complex trauma, which refers to repeated or prolonged exposure to trauma and its aftermath. There is also no mention of neuroplasticity; however, APA (2022) acknowledged that many mental disorders can be caused by a combination of biological, psychological, and environmental factors and that the interplay between these factors is complex. Counselors are advised to consider an individual's cultural background, worldview, and life experiences—to include ACEs—and to use this information to inform their understanding of the individual's symptoms and to develop culturally sensitive and appropriate treatment plans. This includes screening for ACEs and incorporating trauma-informed approaches into treatment. We provide more detail in Chapter 4 of this *Learning Companion.*

Systemic Issues With Diagnosis

One of the most prominent critiques of the *DSM* is that the diagnostic classification system may perpetuate or exacerbate existing health disparities (Deferio et al., 2019; Gaete et al., 2017). Health disparities refer to differences in the quality and access to health and health care due to inequitable access to social, economic, and environmental resources. Health disparities result in unequal access to care, higher rates of disease and illness, and worse health outcomes for individuals experiencing systemic oppression (Deferio et al., 2019). Examples of health disparities also include access to preventive care and treatment.

Historically, Western counseling and psychology have failed to understand the complex and often ongoing experiences of trauma related to and resulting from discrimination, racism, and other systemic oppression. Researchers continue to provide evidence that experiencing racism can lead to negative physical and mental health outcomes, including higher rates of chronic physical (e.g., diabetes, hypertension, obesity) and mental (e.g., depression) health conditions (Carter et al., 2017). Relatedly, scholars and practitioners are continuing to identify how these collective stressors are critical to fully understanding the experiences of individuals, families, and communities (Solheim et al., 2022). While cultural biases often result in a lack of access to appropriate assessments and treatments, a full understanding of how systemic issues contribute to mental illness remains largely absent from the *DSM.*

The *DSM-5-TR* attempts to address the impact of racism and discrimination of individuals and groups more adequately; however, a full understanding of intersectionality remains absent. Intersectionality is a theoretical framework that recognizes and studies the complex interplay of multiple social identities within their related systems of oppression, privilege, and discrimination (Crenshaw, 1989; Walby et al., 2012). The aforementioned limitations of diagnostic assessment for historically marginalized individuals, including the potential for overdiagnosis and misdiagnosis of historically minoritized individuals, do not adequately address the impact of systemic oppression and health disparities inherent to and reflected within current diagnostic nosology.

Despite these criticisms, the *DSM* continues to be widely used in clinical practice and research and is seen as a valuable tool for organizing information about mental health conditions and guiding treatment decisions. Counselors need to be particularly mindful of these intersections and impacts on mental health as they navigate diagnosis. In the next chapter of this *Learning Companion*, we describe a socioecological approach to provide counselors with a more holistic and culturally informed way for diagnosis and treatment planning.

Sociocultural Competency

It is important for counselors to engage in ongoing cultural humility and competency work to facilitate a deeper diagnostic understanding inclusive of clients' background, culture, and values. Counselors should strive to understand how clients' multifaceted and intersecting identities impact how they experience or express mental health concerns. Counselors should also be aware of the potential impact of power dynamics, privilege, and oppression on clients' experience and must be respectful, nonjudgmental, and open-minded when gathering information and making a diagnosis.

To accurately interpret client symptoms within the context of their lived experiences, counselors must learn about cultures and experiences they may not be familiar with so they can properly contextualize symptoms. Counselors should strive to be aware of their own biases to ensure that their diagnosis is based on accurate, culturally sustaining information rather than their own cultural assumptions, stereotypes, and biases. To this end, it is recommended that counselors:

1. Become familiar with the client's culture, identity, and values.
2. Ask open-ended questions and listen carefully to the client's answers.
3. Use an ecosystemic lens and be aware of power dynamics, privilege, and oppression and how they may impact the client's experience.
4. Gather accurate and up-to-date information about the client's condition.
5. Develop a nonjudgmental, respectful, and open-minded attitude.
6. Consider the multiple factors that may be influencing the client's condition.
7. Consider the client's strengths and factors influencing community and individual resilience.
8. Work collaboratively with the client to develop a plan for treatment that is in alignment with their background, values, and beliefs.

When conducting assessments, counselors should use culturally appropriate tools and measures that are sensitive to the unique experiences and perspectives of their clients. They should also be aware of the limitations and biases that may be present in traditional assessment tools and consider alternative methods of assessment, such as cultural formulations (discussed in the next chapter). As part of this process, counselors should collaborate with clients and involve them in the diagnostic process by seeking their input and perspectives. Even beyond considering the cultural context and the ways in which cultural factors can impact mental health experiences and expressions, counselors must use assessments that are accurate, culturally sensitive, and responsive to the client's unique experiences and perspectives.

Reducing Diagnostic Biases

To effectively address diagnostic bias, counselors must continue to educate themselves on cultural diversity, social justice, and intersections of multiple identities. This education can include attending workshops or conferences, reading books and articles, or seeking supervision from mentors with strong expertise in and commitment to culturally sustaining practice. Counselors should be aware of their personal biases and how these biases can affect the diagnostic process. By being self-reflexive, counselors can work to reduce the influence of biases and ensure that their diagnoses are culturally appropriate.

Self-awareness is imperative to working effectively with clients, specifically understanding personal biases and how these biases affect their approach to diagnosis. Strategies for gaining increased self-awareness include taking the time to identify personal biases, understanding personal privilege, and understanding how one's actions and thoughts perpetuate systemic inequalities to maintain or increase personal privilege. Being able to explain the impact of race, gender, ethnicity, cultural group membership, and other sociocultural characteristics on one's views and understanding of clients and counseling practice is important. Finally, continuing to remain aware and to engage in exploration and education around cultural competence is strongly encouraged. All counselors should engage in continued supervision to explore personal biases and clinical practice.

Questions for Consideration

1. How do certain diagnoses disproportionately affect certain groups? What are the impacts?
2. What are some common critiques of the *DSM*?
3. How can counselors use the *DSM* in a culturally competent and socially just manner?
4. What are some examples of health disparities?
5. What are some sociocultural differences in how individuals express distress?

Chapter 4

Culturally Responsive Case Conceptualization and Treatment Planning: Cultural Formulation

Every client has a story. While being human does include existential experiences universal to everyone, clients bring to those experiences their own personalities, nuances in collecting and processing data, approach to the world, ways of making meaning, and methods for getting their needs met. Often, these complex experiences are deeply rooted in their sociocultural environments and interactions with the world. During counseling, one can easily "get lost" in the information received from clients and wonder how to make sense of the client's world and meet their needs. This process can overwhelm counselors' efforts to help. Case formulation and case conceptualization provide frameworks or road maps for understanding the client's point of view and needs, in terms of what happened, why it happened, and the best counseling approach to address clients' needs.

Rationale for Case Formulation and Conceptualization

Formulation refers to the ability to put together the components of something, using a formula. The *DSM-5-TR* authors discuss clinical case formulation as the first item in the chapter, "Use of the Manual" (APA, 2022, p. 21). The location of this information may give an indication of the importance with which the authors view clinical case formulation, because of its link to treatment planning. Underscoring the importance of this, the Council for Accreditation of Counseling and Related Educational Programs (CACREP, 2024) includes understanding the knowledge and skills associated with systemic approaches to conceptualizing clients in their curriculum standards for all entry-level programs. They further require that case conceptualization occur from a "variety of models and approaches" (CACREP, 2024, p. 14) and multiple theoretical perspectives at the doctoral level. The *DSM-5-TR* also places a strong emphasis on the need for thorough evaluation and reliable assessment that go beyond a basic symptom count, while also noting that the manual does not address evidence-based treatment planning. The competencies associated with case formulation, case conceptualization, and evidence-based treatment planning are vital to effective mental health treatment (J. Sperry & Sperry, 2020; Sung & Skovholt, 2019).

Eels (2020) noted that formulation often referred to an informal, less organized process. More recently, the idea of case conceptualization as a more structured, core competency has taken root.

Defining Case Conceptualization

Merriam-Webster (n.d.) defined *conceptualization* as the act of forming a concept or "to form a concept of." Case conceptualization is "a method and clinical strategy for obtaining and organizing information about a client, understanding and explaining the client's situation and maladaptive patterns, guiding and focusing treatment, anticipating challenges and roadblocks, and preparing for successful termination" (L. Sperry & Sperry, 2020, p. 4). Case conceptualization, the intricate process of "focusing" that leads to effective treatment focus, not only takes time to learn but is also related to deliberate practice and reflective practice behaviors (Binensztok, 2019; L. Sperry & Sperry, 2020, p. 60). The basis of any type of conceptualization is the art of gathering, understanding, synthesizing, and making meaning of data. As clients convey their stories, counselors must engage in accurate and thorough assessment, synthesize the information using an appropriate framework, and create a plan that best addresses clients' concerns. When counselors reflect the story accurately, it is much more likely that clients will receive the most effective care. In keeping with this, Bieling and Kuyken (2003) referred to case conceptualization as "the heart of evidence-based practice" (p. 53). When case conceptualization is not utilized or is based on an unreliable framework, biases and judgment errors can occur, ultimately resulting in a lower standard of care and poor counseling outcomes for clients. Cline et al. (2022) noted both the crucial nature and high levels of anxiety reported by both aspiring counselors and their supervisors when it comes to this skill. They also pointed out the level of cognitive complexity needed to synthesize and analyze multifaceted data from multiple perspectives.

Theorists have posited multiple models for case conceptualization, many based in specific theoretical orientations to counseling (Ridley et al., 2017). Some examples include psychoanalytic (McWilliams, 1999), cognitive behavioral (Wright et al., 2006), psychodynamic (Levensen & Strupp, 2007), and Adlerian (Dinkmeyer & Sperry, 2000). These models tend to follow a similar flow or blueprint based loosely on the scientific method of problem solving. Five components are typically included: problem identification through assessment and data collection; identification of the psychological process through data analysis and organization; synthesis of client data; treatment planning and intervention; and reassessment for improvement, obstacles, detection, or termination.

Theorists noted a number of current and ongoing issues associated with clinical case conceptualization. Problems include a lack of consensus when defining case conceptualization, especially as many models currently in use are tied to specific theoretical orientations and not generalizable for those who practice from differing orientations or from a transtheoretical model, such as the wellness theory or development counseling and theory (Ridley & Jeffrey, 2017). Additional problems include the lack of "hands-on" information for implementing case conceptualization and the fact that most models do not cover or promote the crucial impact of culture, with certain exceptions. L. Sperry's (2010) integrative case conceptualization (ICC) model includes cultural considerations both within the framework and the definition (Ridley et al., 2017). Specifically, this model requires that one "identifies level of acculturation, ethnic and gender identification (if relevant); links presentation to culture versus psychological factors; [and] anticipates impact of cultural factors on treatment process" (L. Sperry, 2010, p. 113). Furthermore, Stoupas et al. (2018) identified this model as one of the few that also addresses the spiritual and religious domains. A thorough assessment of clients' cultural realities and related issues when engaging in diagnosis and treatment is essential for ethical practice (ACA, 2014). It is incumbent upon counselors to identify and use a model of case conceptualization that leads to effective treatment planning and outcomes for their clients. In the next section, we describe the ICC model, including its functions, components, and elements, as one such option for counselors.

ICC Model

Consistent with the definition of case conceptualization identified previously in this chapter, the ICC model includes five functions counselors use when engaging in case conceptualization (L. Sperry & Sperry, 2020). The first function is obtaining data and organizing the information into meaningful hypotheses about clients' presenting problems. Initial or Level 1 assessment is a key part of this function. Whereas targeted follow-up and ongoing assessment occur throughout the counseling process, the art of assessment begins immediately. Gill and Freund (2018) noted the crucial nature of assessment in the counseling process and defined assessment as "the act of determining the amount of value or importance an individual assigns to a specific construct" (p. 42). Assessment begins when clients and counselors start the counseling process and assess each other. For effective counseling to occur, counselors must engage in an assessment process mindfully and intentionally with the purpose of developing the most effective treatment plan to meet the client's needs. This includes effective diagnostic, clinical, and cultural formulation interviews. Using the information gathered throughout this process, counselors will form hypotheses regarding the presenting problems, the origins of the problem, maladaptive patterns, and contributors to and perpetuations of the problem. This information assists counselors when engaging in the second function, explaining (L. Sperry & Sperry, 2020).

In explaining, counselors attempt to understand clients' stories as closely as possible. In so doing, they understand client concerns consistent with the clients' individual personalities, needs, sociocultural identities, and worldview, which provide the basis for counseling recommendations and for the third function, guiding and focusing treatment. In this third function, a strong formulation provides the basis for determining evidence-based interventions targeted at resolving client concerns and promoting wellness. The fourth function encourages counselors to anticipate challenges and obstacles to the therapeutic relationship and counseling process. Obstacles could include empathic failures, ruptures in the relationship, commitment to treatment, relapse, and other problems that arise in the process. Finally, counselors include a path for termination throughout counseling. Termination is a normal part of the process, and counselors acknowledge the difficulty some clients may have with this function (L. Sperry & Sperry, 2020). Ethical termination can serve as a model for transition in other relationships as well.

ICC Model Components

First Component: Diagnostic Formulation

In addition to the five functions of case conceptualization, the ICC model endorses four components that must be present (L. Sperry & Sperry, 2020). The first component, diagnostic formulation, attempts to answer the question, "What happened?" Counselors work with clients to understand the presentation, or presenting problem, including any appropriate *DSM-5-TR* diagnoses. Precipitants and triggers associated with the presentation are identified as counselors work to understand clients' patterns of thoughts, feelings, and behaviors. In ICC, the idea of clients' patterns is similar to the Adlerian concept of lifestyle. This refers to a pervasive way of attending to the world that can be either flexible and adaptive or inflexible and maladaptive, leading to ongoing difficulties. Patterns are conceptualized using the way in which clients approach others. Specifically, do they move toward others, against or away from others, or in ambivalent ways? Clients typically engage in one or more of these movements without being fully aware of their behavior. These patterns often have underlying goals, such as feeling safe or getting attention. Understanding clients' patterns inform counselors about the link between presentation and precipitants. Consistent with the Adlerian concept of lifestyle, cultural identities and family-of-origin factors contribute heavily to the development of clients' patterns. For example, Stoupas et al. (2018) described patterns in spirituality, detailing how clients' "God image" can be influenced and how level of faith commitment endorsed by clients may leave clues about underlying patterns. Because of the cultural underpinning associated with these patterns, counselors must conduct a thorough assessment of both pattern and personality within sociocultural context as described later in this chapter.

Second Component: Clinical Formulation

Clinical and cultural formulations are the next two components of this model of case conceptualization. These components rely on and inform each other, as culture cannot be divorced from the clinical presentation and vice versa. The second component, clinical formation, is a counselor's attempt to answer the question, "Why did this happen?" Predisposition and perpetuants serve as the basis for clinical formulation and, in turn, connect diagnosis to treatment (Stoupas et al., 2018). Counselors can determine predisposition, or etiological factors, by identifying sociocultural, biological, and psychological factors that may impact the presenting problem. Psychological factors can include personality, intelligence, self-esteem, and related intrapsychic factors. Sociocultural factors include, but are not limited to, family of origin, family stressors or secrets, abuse or trauma, and support systems. Perpetuants reinforce clients' maladaptive patterns and are often created by clients to maintain behaviors that feel safe to them. Unfortunately, the opposite is often the case, as clients continue to engage in patterns that lead to increased distress (L. Sperry & Sperry, 2020).

Third Component: Cultural Formulation

Cultural formulation is the third components in the ICC model. The authors of the *DSM-5-TR* defined culture as "systems of knowledge, concepts, values, norms, and practices that are learned and transmitted across generations" (APA, 2022, p. 860). Gill and Freund (2018) noted that culture permeates every part of people's lives, but it is not innate. Culture is a system created by groups and passed down through generations with a goal of creating and maintaining connections. Cultural experiences are inherently connected to race, gender, ethnicity, and socioeconomic status.

Changes to the DSM-5-TR. Whereas the *DSM-5* included a stand-alone section dedicated to cultural formulation, the authors of the *DSM-5-TR* added to this idea in their Culture and Psychiatric Diagnosis chapter in Section III (APA, 2022). This chapter is broken down into three parts: Key Terms, Cultural Formulation, and Cultural Concepts of Distress. The Key Terms section provides definitions and foundations for understanding culture, race, and ethnicity. In the Cultural Formulation section, the *DSM-5-TR* authors noted how they expanded upon the information provided in the *DSM-5*. They also highlighted the Cultural Formulation Interview (CFI) as a resource for this process. The third section, Cultural Concepts of Distress, incorporates specifics regarding differing cultural experiences, understanding, and descriptions of mental health symptoms. As we proceed with our description of cultural formulation, we will also cover the information included in the *DSM-5-TR*. This information is relevant to this component of case conceptualization and crucial to understanding clients' worldviews, presenting issues, and pattern development.

Integration with cultural formulation. The *DSM-5-TR* authors provide an assessment framework for making sense of information regarding social and cultural context and history as they relate to clients' mental health (APA, 2022). Likewise, cultural formulation within the ICC model is based on a "systematic review of cultural factors and dynamics" (L. Sperry & Sperry, 2020, p. 54). ICC formulation includes four elements that result in a cultural statement toward determining the role culture plays in the client's presentation: cultural identity, acculturation and acculturative stress, cultural explanation, and culture versus personality.

The *DSM-5-TR* describes cultural identity in terms of age, gender, ethnoracial background, or other sociocultural characteristics. The ICC model frames culture as a sense of belonging (L. Sperry & Sperry, 2020), specifically, the extent to which clients identify with or belong to ethnoracial groups versus assimilating to the majority cultural norms. Acculturation refers to the adaptation to a different culture, typically the majority culture. Because culture permeates every part of daily life, adapting to a different culture will result in varying degrees of stress. Within the cultural formulation of this model, acculturative stress attempts explain the impact of adaptation on clients. This includes stress associated with factors such as learning communication styles and/or languages, managing expectations that are often dramatically different, experiencing negative consequences of discrimination, and being exposed to incidents of racism and systemic racism (L. Sperry & Sperry, 2020). Acculturative stress does not extend solely to race, ethnicity, and gender; it also applies to religious and spiritual beliefs and practices (Stoupas et al., 2018).

Cultural concepts of distress are covered as the third part of the *DSM-5-TR* chapter, Culture and Psychiatric Diagnoses. In this section, cultural concepts of distress refer to clients' personal expression of distress, including the experiences, communication of problems, upsetting thoughts, and emotions. The *DSM-5-TR* authors give a strong rationale for the need to incorporate this information into diagnosis and provide 10 specific examples that may emerge in the therapeutic setting (APA, 2022). Understanding clients' expression of the presentation in terms of cultural context is at the heart of ICC cultural explanation. This portion of the cultural formulation focuses on clients' expression of the problem and extends to their culturally informed beliefs regarding the presenting problem, history of treatment, and expectations (L. Sperry & Sperry, 2020).

Because of the culturally based nature of help-seeking behaviors, these are also explored during this process (APA, 2022). As part of the cultural formulation, counselors must consider the question, "What better explains the problem, cultural factors, and personality patterns described in the diagnostic formulation?" This is often straightforward for clients with lower levels of acculturative stress. However, this can be a difficult task when acculturative stressors are present and acculturative stress plays a major factor in the presenting problem. Counselors attempt to determine if personality dynamics are primarily at play in the presenting problem, if cultural dynamics play the primary role, or if problems are related to both. A thorough and accurate assessment of the impact of culture and the impact of acculturative stress is key here.

Cultural Formulation Interview (CFI). The CFI in the *DSM-5-TR* provides counselors with concrete guidance for engaging cultural assessment. The CFI is a semistructured interview consisting of 16 questions covering domains such as cultural definition of the problem; cultural perceptions of cause, context, and support; cultural factors affecting self-coping and past help seeking; and cultural factors affecting current help seeking. Designed to be completed in about 15 to 20 minutes, the CFI provides concrete direction and tools for bringing culture into diagnostic assumptions. In addition, APA (2013a) provides a series of 12 supplementary modules to be used as adjuncts to the CFI or independent of the CFI. Addressing topics and populations such as needs of immigrants and refugees; coping and help seeking; and spirituality, religion, and moral traditions, the modules provide a foundation upon which culturally sustaining counselors can build.

During a year-long field trial involving the CFI, Aggarwal et al. (2020) identified several barriers to implementing the CFI. From the client perspective, barriers included confusion about how the CFI was different from other assessments, reluctance to discuss the past, confusion over several items, rigidity in conversation, and difficulty participating given the nature of their concerns. Interdisciplinary clinicians sometimes questioned conceptual connections between the CFI and presenting problems, wondered whether the entire interview was helpful, identified instances in which clients may not be able to participate, and worried about being overly structured in delivery of the interview. They also noted concerns regarding the amount of time needed to complete the entire CFI. Even if counselors simply find the CFI helpful as a guide to facilitating conversations about culture, the CFI provides a step forward in helping counselors move from multicultural awareness to skills when thinking diagnostically.

Broaching and cultural humility. Beginning counselors often express insecurity when addressing the impact of acculturative stress with their clients, and seasoned counselors may express discomfort as well. *Broaching* is a method by which counselors intentionally initiate conversations and/or ask direct questions about race, ethnicity, culture, power, and privilege in an open and inviting manner (Day-Vines et al., 2007). King (2021) stated that "broaching is unanimously conceptualized as a counselor's responsibility to initiate conversations about race/ethnicity, culture, and power" (p. 90).

Day-Vines et al. (2020) presented the multidimensional model of broaching behavior, theorized on a continuum of behavior, to aid in understanding how counselors approach race, ethnicity, and culture (REC) with clients. This model incorporates four dimensions to facilitate the counselor's discussion of REC. These dimensions include intracounseling, intraindividual counseling, intra-REC, and inter-REC (Day-Vines et al., 2020), which are used in a fluid, interactive way. The intracounseling dimension refers to a counselor's broaching behaviors in terms of REC and includes the introduction of cultural humility, along with the acknowledgment that the counselor may not fully comprehend the impact of REC on the client (Day-Vines et al., 2020). The intracounseling process is a counselor-initiated examination of cultural similarities and differences within the counseling relationship and addresses REC factors as they arise, referred to as *cultural immediacy.* The intraindividual counseling dimension helps the counselor to understand identity intersectionality and the impact of all REC factors on the client's worldview and presenting problem. Working within this dimension, the counselor will encourage exploration of the impact of multiple intersecting identities on the client's worldview and avoid conceptualizing from one perspective alone (Day-Vines et al., 2020). In the intra-REC dimension, the counselor broaches issues arising from discrepancies with the client's worldview and those of the people in their lives with a similar cultural group or REC. In acknowledging that divergencies occur and are often a source of emotional stress, the counselor discourages compartmentalizing and elicits increased disclosure from the client (Day-Vines et al., 2020). Finally, the inter-REC dimension refers to the counselor's acknowledgment of the personal impact of systemic racism and discrimination on the client's overall wellness, which may in turn lead to advocacy-based interventions. These dimensions align with the Multicultural and Social Justice Counseling Competencies (Ratts et al., 2016), and Day-Vines and colleagues offer specific case examples in their 2020 publication.

Research and practice experience provide support for the positive impact of broaching for the counseling relationship and the therapeutic process (King, 2021; King & Borders, 2019). However, counselors may be reluctant to use this method for a variety of reasons, including fear of offending, what language to use when broaching, and whether issues of culture and power are relevant to the process (King, 2021). Some research suggests that these fears are not valid, and there is support for including broaching as a priority from the beginning of the counseling process (King & Borders, 2019). Scholars also recommend personalizing broaching statements, to include normalizing of the technique, attending to both individual client identity and systemic experiences of racism, and inviting the client to share their perspective (King, 2021). A genuine and ongoing approach to understanding the client's experiences includes attending to cultural opportunities, or the in-session moments that present an opportunity to engage in therapeutic dialog related to the client's culture (Shaw, 2016). Engaging in these opportunities conveys the counselor's commitment to cultural humility.

Cultural humility involves a lifelong process of learning to respect differing cultures and accepting individuals from other cultures. Hook et al. (2017) recognized that approaching culture from an attitude of humility, wherein the counselor focuses on what they do not know, precludes behaviors like making assumptions and stereotyping clients. The interpersonal and intrapersonal dimensions encompass cultural humility. Within the interpersonal dimension, counselors engaging in cultural humility understand that, by its unique nature, their own cultural experience limits their understanding of the cultural experience of the client (Shaw, 2016). The intrapersonal dimension of cultural humility requires that counselors who practice cultural humility do so from an other-oriented stance with openness, respect, and interest, as they invite the client to share, describe, and explore their cultural identity and experience (Shaw, 2016). This calls for counselors to be open to learning about the unique cultural experiences that clients bring to counseling and a willingness to recognize and address issues of power and privilege (Grad, 2022). When embracing cultural humility, counselors continually engage in a reflective process regarding power, privilege, and personal biases (Atkins & Lorelle, 2022). Counselors who are effective in culturally responsive case conceptualization and treatment planning will approach conversations regarding the unique lived experiences of clients from all cultures with a sense of cultural humility and open questioning.

Fourth Component: Treatment Formulation

Treatment formulation and treatment planning are the final component in the ICC model. In this component, counselors attempt to answer the question, "How can it change?" (L. Sperry & Sperry, 2020). The goal is to create an accurate and effective blueprint for counseling approaches resulting in the most effective outcomes for the client. When the diagnostic, clinical, and cultural formulations have high explanatory power, the treatment formulation follows in a logical fashion (Stoupas et al., 2018). The ICC model endorses seven elements as part of the treatment planning process: treatment goals, focus, strategy, intervention, anticipated obstacles, treatment-cultural, and prognosis.

Counselors should focus on coconstructing realistic and measurable treatment goals with clients. Focusing encourages counselors to consistently provide goal-directed and evidence-based interventions consistent with client needs while attending to the influence of culture on the overall process. Treatment strategy refers to action plans cocreated with clients. L. Sperry and Sperry (2020) noted several frequently utilized strategies, including cognitive reprocessing, corrective emotional experiences, exposure, medication, support, and replacement. Interventions are the agreed-upon steps taken by counselors and clients to improve the problem. Accurate intervention flows from a strong assessment of clients' needs, as well as the goals and strategies. Furthermore, a strong treatment plan includes information regarding anticipated obstacles and challenges to progress, such as the impact of pattern, ruptures, relapse, ambivalence, and resistance.

Based on the impact of acculturation and acculturative stress as determined in the cultural formulation, counselors may use culturally responsive theories or sustaining interventions as part of the treatment-cultural element. Multicultural counseling and therapy is a metatheory that includes multiple approaches to counseling and applies the tenets of cultural identity development for both the counselor and the client (Hays & Erford, 2022). As its core, multicultural counseling and therapy has the goal of liberation of consciousness for the individual, family, community, and organization. Additional therapies include relational-cultural theory, feminist theory, and empowerment theory. Examples of interventions include transgenerational genograms that focus on culture or spiritual/religious worldviews (Gill et al., 2020) using third-wave cognitive behavior therapy models that include history, culture, and religion/spirituality. Mindfulness-based self-compassion seeks to discuss and honor cultural backgrounds. Affinity groups may include those of similar cultural backgrounds and experiences. These groups have the goal of increasing common humanity toward building cultural humility (Ivers & Johnson, 2022). Ethical counselors coconstruct these interventions with clients while not engaging in cultural appropriation or reaching beyond their scope of practice. Finally, prognosis is included in the treatment formulations portion. This is informed by the diagnostic, clinical, and cultural formulations.

Family and Group Case Conceptualization

Counselors who work with groups face some similar challenges in case conceptualization as counselors working with individual clients, including the lack of consensus definition, limited utility of the models, and need for infusion of cultural implications. Identifying the "client" when conceptualizing group, couple, and family counseling may also become an issue. In fact, group, couple, and family counseling are all impacted by the discussion of who the "case" focuses on. Sung and Skovholt (2019) noted that group counselors often attempt to elicit group goals rather than individual ones and to use these as the basis for case formulation. They noted that the steps taken by group counselors in terms of conceptualization for groups are similar to patterns used by counselors engaged in individual case conceptualization. Their qualitative study illuminated master group therapists' ability to conceptualize the groups as a whole and as individuals within groups. This ability also extended to movement between individual clients and groups and may improve overall health and wellness of both.

Family counselors face a similar dilemma in that systems theories often see the family as the "client" (Young et al., 2021). However, ethical codes that apply to this type of counseling, such as those of the International Association for Marriage and Family Counseling (2017), require separate documentation for each individual in order to maintain confidentiality. Within the family modality, counselors not only conceptualize individuals but also focus conceptualization on the entire family system (L. Sperry & Sperry, 2022). L. Sperry and Sperry (2022) recommended that individual case conceptualization be created for all members of the family as well as the group. The focus should include the unique context, needs, and resources of each family member and the family unit (Bitter, 2021). In keeping with the ICC model described earlier, counselors will focus on culture, including the family culture, as well as individual and familial patterns of behavior. Family-oriented case conceptualization will include systems dynamics and identify systemic maladaptive patterns for power sharing, negotiating, gaining intimacy, and family rules and themes.

Couples counseling involves similar limitations. When conducting couples counseling, counselors must engage in a thorough and ongoing assessment process at the outset of therapy and throughout the process to minimize these limitations. L. Sperry and Peluso (2019) noted that the counselor must be mindful to answer three specific questions: Are the problems related to individual personality factors or to the system itself? Which modality is optimal therapeutically? If couples counseling is optimal, what strategies, focus, duration, and type of treatment are most effective for this couple? Case conceptualization focuses on both the individuals and the couple as a unit; therefore, three case conceptualizations are recommended. In addition to the elements described previously in this chapter, relational patterns are key to understanding the couple's interactions (L. Sperry & Peluso, 2019). Maladaptive patterns can form as a result of parental models and personality or other factors, impacting all aspects of the relationship (L. Sperry & Peluso, 2019). Counselors must conduct a thorough assessment and engage in high-level case conceptualization to determine the best treatment for addressing these patterns.

Questions for Consideration

1. How does case conceptualization inform diagnosis and treatment planning?
2. What are the pros and cons of the CFI, and how would you use this assessment effectively?
3. What is cultural humility, and how can you incorporate it into your practice?
4. How can you use the ICC model in couples and group counseling?

Chapter 5

Practice Implications for Counselors

In our first few chapters, you have likely deepened your understanding of the history and philosophy of the *DSM*. You also explored sociocultural issues inherent in diagnosis, learned strategies for culturally responsive case conceptualization and treatment planning, and considered how suicidal behavior and nonsuicidal self-injury can occur alongside experiences of mental disorder. You may be wondering about the practicalities of using the *DSM-5-TR* as well as how diagnosing clients fits with your identity as a professional counselor.

Initially, many mental health advocates voiced concerns that the *DSM-5* (APA, 2013b) would lead to rather drastic shifts in the conceptualization of mental disorders, assessment procedures, and diagnostic thresholds. In the end, the manual kept a descriptive categorical system much like previous versions. Still, those involved in revisions of the *DSM-5* laid the groundwork for shifts to neurobiological conceptualizations, removal of boundaries between medical and mental disorders, prescription of assessment measures in attempts to document complexities of mental illness, and revised conceptualization of schizophrenia spectrum and personality disorders. The *DSM-5-TR* continues this tradition with text revisions incorporating the latest science while deepening explicit attention to intersections among diagnosis, suicide behavior, sociocultural context, ethnoracial identity, and gender identity.

In this chapter, we review philosophical implications for the counseling profession and address technical considerations such as how to use other specified and unspecified diagnoses, coding procedures, and assessment tools. We conclude the chapter with reflections regarding counselors' roles in the future of the *DSM*.

Diagnosis and the Counseling Profession

As a profession, counseling is uniquely focused on using an empowerment-based approach "to accomplish mental health, wellness, education, and career goals" (Kaplan et al., 2014, p. 366). Professional counselors should be familiar with philosophical foundations that include a commitment to normal human development; wellness as a primary paradigm (Myers, 1991); and an integrated understanding of systemic, social, and cultural foundations. Concerns about the degree to which diagnosis is consistent with a strong professional counseling identity are not new or unique to the *DSM-5-TR*. Reflecting on risks and realities within *DSM-IV* (APA, 1994), Ivey and Ivey (1998) asked, "We want to define ourselves as concerned with normal development, but how can we face the reality of pathological and deficit models of child development, managed health care, and the omnipresent *DSM-IV*?" (p. 334). Zalaquett et al. (2008) explained,

> It is important to note that this diagnostic nosology represents a medical model that stands in sharp contrast to many counselors' core values and beliefs. The medical model treats counseling concerns and behavioral symptoms as indicators of underlying diseases, emphasizes the client's deficits, leads to a top-down professional attitude, places the client in a passive (recipient) position, emphasizes individual origin of symptoms, and offers medications as the common mode of treatment. The counseling model, in contrast, treats such symptoms as responses to life challenges, emphasizes the client's strengths and assets in dealing with problems, leads to a more egalitarian relationship in the counseling setting, places the client in an active and engaged (agent) position in the treatment process, directs attention to environmental factors that may be linked to the individual's symptoms, and offers nonpsychopharmacological treatments. (p. 364)

The philosophical questions are long-standing. Eriksen and Kress (2006) explored these issues in depth as they worked to balance realities of practice; potential benefits of diagnosis; and key contradictions in values, assumptions, and philosophies of the counseling profession. They proposed strategies counselors may use to enhance understanding of developmental and contextual considerations in an ethical manner. Similarly, Kress et al. (2010) addressed ethical dimensions of diagnosis within clinical mental health counseling. These balanced views address issues of professional identity and practice implications well and will continue to be of use to counselors who seek balance in their diagnostic process. Although most concerns regarding diagnosis and professional identity will remain static, the *DSM-5-TR* continues to present two specific challenges and opportunities relating to professional counseling identity: examining its neurobiological foundations and maintaining a holistic perspective in the context of nonaxial diagnosis.

Neurobiological Foundations

The initial *DSM-5* revision process spawned conversations regarding what constitutes a mental disorder, including new conceptualizations regarding the line between medical disorders and mental disorders. At first, the DSM-5 Task Force proposed a reformulation in the definition of mental disorder in a manner that implied all mental disorders were rooted in psychobiological dysfunction. The proposed revision generated a firestorm of controversy regarding the questionable foundation upon which APA could claim all mental disorders as having psychobiological roots. Ultimately, APA rejected the proposed revision in favor of a more balanced definition carried forward in the *DSM-5-TR*:

> A *mental disorder* is a syndrome characterized by clinically significant disturbance in an individual's cognition, emotion regulation, or behavior that reflects a dysfunction in the psychological, biological, or developmental processes underlying mental functioning. Mental disorders are usually associated with significant distress or disability in social, occupational, or other important activities. An expectable or culturally approved response to a common stressor or loss, such as death of a loved one, is not a mental disorder. Socially deviant behavior

(e.g., political, religious, or sexual) and conflicts that are primarily between the individual and society are not mental disorders unless the deviance or conflict results from a dysfunction in the individual, as described above. (APA, 2022, p. 14)

The *DSM-5-TR* continues to give attention to the neurobiological foundations of disorders. Subtle use of language also reflects a movement toward biological explanations of disorder. Mental disorders are not differentiated from medical disorders in diagnostic formulations. In addition, APA (2022) uses *another medical condition* to denote mental disorders caused by underlying medical concerns. This subtle language implies that mental disorders are medical disorders at their core.

Ivey and Ivey (1998) were astute in their observation that "developmental orientation, however, does not rule out biological factors—rather environment interacts with personal biology. The issue is finding balance between personal and environmental factors" (p. 336). When the *DSM-5* was published, Miller and Prosek (2013) advocated for renewed attention to the impact of this movement toward biological explanations of emotional problems, especially for vulnerable populations. Certainly, emerging neuroscience research holds much promise for facilitating understanding regarding the complexities of the brain, experiences, and disorder. Still, overreliance on biological explanations without attention to the interaction with personal and environmental factors could lead to increased pathologizing, unnecessary pharmacological treatments, and unknown long-term effects on clients. There is also the question within the counseling community whether this focus may cause counselors to stray from the profession's humanistic roots (Montes, 2013).

For now, we urge professional counselors to seek additional training regarding neuroscience and the implications for counseling and to remain alert to opportunities and challenges for our profession. Scholars like Siegel et al. (2021) offer trainings and readings on interpersonal neurobiology that are accessible to professional counselors, consistent with our foundations, and directly relevant to counseling practice. Likewise, a growing body of counseling scholars is working to bring together counseling foundations and neuroscience (e.g., Field, 2017; Field & Ghoston, 2020; Luke, 2015; Luke et al., 2019).

Nonaxial Diagnosis

Diagnosis in the *DSM-5-TR* continues to be nonaxial, representing a shift from the multiaxial system of diagnosis in the *DSM-III* and *DSM-IV* designed to ensure that mental health providers conceptualized clients in a biopsychosocial manner. Axes I and II included psychological disorders, Axis III provided space to note medical conditions, Axis IV required attention to psychosocial and environmental stressors, and Axis V provided space for rating the degree of distress and impairment in functioning. Until the publication of the *DSM-5*, multiaxial diagnosis was a part of everyday diagnostic decisions and conversations. Insurance companies frequently requested notations for each axis and sometimes determined the level of care and client progress based on Global Assessment of Functioning ratings. Scholars concerned with the cultural implications of *DSM* diagnosis, the context of distress, and professional identity frequently pointed to Axis IV as a place where counselors could ensure attention to external and contextual influences on client well-being (Kress et al., 2014).

Regardless of reporting formats, professional counselors should remember that the *DSM* is a diagnostic guide rather than a theoretical framework or treatment manual. A nonaxial diagnostic format need not affect how professional counselors make sense of or respond to client concerns. Rather, counselors can still conceptualize clients consistent with our unique foundations. As noted in previous chapters, we can still bring empowerment, strengths-based, and wellness-oriented approaches to all clients, even those who present with significant disruptions in functioning. Counselors who find the *DSM-5-TR*'s nonaxial diagnostic format incomplete may take steps to incorporate more holistic assessment and case formulation methods in their routine assessment and treatment planning practices. In the next two sections, we attend more specifically to logistics of coding and recording of diagnoses within the *DSM-5-TR*.

Other Specified and Unspecified Diagnoses

Clinicians who work with individuals who do not meet full criteria for more specific disorders within the *DSM-5-TR* have options for issuing other specified and unspecified diagnoses. Counselors should use *other specified* diagnosis to record a concern within a specific diagnostic category alongside a reason why a more specific diagnosis is not provided. In some cases, the *DSM-5-TR* provides a list of other specified diagnoses, including conditions for further study. Other times, clinicians may simply indicate reasons for the other specified diagnosis. For example, a client who meets all criteria for bulimia nervosa except frequency requirements could receive a diagnosis of F50.8 other specified feeding or eating disorder, bulimia nervosa of low frequency.

Counselors should use *unspecified* diagnosis when they are certain about the category of diagnosis but unable or unwilling to provide additional details. For example, a client who presents to an emergency room in an acutely psychotic state may not be able to provide the history necessary for an accurate diagnosis, and the clinician may not have access to information that might indicate if the disturbance was induced by a substance, medication, or another medical condition. In that case, one may render a diagnosis of F29 unspecified schizophrenia spectrum and other psychotic disorder.

Coding and Recording

ICD-10-CM Coding

Consistent with federal practices, the *DSM-5-TR* includes *ICD-10-CM* codes for data collection, insurance coding, and research purposes. The *ICD-10-CM* codes for mental disorders generally begin with the letter F; *ICD-10-CM* codes for psychosocial and environmental factors associated with disorders or of focus in counseling often begin with Z. There may be times that *DSM-5-TR* and *ICD-10-CM* names do not match completely, so counselors should always include both the code and the name of the disorder when documenting diagnoses.

Subtypes and Specifiers

Greater attention to a dimensional diagnostic system in the *DSM-5-TR* means that there are quite a few subtypes and specifiers included throughout the manual. For example, a client who has 2 or more years of depressed mood, including the presence of major depressive episodes within the experience, a degree of anxiety, and intermittent panic attacks, may be diagnosed with F34.1 persistent depressive disorder, with anxious distress, with panic attacks, late onset, with intermittent major depressive episodes, without current episode, moderate.

In most cases, clinicians will include the same diagnostic code regardless of the subtypes and specifiers assigned. There are some notable exceptions, especially regarding substance-related disorders. Although we include an outline of coding notes throughout this book, professional counselors should refer to the *DSM-5-TR* for coding instructions and examples.

Nonaxial Reporting Options

We noted earlier that counselors can and should retain a holistic approach to diagnosis even in the context of nonaxial reporting. Official *DSM-5-TR* diagnoses will include codes for mental health diagnoses, clinically significant psychosocial and environmental concerns, and relevant medical diagnoses that are part of the official record and confirmed by medical professionals qualified to diagnose them. These will be reported in a line-by-line manner.

We assume counselors will list disorders or concerns in order of clinical priority or relevance, with the principal diagnosis and reason for the visit listed first. When the principal diagnosis and reason for the visit are different, APA (2022) advised users to include a parenthetical notation regarding which is which. For example, a child who is referred for counseling because of numerous disciplinary problems at school and is found to meet criteria for ADHD may receive a diagnosis of

- F90.2 attention-deficient/hyperactivity disorder, combined presentation, moderate (principal diagnosis), and
- Z55.9 academic or educational problem (reason for visit).

In contrast, someone who meets criteria for depression, uses alcohol excessively, and is unable to control their diabetes as a result of the disturbance may receive a diagnosis of

- F32.2 major depressive disorder, single episode, severe;
- F10.10 alcohol use disorder, mild; and
- E11 Type 2 diabetes mellitus.

The second example raises an important consideration regarding counselors' scope of practice. A diagnosis of medical conditions alongside mental health disorders makes sense for psychiatrists who are qualified to diagnose and treat both. It also makes sense for mental health professionals who work in interdisciplinary settings where medical diagnoses are a matter of record. Given that counselors are not qualified to diagnose medical conditions, it is wise to refrain from including diagnostic mention of specific medical conditions unless the information is obtained via official medical records. Instead, counselors may include mention of client-reported medical conditions elsewhere in the case notes with a note that the client self-reported the medical concern or counselor recommendations for medical referrals or consultations.

The following points may serve as important reminders regarding rendering nonaxial diagnoses:

- The *ACA Code of Ethics* (ACA, 2014) notes the right to refuse to diagnose should a counselor believe that rendering a diagnosis could be harmful. Refusing to diagnose is different from assigning an inaccurate diagnosis. There are substantial ethical and legal ramifications of upcoding (i.e., assigning a more severe diagnosis so insurance will cover treatment) and downcoding (i.e., assigning a less severe diagnosis to reduce potential stigma). These practices are risky and amount to insurance fraud.
- Counselors who are not yet ready to render a diagnosis may defer diagnosis using the *ICD-10-CM* code R69.
- If they determine no diagnosis is present, counselors may use the code Z03.89 encounter for observation for other suspected diseases and conditions ruled out.

In reality, there should always be a reason for a counseling visit or referral, so we recommend using a more specific Z code from the Other Conditions That May Be a Focus of Clinical Attention chapter in the *DSM-5-TR*.
- When relatively certain that a client meets or will meet criteria for a diagnosis, counselors may note uncertainty by indicating the diagnosis as provisional. *Provisional* should be placed in parentheses following the diagnosis.
- The *DSM-5-TR* includes a long list of contextual issues that may be clinically relevant for clients. We encourage counselors to include the Z codes when they are important to client conceptualization and treatment planning. Counselors may also use supplemental case documentation formats that include space for enhanced attention to psychosocial and environmental considerations alongside notations for client strengths and supports in addition to problems.

The *DSM-5-TR* includes directions that clinicians include "separation notations" for disability. To some degree, counselors will indicate the degree of distress and impairment using the dimensional assessment severity ratings provided throughout the *DSM-5-TR*. The *DSM-5-TR* also includes a more comprehensive assessment, the WHODAS 2.0 (WHO, 2010), as holding promise for documenting functional impairment. Regardless of whether one adopts the WHODAS 2.0, counselors need to consider how to attend to impairment in routine assessment and case documentation practices.

Diagnostic Assessment and Other Screening Tools

The print version of the *DSM-5-TR* includes several assessment tools counselors may find helpful for screening client concerns. These include cross-cutting symptom measures for initial screening; a clinician-rated measure of psychosis severity; and the WHODAS 2.0, a well-validated measure of disability-related concerns. APA (n.d.) also provides a number of supplemental assessment tools in their website. Some of these tools can be helpful for ensuring systematic assessment while also measuring progress.

Cross-cutting symptom measures were "modeled on general medicine's review of symptoms" (APA, 2022, p. 841). Think of Level 1 cross-cutting symptom measures as a very general screening checklist you might complete when you see your general practitioner. It does not lead to a diagnosis, but it is a quick way of signaling areas that need to be further explored. The *DSM-5-TR* includes an adult measure and a child measure to be completed by a caregiver; the supplemental website also includes a self-report measure for youth ages 11 to 17. For example, the adult version of the cross-cutting symptom measure includes 23 questions focused on 13 domains of broad concern to clinicians across settings. Domains include areas such as depression, anger, anxiety, and sleep problems. Clients or informants use a scale from 0 (*none/not at all*) to 4 (*severe/nearly every day*) to rate their concerns over a 2-week period. With the exception of suicidal ideation, psychosis, and substance abuse for which any endorsement warrants follow-up, counselors are advised to further inquire about any domains in which a client endorses items at a level of mild/several days or greater.

To facilitate assessment, most Level 1 domains are associated with Level 2 cross-cutting symptom measures. Level 2 measures for adults include those focused on depression, anger, mania, anxiety, somatic symptoms, sleep disturbance, repetitive thoughts and behaviors, and substance use. These assessment tools and information regarding the development, administration, and psychometric properties are available free of charge via APA's website. Although most Level 2 measures were developed using well-validated instruments, not all formulations have been validated. For these reasons, counselors should use Level 1 and Level 2 measures with caution, considering them just one source of client information.

APA also provides several disorder-specific severity measures to be used with the *DSM-5-TR*. These measures correspond to specific disorders or categories of disorders. Some are designed as self-report measures, and counselors complete other measures following a diagnostic interview. Except for the Clinician-Rated Dimensions of Psychosis Symptom Severity Scale available in the printed version of the *DSM-5*, these scales are all available through the APA website. These scales vary widely in format, quality, and rigor of psychometric validation. For example, APA chose the Patient Health Questionnaire–9, a well-developed instrument in the public domain, as the severity measure for depression. Counselors can easily access information needed to use this scale with a strong degree of integrity. On the other hand, the Severity Measure for Panic Disorder–Adult has face validity but does not include reference to development and validation procedures. Finally, the Clinician-Rated Severity of Oppositional Defiant Disorder measure simply includes one item advising clinicians to rate severity on a 4-point scale based solely on the number of settings in which concerns occur. Counselors who use severity measures in practice are responsible for learning more about the development, validation, and psychometric properties of the measures so they may ensure adherence to ethical (ACA, 2014) and best practice (Lenz et al., 2022) guidelines. See Schmit and Balkin (2014) for a deeper dive into evaluating these measures.

APA endorses the WHODAS 2.0 as a well-validated method for assessing disability related to medical or mental health concerns. The WHODAS 2.0 is a well-established assessment measure appropriate for use with diverse populations and captures the level of functioning in six domains of life:

- Domain 1: Cognition—understanding and communicating
- Domain 2: Mobility—moving and getting around
- Domain 3: Self-care—attending to one's hygiene, dressing, eating, and staying alone
- Domain 4: Getting along—interacting with other people
- Domain 5: Life activities—domestic responsibilities, leisure, work, and school
- Domain 6: Participation—joining in community activities, participating in society. (Üstün et al., 2010, p. 4)

In short, the WHODAS 2.0 may be completed by a client or informant and includes 36 items in which one rates their concerns over the past 30 days on a scale ranging from 1 (*none*) to 5 (*extreme*). It takes 5 to 20 minutes to complete and is appropriate for repeat administration. Extensive information regarding scoring, norms, psychometric properties, and the development process is provided in a manual available in the public domain (Üstün et al., 2010). A version of the WHODAS appropriate for working with children and youth is currently under development.

As you will learn in our chapter on personality disorders (see Chapter 14), APA has been developing a new dimensional-categorical model of personality traits and functioning. APA's website includes brief and full forms of personality inventories appropriate for use with adults, informants, and youth ages 11–17. The scales and subscales in the assessment tools are aligned with facets and domains conceptualized within the alternative model for personality disorders printed in Section III of the *DSM-5-TR*. Those interested in using this assessment tool should refer to Krueger et al. (2012).

APA's provision of assessment tools corresponding to key constructs within the *DSM-5-TR* represents a shift in thinking from the *DSM* as a manual that simply describes experiences to one in which a degree of clinical practice is suggested or prescribed. As noted throughout this section, the measures provided in print and online vary widely in their rigor. The degree to which they are usable in everyday counseling practice will vary in accordance with properties of the specific measure, counselors' work setting and focus, and counselors' theoretical orientation. The instruments are largely deficit based and grounded in a medical model. We do not yet know whether counselors will find these instruments useful for practice and feasible in the world of managed care. Counselors operating from wellness and strength-based models may wish to incorporate assessment tools reflective of this orientation in addition to or instead of the tools provided by APA. To learn more about these assessments in general, refer to Jones (2012). APA may release measures for further study on a rolling basis, so readers may wish to periodically check APA's website for updates.

The Future of the *DSM*

As we discussed in the introduction to this book, the *DSM* is an evolving manual that reflects the particular time in which it was created. Mental health professionals have witnessed the *DSM* shift from explicit psychodynamic foundations in the original document to implicit to a supposedly atheoretical medical model in the third revision to a more dimensional model in the *DSM-5*.

Given the expansion of national priorities regarding brain-based initiatives and neurobiological research on mental disorders, we expect continued efforts around understanding and classifying the etiology of disorders rather than the classification of symptom-based experiences. Certainly, the National Institute of Mental Health noted such a shift in focus when they endorsed the *DSM-5* as the "contemporary consensus standard for how mental disorders are diagnosed and treated" (see Insel & Lieberman, 2013, para. 2) and went on to express plans for "a new kind of taxonomy for mental disorders by bringing the power of modern research approaches in genetics, neuroscience, and behavioral science to the problem of mental illness" (para. 3).

Professional counselors, as one of the largest consumers of the *DSM* (Frances, 2011), are responsible for ensuring they understand and incorporate the latest advances in related professions while advocating for assessment, diagnostic, and counseling approaches that best empower "diverse individuals, families, and groups to accomplish mental health, wellness, education, and career goals" (Kaplan et al., 2014, p. 366) in accordance with ACA's definition of counseling. In the years to come, professional counselors will need to decide whether to advocate for enhanced inclusion in *DSM* revision processes. They may also explore other ways to navigate realities of the managed care system consistent with the philosophical, theoretical foundations and their work as professional counselors.

As you work to understand the information in this book, we ask you to hold the information you learn, often from psychiatry and psychology research, alongside your philosophical commitment to the counseling profession. In doing so, remember that the *DSM* is simply a collection of "tales of suffering and complaint" (Amundson, 1998, p. 1). Although we worked to help a counseling perspective emerge, there will be times the language is quite medically oriented and pathology focused. Remember your strength-based, holistic, and developmental foundations are assets for navigating a healing process with humans who are hurting. Counselors may pull from character strengths, virtues, and environmental resources as assets in addressing adversity (Tomlinson-Clarke & Georges, 2014). In so doing, you can bring your unique preparation and frameworks to help clients grow through relationships, find empowerment, and understand their experiences within a sociocultural context.

Questions for Consideration

1. What are the benefits and drawbacks of considering mental disorders biological conditions?
2. How can counselors keep integrity in diagnostic practice while also retaining the strength-based, developmental, and contextual commitments of the profession?
3. How can you ensure continued attention to medical conditions, life context, and overall functioning within the nonaxial format?
4. To what degree might the cross-cutting symptom measures be useful in your practice?

Part One

References

Aggarwal, N. K., Jarvis, G. E., Gómez-Carrillo, A., Kirmayer, L. J., & Lewis-Fernández, R. (2020). The Cultural Formulation Interview since *DSM-5*: Prospects for training, research, and clinical practice. *Transcultural Psychiatry, 57*(4), 496–514. https://doi.org/10.1177/1363461520940481

Alvarez, J. C., Waitz-Kudla, S., Brydon, C., Crosby, E., & Witte, T. K. (2022). Culturally responsive scalable mental health interventions: A call to action. *Translational Issues in Psychological Science, 8*(3), 406–415. https://doi.org/10.1037/tps0000319

American Counseling Association. (2014). *ACA code of ethics.* https://www.counseling.org/resources/aca-code-of-ethics.pdf

American Psychiatric Association. (n.d.). *DSM-5-TR online assessment measures.* https://www.psychiatry.org/psychiatrists/practice/dsm/educational-resources/assessment-measures

American Psychiatric Association. (1994). *Diagnostic and statistical manual of mental disorders* (4th ed.).

American Psychiatric Association (2013a). *Cultural Formulation Interview supplementary module.* https://www.psychiatry.org/getmedia/aca8f5a2-9b1b-456c-a3b7-f7f852edcf7c/APA-DSM5TR-CulturalFormulationInterviewSupplementaryModules.pdf

American Psychiatric Association. (2013b). *Diagnostic and statistical manual of mental disorders* (5th ed.). https://doi.org/10.1176/appi.books.9780890425596

American Psychiatric Association. (2022). *Diagnostic and statistical manual of mental disorders* (5th ed., text rev.). https://doi.org/10.1176/appi.books.9780890425787

Amundson, J. K. (1998). Tales of suffering and complaint—Asking *DSM-IV* to do more than it was intended for. *Journal of Systemic Therapies, 17*(3), 1–11. https://doi.org/10.1521/jsyt.1998.17.3.1

Anda, R. F., Felitti, V. J., Bremner, J. D., Walker, J. D., Whitfield, C., Perry, B. D., Dube, S. R., & Giles, W. H. (2006). The enduring effects of abuse and related adverse experiences in childhood. A convergence of evidence from neurobiology and epidemiology. *European archives of psychiatry and clinical neuroscience, 256*(3), 174–186. https://doi.org/10.1007/s00406-005-0624-4

Assogna, F., Piras, F., & Spalletta, G. (2020). Neurobiological basis of childhood trauma and the risk for neurological deficits later in life. In G. Spalletta, D. Janiri, F. Piras, & G. Sani (Eds.), *Childhood trauma in mental disorders: A comprehensive approach* (pp. 385–410). https://doi.org/10.1007/978-3-030-49414-8_18

Atkins, K., & Lorelle, S. (2022). Cultural humility: Lessons learned through a counseling immersion. *Journal of Counselor Preparation and Supervision, 15*(1), Article 9. https://digitalcommons.sacredheart.edu/jcps/vol15/iss1/9

Bieling, P. J., & Kuyken, W. (2003). Is cognitive case formulation science or science fiction? *Clinical Psychology: Science and Practice, 10*(1), 52–69. https://doi.org/10.1093/clipsy.10.1.52

Binensztok, V. (2019). *The influence of reflective practice on the case conceptualization competence of counselor trainees* (Publication No. ED602256) [Doctoral dissertation, Florida Atlantic University]. ProQuest Dissertations and Theses Global.

Bitter, J. R. (2021). *Theory and practice of couples and family counseling* (3rd ed.). American Counseling Association.

Bredström, A. (2019). Culture and context in mental health diagnosing: Scrutinizing the *DSM-5* revision. *Journal of Medical Humanities, 40*(3), 347–363. https://doi.org/10.1007/s10912-017-9501-1

Brooks, R. T., & Hopkins, R. (2017). Cultural mistrust and health care utilization: The effects of culturally responsive cognition intervention. *Journal of Black Studies, 48*(8), 816–834. https://doi.org/10.1177/0021934717728454

Carter, R. T., Johnson, V. E., Roberson, K., Mazzula, S. L., Kirkinis, K., & Sant-Barket, S. (2017). Race-based traumatic stress, racial identity statuses, and psychological functioning: An exploratory investigation. *Professional Psychology: Research and Practice, 48*(1), 30–37. https://doi.org/10.1037/pro0000116

Cline, J. L., Sturm, D. C., & Staton, A. R. (2022). Teaching case conceptualization skills to clinical mental health students to enhance clinical competency and cognitive complexity. *Journal of Counselor Preparation and Supervision, 15*(3), Article 1. https://digitalcommons.sacredheart.edu/jcps/vol15/iss3/1

Council for Accreditation of Counseling and Related Educational Programs. (2024). *2024 CACREP standards.* https://www.cacrep.org/wp-content/uploads/2023/06/Combined-version-6.21.23.pdf

Crenshaw, K. (1989). Demarginalizing the intersection of race and sex: A Black feminist critique of antidiscrimination doctrine, feminist theory and antiracist politics. *University of Chicago Legal Forum, 1989*(1), Article 8. http://chicagounbound.uchicago.edu/uclf/vol1989/iss1/8

Cross, D., Fani, N., Powers, A., & Bradley, B. (2017). Neurobiological development in the context of childhood trauma. *Clinical Psychology, 24*(2), 111–124. https://doi.org/10.1111/cpsp.12198

Dailey, S. F. (2018). Counselor self-awareness and counselor communication. In C. S. Gill & R. R. Freund (Eds.), *Spirituality and religion in counseling* (pp. 8–31). Routledge.

Day-Vines, N. L., Cluxton-Keller, F., Agorsor, C., Gubara, S., & Otabil, N. A. A. (2020). The multidimensional model of broaching behavior. *Journal of Counseling & Development, 98*(1), 107–118. https://doi.org/10.1002/jcad.12304

Day-Vines, N. L., Wood, S., Grothaus, T., Craigen, L., Holman, A., Dotson-Blake, K., & Douglass, M. (2007). Broaching the subjects of race, ethnicity, and culture during the counseling process. *Journal of Counseling & Development, 85*(4), 401–409. https://doi.org/10.1002/j.1556-6678.2007.tb00608.x

Deferio, J. J., Breitinger, S., Khullar, D., Sheth, A., & Pathak, J. (2019). Social determinants of health in mental health care and research: A case for greater inclusion. *Journal of the American Medical Informatics Association, 26*(8–9), 895–899. https://doi.org/10.1093/jamia/ocz049

Dinkmeyer, D., & Sperry, L. (2000). *Counseling and psychotherapy: An integrated, individual psychology approach.* Prentice Hall.

Eap, S., Gobin, R. L., Ng, J., & Hall, G. C. N. (2010). Sociocultural issues in the diagnosis and assessment of psychological disorders. In J. E. Maddux & J. P. Tangney (Eds.), *Social psychological foundations of clinical psychology* (pp. 312–328). Guilford Press.

Earnshaw, V. A., Bogart, L. M., Klompas, M., & Katz, I. T. (2019). Medical mistrust in the context of Ebola: Implications for intended care-seeking and quarantine policy support in the United States. *Journal of Health Psychology, 24*(2), 219–228. https://doi.org/10.1177/1359105316650507

Ecks, S. (2015). The strange absence of things in the "culture" of the *DSM-V. Canadian Medical Association Journal, 188*(2), 142–143. https://doi.org/10.1503/cmaj.150268

Eels, T. D. (2020). Foreword. In L. Sperry & J. Sperry (Eds.), *Case conceptualization: Mastering this competency with ease and confidence* (pp. xi–xii). Routledge.

Eriksen, K., & Kress, V. E. (2006). The *DSM* and professional counseling identity: Bridging the gap. *Journal of Mental Health Counseling, 28*(3), 202–217. https://doi.org/10.17744/mehc.28.3.4f39a6wr1n3fceh2

Felitti, V. J., Anda, R. F., Nordenberg, D., Williamson, D. F., Spitz, A. M., Edwards, V., & Marks, J. S. (1998). Relationship of childhood abuse and household dysfunction to many of the leading causes of death in adults: The Adverse Childhood Experiences (ACE) Study. *American Journal of Preventive Medicine, 14*(4), 245–258. https://doi.org/10.1016/S0749-3797(98)00017-8

Field, T. A. (2017). *Neurocounseling: Brain-based clinical approaches.* American Counseling Association.

Field, T. A., & Ghoston, M. R. (2020). *Neuroscience-informed counseling with children and adolescents.* American Counseling Association.

Frances, A. J. (2011, June 3). Who needs *DSM-5*? A strong warning comes from professional counselors. *Psychology Today.* https://www.psychologytoday.com/us/blog/dsm5-in-distress/201106/who-needs-dsm-5

Gaete, J., Smoliak, O., Couture, S., & Strong, T. (2017). *DSM* diagnosis and social justice: Inviting counselor reflexivity. In C. Audet & D. Paré (Eds.), *Social justice and counseling* (pp. 196–211). Routledge/Taylor & Francis. https://doi.org/10.4324/9781315753751-20

Gill, C. S., & Freund, R. R. (2018). Understanding worldview and impact of spiritual systems through assessment: Open and closed faith systems. In C. S. Gill & R. Freund (Eds.), *Spirituality and religion in counseling: Competency-based strategies for ethical practice* (pp. 32–50). Routledge/Taylor & Francis. https://doi.org/10.4324/9781315211046-3

Gill, C. S., Harper, M. C., & Dailey, S. (2020). Assessing the spiritual and religious domain. In C. S. Cashwell & J. S. Young (Eds.), *Integrating religion and spirituality in counseling: A guide to competent practice* (3rd ed., pp. 165–189). American Counseling Association.

Grad, R. I. (2022). Therapeutic alliance and childhood interpersonal trauma: The role of attachment, cultural humility, and therapeutic presence. *Journal of Counseling & Development, 100*(3), 296–307. https://doi.org/10.1002/jcad.12423

Hays, D. G., & Erford, B. T. (2022). *Developing multicultural counseling competence: A systems approach* (4th ed.). Pearson.

Hook, J. N., Davis, D., Owen, J., & DeBlaere, C. (2017). *Cultural humility: Engaging diverse identities in therapy.* American Psychological Association.

Insel, T. R., & Lieberman, J. A. (2013, May 13). *DSM and RDoc: Shared interests.* https://nyspi.org/node/15128

International Association for Marriage and Family Counseling. (2017). *IAMFC code of ethics.* https://www.iamfconline.org/public/IAMFC-Ethical-Code-Final.pdf

Ivers, N. N., & Johnson, D. A. (2022). The relationship between mindfulness and multicultural counseling competence among mental health practitioners. *The Journal of Humanistic Counseling, 61*(1), 43–57. https://doi.org/10.1002/johc.12170

Ivey, A. E., & Ivey, M. B. (1998). Reframing *DSM-IV*: Positive strategies from developmental counseling and therapy. *Journal of Counseling & Development, 76*(3), 334–350. https://doi.org/10.1002/j.1556-6676.1998.tb02550.x

Jaiswal, J., & Halkitis, P. N. (2019). Towards a more inclusive and dynamic understanding of medical mistrust informed by science. *Behavioral Medicine, 45*(2), 79–85. https://doi.org/10.1080/08964289.2019.1619511

Jones, K. D. (2012). Dimensional and cross-cutting assessment in the *DSM-5. Journal of Counseling & Development, 90*(4), 481–487. https://doi.org/10.1002/j.1556-6676.2012.00059.x

Kaplan, D. M., Tarvydas, V. M., & Gladding, S. T. (2014). 20/20: A vision for the future of counseling: The new consensus definition of counseling. *Journal of Counseling & Development, 92*(3), 366–372. https://doi.org/10.1002/j.1556-6676.2014.00164.x

Karatekin, C., & Hill, M. (2019). Expanding the original definition of adverse childhood experiences (ACEs). *Journal of Child & Adolescent Trauma, 12*(3), 289–306. https://doi.org/10.1007/s40653-018-0237-5

Kazda, L., Bell, K., Thomas, R., McGeechan, K., Sims, R., & Barratt, A. (2021). Overdiagnosis of attention-deficit/hyperactivity disorder in children and adolescents: A systematic scoping review. *JAMA Network Open, 4*(4), Article e215335. https://doi.org/10.1001/jamanetworkopen.2021.5335

King, K. M. (2021). "I want to, but how?" Defining counselor broaching in core tenets and debated components. *Journal of Multicultural Counseling and Development, 49*(2), 87–100. https://doi.org/10.1002/jmcd.12208
King, K. M., & Borders, L. D. (2019). An experimental investigation of White counselors broaching race and racism. *Journal of Counseling & Development, 97*(4), 341–351. http://doi.org/10.1002/jcad.12283
Kirmayer, L. J. (2013). The cultural diversity of healing: Meaning, metaphor, and mechanism. *Heart Views, 14*(1), 39–40. https://doi.org/10.4103/1995-705x.107123
Kress, V. E., Barrio Minton, C. A., Adamson, N. A., Paylo, M. J., & Pope, V. (2014). The removal of the multiaxial system in the *DSM-5*: Implications and practice suggestions for counselors. *The Professional Counselor, 4*(3), 191–201. https://doi.org/10.15241/vek.4.3.191
Kress, V. E., Hoffman, R. M., & Eriksen, K. (2010). Ethical dimensions of diagnosing: Considerations for clinical mental health counselors. *Counseling and Values, 55*(1), 101–112. https://doi.org/10.1002/j.2161-007X.2010.tb00024.x
Krueger, R. F., Derringer, J., Markon, K. E., Watson, D., & Skodol, A. E. (2012). Initial construction of a maladaptive personality trait model and inventory for *DSM-5*. *Psychological Medicine, 42*(9), 1879–1890. https://doi.org/10.1017/S0033291711002674
La Roche, M. J., Fuentes, M. A., & Hinton, D. (2015). A cultural examination of the *DSM-5*: Research and clinical implications for cultural minorities. *Professional Psychology: Research and Practice, 46*(3), 183–189. https://doi.org/10.1037/a0039278
Lawrence, J. (2000). The Indian Health Service and the sterilization of Native American women. *American Indian Quarterly, 24*(3), 400–419. https://doi.org/10.1353/aiq.2000.0008
Lenz, A. S., Ault, H., Balkin, R. S., Barrio Minton, C., Erford, B. T., Hays, D. G., Kim, B. S. K., & Li, C. (2022). Responsibilities of Users of Standardized Tests (RUST-4E). *Measurement and Evaluation in Counseling and Development, 55*(4), 227–235. https://doi.org/10.1080/07481756.2022.2052321
Levensen, H., & Strupp, H. (2007). Cyclical maladaptive patterns: Case formulation in time-limited dynamic psychotherapy. In T. D. Eells (Ed.), *Handbook of psychotherapy case formulation* (2nd ed., pp. 164–197). Guilford Press
Luke, C. C. (2015). *Neuroscience for counselors and therapists: Integrating the sciences of mind and brain*. Sage.
Luke, C., Miller, R., & McAuliffe, G. (2019). Neuro-informed mental health counseling: A person-first perspective. *Journal of Mental Health Counseling, 41*(1), 65–79. https://doi.org/10.17744/mehc.41.1.06
McWilliams, N. (1999). *Psychoanalytic case formulation*. Guilford Press.
Merriam-Webster. (n.d.) Conceptualization. In *Merriam-Webster.com dictionary*. https://www.merriam-webster.com/dictionary/conceptualization
Merrick, M. T., Ford, D. C., Ports, K. A., Guinn, A. S., Chen, J., Klevens, J., Metzler, M., Jones, C. M., Simon, T. R., Daniel, V. M., Ottley, P., Mercy, J. A. (2019). Vital signs: Estimated proportion of adult health problems attributable to adverse dhildhood experiences and implications for prevention—25 states, 2015-2017. *Morbidity and Mortality Weekly Report, 68*(44), 999–1005. https://doi.org/10.15585/mmwr.mm6844e1
Merten, E. C., Cwik, J. C., Margraf, J., & Schneider, S. (2017). Overdiagnosis of mental disorders in children and adolescents (in developed countries). *Child and Adolescent Psychiatry and Mental Health, 11,* Article 5. https://doi.org/10.1186/s13034-016-0140-5
Miller, R., & Prosek, E. A. (2013). Trends and implications of proposed changes to the *DSM-5* for vulnerable populations. *Journal of Counseling & Development, 91*(3), 359–366. https://doi.org/10.1002/j.1556-6676.2013.00106.x
Montes, S. (2013, November 1). Facing a rising tide of personality disorders. *Counseling Today*. https://ct.counseling.org/2013/11/facing-a-rising-tide-of-personality-disorders/
Moran, M. (2022, February 22). Impact of culture, race, social determinants reflected throughout new *DSM-5-TR*. *Psychiatric News*. https://doi.org/10.1176/appi.pn.2022.03.3.20
Morgan, P. L., Woods, A. D., & Wang, Y. (2023). Sociodemographic disparities in attention-deficit/hyperactivity disorder overdiagnosis and overtreatment during elementary school. *Journal of Learning Disabilities, 56*(5), 359–370. https://doi.org/10.1177/00222194221099675

Mukhtar, S. (2023). COVID-19 feminist framework and biopsychosocial-spiritual perspective for social workers and mental health practitioners to manage violence, abuse, and trauma against children, women, BIPOC, and LGBTQIA+ during and post-COVID-19. *International Social Work, 66*(1), 93–106. https://doi.org/10.1177/00208728211067158

Myers, J .E. (1991). Wellness as the paradigm for counseling and development: The possible future. *Counselor Education and Supervision, 30*(3), 183–193. https://doi.org/10.1002/j.1556-6978.1991.tb01199.x

O'Hara, C., Chang, C. Y., & Giordano, A. L. (2021). Multicultural competence in counseling research: The cornerstone of scholarship. *Journal of Counseling & Development, 99*(2), 200–209. https://doi.org/10.1002/jcad.12367

Perry, B. L., Neltner, M., & Allen, T. (2013). A paradox of bias: Racial differences in forensic psychiatric diagnosis and determinations of criminal responsibility. *Race and Social Problems, 5*(4), 239–249. https://doi.org/10.1007/s12552-013-9100-3

Porter, C., Palmier-Claus, J., Branitsky, A., Mansell, W., Warwick, H., & Varese, F. (2020). Childhood adversity and borderline personality disorder: A meta-analysis. *Acta Psychiatrica Scandinavica, 141*(1), 6–20. https://doi-org/10.1111/acps.13118

Ratts, M. J., Singh, A. A., Nassar-McMillan, S., Butler, S. K., & McCullough, J. R. (2015). *Multicultural and social justice counseling competencies.* https://www.counseling.org/docs/default-source/competencies/multicultural-and-social-justice-counseling-competencies.pdf?sfvrsn=20

Ridley, C. R., & Jeffrey, C. E. (2017). Thematic mapping in case conceptualization: An introduction to the special section. *Journal of Clinical Psychology, 73*(4), 353–358. https://doi.org/10.1002/jclp.22355

Ridley, C. R., Jeffrey, C. E., & Roberson, R. B. (2017). Case misconceptualization in psychological treatment: An enduring clinical problem. *Journal of Clinical Psychology, 73*(4), 359–375. https://doi.org/10.1002/jclp.22354

Riggs, D. W., Pearce, R., Pfeffer, C. A., Hines, S., White, F., & Ruspini, E. (2019). Transnormativity in the psy disciplines: Constructing pathology in the *Diagnostic and statistical manual of mental disorders* and standards of care. *American Psychologist, 74*(8), 912–924. https://doi.org/10.1037/amp0000545

Schmit, E. L., & Balkin, R. S. (2014). Evaluating emerging measures in the *DSM-5* for counseling practice. *The Professional Counselor, 4*(3), 216–231. https://doi.org/10.15241/els.4.3.216

Schwartz, R. C., & Blankenship, D. M. (2014). Racial disparities in psychotic disorder diagnosis: A review of empirical literature. *World Journal of Psychiatry, 4*(4), 133–140. https://doi.org/10.5498/wjp.v4.i4.133

Schwartz, R. C., & Feisthamel, K. P. (2009). Disproportionate diagnosis of mental disorders among African American versus European American clients: Implications for counseling theory, research, and practice. *Journal of Counseling & Development, 87*(1), 295–301. https://doi.org/10.1002/j.1556-6678.2009.tb00110.x

Shaw, S. (2016, December 27). Practicing cultural humility. *Counseling Today.* https://ct.counseling.org/2016/12/practicing-cultural-humility/

Siegel, D. J., Schore, A. N., & Cozolino, L. J. (2021). *Interpersonal neurobiology and clinical practice.* Norton.

Solheim, C. A., Ballard, J., Fatiha, N., Dini, Z., Buchanan, G., & Song, S. (2022). Immigrant family financial and relationship stress from the COVID-19 pandemic. *Journal of Family and Economic Issues, 43*(2), 282–295. http://doi.org/10.1007/s10834-022-09819-2

Sperry, J., & Sperry, L. (2020, December 7). Case conceptualization: Key to highly effective counseling. *Counseling Today.* https://ct.counseling.org/2020/12/case-conceptualization-key-to-highly-effective-counseling/

Sperry, L. (2010). *Core competencies in counseling and psychotherapy: Becoming a highly competent and effective therapist.* Routledge.

Sperry, L., & Peluso, P. (2019). *Couple therapy: Theory and effective practice* (3rd ed.). Routledge.

Sperry, L., & Sperry, J. (2020). *Case conceptualization: Mastering this competency with ease and confidence* (2nd ed.). Routledge.

Sperry, L., & Sperry, J. (2022). *The 15 minute case conceptualization mastering the pattern-focused approach.* Oxford University Press.

Stoupas, G., Binensztok, V., & Sperry, L. (2018). Understanding the spiritual domain through case conceptualization. In C. S. Gill & R. R. Freund (Eds.), *Spirituality and religion in counseling: Competency-based strategies for ethical practice* (pp. 64–82). Routledge.

Sung, Y., & Skovholt, T. (2019). Master group counselors' case conceptualizations. *The Journal for Specialists in Group Work, 44*(2), 118–137. https://doi.org/10.1080/01933922.2019.1599479

Tomlinson-Clarke, S. M., & Georges, C. M. (2014). *DSM-5*: A commentary on integrating multicultural and strength-based considerations into counseling training and practice. *The Professional Counselor, 4*(3), 272–281. https://doi.org/10.15241/stc.4.3.272

Üstün, T. B., Kostanjsek, N., Chatterji, S., & Rehm, J. (2010). *Measuring health and disability: Manual for WHO Disability Assessment Schedule (WHODAS 2.0)*. World Health Organization Press.

Walby, S., Armstrong, J., & Strid, S. (2012). Intersectionality: Multiple inequities in social theory. *Sociology, 46*(2), 224–240. https://doi.org./10.1177/0038038511416164

Whaley, A. L. (2001). Cultural mistrust: An important psychological construct for diagnosis and treatment of African Americans. *Professional Psychology: Research and Practice, 32*(6), 555–562. https://doi.org/10.1037/0735-7028.32.6.555

World Health Organization. (2010). *WHO Disability Assessment Schedule 2.0–WHODAS 2.0.*

Wright, J., Basco, M., & Thase, M. (2006). *Learning cognitive-behavior therapy: An illustrated guide.* American Psychiatric Press.

Young, M., Klest, D., & Bitter, J. R. (2021). Virtue, ethics, and legality in couples and family practice. In J. R. Bitter (Ed.), *Theory and practice of couples and family counseling* (3rd ed., pp. 79–104). American Counseling Association.

Zalaquett, C. P., Fuerth, K. M., Stein, C., Ivey, A. E., & Ivey, M. B. (2008). Reframing the *DSM-IV-TR* from a multicultural/social justice perspective. *Journal of Counseling & Development, 86*(3), 364–371. https://doi.org/10.1002/j.1556-6678.2008.tb00521.x

Part Two

Changes and Implications Involving Mood, Anxiety, and Stressor-Related Concerns

Introduction

The disorders covered in Part Two are divided into six chapters: Chapter 6, Depressive Disorders; Chapter 7, Bipolar and Related Disorders; Chapter 8, Anxiety Disorders; Chapter 9, Obsessive-Compulsive and Related Disorders; Chapter 10, Trauma- and Stressor-Related Disorders; and Chapter 11, Gender Dysphoria in Children, Adolescents, and Adults. This part includes diagnoses, such as major depressive disorder and posttraumatic stress disorder, that involve affective distress commonly seen by counselors across various work settings and client populations. In each chapter, readers will find a basic description of the diagnostic classification, an overview of specific disorders covered, and highlights and essential features of each disorder (including differential diagnoses and cultural considerations). Comprehensive reviews of specific changes, when applicable, from the *DSM-5* to the *DSM-5-TR* are provided. For disorders commonly seen by counselors, we present case studies to help counselors understand practically how these disorders may present clinically in a wide variety of contexts and client populations. In keeping with our intent to discuss conditions relevant to counselors, we discuss pervasiveness of disorders among the general population as well as etiology and treatment. We also emphasize, from an ecosystemic perspective, special considerations for counselors to better understand individual, social, community, and societal factors that may impact diagnostic assessment and/or treatment. Unless explicitly stated, prevalence rates are based on *DSM-5-TR* criteria.

Major changes to look for in Part Two related to depressive disorders include changes to the wording of Criterion D for major depressive disorder, changes to the wording for persistent depressive disorder, the restoration of unspecified mood disorder, the addition of major depressive episode superimposed to other specified depressive disorder, and updated language for depressive disorder due to another medical condition. For bipolar and related disorders, we have highlighted changes to Criterion B for bipolar I and Criterion C for bipolar II disorders and modified severity specifiers for manic episodes and mood-congruent/mood-incongruent psychotic features. For anxiety and obsessive-compulsive and related disorders, we highlight changes to social anxiety disorder, which removed the term *social phobia*, and the addition of olfactory reference disorder as an example of presentations that can be specified under other specified obsessive-compulsive and related disorders. A discussion of the newly minted disorder, prolonged grief disorder, is presented in Chapter 10, Trauma- and Stressor-Related Disorders. Counselors will also see numerous changes from the *DSM-5* to *DSM-5-TR* that are intended to provide greater clarity and consistency, both for specific disorders and throughout the manual. Changes to look for associated with gender dysphoria reflect attempts by the DSM-5-TR Task Force to reinforce choice language and reduce associated stigma through more accurate, inclusive vernacular. For example, the text was updated with "experienced gender" replacing "desired gender," "gender affirming hormone treatment" replacing "cross-sex medical procedure," and "cross-sex hormone treatment" replacing "gender affirming hormone treatment."

Chapter 6

Depressive Disorders

Depression is a sustained condition of prolonged emotional dejection, sadness, and withdrawal. This persistent affective state "colors a person's perception of the world" (Reid & Wise, 1995, p. 145). Depressive disorders are diagnosed when a person's depressed mood is prolonged enough to interfere with regular daily functioning (APA, 2022a; NIMH, 2021).

Unlike addiction, impulse control, and behavioral concerns, depressive disorders primarily affect individuals through disturbance of mood and anxiety symptoms that are often co-occurring (NIMH, 2021). Worldwide, the prevalence rate for depression is high in comparison with other mental health disorders, with the World Health Organization (WHO, 2023) reporting that 280 million people, or 3.8% of the global population, have a depressive disorder. Because the prevalence of depression among adults in the United States is approximately 4.7%, these diagnoses are frequently the focus of clinical attention for counselors (National Center for Health Statistics, 2020).

Major Changes From *DSM-5* to *DSM-5-TR*

Changes regarding disruptive mood dysregulation disorder (DMDD) include minor text edits and some substantial section changes. The section changes include the new environmental factors consideration under "Risk and Prognostic Factors," the new "Culture-Related Diagnostic Issues" section, and the expansion of "Gender-Related Diagnostic Issues" to include "Sex-" within the header and discussion. Interestingly, the text section for suicide risk was removed for the updated nosology, and the new text section, "Association With Suicidal Thoughts and Behaviors," was not added. The DMDD changes also include research updates relevant to prevalence, development and course, and risk and prognostic factors (i.e., data highlighting age, gender, and genetic factors.)

Major depressive disorder (MDD) changes include Criterion D and an expansion in research data addressing features, prevalence, risk, culture, and gender. The "Culture Related Diagnostic Issues" section contains new text that highlights cross-cultural concerns locally and globally. We now have evidence of sex and gender differences between men and women discussed in the course of illness, a text section for "Association With Suicidal Thoughts or Behavior," updates for other text sections, and additional categories to the "Differential Diagnosis" section.

Changes in the *DSM-5-TR* also include the removal of "dysthymia" from the persistent depressive disorder diagnosis name and criterion sets, in addition to the updated text sections and additional differentials for this diagnosis. All except for two of the seven original specifiers have been removed, leaving only the *with anxious distress* specifier and *with atypical features* specifiers.

Premenstrual dysphoric disorder (PMDD) now includes updated text sections and additional differentials. The authors of the *DSM-5-TR* reinstated the unspecified mood disorder to this section and the bipolar disorders section, stating that this was unintentionally removed in the *DSM-IV-TR* (APA, 2022a). Other specified depressive disorder now includes a fourth example, "major depressive disorder superimposed."

In addition to these changes, in the original edition of the *DSM-5-TR*, the APA released an update, the *Supplement to the Diagnostic and Statistical Manual of Mental Disorders, Fifth Edition, Text Revision* (APA, 2022b), in September 2022, which describes new changes to the criteria for three disorders in this chapter. Specifically, the phrase "commit suicide," found in major depressive disorder Criterion A.9, was removed and replaced with language considered less stigmatizing (APA, 2013a). Additionally, the supplement reported that language was added in the "Differential Diagnosis" section to help clinicians differentiate between major depressive disorder and prolonged grief disorder, specifically, that prolonged grief is marked by a preoccupation with the deceased accompanied by emotional suffering and reduced engagement. Moreover, the symptoms of prolonged grief disorder stem from the grief event, personal loss, and the impact on one's ability to derive meaning from life. This contrasts with major depressive disorder, in which the depressed mood that persists is broad and unrelated to a loss. Prolonged grief is considered when an individual continues to experience a grief response, causing difficulties in functioning for more than 12 months following a death. In cases in which criteria for major depressive disorder and prolonged grief disorder are met, clinicians should use both diagnoses (APA, 2022b). We note that although the supplement reports these changes, we were unable to locate some of them in a *DSM-IV-TR* copy we purchased in 2023. The entire supplement is provided in APA (2022b). We encourage counselors to become familiar with this document.

Differential Diagnosis

Comorbidity is the rule rather than the exception with anxiety and depressive disorders. For example, symptoms of MDD and generalized anxiety disorder converge in several specific areas, including excessive fatigue, difficulty concentrating, and sleep disturbance (Aina & Susman, 2006). Kessler et al. (2015) reported that 45.7% of individuals diagnosed with lifetime depression worldwide also qualified for at least one chronic anxiety diagnosis. The Anxiety and Depression Association of America (ADAA, 2022) posited that nearly 50% of individuals diagnosed with an anxiety disorder also meet the criteria for a depressive disorder. However, there are specific differences among these disorders. For example, individuals who have depressive disorders typically do not display marked fear and uncertainty common with anxiety. Moreover, clients diagnosed with anxiety disorders do not usually display persistent feelings of sadness, hopelessness, and anhedonia typically observed by counselors within the context of depressive disorders. The *DSM-5* introduced a new *with anxious distress* specifier in hopes of capturing overlapping features of depressive and anxiety disorders. The *DSM-5-TR* includes this specifier with no changes from the original concept.

Etiology and Treatment

Most researchers agree that the etiology of depressive disorders is multifaceted, and pertinent aspects include biological factors, personality factors, neurochemistry, developmental processes, and environmental factors (Bains & Abdijadid, 2023; NIMH, 2023b). Treatments for these disorders are most successful when started in the early stages of the disorder. Counselors should always recommend a medical assessment to identify and address physiological causes. Using APA's online resources, counselors can find numerous assessment measures for depressive disorders, such as the Patient Health Questionnaire for adults. These assessments are not meant to be stand-alone diagnostic tools; counselors will find that they provide clarity and enhance clinical decision-making.

The most common and effective forms of treatment for depressive disorders combine medication management and psychotherapy (Bains & Abdijadid, 2023; NIMH, 2021). In terms of psychotherapy treatment outcomes, research indicates that depressive disorders typically respond to psychotherapeutic interventions (NIMH, 2021). NIMH (2021) and the ADAA (2020) have identified cognitive behavior therapy (CBT) and interpersonal therapy as the two most efficacious psychotherapeutic treatment modalities for depressive disorders. CBT assists individuals with restructuring and reframing negative thought processes, and interpersonal therapy helps them understand and work through discordant relationships (Corey, 2022; Ivey et al., 2012). Alternatively, some theorists posit that transtheoretical factors, often referred to as "common factors," including therapeutic alliance and relationship, lead to long-term symptom reductions for clients with mental illness (Mozdzierz et al., 2011).

Implications for Counselors

The counselor's ability to recognize depressive disorders is essential because of the high prevalence rates of depressive disorders found in the United States at any given time (National Center for Health Statistics, 2020). Depressive disorders are nearly twice as prevalent in women than in men. Although persons from any racial or social class background can be affected, these disorders are more commonly diagnosed in individuals who are unemployed or unable to work, previously married, and without health insurance (CDC, 2010). Clients with a family history of depression also present at higher risk, as do individuals of African American or Latino descent (Bailey et al., 2019; McKnight-Eily et al., 2021). Furthermore, the added stressors faced by minority groups during the COVID-19 pandemic disproportionately impacted the depressive symptoms experienced by Latinos and African Americans. McKnight-Eily et al. (2021) reported that lack of access to care, housing instability, food insecurity, and ongoing discrimination occurred at much higher rates for Latinos and African Americans than by White non-Hispanic Americans. They also found that symptoms of depression were higher for Blacks than for Whites and that these symptoms were reported 59% more frequently for Latinos than for White non-Hispanic Americans. Furthermore, the ADAA (2023) reported that LGBTQ+ youth are six times more likely to experience depressive symptoms than their heterosexual peers, as well as higher suicidal thoughts and nonsuicidal self-injury rates.

Depression is the most common mental disorder in the United States, with the prevalence rate increasing; as a result, depression is commonly seen within a typical mental health practice (Goodwin et al., 2022). Counselors often overlook the underlying symptoms of depression, focusing instead on the client's chief complaint, such as problems with mood or adjustment difficulties. Counselors will need to inquire about other problems, such as substance abuse, somatic complaints, or recent changes in medical status. Failure to do so can lead to the assumption that a depressive disorder is the only presenting problem for the client.

To help readers better understand changes from the *DSM-5* to the *DSM-5-TR*, the remainder of this chapter outlines each disorder within the Depressive Disorders chapter of the *DSM-5-TR*. Readers should note that we discuss changes in the text revision of this nosology; however, this is not a stand-alone diagnostic resource. Although a summary and special considerations for counselors are provided for each disorder, when diagnosing clients, counselors need to reference the *DSM-5-TR*. The diagnostic criteria and features, subtypes, specifiers (if applicable), prevalence, course, and risk and prognostic factors for each disorder must be clearly understood before diagnosis.

Disruptive Mood Dysregulation Disorder (F34.81)

> No one gets me, especially my dad. I do the right thing, and I get in trouble. That's why I get mad all the time, and sometimes I get in fights. My little sister is so stupid that I can't help but get mad at her. When she does dumb stuff, I yell at her, and sometimes I yell at my teachers too. I shouldn't have to do homework because I know all this stuff anyway, and I get so mad when they try to make me. They keep telling me I yell all the time, but it's not my fault. They just don't understand.—Barry

Disruptive mood dysregulation disorder (DMDD) was added to the *DSM-5* as a response to the rise in children diagnosed with bipolar disorder (Blader & Carlson, 2007; Moreno et al., 2007). When this diagnosis was initially discussed, clinicians voiced support for its inclusion because of the overdiagnosis of bipolar disorder in young adults and concern over whether severe nonepisodic irritability was developmental rather than a diagnosable pathological disorder. This concern persists, along with concerns regarding the conceptual basis and the validity of this disorder as a stand-alone construct (Hatchett, 2022). The inclusion of DMDD aimed to clarify these issues and allow for an appropriate diagnosis of children who do not fit well into the diagnosis of either conduct disorder or bipolar disorder.

Many research studies have been conducted following the inclusion of DMDD in the *DSM-5*. Therefore, our understanding of this disorder's prevalence, risk factors, and treatment has increased. The *DSM-5-TR* includes this updated research in the "Prevalence" and "Development and Course" sections (APA, 2022a, p. 179). In short, researchers indicate that although the prevalence rate of the general public is unclear, one study reported a rate of 2.5% within a cohort of Brazilian 11-year-olds. Gender differences are not reported; however, clinic trends indicate that most individuals reporting symptoms are males as young as 6 years of age (APA, 2022a, p. 179). To this end, researchers tend to conceptualize DMDD along with other externalizing disorders, which are more frequently diagnosed in males (Hatchett, 2022). The *DSM-5-TR* authors have identified risk factors related to adverse childhood experiences (ACEs), malnutrition, irritable temperament, and a family history of depression (APA, 2022a).

Although there is limited evidence of the effectiveness of treatments for DMDD, some evidence supports the use of CBT, dialectical behavioral therapy for children, and interpersonal psychotherapy for mood and behavior dysregulation (Hatchett, 2022). Theorists propose treatments such as Adlerian play therapy (Meany-Walen et al., 2014) and the combination of Adlerian therapy and equine therapy (Sauer & Gill, 2020). It is not uncommon to combine these modalities with psychopharmacology, including mood stabilizers, stimulants, and antipsychotics (Gilea & O'Neill, 2015).

Major Changes From *DSM-5 to DSM-5-TR*

The DMDD changes include minor text edits and more substantial section changes. Such section changes include the new "environmental factors" consideration under the "Risk and Prognostic Factors" section, the new "Culture-Related Diagnostic Issues" section, and the expansion of "Gender-Related Diagnostic Issues" to include "Sex-" within the header and discussion. Interestingly, the text section for "Suicide Risk" was removed for the updated nosology, and the new text section, "Association With Suicidal Thoughts and Behaviors," was not added. The DMDD changes also include research updates relevant to "Prevalence," "Development and Course," and "Risk and Prognostic Factors" (i.e., data highlighting age, gender, and genetic factors; APA, 2022a).

Essential Features

DMDD is a depressive disorder diagnosis intended for children and adolescents between the ages of 6 and 18, with onset before age 10 (APA, 2022a). The disorder is marked by severe, recurrent outbursts of temper, either verbal or behavioral, that are significantly out of proportion in intensity and duration with situational factors and the individual's developmental stage. The individual's mood between temper outbursts is persistently irritable or angry. Frequency must average at least three times per week for at least 12 months or more, and the behavior must be observable by others (e.g., parents, teachers, peers). The behaviors will occur in at least two settings (e.g., school and home) and be severe in at least one. The individual cannot be free from severe recurrent temper outbursts for longer than 3 months (APA, 2022a). Counselors should not give this diagnosis before the age of 6 or for the first time after 18, and history or observation of symptoms has an age of onset prior to 10 years old. If symptoms consistent with hypomania or mania occur for more than a day, another diagnosis is warranted. Counselors are cautioned to differentiate between appropriate childhood excitement or celebrations and hypomanic or manic symptoms. For a DMDD diagnosis, symptoms cannot occur only during a major depressive episode or be better explained by another disorder, and they cannot be related to medical or neurological conditions or substance use (APA, 2022a).

Special Considerations

Counselors diagnosing DMDD need to consider whether symptoms of an abnormally elevated or expansive mood have ever been present most of the day, for 1 day, or have a duration of longer than 1 day. If so, counselors need to consider the presence of grandiosity or inflated self-esteem, decreased need for sleep, pressured speech, flight of ideas, distractibility, increase in goal-directed activity, or excessive involvement in activities with a high potential for painful consequences. If these symptoms are present, counselors should consider a diagnosis of bipolar disorder. Counselors must take special care to differentiate abnormally elevated mood from developmentally appropriate mood elevation because the latter could occur in the context of anticipation or participation in a special event.

> ***Note:*** Although initially proposed, criteria regarding hyperarousal were removed because these symptoms could be accounted for by assigning an additional diagnosis of ADHD.

Cultural Considerations

DMDD tends to be diagnosed more frequently in males. The *DSM-5-TR* discussed this in relation to irritability and childhood development, suggesting that patterns of irritability may differ between genders. "Culture-Related Diagnostic Issues" is a new text section in the *DSM-5-TR*. The *DSM-5-TR* authors note that limited data are available regarding culture and the diagnosis of DMDD. They also note that adaptive responses to trauma, including long-standing racism and discrimination, must be considered when determining whether DMDD is appropriate (APA, 2022a). Compared with White youth, racial/ethnic minorities are much more likely to be diagnosed with DMDD than other differentials, such as ADHD. Fadus et al. (2020) warned of the risk of unconscious bias in diagnosing this disorder. Misdiagnosis can lead to inappropriate treatment planning and poor outcomes.

Because counselors are not immune to implicit biases, they can take steps to improve cultural competency by participating in multicultural training that includes dispositional mindfulness and reflective practices (Ivers et al., 2021).

Differential Diagnosis

DMDD cannot be diagnosed if behavioral concerns are exclusively present during a major depressive episode or are better accounted for by another diagnosis. Additionally, DMDD cannot be diagnosed alongside oppositional defiant disorder (ODD) or bipolar disorder, although it can coexist with ADHD, conduct disorder, and substance use disorder. If the client meets the criteria for this disorder and ODD, counselors should only assign DMDD. Finally, counselors must ensure that no other explanation, such as a medical or neurological condition, better accounts for the behavior. Fadus et al. (2020) underscored the difficulty in differentiating DMDD from ODD, ADHD, and conduct disorder. Few standardized instruments are available that capture the symptoms of DMDD; therefore, counselors must conduct a thorough and accurate assessment of symptoms. As noted above, counselors must maintain an awareness of potential bias based on race and ethnicity while moving toward accurate diagnosis and subsequent treatment. Counselors can consider using the cross-cutting measure found in Section III of the *DSM-5-TR* (Hatchett, 2022).

> ***Note:*** If an individual has ever experienced a manic or hypomanic episode, the diagnosis of DMDD should not be assigned.

Coding, Recording, and Specifiers

The *DSM-5-TR* now lists the diagnostic code for DMDD as F34.81. There are no specifiers for this diagnosis.

Case Example

> Angelo is a 16-year-old Latino American high school student living with his biological, married parents in a middle-class urban environment. He has no siblings and reports feeling particularly close to his mother. Angelo's dad has traveled extensively for work for the past 7 years, and Angelo reports not having a close relationship with him. Angelo presents as physically healthy, although slightly underweight and generally small in stature. His physical appearance is unkempt, his clothes are soiled, and he appears to have problems with personal hygiene. His mother states that getting Angelo to complete daily living activities is often very difficult; she does not push him unless she feels it is very important. When asked about his personal hygiene, Angelo reports that showering is stupid because he is just going to get dirty again, and he feels he looks fine. Aptitude testing suggests Angelo is of above-average intelligence. However, he is in danger of not passing the 11th grade because he refuses to turn in homework and fails to attend class. Angelo states that school is pointless because he will never use the information in real life. He frequently gets into verbal conflicts with his teachers.
>
> Angelo reports that he has had many acquaintances over the years, but none are long-term friends. When asked why, he reports that "they are idiots and don't do what I tell them to do, so I stop hanging out with them." Angelo admits to wanting to hit people when they make him angry. He has been suspended from school for fighting. Angelo is active in sports and excels in baseball, for which he has a high batting average. However, school reports indicate he is frequently left out of the lineup or removed from the game because of excessive anger and verbal aggression toward other players. His coach states that he could have a

future in baseball, but his reputation for poor sportsmanship prohibits him from progressing in the sport. He is not friends with any of his teammates.

Angelo's mother states that Angelo began showing signs of excessive irritability and outbursts when he was about 9 years of age. These outbursts included yelling, throwing objects, and refusing to engage in social or daily living activities. This behavior occurred both at home and at school. Over the past year, Angelo's outbursts have occurred at least three times per week, with 3 weeks being the longest Angelo has gone without an outburst. He has been required to speak to the school counselor twice over the year because of his outbursts. When asked about his mood, Angelo reports feelings of sadness, helplessness, and hopelessness but denies any thoughts of harm to himself. Angelo has never experienced symptoms of a manic episode, and he has no history of previous clinical diagnosis or substance utilization.

Diagnostic Questions

1. Do Angelo's presenting symptoms meet the criteria for a depressive disorder? If so, which disorder?
2. Based on the disorder identified in Question 1, which symptom(s) led you to select that diagnosis?
3. What would be the reason(s) a counselor may not diagnose Angelo with ODD?
4. Would Angelo be more accurately diagnosed with bipolar disorder? If so, why? If not, why not?
5. What rule-outs would you consider for Angelo's case?
6. What culturally relevant data would be helpful, and how might you gather this information?
7. What other information may be needed to make an accurate clinical diagnosis?

Major Depressive Disorder, Single Episode (F32._) and Recurrent Episodes (F33._)

> I just didn't want to live anymore. The feeling of worthlessness and hopelessness was overwhelming. I couldn't get off the sofa. The exhaustion was crushing, and all I wanted to do was sleep. I lost a lot of weight because I just didn't care about food or much of anything else anymore. This went on for days, and nothing seemed to help. I just felt depressed.—Angela

Major depressive disorder (MDD) has a long history of inclusion in the *DSM* diagnostic system and is one of the most frequently diagnosed mental disorders among health professionals (NIMH, 2023b). Although the NIMH (2023b) estimated that 8.3% of the U.S. adult population suffered from MDD in 2020, it reported that only 61% received treatment versus 66% who sought treatment.

MDD is characterized by nearly universal—meaning every day, nearly all day—feelings of sadness and loss of interest in previously enjoyed activities. Many individuals will experience loss of appetite, fatigue, problems with sleep, and suicidal ideation. Others may also experience agitation, trouble with concentration, and excessive feelings of guilt. Because feelings of worthlessness predominate for individuals with MDD, low self-esteem and excessive guilt (either real or imagined) are not uncommon (APA, 2022a). Major depression is considered a chronic illness that can lead to various emotional and physical problems that may require long-term mental health and psychopharmaceutical treatments.

Major Changes From *DSM-5* to *DSM-5-TR*

The authors of the *DSM* recommended changing the language for Criterion D for MDD when they originally drafted the *DSM-5*. This language change from the *DSM-IV-TR* to the *DSM-5* caused some confusion for clinicians. As a result, Criterion D now reads as it did in the *DSM-IV-TR*, clarifying that even if only one major depressive episode is not accounted for by schizoaffective disorder, then clinicians can diagnose MDD. Furthermore, when at least one major depressive episode occurs, and the individual has another psychotic diagnosis without a mood component, MDD can be "superimposed on" the existing psychotic disorder (APA, 2022c).

Throughout the text sections of the *DSM-5-TR*, changes were made to reflect the growing knowledge base around gender differences in the course and the prevalence of MDD. For example, women tend to experience depression in the form of sleep and appetite disturbances, as well as relationship difficulties and gastrointestinal problems. Their experience of comorbidity is more likely with anxiety, bulimia, and somatoform disorders, whereas men experience comorbidity more often with substance abuse. Men tend to report more risk taking, drug abuse, and decreased impulse control (APA, 2022a). The *DSM-5-TR* includes additional information in the environmental portion of the text section "Risk and Prognostic Factors," acknowledging the disproportionate amount of ACEs women encounter. The manual reports that ACEs, and other social determinants such as racism, low income, discrimination, and lack of education, are risk factors for depression.

In the *DSM-5-TR*, a text section titled "Association With Suicidal Thoughts or Behavior" was added. This section takes the place of "Suicide Risk" in the previous manual and underscores the fact that individuals with MDD have a 17-fold increased risk for suicide compared with their peers. The *DSM-5-TR* authors report anhedonia as having a strong association with suicide; other factors, such as ACEs, social disconnection, living alone, access to guns, impairment in decision-making, and hopelessness, play a role.

Finally, the *DSM-5-TR* authors acknowledge the growing number of differentials that are associated with MDD by adding text subsections for eight new categories: bipolar I disorder, bipolar II, or other specified bipolar and related disorder; persistent depressive disorder; premenstrual dysphoric disorder; disruptive mood dysregulation disorder; major depressive episodes superimposed on schizophrenia, delusional disorder, schizophreniform disorder, or other specified or unspecified schizophrenia spectrum and other psychotic disorder; schizoaffective disorder; bereavement; and prolonged grief disorder.

Essential Features

MDD can be diagnosed at any age, and the likelihood of onset increases significantly once an individual reaches puberty (APA, 2022a). Although prevalence rates in the U.S. population peak for people in their early 20s, it is not uncommon for the first episode of major depression to occur in mid- or later life. The disorder is marked by a single or recurrent major depressive episode, which must consist of at least five of nine criteria. These criteria differ from an individual's normal functioning and include

- depressed mood almost every day, with an irritable mood, more often noted in children and adolescents
- a marked diminished interest or pleasure in activities almost every day
- a significant change in daily appetite or a significant weight change, gain, or loss of more than 5% body weight in 1 month, not due to dieting, and in children, failure to make expected weight gains is also considered
- sleep disturbance, either insomnia or hypersomnia, nearly every day

- a change in normal physical pace, either psychomotor agitation or retardation, that others must observe in addition to self-report
- noteworthy energy loss or fatigue almost every day
- excessive or inappropriate guilt, which can be delusional, or feelings of worthlessness, not including guilt or self-blame related to being ill
- reduced ability to concentrate, focus, or make decisions almost daily, as reported by self or others
- frequent thoughts of death or suicidal ideation with or without a specific plan or attempting suicide. (APA, 2022a)

The symptoms must persist for a 2-week period. Counselors should not include symptoms related to another medical condition when diagnosing (e.g., difficulty concentrating because of a traumatic brain injury).

Note: Depression is one of the most common complications of chronic illness; many people with chronic illness experience depression. It is estimated that up to one third of individuals with severe medical conditions experience symptoms of depression.

Special Considerations

MDD is associated with high rates of mortality. As many as 40.3% of individuals diagnosed with MDD within a calendar year considered suicide, and there is a 15% suicide risk rate (Orsolini et al., 2020). Indeed, it is critical that counselors understand issues and criteria related to this condition, particularly when developing and implementing evidence-based treatments for reducing symptoms.

Counselors who work with clients at risk for MDD should use depression screening and suicide assessment instruments to closely monitor clients with moderate to severe depressive symptoms. Counselors must know the risk and protective factors unique to each client struggling with MDD. Should a higher level of care, such as inpatient hospitalization, be warranted, counselors must be aware of their ethical obligations per the *ACA Code of Ethics* (ACA, 2014), organization policies for accessing care, and related laws and procedures in their local practice areas. Such regulating bodies outline a continuum of care and the necessity of recommending the appropriate level of care to ensure clients are not undertreated.

A higher prevalence of MDD is observed among those affected by COVID-19, making it ever more pertinent to consider the pandemic's impact on mental health and wellness. One study exploring the prevalence of MDD among COVID-19 patients at a tertiary care center in India found that of 440 patients hospitalized for COVID-19, 30.90% met criteria for MDD at discharge, and 19.5% continued to qualify for MDD 30-day postdischarge based on admission and discharge data (Kaur et al., 2021). Furthermore, during the pandemic, frontline health care workers were vulnerable to developing MDD, especially between 2020 and 2021. Wild et al. (2022) reported that out of a sample of 103 frontline health care workers across four medical facilities in England, 39% met the criteria for MDD, which likely developed during the occupational stressors of the pandemic based on self-reporting interview using the Patient Health Questionnaire–9. Wild et al. postulated that the rates of MDD were higher than the published data. These findings underscore the pandemic's impact on our culture and the importance of exploring the onset of symptoms in relation to COVID-19 experiences.

Cultural Considerations

In a postmodern, multicultural society, identifying cultural norms for how different communities experience any depressive disorder is challenging. Despite this, we can provide counselors with general guidelines that can be used to better understand culture's role when diagnosing MDD (or any depressive disorder). First, counselors must understand that many people recognize depression as a physical rather than a psychological problem. Patterns of somatization are common among Latinos, Mexican Americans, and Puerto Ricans (Escovar et al., 2018). In many ways, however, the somatic experience of symptoms is universal across cultures. For example, the inability to sleep and feelings of fatigue are commonly reported and included in diagnostic criteria. Depressive symptoms in many Asian cultures are experienced as physical rather than psychological ailments (Kong et al., 2019). Many Asian clients do not express sadness or tearfulness; instead, they report dullness, uneasiness, feelings of inner pressure, physical aches, dizziness, or feeling tired. Counselors may also discover that some Asian immigrants regard mental illness as morally offensive and futile (Kong et al., 2019). Although this cultural pattern may depend on one's level of acculturation, counselors should be aware of how depressive symptoms manifest and are reported among diverse cultural groups.

Depression tends to be more prevalent in women, with 10.5% of adult women experiencing depression in 2020 (NIMH, 2023b). Depression is on the rise among young adults, with the CDC reporting that 21% of those ages 18 to 29 experience depressive symptoms (Villarroel, 2020). Depression is noted as the most significant mental health issue of later life (Myers & Harper, 2004). Almost 13.5% of adults receiving in-home care and 11.5% of hospitalized patients report depressive symptoms (CDC, 2022). Income inequality is related to higher levels of depression, according to the *DSM-5-TR*. Furthermore, the ADAA (2020) argued that MDD may be underreported or underdiagnosed among African Americans because of stigma, stereotypes, and socioeconomic barriers, which may lead to misdiagnosis or underdiagnosis for this population. The authors of the *DSM-5-TR* underscore this conclusion, stating that for African Americans and Caribbean Americans, the impact of racism, discrimination, increased social adversity, and lack of resources may heavily influence the chronic nature of depressive symptoms (APA, 2022a). Finally, the NIMH (2023b) demonstrated that those who endorsed two or more races also reported the highest level of depressive symptoms, compared with other racial groups, at 13.9%.

Counselors must understand that culture influences clients' experience of symptoms, the language used to report them, and how they will approach treatment. Furthermore, it is important to note how culture may affect the likelihood of clients' risk-taking or suicidal behavior, which can influence how clients interact with mental health professionals. First-generation immigrants may be uncomfortable with a client-directed counseling model and may need a more directive, hierarchical therapeutic relationship. Finally, whether working with depression, trauma, or any mental health disorder, counselors must be sensitive to institutional racism and be aware that mental health professionals can unintentionally project a sense of stigma onto clients. Counselors can avoid this by understanding their biases and refraining from stereotypical behavior. Counselors can increase their multicultural competence and intellectual humility by continually attempting to be curious and open to understanding the client's cultural worldview.

The authors of the *DSM-5* removed the bereavement exclusion, found in the *DSM-IV-TR*, for individuals who experienced depression for up to 2 months after the death of a loved one. Researchers and the DSM-5 Task Force reasoned that bereavement-related depression does not differ significantly from other stressor-related depressive episodes involving a form of loss, such as a divorce or job loss (APA, 2013c, 2013d). This change is consistent with long-standing *ICD* criteria for depression and remains in the *DSM-5-TR*.

Kendler et al. (2008) compared the responses of those reporting bereavement-related depressive episodes with those who reported other life events as triggers. The results did not differ significantly in frequency and duration of symptoms or in the number of depressive (i.e., Criteria A) symptoms identified. Participants with bereavement-related depressive symptoms are more likely to be women and tend to be older (average of 72 years) at the onset of symptomatology. These participants tend to seek treatment less frequently and express more fatigue and loss of interest. However, they experience less guilt than peers endorsing depression relating to another stressful event unrelated to bereavement. The *DSM-5-TR* authors attempt to clarify that bereavement does not always lead to a diagnosis of MDD. Although a natural grieving process can occur without a diagnosis of MDD, individuals who experience clinically significant and impairing symptoms deserve appropriate care for concerns related to bereavement and depression. The *DSM-5-TR* retains language that advises practitioners to carefully differentiate the natural process of grieving from MDD (APA, 2022a).

Differential Diagnosis

In addition to the inclusion of bipolar disorders, the authors of the *DSM-5-TR* added major depressive episodes superimposed on schizophrenia, schizoaffective disorder, delusional disorder, schizophreniform disorder, or other specified or unspecified schizophrenia spectrum and other psychotic disorders. They added bereavement, schizoaffective disorder, depressive disorder due to another medical condition, persistent depressive disorder, premenstrual dysphoric disorder, and disruptive mood dysregulation disorder. With the September 2022 supplement, they also added prolonged grief disorder (APA, 2022b), for a total of nine new differentials.

Individuals experiencing MDD will have clinically significant distress or impairment in at least one area of daily functioning, such as social, occupational, or other vital areas (APA, 2022a), not resulting from a medical condition or substance use. Additionally, the symptoms are not more consistent with another diagnosis, such as schizoaffective disorder, and are not masking another disorder, such as delusional disorder or other specified schizophrenia spectrum or psychotic disorder. If clients have previously experienced manic or hypomanic episodes unrelated to medication, substance, or a medical condition, a diagnosis of bipolar disorder may be more appropriate (APA, 2022a). When differentiating MDD relating to a stressor from adjustment disorders with depressed mood, counselors can take caution by ensuring that the full criteria for MDD are met.

Coding, Recording, and Specifiers

Coding and recording for MDD are contingent on single or recurrent episodes and severity, such as *mild*, *moderate*, *severe*, and *with psychotic features*, as well as specifiers to note unique features and course. The diagnostic code for a single MDD episode is F32._ and for recurrent episodes is F33._ (the blank spaces indicate specifiers that the counselors must select prior to giving a diagnosis of MDD). Note that the *ICD-10-CM* code is the same for both single and recurrent episodes. Because these specifiers apply to all depressive disorders, we discuss them (and their associated codes) at the end of this chapter. Readers will note, however, that to be considered recurrent, there must be two consecutive symptom-free months between episodes during which the criteria are not met. The number of episodes, severity, and course specifiers are always listed following the MDD diagnosis code. Note that there are specifiers without codes that may be used as applicable (APA, 2022a). These are also listed at the end of this chapter.

Persistent Depressive Disorder (F34.1)

> I remember being very happy at times as a teenager, but that was years ago. I'm sad most days now. Sometimes I just eat and eat and can't stop myself. I don't like the way I look or act, and I feel tired most of the day. Naps don't help even though I take a lot of them. I have a part-time job, but it doesn't pay much so I still live at home. Mom tells me I'm just a melancholy person and that's OK.—Maria

Persistent depressive disorder (PDD), known in the *DSM-IV-TR* as dysthymic disorder, was initially called neurotic depression and then relabeled dysthymic disorder in the *DSM-III* (Sprock & Fredendall, 2008). In reality, PDD consolidates the *DSM-IV-TR* chronic MDD and dysthymia. A person with PDD presents with a depressed mood almost all day, more days than not (APA, 2022a). The disorder can appear as a chronically irritable mood for children, and the mood disturbance must last 1 year or more. Counselors should note that it is not uncommon for MDD to precede PDD, as one criterion for PDD is that MDD may be continuously present for more than 1 year. This will be noted in the "Coding, Recording, and Specifiers" section.

Major Changes From *DSM-5* to *DSM-5-TR*

As noted above, the authors of the *DSM-5* changed the name of this disorder from dysthymic disorder to persistent depressive disorder, leaving the word "dysthymia" in parentheses, which was removed in the *DSM-5-TR*, reflecting the permanent name change. Five specifiers were removed from the criteria section, leaving *with anxious distress* and *with atypical features*. The *DSM-5-TR* authors argue that the specifiers they removed were extraneous (APA, 2022d). The text sections "Culture-Related Diagnostic Issues" and "Association With Suicidal Thoughts or Behavior" were added, as were the differentials of other specified depressive disorder, bipolar I and bipolar II disorder, and cyclothymic disorder (APA, 2022a).

Essential Features

For a diagnosis of PDD to be assigned during the experience of the depressed mood, the individual will report at least 2 years of depressed mood in which they experience at least two symptoms among the following: (a) poor appetite or overeating, (b) insomnia or hypersomnia, (c) low energy or fatigue, (d) low self-esteem, (e) poor concentration or difficulty making decisions, or (f) feelings of hopelessness (APA, 2022a). However, clients may experience symptoms beyond these minimal criteria. In children, the disturbance may include an irritable rather than depressed mood, which lasts 1 year to meet the criteria. In either case, the individual may not be free of symptoms for more than two consecutive months. The age of onset is typically in childhood, adolescence, or early adulthood (APA, 2022a).

Special Considerations

We have noted many similarities between PDD and MDD, and counselors should be aware of distinct differences in the diagnostic criteria. The most notable discrepancy is that PDD is a chronic, ongoing condition rather than an episodic experience. Previously, the depressive symptoms experienced in PDD were considered less severe compared with major depressive episodes. This is no longer true, given the significant revision to this disorder.

Cultural Considerations

PDD is based on criteria for both dysthymic disorder and chronic MDD. The *DSM-5-TR* reports prevalence rates for these disorders separately rather than reporting a rate for PDD specifically. However, the NIMH (n.d.-c) reported that PDD affects 1.5% of the population, noting that higher rates were diagnosed for women and in higher income countries (APA, 2022a). Individuals with borderline personality disorder are at higher risk for PDD (APA, 2022a). Furthermore, dysthymia is frequently observed during counseling sessions, with a high prevalence of this disorder noted among older adults (Zalaquett & Stens, 2006) and in the African American community (Vontress et al., 2007). Vontress et al. (2007) underscored the importance of noting culturally relevant factors when conceptualizing this disorder among African Americans. Of additional importance is the elevated risk of suicidality associated with this disorder. Wolf et al. (2022) conducted research that identified a cognitive behavioral analysis system of psychotherapy as a technique to reduce suicidal ideation in an inpatient sample, maintaining that suicidal behavior is related to thoughts of loneliness for individuals with PDD. Similarly, Sabaß et al. (2022) demonstrated that childhood maltreatment and loneliness are reported at higher rates among those with PDD, maintaining that avoidant attachment style plays a role in a sustained sense of loneliness in this population.

Differential Diagnosis

The diagnosis of dysthymia in the *DSM-IV-TR* required that the individual be free of any major depressive episodes in the first 2 years of the experience. However, changes to PDD criteria in the *DSM-5* stipulate that the disorder may involve the presence of a major depressive episode at any point in the experience. The *DSM-5-TR* also follows this guidance and provides extensive guidelines for differentiating between MDD and PDD, and it includes numerous specifiers in which the major depressive episode is or is not present alongside the disorder (see APA, 2022a, pp. 193–194). The authors of the *DSM-5-TR* added other specified depressive disorder and bipolar I and bipolar II disorder to the differentials for this diagnosis. Unlike bipolar disorders, which are characterized by at least one manic or hypomanic episode, PDD is a sustained experience of depression most days for at least 2 years.

PDD cannot be diagnosed if symptoms occur only during the course of schizophrenia spectrum or other psychotic disorders or if a client has ever experienced a manic episode, hypomanic episode, or cyclothymic disorder. Clinically significant impairment or distress in critical areas of functioning must be evident, such as problems with interpersonal relationships or maintaining employment. Additionally, the symptoms are not better accounted for by the direct effects of a substance or medication use. Finally, counselors need to be sure there is no other explanation for the behavior, such as another medical or neurological condition.

Coding, Recording, and Specifiers

There is one diagnostic code for PDD (dysthymia): F34.1. Counselors are required to indicate the current severity of *mild*, *moderate*, or *severe* and other specifiers in writing. It is essential that counselors note there are now two specifiers to describe the client's chronic mood state (i.e., *with anxious distress* and *with atypical features*) and the ability to indicate if the client is in *partial remission* or *full remission*. Counselors will also identify if the client is *early onset* (i.e., before the age of 21) or *late-onset* (i.e., after the age of 21) and whether the following applies: *with pure dysthymic syndrome, with persistent major depressive episode, with intermittent major depressive episodes, with current episode, with intermittent major depressive episodes,* or *without current episode* (APA, 2022a).

Case Example

> Anthony is a 37-year-old African American man who is attending counseling for the first time at the insistence of Willa, his wife of 10 years. Willa states that she has been dealing with Anthony's "chronic negativity" for at least 6 years and that he "wasn't always like this." It has been much worse recently, and she says she has had enough. She has told Anthony that if he does not get help, she is not going to stay in the marriage. As a result, Anthony has made an appointment for an intake, during which he tells you, "Nothing is going to help."
>
> Anthony presents as underweight, neatly dressed, and unshaven. His affect is blunted, and he speaks only to answer direct questions. During the intake,

he appears to be thinking about other things and is frequently distracted. He reports that he is tired a lot and doesn't want to waste his energy on things that aren't important, such as shaving and showering. He does these things when his wife "nags" at him, which he states she does a lot, particularly when he doesn't feel like eating. Anthony reports working the same full-time job for the past 10 years. He has never put in for a raise or promotion because "it's a lot of effort and very competitive." He frequently leaves work early or uses sick time because he feels "down" and needs a break.

Anthony can recall a time when he had more energy and was at an average weight. He states this was about 5 years ago, and then he went through a time when "things were horrible." When asked about this period, Anthony states he never had thoughts of hurting someone else and did think about killing himself. He reports feeling so depressed that he just didn't want to live anymore. His wife reports that he had difficulty getting out of bed during this time and lost a lot of weight. She reports that he had no sexual interest in her and would say negative things about himself. She states she should have "made" him get help at the time, but he seemed to be getting better, so she just "let it go."

When asked, Anthony states that he does have friends, and most of them are lifelong. He says he doesn't spend a lot of time with them because he is tired and feels down. He reports that they call him "Eeyore," and he says they are probably right. He is currently well-oriented and denies thoughts of harm to himself or anyone else. A recent medical workup indicates that he is in good health. He reports drinking the occasional beer with his friends and denies other substance use. He states he wants to become more positive and have more energy so that his wife won't leave him.

Diagnostic Questions

1. Do Anthony's presenting symptoms meet the criteria for a depressive disorder? If so, which one?
2. What would be the reason(s) a counselor would not diagnose Anthony with PDD?
3. Would Anthony be accurately diagnosed with major depressive episodes?
4. What rule-outs would you consider for Anthony's case?
5. What culturally relevant data would be helpful, and how might you gather this information?
6. What other information may be needed to make an accurate clinical diagnosis?

Premenstrual Dysphoric Disorder (F32.81)

> I learned to count the days and dread that time of the month. I wouldn't make plans around the time I would have my period. I would avoid family and friends because I was so afraid of what I would say. My boyfriend dreads it because I am so sensitive, depressed, and angry. I couldn't concentrate at work and wanted to eat all the time. I felt horrible and was often so swollen I couldn't even put my jewelry on.—Molly

Premenstrual dysphoric disorder (PMDD) is a depressive disorder exclusive to women. It is characterized by intense emotional and physical symptoms that occur in the days prior to the onset of menses and often continue into menstruation (Daw, 2002). Originally included in the *DSM-III-R* (APA, 1987) as "late luteal phase dysphoric disorder," this disorder was changed to premenstrual dysphoric disorder in the *DSM-IV* (Cunningham et al., 2009), where it was listed and coded as depressive disorder not otherwise specified (NOS). For most women, mild physical and emotional symptoms can occur near and during menstruation, frequently referred to as premenstrual syndrome or PMS. Prevalence rates of this disorder are reported at 5.8% in a German sample and 1.3% in the United States; however; these estimates likely vary by age, occurring more frequently for adolescent girls (APA, 2022a).

Major Changes From *DSM-5* to *DSM-5-TR*

Although previous editions of the *DSM* included reference to PMDD within the NOS category, PMDD appeared as an official disorder for the first time in the *DSM-5*. The *DSM-5-TR* authors made minor changes to this diagnosis by updating some text sections, including suicidal thoughts as a text section and "other medical conditions" as part of the Differential Diagnosis section.

Essential Features

PMDD symptoms typically begin the week before menstruation, improve in the days after menstruation starts, and dissipate as menstruation ends. The individual must experience at least five symptoms, including at least one of the following: (a) severe mood swings (affective lability), which include feeling suddenly sad or tearful or becoming overly sensitive to rejection; (b) increased interpersonal conflicts, significantly increased anger, or irritability; (c) feelings of hopelessness, self-critical thoughts, or distinctly depressed mood; or (d) noticeable anxiety, tension, or feeling of edginess (APA, 2022a).

Additional symptoms that can be considered include a lack of interest in normal activities, self-reported problems with concentration, fatigue, changes in eating habits (under- or overeating and cravings), sleep disturbance, feeling a loss of control, being overwhelmed; physical symptoms include tenderness in the breasts, pain in the muscles or joints, swelling, bloating, or weight gain (APA, 2022a). Moreover, the symptoms must occur in most menstrual cycles the year before this diagnosis is given, resulting in clinically significant impairment in social, work, school, or usual activities. These symptoms result in clinically significant distress or hinder daily activities such as work, school, and social interactions. This distress does not relate to another disorder. Although they may be comorbid with panic disorder, major depression, or personality disorder, the symptoms of PMDD are distinct. Daily ratings for two symptoms cycles are used to verify the diagnosis, which can be provisional prior to data collection. As with other diagnosis, the symptoms are not related to substance use/abuse or other medical condition (APA, 2022a).

Special Considerations

Concerns regarding the inclusion and diagnosis of PMDD in the *DSM* have been part of the research and discourse process since its inception (Daw, 2002). These concerns include stigmatizing or targeting women for their normal biological functions, pathologizing normal reproductive functioning (APA, 2013c), and relying on medication therapy for treatment (Daw, 2002). The *DSM-5* Mood Disorders Work Group responded to the concerns, stating that statistics on the prevalence indicate that PMDD affects a small portion of women and that symptoms should not be generalized to all women. Furthermore, in acknowledging this as a diagnosis, APA believes this conveys that PMDD does not typically occur for menstruating women and is only clinically impairing for a few days (APA, 2013c). Certainly, counselors must be careful about stigma and inherent biological processes. In addition, there is a link between abuse history and the prevalence of PMDD; therefore, counselors are encouraged to consider the likelihood of abuse and adjust assessment treatment for this factor as needed.

Cultural Considerations

A portion of the etiology of PMDD can be attributed to a combination of physiological factors, including hormones, neurotransmitters, and variations in a specific estrogen receptor (Cunningham et al., 2009; Girdler et al., 2007; Pearlstein & Steiner, 2008). However, a growing body of research links these physiological factors to stress, particularly from physical abuse, emotional abuse, and sexual abuse in childhood (Azoulay et al., 2020; Hantsoo & Epperson, 2015; Kulkarni et al., 2022). When examining the trauma spectrum and premenstrual symptoms, Pilver et al. (2011) found that women diagnosed with PTSD were most likely to experience PMDD symptoms. Girdler et al. (2007) reported that women diagnosed with PMDD were at least 60% more likely to have experienced physical or sexual abuse over their lifetime when compared with women who had not received this diagnosis. They posited that traumatic events, particularly early life trauma, could contribute to dysregulation in stress-responsive systems, which may be a risk factor for PMDD. Because racial/ethnic minority women are more likely to experience abuse, cultural considerations are important. For instance, Pilver et al. (2011) found a relationship between symptoms of PMDD and lifetime racial, gender, age, or other types of discrimination. Azoulay et al. (2020) acknowledged the role of emotional regulation in the relationship between premenstrual dysphoria and childhood trauma. Their research highlights the need for counselors to use techniques to improve these individuals' emotional regulation abilities. Additional treatment recommendations include medication, such as antidepressants, hormones, and CBT (Hantsoo & Epperson, 2015).

Differential Diagnosis

When diagnosing PMDD, counselors should ensure that its symptoms are not better explained by normal hormonal fluctuations or exacerbation of symptoms related to another previously diagnosed disorder. Counselors should also clarify that symptoms are not directly related to substance use or other medical issues. The symptoms of PMDD are primarily affective or anxiety related, so counselors should not give this diagnosis when an underlying depressive, anxiety disorder, or medical condition exists and better accounts for the premenstrual exacerbation. Instead, the premenstrual exacerbation of anxiety and depression may be accounted for by an already existing disorder that commonly occurs with PDD, panic disorder, and generalized anxiety disorder (Pearlstein & Steiner, 2008). This can be a complicated issue because women diagnosed with PMDD are more likely than other women to have co-occurring disorders such as PTSD or anxiety disorder. Furthermore, comorbidity is complicated by symptom overlap for some disorders, which makes diagnosis even more challenging (Cunningham et al., 2009).

Coding, Recording, and Specifiers

There is only one diagnostic code for PMDD: F32.81. While there are no specifiers, if there has not been a daily rating of symptoms for at least two cycles, a provisional diagnosis must be noted after the name (APA, 2022a).

Case Example

> Shara is a 32-year-old Asian American woman who presents to counseling services at the insistence of her girlfriend, Dani. Shara reports that they have a good relationship for the most part, although they get into horrible fights once a month. She states that she is aware that she has always had difficulty around the time of menstruation, and lately, she has become more aware of the impact this has on her life.

Shara reports that she becomes physically uncomfortable before her period, stating that she experiences pain and swelling. At that point, she becomes tearful, easily stressed out, and may "snap off at people" at any moment. She occasionally leaves work early and refuses to leave her house or talk to anyone because she fears what she may do or say. Shara reports these symptoms have been consistent since her early 20s and, for some reason, seem to be getting worse.

Diagnostic Questions

1. Do Shara's presenting symptoms meet the criteria for PMDD?
2. What would be the reason(s) a counselor would not diagnose her with PMDD?
3. What treatment approaches could a counselor use when working with Shara?
4. What rule-outs would you consider for her case?
5. What other information may be needed to make an accurate clinical diagnosis?

Substance/Medication-Induced Depressive Disorder

Substance/medication-induced depressive disorder is a depressive disorder in which there is evidence that a substance or medication physiologically causes the onset of depressive symptoms. The symptoms must be more than what is expected given the use of the substance and must last a month or more after substance intoxication or withdrawal. The *DSM-5-TR* includes an additional specifier, *with onset after medication use*, and language clarifying how to use this specifier in the criterion section (APA, 2022a). Additionally, the *DSM-5-TR* authors note in the "Diagnostic Features" section that there are two categories of substances that would most likely result in this condition: depressants and stimulants. They also list examples stating that new drugs are likely to be added (APA, 2022a). Updates were made to text sections for prevalence, development and course, risk and prognostic factors, diagnostic markers, and differential diagnosis. Finally, the authors added "Sex" to "Gender-Related Diagnostic Issues" and the text section "Association With Suicidal Thoughts and Behavior."

Essential Features

Substance/medication-induced depressive disorder presents symptoms consistent with those of a depressive disorder. However, evidence demonstrates that symptoms for this disorder develop during or within a month of use or withdrawal from a particular substance known to produce depressive symptoms. Verification can be produced by using history, laboratory findings, or physical examination of the client (APA, 2022a).

Clinicians should not diagnose this disorder if depressive symptoms precede the onset of substance use or withdrawal. If the symptoms continue for a month or more after cessation of the substance use or at the end of the withdrawal period, the symptoms may be better accounted for by an independent mood disorder (APA, 2022a). Moreover, the depressive symptoms should not occur concomitant with delirium alone and must result in clinically significant impairment in key functional areas.

Special Considerations

Given the presumed physiological connection between substance use and the development of depressive episodes, this diagnosis should be made by a physician or in consultation with a physician with expertise to determine the etiology. According to APA (2022a), individuals with alcohol or stimulant use disorders are at least 40% more likely to experience this disorder. In comparison, for those who do not abuse these substances, the overall prevalence rate of this disorder is 0.26% of the U.S. population (APA, 2022a). Counselors should be aware that substance/medication-induced depressive disorder, which involves alcohol, heroin, or cocaine use, has specific implications for treatment. For example, Samet et al. (2012) found that individuals with substance-induced depressive disorders had a much greater relapse risk than those diagnosed with MDD. These authors reported their findings were consistent with neurobiological research on addiction, positing that brain changes that occur during dependence, presenting as depressive symptoms, can linger long after withdrawal and well into the maintenance stage. Therefore, counselors working with clients who meet the criteria for this disorder should be aware of the high risk of relapse. Evidence-based treatments for addressing mood concerns, treating substance use disorders, and teaching relapse-prevention and coping skills are essential. Informing clients about the symptoms and implications of this disorder and developing relapse prevention plans and strategies for coping with relapse are also important.

Individuals diagnosed with certain other mental disorders, such as bipolar, antisocial personality, and schizophrenia, are at higher risk of experiencing this disorder, as are those who experience stressful life events in the year prior to the onset of symptoms and those who have a family history of substance abuse. It is important to note that added stressors such as racism, poverty, and marginalization could increase the risk, but gender does not. The *DSM-5-TR* authors also note that, as with other groups who abuse alcohol, the risk of suicide increases for those with this disorder who abuse alcohol (APA, 2022a).

Differential Diagnosis

Substance/medication-induced depressive disorder should be diagnosed instead of substance intoxication and substance withdrawal only when depressive symptoms are prominent and the condition is clinically impairing for the client. In addition, counselors must be careful to assess for co-occurring substance use disorders. If depressive disorder symptoms occur at times when a substance is not used, counselors should consider an independent depressive disorder.

Coding, Recording, and Specifiers

In addition to variation based on substance class, the *ICD-10-CM* further differentiates coding procedures based on whether a comorbid substance use disorder is present for the same class of substance. Specifiers for this disorder include *with onset during intoxication*, *with onset during withdrawal*, and *with onset after medication use*, which is newly added. For example, a woman experiencing depressive symptoms during withdrawal of a severe alcohol use disorder would receive a diagnosis of F10.24 severe alcohol use disorder, with alcohol-induced depressive disorder. An additional diagnosis of a severe alcohol use disorder, severe, is not recorded. However, when the depressive symptoms related exclusively to a substance occur without a substance use disorder, the diagnosis of substance/medication-induced depressed disorder is given, followed by the appropriate specifier. For example, a young adult experiencing depressive symptoms while drinking heavily would receive a diagnosis of F10.94 alcohol-induced depressive disorder, with onset during intoxication.

Counselors will list each substance separately when more than one substance class is considered clinically significant. When recording substance/medication-induced disorders, counselors must reference the criteria set and the corresponding recording procedures for the specific substance-specific codes, also being sure to record the name of the substance. For substances that do not fit into any category, counselors should use the code of other substances. Likewise, if counselors are unaware of the name of the substance, the code for an unknown substance should be used. The codes for both classes are the same, and counselors do need to specify whether the substance is other (meaning it is not included in the listing) or unknown.

Depressive Disorder Due to Another Medical Condition (F06._ _)

Depressive disorder due to another medical condition differs from substance/medication-induced depressive disorder because the former diagnosis applies when symptoms are consistent with MDD and are presented as exclusively relating to a medical condition (APA, 2022a). There are no changes in the diagnostic criteria for this section from the *DSM-5* to the *DSM-5-TR*.

Essential Features

During a depressive disorder due to another medical condition, the individual will typically present with a significant mood change, which can be connected directly to a medical condition through physical examinations, laboratory findings, or history that gives evidence linking the two conditions (APA, 2022a). The mood change will include a noticeable depressed mood or diminished interest in usual pleasures. Another condition or mental disorder cannot better explain the symptoms, and there must be clinically significant impairment, distress, mental health hospitalization, or psychotic features. The symptoms cannot occur only during delirium (APA, 2013a).

Special Considerations

For diagnosis of this disorder, it is crucial to ensure that the related medical condition can cause depressive symptoms. This determination should be made by a qualified physician who can diagnose the medical condition and determine the etiology. Some medical conditions associated with depressive symptoms include hypothyroidism, stroke, Huntington's disease, Parkinson's disease, and traumatic brain injury. Depressive symptoms can present as early as 1 day after a stroke and occur early in conjunction with Huntington's disease. The symptoms tend to precede impairments related to the advancement of Parkinson's disease and Huntington's disease. The *DSM-5-TR* authors added a text section to address the prevalence of this disorder, noting that sex differences with this disorder are consistent with the sex difference related to the underlying medical condition (APA, 2022a). They added information regarding development and course, as well as the text section "Association With Suicidal Thoughts or Behavior," indicating that clinicians can assume the same level of suicidal risk or higher with this disorder as with MDD.

Cultural Considerations

Although considerable data suggest a link between physical illness and depression (Østergaard & Foldager, 2011), there is limited research on depressive disorder due to another medical condition and culture, perhaps because of the difficulty in assessing, diagnosing, and determining the actual etiology of depressive symptoms. Gender as a cultural consideration can play a diagnostic role in understanding and determining the overlap between depression and medical conditions. APA (2022a) notes that, in some cases, certain diseases run along gender lines. One such medical condition is the occurrence of strokes, which occur more often in men and are known to be more likely to cause depressive symptoms (APA, 2022a). Clinicians should consider gender in relation to common medical conditions and related mental health trends, such as depression.

Differential Diagnosis

Differentiating this disorder from a depressive disorder not related to a medical condition is challenging. Counselors need to determine if a depressive episode has ever occurred or if this episode began before the onset of the medical condition. It is also important to ensure that the medical condition the client is experiencing can cause the symptoms of a depressive disorder. Furthermore, monitoring the course of the symptoms can confirm that the diagnosis is related to a medical condition, especially if the symptoms lessen or disappear as the medical condition resolves (APA, 2022a). Finally, the *DSM-5-TR* includes two new differential diagnoses: delirium and major or mild neurocognitive disorders and demoralization. Clinicians should note that demoralization, rather than the medical condition, may account for depressive symptoms after certain medical events. The anhedonia often associated with depression does not occur in demoralization; rather, individuals may experience helplessness, hopelessness, and the desire to quit.

Because most medical conditions that could create depressive symptoms are also treated with medication that may do the same, counselors should consider medication-induced depressive disorder in the differential. Certain medical conditions (such as a stroke) can present significant life stressors for individuals. Adjustment disorders should be considered as an additional diagnosis if the medical condition is known to have caused the depression *and* the client is experiencing difficulty adjusting to the diagnosis. However, suppose the depression is a response to the medical diagnosis and its implications and full criteria for another depressive disorder are not met. In that case, adjustment disorders may be the more appropriate diagnosis.

Coding, Recording, and Specifiers

The coding for each condition depends on the specifier, such as F09.31, depressive disorder due to (list condition) *with depressive features*. The specifiers may also include F09.32, *with major depression-like symptoms*, or F09.34, *with mixed features* (APA, 2022a). Clinicians must include the medical condition after "due to" and the medical code for the illness listed before this disorder.

Other Specified and Unspecified Depressive Disorders: (F32.89/F32.A)

The other specified depressive disorder (F32.89) category is provided for symptom presentations that lead to clinically significant distress or impairment and do not meet the full criteria for a specific depressive disorder. The *DSM-5* allowed the counselor to specify one of the three types: recurrent brief depression, short-duration depressive episode (4–13 days), and depressive episode with insufficient symptoms (APA, 2013a). The *DSM-5-TR* adds "major depressive episode superimposed" on schizophrenia and schizophrenia spectrum-related disorders unless the major depressive episode is part of a schizoaffective disorder (APA, 2022a). There is one code for this diagnosis (F32.89). The counselor should indicate this code, followed by the disorder name and the specific designation, such as short-term depressive episode (APA, 2022a).

The unspecified depressive disorder (F32.A) diagnosis can be assigned when an individual presents with symptoms of a depressive disorder and the counselor does not have access to more specific diagnostic information or chooses not to diagnose a specific depressive disorder.

Unspecified Mood Disorder (F39)

Unspecified mood disorder (F39) was removed from the *DSM-IV-TR* and then added back to the *DSM-5-TR*. The diagnosis aims to indicate that symptoms of bipolar or depressive disorder are identified, but they do not rise to a full diagnosis in either classification. Furthermore, the clinician may not have enough information to identify which diagnostic class exists.

Specifiers for Depressive Disorders

The following is an all-inclusive listing of specifiers for depressive disorders. We have chosen to include these because of the requirement for counselors to accurately identify and list specifiers to clarify further the course, severity, or special features of the identified depressive disorder. This section also discusses the term *maternity blues* included in the *DSM-5-TR* to better assist clinicians in distinguishing this from postpartum features. Additionally, there are minor text changes in this section, although the overall content and discussion of specifiers are similar between editions.

Severity specifiers are used throughout the Depressive Disorders chapter of the *DSM-5-TR*. These specifiers are based on the most recent episode and are identified by the number of symptoms, symptom severity, and degree of impairment. For a specifier of *mild*, few additional symptoms are noted, they are manageable, and they only result in minor impairment. For *severe*, there are multiple excesses of intensely distressing and unmanageable symptoms and marked interference with functioning. *Moderate* occurs when symptom number, intensity, and impairment fall between mild and severe (APA, 2022a).

For diagnoses of MDD and PDD, the *DSM-5-TR* allows for the specifier *with anxious distress* if, during most days of a current or most recent experience of MDD or PDD, two of the following symptoms are reported: being keyed up or tense, increased restlessness, excessive worry that leads to difficulty concentrating, irrational fear that something negative is about to occur, and fear of loss of self-control. Symptom severity can be identified for this specifier. If two symptoms are noted, *mild* severity is indicated. For three symptoms, *moderate* is indicated; if four or more symptoms are present, *moderate-severe* is used.

Another specifier clinicians can combine with MDD is *with mixed features*. For this specifier to be given, the individual must experience three manic/hypomanic symptoms almost every day during the depressive episode. These include inflated self-esteem or grandiosity; elevated mood; pressured speech or increased talkativeness; racing thoughts or flight of ideas; increased energy or goal-directed activity; involvement in high-risk, high-consequence behaviors; and decreased need for sleep (APA, 2022a). These symptoms are not related to medication or substance use and must be noticeable to others. If symptoms meet the full criteria for either mania or hypomania, the appropriate bipolar disorder diagnosis should be given. In the *DSM-5-TR*, this specifier was removed for PDD (APA, 2022a).

Note: It is important to note the specifier where appropriate because of the strong link between these specific features and a future diagnosis of bipolar disorder.

For the specifier *with melancholic features* to be applicable, during the most severe period of the episode, the individual must experience a lack of pleasure in all or almost all activities or have a lack of response to pleasurable events. Three or more additional symptoms must be experienced from the following: distinct depression that may include deep despondency, despair, glumness, or empty mood; increased depression in the morning that can be accompanied by early waking, at least 2 hours earlier than normal; noticeable slowing or psychomotor agitation; significant weight fluctuation; and overwhelming guilt. The changes are noticeable, and psychomotor changes are almost always present. In addition, the condition occurs more frequently in individuals who also experience psychotic features and is more likely to occur in severe depressive episodes requiring inpatient treatment (APA, 2022a). The specifier *with melancholic features* cannot be met during the same episode as *with catatonia* (APA, 2022a).

The specifier *with atypical features* is applicable when the individual spends most days of the current or most recent major depressive episode experiencing mood reactivity and two or more additional features, which include significant weight gain or increased appetite, constant daytime sleepiness, feeling of heaviness in the arms or legs, and a history of social or occupational issues related to extreme sensitivity to being rejected. This sensitivity to rejection begins early in life and can occur even when the individual is not experiencing depressive symptoms but can be worse during a depressive episode.

For the specifier *with psychotic features* to be given, the individual will experience delusions or hallucinations at any time during the depressive episode. *With mood-congruent psychotic features* or *without mood-congruent psychotic features* should be diagnosed if psychotic features are present. When the psychotic features are mood-congruent, they will be consistent with the depressive themes (e.g., guilt, death, punishment). When this does not occur, or when the content is mixed, a specifier *with mood-incongruent psychotic features* should be included (APA, 2022a).

With catatonia is specified when catatonic features are present during most of the episode for a depressive episode. Criteria for catatonia associated with a mental disorder are given in the Schizophrenia Spectrum and Other Psychotic Disorders chapter.

The specifier *with peripartum onset* can be used when mood symptoms begin during pregnancy or in the 4 weeks after delivery, with a prevalence rate of about 9%. Whereas mood episodes can begin before or after delivery, about half of women begin experiencing these symptoms before delivery, and as such, the specifier is *peripartum*. Symptoms associated with this can be severe. For some women, this includes anxiety, panic attacks, and psychotic features, which can be extreme and include command hallucinations to harm or kill the child; however; the *DSM-5-TR* authors report this is very rare. Between one in 500 and one in 1,000 women experience postpartum episodes with psychotic features (APA, 2022a). The risk of experiencing peripartum or postpartum symptoms increases with prior history of symptoms, family history, and history of depressive or bipolar diagnosis (APA, 2022a). New to the *DSM-5-TR* is information differentiating peripartum depressive disorders from the "baby blues" and information regarding other medical conditions that may increase the risk of perinatal depression.

> ***Note:*** The APA (2022a) reports that about 7% of women will experience a depressive episode between the birth of a child and 1 year.

When an MDD, recurrent, occurs in a pattern over the life span, coinciding with a specific season, the specifier *with seasonal pattern* may apply. The depressive episode will have a consistent temporal relationship to a particular time of year, unrelated to outside stressors such as difficult holiday events. Moreover, it will not occur outside the seasonal pattern for at least 2 years. The symptomatology may diminish or change as the seasons change, and the seasonal episodes will outnumber the nonseasonal episodes over the life span. In MDD, recurrent, *with seasonal pattern*, the depressive episodes tend to occur more often in fall and winter and are not typical in the summer. The symptoms appear more often in younger individuals who live in higher latitudes (APA, 2013a).

If the symptoms of the current episode are still ongoing and do not meet full criteria, or if the individual has experienced no significant symptoms for 2 months, *in partial remission* can be specified. If there are no significant symptoms, the specifier *in full remission* is applicable.

Questions for Consideration

1. What short-term impact did the COVID-19 pandemic have for depressive disorders, and what do you anticipate the long-term effects may be?
2. What are the major strategies counselors use to address MDD?
3. Consider the pros and cons of diagnosing premenstrual dysphoric disorder. Does this diagnosis pathologize menstruation? When is it appropriate to give the diagnosis?

Chapter 7

Bipolar and Related Disorders

Bipolar refers to fluctuations of mood (APA, 2022a; NIMH, n.d.-b) between two extremes from the highs of mania to the lows of depression. These swings can sometimes be quite severe and debilitating. Although not officially included in the *DSM* until the third edition (APA, 1980), writers as far back as the ancient Greeks referred to *melancholia* and *mania*. Aretaeus of Cappadocia wrote of individuals who displayed high levels of energy and euphoria followed by periods of melancholy (Burton, 2012). During the 19th century, psychiatric professionals used terms such as *manic depressive* and *affective psychosis* to describe this phenomenon (APA, 2013a). Kraepelin (1921) theorized that these symptoms were separate from psychosis and conceptualized them on a spectrum, emphasizing outcome as a criterion. Originally termed *manic depressive illness* in the first *DSM*, the diagnosis was renamed bipolar disorder in the *DSM-III* because of the stigma associated with manic depression and the attempt to explain the polarity of disorder rather than simply focus on symptomatology. Theorists have also debated the need for conceptualization of bipolar disorder on a spectrum (Merikangas et al., 2007; Paris, 2009).

Since the *DSM-III*, the diagnosis of bipolar disorder has increased rapidly, particularly for adolescents, for whom claims of increase were between 10% and 40% (Jenkins et al., 2011). However, Van Meter et al. (2019) found a U.S. prevalence rate of 3.9% in the pediatric bipolar spectrum, which is consistent with that of other Western countries. Miller and Black (2020) reported that the prevalence of these disorders collectively could be as high as 5% in the United States when considering all diagnoses on the bipolar spectrum, and NIMH (n.d.-b) reported that 82.9% of cases are diagnosed as severe. Furthermore, bipolar disorder is the sixth leading cause of disability worldwide (Akinhanmi et al., 2018). Individuals diagnosed with bipolar disorder have the highest rates of suicide and premature death related to medical disorders, with a 10 to 20 times increased risk of suicide compared with the U.S. population in general (Miller & Black, 2020).

Major Changes From *DSM-5* to *DSM-5-TR*

The major changes to the Bipolar and Related Disorders chapter in the *DSM-5-TR* include updated information for text sections, particularly relating to bipolar disorder and children; the role of environment in risk factors; cultural factors; and clarification for differentials. Additionally, the new text section, "Association With Suicidal Thoughts or Behavior," was added to bipolar I and bipolar II disorders. Clarification for coding was added to these disorders as well as certain specifiers. Additionally, the "Unspecified Mood Disorder" section, which was unintentionally removed from the chapter and from the Depressive Disorders chapter of the *DSM-IV-TR*, was reinstated in both sections.

In addition to these changes, which appear in the original edition of the *DSM-5-TR*, the APA released an update, the *Supplement to the Diagnostic and Statistical Manual of Mental Disorders, Fifth Edition, Text Revision* (APA, 2022b), in September 2022, which describes new changes to the criteria for three disorders in this chapter. Specifically, the phrase "commit suicide" was removed and replaced with language considered less stigmatizing. Also, the language for bipolar I major depressive episode, Criterion A9; bipolar II major depressive episode, Criterion A9; and bipolar specifiers, manic or hypomanic episode, with mixed features, Criterion A6, no longer includes "a suicide attempt or specific plan for committing suicide." The updated criteria now state, "Recurrent thoughts of death (not just fear of dying), recurrent suicidal ideation without a specific plan, a specific suicide plan, or a suicide attempt." We note that although the 2022 supplement reports these changes, we were unable to locate some of them in a *DSM-IV-TR* copy purchased in 2023.

Differential Diagnosis

As with depressive disorders, comorbidity seems to be the rule rather than the exception for bipolar and related disorders. Because individuals tend to seek treatment more frequently when they are experiencing depression, bipolar and related disorders are often mistaken for depression or anxiety (McIntyre et al., 2022). Furthermore, symptoms consistent with hypomania are usually unreported or misdiagnosed as anxiety (APA, 2022a). Together, it is estimated that between 20% and 30% of individuals being treated for depression and anxiety symptoms have bipolar disorder (Manning, 2010). Psychotic symptoms that can occur during a manic episode or in a depressive episode related to bipolar disorders are frequently mistaken for schizophrenia, schizoaffective disorder, or substance-induced psychotic disorder. When this happens, the client does not receive a timely diagnosis of the appropriate bipolar disorder, resulting in poorer treatment outcomes (Altamura et al., 2015). In other cases, bipolar disorder may go completely unrecognized. Das et al. (2005) screened individuals at a primary care facility for bipolar disorder. Of the 81 individuals who qualified for a bipolar disorder diagnosis, just 9% were diagnosed with bipolar or related disorders. Remaining participants were undiagnosed or carried depressive, substance use, and anxiety disorder diagnoses. Manning (2010) posited that a thorough history, accurate assessments, and a good therapeutic alliance, including multiple contacts with the client, might be key to accurately diagnosing bipolar and related disorders.

Etiology and Treatment

Although no one single explanation can be given, researchers and theorists posit a variety of contributors to bipolar disorder, including genetic predisposition, neurobiological factors, brain structure, ion activity, and impaired executive functioning (Alloy et al., 2009; R. J. Comer, 2022; Hankin, 2009). Understanding the factors that contribute to bipolar symptoms can inform well-rounded, evidence-based treatments. Childhood adversity, family conflict, early emotional trauma, and life stressors are also risk factors (APA, 2022a).

The *DSM-5-TR* authors note that relapsing depressive symptoms seem related to recent life stress and negative life events, and manic symptoms seem related to goal attainment (APA, 2022a). Substance use and/or abuse may play a role in increased manic symptoms.

Traditionally recommended treatment for bipolar and related disorders includes psychotherapy in conjunction with mood-stabilizing medication. Psychoeducation, CBT, family-focused therapy, and interpersonal and social rhythm therapy have been shown to be effective in treating the symptoms of bipolar disorder (Steinkuller & Rheineck, 2009). Lithium and other mood stabilizers have had high success rates in decreasing manic episodes and symptoms; however, individuals who discontinue medication are at very high risk of relapse (R. J. Comer, 2022). Psychoeducation can emphasize the importance of lifestyle management and regular medication use and assist with social skills and relationship building. Medication and other drugs are more effective when combined with therapy (R. J. Comer, 2022). Mindfulness-based interventions have shown promise for symptom reduction and improved executive functioning (Stange et al., 2011), and there is evidence that dialectical behavior therapy (DBT) group skills training may provide increased overall well-being, emotional regulation, distress tolerance, and symptom reduction when used to treat those who have bipolar disorders (Eisner et al., 2017; Van Dijk et al., 2013).

Implications for Counselors

Because of the impact of bipolar disorder on the individual, family, and community, it is critical that counselors are able to recognize the disorder. Individuals with bipolar disorder tend to have more health problems, experience relationship issues, and are at risk for suicidal ideation and attempts (Miller & Black, 2020; Steinkuller & Rheineck, 2009). Because of issues with comorbidity, many clients in mental health centers may not be fully treated for the symptoms of bipolar disorder (Altamura et al., 2018; Manning, 2010). Rather than attend solely to initial presenting problems (which may be depressive or anxious in nature), counselors need to attend to the possibility of bipolar disorder through a full and complete assessment, which may be over several sessions.

To help readers better understand changes from the *DSM-5* to *DSM-5-TR*, the rest of this chapter outlines each disorder addressed in the Bipolar and Related Disorders chapter of the *DSM-5-TR*. Readers should note that we have focused on major changes from the *DSM-5*; however, this is not a stand-alone resource for diagnosis. Although a summary and special considerations for counselors are provided for each disorder, when diagnosing clients, counselors need to reference the *DSM-5-TR*. It is essential that the diagnostic criteria and features, subtypes and specifiers (if applicable), prevalence, course, and risk and prognostic factors for each disorder are clearly understood prior to diagnosis.

Bipolar I Disorder (F31. _ _)

> The constant energy was amazing. It felt like I was connected to everything and everyone all at once. Everything I saw was beautiful and I bought everything I wanted. But after about a week or so, the crash would come and I would be miserable. The misery would increase over time until I didn't want to live anymore. No one understood. My wife eventually left, and I can't pay for all things that I bought.—Richard

With a lifetime prevalence of 1.5% (APA, 2022a), bipolar I disorder is characterized by the presence of at least one manic episode. This episode can precede or follow major depressive or hypomanic episodes. Most individuals who meet full criteria for manic episodes also experience major depressive episodes. Although major depressive episodes are not required for diagnosis, it is atypical for manic episodes to occur without a history of depression (APA, 2022a).

Essential Features

At least one episode of mania is required for a bipolar I disorder diagnosis. Symptoms of a manic episode will occur for at least a week, almost every day, with symptoms being present most of the day. During this time, the individual will experience abnormally increased goal-directed activity or heightened energy levels along with persistently elevated, irritable, or expansive mood (APA, 2022a). The individual will experience some additional symptoms that represent a noticeable change from usual behavior. If the mood is irritable only, the individual will experience at least four of the following symptoms (for other mood presentations, three or more of the following are required): exaggerated self-esteem or grandiosity; limited need for sleep; pressured speech or abnormally talkative self-report of racing thoughts or flight of ideas; inability to concentrate or easily distractible as indicated by self or others; significant increase in psychomotor agitation or goal-directed activity that is often social, work, or sexually related; and increased involvement in high-risk behavior or activities that could result in painful consequences (APA, 2022a).

In addition to the current or historical presence of a manic episode, individuals with bipolar I disorder often have histories involving major depressive and hypomanic episodes. Contrary to popular belief regarding the nature of bipolar disorder as involving rapid mood swings, mood episodes may go on for weeks or months at a time, resolve, and then be followed several months (or more) later with another mood episode.

Special Considerations

As with MDD, bipolar I disorder is associated with high rates of lethality. Some researchers speculated that between 25% and 50% of individuals with this disorder attempt suicide (Jamison, 2000), and Miller and Black (2020) estimated the suicide risk to be 20–30 times that of the general population. The *DSM-5-TR* estimates that 5% to 6% of those diagnosed with bipolar disorder will die by suicide (APA, 2022a). The length of depressive episodes and previous suicide attempts are related to elevated risk, as are the higher rates of alcohol use disorder, which is often comorbid with bipolar disorder (APA, 2022a). In addition, individuals who are experiencing a manic episode often engage in risky, even life-threatening, behaviors as part of the course. Counselors need to be particularly aware of these risk factors and engage clients who have bipolar disorder in risk assessments and crisis planning.

The *DSM-5-TR* now includes additional language to address and clarify a diagnosis of bipolar disorder in children. They note that although the typical age of onset is between 20 and 30 years of age, children are diagnosed with this disorder. When considering a bipolar diagnosis for children, counselors should carefully consider whether the symptoms reported or observed differ greatly from the child's baseline or developmental level, and concerning symptoms must include persistently increased behavioral activity that is typical for that child (APA, 2022a).

Counselors also need to be aware of the impact of bipolar I disorder on the family system. R. J. Comer (2022) noted that the "roller coaster ride" (p. 216) of bipolar emotions results in dramatic impact on the individual's friends and family. Health care costs for an individual with bipolar I disorder are three times higher than costs for other individuals because there are significantly more hospital visits, doctor visits, and medications (Chatterton et al., 2008). As a result of their symptoms, individuals with this disorder are less likely to be married and may experience higher divorce rates and chronic relationship instability (APA, 2022a). They are more likely to experience economic problems, such as decreased productivity and excess unemployment, and health problems, such as diabetes and cardiovascular disease (Miller & Black, 2020). Because of this disruption and the impact on functioning, family members should be included in the therapeutic process whenever possible (Steinkuller & Rheineck, 2009).

Although lifelong management may be required, there are effective treatments for bipolar I disorder. Mood-stabilizing and antipsychotic medications have been shown to be effective for treatment, and many researchers agree that a combination of psychotherapy and medications is the most effective treatment (R. J. Comer, 2022; Culver et al., 2007; Miller & Black, 2020; Steinkuller & Rheineck, 2009). Evidence-based interventions for treating bipolar I disorder include psychoeducation, CBT (Chiang et al., 2017), family-focused therapy, and interpersonal and social rhythm therapy (Steinkuller & Rheineck, 2009). There is evidence to support the integration of mindfulness techniques and DBT skills group into therapeutic practices toward improving well-being for those with bipolar symptoms (Eisner et al., 2017; Stange et al., 2011; J. M. Williams et al., 2008). Counselors can use these interventions for assisting clients with bipolar I disorder.

Cultural Considerations

Although bipolar I disorder occurs as frequently in women as in men, women tend to experience more rapid cycling and depressive episodes than men (APA, 2022a; R. J. Comer, 2022; Ketter, 2010). Concurrent with bipolar I, women also experience higher rates of eating disorders and substance use disorders (APA, 2022a). In terms of cultural variation, individuals diagnosed with bipolar I disorder often have lower socioeconomic status, higher rates of disability, and lower life expectancy (Miller & Black, 2020). The *DSM-5-TR* authors note that certain symptoms of bipolar disorder, such as psychotic features, may vary by culture, particularly in terms of flight of ideas and types of delusions. They posit that cultures that tend to be more individualistic and are reward based in nature have higher rates of bipolar disorder (APA, 2022a). Researchers identified racial disparities in the diagnosis of bipolar disorder, with individuals of African descent being misdiagnosed with another disorder, such as schizophrenia, rather than bipolar disorder more frequently than non-Latinx Whites. As a result, African Americans are at greater risk of receiving inappropriate treatment and poor outcomes (Akinhanmi et al., 2018; APA, 2022a).

Differential Diagnosis

Counselors should take care when considering a diagnosis of unipolar depression versus bipolar disorder. Clients who present during a major depressive episode may actually have bipolar disorder but seek treatment during the depressive phase. Depressive symptoms are often the first to appear, and they may persist longer or occur more frequently than manic symptoms (APA, 2022a). A thorough and accurate assessment of the symptoms is crucial to an appropriate diagnosis. Some factors that counselors should consider include a family history of depression, presence of psychotic symptoms, onset in the 20s, resistance to antidepressants, and multiple major depressive episodes (APA, 2022a).

For a bipolar I disorder diagnosis, the manic episodes cannot be better explained by substance use or a medical condition and must be severe enough to result in significant impairment in functioning, include psychotic features, or require hospitalization. The APA (2022a) notes that if an individual experiences a manic episode while receiving antidepressant treatment, the diagnosis is warranted as long as the episode continues with full criteria met after the effects of the treatment are over. Symptoms of bipolar I disorder must present in an episode and represent a marked difference in one's baseline functioning, thus differentiating bipolar I disorder from symptoms of a personality disorder. A personality disorder should never be diagnosed during a manic episode (APA, 2022a).

Moreover, symptoms of mania or hypomania can occur along with MDD. If the episodes are shorter in duration than required or have fewer symptoms than is necessary for a bipolar I disorder diagnosis to be given, MDD or bipolar II disorder can be diagnosed. Anxiety disorder and panic symptoms should be explored through careful determination of the episodic nature of the client's symptoms. Gathering a thorough history of symptoms can be crucial to helping differentiate panic or anxiety from a true experience of mania (APA, 2022a).

Because onset for this disorder can occur between 15 and 44 years of age (Van Meter et al., 2019), counselors will need to differentiate between mania and ADHD, especially in adolescents (APA, 2022a). Whereas ADHD symptoms are continuous, bipolar I symptoms occur episodically, which will help counselors to differentiate between the two. Severe irritability can present a similar challenge, particularly in children; a diagnosis of DMDD may be more appropriate if an episode of mania is not clearly present (APA, 2022a).

Coding, Recording, and Specifiers

The diagnostic code for bipolar I disorder is F31. Coding for bipolar I disorder is based on the current or most recent episode only. Counselors must also specify severity, whether psychotic features are present, and whether the client is in partial or full remission. If psychosis is present, the specifier *with psychotic features* is given. If the episode includes psychotic features, that code is given rather than specifying severity. Severity indicators are listed as mild, moderate, or severe. Remission status includes in partial remission or in full remission. An unspecified episode specifier may also be given (APA, 2022a). As shown in the table on pages 142–143 of the *DSM-5-TR*, all coding numbers for these specifiers are based on whether the most recent or current episode is manic, hypomanic, or depressed. When the name of the diagnosis is given, bipolar I is stated or written first, followed by the type of episode (i.e., manic, hypomanic, or depressed), and finally any and all the noncoded specifiers that apply. We discuss additional specifiers for bipolar and related disorders at the end of this chapter. Readers can also refer to pages 169–175 in the *DSM-5-TR* for more information regarding specifiers for bipolar and related disorders.

Case Example

> Vincent is a 28-year-old African American man who has just completed a major work project. He and his team were contracted to complete the project within a 2-month time frame. Vincent bragged, however, that he is good enough to get the work done in half the time. About 2 weeks into the project, his energy level "went on high" as it has done in the past. Vincent states that he slept a couple of hours a day, working at fevered pitch. He states that he was the best contractor ever hired and that, even though his colleagues told him he was edgy and difficult most of the time, he knew this was not the case because women were "all over him." In fact, he bragged about taking a different woman home almost every night. After a little over a week, his energy level slowly returned to normal and the work was completed, early as he predicted, making his employer very happy.
>
> Because he had done such a great job and received a sizable bonus, Vincent's coworkers were surprised when he began missing work. He told them he wasn't feeling well and didn't want to get out of bed. When his family didn't hear from him in over a week, his sister stopped by to check on him. She found him unkempt; he had eaten very little in a week and had considered ingesting a bottle of aspirin. Vincent explained this to you as you complete his intake at the inpatient psychiatric facility where you work. He stated that he has experienced elevated energy levels before but never felt this sad afterward. He doesn't want to live if he has to feel like this again.

Diagnostic Questions

1. Do Vincent's presenting symptoms meet the criteria for bipolar disorder? If so, which one?
2. What would be the reason(s) a counselor would not diagnose Vincent with bipolar I disorder?

3. Would Vincent be accurately diagnosed with manic episodes?
4. What rule-outs would you consider for Vincent's case?
5. What other information may be needed to make an accurate clinical diagnosis?
6. Are there any assessments available that might help you determine symptom severity?

Bipolar II Disorder (F31.81)

> The extra boost of energy was great. While my colleagues were downing coffee and energy drinks, I could easily handle all the workload and then some. I didn't need as much sleep either, so I could get up early to work as well. I was so much better at my job than they were, and my boss would be so happy with me. But the downside was that blues would get really bad at times, and I lost my last job because I was so sad I couldn't leave the house for days.—Cecilia

Bipolar II disorder is characterized by at least one hypomanic episode and at least one major depressive episode and has been recognized as a unique diagnosis since the 1970s (Swartz et al., 2012). Although bipolar II disorder is conceptualized as a mild bipolar disorder or mild mania, this disorder is phenomenologically distinct from bipolar I disorder (APA, 2022a; Swartz et al., 2012). There is no experience of full mania or psychosis; however, the lifelong impact can include poor health-related outcomes, higher rates of suicide, and significant psychosocial impairment (Swartz et al., 2012). Furthermore, individuals with a family history of bipolar II disorder represent about one third of this population, perhaps indicating a genetic link. Changes from the *DSM-5* to *DSM-5-TR* include updates to text sections and the introduction of "Association With Suicidal Thoughts or Behavior" as a new text section (APA, 2022a). The *DSM-5-TR* supplement also removes the language "commit suicide," adding the more sensitive statement "a specific suicide plan, or a suicide attempt" (APA, 2022b).

Essential Features

Bipolar II disorder requires an individual to experience at least one hypomanic episode and one major depressive episode in the absence of any history of manic episodes. A hypomanic episode is described as a period of time lasting at least 4 consecutive days in which the person will present with an abnormal mood described as persistently elevated, expansive, or irritable. During this time, the person will experience heightened energy or unusually increased activity (APA, 2022a). Although the specific symptoms for hypomania are identical to those for mania with the expectation of the minimum time period required, the hypomanic symptoms cannot cause marked impairment, be associated with hospitalization, or involve psychotic symptoms. Because these symptoms may be more subtle, they must be observable to others and not simply a return to normal mood. Counselors should note that bipolar II is not a milder form of bipolar I, because both cause significant impairment within individuals.

Special Considerations

Counselors need to keep in mind some unique circumstances surrounding bipolar II disorder. Whereas the 12-month prevalence rate of this disorder is 0.08% in the United States, hypomanic episodes may go undiagnosed for a long period of time, creating what the *DSM-5-TR* refers to as "more than a 10-year lag" (APA, 2022a, p. 155) between onset and proper diagnosis, even though hypomanic episodes are highly recurrent. Individuals experiencing bipolar II disorder tend to have higher rates of "rapid cycling" than do those with bipolar I disorder (Swartz et al., 2009), and these cycles occur more frequently in women than in men (APA, 2022a). Rapid cycling occurs when the individual experiences four or more mood episodes, either hypomanic or depressed, within a 12-month period, and this occurs in 5% to 15% of cases. Rapid cycling often indicates poorer outcomes, and when these cycles begin to occur more closely, counselors must watch closely for overall increased symptomatology (APA, 2022a).

As with bipolar I disorder, interpersonal relationships and occupational status may be difficult for individuals with bipolar II to maintain, with up to 15% of these individuals continuing to experience some level of dysfunction between episodes (APA, 2022a). Furthermore, high rates of suicidal ideation occur in both groups (Weinstock et al., 2009). APA (2022a) reports that one third of individuals who have this disorder will attempt suicide; people with bipolar II disorder tend to make more lethal attempts than those diagnosed with bipolar I disorder. The length of depressive episode and having a first-degree family member with the same diagnosis are indicators of higher suicide risk (APA, 2022a). As a result, counselors must be vigilant with risk assessment and prevention when working with these individuals.

As with bipolar I disorder, co-occurring disorders are more likely than not for bipolar II disorder. Counselors should note that about 60% of individuals diagnosed with bipolar II disorder have three or more comorbid mental disorders (APA, 2022a). Anxiety is the highest co-occurring disorder, but substance use disorders are frequent as well, specifically alcohol use disorder and cannabis use disorder. These individuals may struggle with eating disorders, with binge-eating disorder being prominent. Women with this diagnosis may also struggle with premenstrual syndrome and PMDD. Both men and women report multiple co-occurring medical disorders, some of which are debilitating, resulting in lifelong struggle and potential early death (APA, 2022a).

Whereas there are few evidence-based treatments specifically for bipolar II disorder, mood stabilizing medications are often used in conjunction with psychological interventions (Fisher et al., 2018). Evidence-based treatments for individuals who have bipolar II disorder include cognitive therapy, CBT, psychoeducation, family-focused therapy, and case management, in conjunction with medication (Swartz et al., 2012). Swartz et al. (2012) also found preliminary evidence that interpersonal and social rhythm therapy can be effective for working with this population. Furthermore, DiRocco et al. (2020) reported that an adapted version of DBT served as a promising intervention in a sample that included individuals with both bipolar I and bipolar II disorders.

Cultural Considerations

Some research suggests that bipolar II disorder is more common in women than in men, but this is not definitive. Rapid cycling with mixed depressive features do occur more often for women, and childbirth and early postpartum could prompt these symptoms. Additionally, perimenopause may produce symptoms of mood instability that counselors could have difficulty differentiating from bipolar II disorder (APA, 2022a). A medical examination is important to assist in accurate diagnosis in this population as well as in older adults. The average age of onset for this disorder is somewhat later than that for bipolar I disorder (APA, 2022a). Bipolar II disorder has a more chronic course (Swartz et al., 2012). This is likely because episodes of hypomania have seemingly less severe consequences, such as hospitalization, which are customary to bipolar I disorder. The misconception that bipolar II disorder is a milder form of bipolar disorder (Akiskal, 2002) needs to be clarified by mental health professionals, so laypersons and individuals diagnosed with this disorder are better educated about manifestations of this illness and courses of treatment. Also relevant is a thorough understanding of the cultural context in which the client reports symptoms.

As stated previously, individuals diagnosed with mental disorders experience symptoms grounded within the framework of their cultural beliefs, values, and norms (Hays & Erford, 2018; Warren, 2007). Misunderstanding a client's worldview can lead to high rates of misdiagnosis, delayed diagnosis, or a lack of recognition and treatment of comorbid conditions. Aside from clients not receiving proper treatment, these problems negatively affect the way in which they are able to function and interact with others (Vázquez et al., 2011). These problems also can lead to psychosocial issues, such as high rates of unemployment and problems with physical health. All of these contribute to stigma, especially among different cultural groups. Mental health settings that are incompatible with the cultural background of the clients they serve deter these clients from seeking mental health support services or following through with treatment (Hays & Erford, 2018).

Differential Diagnosis

For a diagnosis of bipolar II disorder, the symptoms must represent a distinct change from the individual's normal functioning; must cause clinically significant impairment in social, occupational, or other important areas of functioning; and must be observable by others. If a person experiences a hypomanic episode during antidepressive treatment, the symptoms must continue beyond the effects of the treatment to be considered for this diagnosis. Symptoms cannot be better explained by another medical condition or abuse of a substance. They cannot be better explained by schizoaffective disorder, schizophrenia, schizophreniform, delusional, or any other disorder on the schizophrenia spectrum (APA, 2022a). Although psychosis may occur during a major depressive episode, psychotic features cannot occur within hypomania. The symptoms of a hypomanic episode will not be severe enough to warrant hospitalization, nor will they result in marked impairment in social or work functioning (APA, 2022a).

Mental health professionals may struggle to differentiate bipolar II disorder from MDD or bipolar I disorder. Determining whether the specific episode meets full criteria and length for hypomania will assist the counselor in determining an accurate diagnosis. Recognizing symptoms as part of a specific episode, rather than chronic irritability associated with depression only, occurs more effectively when a thorough evaluation of symptoms is given. A diagnosis of cyclothymic disorder may be more appropriate if hypomanic and depressive episodes are noted but the individual does not meet full criteria for major depressive and hypomanic episodes (APA, 2022a). Psychotic features can occur along with the symptoms of bipolar II disorder but do not occur outside of a mood episode, such as a major depressive episode.

Coding, Recording, and Specifiers

There is only one diagnostic code for bipolar II disorder, F31.81, unless the specifier *with catatonia*, 293.89 (F06.1), is appropriate. However, counselors can indicate current severity (i.e., mild, moderate, or severe), course, and other specifiers in writing. For example, for a client who presents with severe bipolar II disorder with catatonic features, the diagnostic code would be written as "F06.1 bipolar II, with catatonia, severe." Unlike bipolar I disorder, severity and course specifiers do not have specific codes associated with them. The most recent episode (either hypomanic or depressed) should be given, as well as severity and all the following specifiers that apply: *with anxious distress*, *with mixed features*, *with rapid cycling*, *with mood-congruent psychotic features*, *with mood-incongruent psychotic features*, *with peripartum onset*, and *with seasonal pattern* (APA, 2022a). We discuss additional specifiers for bipolar and related disorders at the end of this chapter. See pages 169–175 in the *DSM-5-TR* for more information regarding specifiers for bipolar and related disorders.

Case Example

> Sue is a 24-year-old Caucasian elementary school teacher who started coming to see you for counseling 3 months ago because she was experiencing moderate depressive symptoms. When she originally presented for counseling, she

reported a history of depression. You have been working with her using CBT and teaching her coping skills for depression. Sue came in for her regularly scheduled appointment and was accompanied by her husband, Zion, who is extremely worried about her.

Sue's husband states that for several days, including this weekend, she was not herself. He reports that she didn't sleep much but wasn't tired. She was highly "keyed up," talking constantly. Zion reports that she couldn't seem to focus on anything and was fixated on the idea that something awful was going to happen. She told him she doesn't want him or the children out of sight. Zion states that there is no reason to think that this is the case, but Sue was too upset and distracted to listen to reason. When pressed, he states that her symptoms lasted all day for 4 days but not for a full week. Sue has never used drugs and is not on medication.

Diagnostic Questions

1. Do Sue's presenting symptoms meet the criteria for a bipolar disorder? If so, which one?
2. What would be the reason(s) a counselor would not diagnose Sue with bipolar I disorder?
3. Would Sue be accurately diagnosed with manic episodes? Why or why not?
4. What rule-outs would you consider for Sue's case?
5. Are there any specifiers that apply?
6. What other information may be needed to make an accurate clinical diagnosis?

Cyclothymic Disorder (F34.0)

Ever since my mid-20s, I've been described as moody. My friends and family members seem to test the waters before hanging out with me, and I know it's because they want to avoid me when I'm down. When I'm happy and energetic, we always have good times. But I cycle through the energy and start feeling down pretty regularly. I wish I could control it.—Justin

Cyclothymic disorder, originally introduced in the *DSM-II* (APA, 1968) as an affective personality disorder, was reported under bipolar disorder when this category was renamed in the *DSM-III* (APA, 1980). Having been noted as far back as the 1880s when German psychiatrist Karl Kahlbaum coined the term *cyclothymia* (Van Meter et al., 2012), this subthreshold form of bipolar disorder is characterized by cycles of hypomanic symptoms and depressive symptoms that occur at distinctly different times within at least a 2-year period for adults and a 1-year period for children. The lifetime prevalence of this disorder is about 0.4% in the U.S. general population (APA, 2022a). However, theorists argue that this is actually the most common mood disorder and goes underdiagnosed due to the ambivalent language (Van Meter et al., 2017). Individuals rarely seek treatment for cyclothymic disorder; when they do, it is typically during a depressive cycle (Van Meter et al., 2012). The disorder usually presents in late adolescence or early adulthood and can be a precursor to other mood disorders (APA, 2022a).

Essential Features

Cyclothymic disorder is diagnosed when, over the course of 2 years for adults or 1 year for children and adolescents, the individual experiences multiple periods of depressive symptoms that do not meet criteria for depression and multiple periods of elevated mood that do not meet criteria for hypomania (APA, 2022a). During this time frame, the individual cannot be symptom free for more than 2 months, and the symptoms must be present more days than not. The disorder should not be diagnosed if the symptoms can be better explained by another medical condition or substance use. In addition, the symptoms cannot be better explained by another bipolar or related disorder, schizoaffective disorder, schizophrenia, schizophreniform, delusional, or any other disorder on the schizophrenia spectrum (APA, 2022a).

Special Considerations

Although individuals with cyclothymic disorder tend to seek treatment more frequently when experiencing depressive symptoms, counselors need to be aware that both mood presentations have a significant impact on the client's functioning. The depressive symptoms can include irritability, explosive episodes, low self-esteem, and guilt. Although the description of the disorder appears mild, cyclothymia may be more treatment resistant than MDD or bipolar II disorder (Van Meter et al., 2012). Furthermore, hypomanic symptoms associated with this disorder can include impulsivity and uninhibited friendliness. Suicidality is a critical issue with individuals diagnosed with cyclothymic disorder, and these clients should be monitored carefully. Because of the chronic change in mood presentation, social functioning can be severely affected (Fava et al., 2011; Van Meter et al., 2012). Therapies, including CBT and CBT in conjunction with well-being therapy, have been shown to reduce mood instability and increase quality of sleep (Fava et al., 2011; Van Meter et al., 2012). Cultural considerations for individuals with cyclothymic disorder do not vary considerably from those for individuals with MDD. Although the prevalence is the same, more women than men get treatment (APA, 2013a).

Cultural Considerations

In the general population, there is no significant difference in lifetime prevalence of cyclothymic disorder according to gender (APA, 2013a). Studies investigating cyclothymic disorder in children are rare. Van Meter et al. (2012) examined individuals with familial patterns of cyclothymic and bipolar disorders and found that individuals with cyclothymic disorder experienced greater irritability and were more likely to have a family history of bipolar disorder. In a study of cyclothymic temperament in adults with ADHD, researchers discovered individuals were more likely to have lower levels of education and higher levels of occupational problems (Landaas et al., 2012).

Because the symptoms of cyclothymic disorder are similar to those of bipolar disorders, clients must describe fluctuations in mood and behavior. As described previously in the "Cultural Considerations" section of bipolar II disorders, counselors must be aware of cultural innuendos regarding mania, hypomania, and depression to accurately understand what the client is experiencing. Descriptions of these symptoms can vary significantly depending on a client's culture, so counselors should be sure to investigate the client's cultural worldview and consider these in diagnosis and treatment planning.

Differential Diagnosis

When diagnosing cyclothymic disorder, counselors should ensure that the client does not meet the criteria for MDD, mania, or a full hypomanic episode. In addition, counselors should differentiate this disorder from the rapid cycling presentation of bipolar I and II disorders; because of frequent shifts in rapid cycling, both of these disorders may resemble cyclothymic disorder. A thorough assessment of presenting symptoms and history will assist counselors in determining whether full criteria for a depressive episode, manic episode, or hypomanic episode have been met. If at any point the full symptoms of these episodes have been met, the cyclothymic disorder diagnosis can be dropped and the more appropriate mood disorder assigned (APA, 2013a).

Because this disorder was originally included in the chapter on personality disorders, referred to as cyclothymic temperament, it can be confused for borderline personality disorder (Van Meter et al., 2012). APA (2022a) acknowledges this change and suggests that marked shifts in mood can be associated with both disorders, and both disorders can be diagnosed if the full criteria for each have been met. APA (2022a) also notes that the mood elevation, increased energy, and even euphoria often associated with cyclothymia is not typical of borderline personality disorder.

Coding, Recording, and Specifiers

There is only one diagnostic code for cyclothymic disorder: F34.0. If applicable, coding is recorded along with the specifier *with anxious distress*. See the end of this chapter for more information on this specifier. Because mood symptoms are considered mild by nature, there is no specifier for mild, moderate, and severe.

Substance/Medication-Induced Bipolar and Related Disorder (__.__)

This is a diagnosis that presents with the same essential features as those of manic, hypomanic, and depressive episodes. The symptoms are very similar to those of a bipolar disorder; however, they are related directly to the use of a substance or a medication and subside when those factors are removed. If an individual continues to experience symptoms of mania or hypomania after the effects of medication, treatments, or substance have subsided, a bipolar or related disorder may be diagnosed (APA, 2022a)

Essential Features

Substance/medication-induced bipolar disorder is characterized by clinically significant changes in mood that include elevated, expansive, or irritable mood or lack of interest in pleasurable activities or all activities. This may or may not include depressive symptoms. The mood disturbance must occur during or soon after substance intoxication or withdrawal or after taking medications. The substance or medication must be able to cause the symptoms, and the disturbance does not only occur when the individual is experiencing delirium (APA, 2022a). Furthermore, the symptoms must result in clinically significant distress or impairment in functioning.

Special Considerations

Etiology is the key to understanding this distinct disorder. As a result, when making this diagnosis, counselors should take steps to ensure that an independent bipolar or related disorder does not exist and should better explain the observed symptoms. This will almost always involve a consultation with a physician who is qualified to determine etiology of symptoms. If the symptoms occurred before the substance or medication was ingested or continued for a month or more afterward, it is likely that the condition is not related to substance use or medication (APA, 2022a).

Differential Diagnosis

The side effects of some psychotropic medications can account for symptoms consistent with mania and hypomania. Unless the person meets the full criteria for a bipolar disorder, independent of these medications or treatments, a bipolar diagnosis is not warranted (APA, 2022a). If mania occurs while the person is receiving treatments but extends well beyond the cessation of treatment, bipolar I disorder can be diagnosed. However, in the case of hypomanic symptoms that extend well beyond the end of treatment, a depressive episode must have occurred previously for bipolar II disorder to be diagnosed (APA, 2022a).

Coding, Recording, and Specifiers

For substance/medication-induced bipolar and related disorder, the *ICD-10-CM* codes are used. The name of the substance causing the symptoms is used to identify the code and is in the written name as well. The code can include .1, .2, or .9 to indicate *with use disorder, mild*; *with use disorder, moderate*; or *without use disorder*, respectively. Additionally, specifiers *with onset during intoxication* and *with onset during withdrawal* should be indicated after the code and name (APA, 2022a). The authors of the *DSM-5-TR* added an additional specifier to this list, *with onset after medication use*. See page 163 of the *DSM-5-TR* for more information.

Bipolar and Related Disorder Due to Another Medical Condition (F06.3)

Differing from substance/medication-induced bipolar and related disorders, the diagnosis of bipolar and related disorders due to another medical condition applies when symptoms consistent with mania present related exclusively to a medical condition. Typically, the symptoms are seen on the onset of the medical condition but can occur as part of the relapse of a medication condition or as the course of the condition intensifies (APA, 2022a).

Essential Features

In bipolar disorder due to another medical condition, the individual will typically present with a significant mood change, which can be connected directly to a medical condition through physical examinations, laboratory findings, or history with evidence linking the two conditions (APA, 2022a). The mood change will include unusually elevated or expansive mood or chronic irritability, along with increased energy levels or activities. Another condition or mental disorder cannot better explain the symptoms, and there must be clinically significant impairment, distress, mental health hospitalization, or psychotic features. The symptoms cannot occur only during delirium (APA, 20a).

Special Considerations

Consistent with substance/medication-induced bipolar and related disorders, etiology is the key to diagnosing this disorder. Although these individuals are most often seen in medical settings first, counselors need to be aware that certain medical conditions can cause bipolar symptoms (e.g., multiple sclerosis, stroke, Cushing's disease; APA, 2022a). Furthermore, because symptoms are consistent with mania, counselors should monitor carefully for suicidal ideation and collaborate with physicians who are qualified to make diagnoses related to etiology of the condition.

Differential Diagnosis

Because medical conditions that can induce manic symptoms may be treated by medications that do the same, it is important to determine the etiology when differentiating the two (APA, 2022a). An assessment that assists in identifying the timing of symptom onset can be helpful. In addition, presence of symptoms for delirium, catatonia, and acute anxiety should be noted as well when considering a differential diagnosis.

Coding, Recording, and Specifiers

The coding for this disorder is determined through the *ICD-10-CM* and are codes related to the specifier (APA, 2022a). These include F06.33, *with manic features*; F06.33, *with manic- or hypomanic-like episode*; or F06.34, *with mixed features*. As with all diagnostic coding related to instances in which another medical condition is clinically significant, the name of the medical condition should be included in the name of the disorder. In addition to the mental disorder, the medical condition should also be coded and listed immediately before the mental disorder. For example, if a client has bipolar disorder due to hyperthyroidism, with manic features, clinicians would use the codes E05.90 hyperthyroidism; F06.33 bipolar disorder due to hyperthyroidism, with manic features. Of course, counselors are not going to be diagnosing medical conditions; however, knowledge regarding placement is critical for interdisciplinary communication and enhanced client care.

Other Specified and Unspecified Bipolar and Related Disorders: (F31.89/F31.9)

The other specified bipolar and related disorder (F31.89) category may be used for diagnosis if the counselor wants to identify the specific reason that the full diagnosis for a bipolar or related disorder is not met. There are five specifiers for this diagnosis: *short-duration hypomanic episodes and major depressive episodes*, *hypomanic episodes with insufficient symptoms and major depressive episodes*, *hypomanic episode without prior major depressive episode*, *short-duration cyclothymia (less than 24 months)*, and the newly added *manic episode superimposed on schizophrenia, schizophreniform disorder, delusional disorder, or other specified and unspecified schizophrenia spectrum and psychotic disorder* (APA, 2022a). There is one code for this diagnosis (F31.89). The counselor should indicate this code, followed by the disorder name, and finally the specific designation, such as short-term cyclothymia. The unspecified bipolar and related disorder (F31.9) diagnosis can be given when an individual presents with symptoms of a bipolar or related disorder but does not meet the full criteria, and the counselor does not have the information to diagnose other specified bipolar and related disorder.

Unspecified Mood Disorder (F39)

Unspecified mood disorder (F39) was removed from the *DSM-IV-TR* but added back to the *DSM-5-TR*. The purpose of the diagnosis is to indicate that symptoms of either a bipolar or depressive disorder are identified but they do not rise to a full diagnosis in either classification. Furthermore, the clinician may not have enough information to identify which diagnostic class exists. This diagnosis is also listed for depressive disorders.

Specifiers for Bipolar and Related Disorders

The following is an all-inclusive listing of specifiers for bipolar and related disorders. We have chosen to include these because of the requirement for counselors to accurately identify and list specifiers to further clarify the course, severity, or special features of the identified bipolar disorder. The major change to this section includes the addition of *with anxious distress* and *with mixed features* as specifiers.

Essential Features

If the symptoms of the current episode are ongoing but do not meet full criteria, or if the individual has experienced no significant symptoms for 2 months, *in partial remission* can be specified. If there are no significant symptoms, *in full remission* is applicable. Severity specifiers can also be identified based on the number of symptoms, symptom severity, and degree of impairment. For the specifier *mild*, few additional symptoms are noted, they are manageable, and they result in only minor impairment. For *severe*, there are multiple excess symptoms, they are intensely distressing and unmanageable, and there is a marked interference with functioning. *Moderate* occurs when symptom number, intensity, and impairment fall between mild and severe (APA, 2013a).

For the diagnosis of bipolar and related disorders, counselors can identify specifiers as appropriate. The *DSM-5* allows for the specifier *with anxious distress* if, during most days of a current or most recent episode of mania, hypomania, or depression, two of the following symptoms are reported: feeling keyed up or tense, increased restlessness, excessive worry that leads to difficulty concentrating, irrational fear that something negative is about to occur, and fear of loss of self-control. Symptom severity can be identified for this specifier as well. If two symptoms are noted, *mild* severity is indicated. For three symptoms, *moderate* is indicated, and *moderate-severe* is indicated if four or more symptoms are present.

> ***Note:*** The specifier *with anxious distress* has been added to both MDD and bipolar disorder because of its prominence in mental health and special care settings. Anxious distress has been related to higher risk of suicide. APA (2013a) encourages clinicians to be aware of severity levels, assess, and plan appropriately.

Another specifier associated with the manic, hypomanic, or depressive episode of bipolar I and II disorders is *with mixed features*. The criteria for the *with mixed features* specifier differ depending on the current mood episode. For this specifier to be given as a *manic or hypomanic episode, with mixed features*, the individual will have experienced a full manic or hypomanic episode, and during the majority of days this occurs, the individual also experiences at least three of the following additional symptoms: lack of interest or pleasure in all or almost all activities; depressed mood or noticeable dysphasia; noticeable slowing of movement or psychomotor retardation; lack of energy or constant fatigue; guilt or feeling of being worthless; and unusual preoccupation with dying, thoughts of suicide, a plan for suicide, or an attempt. Clinicians should note that in the *DSM5-TR* the supplement (APA, 2022b), the language for Criterion 6 was changed to reflect less stigmatizing language. This change removed the language "commit suicide" to "a specific suicide plan, or a suicide attempt." However, we note that although the supplement reports these changes, we were unable to locate some of them in a *DSM-5-TR* copy purchased in 2023. These symptoms are not related to medication or substance use and must include change that is noticeable to others. If the individual meets all the criteria for both mania and depression at the same time, manic episode with mixed features should be assigned.

For the specifier *depressive episode, with mixed features* to apply, the individual will have met all the criteria for a major depressive episode with a minimum of three of the manic/hypomanic symptoms occurring most days during the episode. The manic/hypomanic criteria include exaggerated self-esteem or grandiosity; expansive or increase mood; limited need for sleep; pressured to speak or abnormally talkative; self-report of racing thoughts or flight of ideas; inability to concentrate or easily distractible as indicated by self or others; significant increase in psychomotor agitation or goal-directed activity that is often social, work, or sexually related; and unusually increased involvement in high-risk behavior or activities that could result in painful consequences (APA, 2013a). Furthermore, the symptoms are not related to a medical condition, medication, or substance and must differ from typical behavior in a way that is noticeable to others.

The specifier *with rapid cycling* may be present in both bipolar I and II disorders. The individual will have at least four mood episodes within a 12-month period, and these will meet the criteria for manic, hypomanic, or major depressive episodes. These episodes can switch polarity (mania and hypomanic are on the same pole) and will have either partial or full remission for at least 2 months. The episodes may occur in any order and meet the time frames and full criteria for manic, hypomanic, or major depressive episodes, with the only difference being that rapid cycling episodes occur more frequently. The episodes cannot be influenced or better accounted for by substance use (APA, 2013a).

For the specifier *with melancholic features* to be applicable, during the most severe period of the major depressive episode, the individual must experience lack of pleasure in almost all or all activities or lack of response to pleasurable events. Three or more additional symptoms must be experienced from the following: distinct depression that may include deep despondency, despair, glumness, or empty mood; increased depression in the morning that can be accompanied by early waking, at least 2 hours earlier than normal; noticeable slowing or psychomotor agitation; significant weight fluctuation; and overwhelming guilt. The changes are noticeable, and the psychomotor changes are almost always present. Furthermore, the condition occurs more frequently in individuals who also have psychotic features and are more likely to occur in severe depressive episodes requiring inpatient care (APA, 2013a).

The specifier *with atypical features* is applicable when the individual spends most days of the current or most recent major depressive episode experiencing mood reactivity and two or more additional features. The additional features include significant weight gain or increased appetite, constant daytime sleepiness, feeling of heaviness in the arms or legs, and a history of social or occupational issues related to extreme sensitivity to being rejected. This sensitivity to rejection begins early in life and can occur even when the individual is not experiencing depressive symptoms but can be worse during a depressive episode.

> ***Note:*** Although the term *atypical depression* was historically acknowledged as the traditional presentation of depressive symptoms, depression is no longer a rarely diagnosed condition, as the name may imply.

For the specifier *with psychotic features* to be given, the individual will experience delusions or hallucinations during the episode. The specifier *with mood-congruent psychotic features* or *without mood-congruent psychotic features* should be diagnosed if psychotic features are present. When the psychotic features are mood-congruent, they will be consistent with the manic themes (e.g., grandiosity), but there may also be paranoia surrounding whether others believe the grandiose statements or the individual's capacities. When this does not occur, the specifier *with mood-incongruent psychotic features* should be included. The *DSM-5-TR* also breaks the mood-congruent and incongruent psychotic features apart by whether they occur in a current or most recent manic episode or major depressive episode (APA, 2022a). This language is clarifying and more specific to the content of these psychotic features.

The specifier *with catatonia* is specified when catatonic features are present during most of the episode for either a manic or a major depressive episode. Criteria for catatonia associated with a mental disorder are given in the Schizophrenia Spectrum and Other Psychotic Disorders chapter.

The specifier *with peripartum onset* can be used when the beginning of mood symptoms is during pregnancy or in the 4 weeks after delivery for current or most recent episode of mania, hypomania, or major depression in bipolar I or bipolar II disorder. Whereas mood episodes can begin before or after delivery, about half of women begin experiencing these symptoms prior to delivery and, as such, the specifier is *with peripartum onset.* Symptoms associated with this can be severe, and for some women this includes anxiety, panic attacks, and psychotic features that can be extreme and include command hallucinations to harm or kill the child. Of note is that 50% of these depressive episodes begin during the pregnancy, and between conception and birth, an estimated 9% of women will experience this disorder. Furthermore, caution should be taken not to confuse this disorder with typical "baby blues" which may present more as mood changes due to physiological changes after childbirth. Pregnancy-related thyroid changes can also be an issue here, and a full medical examination is warranted for accurate diagnosis (APA, 2022a).

When a mood episode, whether manic, hypomanic, or depressive, occurs regularly over the life span, in conjunction with a specific season, the specifier *with seasonal pattern* may apply. Although other mood episodes can occur, the type of episode referred to by this specifier has a consistent temporal relationship to a particular time of year, unrelated to outside stressors (such as difficult holiday events), and it will not occur outside the seasonal pattern for at least 2 years. The symptomatology may either diminish or change as the seasons change, and the seasonal episodes will outnumber the nonseasonal episodes over the life span. In the *DSM-5-TR,* severity specifiers associated with seasonal pattern are now delineated by whether the individual is experiencing a manic episode or major depressive episode, for a more accurate report (APA, 2022a).

Questions for Consideration

1. What cultural factors should counselors be aware of when considering whether a diagnosis of bipolar I disorder is appropriate?
2. Can children be diagnosed with bipolar disorder and, if so, what should counselors keep in mind when contemplating this diagnosis?
3. What treatments are typically used by counselors who are working with clients diagnosed with bipolar disorder?
4. Bipolar disorder is associated with elevated risk of suicidal thoughts and behaviors. What steps might a counselor engage in to protect clients with this diagnosis?

Chapter 8

Anxiety Disorders

Anxiety is "a state of apprehension, uncertainty, and fear focused on the anticipation of a realistic or fantasized threatening event or situation, often impairing physical and psychological functioning" (*American Heritage Dictionary*, n.d.). The APA (2022a) purports that each of the anxiety disorders shares features of fear and anxiety, which it defined as follows: "*Fear* is the emotional response to real or perceived imminent threat, whereas *anxiety* is anticipation of future threat" (p. 215). People who experience anxiety often have physiological symptoms such as muscle tension, heart palpitations, sweating, dizziness, or shortness of breath. Emotional symptoms include restlessness, a sense of impending doom, fear of dying, fear of embarrassment or humiliation, or fear of something terrible happening. People with anxiety disorders worry more than others and display excessive or persistent fear and anxiety (Byrd-Bredbenner et al., 2020).

Prevalence of anxiety among the general population is high. Each year, anxiety disorders affect approximately 40 million, or 18%, of adults in the United States (NIMH, n.d.-a). Anxiety disorders have a lifetime prevalence of approximately 30%. Close to 50% of individuals diagnosed with an anxiety disorder also meet the criteria for a depressive disorder. Anxiety disorders in themselves are highly comorbid and share genetic predispositions (Byrd-Bredbenner et al., 2020). It is important for counselors to accurately diagnose anxiety disorders as they respond to clinical interventions (ADAA, 2022).

Anxiety manifests in multiple ways, including fear for the future on a cognitive level, muscle tension on a somatovisceral level, and situational avoidance on a behavioral level. These experiences can have a pervasive impact on individuals' daily functioning, including varying degrees of difficulty in establishing and maintaining interpersonal relationships (Hickey et al., 2005). Anxiety disorders often persist over time, thus representing ongoing challenges for the many people living with them (APA, 2022a; Takeshima et al., 2021). Because the prevalence of anxiety disorders in the general population is so high, they are frequently the focus of clinical attention for counselors and are often diagnosed within counseling settings (ADAA, 2022; Kress & Paylo, 2018).

Major Changes From *DSM-5* to *DSM-5-TR*

There are no major changes to the anxiety disorders from the *DSM-5* to the *DSM-5-TR*. The only modification to this section is the removal of the parenthetical "social phobia" from social anxiety disorder because there was no evidence of clinical utility for continued use of the term (APA, 2022a).

Differential Diagnosis

APA (2022a) posits that clinical attention should focus on the discernment of disorders enumerated within the Anxiety Disorders chapter in the *DSM-5-TR*. Perhaps the best way for counselors to accurately diagnose anxiety disorders is to have a clear framework for the specifics of each diagnosis as well as common differential and comorbid diagnoses. Differential diagnosis of anxiety disorders can be challenging, especially considering the comorbidity of anxiety disorders with depressive disorders. One way to differentiate the two is for counselors to keep in mind that depressive disorders are sometimes viewed as anxious-misery with high incidences of sadness and anhedonia; this distinguishes them from anxiety disorders that often include anxious anticipation, uncertainty, and fear (Byrd-Bredbenner et al., 2020). Anhedonia and lowered affect are more commonly symptoms of depression than anxiety, whereas sleep disturbance, overall fatigue, and difficulty with concentration can be symptoms of both (APA, 2022a). The high comorbidity rates between depression and anxiety often make discernment a difficult task for counselors and researchers alike. Clear understanding of distinctions across disorders can assist with accurate differential diagnosis.

Counselors can also consider the propensity of individuals with anxiety disorders to worry more about future events and individuals with depressive disorders to be generally sad or morose. Across the spectrum of anxiety disorders, there are heightened responses to threats (real or perceived), increased responses to stress, and reactivity of the amygdala. Common overarching features of anxiety and depressive disorders include inability to focus, appetite or sleep disturbance, and negative impact on self-efficacy (ADAA, 2022; APA, 2022a).

Etiology and Treatment

Individuals diagnosed with anxiety disorders are at risk for comorbid depressive disorders (ADAA, 2022). Because of their high prevalence rate, these diagnoses are frequently the focus of clinical attention for counselors. Over the course of a lifetime, an individual's diagnosis can migrate from anxiety to depression and vice versa. Therefore, it is important for counselors to view the treatment of these disorders from a longitudinal perspective (Batelaan et al., 2010).

Anxiety disorders contain myriad psychobiological factors that include genetic predisposition, social and cultural contexts, and life events. Kessler et al. (2012) discussed the lifetime morbid risk, or portion of people who will eventually develop the disorder at some time in their life, regardless of risk factors such as comorbid diagnoses. In the United States, specific phobia (18.4%) and social phobia (13.0%) have the highest lifetime morbid risk, and agoraphobia has the lowest (3.7%). Women are more likely than men to have coexisting anxiety and depression (APA, 2022a). Additionally, anxiety disorders are the most common disorders among youth (Sood et al., 2012; Watkins et al., 2022) and have a median age of onset of 11 years.

Implications for Counselors

Because anxiety disorders are often diagnosed in counseling settings, it is important for counselors to focus on ongoing assessment and monitoring in addition to remaining abreast of evolving empirically supported interventions. Counselors working with individuals living with an anxiety disorder should address psychosocial implications such as social isolation or declining academic/career development. Support and guidance for these clients can help with anxiety management and positive treatment outcomes. It is important for counselors to note that anxiety disorders present increased risk for suicidality (APA, 2022a); therefore, assessment of suicide risk should be incorporated into treatment for all clients.

Counselors can access an array of evidence-based interventions that assist with positive treatment outcomes. Individuals with anxiety disorders generally respond to CBT, behavior therapy, mindfulness, and relaxation training (ADAA, 2022). Emotion-focused therapy, acceptance and commitment therapy, and sensation-focused intensive treatment have shown efficacy for anxiety disorder treatment. With medical supervision, psychopharmacology and exercise can demonstrate ongoing positive effects (Kress & Paylo, 2018).

The remainder of this chapter enumerates the anxiety disorders as listed in the *DSM-5-TR*. Although a summary and special considerations for counselors are provided for each disorder, when diagnosing clients, counselors should reference the *DSM-5-TR*. It is essential that the diagnostic criteria and features, subtypes and specifiers (if applicable), prevalence, course, and risk and prognostic factors for each disorder are clearly understood prior to diagnosis.

Separation Anxiety Disorder (F93.0)

> I know it is irrational but every time my partner begins to get ready for work, I start to feel horrible. I am certain that something bad will happen as soon as he leaves. It may be a car wreck or a heart attack, but I just know something bad will happen. I get physically ill. Sometimes I throw up. Often, I go to work with him. It's causing problems for him, and he has become very frustrated because this has gone on for so long.—Benjamin

Separation anxiety disorder was moved from the Disorders Usually First Diagnosed in Infancy, Childhood, or Adolescence chapter of the *DSM-IV-TR* to the Anxiety Disorders chapter of the *DSM-5*, and the age-of-onset requirement ("before age 18 years") was dropped, thus allowing for diagnosis of separation anxiety disorder in adults (Mohr & Schneider, 2013). Criteria and coding remain unchanged in the *DSM-5-TR*.

Essential Features

The essential feature for separation anxiety disorder includes developmentally inappropriate nervousness and fear related to separation from the primary caregiver. In addition to fear and anxiety, physical symptoms can include headaches, stomachaches, and cardiovascular symptoms in adolescents and adults. These emotional and somatic symptoms can develop in childhood and persist into adult life. The fear or worry is focused on potential harm to attachment figures. This leads to reluctance to be alone or away from loved ones. Typical behaviors are "clinging" or "shadowing" (APA, 2022a, p. 217), with sleep disturbances commonly affecting children and adults.

Special Considerations

Separation anxiety disorder can be extant through the life course, although it must last 6 months or longer for diagnosis in adults. For children, there is a minimum duration of 1 month. Prevalence rates are 4% for children, 1.6% for adolescents, and 0.9% to 1.9% for adults. Separation anxiety disorder is the most prevalent anxiety disorder in children, with girls more susceptible than boys. Functionality in school, work, or social settings is often impaired (APA, 2022a).

Separation anxiety disorder also affects adults, with the key features similar across the age spectrum: fear of separation from or harm befalling loved ones (APA, 2022a). Adults with separation anxiety disorder typically display more covert behaviors, such as staying home or close to loved ones as well as engaging in frequent check-ins (Marnane & Silove, 2013).

Expectations for physical and emotional closeness in relationships are culturally linked, and counselors must be careful not to pathologize behaviors of individuals from collectivist cultures in which parents and children are rarely separated. Sood et al. (2012) studied help seeking among Indian American, Puerto Rican, and European American mothers of children diagnosed with separation anxiety disorder. Puerto Rican mothers were more likely to view the symptoms as resulting from a physical health condition and were thus less likely to seek psychological treatment. Acculturation was directly correlated with help-seeking behaviors, and those with strongly held religious beliefs were more likely to seek assistance from religious leaders. Sood et al.'s study highlights the need to consider cultural variables in addressing perception and treatment. There are also broad differences cross-culturally for cases when youth live independently and in the perceived value of intergenerational households.

Differential Diagnosis

When considering separation anxiety disorder, counselors must distinguish between developmentally and culturally appropriate reactions to separation and abnormal reactions to separation. Common differential diagnoses for separation anxiety disorder include generalized anxiety disorder (GAD), panic disorder, agoraphobia, conduct disorder, PTSD, illness anxiety disorder, bereavement, depressive and bipolar disorder, ODD, psychotic disorder, and personality disorder. With separation anxiety disorder, the thrust of the anxiety is focused on separation from attachment figures (APA, 2022a). It is different from GAD and social anxiety disorder in this regard. GAD's predominant features are diffuse anxiety, whereas social anxiety disorder is specific to social situations.

Panic disorder, with its unexpected panic attacks, is distinguishable from separation anxiety disorder in that the unexpected and incapacitating panic attacks are not extant. PTSD centers around intrusive thoughts about and avoidance of memories related to the traumatic event; the worries central to separation anxiety disorder are related to harm to loved ones. With illness anxiety disorder, depressive disorder, bipolar disorder, and ODD, there is no predominant concern in being separated from attachment figures. Psychotic disorders contain hallucinations, which are not an evident feature of separation anxiety disorder (APA, 2022a).

Coding, Recording, and Specifiers

There is only one diagnostic code for separation anxiety disorder: F93.0. There are no specifiers for this diagnosis.

Selective Mutism (F94.0)

> Camilla didn't speak to anyone but me for 2 months after the accident. No one knew what to do. Clearly, she had the ability to talk but she just refused to do so. I didn't want to punish her, which didn't seem to help anyway. I promised her rewards, but she didn't respond to that either. The students in her kindergarten class really teased her.—Jules (Camilla's mom)

Selective mutism represents the voluntary refusal to speak (typically occurring outside of the home or immediate family). Selective mutism was a new diagnosis in the Anxiety Disorders chapter of the *DSM-5*, because of the restructuring of the chapters and the removal of the chapter on disorders usually first diagnosed in infancy, childhood, or adolescence (APA, 2013a). The criteria and coding for selective mutism remain unchanged in the *DSM-5-TR*.

Essential Features

The essential feature of selective mutism is a refusal to verbally communicate outside of the home or with people other than immediate family members or caregivers not due to speech or language difficulties. Children with selective mutism may speak only to immediate family members and will sometimes communicate with nonverbals such as nodding or grunting; these children do not usually possess language deficits. Selective mutism typically has an age of onset of under 5 years and is often first noticed in school settings (APA, 2022a).

Special Considerations

Selective mutism can manifest in adolescents and adults but more frequent in children (APA, 2022a). Excessive shyness is a personality trait often seen with selective mutism. Children diagnosed with selective mutism have high diagnostic comorbidity with other anxiety disorder, most frequently social anxiety disorder (APA, 2022a). Children with selective mutism frequently have significant impairment in social and school situations. Social isolation and academic impairment both occur.

Cultural formulations play a critical role in the diagnosis of selective mutism. There is risk of misdiagnosis when culture is not integrally considered in diagnosing selective mutism. As with all diagnoses, clinicians should consider any possible cultural factors and integrate these into assessment protocols. It is important to assess language acquisition (especially if a child is living in a country whose native language is not their own). Further research on the cultural contexts and diagnosis of selective mutism is needed (APA, 2022a).

Differential Diagnosis

Counselors who are considering a diagnosis of selective mutism must examine the child's developmental and contextual functioning so they do not pathologize normal developmental transitions and adjustments. Common differential diagnoses for selective mutism include communication disorders, neurodevelopmental disorders, schizophrenia and other psychotic disorders, and social anxiety disorder. It is important to note that with selective mutism, the communication disorders are not specific to social situations and are more pervasive. Selective mutism should be diagnosed only when a child has readily demonstrated speaking ability in certain situations such as the home environment. This is distinct from neurodevelopmental disorders, schizophrenia, and other psychotic disorders for which there may be impairment in communication regardless of the setting. Finally, it is not uncommon for social anxiety disorder to occur alongside selective mutism; when this occurs, both diagnoses should be given (APA, 2022a).

Coding, Recording, and Specifiers

There is only one diagnostic code for selective mutism: F94.0. There are no specifiers for this diagnosis and no coding or recording changes in the *DSM-5-TR*.

Specific Phobia (F40._ _ _)

> Ever since I was a child, I've been terrified of needles. My friends got their ears pierced but I refused to go near the salon. I avoid the doctor for the same reason, even when I know I should go. Last time I got sick, I waited until the last minute to go in. When the nurse started talking about taking my blood, my stomach started hurting, my heart started pounding in my ears, and I got light-headed. I refused to let her draw blood. It's been so long since I had blood work, I just am so afraid to do it.—Marin

Specific phobias represent the existence of fear or anxiety in the presence of a specific situation or object. This is called the "phobic stimulus" (APA, 2022a, p. 225). This fear or anxiety must be markedly stronger than the actual threat of the object or situation (e.g., likelihood of being stuck on a well-maintained elevator). Specific phobias carry a 12-month community prevalence rate of 9.0% to 12.0% (APA, 2022a).

Essential Features

The main feature of specific phobia is an inappropriate fear response to a specific object or situation that is incongruent with the danger or threat and out of proportion to the danger posed. Specific phobias can develop after a traumatic event or from witnessing traumatic events. Individuals with a specific phobia will avoid situations of exposure to the stimulus. The fear or anxiety happens every time the person is exposed to the stimulus and may include symptoms of a panic attack. The median age of onset for a diagnosis of specific phobia is 7 to 11 years (APA, 2022a).

Special Considerations

Physiological arousal responses resulting from specific phobia may include feeling faint, accelerated heart rate and blood pressure, and hyperarousal. Quality of life is negatively affected, and impairment in overall functioning is common. Early intervention is key because the recovery rate for specific phobia in children can be as high as 60% after CBT (Mohr & Schneider, 2013).

It is important to take sociocultural context into account when assessing specific phobia. In some contexts, fear of a stimulus is real and proportionate (e.g., being bitten by a poisonous snake in certain geographic locations). Black Americans and White Americans have higher incidence of specific phobias than Asian Americans and Latinx individuals, and further research is needed for additional understanding (APA, 2022a).

Differential Diagnosis

When considering whether to diagnose a specific phobia, counselors are wise to consider the degree to which the fear and response to the fear are consistent with one's developmental level and cultural context. This diagnosis should not be made if the fear is seen as culturally appropriate. Similarly, counselors must consider the degree of distress and impairment associated with the phobia. Common differential diagnoses for specific phobia include agoraphobia, social anxiety disorder, separation anxiety disorder, panic disorder, obsessive-compulsive disorder (OCD), trauma and stressor-related disorders, eating disorders, and schizophrenia spectrum and other psychotic disorders. Agoraphobia has many fears that overlap with specific phobias. Counselors should diagnose agoraphobia when more than one condition/situation is feared. Social anxiety disorder should be diagnosed instead of specific phobia when social situations are the cause of the fear. Panic attacks can occur in conjunction with specific phobia; however, the diagnosis of panic disorder would supersede the diagnosis of specific phobia if the panic attacks are unexpected. A diagnosis of specific phobia would not be given if the fear results from delusional thought processes such as those disorders in the schizophrenia spectrum and other psychotic disorders (APA, 2022a).

Coding, Recording, and Specifiers

Specifiers for specific phobia include *animal, natural environment, blood-injection injury, situational,* and *other.* Blood-injection injury includes four subtypes: *fear of blood, fear of injections and transfusions, fear of other medical care,* and *fear of injury.* Approximately 75% of individuals diagnosed with specific phobia fear more than one object. When this occurs, more than one diagnosis is given. The following is a complete list of codes and specifiers for specific phobia.

F40.218 Animal
F40.228 Natural environment
F40.23x Blood-injection injury
F40.230 Fear of blood
F40.231 Fear of injections and transfusions
F40.232 Fear of other medical care
F40.233 Fear of injury
F40.248 Situational (e.g., airplanes, elevators, enclosed places)
F40.298 Other (e.g., situations that may lead to choking or vomiting; in children, e.g., loud sounds or costumed characters)

In cases in which individuals experience panic attacks in response to their phobia, counselors should add *with panic attacks* to the diagnosis.

Social Anxiety Disorder (F40.10)

> I was so relieved when I was told I could work from home. Even though my job is working on computer programs, the anxiety around interacting with the people in the office was overwhelming. I don't think they liked me anyway because I always said the wrong things. I thought my boss was going to fire me because I had such a hard time going into work but I am good at my job so they made this arrangement. My family members seem concerned though because I almost never leave my house.—Rhijad

Social phobia was renamed social anxiety disorder in the *DSM-5,* and social phobia is no longer a clinically utilized term (APA, 2013a). Social anxiety disorder is one of the most common mental disorders with a lifetime prevalence rate of slightly greater than 10%; the majority of diagnoses are made during childhood or early adolescence (Kerns et al., 2013). Social anxiety disorder is often seen in conjunction with MDD, other anxiety disorders, and substance-related disorders (APA, 2022a).

Essential Features

The main feature of social anxiety disorder is ongoing fear and worry surrounding myriad social situations (Byrd-Bredbenner et al., 2020; Goetter et al., 2020). Individuals with social anxiety disorder often fear negative evaluation (e.g., being humiliated, embarrassed, or rejected) by others (either unfamiliar or familiar) in performance, interaction, or observation situations. A *performance only* specifier was added for social anxiety disorder in the *DSM-5* and includes a minimum duration of 6 months. Children, adolescents, and adults share the same criteria for duration (APA, 2022a; Mohr & Schneider, 2013).

Special Considerations

Women tend to be diagnosed with social anxiety disorder more often than men, but both genders may experience lifelong consequences. Individuals with social anxiety disorder may drop out of school, have difficulties maintaining continuous employment, and experience low socioeconomic status. Although individuals may seek mental health care after living 15 to 20 years with this disorder, being unemployed is frequently a trigger for initiating treatment (APA, 2022a).

The United States reports among the highest prevalence rates of social anxiety disorder in the world. Counselors should keep in mind cultural implications that can be misconstrued as social anxiety, such as variations in eye contact. As with all areas of clinical work, it is important for counselors to carefully assess social constructs in diagnosing social anxiety disorder (ADAA, 2022; APA, 2022a).

Differential Diagnosis

Common differential diagnoses of social anxiety disorder are normative shyness, agoraphobia, panic disorder, GAD, separation anxiety disorder, specific phobias, selective mutism, MDD, body dysmorphic disorder, delusional disorder, autism spectrum disorder (ASD), personality disorder, and ODD. It is important to note that shyness is a personality trait and is not pathological in nature; a diagnosis of social anxiety disorder is unwarranted unless there is impairment in functioning. Individuals with social anxiety disorder are fearful of negative evaluation from others; they are not fearful of, nor do they worry about, separation from loved ones as seen in separation anxiety disorder. Conversely, individuals with specific phobias do not typically worry about being judged in social situations (C. H. Ko et al., 2021).

Selective mutism is differentiated from social anxiety disorder in that individuals diagnosed with selective mutism are not fearful in social situations in which they are not required to speak. For individuals with body dysmorphic disorder, fear and avoidance are specifically caused by thoughts about their own appearance. In contrast to individuals diagnosed with ASD, individuals with social anxiety disorder display a capacity for age-appropriate interactions and social relationships; however, they avoid them or endure them with intense distress. Finally, a key differentiating feature of individuals with social anxiety disorder from those with delusional disorder is that individuals diagnosed with social anxiety disorder typically display insight into the disproportionate fear or worry they have in social situations (APA, 2022a).

Coding, Recording, and Specifiers

There is only one diagnostic code for social anxiety disorder: F40.10. Social anxiety disorder has a *performance only* specifier, which is given if anxiety is specific to speaking or performing in public. Individuals diagnosed with the *performance only* specifier are mainly impaired in their occupational environments or in school situations in which public speaking is a requirement. These individuals are not afraid of and do not avoid other social situations. If individuals experience panic attacks in conjunction with social anxiety disorder, the specifier *with panic attacks* should be added to the diagnosis.

Case Example

Adam is an 11-year-old fifth grader who is the fourth of seven children born into an Orthodox Jewish family. Adam is one of five boys in his family. His father is loving and attentive but also works a lot; Adam's mother does most of the hands-on parenting. At home, Adam is quiet and serious but takes time to read to his younger siblings and occasionally plays outside with his brothers. At school, Adam stays by himself and rarely interacts with his classmates. Adam will make excuses to stay in the classroom during recess (such as wanting extra time to study) and prefers to study after school in lieu of extracurricular activities.

Adam is a quiet, serious child who obeys the rules and rarely displays upset emotions or anger. Adam's mom is busy raising seven children and is grateful that Adam has no disciplinary issues and performs well academically. She does not see a problem with his behaviors. His teacher has referred Adam to the school counselor because of his reluctance to work on any group projects or engage with peers. Adam tells his counselor that he has no friends other than his siblings and that he doesn't want any. He says that he enjoys studying and playing games with his brothers but "doesn't have time for friends." Upon questioning, Adam discloses that he has never had any peer friendships and gets nervous in most situations outside of his home. Unlike his siblings, he does not look forward to religious services although he enjoys his religious studies.

Adam generally avoids social interactions and is afraid to travel outside of his hometown. He reports feeling sick to his stomach when his routine changes. At home, although quieter than his brothers, Adam laughs, jokes, and interacts with all his siblings. He tells his counselor that he would like to have one or two close friends to hang out with but also is "fine" the way things are.

Adam's presenting symptoms include worry that he will embarrass himself, freezing in unfamiliar situations, avoidance of social situations, and emotional distress outside of his home environment. These feelings and behaviors have been extant since he began elementary school and have increased in severity over the course of the past year.

Diagnostic Questions

1. Do Adam's presenting symptoms meet the criteria for an anxiety disorder? If so, which one?
2. Based on the disorder identified in Question 1, which symptom(s) led you to select the diagnosis?
3. What would be the reason(s) a counselor may not diagnose Adam with GAD?
4. Would Adam be more accurately diagnosed with ASD? Why or why not?
5. What rule-outs would you consider for Adam's case?
6. What other information may be needed to make an accurate clinical diagnosis?

Panic Disorder (F41.0)

I never knew when it was going to hit me and that made it even worse. My heart would start pounding, my hands would shake, and I would start sweating. I couldn't breathe. I felt like the world was going to end and I was going to die at any moment. I felt like I was going crazy.—Mabel

Panic disorder involves recurrent, unexpected panic attacks. The median age of onset ranges from 20 to 24 years, with a small percentage of individuals first diagnosed in childhood. Panic disorder is not usually first seen in individuals over the age of 45. There is an annual U.S. prevalence rate of 2.1% to 2.8%; this is one of the highest prevalence rates worldwide (APA, 2022a).

Essential Features

The essential features of panic disorder are persistent fear or concern of inappropriate fear responses, with recurrent and unexpected panic attacks including physiological changes such as accelerated heart rate, sweating, dizziness, trembling, and chest pain. Worry and behavioral changes may also accompany the diagnosis. Panic disorder has physical and cognitive symptoms and involves numerous, unexpected panic attacks (although it is important to note that individuals with panic disorder can have expected panic attacks, too). Worry typically focuses on physical symptoms or concern about mental functioning such as losing control (APA, 2022a).

Special Considerations

The global lifetime prevalence ranges from 1.7% to 2.7%. Childhood abuse (sexual and physical) is a risk factor. There is scientific evidence of genetic predisposition, with women being more likely to receive the diagnosis of panic disorder than men (APA, 2022a).

Individuals with panic disorder display specific variations in physical symptoms based on cultural contexts. Cultural expectations can lead to the experience of panic attack, such as *ataque de nervios* ("attack of nerves"; APA, 2022a, p. 871, "Appendix: Glossary of Cultural Concepts of Distress") in Latin Americans that involves trembling, screaming, crying, aggression, depersonalization, and possible suicidal behavior. African American and Afro-Caribbean groups generally have lower rates of panic disorder. Fears related to the symptoms of panic disorder vary across cultures. Although White Americans have a higher prevalence rate of panic disorder, they typically have less functional impairment than Black Americans; this lends to the need for counselors to carefully assess severity with Black American clients (APA, 2022a).

Differential Diagnosis

By themselves, panic attacks are not a diagnosable condition; a diagnosis of panic disorder is only made if one's response to unexpected panic attacks includes persistent worry or behavioral changes associated with the attacks. Common differential diagnoses for panic disorder are other specified or unspecified anxiety disorder, anxiety disorder due to another medical condition, substance/medication-induced anxiety disorder, and other mental disorders with panic attacks as an associated feature. Illness anxiety disorder, formerly known as hypochondriasis, often shares features with or is comorbid with panic disorder (Byrd-Bredbenner et al., 2020). It is the unexpected nature of the panic attack that makes panic disorder distinct from panic attacks occurring within the context of another anxiety disorder. If an unexpected panic attack has not occurred, the diagnosis of panic disorder is not appropriate and is also not diagnosed if the panic attack results from a medical condition or utilization of a substance (APA, 2022a).

Coding, Recording, and Specifiers

There is only one diagnostic code for panic disorder: F41.0. However, there is extensive information about the single specifier, *panic attack*. See the next section regarding the *panic attack* specifier. Note that the *panic attack* specifier is not a mental disorder and is not assigned a diagnostic code.

Panic Attack Specifier

Panic attack is not classified as a mental disorder and does not have a diagnostic code. Panic attacks are abrupt surges of intense fear; they can occur with mental disorders such as depressive and anxiety disorders and be extant with physical disorders. *Panic attack* is a specifier for both mental and physical disorders; however, the elements of panic attack are contained within the criteria for panic disorder, so it is not a specifier for that diagnosis. An example of panic attack used as a specifier is social anxiety disorder, *with panic attack* (APA, 2022a).

Essential Features

Panic attacks represent intense fear or discomfort that occurs abruptly and peaks rapidly. Physical symptoms predominate and must include a minimum of four out of the 13 identified symptoms. These mostly physical symptoms occur and reach their peak within minutes. Panic attacks have a 9.5% to 11.2% annual prevalence rate in the general U.S. population (APA, 2022a). See page 242 of the *DSM-5-TR* for a list of physical symptoms.

Special Considerations

The rapid time to reach peak intensity distinguishes panic attacks from general or ongoing anxiety. Panic attacks are associated with higher rates of suicidal ideation and behaviors. As such, individuals presenting with panic attacks should be carefully screened for suicide risk. Panic attacks are rare in young children and occur more frequently in women than men (APA, 2022a).

There are culturally distinct symptoms that do not count toward four of the 13 symptoms needed for use of the *panic attack* specifier. Cultural context can lend to the difference between expected and unexpected panic attacks and may also cause fear of specific situations. The *DSM-5-TR* includes an Appendix titled the "Glossary of Cultural Concepts of Distress" that provides specific information about the cultural syndromes (APA, 2022a).

Differential Diagnosis

Common differential diagnoses for the *panic attack* specifier include other paroxysmal episodes, anxiety disorder due to another medical condition, and substance/medication-induced anxiety disorder. For appropriate application of the *panic attack* specifier, abrupt surges of intense fear or discomfort must occur in the individual. This distinguishes panic attack from emotional reactions such as grief or anger. Multiple medical conditions, as well as myriad substance intoxication and withdrawal, can cause panic attacks. If the age of onset for panic attack is older than 45 years or if there are unusual symptoms occurring during the panic attack, it is important to carefully consider the possibility of the panic attack being caused by a medical condition or substance use (APA, 2022a).

Agoraphobia (F40.00)

> I didn't leave my condo for 2 months. I had everything delivered. The fear has been bad for years but that was the worst. Obviously, I lost my job. But I was certain that if I went out, something awful would happen.—Devin

Agoraphobia represents an intense fear that results from real or imagined exposure to a wide range of situations. There is a 1.7% prevalence rate for the diagnosis of agoraphobia for adolescents and middle-age adults; it is less prevalent (0.4%) in young children and older adults (APA, 2022a). The mean age of onset of agoraphobia is 17 years, and onset during childhood is rare. Females are twice as likely to be diagnosed with agoraphobia than males. Agoraphobia leads to moderate to severe impairment in functioning, with more than 33% of individuals diagnosed with agoraphobia restricted to home environments (APA, 2022a).

Essential Features

Agoraphobia represents fear of situations in which escape from bad things is difficult. The fear may fluctuate depending on exposure to the event; it may also result from anticipation of an event. This response happens almost every time an individual is exposed to the situation or event (it is not agoraphobia if the response occurs only some of the time). Avoidance of the event or situation must also be present and can include cognitive or behavioral aspects (APA, 2022a).

Special Considerations

A diagnosis of agoraphobia is given regardless of whether the individual meets the criteria for panic disorder. If criteria for both conditions are met, both diagnoses are given. It is important to note that agoraphobia can impair functioning to the level that an individual becomes homebound. Most people who are given the diagnosis of agoraphobia have comorbid mental disorders, including a higher likelihood of other anxiety disorders (APA, 2022a).

There is a need for research focusing on the cultural considerations of agoraphobia. The *DSM-5-TR* does not include cultural information specific to the diagnosis. Barzegar et al. (2021) mentioned the challenges in identification and diagnosis across the world, which lead to many individuals missing out on access to treatment.

Differential Diagnosis

Common differential diagnoses for agoraphobia include the following: specific phobia, separation anxiety disorder, social anxiety disorder, panic disorder, acute stress disorder, PTSD, MDD, and other medical conditions. A diagnosis of agoraphobia can be given in conjunction with that of another disorder if the criteria for both are met unless the fears result from the sequelae of another disorder. MDD can leave an individual homebound, but this is predominantly from apathy or anhedonia. One of the main challenges is differentiating agoraphobia from specific phobia. Acute stress disorder and PTSD can be distinguished from agoraphobia in that the avoidance occurs only from situations that trigger a memory of the traumatic event, such as a driving or riding in a car after a motor vehicle accident (APA, 2022a).

Coding, Recording, and Specifiers

There is only one diagnostic code for agoraphobia: F40.00. The specifier *with panic attacks* may be added if individuals experience panic attacks associated with agoraphobia.

Case Example

> Daryl is a 40-year-old woman of Navajo descent and a married mother of two teenage sons. Over the course of her 19-year marriage, she has rarely worked outside of the home. During the past 5 years, Daryl has gradually given up engaging in most of the leisure and social activities she previously enjoyed, such as painting, making pottery, and attending concerts. She has developed feelings of worry about many bad things happening to her if she leaves her home, including car accidents, robbery, becoming lost, and falling ill. These feelings have increased in intensity and frequency over the past 13 months. Daryl has relied on her husband and children to purchase groceries and household necessities. She no longer paints and has not used her outdoor pottery kiln, a lifelong

hobby and a source of income, in over a year. Although she regularly engages in yard work, she no longer receives the enjoyment from it she previously did.

Daryl's husband is worried about her, and her relationships with her sons have suffered because she no longer attends their extracurricular events. Despite repeated attempts at various relaxation and calming techniques, Daryl cannot force herself to reengage in any of these activities.

Daryl reports that she fears situations that include being outside of her home or yard, being in a crowd, standing in a line, crossing a bridge, and driving or riding in a car. Daryl has no prior history of panic attacks or previous trauma.

Diagnostic Questions

1. Do Daryl's presenting symptoms meet the criteria for an anxiety disorder? If so, which one?
2. Based on the disorder identified in Question 1, which symptom(s) led you to select the diagnosis?
3. What would be the reason(s) a counselor may not diagnose Daryl with GAD?
4. Would Daryl be more accurately diagnosed with a depressive disorder? Why or why not?
5. What rule-outs would you consider for Daryl's case?
6. What other information may be needed to make an accurate clinical diagnosis?

Generalized Anxiety Disorder (F41.1)

I constantly felt tense and jumpy. For months I lived with excessive worry and fears that something was wrong or something bad was going to happen. My friends described me as high-strung. I just wished could sleep through the night.—Trey

Generalized anxiety disorder (GAD) is one of the most common of all mental disorders, with an annual prevalence rate of 2.9% among adults in the United States and a lifetime risk of 9% (APA, 2022a; J. S. Comer et al., 2012; C. H. Ko et al., 2021). Excessive worry or anxiety about a number of events is the key feature of GAD, with the experience of the anxiety or worry in discord with the actual or expected event.

Essential Features

Essential features include anxiety or worry that takes place across a number of settings and more days than not for at least 6 months. Individuals with GAD find it difficult to control the worry and experience at least three characteristic symptoms, including restlessness or feeling keyed up or on edge, being easily fatigued, difficulty concentrating or mind going blank, muscle tension, irritability, and sleep disturbance (APA, 2022a).

Special Considerations

The predominant symptom of GAD is chronic worry. The intensity of the worry and its resultant impairment in functioning distinguishes GAD from nonclinical levels of anxiety. These worries can be consuming, marked, and cause considerable concern to the individual. Physical and somatic symptoms often accompany GAD; these include muscle tension, sweating, nausea, diarrhea, accelerated heart rate, and dizziness. As with other disorders in this chapter, women are more likely than men to receive the diagnosis (Friborg et al., 2013; C. H. Ko et al., 2021).

Cultural considerations include previous exposure to traumatic events occurring environmentally or geographically. In the United States, GAD is highest among Native Americans and White Americans; this is most notable in younger individuals. Asian, Latinx, African, and Caribbean Black populations have lower rates of GAD. Although it may manifest differently, the overall worry and anxiousness associated with GAD is extant across all cultures, and there is a need for additional research in this area (APA, 2022a; Goetter et al., 2020).

Differential Diagnosis

Differential diagnoses for GAD include anxiety disorder due to another medical condition; substance/medication-induced anxiety disorder; social anxiety disorder; OCD; PTSD; adjustment disorders; and depressive, bipolar, and psychotic disorders. The clear distinction between GAD and anxiety disorder due to another medical condition is that the substance must be etiologically related to the anxiety. Those with GAD have diffuse worry that focuses on events that have yet to happen; this separates individuals with GAD from individuals living with social anxiety disorder, PTSD, OCD, and adjustment disorders. Adjustment disorders also do not persist for 6 months or more beyond the termination of the stressor or its consequences. If inordinate worry occurs only during the course of depressive, bipolar, and psychotic disorders, GAD should not be diagnosed (APA, 2022a).

Owing to lack of specificity in the criteria, differential diagnosis can be a challenge. Many of the anxiety disorders outlined in this chapter along with OCD, PTSD, adjustment disorders, depressive disorders, and psychotic disorders possess similar features to GAD. It is likely that individuals with GAD have, have had, or will develop other anxiety or depressive disorders (APA, 2022a; Byrd-Bredbenner et al., 2020).

Coding, Recording, and Specifiers

There is only one diagnostic code for GAD: F41.1. There are no specifiers for this diagnosis, although counselors may choose to use the specifier *with panic attack* if appropriate.

Case Example

> Jean is a 65-year-old, African American divorced mother and grandmother. She has a successful career in real estate and enjoys good physical health. Throughout her childhood and adulthood, Jean has been characterized as a nervous and high-strung person. She typically worries excessively about all aspects of her life and often lets her fear of the worst keep her from enjoying activities. Jean is very good at putting on a "game face" and masking her anxiety with humor and good cheer. However, Jean's fear and worry keep her from traveling to family reunions and impede her ability to relax.
>
> Over the past year, Jean's worries have increased in intensity and frequency. She has been canceling appointments on occasion in order to "not have to deal with the stress." Never one to drink much alcohol, Jean will have a glass of wine before bed several times a week to "take the edge off." She has also experienced some physical symptoms, such as difficulty falling asleep, needing to urinate frequently, and muscle tension.
>
> Jean's emotional symptoms include worrying about many things, difficulty concentrating, and irritability occurring multiple times daily. She tires easily and sometimes feels so overwhelmed she does not want to get out of bed. Jean states she has trouble stopping her worrisome thoughts and reports that her family is concerned about her and has encouraged her to see a counselor. Although Jean would like to feel better, she expressed doubt that counseling could be helpful and believes this is just "the way she is." Jean has been treated for depression in the past and reports that she doesn't feel "depressed" now.

Diagnostic Questions

1. Do Jean's presenting symptoms meet the criteria for an anxiety disorder? If so, which one?
2. Based on the disorder identified in Question 1, which symptom(s) led you to select the diagnosis?
3. What would be the reason(s) a counselor may not diagnose Jean with agoraphobia?
4. Would Jean be more accurately diagnosed with a depressive disorder? Why or why not?
5. What rule-outs would you consider for Jean's case?
6. What other information may be needed to make an accurate clinical diagnosis?

Substance/Medication-Induced Anxiety Disorder

Anxiety caused by substance use is the primary criterion for the diagnosis of substance/medication-induced anxiety disorder. Panic or anxiety must have developed during or soon after substance/medication usage and exceed what would be expected to be associated with intoxication or withdrawal from that specific substance. Prevalence rates for this disorder are reportedly low (0.002%), although it is difficult to assess accurate rates because of diagnostic challenges in differentiating this disorder from other anxiety or substance disorders. It is important for counselors to tease out substances used to self-medicate anxious symptoms with anxiety resulting from substance use or withdrawal (APA, 2022a).

Essential Features

Essential features of substance/medication-induced anxiety disorder are that the symptoms occur during intoxication, during withdrawal, or after medication use but persist long after physiological intoxication or withdrawal is present. The anxiety must be severe enough to cause a need for clinical intervention.

Special Considerations

Laboratory tests (e.g., urinalysis) can be helpful in assessing substance/medication-induced anxiety disorder. Several medications can cause symptoms of anxiety. These include, but are not limited to, antidepressant medications, antihypertensive and cardiovascular medications, corticosteroids, anticonvulsants, antihistamines, oral contraceptives, insulin, and bronchodilators. Counselors should consult with physicians to determine whether an anxiety disorder may be physiologically caused by use of a substance or medication. Working in conjunction with the client's health care provider can aid counselors in clarifying these issues and assist with accurate diagnostic screening for anxiety disorders.

Differential Diagnosis

Common differential diagnoses for substance/medication-induced anxiety disorder include substance intoxication and substance withdrawal, anxiety disorder not induced by a substance/medication, delirium, and anxiety disorder due to another general medical condition. A diagnosis of substance/medication-induced anxiety disorder is only used when anxiety symptoms are predominant. If panic or anxiety symptoms occur exclusively during the course of delirium, they are not separately addressed.

Coding, Recording, and Specifiers

Counselors should not make this diagnosis without confirmation from a medical professional that the anxiety disorder is substance related. The extensive coding chart for substance/medication-induced anxiety disorder can be found on page 256 of the *DSM-5-TR*. When using this chart, counselors will notice specifiers for substance/medication-induced anxiety disorder, including *with onset during intoxication*, *with onset during withdrawal*, and *with onset after medication use*, with severity indicators of accompanying substance use disorder. Again, counselors may use the specifier *with panic attack* at their discretion. The specifier follows the name of the disorder, for example, F11.188 mild opioid use disorder with opioid-induced anxiety disorder *with onset during intoxication* (APA, 2022a).

Anxiety Disorder Due to Another Medical Condition (F06.4)

Medical conditions can cause the development of an anxiety disorder, but they must cause clinically significant distress. APA (2022a, p. 259) reports "unclear" prevalence rates of anxiety disorder due to another medical condition because of the extreme difficulty with differential diagnosis for this category. It is especially important for counselors to carefully rule out differential diagnoses and consult with a physician before using the diagnosis of anxiety disorder due to another medical condition.

Essential Features

Marked anxiety attacks occur and can be directly attributed to an existing medical condition. The development of the anxiety can parallel the course of the illness. Examples of medical conditions that can cause anxiety disorder due to another medical condition include endocrine disease, cardiovascular disorders, respiratory illness, metabolic disturbance, and neurological illness (APA, 2022a).

Special Considerations

Because prevalence rates are not clear for this disorder, it is important to track the course of the illness to be able to chart the concomitant course of the anxiety. This is a key consideration for work with older adults because they are at higher risk of chronic illnesses. Counselors also need to be aware of the possibility of the development of anxiety disorder not related to physical illness (Byrd-Bredbenner et al., 2020).

Differential Diagnosis

Common differential diagnoses are substance intoxication, substance withdrawal, delirium, anxiety disorder due to another medical condition, and adjustment disorders. Anxiety symptoms, such as panic, must be predominant and demand separate clinical assessment. It is important for counselors to rule out the existence of anxiety disorders that have developed during the course of a medical condition but are not resultant from direct effects of the medical condition. Anxiety that occurs during a delirium does not qualify the individual for the diagnosis of anxiety disorder due to another medical condition. The key to discerning anxiety disorder due to another medical condition is that the anxiety symptoms must be attributed to the physiological effects of the medical condition (APA, 2022a). In other words, a medical condition *causes* the anxiety and is not simply anxiety or worry about a medical condition.

Coding, Recording, and Specifiers

There is only one diagnostic code for anxiety disorder due to another medical condition: F06.4. Although counselors may specify *with panic attacks*, there are no other specifiers for this diagnosis.

Other Specified and Unspecified Anxiety Disorders: (F41.8/F41.9)

The final listings for the anxiety disorders chapter are other specified and unspecified anxiety disorders. Other specified anxiety disorder, F41.8,

> applies to presentations in which symptoms characteristic of an anxiety disorder that cause clinically significant distress or impairment in social, occupational, or other important areas of functioning predominate but do not meet the full criteria for any of the disorders in the anxiety disorder diagnostic class. The other specified anxiety disorder category is used in situations in which the clinician chooses to communicate the specific reason that the presentation does not meet the criteria for any specific anxiety disorder (e.g., "generalized anxiety not occurring more days than not"). (APA, 2022a, p. 261)
>
> The unspecified anxiety disorder, F41.9, is used in situations in which the clinician chooses *not* to specify the reason that the criteria are not met for a specific anxiety disorder, and includes presentations in which there is insufficient information to make a more specific diagnosis (e.g., in emergency room settings). (APA, 2022a, p. 261)

Questions for Consideration

1. How might the physiological nature of anxiety impact accurate diagnosis?
2. What are commonalities for those living with an anxiety disorder or disorders?
3. How can biopsychosocial information assist with differential diagnosis for anxiety disorders?
4. What might be a common treatment recommendation(s) for someone diagnosed with an anxiety disorder?

Chapter 9

Obsessive-Compulsive and Related Disorders

The term *obsessive-compulsive* is characterized by unwanted and repeated mental rituals, including thoughts, feelings, ideas, and sensations, or observable behaviors (i.e., obsessions) that make an individual feel driven to do something (i.e., compulsions; Reghunandanan et al., 2015; Stein et al., 2016). Examples of obsessions and compulsions include excessive counting, skin picking, ruminating about physical flaws, and hoarding (see Table 9.1). Rituals are very common among individuals diagnosed with obsessive-compulsive disorder (OCD) and may include frequent checking of doors or locks, recurrent hand washing, avoidance of certain situations, or mental acts such as counting. An example would be a person who has persistent and uncontrollable thoughts that he is soiled, polluted, or otherwise unclean. To mitigate stress, he washes his hands numerous times throughout the day, gaining temporary relief from these thoughts. For his behavior to be considered

Table 9.1
Common Obsessions and Compulsions

Obsessions	*Commonly Associated Compulsions*
Fear of contamination	Washing, cleaning
Need for symmetry, precise arranging	Ordering, arranging, balancing, straightening until "just right"
Unwanted sexual or aggressive thoughts or images	Checking, praying, "undoing" actions, asking for reassurance
Doubts (e.g., gas jets off, doors locked)	Repeated checking behaviors
Concerns about throwing away something valuable	Hoarding

an OCD, it must be disruptive to his everyday functioning, such as washing to the point of excessive irritation of his skin.

Disorders listed in this chapter include OCD, body dysmorphic disorder (BDD), hoarding disorder, trichotillomania (TTM; hair-pulling disorder), excoriation (skin-picking) disorder, substance/medication-induced obsessive-compulsive and related disorder, obsessive-compulsive and related disorder due to another medical condition, and both other specified and unspecified obsessive-compulsive and related disorders. These disorders have the common feature of obsessive preoccupation and engagement in repetitive behaviors that are unique to individuals with obsessive-compulsive and related disorders (OCRDs) and are nearly homogeneous across different cultural groups (Pascual-Vera et al., 2019). Considered similar enough to be grouped in the same diagnostic classification but distinct enough to subsist as separate disorders, some disorders in this chapter have historically been considered a part of the "obsessive-compulsive spectrum."

The debilitating nature of these disorders for individuals and families and the complexity in which these disorders can present in clinical practice (Reghunandanan et al., 2015) make it imperative that counselors understand that obsessions and compulsions are different from daily worries, concerns, or habits. All individuals have momentary concerns, and many individuals have experienced circumstances in which they have extreme worry. The marked difference for individuals diagnosed with an OCRD is the persistent pattern of unwanted thoughts, images, or impulses (obsessions) and the ritualistic nature of their attempts (compulsions) to neutralize these thoughts or emotions (Clark & Radomsky, 2014).

Counselors should also understand that people experiencing OCRD symptoms do not always recognize their obsessions or compulsions as unreasonable or excessive. Although clients must realize the obsessive thoughts, mental images, or urges are a product of their own minds, it is not required that they understand their behavior or mental rituals are excessive. OCRDs should also be distinguished from developmentally appropriate fixations (APA, 2022a). Furthermore, counselors should understand that OCRDs are considered neuropsychological disorders (Reghunandanan et al., 2015).

Major Changes From *DSM-5* to *DSM-5-TR*

Aside from overarching changes found throughout the *DSM-5-TR*, there is only one specific change from the *DSM-5* to the *DSM-5-TR* within the Obsessive-Compulsive and Related Disorders chapter. Olfactory reference disorder (olfactory reference syndrome) was added as an example of presentations that can be specified under an "other specified" designation for other specified obsessive-compulsive and related disorder. Furthermore, excessive showering, while not included as a descriptive reference in the *ICD-10-CM*, is included in the *DSM-5-TR* because this is a widely recognized repetitive behavior (compulsion; APA, 2022a). Counselors should remember that there are coding changes unique to the *DSM-5-TR*, so paying close attention to these codes and relevant changes is important for documentation and billing.

Counselors relatively new to the *DSM* should understand the history of this diagnostic category that, fairly recently, with the release of the *DSM-5* and *ICD-10-CM*, grouped these disorders into one classification. Prior iterations of the *DSM* did not include hoarding disorder and excoriation (skin-picking) disorder, which were added as new disorders in the *DSM-5* (APA, 2013a) under the OCRD diagnostic category. OCD, BDD, and TTM were previously included in the *DSM-IV-TR* under anxiety disorders, somatoform disorders, and impulse-control disorders, respectively. Substance/medication-induced obsessive-compulsive and related disorder and obsessive-compulsive and related disorder due to another medical condition were also newly introduced in the *DSM-5*. All these disorders, with the exclusions noted above, have remained unchanged from the *DSM-5* to the *DSM-5-TR*.

History of OCRDs and the *DSM*

The fundamental features of obsession and compulsion, rather than anxiety, served as the driving force for moving OCD and other related disorders to a separate chapter under the *DSM-5* (APA, 2013a). This also follows revisions within the *ICD-10-CM* that classifies OCD separately from anxiety disorder. As with the *ICD-10-CM*, which keeps OCD and anxiety disorder in the same larger category, the sequential order of the Obsessive-Compulsive and Related Disorders chapter within the *DSM* reflects the close relationship between OCD and anxiety disorder. Following the release of the *DSM-5*, separating obsession and compulsion from anxiety received more support from psychiatrists than other mental health professionals, with only 40% to 45% of other mental health professionals supporting the move (Mataix-Cols et al., 2007). Some counselors opposed the move because treatment protocols are similar for anxiety and ORDCs, and, just like anxiety and depression, comorbidity is more often the rule than the exception (Stein et al., 2010). While neurocircuit-based taxonomies for obsessive-compulsive symptoms suggest linkages to broader concepts, such as compulsivity and anxiety (Gillan et al., 2017; Stein et al., 2019; van den Heuvel et al., 2016), we argue that neurological evidence points to an even greater need for diagnostic specificity.

Dysregulated fear, for example, is very common in clients diagnosed with OCD *and* anxiety, but treatment approaches must target different symptoms and circumstances. Fear responses to specific stimuli, mediated by fronto-limbic circuitry, can be assessed using the Intolerance of Uncertainty Scale (Freeston et al., 1994) and treated by supporting executive function training associated with the targeted stimulus (Shephard et al., 2021). Even generalized OCD symptoms such as seeking control, which is marked by an intolerance of uncertainty, require differentiated treatment than anxiety disorders. A client with social anxiety disorder who also exhibits an intolerance of uncertainty could be assessed using the Liebowitz Social Anxiety Scale (Liebowitz, 1987), and treatment would focus on the client's pronounced symptoms of excessive fear and anticipation of social situations related to negative evaluation or scrutiny.

Culture-specific designations mentioned in the *DSM-5-TR* include *kufungisisa*, native to the Shona of Zimbabwe, and *taijin kyofusho*, a Japanese reference to "interpersonal fear disorder" (APA, 2022a). Kufungisisa, or "thinking too much" (APA, 2022a, p. 876), is marked by overthinking that leads to considerable psychological distress. Although it is not specifically mentioned in the Obsessive-Compulsive and Related Disorders chapter of the *DSM-5-TR*, we believe this is an important cultural consideration. Taijin kyofusho, discussed under BDD, is distinguished by a feeling that one's appearance is inadequate or offensive, resulting in anxiety and avoidance of interpersonal situations (APA, 2022a). Not specific to only OCRDs, both should be examined for a wide range of diagnostic considerations, including anxiety, panic attacks, mood disorders, and trauma-related disorders.

Differential Diagnosis

The decision to cluster OCRDs in one chapter, separate from anxiety and trauma and stressor-related disorders, influences differential diagnosis. Common differentials for OCRDs include anxiety disorders, MDD, eating disorders, and psychotic disorders (APA, 2022a; Reghunandanan et al., 2015). Clinical attention should also focus on the discernment of the different disorders enumerated within this chapter (Stein et al., 2011). Given the variation in which individuals recognize their beliefs or behaviors are excessive, it can be very difficult for counselors to differentiate OCRDs from symptoms of excessive fear and anxiety that characterize anxiety disorders. One way to differentiate OCRDs is the common feature of obsessive preoccupation and repetitive behaviors. Once either one of these characteristics (or both) have been established, counselors can then distinguish between the different disorders in this chapter.

> **Note:** To help differentiate between OCRDs and anxiety disorders, counselors can ask clients, "Do you ever have thoughts or images that you can't get out of your mind?" and "Are there things that you can't resist doing over and over again?"

Differential diagnosis of OCRDs is challenging because of comorbidity with other diagnoses. It is not uncommon for individuals diagnosed with an OCRD to also exhibit symptoms that meet the clinical threshold for depressive and anxiety disorders, bipolar disorders, somatic symptom disorder, illness anxiety disorder, eating disorders, impulse-control disorders, and ADHD (Fineberg et al., 2013; Pallanti et al., 2011). There is also a significant amount of literature dedicated to comorbidity between OCD and tic disorders. In a clinical population of children ages 6 to 18 years diagnosed with tic disorder, Tanidir et al. (2015) found approximately 19% also met diagnostic criteria for OCD. A population-based study of children and adolescents in Iran with a lifetime tic disorder found 13.9% had comorbid OCD (Mohammadi et al., 2021).

In terms of commonality, counselors should look for mood disorders, specifically depression, social and simple phobias, eating disorders, panic disorders, and tic disorders. Counselors should be aware that comorbidity with schizophrenia and other psychotic disorders is relatively uncommon; in cases in which a client is unable to recognize that the obsession is a product of their own mind, the obsession may be better classified as a delusion. In that case, a schizophrenia spectrum or other psychotic disorder may be a more appropriate diagnosis.

Etiology and Treatment

Exact etiology for OCRDs has not been determined; however, for many years, OCRDs have been considered a "model neuropsychiatric disorder" (S. M. Ko, 1996, p. 186). Earlier research noted abnormalities in serotonin (5-HT) and dopamine neurotransmission and attributed these as responsible for mental rituals and compulsive behaviors (Bloch et al., 2006; Greist et al., 1995). Clinical trials attempting to balance these systems using selective serotonin reuptake inhibitors (SSRIs) yield mixed results (see Shephard et al., 2021). More current investigations have supported the idea that individuals with OCRDs have notable alterations in cortico-striatal-thalamic-cortical circuits (Milad & Rauch, 2012) but also demonstrate dysfunction within the fronto-limbic, fronto-parietal, and cerebellar neurotransmitter systems (Shephard et al., 2021; Stein et al., 2019). The fronto-limbic circuit is responsible, among other things, for processing fearful or threatening stimuli (amygdala) and evaluating (ventromedial prefrontal cortex) an appropriate emotional response. The ventromedial prefrontal cortex, or the "evaluation center" of the brain, is a robust neural network responsible for memory, decision-making, self-perception, and social reasoning (Gage & Baars, 2018). Studies on twins have also suggested a strong genetic influence (van Grootheest et al., 2005), and a considerable amount of literature supports the idea that OCRDs are stress responsive, meaning symptoms increase with stress. However, stress in and of itself is not seen as an etiologic factor (Abramowitz et al., 2008; Lin et al., 2007).

The most commonly reported treatment for OCRDs involves a combination of psychopharmacological treatments, primarily SSRIs, and psychotherapy (Reghunandanan et al., 2015; Simpson et al., 2008; Tenneij et al., 2005; Tolin et al., 2004). Counselors seeking to understand pharmacological specificity for these disorders should refer to Fineberg et al. (2013). CBT has been identified as more effective than drug treatment alone (Fineberg et al., 2020; Melville, 2013) or as a suitable replacement once medication has reduced symptomatology (Tundo et al., 2007). The International Obsessive-Compulsive Disorder Foundation specifically recommends exposure and response prevention (ERP; Abramowitz, 2018), a type of CBT, citing that ERP may reduce symptoms by 60% to 80% if clients are active participants in treatment (Jacoby & Abramowitz, 2016; Melville, 2013).

ERP confronts thoughts, images, objects, and situations that make a person experience anxiety and uses "response prevention" to encourage clients to choose not to engage in a compulsive behavior. While not inherently included within the ERP protocols, there is a strong need for the counselor-client alliance to be established, as well as a sense of safety prior to engaging in any type of exposure therapy (Buchholz & Abramowitz, 2020). Mindfulness-based interventions, specifically mindfulness-based cognitive therapy and acceptance and commitment therapy, are also emerging as some of the most promising interventions for OCRDs (Reddy et al., 2021). Given the varied level of insight and insight specifiers for most disorders within this chapter, treatment approaches that target increased awareness are encouraged.

Implications for Counselors

The ability of counselors to recognize OCRDs is important because studies have indicated that nearly one in 100, or approximately 2 to 3 million adults, currently have OCD (Abramowitz, 2018; Ruscio et al., 2010). Numbers for children are also alarming, with nearly one in 200, or 500,000 children and adolescents, diagnosed with OCD (Ruscio et al., 2010). These numbers only apply to OCD and do not include other related disorders. Rates of BDD among community samples are between 0.7% and 2.4% of the general population (Koran et al., 2008; Phillips, 2004). Hoarding affects 1.7% to 3.6% of the general population (Postlethwaite et al., 2019). TTM prevalence rates for the United States are approximately 1.7% (Grant et al., 2020), and studies have indicated 3.1% to 3.8% of college students exhibit signs of excoriation (Grant & Chamberlain, 2020; Misery et al., 2012).

The rest of this chapter outlines each disorder within the Obsessive-Compulsive and Related Disorders chapter of the *DSM-5-TR* to help readers better understand the disorders. Readers should note this is not a stand-alone resource for diagnosis. Although a summary and special considerations for counselors are provided for each disorder, when diagnosing clients, counselors need to reference the *DSM-5-TR*. It is essential that the diagnostic criteria and features, subtypes and specifiers (if applicable), prevalence, course, and risk and prognostic factors for each disorder are clearly understood prior to diagnosis.

Obsessive-Compulsive Disorder (F42.2)

> I couldn't do anything without counting. It invaded every aspect of my life and really bogged me down. I would wash my hair three times as opposed to once because 3 was a good luck number and 1 wasn't. It took me longer to read because I'd count the lines in a paragraph. When I set my alarm at night, I had to set it to a number that wouldn't add up to a "bad" number.—Cathey

Obsessive-compulsive disorder (OCD) is characterized by "recurrent, persistent, and intrusive anxiety-provoking thoughts or images (obsessions) and subsequent repetitive behaviors (compulsions)" (den Braber et al., 2008, p. 91). These thoughts, beliefs, ideas, or mental rituals dominate an individual's life. Compulsions are the acts that relieve this distress and can be simple (e.g., thinking of a word) or extraordinarily complex (e.g., engaging in an elaborate washing routine that takes hours to complete). Most individuals with OCD have both obsessions and compulsions, although it is not unheard of for clients to report obsessions only. Once considered a rare and eccentric disorder, OCD has risen considerably in visibility since the National Institute of Mental Health conducted a study in 1988 that recognized a 2.5% lifetime prevalence of OCD in the U.S. population (Karno et al., 1988). A unique feature of OCD, and other disorders within this chapter, is the relative homogeneity of symptoms across different nationalities, spiritual and/or religious identities, and cultural contexts (Pascual-Vera et al., 2019). There have been no major changes to this disorder in the *DSM-5-TR*.

Essential Features

The most common pattern of obsessions and compulsions is persistent doubt, such as "Did I lock the door?" that leads a person to repetitively check the locks (Ruscio et al., 2010). Also common is a fear of contamination, which causes excessive washing of one's hands or body (APA, 2022a; Gan et al., 2021). In addition, there is a strong need to have things in a particular order, which causes significant distress when objects are perceived as disorganized. These thoughts and behaviors significantly influence clients' lives, sometimes to the point of interfering with work, school, family relationships, or social obligations. Impairment, unfortunately, is not emphasized in the literature, but it should be noted that most individuals diagnosed with OCD experience symptoms for 8.9 years and, on average, have been reported to experience obsessions and compulsions for 5.9 and 4.6 hours per day, respectively (Ruscio et al., 2010). These numbers demonstrate the extreme burden of OCD symptoms on individuals, their families, and society. Individuals exhibiting symptoms of OCD often realize that these thoughts and behaviors are irrational and often have a strong desire to resist the obsessive thoughts and compulsive behaviors. Because of a lack of cognitive awareness, children have never been required to recognize obsessive-compulsive behaviors as unreasonable.

Special Considerations

Having some degree of obsessive thoughts or compulsive behaviors is not rare; in fact, up to 94% of individuals within the general population at some point over their lifetime experience unwanted intrusive thoughts, impulses, or images (Clark & Radomsky, 2014). A clinical diagnosis of OCD, however, requires substantial distress or impairment. Counselors should pay close attention to whether the symptoms significantly interfere with a person's daily routine. For example, clients can have a fear of blurting out obscenities or insults, but until this fear prevents them from engaging in activities of daily living or from engaging in a regular routine at work, home, or school or in social situations, it cannot be diagnosed as OCD.

Counselors should be aware that the level of insight among adults, and even children, varies considerably. The specifier *with poor insight* can be applied to this diagnosis, but it is not unusual for adults to vary considerably in their ability to recognize a mental ritual or behavior as unreasonable (APA, 2022a). This is particularly common when the disorder coexists with another psychological disorder such as MDD or social anxiety disorder, and poor levels of insight is associated with more severe symptoms and a lower chance of recovery following treatment (Gan et al., 2021). Because avoidance of certain situations, such as one that might make an individual dirty, is common, evading objects or scenarios that provoke obsessions or compulsions may begin to seem ordinary as opposed to excessive (Shephard et al., 2021). Counselors who work with individuals diagnosed with OCD must be on the lookout for situations that restrict functioning severely. There remains a large treatment gap for OCD. In a study of individuals who had a lifetime prevalence of OCD, only 29.2% received treatment specifically targeted for their OCD symptoms (Ruscio et al., 2010).

Cultural Considerations

As stated previously, prevalence of OCD is worldwide (APA, 2022a), with considerable cross-cultural homogeneity for both unwanted mental intrusions and ritualistic, repetitive behaviors. Noting that most studies on OCRDs were limited to only European or American samples, Pascual-Vera et al. (2019) conducted a general population (nonclinical) study of the prevalence and nature of intrusive thoughts among 1,473 individuals from seven countries in Europe, the Middle East, and South America. Results indicated there were no significant differences in terms of prevalence, but Iranian and Turkish respondents showed slightly higher frequencies of unwanted intrusive thoughts. Individuals from Spain and Portugal experienced higher levels of discomfort associated with their symptoms. While cross-cultural prevalence is an important component of clinical utility, it should not be assumed that cultural variations in symptom expression or disclosure are similar. For example, in an investigation of obsessive thought content, Medeiros et al. (2017) found religious obsessions were more frequent among individuals from Middle Eastern countries, whereas Brazilians more commonly reported aggression-based intrusive content. Reports of contamination symptoms among African Americans are nearly two times those reported by European Americans (Wheaton et al., 2013; M. T. Williams et al., 2012). Culture can also strongly influence rates of endorsement of certain symptoms, and racial microaggressions have been significantly associated as a primary barrier of care for minoritized Americans (M. Williams & Halstead, 2019).

Culturally appropriate ritualistic behavior, such as rituals to ward off bad luck, may have distinct parallels to OCD but are not indicative of OCD unless the behavior exceeds cultural norms. Counselors must be sure that they are familiar with the cultural context of the client before determining that a ritualistic behavior is obsessive-compulsive and review resources specific to cultural competency and OCD treatment (M. T. Williams et al., 2020). OCD will typically manifest before the age of 25, with 19.5 years reported as the mean age of onset in the United States (APA, 2022a). Symptoms become more prevalent as the individual ages (Morrison, 2006). Many clients will report that obsessive hand washing, for example, began with a 3- to 4-minute wash routine using only soap. Gradually, however, clients may report that they began to use nail brushes, surgical soap, and washing for 15 minutes per arm numerous times per day.

Gender does not seem to be an indicator of prevalence. In children, however, OCD is more common in boys than in girls. Whereas the *DSM-5-TR* states that the age of onset is earlier for men, research has indicated a wider age of onset, with symptoms appearing between ages 6 and 15, and women typically first experience symptoms between the ages of 20 and 29 years (Mancebo et al., 2008). Familial patterns for OCD are higher in first-generation biological relatives than in the general population. Pathophysiologic findings provide evidence of a familial pattern with OCD; studies of monozygotic twins have revealed concordance rates as high as 87% and nearly half that for dizygotic twins (den Braber et al., 2008). Symptoms may fluctuate and increase with emotional stressors. For example, during flu season, a client may experience constant worry about becoming contaminated and exhibit persistent OCD symptoms, but these symptoms may decrease or even disappear during the summer months.

Differential Diagnosis

Common differentials for OCD include mood disorders, anxiety disorders, eating disorders, and psychotic disorders (APA, 2022a; Reghunandanan et al., 2015). As discussed previously, it is important for counselors to identify the presence of unwanted intrusive thoughts or ritualistic repetitive behaviors prior to diagnosing OCD. However, this is undoubtedly challenging given that the level of insight can vary and presentation in children is not uncommon. Obsessions and compulsions for children, for example, will contain different content, and children may lack the ability to explain the rationale behind performing a behavior or ritual. The presence of obsessions and/or compulsions that cause clinically significant distress or impairment remains constant for both children and adults (APA, 2022a).

Counselors must be sure to distinguish OCD from anxiety disorder due to another medical condition. For example, counselors working with children experiencing a sudden onset of obsessions, compulsions, or tics need to work with a medical professional to rule out pediatric autoimmune neuropsychiatric disorder associated with streptococcal infections. If a substance is the source of the obsession or compulsion, counselors need to rule out substance/medication-induced anxiety disorder. Counselors should be aware that OCD could occur within the context of other psychological disorders. However, if content is distinctly related to another disorder, such as fixation with one's appearance as in BDD or preoccupation with a fear-based object or situation as in specific phobia or social anxiety disorder, OCD cannot be diagnosed unless there are symptoms that are unrelated to the other disorder. In this case, both disorders would be diagnosed. Finally, an important criterion that distinguishes OCD from psychotic disorders is the ability of the individual to recognize, at some point, that the obsessions or compulsions are unreasonable. Although levels of insight occur on a continuum, counselors who detect a presence of psychotic features should consider assessing for schizophrenia spectrum and other psychotic disorder instead of or in addition to OCD.

The following questions can help counselors distinguish OCD from other mental health disorders:

- Do you have frequent unwanted thoughts?
- Have you ever tried to get rid of these thoughts? If so, what did you do?
- Do you have certain rituals or behaviors that you repeat frequently during the day?
- Do you check things over and over again?
- Do you often put things in order or feel overly concerned with symmetry?
- Does doing any of these things trouble you?

Note: As many as half of individuals diagnosed with OCD have a comorbid psychiatric disorder. It is not uncommon for clients to only display OCD symptoms when they are experiencing a major depressive episode. Counselors should be careful to assess for accompanying disorders.

Coding, Recording, and Specifiers

There is only one diagnostic code for OCD: F42.2. However, there are two specifiers. The first specifier indicates the client's current level of insight (*with good or fair insight*, *with poor insight*, or *with absent insight/delusional beliefs*). The second specifier, *tic-related*, denotes whether an individual has a current or history of a tic disorder. These specifiers do not have specific codes associated with them.

Note: With the release of the *DSM-5-TR*, the diagnostic code for OCD is no longer the same as for hoarding disorder. Hoarding was a new disorder in the *DSM-5* and was not listed as a diagnosable disorder in the *ICD-9-CM*, so the *DSM-5* used the same diagnostic code for both OCD and hoarding disorder. The *ICD-10-CM* now includes hoarding, which is coded under F42.3.

Case Example

Anuj is a 15-year-old Indian American boy who lives with his mother in a lower-middle-class neighborhood bordering a major metropolitan area. He is the only child and attends the 10th grade at a local public high school. Anuj recently had a full physical for school and the doctor reported no medical problems. His mother states that Anuj has a great deal of difficulty concentrating on and completing any of his schoolwork.

Anuj reports he is constantly distracted by powerful and strange thoughts, such as counting how many times he blinks and how many steps it takes to get to the hallway. He feels compelled to avoid stepping on any floor tiles with dirt on them because he does not want to get germs on his feet. The possibility that germs could be on door handles or windows also forces him to avoid touching them unless he first uses a cloth (which he always carries with him) to clean them off. In fact, if he misplaces or forgets to bring a clean cloth with him, he feels a great deal of anxiety, feels paralyzed, and may get physically ill.

Anuj realizes that his behavior does not make sense, and it frustrates him that he cannot overcome these powerful thoughts. Although he has always had a lot of unusual fears and behaviors associated with cleanliness, his behaviors have become increasingly frequent over the past 2 years. Other classmates make fun of him and call him crazy.

Anuj has been staying home from school because he is embarrassed and upset with himself. His mother is concerned about his absences from school but does not know how to make him go to school. His teachers are concerned about his absences and poor academic performance. They support Anuj as much as they can, but they do not understand his behavior either.

Diagnostic Questions

1. Do Anuj's presenting symptoms meet the criteria for an OCRD? If so, which disorder?
2. Based on the disorder identified in Question 1, which symptom(s) led you to select that diagnosis?
3. What would be the reason(s) a counselor may not diagnose Anuj with the disorder identified in Question 1?
4. Would Anuj be more accurately diagnosed with obsessive-compulsive personality disorder? If so, why? If not, why not?
5. What rule-outs would you consider for Anuj's case?
6. What other information may be needed to make an accurate clinical diagnosis?

Body Dysmorphic Disorder (F45.22)

> You could say that all my life I've been semi-obsessed with being perfect. I often did not think I looked pretty enough. What's amazing to me is that I know that I am very attractive, and yet whenever I glance at myself in public or something, I kind of see everything wrong with me. It's very frightening. Most of all, I fear that people are judging me for the imagined flaws that I see staring back at me.—Ester

Body dysmorphic disorder (BDD), which was moved from the somatoform disorders section of the *DSM-IV*, involves excessive concern about how one looks, specifically with the shape or appearance of one's body or a specific body part. Common concerns often involve breasts, genitalia, hair, nose, or some other portion of the face. Distress is not focused on worries about the presence of an unknown medical condition, as with illness anxiety disorder, or excessive concern with body weight, as with eating disorder. Historically, this disorder was referred to as dysmorphophobia, but this was changed in the *DSM-IV* because the term implied a phobia rather than an OCD. Specific phobias within the *DSM-5-TR* require a client to experience anxiety and fear associated with a specific stimulus, such as a specific animal (spider), environmental conditions (heights), or situations (enclosed spaces; APA, 2022a). Because individuals diagnosed with BDD do not present with persistent and irrational fear of their bodies or body parts, a more accurate term is *dysmorphia*, which refers to preoccupation rather than irrational fear.

Note: When working with clients who have concerns about their bodies, counselors should carefully consider whether a delusional disorder, illness anxiety disorder, or feeding or eating disorder is present.

Essential Features

Common concerns for individuals with BDD are skin imperfections such as wrinkles, scars, or acne. Hair concerns can be due to the lack of hair or too much hair. Individuals may also obsess about their weight, height, or the shape of a body part. Although most individuals can point out some feature of their appearance that they would like to change, BDD is a devastating disorder in which individuals repeatedly obsess about their body or a part of their body. For example, they will spend hours a day engaged in activities to camouflage their "defect" or repeatedly check themselves in a mirror. Clients may report feeling "hideous" and "deformed" and engage in repetitive behaviors (e.g., checking a mirror) or mental acts (e.g., comparing self to others) in response to these feelings. Perce ived flaws may not be unobservable or seem like minor physical characteristics to others. It is not uncommon for some clients to seek out surgical interventions to correct perceived flaws; however, these individuals seldom feel satisfied with the results of surgery and often attempt other surgical procedures or look for other ways they can modify the perceived imperfection (Bjornsson et al., 2010). Obsessions can focus on one or more body areas, but the skin, hair, and facial features (nose) are most common (APA, 2022a).

BDD is an underrecognized yet relatively common disorder, affecting 2.5% of women and 2.2% of men in the general population (Bjornsson et al., 2010; Koran et al., 2008). Prevalence of BDD in clinical settings is high, including 9% to 12% of individuals in dermatological settings and up to 53% of clients seen by cosmetic surgeons. For individuals with BDD, ritualistic behaviors and mental acts are exhausting and time consuming, sometimes leading them to constantly seek reassurance from others (APA, 2022a). Ideas or delusions of reference may be present, meaning the individual believes others are mocking them or viewing them negatively because of how they look (Bjornson et al., 2010). Compulsions, such as touching, styling, or cleaning areas of focus, can cause damage and lead to additional stress and impairment. Trying to hide an area of concerns, such as wearing baggy clothes or applying makeup, is common. There have been no major changes to this disorder in the *DSM-5-TR*.

Special Considerations

BDD is strongly linked to suicidal ideation. Angelakis et al. (2016) found that BDD was a stronger predictor of suicidality than any other disorder, including OCD and anorexia nervosa. BDD is associated with increased occupational and social impairment, hospitalization, and problems with executive functioning, specifically emotional recognition and attention (APA, 2022a). Counselors should not assume BDD is simply a symptom of depression or, in the case of adolescents, developmental "fixation" on one's appearance. Although this diagnosis often coexists with depression, it should always be considered a stand-alone diagnosis if diagnostic criteria are met.

Muscle dysmorphia, a specifier for BDD in which the focal area is the size or shape of an individual's body, has a much higher prevalence rate in men and boys (APA, 2022a). Many individuals will diet or exercise or take supplements to change the composition of their bodies. Individuals with BDD who present with little to no insight or delusional beliefs are at a high risk for suicide, severe impairment (e.g., dropping out of school, hospitalization), and severe deficiency in their quality of life.

Social and Cultural Considerations

First coined by Italian psychiatrist Enrico Morselli as "dysmorphophobia," a derivative of "dysmorphia," a Greek word meaning ugliness, BDD has a global presence. Usually beginning in early adolescence, BDD has an age onset of 16 to 22 years (Bjornsson et al., 2013; Mancebo et al., 2008). This diagnosis affects males and females equally but with different manifestations. Males are more likely to be preoccupied with their physique, genitals, and loss of hair (Pope et al., 2005), whereas females are more likely to have a comorbid eating disorder, hide perceived defects with various camouflaging techniques, frequently check mirrors, and pick their skin as a symptom of BDD (Phillips et al., 2006). Malcolm et al. (2021) noted increased levels of concern in women regarding their legs and lower levels of insight, whereas concerns in men were over their muscularity/build. For both women and men, skin remained the primary area of concern. In terms of psychosocial functioning, males fared worse than females and were more likely to be unemployed and receiving disability payments.

While symptom characteristics may be shared cross-culturally, cultural values and preferences can influence symptom content and focus. Taijin kyofusho, a Japanese reference commonly associated with social anxiety disorder, is marked by a feeling of shame or offensiveness to others based on inadequacies in one's appearance (APA, 2022a). Individuals belonging to cultures with a collectivist focus may feel that their perceived flaws or defects bring shame to others (APA, 2022a). There is a lack of research on cultural manifestations of BDD specifically (A. R. Singh & Veale, 2019), but there is evidence to support the idea that racial teasing due to facial features, body image, and skin tone is associated with increased BDD symptoms (Pillai & Sündermann, 2020; Schooler, 2007) and higher instances of body image distortions among historically marginalized groups, including the LGBTQ+ population and the overrepresentation of "idealized" Caucasian individuals on social media. Morgan-Sowada and Gamboni (2021) described the intersection of BDD and affectional identity, noting contradictory messages reported among gay men who felt "the push and pull to be 'perfect,' 'manly,' but not 'too manly,' . . . effeminate . . . but 'not too effeminate'" (p. 15). This description uniquely captures the intersection of BDD and the importance of understanding a client's multiple identities.

Differential Diagnosis

For a diagnosis of BDD, the symptoms must represent disproportionate concerns about real or imagined flaws related to one's appearance (APA, 2022a). Counselors should consider the degree to which one's concern with appearance may be culturally or developmentally expected (even if unhealthy). Counselors must rule out eating disorders when a client is only concerned with weight and feeling "fat." Counselors should also strongly consider depressive, anxiety, psychotic, and other OCRDs such as OCD (Frances, 2013). Determining that the client's obsessions and symptomatology focus only on appearance will help ensure accurate diagnosis (APA, 2022a).

Coding, Recording, and Specifiers

There is only one diagnostic code for BDD: F45.22. However, there are two specifiers, the first of which indicates extreme preoccupation with one's body build and the second an individual's level of insight. Counselors should use the specifier *with muscle dysmorphia* if clients are significantly troubled by the idea that their body build is too small. This specifier is also used if the clients are preoccupied with other body areas, such as their breasts. Counselors should indicate current insight (*with good or fair insight*, *with poor insight*, or *with absent insight/delusional beliefs*) specifiers assessing the degree to which clients accept their beliefs as true.

Case Example

Becca, a 26-year-old single Hispanic woman, had been ashamed of her "grotesque" nose and "acne-scarred" skin since junior high school. She reported being "absolutely convinced" that she looked "deformed and atrocious." When she started to date in high school and was called "pretty" by a potential boyfriend, she remembers feeling like he was making fun of her. When her family members tried to tell her she was pretty, she would get angry and feel they were lying to her. Becca was convinced that others talked about her "hideous" nose and "monstrous" skin. Because of her self-loathing, Becca began to isolate herself and dropped out of school. She has not been able to keep a job, aside from working as a remote call center worker. She has become severely depressed, withdrawn, and anxious whenever she needs to leave her home. She has a history of two suicide attempts and was hospitalized after both attempts.

Although her friends and family strongly advised against it, Becca received two rhinoplasties for a nose that outwardly appeared normal. She also received a course of isotreninoin (Accutane). These treatments left Becca even more obsessed with her appearance and feeling more depressed because her "last hopes" had not cured her perceived ugliness.

Diagnostic Questions

1. Do Becca's presenting symptoms meet the criteria for BDD? Which symptom(s) led you to select that diagnosis?
2. What rule-outs would you consider for Becca's case?
3. What course of treatment would you recommend for Becca?

Hoarding Disorder (F42.3)

I've always had trouble throwing things away. Magazines, newspapers, old clothes. What if I need them one day? I don't want to risk throwing something out that might be valuable. The large piles of stuff in our house keep growing so it's difficult to move around and sit or eat together as a family. My wife is upset and embarrassed, and we get into horrible fights. I'm scared when she threatens to leave me. My children won't invite friends over, and I feel guilty that the clutter makes them cry, but I get so anxious when I try to throw anything away. I don't know what's wrong with me, and I don't know what to do.—Ben

Hoarding is defined as "persistent difficulty discarding or parting with possessions, regardless of their actual value" (APA, 2022a, p. 277). Historically referred to as pathological or compulsive hoarding, this disorder has extremely detrimental emotional, social, and financial effects on individuals and their loved ones. Because of their avoidance of or difficulty with getting rid of possessions, individuals diagnosed with hoarding disorder are consumed with fears related to losing important information or objects of emotional significance (Abramowitz, 2018).

Major Changes From *DSM-5 to DSM-5-TR*

There have been no changes to the diagnostic criteria for hoarding disorder in the *DSM-5-TR*. However, similar to TTM in the next section of this chapter, only recently has hoarding disorder been considered a distinct disorder. Hoarding was previously listed in the *DSM-IV-TR* as one of eight concurrent criteria for obsessive-compulsive personality disorder (OCPD). The DSM-5 Task Force made the decision to list hoarding as a discrete disorder because individuals with hoarding symptoms may not display any other symptoms of OCD and are often nonresponsive to traditional treatments for OCD or OCPD, such as exposure therapy or psychopharmaceutical treatments (Bloch et al., 2014). Moreover, correlational studies identify only a small to moderate relationship between hoarding and OCD (Abramowitz et al., 2008; Wu & Watson, 2005). Invasive and uncomfortable thoughts or images are atypical for individuals with hoarding disorder. This is likely due to a lower level of reported insight regarding their behavior as excessive or unpleasant (APA, 2022a; Nakao & Kanba, 2019). From a behavioral lens, compulsive behaviors related to OCD are negatively reinforced, meaning obsessive behaviors and mental rituals help the individual avoid physical or emotional pain. Conversely, individuals diagnosed with hoarding disorder hold strong emotional attachments to possessions that positively reinforces hoarding behavior. Other strong indicators that hoarding is a distinct disorder rather than a component of OCD are that hoarding is the only OCD symptom that increases with age and that distress and disability often appear late in the course of the disorder (Ayers et al., 2010; Nakao & Kanba, 2019).

Essential Features

Individuals with hoarding disorder typically have living spaces and personal surroundings cluttered to the point of being useless for their intended purpose (e.g., a bathroom or a bedroom). Hoarding behaviors often cause a considerable amount of distress for the individual and family members, caregivers, neighbors, and friends who attempt to clear spaces. It is important to note that the diagnostic criteria for hoarding, like other OCRDs, include symptoms that cause significant impairment in social, occupational, or other essential areas of functioning.

Prevalence of hoarding among the general population is 2% to 5%, with older adults more likely to exhibit hoarding behaviors. Hoarding typically manifests in childhood and worsens as clients become older. Some researchers claim that as the geriatric population increases, so will the number of adults diagnosed with hoarding disorder (Ayers et al., 2010; Cath et al., 2017). Symptoms often are associated with other psychological disorders such as depression, anxiety, and substance abuse. Although epidemiological research is limited, some researchers have identified a familial pattern (Samuels et al., 2008).

Special Considerations

A client's ability to maintain a safe living environment, free of any public health consequences, is often a major indicator for counselors considering this diagnosis. Counselors should not diagnose hoarding simply because a person owns an abnormal amount of things. Counselors should keep in mind the following three behaviors regarding hoarding: (a) acquisition of numerous possessions (many of little value), (b) difficulty discarding these possessions, and (c) significant difficulty organizing possessions. In contrast to people with hoarding problems, people who collect items often keep their property well organized. Collectors often display items for others to appreciate, whereas hoarders overrun living areas with items and can create problems such as financial obligations of paying for storage space.

When collecting behaviors lead to health or safety problems or cause significant distress, hoarding becomes a diagnosable disorder. For example, a major feature of hoarding is the large amount of disorganized clutter that creates chaos in the home or office. Individuals diagnosed with hoarding disorder often have rooms that can no longer be used as they were intended, create challenges for others while moving around the home, have homes with blocked exits, and make life inside the home difficult (Frances, 2013; Nakao & Kanba, 2019). Counselors should pay close attention to health and safety concerns, especially in older adult clients. Client safety (e.g., falling over items in one's home or illnesses due to contaminated food or infestation) is the number one concern for counselors working with individuals diagnosed with hoarding disorder.

One significant manifestation of hoarding disorder is animal hoarding. Although there is currently no percentage estimate of commonality as animal hoarding itself has only recently been recognized, and therefore research is minimal, animal hoarding in particular has the highest fatality rate of all types of hoarding. This is due to the animals kept as part of the hoard often dying because of neglect or disease (B. Williams, 2014).

Social and Cultural Considerations

Although people with hoarding disorder are typically older, most have had trouble discarding items early on in their lives. They are also less likely to be married, which may relate to functional impacts associated with the disorder. Although there is limited transcultural research of hoarding disorder, Nordsletten et al. (2018) investigated individuals presenting with hoarding disorder symptoms across four countries (United Kingdom, Spain, Japan, and Brazil) and determined that diagnostic features and severity of hoarding disorder remained stable. However, as with many disorders in the *DSM-5-TR*, a large majority of epidemiological and treatment investigations for hoarding disorder have been conducted within the United States with notable exclusions of non-White persons. In a systematic review of hoarding disorder treatment studies, De La Cruz et al. (2016) reported approximately 90% of hoarding disorder investigations used a White/Caucasian sample.

Hoarding disorder is not uncommon in individuals who have a history of trauma or have experienced significantly stressful life events (Chia et al., 2021). Although some researchers have identified material deprivation (e.g., lack of money, food, adequate clothing, or shelter during their lifetime) as an environmental risk factor, consensus among scholars is that there is no clear link between a lack of material items and hoarding disorder (Landau et al., 2011). Studies of childhood adversity and emotional attachment difficulties point to strong correlates of hoarding behavior and poor attachments. Moreover, researchers have found individuals who have experienced multiple traumas report higher levels of hoarding symptom severity, which supports the position that cumulative events rather than a particular traumatic event may be associated with increased hoarding disorder prevalence (Kehoe & Egan, 2019). Frost et al. (2011) posited that hoarding behavior serves as a coping mechanism and a way to seek control over one's environment. Low levels of comorbidity between hoarding disorder and PTSD, despite similar reports of trauma exposure, support this position (Kehoe & Egan, 2019).

Differential Diagnosis

Researchers have identified important phenomenological differences between hoarding and prototypical OCD symptoms, which can help counselors differentiate between hoarding disorder and OCD (Landau et al., 2011). Thoughts associated with hoarding are not intrusive and, typically, no ritualistic attributes are associated with hoarding behaviors. Researchers have also discovered that failure to discard possessions is more of a passive behavior than an active attempt to neutralize unwanted thoughts, images, or impulses (Nakao & Kanba, 2019; Pertusa et al., 2010). Counselors must be sure to rule out MDD, schizophrenia, or any neurocognitive disorder such as autism spectrum disorder because the presentation of any one of these could result in an inability for a client to be able to get rid of objects or clear clutter (APA, 2022a; Frances, 2013). Medical conditions that cause secondary hoarding, such as brain injury or disease and Prader-Willi syndrome, are excluded. Hoarding is often comorbid with autism spectrum disorder and ADHD-inattentive type (Hartl et al., 2005; Nakao & Kanba, 2019).

Coding, Recording, and Specifiers

There is only one diagnostic code for hoarding disorder: F42. Because hoarding was not directly mentioned in either the *ICD-9* or the *ICD-10*, the diagnostic code for OCD (300.3) was previously included in the *DSM-5* but has been removed from the *DSM-5-TR*. There are two specifiers, the first of which indicates extreme hoarding and the second an individual's level of insight. Counselors should use the *with excessive acquisition* specifier if attainment of items is extreme and individuals are unable to discard large numbers of possessions. In addition, counselors should use insight specifiers (e.g., *with good or fair insight*, *with poor insight*, or *with absent insight/delusional beliefs*) to indicate the degree to which the individual is able to understand the hoarding beliefs and behaviors as problematic. These specifiers do not have specific codes associated with them.

Case Example

Barrett, an articulate 69-year-old Caucasian male retiree, first came to the attention of the Community Services Board when a neighbor complained to the police about the mounds of trash she could see through Barrett's windows. A staff person from the fire department visited Barrett but was unable to investigate the complaint because he would not allow the investigator to enter his home. The fire official was able to persuade Barrett to meet with a case manager from Adult Protective Services, who evaluated Barrett and found him to be competent and able to refuse services. Over the next 10 years, neighbors complained about Barrett's hoarding behavior approximately every 2 years. Complaints included references to a car that was so stuffed full of items that it was unsafe to drive, rodents on the property, and trash piled up in the backyard.

When Barrett was not seen at his volunteer job for several days, his supervisor requested that police check on his welfare. Police found Barrett unconscious in a corner of his bedroom where he had landed after tripping over a pile of papers. Barrett was hospitalized and received treatment for an infection of both legs. During this time, the fire marshal condemned his home. In the hospital, a counselor met with Barrett to help him cope with being removed from his home and begin exploring a plan for moving forward.

Diagnostic Questions

1. Do Barrett's presenting symptoms meet the criteria for an ORCD? If so, which disorder?
2. Based on the disorder identified in Question 1, which symptom(s) led you to select that diagnosis?
3. What would be the reason(s) a counselor may not diagnose Barrett with OCD or OCPD?
4. Would Barrett be more accurately diagnosed with an anxiety disorder? If so, why and which one? If not, why not?
5. What rule-outs would you consider for Barrett's case?
6. What other information may be needed to make an accurate clinical diagnosis?

Trichotillomania (Hair-Pulling) Disorder (F63.3)

> I eat my hair. I know I am a freak but I don't even realize I am doing it. I just pull at my hair and, one day, just started swallowing it. I have tried to stop but I cannot. Even the thought of trying to stop again makes my heart start racing.—Allyia

Previously identified in the *DSM-IV-TR* as an impulse-control disorder, trichotillomania (TTM), or hair-pulling disorder, is characterized by the compulsive urge to pull out, and sometimes ingest, one's own hair (APA, 2022a). TTM leads to noticeable hair loss and, as characteristic of all OCRDs, causes distress or functional impairment (APA, 2022a; Farhat et al., 2020). The *ICD-10-CM* classifies TTM as a habit and impulse disorder in the section on disorder of adult personality and behavior. Both the *ICD* and the *DSM* describe TTM as recurrent and noticeable by others.

Essential Features

Hair pulling often occurs without focused attention, which means individuals are typically not aware they are doing it (APA, 2022a). This is different from OCD, in which people may have a high level of insight into their behavior (Chamberlain et al., 2007). TTM results in noticeable hair loss, which is associated with feelings of shame and withdrawal from social and occupational activities. Additionally, it causes moderate perceived disability and significantly alters quality of life (Farhat et al., 2020). Hair-pulling methods vary, but most individuals report removing hair from the scalp with their thumb and forefinger, but sometimes items such as tweezers can be used (Woods & Houghton, 2014). Characteristic of OCRDs, rituals or patterns often precede hair removal and may include visual searching, combing, or touching. Hair pulling occurs in response to a wide range of negative moods, such as anger, boredom, sadness, or stress (Christenson & Mackenzie, 1995; Jafferany & Osuagwu, 2018). Although the research is limited, environmental variables associated with TTM include watching television, reading, studying, and grooming (Flessner et al., 2008). Many people report specific emotional states (e.g., stress or anxiety), a sense of tension, or an urge to pull preceding an episode, which in turn is alleviated after pulling (Woods et al., 2006).

The hallmark feature of TTM is pleasure, gratification, or relief experienced by the client as a result of pulling out one's hair (APA, 2022a; Woods & Houghton, 2014). In the *ICD-10*, this disorder is described as "preceded by mounting tension and is followed by a sense of relief or gratification" (WHO, 2019, "Trichotillomania" section). It is the defining characteristic of relief, as opposed to pleasure, that caused this disorder to be recategorized. Impulse disorders, such as pyromania and kleptomania, give pleasure to the person and are not typically carried out for the purpose of relief (Gershuny et al., 2006; Stein et al., 2006). Prevalence of TTM is 1% to 2% of adults and adolescents in the general population (APA, 2022a).

Special Considerations

Counselors should be aware that the reference to "mania" in TTM implies an interest or enthusiasm for the hair-pulling behavior. Since this is not the case, a more neutral reference to hair-pulling disorder has been included in the *DSM-5*. The typical age of onset is between 12 and 13, and the disorder affects mostly females (APA, 2022a; Jafferany & Patel, 2018). Cases of TTM in toddlers and young children, referred to as pediatric TTM, have been reported with onset between the ages of 18 months and 4 years. Pediatric TTM is often short term, but TTM in older children and adolescents may persist through adulthood without intervention (Tolin et al., 2007). There is little empirical evidence around etiology for TTM, but consistent with other OCRDs, there is preliminary support for functional brain abnormalities and neuropsychological deficits (Woods & Houghton, 2014). Common treatment approaches include CBT (Abramowitz et al., 2017), habit reversal therapy (Morris et al., 2013), acceptance and commitment therapy (Hayes et al., 1999), monitoring devices that promote awareness (Himle et al., 2018), and response inhibition training (Lee et al., 2018). SSRIs have also been found to be effective for the treatment of TTM (Chamberlain et al., 2007; Melville, 2013). For a review of these and other treatment approaches, see Jafferany and Patel (2018).

Given potential dermatological complications, in addition to conducting a behavioral and functional assessment, counselors should encourage clients to have a medical examination because hair follicles can be permanently damaged, injured, or inflamed (Jafferany & Patel, 2018). Clinician rating scales such as the Yale-Brown Obsessive-Compulsive Scale–

Trichotillomania (Stanley et al., 1999) and client report scales such as the Massachusetts General Hospital Hairpulling Scale (Keuthen et al., 1995) may yield additional insight.

Social and Cultural Considerations

Very few studies have investigated cultural considerations and features of TTM. Using a cross-sectional design of persons diagnosed with TTM, Neal-Barnett et al. (2010) found that individuals from historically minoritized racial and ethnic groups reported greater problems related to home management. Additionally, there were fewer reported instances of seeking treatment and lower levels of reported distress prior to engaging in hair pulling. White/Caucasian individuals reported an increase in academic and occupational stressors and higher frequency of pulling at eyelashes and eyebrows. More women than men are reported as being diagnosed with TTM, with some reports indicating a ratio of 9:1 (Snorrason et al., 2012). Counselors are cautioned against underdiagnosing TTM in men, as this ratio could be better explained by men being less likely to seek treatment or to explain hair loss to baldness or shaving (Woods & Houghton, 2014). Excoriation is also associated with dementia and Alzheimer's disease in older clients, often as an inadvertent way to convey stress or other issues in their environment (Ikoma et al., 2020; Johansson et al., 2004).

Differential Diagnosis

It may be difficult to differentiate TTM from other OCRDs, specifically OCD and BDD. Counselors can assess a client's level of pleasure in engaging in hair pulling, which would be more indicative of TTM, because individuals with OCD generally seek relief, not pleasure, when performing behavior rituals. Counselors can also assess the client's level of fixation (obsession), assessing whether there is extreme dislike/disgust (BDD) or physical gratification (TMM). A TTM diagnosis should not be made if there is a preexisting dermatological problem, another medical condition, or if the hair pulling is in response to a delusion, hallucination, or another mental health disorder (APA, 2022a). TTM has a high rate of comorbidity, with some studies reporting up to 60% of individuals diagnosed with TTM having another mental health disorder (Chamberlain et al., 2007). It is not uncommon for individuals to also be diagnosed with MDD, GAD, social phobia, OCD, or other impulse-control disorder and substance use disorder. Evidence of comorbidity with excoriation, with similar risk factors, and other topical behaviors such as nail, lip, and cheek chewing; nose picking; and thumb sucking has been reported (Snorrason et al., 2012; Woods et al., 2006).

Coding, Recording, and Specifiers

There is only one diagnostic code for TTM (hair-pulling) disorder: F63.3. There are no specifiers for this disorder.

Excoriation (Skin-Picking) Disorder (F42.4)

> First it was occasional picking at scabs and acne on my face. Then I started just sitting at home picking at my fingers and arms. Now, I spend hours nearly every day obsessed with picking the skin on my face, arms, and hands. I think about it all the time. I can't even go to work sometimes because I am either embarrassed about the scabs and scars on my skin or because I am so consumed with the need to keep picking at myself.—Meagan

Excoriation (skin-picking) disorder is characterized by repetitive and compulsive picking of skin, resulting in tissue damage (Grant & Chamberlain, 2020). Sometimes called neurotic excoriation, compulsive skin picking, dermatillomania, or psychogenic skin picking, symptoms of excoriation can also include skin rubbing, squeezing, lancing, and biting (APA, 2022a; Lochner et al., 2017). Individuals with excoriation disorder may use their fingers, fingernails, tweezers, or other objects. These individuals spend a considerable amount of time picking, and the disorder can continue for months or years. This disorder may be accompanied by a range of behaviors or rituals, typically does not occur in the presence of other people, and has the potential to cause significant distress in several areas of functioning (APA, 2022a).

Major Changes From *DSM-5* to *DSM-5-TR*

There have been no changes to the diagnostic criteria for excoriation disorder within the *DSM-5-TR*. Prior to the release of the *DSM-5*, symptoms of excoriation disorder were previously classified by clinicians as impulse-control disorder not otherwise specified because there was no other appropriate diagnostic classification. When the *DSM-5* was being developed, there were serious deliberations as to whether this disorder should be included as an impulse-control disorder or as a body-focused repetitive behavioral disorder (Stein et al., 2010). Before inclusion in the *DSM-5*, excoriation was considered clinically similar to substance abuse or impulse-control disorders rather than a disorder related to obsessive-compulsive behavior. However, like TTM, the core feature of excoriation is repetitive feelings of tension, anxiety, or agitation immediately preceding the picking episode (i.e., obsessive) and feelings of relief during or following picking (i.e., compulsive). Thus, the diagnosis was included within the Obsessive-Compulsive and Related Disorders chapter.

Essential Features

Six core features characterize excoriation: (a) recurrent and repetitive picking resulting in noticeable tissue damage; (b) intrusive urges to pick skin; (c) feelings of tension, anxiety, or agitation immediately preceding the picking episode; (d) feelings of pleasure, relief, or satisfaction during or after picking; (e) the picking cannot be accounted for by another medical issue (e.g., scabies, eczema) or mental disorder (e.g., cocaine or amphetamine use disorders); and (f) the individual suffers significant distress or social or occupational impairment as a result of the picking behavior (APA, 2022a). Clients most frequently report picking at the face, but the fingers, arms, torso, hands, legs, back, and stomach are also common areas for picking.

Special Considerations

Counselors should be sensitive to the needs of clients who engage in skin picking. Possible medical concerns include infections, scarring, and even serious physical deformities (e.g., disfigurement). This behavior may result in skin discoloration or scarring. In more serious cases, severe tissue damage and visible disfigurement can result. Although skin picking is typically not related to other physical or mental disorders, it is essential for counselors to help clients identify whether picking is a symptom of another problem, for example, dermatological disorders, autoimmune problems, BDD, or psychosis. Because clients are often embarrassed about their problems, they may avoid treatment (Flessner & Woods, 2006). In a study of 31 patients with pathological skin picking, only 14 had ever sought treatment, and only six had ever received dermatological treatment. The largest concern for counselors is significant medical complications such as scarring and infection. As with TTM, common interventions include cognitive behavioral approaches (i.e., awareness and habit reversal) and psychopharmaceutical treatments, with habit reversal therapy showing the most promise. In a small randomized controlled trial for excoriation disorder ($N = 34$), Schuck et al. (2011) found habit reversal therapy was effective at decreasing excoriation disorder symptoms at 4-week, 6-week, and 2-month follow-ups. A similar study conducted by Teng et al. (2006) confirmed these findings.

Note: Clients are typically embarrassed about hair-pulling or skin-picking disorders. Therefore, if you do not see evidence of the disorder, you are not likely to hear about associated symptoms.

Social and Cultural Considerations

Prevalence of excoriation disorder in a general U.S. population sample has been reported as 3.1%, with a slight female majority (54.1%; Grant & Chamberlain, 2020). This is similar to previous epidemiological studies that report prevalence rates of excoriation ranging from 1.4% to 5.4% in the general population (Odlaug & Grant, 2010). Age of onset is bimodal, beginning in either young adulthood or between the ages of 30 and 45. Lifetime prevalence of excoriation disorder and associated diagnostic presentations of skin picking have been reported as similar across different age cohorts and cultural groups in different countries, including Europe (Bohne et al., 2002), Africa (Lochner et al., 2002), North America (Tucker et al., 2011), South America (Ferrão et al., 2006), and the Middle East (Calikusu et al., 2012; Leibovici et al., 2015). However, despite similarity in symptoms, counselors are advised to remember that similar to TTM, individuals with excoriation disorder experience significant shame and isolation and may, depending on their culture of origin, feel they are bringing shame to others.

Differential Diagnosis

Similar to TMM, comorbidity with other OCRDs such as OCD, BDD, and TTM is common for excoriation disorder (Lochner et al., 2017). In fact, excoriation disorder was originally included within the OCRD chapter of the *DSM-5* due to the comorbidity of excoriation and OCD and the similarity of treatment for these disorders (Stein et al., 2010). In an examination of clients with BDD, 44.9% reported skin-picking behaviors (Grant et al., 2006). Also common is the existence of another body-focused repetitive behavior such as excessive washing seen in individuals diagnosed with OCD. Somatic symptoms, such as a factitious disorder, should be ruled out, as should any other substance-/medication-induced disorder (APA, 2022a).

Individuals with excoriation disorder report elevated rates of GAD and/or depression. Using a general population convenience sample of 10,169 adults in the United States, Grant and Chamberlain (2020) found that approximately 25% of individuals who reported a lifetime occurrence of excoriation disorder also reported having a panic disorder, PTSD, OCD, or ADHD. Within the same sample, 10% to 20% reported have an eating disorder, addiction, TTM, or bipolar disorder. The high level of comorbidity for excoriation disorder not only points to the high burden of this disorder for clients, but also points to the critical need for counselors to conduct a full psychosocial assessment for individuals reporting this disorder.

Counselors working with children should consider the possibility of Prader-Willi syndrome or a pervasive developmental disorder. While rare, Prader-Willi syndrome is a genetic disorder associated with hyperphagia, hypogonadism, and skin picking (Grant & Chamberlain, 2015).

Coding, Recording, and Specifiers

There is only one diagnostic code for excoriation (skin-picking) disorder: F42.4. There are no specifiers for this disorder. Readers will note that earlier editions of the *DSM-5* coded excoriation disorder using the *ICD-10* code for excoriation that began with an "L" as opposed to the commonly seen "F." The reason is because it was only in October 2017 that the *ICD* had a specific listing for excoriation disorder. In *ICD-10*, this disorder was coded as factitial dermatitis (L98.1) and the "L" was classified under "other disorders of skin and subcutaneous tissue, not elsewhere classified" (WHO, 2007). However, since the publication of the *ICD-11*, the WHO (2021) added excoriation (skin-picking) disorder as a new category under OCD.

Case Example

Adrianne, a 38-year-old European American single woman, picks her arms daily. Although she had previously picked at her face, particularly her nose, her arms have been her main focus for the past 2 years. Her picking sometimes lasts as long as 3 hours each day and is so intense that her arms are scarred and covered with scabs. When she touches her arms, she has an irresistible urge to pick. Adrianne reports that sometimes when she walks and her hands touch her thighs, this would cause her to stop walking and pick.

Adrianne started picking her face when she was 14 years old. Because of the time she spent picking, she missed a significant amount of high school and could not graduate. Since then, because of the facial scarring, Adrianne started focusing on her arms. Scarring and the consistent bleeding caused Adrianne to avoid going out in public, working, or socializing. She lives alone on medical disability. She had never sought help for her picking until just recently when she was hospitalized for septicemia, a life-threatening infection caused by her skin picking.

Diagnostic Questions

1. Do Adrianne's presenting symptoms meet the criteria for excoriation (skin-picking) disorder?
2. Which symptom(s) led you to agree with this diagnosis?
3. What rule-outs would you consider for Adrianne's case?
4. What other information may be needed to make an accurate clinical diagnosis?

Substance/Medication-Induced Obsessive-Compulsive and Related Disorder

Substance/medication-induced obsessive-compulsive and related disorder is characterized by obsessive-compulsive symptoms as a direct result of substance use (APA, 2022a). For an individual to meet the criteria for this disorder, symptoms must have occurred during or soon after substance or medication intoxication or withdrawal; must be in excess of what is expected during intoxication or withdrawal for the specific substance; and must subside after the effects of the medication, treatments, or substance have been removed.

Major Changes From *DSM-5* to *DSM-5-TR*

The *DSM-IV-TR* included a specifier *with obsessive-compulsive symptoms* in the diagnoses of substance-induced anxiety disorder, but the *DSM-5-TR* classifies this as a distinct disorder given that OCRDs are now a distinct category. This change is consistent with the intent of *DSM-IV-TR* and reflects the recognition that substances, including medications, can present with symptoms similar to primary OCRDs.

Special Considerations

Counselors should ensure that the substance or medication deemed to be responsible for symptoms directly caused the disturbance; this effect does not only occur when the individual is experiencing delirium (APA, 2022a). Moreover, the symptoms must in some way result in clinically significant distress or impairment to functioning.

Coding, Recording, and Specifiers

Similar to all substance/medication-induced disorders in the *DSM-5-TR*, the *ICD-10-CM* codes are used. An extensive coding chart for substance/medication-induced obsessive-compulsive and related disorder can be found on page 288 in the *DSM-5-TR* (APA, 2022a). As with all substance/medication-induced disorders, the name of the substance causing the symptoms is used to identify the appropriate code and is included in the written name of the disorder. Associated severity specifiers should also be used. For example, F15.188 mild cocaine-induced obsessive-compulsive and related disorder would be used to document a client who presents with a specific substance-induced obsessive-compulsive and related disorder with mild symptoms.

Three different types of substances are classified as applicable to OCRDs. These are amphetamines/stimulants, cocaine, or other/unknown substance. Specifiers indicating *with onset during intoxication*, *with onset during withdrawal*, or *with onset after medication use* can be indicated after the code and name but, as with all specifiers in this chapters, do not have specific codes associated with them (APA, 2022a). Counselors using the *ICD-10-CM* diagnostic codes should note specific coding procedures when there is a co-morbid substance use disorder present for the same class of substance. For example, if a mild substance use disorder is comorbid with the substance/medication-induced obsessive-compulsive related disorder, the fourth position character should be a "1" (e.g., F15.188). If the comorbid substance use disorder is considered heavy, the fourth position character should be a "2." If there is no comorbid disorder, the fourth position character should be a "9," and only the substance-induced obsessive-compulsive and related disorder would be recorded (APA, 2022a).

Note: Counselors should reference page 545, Table 1, Diagnoses Associated With Substance Class, in the Substance-Related and Addictive Disorders chapter of the *DSM-5-TR* to fully understand which mental health diagnoses are associated with specific substance classes.

Obsessive-Compulsive and Related Disorder Due to Another Medical Condition (F06.8)

Medical conditions can cause the development of an OCRD, but symptoms must cause clinically significant distress to be diagnosed. Symptoms can include a wide range of obsessive-compulsive features (e.g., obsessions, compulsions, preoccupation with appearance, hoarding, skin picking), but there is direct pathophysiological evidence of a medical condition. The characteristic features of an obsessive-compulsive and related disorder due to another medical condition is that symptoms are not better explained by another OCRD and are deemed to be the result of direct pathophysiological consequence of a medical condition (APA, 2022a).

Major Changes From *DSM-5* to *DSM-5-TR*

Obsessive-compulsive and related disorder due to another medical condition was introduced as a distinct disorder in the *DSM-5*. It was previously a specifier in the diagnoses of anxiety disorder due to a general medical condition in the *DSM-IV-TR*. This reflects the recognition that medical conditions can present with symptoms similar to OCD. No changes have been made to this disorder in the *DSM-5-TR*.

Essential Features

A medical condition, as evidenced by laboratory findings, physical examination from a medical professional, or physical health history, must be present when diagnosing a client with obsessive-compulsive and related disorder due to another medical condition. Furthermore, the condition cannot be better explained by another medical condition or use of a substance/medication. As with any OCRD, symptoms must cause significant impairment to social, occupational, or other essential areas of functioning.

Special Considerations

Two medical conditions that are of significance are (a) pediatric autoimmune neuropsychiatric disorder associated with streptococcal infections (PANDAS), with the rapid onset of OCD symptoms or tics due to strep throat or scarlet fever; and (b) pediatric acute-onset neuropsychiatric syndrome, a broader condition similar to PANDAS but not related to a strep infection (APA, 2022a). Clients with a history of these disorders are prone to obsessive-compulsive traits.

Social and Cultural Considerations

There is limited information on cultural considerations for this disorder because these are typically relevant to the underlying medical illness rather than the psychiatric diagnosis. However, as with any medical disorder, counselors should consult with health professionals for information related to the development and course of the medical disorder as it relates to the client's cultural background.

Differential Diagnosis

It is especially important for counselors to rule out differential diagnoses, such as a primary diagnosis of OCD or an illness anxiety disorder (i.e., hypochondriasis), and consult with a physician to determine physiological etiology before using the diagnosis of obsessive-compulsive and related disorder due to another medical condition.

Coding, Recording, and Specifiers

There is only one diagnostic code for obsessive-compulsive and related disorder due to another medical condition: F06.8. When coding this disorder, counselors should be sure to indicate the medical condition alongside the diagnosis (e.g., obsessive-compulsive and related disorder due to PANDAS). There are five specifiers associated with this diagnosis that are relatively self-explanatory because they relate to the diagnoses found within this chapter. These include *with obsessive-compulsive disorder–like symptoms*, *with appearance preoccupations*, *with hoarding symptoms*, *with hair-pulling symptoms*, and *with skin-picking symptoms*. There are no specific codes assigned to these specifiers.

Note: Proper recording procedures should include the separate coding and listing of the medical condition immediately before the obsessive-compulsive and related disorder due to another medical condition diagnosis.

Other Specified and Unspecified Obsessive-Compulsive and Related Disorders (F42.8/F42.9)

The other specified obsessive-compulsive and related disorder (F42.8) category, along with the unspecified criterion (F42.9), replaced the not otherwise specified category in the *DSM-IV-TR*. This disorder may include conditions such as body-focused repetitive behavior disorder and obsessional jealousy. Body-focused repetitive behavior disorder, for example, is characterized by recurrent behaviors other than hair pulling and skin picking (e.g., nail biting, lip biting, cheek chewing) and repeated attempts to decrease or stop the behaviors. Obsessional jealousy is characterized by nondelusional preoccupation with a partner's perceived infidelity.

The other specified obsessive-compulsive and related disorder category is used in situations in which the counselor chooses to communicate the specific reason the presentation does not meet the criteria for any specific anxiety disorder (e.g., "body dysmorphic-like disorder with actual flaws"; APA, 2022a, p. 294). The example given would indicate BDD, except the client's preoccupation involves a physical imperfection that *is* evident to other people. When coding other specified obsessive-compulsive and related disorder, counselors no longer use one diagnostic code; instead, unique codes are used for each disorder. Other specified obsessive-compulsive and related disorder should be coded using F42.8, and unspecified obsessive-compulsive and related disorder should be coded using F42.9.

As with other unspecified designations, if the counselor chooses *not* to specify the reason the criteria are not met, then the unspecified obsessive-compulsive and related disorder (F42.9) category is used. In either case, symptoms cause clinically significant impairment or distress. This diagnosis is also commonly used when counselors are unable to distinguish whether a medical illness or substance has played a causal role in the manifestation of obsessive-compulsive symptoms.

Note: The diagnostic code for specified and unspecified obsessive-compulsive and related disorder is no longer the same.

Major Changes From *DSM-5* to *DSM-5-TR*

One notable change from the *DSM-5* to the *DSM-5-TR* is the addition of olfactory reference disorder (olfactory reference syndrome) as an example of presentations that can be specified under an "other specified" designation for other specified obsessive-compulsive and related disorder. Formerly referred to as "jikoshu-kyofu" in the *DSM-5*, the *DSM-5-TR* included this reference as an example under olfactory reference syndrome due to the faulty assumption by some clinicians that olfactory references (characterized by the belief that one emits a foul odor) are specific to Japanese culture. Globally recognized as a disorder impacting individuals from various cultural and social backgrounds, olfactory reference disorder has also been added to the *ICD-11* (it is not in the *ICD-10-CM*). Excessive showering, while not included as a descriptive reference in the *ICD-11*, is included in the *DSM-5-TR* as this is a widely recognized repetitive behavior (compulsion).

Questions for Consideration

1. How are obsessions and compulsions different from daily worries, concerns, or habits?
2. What factors should counselors consider when differentiating OCD from an anxiety disorder?
3. Can children be diagnosed with OCD and, if so, what should counselors keep in mind when contemplating this diagnosis?
4. BDD is associated with elevated risk of suicidal thoughts and behaviors. What steps might a counselor engage in to protect clients with this diagnosis?
5. What treatments are typically used by counselors who are working with clients diagnosed with excoriation (skin-picking) disorder?

Chapter 10

Trauma- and Stressor-Related Disorders

The term *trauma* has historically been referred to as an emotional response to a severely distressing event, such as combat, sexual assault, severe accidents, abuse, or exposure to a natural or human-caused disaster (Norris & Elrod, 2006; Tramontin & Halpern, 2007; Ursano et al., 1994). While many within the mental health profession continue to treat psychological trauma as an emotional response to a specific event, an overwhelmingly extensive body of literature highlights the neurobiology of trauma in response to one or more event(s) or circumstance(s). There is also a growing body of literature that points to the transgenerational nature of trauma exposure for some individuals, which means that the traumatic experiences of one generation are passed down to another (R. D. Goodman & West-Olatunji, 2008; Yehuda & Lehrner, 2018). Traumatic events are considered physically or emotionally injurious or life threatening and, without treatment, can result in a long-lasting, pervasive impact on all aspects of an individual's functioning. The Substance Abuse and Mental Health Services Administration (SAMHSA, 2014) defines trauma as a "series of events or set of circumstances that is experienced by an individual as physically or emotionally harmful or life threatening and that has lasting adverse effects on the individual's functioning and mental, physical, social, emotional, or spiritual well-being" (p. 7). Examples include physical, sexual, and emotional abuse or neglect; sudden, unexplained separation from a caregiver or loved one; poverty; racism, discrimination, and oppression; and community-based violence.

Major Changes From *DSM-5* to *DSM-5-TR*

The Trauma- and Stressor-Related Disorders chapter in the *DSM-5-TR* includes PTSD, acute stress disorder, adjustment disorders, reactive attachment disorder (RAD), disinhibited social engagement disorder (DSED), and a new diagnosis of prolonged grief disorder (PGD). As a relatively new diagnostic chapter, the most significant change within the *DSM-5-TR* for this section is the addition of PGD, originally proposed under Section III of the *DSM-5*.

Other notable changes are the removal of the "note" under PTSD Criterion A.2. for children under the age of 6, which was considered redundant. This note reiterated, as indicated under the PTSD Criterion A.2 for children 6 years and younger, that witnessing an event via electronic media, television, movies, or pictures should not be considered. Although this is a minor change, changes from the *DSM-IV-TR* to the *DSM-5* were significant for disorders marked by exposure to a traumatic event.

In the *DSM-IV-TR*, PTSD and acute stress disorder were categorized as anxiety disorders; RAD was categorized as disorders usually first diagnosed in infancy, childhood, and adolescence; and adjustment disorders had their own diagnostic category. The *DSM-5* placed these disorders together based on their common roots in external events or triggers (APA, 2013a). Categorizing these disorders according to common etiology (i.e., trauma or psychological stressors preceding the disorder), as opposed to common phenomenology, has both clinical utility and heuristic value (First, 2010; First et al., 2004). Because many of these disorders are similar enough to be grouped together but distinct enough to subsist as separate disorders, counselors can more easily distinguish them from one another. For example, including PTSD and adjustment disorders in the same diagnostic classification allows counselors to identify marked differences more easily between these diagnoses. Furthermore, because these disorders are grouped according to cause as opposed to symptoms and all have demonstrated neurobiological homogeneity, researchers can easily create testable theoretical explanations for trauma-based disorders (Friedman et al., 2011).

Essential Features

Potentially traumatic events include combat, sexual and physical assault, robbery, being kidnapped or taken hostage, terrorist attacks, torture, disasters, severe automobile accidents, child abuse, and life-threatening illnesses (APA, 2022a; Benjet et al., 2016; NIMH, 2023a). Trauma also extends to witnessing death or serious injury by violent assault, accidents, war, racism, oppression, and community-based violence. Two disorders in this chapter address severe social neglect in childhood, separated into two distinct disorders: RAD and DSED. Both require an absence of adequate caregiving during childhood but are marked by internalizing (RAD) versus externalizing (DSED) symptoms (APA, 2022a). PGD, a new disorder, addresses bereavement-specific trauma that is characterized by debilitating symptoms of longing for the deceased that are atypically persistent and significantly impair functioning (APA, 2022a; Prigerson et al., 2021). References to stressor-related events in the *DSM-5-TR* also include circumstances that cause less adverse emotional effects for a shorter period of time (APA, 2022a). Whereas these events cause a distinct disturbance for an individual, sometimes to the point of social or occupational impairment, adverse emotional effects decrease once the stressor is removed (APA, 2022a). Examples of stressor-related events include relationship breakups, business difficulties or loss of a job, or marital problems. Developmental events, such as going away to school or retiring, can also cause serious stress.

Most people will experience a traumatic event within their lifetime. While trauma exposure is higher in lower income countries, with postconflict zones reporting the highest exposure risk, global epidemiological surveys demonstrate stability in terms of the types of events reported. Using a combined sample of 68,894 adults across 24 countries, Benjet et al. (2016) found accidents/injuries (36.3%), unexpected death of a loved one (31.4%), witnessing death or serious injury (36.9%), collective violence (9.4%), and life-threatening illness (5%) were the most frequently reported traumatic events, making up 51% of traumatic event reports across the seven continents investigated. These findings align with U.S.-based population studies on event type (Ogle et al., 2013). Also consistent across the literature are associations between trauma exposure and sociodemographic factors, such as gender, racial and ethnic identity, poverty, unemployment, lower levels of income and education, and access to affordable health care (Atwoli et al., 2015). Trauma is especially common in the lives of people with mental and substance use disorders. The Office of Disease Prevention and Health Promotion's (n.d.) even includes exposure to trauma as a social determinant of health. Therefore, the need to adequately assess, diagnose, and treat trauma is a vital part of the healing and recovery process. A part of this is understanding that different people will react differently to similar events. One person may experience an event as traumatic whereas another person may not suffer trauma from the same event.

As with many disorders found within Part Two of this book, prevalence of trauma-based disorders among the general population is high (APA, 2022a; Woolgar et al., 2022). According to the National Comorbidity Survey Replication (Kessler et al., 2005), the past year prevalence of PTSD was 3.5%, with a 3.6% lifetime prevalence among men and 9.7% prevalence among women (Schnurr, n.d.). Children and adolescents who have been exposed to traumatic events are 16% more likely to be diagnosed with PTSD. There are limited data on the prevalence of acute stress disorder, especially in the general population. Due to the nature of acute stress disorder, prevalence measurements are highly variable based on the assessment measure used and the nature of the trauma (Fanai & Khan, 2023). General prevalence statistics for acute stress disorder following a traumatic event range from 6% to 33% (Bryant, 2022). The prevalence of RAD is estimated to be 0.9% in children age 1.5 years (Skovgaard, 2010) and 1.40% in children ages 6 to 8 years (Minnis et al., 2013). Children who are orphaned or placed in foster care at an early age have a higher chance of developing RAD. The prevalence of adjustment disorders has been reported to be 0.9% in a general population sample (age range of 14 to 93 years old) that fulfilled the criterion of clinically significant impairment. Additionally, 1.4% of the sample was diagnosed with adjustment disorder without fulfilling the impairment criterion (Maercker et al., 2012). Between 3% and 10% of primary care patients have adjustment disorders (Fernández et al., 2012; Sundquist et al., 2017). Prevalence in patients in outpatient mental health treatment ranges from 5% to 20%. Individuals with high socioeconomic status backgrounds have lower levels of symptoms of adjustment disorder because they have more access to buyable resources (Lotzin et al., 2021) and a sense of stability and belonging to society (Mimoun et al., 2020).

Counselors should note that different people will react differently to similar events. One person may experience an event as traumatic whereas another person would not suffer trauma from the same event. Not all people who experience a potentially traumatic event will become psychologically traumatized. Counselors are advised to pay close attention to the neurological responses associated with trauma exposure, the impact of adverse childhood experiences on social determinants of health, and intersectional trauma. All of these are discussed in this chapter, and counselors who lack a clear understanding of these concepts are at risk of making grave diagnostic and case conceptualization errors.

Differential Diagnosis

The onset of trauma related to disorders in this chapter can be associated with increased risk of anxiety, depression, disordered eating, sleep disturbances, substance use problems, and suicidal ideation (APA, 2022a; Frommberger et al., 2014). It is not uncommon for individuals diagnosed with a traumatic disorder to also exhibit symptoms of somatic symptom disorder, impulse-control disorder, bipolar disorder, and ADHD. Symptoms of these disorders have also been linked to dissociative disorders. Many survivors of traumatic events, especially children, are often misdiagnosed with ADHD (Frommberger et al., 2014; Gibson, 2007). Children diagnosed with RAD or DSED are often mistaken for children with autism spectrum disorder (ASD), ADHD, or ODD and often have behavioral problems during childhood and adolescence (APA, 2022a; Davidson et al., 2015; Zeanah & Gleason, 2015). Cognitive and language delays or impairments often co-occur with RAD and DSED (Bruce et al., 2019; Gleason et al., 2011).

Etiology and Treatment

Given that the identification of a traumatic event is a requirement for any disorder in this chapter, we start the discussion of etiology and treatment with an explanation of how the definition of a traumatic event and subsequent examples within the nomenclature have changed. We believe it is important for counselors to understand this history, because it was only since 1980 that severe emotional disturbance as a direct result of trauma exposure was even considered a diagnosable disorder. Even then, only once—with the publication of the *DSM-5*—has the diagnostic criteria been significantly modified to reflect relevant research and clinical observations. As such, we strongly encourage counselors to fully understand relevant research on trauma and how symptoms manifest in the many varied client populations counselors serve. Plainly speaking, understanding the *DSM-5-TR* criteria is simply not enough. While this can be said about all disorders, it is particularly relevant to disorders found in this chapter.

Trauma and the *DSM*

In the *DSM-I* (APA, 1952), individuals were diagnosed with gross stress reaction resulting from psychological problems that arose as a result of military or civilian experiences (Friedman et al., 2011). However, the concept of gross stress reaction was criticized for not providing a solid foundation for diagnosing criteria. The *DSM-II* (APA, 1968) disposed of that diagnosis and developed the alternative diagnosis, situational reaction. Clinicians felt this diagnosis captured both traumatic and unpleasant events resulting from traumatic exposure. Both gross stress reaction and situational reaction were identified as being reversible and temporary disorders. However, in the late 1970s, mental health clinicians noticed patients were presenting with severe, chronic, and irreversible symptoms from exposure to traumatic events. This resulted in the *DSM-III* (APA, 1980) diagnostic criteria for PTSD that remained in existence until the publication of the *DSM-5*. Through the development of the diagnostic criteria for PTSD in the *DSM-5*, the possible symptoms increased from 12 to 17, the symptom clusters shifted, and more explicit attention to what represents and does not represent a traumatic event was evident (Friedman et al., 2011).

The addition of a fourth diagnostic cluster within the *DSM-5* criteria for PTSD was also significant. The change is a result of splitting up *DSM-IV-TR* Criterion C, avoidance and numbing, into two criteria: avoidance (Criterion C) and negative alterations in cognitions and mood (Criterion D). Avoidance and numbing were separated because of empirical evidence and clinical experiences that indicated at least one avoidance symptom (e.g., evasion of activities, thoughts, feelings, or conversations related to the event) was needed for an accurate PTSD diagnosis (Friedman et al., 2011). The cognition and mood criterion was added to the *DSM-5* because research indicates that shifts in cognition and emotion dysregulation are common to all individuals diagnosed with PTSD. See Table 10.1 for a breakdown of the four clusters and associated examples.

Neurobiological Explanations for Trauma

Traumatic events alter the brain's circuitry that causes the brain to attempt to protect the individual from further harm. Referred to by some as "survival mode," the commonly understood reference is an individual's fight, flight, or freeze response. This is an excellent yet simplistic example of the neurobiological response whereby an individual is presented with a traumatic stressor (i.e., being at gunpoint) and their brain, guided by the amygdala,

Table 10.1
Diagnostic Criteria of Posttraumatic Stress Disorder (PTSD)

PTSD Diagnostic Clusters	*Commonly Associated Examples*
Exposure (Criterion A): Direct experience; witnessing the event(s) in person; learning that a friend or close family member was directly affected by a traumatic event; repeated exposure to averse details of a traumatic event (exposure to electronic media is not considered repeated exposure).	
Cluster 1 (Criterion B): Intrusion	Recurrent, involuntary, and intrusive distressing memories or dreams of the traumatic event and dissociative reactions (i.e., flashbacks). In children, trauma-specific reenactment may occur in play. Intense distress or marked physiological reactions because of exposure to internal or external cues that symbolize or resemble an aspect of the traumatic event.
Cluster 2 (Criterion C): Avoidance (one or both)	Avoidance or attempts to avoid distressing memories, thoughts, or feelings or external reminders about or closely associated with the traumatic event.
Cluster 3 (Criterion D): Negative alterations in cognitions or mood (two or more)	Inability to recall an important aspect of the traumatic event, persistent negative beliefs of oneself, persistent distorted cognitions about the cause or consequences of the traumatic event, persistent negative emotional state, diminished interest in significant activities, or persistent inability to experience positive emotions. Represents myriad feelings a survivor can experience. Includes, but is not limited to, persistent and distorted sense of blame of self and others, estrangement, markedly diminished interest in activities, and problems remembering.
Cluster 4 (Criterion E): Arousal and reactivity (two or more)	Irritability and angry outbursts, recklessness, hypervigilance, exaggerated startle response, problems with concentration, or sleep disturbances.

commands the individual—either physically or verbally—to confront, flee/avoid, or become immobile (Baxter & Croxson, 2012). Neurobiological responses cause alterations in the way the limbic system functions, activation within the hypothalamic-pituitary-adrenal (HPA) axis resulting in cortisol level changes, and neurotransmitter dysregulation of arousal and endogenous opioid systems.

One function of the limbic system is to be responsible for emotional and behavioral responses, serving as a trauma "storage" center for the purpose of self-protection. For example, a child touches a hot stove and gets burned, so the limbic system captures data to avoid being hurt again. Cortisol is the body's "stress hormone," which is produced via interactions between the hypothalamus, pituitary gland, and adrenal glands, also known as the HPA axis. The HPA axis has an essential role in determining how the body responds to a traumatic stressor by serving as the pathway center for cortisol production. The HPA axis, for example, may be activated when an individual experiences a stressor, such as hearing a fire alarm and smelling smoke. A quick rise in cortisol levels can increase glucose (sugar) in the bloodstream and shut down nonessential functions, helping the body to focus on the immediate danger. This focused response would most likely be to get oneself and others to safety with all other body systems taking a "back seat" until the immediate danger is resolved. The endogenous opioid system regulates affective processing, including pleasure, reward, and pain, and can be thought of as the mechanism that shuts down pain so an individual can effectively respond to acute stress. For example, if an individual is physically hurt trying to escape a fire, their body may shut down pain receptors for the purpose of escaping additional harm.

While the term fight, flight, or freeze—or our own example—infers a neurological response to a specific event, trauma-informed counselors understand the depths by which a person's survival response can manifest emotionally, behaviorally, cognitively, physically, and spiritually to one or more events or circumstances. Limbic system dysfunction can cause misattribution of seemingly benign events. Blunted HPA axis dysfunction can lead to an inability for the body to properly regulate stress. Prolonged release of endogenous opioids can lead to flashbacks and intrusive thoughts. These are just a few examples of how traumatic or stressful events or circumstances may be physically or emotionally harmful to an individual and can involve a single experience or a long-lasting or repetitive event or events. Stated previously, trauma affects everyone differently (SAMHSA, 2014). However, there is one common factor encompassing all traumatic experiences: Traumatic events overwhelm a person's ability to cope and have both a physiological and psychological impact (Norris & Elrod, 2006; Tramontin & Halpern, 2007). Counselors working with clients who have experienced a trauma (or traumas) need to understand both the emotional and the behavioral manifestations of trauma, as well as the physiological impact of trauma within the body (Bicknell-Hentges & Lynch 2009; Rothschild, 2017).

Although a further review of the impact of trauma is outside the scope of this book, we do want to highlight that while trauma can occur at any age, it has particularly debilitating long-term impact on the developing brain of children and adolescents. We encourage all counselors to become intimately familiar with the impact of adverse childhood experiences on an individual's development and life span, associations between trauma and health risk, and the impact of trauma on inter- and intrapersonal relationships. We emphasize that protective factors are essential and, as discussed in Chapter 4 of this *Learning Companion*, being trauma-informed is best supported by a socioecological approach to client diagnosis and case conceptualization.

Case Conceptualization and Treatment

Having explained the research on the neurobiology of trauma and the historical shifts to the diagnostic nomenclature for trauma- and stressor-related disorders, we want to highlight that case conceptualization and treatment for trauma should focus on what "happened to" rather than what is "wrong with" a trauma survivor. Understanding this difference through a developmental, ecological, and neurobiological lens can better inform diagnostic assessment and associated treatment recommendations. To this end, the client's race, ethnicity, culture, and all other identities play a significant role in their experience of, exposure to, and recovery from interpersonal trauma (Bryant-Davis, 2019).

Trauma survivors hold multiple identities, and treatment must take an intersectional trauma approach. Intersectional trauma is a framework that includes sociostructural sources of trauma and stress, such as discrimination or historical trauma, that are sometimes ignored or overlooked in mental health practice (Ezell et al., 2021; K. S. Goodman, 2014; Kira et al., 2021). For decades, scholars of Indigenous communities have demonstrated that social determinants of health are rooted in historical trauma and systemic discrimination and oppression (Evans-Campbell et al., 2006; Williams-Washington & Mills, 2018). Historical trauma is a multigenerational social determinant of health emanating from mass cumulative harm to a specific cultural group. This is different from collective trauma, which can be defined as a shared traumatic experience, such as the global impact of the COVID-19 pandemic, across groups of people and/or communities (Watson et al., 2020).

Both historical and collective trauma can be carried forth to subsequent generations, but historical trauma is targeted at a specific cultural group. Using an intersectional approach, counselors must consider how clients' multiple ethnoracial, social, and personal contexts intersect with their experience of current and historical oppression.

Using an intersectional lens with our example of COVID-19 as a collective trauma explains why Black, Indigenous, and people of color (BIPOC) communities were more vulnerable than nonminority groups during the early months of the pandemic. The United States reported higher fatality rates and greater levels of economic uncertainty among the BIPOC communities (Dailey et al., 2022; Hooper et al., 2020; Yancy, 2020). Relative to European Americans, who had a mortality rate of 54.4 deaths per 100,000, the mortality rate for African Americans was 108.4 deaths per 100,000 and 73.5 for Latinx Americans. In March 2020, the same month that COVID-19 was declared a pandemic, 29 states and the District of Columbia reported statistically significant increases in unemployment, with higher reported disparities among low- or hourly-wage workers, women, and minorities (Solheim et al., 2022). Increased risk and vulnerability can be directly attributed to systemic health disparities, which existed well before the pandemic, and includes higher rates of comorbid medical conditions, lower levels of income and wealth, and limited access to health care (Hooper et al., 2020; Yancy, 2020). Although this is just one example, we cannot overemphasize the need for counselors to consider every client's cultural worldview and socialization when diagnosing and treating trauma- and stressor-related disorders.

The most common and empirically supported forms of treatment for trauma- and stressor-related disorders are cognitive behavioral approaches, including trauma-focused CBT (Cohen et al., 2006), mindfulness-based cognitive therapy (Segal et al., 2002), cognitive processing theory (Resick et al., 2016), and prolonged exposure therapy (Foa et al., 2019). There is also substantial evidence to support the use of mindfulness-based stress reduction (Kabat-Zinn, 2003), acceptance and commitment therapy (Hayes & Lillis, 2014), and eye movement desensitization and reprocessing (Shapiro, 2017). This is not an exhaustive list but only a reference point, and readers will note we have provided disorder-specific treatment recommendations within each section of this chapter.

Finally, regardless of their approach, counselors are encouraged to focus on the ways in which individuals cope with trauma, known as posttraumatic growth, which can be essential for understanding client healing and recovery (Tedeschi & Calhoun, 1996). Not only does this focus on the client's innate abilities to move through adversity, but it is also in direct alignment with the counselor's professional identity of promoting growth and well-being through the life span (ACA, 2014).

Implications for Counselors

It is important that counselors understand that the fundamental feature of trauma, rather than anxiety, serves as the driving force for the movement of trauma- and stressor-related disorders into a separate chapter. This follows the *ICD-10*, which also separates trauma from anxiety disorder (WHO, 2007). However, unlike the *ICD-10-CM*, which keeps trauma and anxiety disorder in the same larger category, the sequential order of this chapter in the *DSM-5-TR* following anxiety disorders and obsessive-compulsive and related disorders reflects the close relationship between trauma and anxiety. In addition to diagnostic similarities, these disorders are also grouped together in an effort to increase clinical utility (First, 2010).

Counselors must closely examine traumatic and stressor-related experiences and closely evaluate diagnostic criteria to accurately assess trauma and stressor-related impairments. With the lower diagnostic threshold for acute stress disorder and PTSD reflected in the *DSM-5* and *DSM-5-TR*, counselors need to be careful about diagnostic inflation, especially in children under the age of 6 (Frances, 2013). Counselors should note the *DSM-5-TR* is the first edition to mention that exposure to racism and discrimination and health disparities may be associated with increased prevalence and environmental conditions associated with PTSD. No other diagnostic category adequately associates historical trauma or systemic oppression to the manifestation of trauma- and stressor-related disorders, but we encourage counselors to consider changes made throughout the manual regarding culture, racism, and discrimination (see "Cultural and Social Structural Issues"; APA, 2022a, pp. 16–19). These changes and acknowledged limitations are particularly relevant to disorders in this chapter.

To help readers better understand disorders discussed in this chapter and associated diagnostic criteria, we outline each disorder within the Trauma- and Stressor-Related Disorders chapter of the *DSM-5-TR*. Readers should note that we have focused on general diagnostic considerations and criterion for each disorder; however, this is not a stand-alone resource for diagnosis. Although a summary and special considerations for counselors are provided for each disorder, when diagnosing clients, counselors need to reference the *DSM-5-TR*. It is essential that the diagnostic criteria and features, subtypes and specifiers (if applicable), prevalence, course, and risk and prognostic factors for each disorder are clearly understood prior to diagnosis.

Reactive Attachment Disorder (F94.1)

> We adopted John when he was 6 years old. He never knew his birth parents and, prior to our adoption, was shuffled from institution to institution. After having been with us for 1 year, John continues to be severely withdrawn, refusing any forms of affection even when he is upset. He doesn't seem to interact with any other children and seems fearful of anyone getting close to him. Even when others try to interact with him or comfort him, he doesn't respond.—Emma (John's mom)

Reactive attachment disorder (RAD) is characterized by markedly disturbed and developmentally inappropriate social relatedness in children before the age of 5 (APA, 2022a; Pritchett et al., 2013; Sadiq et al., 2012). There is broad consensus among clinicians that this disorder results from an extremely inadequate caregiving environment and is directly associated with grossly pathological care. Children diagnosed with RAD continuously fail to initiate or respond to social interactions.

Essential Features

Typically seen before the age of 5, children diagnosed with RAD have not had the opportunity to form stable attachments and have experienced persistent disregard of their basic physical and emotional needs for comfort, stimulation, and affection (APA, 2022a; Schechter & Willheim, 2009; Widom et al., 2009). Symptoms of RAD include detachment, unresponsiveness, or resistance to comforting, holding back emotions, withdrawal from others, and a mixture of approach and avoidance behaviors (APA, 2022a; Zeanah & Gleason, 2015). Children diagnosed with RAD have no developmental delays. Limited epidemiological data exist for this disorder, but it is relatively uncommon. Only a minority of children with severe caretaking deficiencies or abnormalities develop RAD.

Major Changes From *DSM-5 to DSM-5*-TR

Excluding text revisions made throughout the entire manual, there are no changes from the DSM-5 to the DSM-5-TR for RAD. However, in the DSM-IV-TR, RAD was located within the Disorders Usually First Diagnosed in Infancy, Childhood, or Adolescence chapter and included two specifiers: *inhibited* and *disinhibited type*. Disinhibited type, characterized by indiscriminate social skills marked by a child's inability to exhibit appropriate attachments, is no longer included as a criterion for this disorder (APA, 2022a; Zeanah & Gleason, 2010).

Upon release of the DSM-5, this specifier was moved to a separate disorder, disinhibited social engagement disorder (see next section).

Special Considerations

RAD is not diagnosed when children, despite abuse or maltreatment, can still form attachments and are not markedly maladjusted (Schechter & Willheim, 2009; Zeanah & Gleason, 2010). RAD should be differentiated from ASD, which can develop within a relatively supportive setting (APA, 2022a). Although RAD can present like ADHD, it is different because children who are diagnosed with ADHD will form attachments (Zeanah & Gleason, 2010). RAD is not applicable to children with developmental delays or neurological damage. Finally, RAD does not apply to rebellious behavior, which develops in preadolescent and adolescent children who previously had strong attachments with caregivers. Critics of this diagnosis point to limited research with contradictory findings (cf. Allen, 2016; Chaffin et al., 2006).

Common approaches to treating RAD are based on attachment theory and concentrate on increasing the responsiveness and sensitivity of the caregiver, or if that is not possible, placing the child with a different caregiver (Prior & Glaser, 2006). Prevention programs are also important, especially to target problematic early attachment behaviors in both children and caregivers. Cohen et al. (2010) identified the parameters mental health practitioners should focus on when working with children diagnosed with RAD. The first goal is to ensure the child is in a safe and stable environment that can provide for physical and emotional needs. The second goal focuses on how the child can begin to develop an appropriate, healthy attachment with their primary caregiver(s).

Counselors should be aware that neglected children are often at risk for developmental delays, dialectical deficits/disorders, and neglect of medical concerns (Prior & Glaser, 2006). Counselors must remember that all cases of abuse, neglect, and exploitation must be reported. Therefore, counselors need to be familiar with their local and state laws regarding mandated reporting, and their actions need to be in compliance with the *ACA Code of Ethics* (ACA, 2014).

Social and Cultural Considerations

As stated previously, there has been little research on RAD (APA, 2022a; Zeanah & Gleason, 2010). This means that counselors should pay particular attention when making a diagnosis of RAD, especially for cultural groups in which attachment has not been thoroughly studied (APA, 2022a). Because attachment behavior varies greatly from one cultural group to another, counselors must use caution to determine that the child's attachment behavior is markedly disturbed and developmentally inappropriate as defined by the child's cultural norms before making a diagnosis of RAD.

Differential Diagnosis

Pervasive developmental disorders or developmental delays, particularly ASD and intellectual developmental disorder, are commonly considered differential diagnoses (APA, 2022a). Criticisms of RAD are that previous criteria from the *DSM-IV-TR* focused too much on social behavior and not attachment behavior; for example, how a child seeks comfort, support, nurturance, and protection from a preferred attachment figure in times of fear or distress. Focusing on social behavior runs the risk of overlapping with ASD rather than an attachment disorder. Counselors should carefully assess for history of severe neglect, even if this can be difficult given symptom presentation and recall in children as well as absence of repetitive behavior and selective impairments in social communication, both of which are characteristic of ASD (APA, 2022a). In terms of intellectual functioning, children with RAD demonstrate parallel communicative and intellectual functioning.

Coding, Recording, and Specifiers

There is only one diagnostic code for RAD: F94.1. There are two specifiers for this disorder: *persistent*, which is used when the disorder has been present for more than 12 months, and *severe*, when there is evidence of all symptoms, and each has a relatively high level of occurrence. There are no codes associated with these specifiers.

Disinhibited Social Engagement Disorder (F94.2)

> We don't know what to do. Jamaal runs up to strangers and is willing to run away with anyone. One day he even got into a stranger's car while we were at the supermarket. He is distant from us and has been ever since we adopted him 1 year ago. I worry about his safety while at school or away from my partner and I.—Jamaal's father

Disinhibited social engagement disorder (DSED) is a relatively new diagnosis and was first presented as an independent disorder in the *DSM-5* (APA, 2022a). This disorder represents the indiscriminate *social/disinhibited* subtype of the *DSM-IV-TR* childhood diagnosis of RAD (Zeanah & Gleason, 2010). Now considered a distinct disorder, DSED is characterized by a pattern of behavior in which the child actively approaches and interacts with unfamiliar adults (APA, 2022a; Zeanah & Gleason, 2010).

Essential Features

Children diagnosed with DSED do not exhibit developmentally appropriate discretion with unfamiliar adults and may engage in overly familiar behavior with strangers (APA, 2022a; Zeanah & Gleason, 2010). In familiar or unfamiliar settings, these childre n may venture away from a primary caregiver and often are willing to go off with an unfamiliar adult with minimal or no hesitation. Like RAD, the origin of these symptoms is grossly inadequate caregiving that failed to meet the child's basic emotional or physical needs and safety (Schechter & Willheim, 2009; Widom et al., 2009). Risk factors for DSED include repeated changes in caregivers or being raised in unconventional settings, such as an orphanage or institution that severely limited the child's ability to form secure attachments.

Special Considerations

Counselors need to be careful not to overdiagnose RAD or DSED in children who are adopted, living in a foster home, or have been mistreated by their caregiver (APA, 2022a). Children with RAD and DSED are presumed to have grossly disturbed internal models for relating to others; therefore, treatment should involve both the caretaker and the child (Prior & Glaser, 2006). Counselors should not attempt to change the child but rather should focus on changing the child's surroundings and creating positive interactions with caregivers. As with RAD, counselors must be sure the child with DSED is in a safe and stable environment where they can get appropriate care, and counselors should always be aware that neglected children are often at risk for developmental delays, dialectical deficits/disorders, and neglect of medical concerns (Prior & Glaser, 2006). All cases of abuse, neglect, and exploitation must be reported, and counselors need to be familiar with mandated reporting laws as well as the *ACA Code of Ethics* (ACA, 2014).

Social and Cultural Considerations

There has been little research on DSED (APA, 2022a; Zeanah & Gleason, 2010). Similar to RAD, counselors should pay particular attention when making a diagnosis of DSED in cultures in which attachment has not been studied. Because attachment behavior varies greatly from one cultural group to another, counselors must use caution and determine that the child's attachment behaviors are inappropriate as defined by the child's cultural norms before making a DSED diagnosis.

Differential Diagnosis

DSED can be mistaken for ADHD (APA, 2022a; Frances, 2013). Although the symptoms of DSED are inattentiveness and impulsivity, the etiology of DSED—inadequate caregiving and neglect—is what differentiates this disorder from other impulse-control disorders or ADHD (Zeanah & Gleason, 2010). Similar to RAD, counselors must be sure to distinguish DSED from pervasive developmental disorders (Zeanah & Gleason, 2010). Counselors should also be sure the client does not have the genetic disorder Williams syndrome, characterized by mild to moderate intellectual disability (Zeanah & Gleason, 2010). Children with Williams syndrome have unique facial features and distinct personality traits of overfriendliness, anxiety, and high levels of empathy (Mervis & John, 2008).

Note: Counselors must be careful to differentiate RAD and DSED from PTSD. To do so, look for emotional regulation problems and aggression, as these are not core symptoms of either RAD or DSED. Whereas maladaptive care can be defined as trauma, problems with attachment to caregiver prior to 5 years old are distinct features of RAD and DSED and should not be misdiagnosed with PTSD.

Coding, Recording, and Specifiers

There is only one diagnostic code for DSED: F94.2. Counselors will note the *DSM-5* used the same *ICD-9-CM* code for RAD and DSED (i.e., 313.89), but each disorder has a separate diagnostic code in the *DSM-5-TR*. A similar code, with .2 as opposed to the .1 given for RAD, is listed under the *ICD-10-CM*. The reason these are the same in the *ICD-9-CM* but not the *ICD-10-CM* is because the *disinhibited type* specifier was listed under RAD in the *DSM-IV-TR*. When the *DSM-5* and the *ICD-10-CM* were published, DSED was listed as a separate diagnosis. There are two specifiers for this disorder. The specifier *persistent* is used when the disorder has been present for more than 12 months, and *severe* is used when there is evidence of all symptoms, and each has a relatively high level of occurrence. There are no codes associated with these specifiers.

Posttraumatic Stress Disorder (F43.10)

> About a year ago, I was in a major car accident. Although I sustained only minor injuries, two of my friends were killed. At first, the accident seemed like just a bad dream. Then the nightmares started. Now, the sights and sounds of the accident haunt me all the time. I have trouble sleeping at night, and during the day I feel "on edge." I jump whenever I hear a siren or screeching tires, and I avoid TV altogether as I might find a program that shows a car chase or accident scene. I avoid driving when possible.—Amanda

Posttraumatic stress disorder (PTSD) applies only if someone has been exposed to one or more traumatic or stressful events or circumstances. Without severe trauma, a diagnosis of PTSD cannot be made. A *traumatic stressor* is defined in the *DSM-5-TR* as "any event (or events) that may cause or threaten death, serious injury, or sexual violence to an individual, a close family member, or a close friend" (APA, 2022a, p. 830). Critics have argued that this definition does not include nonviolent trauma such as emotional abuse; therefore, counselors should be careful if considering traumas such as emotional neglect and verbal abuse as triggering stressors for PTSD (Frances, 2013).

As mentioned earlier, the past-year prevalence of PTSD was 3.5%, with a 3.6% lifetime prevalence among men and 9.7% among women. No population-based epidemiological studies have been conducted to examine the prevalence rates in children; however, children who have been exposed to specific traumatic events are at greater risk of prevalence of PTSD.

Major Changes From *DSM-5* to *DSM-5-TR*

The *DSM-5-TR* retains the same criteria as the *DSM-5*, with only one major modification to diagnostic criteria that removed a redundant "note" under the diagnostic criteria for PTSD in children 6 years and younger. However, before highlighting this very minor change and reviewing each disorder, we provide a detailed history of the first time, since being introduced into the diagnostic nomenclature, that the criteria set for PTSD was modified under the *DSM-5*. We believe this history provides more context for counselors and better explains future efforts for continued research and understanding of diagnostic concerns related to trauma exposure.

Previously classified in the *DSM-IV-TR* as an anxiety disorder, PTSD underwent substantial changes in the *DSM-5*. Compared with the *DSM-IV-TR*, *DSM-5-TR* diagnostic criteria for PTSD include more explicit attention to what represents, and does not represent, a traumatic event. Within the diagnostic features description, APA (2022a) lists exposure to war as a combatant or civilian, childhood physical abuse, and threatened or actual sexual violence, with a wide range of examples to give a clearer picture of traumatic exposure. References to concentration camps and being diagnosed with a life-threatening illness were removed, but the *DSM-5-TR* does clarify that medical illnesses in which a shocking or catastrophic event occurs (e.g., waking during surgery or anaphylactic shock) may be considered traumatic (APA, 2013a, 2022a; Frances, 2013). The *DSM-5-TR* also offers clarification in Criterion A.3, which states that accidental or violent traumatic events, such as automobile fatalities in which a close family member or friend is involved, can be traumatic (APA, 2013a, 2022a). This clarification, although technically not new to the *DSM*, is controversial because of the potential for exploitation in forensic proceedings, which often use the diagnosis of PTSD for determination of disability or damages compensation. Because the symptoms of PTSD are entirely based on client self-reports, counselors should caution against the misuse of the PTSD diagnosis in forensic settings (Frances, 2013).

New to the *DSM-5*, and retained in the *DSM-5-TR*, is Criterion A.4, which includes recurring or intense exposure, such as extreme traumas frequently witnessed by police officers and first responders (APA, 2013a, 2022a). The addition of this criterion is in response to research that supports the idea that individuals who have regular exposure to traumatic events, such as persons who handle the deceased and other first responders, are at risk for developing PTSD (Tramontin & Halpern, 2007; Ursano, 2004). Although this criterion does not apply to media, television accounts, photos, or movies, *occupational* exposure to events (e.g., exposure of reporters to traumatic events) is included.

Another major change from the *DSM-IV-TR* to the *DSM-5-TR* is the introduction of four, as opposed to three, diagnostic clusters. As discussed, the change is a result of splitting up *DSM-IV-TR* Criterion C, avoidance and numbing, into two criteria: avoidance (Criterion C) and negative alterations in cognitions and mood (Criterion D). Avoidance and numbing were separated because of empirical evidence and clinical experiences that indicated at least one avoidance symptom (e.g., evasion of activities, thoughts, feelings, or conversations related to the event) is needed for an accurate PTSD diagnosis (Friedman et al., 2011). The cognition and mood criterion was added because research indicates that shifts in cognition and emotion dysregulation are common to all individuals diagnosed with PTSD. See Table 10.1 for a breakdown of the four clusters and associated examples.

Other changes to PTSD are related to subtypes. The *DSM-5* includes two new subtypes, the *dissociative* subtype and the *preschool* subtype (APA, 2013a, 2022a), and these are retained in the *DSM-5-TR*. The dissociative subtype is used when PTSD is seen with prominent dissociative symptoms, which are categorized as either depersonalization or derealization. *Depersonalization* includes feelings of detachment from one's own mind or body, "as if one were an outside observer of one's mental processes or body" (APA, 2022a, p. 272). *Derealization* includes experiences in which the world seems unreal, illusory, or distorted. Sometimes referred to as "complex PTSD," this subtype would most likely be seen when an individual has been exposed to multiple traumas, particularly in childhood, that result in a complex range of symptoms.

The preschool subtype is used for children under 6 years old. Not previously recognized within the *DSM* nomenclature, the inclusion of PTSD criteria for children 6 years and younger represents one of the most significant changes from the *DSM-IV-TR* to the *DSM-5*. In general, the diagnostic threshold is lowered for children and exposure is associated with different types of events. The criteria for children 6 years and younger emphasize the impact of traumatic events on children when primary caregivers are involved (see Criterion A.2 for children 6 years and younger), clarify that play reenactment may serve as a catalyst for recurrent or intrusive memories, and only require that either persistent avoidance of stimuli or negative alterations in cognitions and mood be present. This contrasts with the diagnostic criteria for individuals over the age of 6, which require that individuals avoid stimuli and have negative alterations in cognition and mood. The criteria for children under 6 also remove references related to recollection of the event and negative beliefs of self. Children under 6 are not necessarily capable of expressing feelings related to their negative beliefs or expectations of self. Problems such as work-related events and reckless, self-destructive behavior were also not included in this diagnostic set because they are not applicable to children. The inclusion of this new criteria set in the *DSM-5*, and retained in the *DSM-5-TR*, markedly expanded the possibilities for counselors working with children exhibiting traumatic stress and symptoms to include access to health and behavioral health care and increased research regarding prevalence, symptom manifestation, and treatment efficacy.

Another significant change in the *DSM-5* and carried forward in the *DSM-5-TR* is the removal of what was formerly known in the *DSM-IV-TR* as Criterion A.2. This criterion mandated that a response of intense fear, helplessness, or horror to the event must be present for a diagnosis of PTSD. This language has been deleted because the reactions of intense fear, helplessness, or horror do not predict the onset of PTSD (APA, 2013c). Understanding a person's reaction to trauma is a complex task because emotional responses, like traumatic events, vary considerably; counselors should never attempt to identify a "normal" reaction to traumatic stress. Ursano et al. (1994) summarized this exposure well by stating, "Overall, most individuals exposed to traumatic events and disasters do quite well . . . but for some psychiatric illness, behavioral change, or alterations in physical health result. Certainly, no one goes through profound life events unchanged" (p. 5). Finally, what *DSM-IV-TR* called delayed onset is now called *delayed expression*.

Essential Features

Characteristic PTSD symptoms include daytime memories, images, or flashbacks of the event or events (APA, 2022a). Individuals may experience physiological or emotional stress when they encounter reminders of the event, and any potential triggers, even if only remotely related to the event, must be avoided. Many persons with PTSD also become disconnected from others, find little meaning in life or the future, are indifferent in their relationships, have trouble sleeping and concentrating, and may seem to be constantly tense or "on guard." Nightmares and survivor guilt are also common. Symptoms must be present for more than 1 month and, like most clinical diagnoses, cause significant impairment or distress.

> ***Note:*** For a diagnosis of PTSD, there must be exposure to severe trauma. In addition, stress must be relived in some fashion, and clients must attempt to avoid stimuli associated with the trauma, including memories or external reminders of the trauma. Clients must also have cognitive problems and marked changes in their emotional state. Symptoms must last over 1 month, and stress must cause significant distress or impairment. None of these issues may be due to a substance or medical condition.

Counselors should pay particular attention to ensure that all criteria are met for PTSD, not just exposure to an extreme stressor. These additional criteria, as stated previously, include intrusion, avoidance, negative alteration in cognitions and mood, and alterations in arousal and reactivity. These additional criteria are often referred to as "clusters" and are discussed in detail in the next section and outlined in Table 10.1.

Special Considerations

The new Trauma- and Stressor-Related Disorders chapter in the *DSM-5-TR* requires counselors to closely examine premorbid experiences and the new diagnostic criteria to categorize distress and functional impairments. Because all individuals respond to trauma differently, it is important that counselors understand that symptoms of PTSD manifest in various ways. Some clients will reexperience the trauma through nightmares and violent flashbacks, others will be unable to experience pleasure or will have negative core beliefs about themselves, and some others will display a combination of symptoms.

An important consideration for counselors are the risk and prognostic factors in the *DSM-5-TR*, which indicate a predictable pattern of elements that either place clients at risk or serve as protective factors. Separated by pre- and posttrauma, these include emotional, environmental, and genetic or physiological factors. Pretraumatic emotional factors include temperamental or psychiatric problems. Environmental factors include socioeconomic status, education level, and previous exposure to trauma. Genetic factors include gender and age. Inclusion of these elements is based on research that indicates that factors such as age (B. L. Green & Solomon, 1995), gender (Rubonis & Bickman, 1991), ethnicity (Perilla et al., 2002), socioeconomic status (Bolin, 1986; Epstein et al., 1998), and marital and familial status (Gleser et al., 1981; Solomon & Smith, 1994) can be predictive of survivor mental health outcomes. For example, ethnoracial groups, females, younger adults, and individuals with a history of trauma often do not fare as well as their counterparts (B. L. Green, 1990; Norris & Elrod, 2006). It is important to note that these populations are also more frequently exposed to stressors such as rape, domestic violence, and acculturative stress.

Social and Cultural Considerations

In addition to the risk and prognostic factors described previously, counselors should also carefully consider culture-related variations in the type of exposure, severity, and clinical expression of symptoms, as well as the ongoing sociocultural context in relation to the client's diagnosis. Counselors must not forget that clinical presentation of symptoms is culturally specific and may significantly affect clinical expression, particularly with respect to avoidance/numbing and somatic symptoms (Hinton & Lewis-Fernández, 2010). For example, Hinton and Lewis-Fernández (2010) reported that post-9/11 studies found higher rates of panic attacks for Latino Americans (13.4% to 16.8%), a risk factor for PTSD, compared with non-Latinos (5.5%). This can primarily be explained by *ataque de nervios* (attack of nerves), a relatively common manifestation of distress among Latino Americans. Commonly reported symptoms include uncontrollable shouting, attacks of crying, and trembling. Also common are dissociative symptoms; seizure-like or fainting episodes and suicidal gestures are also prominent. Moreover, there is a cultural perception among some Latino Americans that older members of the community need to always maintain control of their emotions; this may account for instances of dissociation regarding emotional responses. For example, when asked about emotional responses to trauma, some Latino clients will respond "*ese no era yo*," which translates to "that was not me" (Lewis-Fernández et al., 2005). Other examples include mental health clinicians working with Cambodians who experienced the torture and brutality inflicted by the Khmer Rouge regime (Van de Put & Eisenbruch, 2004). Some of the survivors described themselves as "thinking too much" (Van de Put & Eisenbruch, 2004, p. 137), which later was described as "Cambodian sickness" (p. 137). Although this study was conducted in the early 1980s, clinicians later noted the symptoms bore similarities to PTSD (Van de Put & Eisenbruch, 2004). Studies such as these reveal how imperative it is for counselors to develop multicultural expertise when working with trauma survivors and to include cultural considerations in all diagnostic assessments.

Differential Diagnosis

PTSD cannot be diagnosed if symptoms are present for less than 1 month. Instead, a diagnosis of acute stress disorder is made if symptoms are present for less than a month. Adjustment disorders should be assigned for clients who have experienced traumatic stress but do not express all other diagnostic criteria for a diagnosis of PTSD or, conversely, if a client presents with PTSD criteria but the stressor is not extreme enough to meet Criterion A (e.g., divorce, losing one's job, business difficulties). Counselors should also consider other anxiety, depressive, dissociative, or psychotic disorders or traumatic brain injury. In terms of comorbid diagnoses, clients with PTSD are 80% more likely to meet diagnostic criteria for other psychiatric diagnoses (Kessler et al., 1995). Substance use disorder and conduct disorders are common, and co-occurrence of PTSD is 48% among those who have experienced traumatic brain injury. Comorbidity is also high in children with PTSD, with ODD and separation anxiety disorder most frequently seen. Finally, counselors should look for neurocognitive disorders because clients who experience head injuries may experience a number of overlapping symptoms (APA, 2022a).

Coding, Recording, and Specifiers

There is only one diagnostic code for PTSD: F43.10; however, counselors must indicate whether the diagnosis is for an adult or for a child under 6 in the written name of the disorder. Counselors may also select two specifiers, as applicable, for both adults and children under 6 years old. The first specifier indicates whether an individual has persistent and recurrent symptoms of dissociation. When indicating *with dissociative symptoms*, counselors will also identify a subtype of depersonalization or derealization. The specifier subtype will be indicated in the written name of the disorder, for example, F43.10 PTSD for children 6 years and younger, *with dissociative symptoms, depersonalization*. The second specifier for PTSD is *with delayed expression*, formerly known as delayed onset. Whereas the typical course of symptoms begins within the first 3 months, this newly renamed specifier recognizes that there may be a delay of months or even years before full criteria for PTSD are met. For counselors, this means that in the aftermath of the trauma, an individual may meet the criteria for acute stress disorder (see next section) rather than PTSD. There are no codes assigned to either of these specifiers. If panic attacks are present with PTSD, counselors may add the specifier *with panic attacks*.

Diagnostic Criteria

Diagnostic criteria for PTSD in adults, adolescents, and children older than 6 years require the individual to have been exposed to actual or threatened death, serious injury, or sexual violation. They may have directly experienced the traumatic event(s), witnessed it happening to others, or learned that it happened to a close family member or friend (APA, 2022a). Additionally, they may have experienced repeated or extreme exposure to aversive details of the event(s). The presence of intrusion symptoms is important, such as distressing memories, nightmares, flashbacks, or intense psychological distress when exposed to reminders of the event or events (APA, 2022a). Persistent avoidance of stimuli associated with the trauma, such as memories or external reminders, is another criterion (APA, 2022a). Negative alterations in cognitions and mood, such as distorted beliefs, persistent negative emotions, detachment, or inability to experience positive emotions, are assessed. Marked alterations in arousal and reactivity, including irritability, hypervigilance, concentration difficulties, and sleep disturbances, are considered. The duration of symptoms should persist for more than 1 month and cause significant distress or impairment in functioning (APA, 2022a). It is crucial to rule out symptoms attributable to substance use or other medical conditions.

Additional specifications of *with dissociative symptoms* or *with delayed expression* can be made. The *with dissociative symptoms* specifier is appropriate if individuals also experience persistent or recurrent symptoms of depersonalization (feeling detached from one's mental processes or body) or derealization (feeling the world is unreal or distorted; APA, 2022a; Hyland et al., 2018). If the full diagnostic criteria are not met until at least 6 months after the traumatic event(s), the *with delayed expression* specifier is appropriate, even for cases in which some symptoms appear immediately (APA, 2022a). These criteria are used to diagnose PTSD in adults, adolescents, and children older than 6 years. Different criteria apply to children 6 years and younger.

The diagnostic criteria for PTSD in children 6 years and younger require the child to have been exposed to actual or threatened death, serious injury, or sexual violence by directly experiencing the traumatic event(s), witnessing it happening to others (especially primary caregivers), or learning that it happened to a parent or caregiver (APA, 2022a). Intrusion symptoms associated with the trauma include distressing memories, distressing dreams, dissociative reactions, intense distress when exposed to reminders of the event, and marked physiological reactions. Persistent avoidance of stimuli associated with the event(s) or negative alterations in cognitions and mood are observed, such as avoiding activities or physical reminders, reduced interest in activities, socially withdrawn behavior, and diminished expression of positive emotions. Alterations in arousal and reactivity are also present, including irritable behavior, hypervigilance, exaggerated startle response, concentration problems, and sleep disturbances. The duration of the disturbance should be more than 1 month and cause clinically significant distress or impairment in relationships or school behavior (APA, 2022a). The disturbance should not be due to substance use or another medical condition. Additional specifications can be made for dissociative symptoms (depersonalization and derealization) and delayed expression of symptoms. It is important to note that the dissociative and preschool subtypes can co-occur, and the diagnosis of PTSD is recommended only when the child has directly experienced the traumatic event or events (APA, 2022a; Hyland et al., 2018).

Case Example

> Officer Teixeira was referred to mental health support services by her husband, who is concerned about her "unpredictable mood swings" and nightmares. He stated that these have been going on for about 9 months and seem to be getting worse. In addition, although no formal action has been taken, Officer Teixeira has had two complaints of using unwarranted force in apprehending offenders. When she comes into counseling, she reports she is seriously at risk of losing her current position. When asked if there are any recent events that might have contributed to her rapid change in behavior, she states she just hasn't been herself since one "horrific case" that took place 9 months ago involving a teenage girl.
>
> Officer Teixeira vividly recalls the details of this case. "She was only 15 when she was attacked by a group of men on the way home from school. They took turns screaming abuse at her and then they each raped her. Finally, they tried

to stab her to death and would almost certainly have succeeded had we not arrived on the scene. I don't know what is worse, the fact that this happened to her or the fact that this is by no means the worst case I have seen."

Officer Teixeira reports being unable to keep the memories of the attack out of her mind. At night, she has terrible dreams of rape and often wakes up screaming. She has had significant difficulty policing her route, especially those areas where she has seen violence. Because of this, she has volunteered to take a desk job, something she never thought she would do. She also avoids any cases in which the victims have been raped, beaten, or abused. Despite these actions, she still feels as if her emotions are numb and that she has no real future in the police force. At home, she is anxious, tense, and easily startled. She is unable to concentrate on anything and reports feeling helpless and shamed that she can't do more to help these victims.

Diagnostic Questions

1. Do Officer Teixeira's presenting symptoms meet the criteria for PTSD?
2. Which symptom(s) led you to select that diagnosis?
3. What rule-outs would you consider for Officer Teixeira's case?
4. What other information may be needed to make an accurate clinical diagnosis?

Acute Stress Disorder (F43.0)

> I just don't know what has happened to Marie. A week ago, she was completely normal, then all of a sudden she is a mess! Ever since she saw that apartment on fire, she has been a complete wreck. She can't sleep, she can't work, and she seems like she is in a daze all the time.—Ronald (Marie's husband)

Introduced in the *DSM-IV* (APA, 1994), acute stress disorder identifies individuals experiencing acute stress responses, as opposed to transitory stress, as a result of exposure to a traumatic event. The inclusion of acute stress disorder was a major diagnostic landmark in the early 1990s because, for nearly a century, the presentation of trauma-like symptoms was referred to only in military populations. Terms such as "shell shock," "war hysteria," or "war neurosis" (Van der Kolk et al., 1996) were commonly used to describe soldiers' reactions to combat.

In addition to identifying acute stress reactions, the overarching goal of acute stress disorder in the *DSM-IV-TR* was to identify people who may be at risk for PTSD. More recent studies, however, have questioned the capacity of acute stress disorder to sufficiently identify persons at risk for PTSD (Bryant et al., 2011). Therefore, counselors should not assume that acute stress disorder is a predictor of PTSD and instead use the criteria presented to help identify acute stress reactions and people who may benefit from early intervention. Research showing that acute stress disorder does not necessarily predict PTSD as well as evidence that acute posttraumatic reactions are exceedingly heterogeneous fueled changes to acute stress disorder in the *DSM-5-TR*.

Major Changes From *DSM-5* to *DSM-5-TR*

As is the case with PTSD, the exposure criterion (Criterion A) for acute stress disorder has changed from the *DSM-IV-TR* to *DSM-5* and is retained in the *DSM-5-TR*. A diagnosis of acute stress disorder requires that exposure to an extreme stressor must meet one of the following criteria: experiencing the event directly; witnessing the event in person; learning that an event occurred to a close family member or friend; or having repeated, first-hand experience with trauma that is not the result of nonwork-related media, pictures, television, or movies (APA, 2022a). As with PTSD, Criterion A for acute stress disorder includes repeated or extreme exposure.

Because of evidence that acute posttraumatic reactions are significantly varied, acute stress disorder requires the presence of nine out of 14 symptoms within five categories (APA, 2022a). Prior iterations of the diagnostic criteria for acute stress disorder within the *DSM-IV-TR* were overly restrictive, requiring that individuals have three or more dissociative symptoms. First and foremost, this was very concerning to mental health professionals given that research on dissociative symptoms as a predictor of PTSD is not conclusive (Breh & Seidler, 2007; Van der Velden et al., 2006). Second, requiring dissociative symptoms disregarded other high-risk persons from being identified, thus limiting services that may be available (Bryant et al., 2011). Third, there is significant literature that highlights dissociative symptoms as a common transient stress response not indicative of psychopathology (Bryant, 2007; Bryant et al., 2011). This argument is also applicable to arousal, which is often observed as a normal stress response and not pertinent to either acute stress disorder or PTSD. As such, we emphasize that counselors—particularly those trained using the *DSM-IV-TR* and earlier iterations—refrain from focusing too much on disassociation. As such, we emphasize that counselors refrain from focusing too much on disassociation or arousal and focus more fully on the client's experience and associated symptoms.

Finally, like other modifications made to the *DSM-5* and carried over to the *DSM-5-TR*, the criteria for this disorder more closely match the definition of acute stress reaction in the *ICD-10-CM*. This more comprehensive description of acute stress is believed to be more useful because the focus is on symptoms rather than specific clusters, which may warrant intervention (e.g., sleep disturbances) but not necessarily predict PTSD. The *ICD-10-CM* goes further to claim that acute stress reactions cannot be categorized into specific response sets (Bryant et al., 2011); therefore, clusters are not useful in the detection of acute posttraumatic stress.

Essential Features

The clinical presentation for acute stress disorder is equivalent to PTSD with two exceptions. First, symptom duration of acute stress disorder is more than 3 days but less than 1 month (APA, 2022a). Second, acute stress disorder does not require symptom clusters. Although clinical presentation varies from person to person, it is not uncommon for those diagnosed with acute stress disorder to have some form of reexperiencing (e.g., flashbacks) or hypervigilance. Detachment or strong reactivity, whether physiological or emotional, is typical when survivors are exposed to reminders of the event. Others can experience reactivity in the form of heightened emotional responses, such as anger, aggression, grief, or problems with concentration (Bryant et al., 2011). Because of the short duration, acute stress disorder has no specifiers; it can be diagnosed in both children and adults.

Special Considerations

Recognizing the heterogeneity of stress responses among individuals, the *DSM-5-TR* diagnosis of acute stress disorder serves to help practitioners differentiate between transient stress responses, which are normal, and acute stress reactions, which may require clinical attention. Counselors must remember that strong emotional, behavioral, cognitive, physiological, and spiritual responses are common among survivors of traumatic events. Although these responses vary significantly from individual to individual, feelings of distress are common and are often normal reactions to a catastrophic event. Differentiating what is a normal reaction from an abnormal one can help counselors better determine which clients may require interventions or, in some cases, be at risk for developing PTSD.

Social and Cultural Considerations

Children and adolescents diagnosed with acute stress disorder have been found to have a greater range of emotional difficulties when they experience a trauma (Salmond et al., 2011). There may also be a difference in the level or duration of trauma between Western and non-Western studies. Western studies often focus on one-time events such as an accident or some similar event in which the sample is selected from a hospital, whereas many non-Western studies tend to focus on events that might be ongoing and do not have a specific start and stop time. The situations and environments between Western and non-Western studies are likely to lend themselves to looking at trauma from different perspectives (Bryant et al., 2011).

Differential Diagnosis

Counselors who work with clients who have experienced a brain injury in the context of the traumatic event will need to ensure symptoms are not better accounted for by a diagnosis of neurocognitive disorder attributable to traumatic brain injury. Panic attacks are not uncommon in clients who present with acute stress. If these attacks are unexpected and there is considerable anxiety about future attacks, then counselors will want to consider whether a diagnosis of panic disorder better accounts for the client's symptom profile.

It is also important to consider both duration of symptoms and the type of stressor when diagnosing acute stress disorder. In doing so, counselors must consider whether symptoms have been present for more than 1 month so as to rule out PTSD. Counselors must also consider whether the associated stressor meets the criteria for acute stress disorder as opposed to an adjustment disorder. The diagnosis of adjustment disorder is used when the stressor does not meet Criterion A for exposure to actual or threatened death, serious injury, or sexual violence. For example, a person losing their job would not meet Criterion A for acute stress disorder. Acute stress symptoms (as described in Criterion B) may be more appropriately diagnosed as an adjustment disorder when an individual does not meet or exceed the symptom profile for acute stress disorder. This is especially true for anger, guilt, and depressive symptoms, which are common to both acute stress disorder and adjustment disorders (APA, 2022a).

Coding, Recording, and Specifiers

There is only one diagnostic code for acute stress disorder: F43.0. There are no specifiers associated with this disorder; however, counselors may add *with panic attacks* if the client experiences panic attacks concurrent with acute stress disorder.

Case Example

> Vanessa, a 46-year-old television reporter, was part of a small group of journalists who were chosen to witness an execution by lethal injection. For several years, she had been following stories of capital punishment. This particular story was very personal to her because she had interviewed members of the victim's family and covered their experiences as the inmate approached execution.
>
> When asked to describe the experience, she stated it was ghastly. "His face turned an ash color, then purple. He seemed to be gasping for air and grimacing. At one point his body convulsed. It took approximately 20 minutes. All of which I will never forget." Vanessa reported she was hoping she could remain objective since she was a reporter and had been covering capital punishment for quite some time.

Vanessa reported that since the execution nearly 2 weeks ago, she has had problems concentrating on her work. She can't stop thinking about the execution and finds herself replaying the scene where the person grimaced over and over in her mind. She has felt detached, almost like she was in a dream watching herself. She has problems sleeping and also problems getting along with her husband. "He just doesn't understand that I need to be left alone right now."

Diagnostic Questions

1. Do Vanessa's presenting symptoms meet the criteria for a stress disorder? If so, which disorder?
2. Based on the disorder identified in Question 1, which symptom(s) led you to select that diagnosis?
3. Would Vanessa be more accurately diagnosed with an adjustment disorder? If so, why? If not, why not?
4. What rule-outs would you consider for Vanessa's case?
5. What other information may be needed to make an accurate clinical diagnosis?

Adjustment Disorders (F43. _)

> Two months ago was when it happened. My department announced budget cuts, and five out of eight of us were asked to leave. After 13 years, I was just asked to go. No party, no compensation package, not even a good-bye. I don't know what I am going to do. I can't seem to do anything now; even getting out of bed is useless. I just sit around all day and cry. The rejection is unbearable. Getting another job and even being able to pay my mortgage just seem hopeless.—Patrick

Introduced in the *DSM-III* (APA, 1980) to describe individuals who did not meet the criteria for a mental disorder but experienced marked distress and impairment because of a life stressor, adjustment disorders focus on individuals who have difficulty coping with a particular source of stress. The stressor can include major life changes, such as retirement or going to school, or loss of something, such as the ending of an important relationship. Events that do not meet the criteria for acute stress disorder or PTSD but still cause marked distress, such as a business crisis or marital problems, are also included.

Major Changes From *DSM-5* to *DSM-5-TR*

Previously listed as a separate chapter in the *DSM-IV-TR*, adjustment disorders are now integrated in the *DSM-5-TR* with other disorders in which an identifiable stressor precedes symptom onset. What differentiates adjustment disorders from other stressor-related disorders is that the identifiable stressor is not considered traumatic. The stressor may be a sole occurrence, such as losing one's job or ending a relationship, or may be a continuous set of stressful circumstances such as relationship or occupational problems. Similar to acute stress disorder, adjustment disorders may be predictive of subsequent impairment. Therefore, the new location of this diagnosis helps increase clinical utility simply by its placement in the *DSM-5-TR*.

Essential Features

Individuals diagnosed with adjustment disorders have impaired relationships in their personal or occupational life or have stress symptoms that exceed what would be expected as a result of the stressor. Reactions need to be somewhat inflated but temporary, with symptom reduction within 6 months once the stressor and its consequences have been removed.

Note: There is no "normal" reaction to a traumatic event. Counselors must remember that adjusting to life stressors is not indicative of mental illness. This category should only be used when an individual encounters a difficult life event and criteria of marked distress and significant impairment are met.

Adjustment disorders occur at all ages; however, symptomatology differs in children and adolescents. These differences are noted in the symptoms experienced, severity and duration of symptoms, and the outcome. Adolescent with adjustment disorders tend to have more behavioral symptoms, such as conduct problems and temper tantrums, whereas adults experience more depressive symptoms, such as tearfulness and loss of pleasure in previously enjoyed activities.

Special Considerations

A major limitation of the diagnostic criteria for adjustment disorders is the amount of ambiguity within diagnostic criteria. Critics posit that there is too much room for interpretation (Frances, 2013; Paris et al., 2013). Therefore, counselors need to approach assigning a diagnosis of adjustment disorder with caution. Counselors should also keep in mind that adjustment disorders can accompany many mental disorders as well as medical illnesses. For example, individuals with adjustment disorders often have symptoms of tearfulness, feel loss of hope, and experience a lack of interest in work or social activity. Although many of these symptoms mirror MDD, unlike MDD, adjustment disorders are always triggered by an outside stressor and generally go away once the individual is able to cope with the situation or the stressor has been removed.

Social and Cultural Considerations

Stressors and the signs associated with the stressor will vary on the basis of the client's cultural influences. Individuals who routinely experience a high level of stress may be at greater risk for an adjustment disorder.

Differential Diagnosis

Adjustment disorders can be differentiated from acute stress disorder or PTSD because the stressor does not include exposure to actual or threatened death, serious injury, or sexual violence (Criterion A for PTSD and acute stress disorder). Counselors also need to consider MDD, personality disorder, or any other mental illness or medical condition that would reduce a client's ability to cope with life stressors. If clients meet criteria for more stringent mental disorders, even in the face of a known stressor, counselors should diagnose the more stringent disorder. Counselors should also consider whether the symptom profile is a normative reaction to an unfortunate event. If the client's reaction is normative and expected, adjustment disorders should not be diagnosed.

Coding, Recording, and Specifiers

There is no diagnostic code for adjustment disorders. Coding and recording are contingent on the counselor choosing one of six specifiers: F43.21 *with depressed mood*, F43.22 *with anxiety*, F43.23 *with mixed anxiety and depressed mood*, F43.24 *with disturbance of conduct*, F43.25 *with mixed disturbance of emotions and conduct*, and F43.20 *unspecified*. Because depressed mood, anxiety, and disturbance of conduct are common to clients diagnosed with adjustment disorders, counselors must assign one of these specifiers to an adjustment disorder diagnosis. If an individual experiences mixed anxiety and depression, the counselor would choose the *mixed* specifier. Similarly, if an individual (most likely a child or adolescent) experiences mixed disturbance of conduct and emotion, the counselor would indicate these symptoms using the *mixed* specifier. For reactions that do not meet any of the aforementioned specifiers, the counselors would choose *unspecified*.

Because adjustment disorders are associated with a known stressor, counselors should also include reference to the stressor by using *ICD-10-CM* Z codes located in Other Conditions That May Be a Focus of Clinical Attention chapter of the *DSM-5-TR*. For example, an adolescent experiencing depression and anxiety related to an unexpected pregnancy may be diagnosed with F43.23 adjustment disorder with mixed anxiety and depressed mood and Z64.0 problems related to unwanted pregnancy.

Prolonged Grief Disorder (F43.8)

Prolonged grief disorder (PGD) is a disorder exclusive to individuals who have lost a loved one and is characterized by symptoms of intense yearning for and/or persistent thoughts of the deceased that persist for at least 12 months after the loss. PGD includes other grief-related symptoms, such as emotional numbness, intense emotional pain, and avoidance of reminders that the person is deceased, that are sufficiently severe enough to cause functional impairment (APA, 2022a). PGD was originally proposed in the *DSM-5* as "persistent complex bereavement disorder" in the Section III chapter, Conditions for Further Study (APA, 2013a) and later approved for inclusion in the *DSM-5-TR* in 2022. It was not until 2019 that this disorder was included in the *ICD-11* and, like PTSD, can be found under "disorders specifically associated with stress."

Historically referred to as "complicated grief" (Zordan et al., 2019), "traumatic grief" (Mutabaruka et al., 2011), "persistent bereavement" (APA, 2013c), and even "pathological grief" (Gort, 1984), the inclusion of PGD within the *DSM* is not without controversy. Early critics regard grief as a normal reaction that has a unique course for every individual and should not be pathologized (Breen & O'Conner, 2007). Bryant (2013) stated, "Because grief is nearly ubiquitous among all people, the distress of losing a loved one is normal and accordingly should not be medicalized" (p. 42). Critics also highlight the danger of diagnostic bias, noting cross-cultural understanding of grief is lacking, and the potential for overreliance on psychotropic medication to treat normative grief symptoms (Bryant, 2013). Others point to the need for a distinct recognition of prolonged grief reactions due to the physical, emotional, and social impairment experienced by approximately 6.8% to 14% of bereaved persons (Lundorff et al., 2017) and research that links poorer health outcomes for these individuals (Shear et al., 2011). Consistent with both positions is that grief is a normative process, notably one of the most difficult circumstances an individual can endure.

Age, gender, and mental health history are the most well-documented risk indicators (Lundorff et al., 2017). Manner of death has been linked to prevalence, with individuals whose loved one died because of violence more likely to be diagnosed with PGD (Currier et al., 2007). PGD is also more prevalent when the death is by a violent method such as homicide or suicide, with an estimated 70% of those with PGD having been exposed to bereavement by a violent method (Djelantik et al., 2020). High levels of comorbidity with somatic symptom disorders, depression, anxiety, and PTSD have been found. Individuals who would historically have met the criteria for PGD are at greater risk for suicide (Latham & Prigerson, 2004; Maciejewski et al., 2007).

Major Changes From *DSM-5* to *DSM-5-TR*

Although the *DSM-5* included a category of persistent complex bereavement disorder as a "Condition for Further Study" in Section III of the manual, this is the first time PGD appears as an official disorder within the *DSM*.

Essential Features

Individuals with PGD present with symptoms occurring for more than 12 months in adults, 6 months in children, following the loss of a loved one. The individual must experience either intense yearning for the deceased or persistent preoccupation with thoughts of the deceased, although the presence of both are not uncommon.

Special Considerations

Social and Cultural Considerations

When diagnosing PGD, counselors should consider cultural factors that may affect the expression and experience of grief. Cultural norms may include rituals or ceremonies that are associated with the loss of a loved one. These cultural practices, for those who are unfamiliar with them, may give the illusion that the period of grief is extended. Counselors must not only acknowledge and honor the importance of these practices for clients but also avoid the assumption that these circumstances would be indicative of PGD. Similarly, cultural norms and values influence how a client expresses grief. Some cultures may place high value on stoicism and may not openly express feelings of bereavement, whereas others may emphasize the importance of grief expressions. The experience of loss and grief may also have different cultural norms based on gender identity, social class, age, or relationship status. Counselors should be aware of these cultural differences and never assume that a lack of expression of grief is indicative of a client not experiencing grief or, conversely, assess grief symptoms as "marked distress" when symptom severity and presentation may be considered appropriate within the client's cultural worldview.

In addition to being aware of cultural factors that may affect the expression and experience of grief when diagnosing PGD, counselors should consider the cultural context of the individual when assessing symptoms and providing support. A client's beliefs, values, and cultural context can affect how they seek help and the level of disclosure they feel comfortable sharing. For example, some individuals may not consider it appropriate to seek help or talk about their grief, whereas others may actively seek out support. A counselor should be aware of these cultural differences and be prepared to provide appropriate and sensitive support to clients from diverse cultural backgrounds.

Differential Diagnosis

PGD is a relatively new diagnosis, and common differential diagnoses have yet to be fully validated. However, differential diagnoses that may be considered when assessing for PGD include MDD, adjustment disorder, persistent depressive disorder (formerly referred to as dysthymia), and borderline personality disorder. MDD and adjustment disorder are the most common differential diagnoses, as PGD and MDD share similar symptom presentation, such as feelings of sadness, loss of interest in activities, and difficulty functioning. However, PGD is specifically related to the loss of a loved one, whereas MDD can occur in response to a variety of stressors. Similarly, adjustment disorder is a condition that can occur in response to a significant life stressor, such as the loss of a loved one. Although PGD and adjustment disorder share some symptoms, such as difficulty functioning, PGD is a more severe and prolonged response to the loss, as specifically required by Criterion D under adjustment disorders, which states "the symptoms do not represent normal bereavement and are not better explained by prolonged grief disorder" (APA, 2022a, p. 319).

Coding, Recording, and Specifiers

There is only one diagnostic code for PGD: F43.8. There are no specifiers for this disorder.

Other Specified and Unspecified Trauma- and Stressor-Related Disorders: (F43.89/F43.9)

Other specified trauma- and stressor-related disorder (F43.89), along with the unspecified criterion (F43.9), replaces the NOS category in the *DSM-IV-TR*. The other specified category may now be used for diagnosis if the counselor wants to identify the specific reason that the full diagnosis is not met, for example, F43.8 other specified trauma- and stressor-related disorder, *ataque de nervios*.

The unspecified trauma- and stressor-related disorder (F43.9) diagnosis is used when clients have prominent trauma- and stressor-related symptoms but do not meet criteria for any of the specific disorders listed in this chapter. This diagnosis is also used in situations when the counselor chooses not to specify the reason that the criteria are not met. In either case, symptoms cause clinically significant impairment or distress. This diagnosis is also commonly used when counselors are unable to distinguish whether a medical illness or substance has played a causal role in the manifestation of symptoms.

> ***Note:*** The diagnostic codes for unspecified trauma and stressor-related disorder (F43.9) and unspecified adjustment disorder (F43.20) are no longer the same and should be coded differently using the associated codes.

Questions for Consideration

1. What are pre- and posttrauma risk and prognostic factors? Why are these factors important to consider when diagnosing trauma- and stressor-related disorders?
2. What treatments are typically used by counselors working with clients diagnosed with acute stress disorder?
3. PGD is associated with elevated risk of suicidal thoughts and behaviors. What steps might a counselor engage in to protect clients with this diagnosis?
4. What cultural factors should counselors consider when determining the suitability of an adjustment disorder diagnosis?"
5. How do you provide holistic care and mitigate bias when counseling persons who have a history of trauma?

Chapter 11

Gender Dysphoria in Children, Adolescents, and Adults

> I was taught early on what I "should" be doing as a boy. I remember asking my mother why God made me look like a boy when I was a girl. She took me to a counselor who told me I was too young to know what I wanted. He simply gave me medication for anxiety and suggested I participate in team sports. That was years ago. Since then, I have not talked to anyone about what it's like to be in this body. I feel so alone and isolated.—Jacob

Gender is a term derived from the Latin word *genus*, meaning "type" or "kind" (Riggs et al., 2015). This expression is typically used to describe a social construct that is originally based on the notion of two genders, male and female (The Trevor Project, 2019). Although the idea of two genders is not accurate, much of our culture is formed around notions of binary sex and gender identity. For many individuals, strong expectations to align their behaviors and expression with sex assigned at birth begin before they are even born. Individuals who feel discrepancies between their sex assigned at birth and their experienced gender often experience distress that is further compounded by responses from their family and social systems. When discrepancies result in distress for the individual, the term *dysphoria*, derived from the Greek idea of difficult to bear (Davy & Toze, 2018), may apply (APA, 2022a).

It is important to note that the distress referred to in a clinical diagnosis of gender dysphoria is not the same as the distress resulting from the multiple societal stressors faced by this population. Factors such as discrimination and stigma can have a deleterious impact on mental health; however, APA (2022a) sees responses to discrimination and stigma as discrete from the distress experienced in gender dysphoria. Furthermore, counselors must have a holistic understanding of the real-world implications associated with a gender dysphoria diagnosis. Individuals who are struggling with the impact of systemic oppression and discrimination resulting from not "fitting into" the gender stereotypes of an abusive society need affirming care to address the mental health consequences of these stressors. Assignment of gender dysphoria can be considered pathologizing and harmful for these individuals. However, because of the difficulty accessing medical and other care without a diagnosis, counselors may use this diagnosis as circumstances warrant, with the fully informed consent of the client, who needs insurance access. Moreover, information from The Trevor Project (2021a), which focuses on eliminating suicidality among LGBTQ+ young people, indicates that transgender youth experience suicidal ideation at much higher rates than do their heterosexual peers. The Trevor Project also notes that gender-affirming health does result in lower suicide rates and points to a recent study in which gender-affirming hormone therapy was associated with lower rates of depression and suicidality (A. E. Green et al., 2021). Furthermore, the Society for Sexual, Affectional, Intersex, and Gender Expansive Identities (SAIGE; formerly the Association for Lesbian, Gay, Bisexual, Transgender Issues in Counseling) standards of care state that the counselor understands that

> the diagnosis of gender dysphoria is only relevant when a client wishes to access medical treatments related to the transition process and is required by insurance. They also explore with the client the systemic oppression related to the medical requirement to have the diagnosis to obtain access to the requested treatment. (Goodrich et al., 2017, p. 207)

Counselors are aware that this is an evolving issue in society, and they consult with ACA and SAIGE to ensure that they have the latest, best information for their clients.

According to the World Professional Association for Transgender Health (WPATH, 2011; see also Coleman et al., 2022), *gender identity* refers to one's deeply felt intrinsic sense of gender. The *DSM-5-TR* describes this as a "category of social identity and refers to an individual's identification as male, female, some category in between (i.e., gender fluid), or a category other than male or female (i.e., gender neutral)" (APA, 2022a, p. 511). The Competencies for Counseling With Transgender Clients (see Burnes et al., 2010) note that gender identity is in "no way" (p. 138) a disorder and highlight the historical marginalization experienced by the population in diagnostic assessment and systems. Within these competencies, gender is discussed in terms of a range or expression of identity, as nonbinary and gender-fluid. *Cisgender* refers to those whose sex assigned at birth is consistent with their expressed gender, and *transgender and gender nonconforming* refers to individuals whose expressed gender does not fit societal expectations of the sex assigned at birth (A. A. Singh & Mingo, 2018). Whereas gender binary refers to a dichotomous belief that one is categorically either male or female, nonbinary individuals conceptualize a continuum that does not require one category or another. Often referring to themselves as "enby," these individuals include those who identify as genderqueer, gender diverse, genderfluid, demigender, bigender, and agender (Coleman et al., 2022). *Gender expression* refers to the manner in which individuals convey their gender in their daily lives (Coleman et al., 2022; A. A. Singh & Mingo, 2018).

In addition to the growth in nomenclature toward inclusiveness, counselors should be aware of confusion and controversy surrounding the terms *sex* and *gender*. *Sex* is characterized as the biological indicators of male and female, typically within a reproductive context, such as testes in males and ovaries in females (APA, 2022a; Crooks & Baur, 2013). Counselors must understand and use the term sex in its proper context, which is to describe biological and medical examples. *Gender* is used to describe more cultural situations and contexts (Riggs et al., 2015; A. A. Singh & Mingo, 2018). Gender incongruence is a diagnostic term (Coleman et al., 2022) and is defined as a "condition in which the gender identity of a person does not align with the gender assigned at birth" (Claahsen-van der Grinten et al., 2021, p. 1349). Individuals who experience a conflict between their expressed gender (i.e., gender identity) and birth-assigned gender, or gender incongruence, may self-identify as transgender.

To help readers better understand diagnostic categories of gender dysphoria in adults and gender dysphoria in children and adolescents, as well as the changes from the *DSM-5* to the *DSM-5-TR*, we have included these changes at the beginning of this chapter.

As with other chapters of this *Learning Companion*, we then present essential features, special considerations, implications for counselors, differential diagnoses, and two case examples to facilitate a better understanding of gender dysphoria among all age ranges.

Major Changes From *DSM-5* to *DSM-5-TR*

Gender dysphoria replaced the previous term *gender identity disorder* in the *DSM-IV-TR*. Although debate continues surrounding gender dysphoria (Davy & Toze, 2018; Riggs et al., 2015), APA (2013b) advocated that retaining this as a mental disorder will promote treatment: "To get insurance coverage for the medical treatments, individuals need a diagnosis. The Sexual and Gender Identity Disorders Work Group was concerned that removing [gender dysphoria] as a psychiatric diagnosis—as some had suggested—would jeopardize access to care" (p. 2). For example, clients can advocate for hormonal and surgical treatments such as gender reassignment surgery because of the clinically significant distress associated with gender dysphoria (APA, 2013b).

Although the specific changes to this section are not extensive, the authors of the *DSM-5-TR* sought to reinforce choice language and reduce associated stigma through more accurate, inclusive vernacular. As a result, the text was updated with "experienced gender" replacing "desired gender," "gender affirming hormone treatment" replacing "cross-sex medical procedure," and "cross-sex hormone treatment" changed to "gender affirming hormone treatment." "Natal male" and "natal female" are more accurately stated as "individual assigned male at birth" and "individual assigned female at birth," respectively. Finally, "difference in sex development" is offered as an alternative term for "disorder of sex development" (APA, 2022a).

Essential Features

A person with gender dysphoria experiences a "mismatch" or incongruency between assumed gender based on sex assigned at birth and gender identity, and this incongruency is associated with clinical distress (Davy & Toze, 2018). A main feature of gender dysphoria is distress and clinical impairment related to the marked incongruence between the gender one is assigned at birth and the gender one experiences (Davy & Toze, 2018; Lindley & Galupo, 2020). APA (2022a) described gender dysphoria as "the distress that may accompany the incongruence between one's experienced or expressed gender and one's assigned gender" (p. 511). The distress experienced must be visible, meaning there is an evident difficulty in social, occupational, or other significant areas of functioning (APA, 2022a).

Children experiencing gender dysphoria will have a noticeable incongruence between their experienced gender and the gender assigned at birth for at least 6 months with at least six of these criteria accompanying the incongruence: strong desire or insistence that one is an alternative gender to that assigned at birth (must be present); a strong preference for wearing the attire typical of a gender not assigned at birth; strong desire for gender roles that differ from those assigned at birth whether in fantasy or make-believe play; strong preference for the activities, games, or toys associated with the gender not assigned at birth; desire to play with others who also identify with the child's experienced gender; rejection of the stereotypes associated with birth-assigned gender, including style of play, typical activities, and toys; strong aversion to sexual anatomy; and desire for the sexual characteristics of one's expressed gender rather than assigned gender (APA, 2022a). As noted above, clinically significant distress occurs for the child, negatively impacting functioning in key areas such as school or social interactions (APA, 2022a).

The criteria for gender dysphoria in adolescents and adults include some noteworthy differences, reflecting the impact of gender dysphoria at different ages. The individual must experience at least 6 months of marked incongruence and distress related to their experienced gender versus the assigned gender. To diagnose this disorder in adolescents and adults, only two of the following criteria must be met rather than the six required for children: pronounced incongruence between their experienced gender and physical sexual characteristics or anticipated secondary sex characteristics; strong desire to get rid of or prevent the development of sex characteristics associated with the gender assigned at birth due to the incongruence with experienced gender; yearning for the sexual characteristics associated with the individual's experienced gender; yearning to be a gender differing from that assigned at birth; strong desire for treatment associated with a gender differing from that assigned at birth; and certainty that the individual's feelings and reactions are those typically associated with a gender differing from that assigned at birth. As with children, the condition results in clinically significant distress, negatively impacting functioning in key areas such as occupational or social interactions (APA, 2022a).

At any age, individuals diagnosed with gender dysphoria often have a continuous discomfort with their gender assigned at birth and feel like they were born the wrong sex, alongside a sense they are different from their peers. They often feel misunderstood; have challenges accessing appropriate mental health care treatment; and have difficulties with social, occupational, and legal issues.

Children

Gender dysphoria, cutting across all age ranges and genders, presents in different ways. For example, girls who have not yet gone through puberty may state that they wish to be boys or insist that they are boys. They will want to wear clothing typically associated with masculine gender expression rather than clothing typically associated with a more feminine gender expression despite their parents' insistence (APA, 2022a). Diagnosing a child with gender dysphoria can help the child receive gender-affirming care to help decrease incongruence between their assigned and expressed gender (Claahsen-van der Grinten et al., 2021).

The timeframe when children are developing behaviors and interests related to their expressed gender is between the ages of 2 and 4. These behaviors include typical and atypical gender role expression. A person who experiences gender dysphoria in childhood may not necessarily experience symptoms of gender dysphoria until adolescence or adulthood. Prevalence rates reported for those experiencing gender dysphoria are limited by data collection methods, as many individuals who meet the criteria do not seek treatment at specialty clinics, making their inclusion in the data unlikely and persistence rates artificially low (APA, 2022a). However, Claahsen-van der Grinten et al. (2021) reported that 0.6% to 1.7% of children and adolescents struggle with gender dysphoria, noting that these numbers may vary in different studies because of assessment methods. Furthermore, The Trevor Project (2019) documented 1.8% of youth overall identifying as transgender, and Claahsen-van der Grinten et al. noted that the numbers of younger individuals seeking treatment has increased dramatically over the past few years, especially among individuals assigned female at birth.

Individuals who experience differences of sex development as well as gender dysphoria often seek medical treatment and attention at an early age (APA, 2022a). These differences are usually related to gender-atypical behavior that starts in early childhood. It is important to remember that differences in sexual development do not always lead to gender dysphoria (APA, 2022a) and that controversy surrounds this diagnosis as well. For example, individuals with differences of sex development, such as ambiguous genitalia, may require medical intervention and gender assignment at an early age. These individuals may or may not experience distress related to incongruence between their experienced gender and the gender assigned at birth. However, some do experience uncertainty regarding their gender as they learn about their medical history (APA, 2022a). Congenital adrenal hyperplasia is a disease that affects the endocrine system, creating a deficiency or overproduction of sex hormones (Dreger et al., 2012). In effect, this disease can alter the development of primary and secondary sex characteristics. Androgen insensitivity syndrome involves the development of biological sex either before birth or during puberty (Gottlieb et al., 2012). Sex development disorders such as these must be diagnosed by a medical professional. Infertility is not uncommon in this population.

Adults

Complexities in gender identity and gender dysphoria alongside disparities in access to care make it difficult to capture the prevalence of gender dysphoria. The authors of the *DSM-5-TR* noted that 0.5% to 0.6% of the population in the United States and Europe identify as transgender and that 0.6% to 1.1% express experiencing gender incongruency (APA, 2022a). Additionally, 2.1% to 2.6% of individuals feel that they are a person of a different sex, and about 0.2% to 0.6% of the population endorses a desire to undergo medical treatment (APA, 2022a). Adults who have gender dysphoria regularly experience a desire to be rid of their primary and secondary sex characteristics. A strong desire to live as another gender must be present in adults for at least 6 months. As stated previously, this is no longer a requirement for children. Most individuals experiencing gender dysphoria try to reduce the incongruence by living in their expressed gender or incorporating a nontraditional gender role (APA, 2022a). Some adults will have the opportunity for gender reassignment surgery. In these instances, the specifier *posttransition* is used.

Adolescents with gender dysphoria may present with characteristics of either children or adults, depending on where they are in their development. Certain physical changes, such as developing secondary sex characteristics as a result of puberty, can cause increased gender dysphoria (APA, 2022a). Prevalence rates for adolescents reporting gender diversity have been increasing recently, with 1.2% identifying as transgender. More adolescents who were assigned female at birth seek gender-affirming treatment than adolescents who were assigned male at birth (Coleman et al., 2022).

Special Considerations

A text section titled "Association With Suicidal Thoughts and Behaviors" is new to the *DSM-5-TR*. This section is included as appropriate for any diagnosis in the nosology. For gender dysphoria, this section is especially important. Individuals with gender incongruency or dysphoria experience notably higher rates of suicidal ideation and behaviors than their cisgender peers, particularly in adolescence (APA, 2022a). Using data from the CDC's Youth Risk Behavior Survey, The Trevor Project (2019) determined that 35% or about one in three youth identifying as transgender attempted suicide in the last year, and nearly half seriously considered suicide. One third of transgender youth reported sexual victimization within the past year, and a similar number had been threatened physically and were afraid to go to school. Peterson et al. (2017) found that over 40% of transgender youth engage or have engaged in nonsuicidal self-injury, and over 50% of transgender youth have at least one comorbid mental health disorder, with depression and anxiety being the most common. Peterson et al. also noted that over 35% of these youth expressed body dissatisfaction, with the majority believing they are too big. Many individuals with gender dysphoria feel negatively about their bodies, and dissatisfaction may be a contributing factor to body dysmorphic disorder (Balleur-van Rijn et al., 2012). Body dissatisfaction is compounded by the fact that these individuals are identifying more with bodies related to their experienced gender than to their sex assigned at birth.

Lifelong instances of maltreatment are prevalent in the transgender population. The authors of the 2015 U.S. Transgender Survey Executive Summary by the National Center for Transgender Equality (NCTE, 2016) described

> disturbing patterns of mistreatment and discrimination and startling disparities between transgender people in the survey and the U.S. population when it comes to the most basic elements of life, such as finding a job, having a place to live, accessing medical care, and enjoying the support of family and community. (p. 2)

Individuals with gender dysphoria experience high rates of stigmatization, discrimination, violence, unemployment, and lack of family and social support (APA, 2022a). By living life in their experienced gender, individuals often must deal with considerable stressors from family, society, and oppressive forces, which may perpetuate symptoms of anxiety or depression (Chodzen et al., 2019; R. J. Comer, 2022). In addition to external factors such as the ones mentioned above, internalizing factors of distress related to body and gender incongruence can result in high levels of stress. Balleur-van Rijn et al. (2012) pointed out that individuals who internalize a negative self-perception often experience feelings of doubt and worthlessness that may lead to depressive disorders. Lindley and Galupo (2020) discussed these experiences in terms of the minority stress model (Meyer, 1995) and attempted to demonstrate the relationship between the high rates of stress associated with gender dysphoria and mental health consequences for these individuals. It is not unexpected that those who endorsed high levels of internalized transphobia, anticipated stress, and gender identity concealment also experienced high levels of gender dysphoria (Lindley & Galupo, 2020). These authors argued for a treatment focus that views the stress transgender individuals experience as a result of navigating cisnormative culture as the basis for mental and physical health disparities.

Cultural Considerations

Gender incongruence and dysphoria occur across various countries and cultures (APA, 2022a). What is considered gender appropriate may vary significantly among different individuals and groups. Additionally, gender roles have changed significantly over the years, and roles that may have been viewed as inappropriate years ago are now considered socially acceptable (Zhu & Chang, 2019). Furthermore, gender roles are dependent on the way in which society views expectations for men and women. Multicultural awareness is critical for counselors working with these clients and their families; therefore, counselors should remember it might be ineffective to use traditional roles of men and women as a foundation on which to identify and define gender (A. A. Singh & Mingo, 2018). Co-occurring mental health problems are not uncommon for this population, but rates do vary between cultural groups, possibly related to accepting and affirming attitudes regarding gender-variant behavior (APA, 2022a).

Negative life experiences, such as abuse and discrimination, that are common to transgender people occur more often for underrepresented populations. The NCTE (2016) documents that people of color are at even higher risk than their White transgender peers and are three times more likely to be in poverty when compared with the U.S. population. Middle Eastern, American Indian, multiracial, Latinx, and Black respondents reported higher rates of unemployment compared with their White peers. Individuals who are undocumented and individuals with disabilities are also disproportionately negatively affected, experiencing very high rates of homelessness, economic hardship, violence, and mental health issues (NCTE, 2016). Transgender individuals reported living with HIV at three times the rate of the general population, and 19% of Black transgender women reported having been diagnosed with HIV (NCTE, 2016). The SAIGE standards of care (Goodrich et al., 2017) direct counselors to consider the impact of cultural and multiple intersecting identities when assessing, diagnosing, and treating these clients.

Differential Diagnosis

APA (2022a) included common differential diagnoses for gender dysphoria as nonconformity to gender roles, transvestic disorder, body dysmorphic disorder, autism spectrum disorder, schizophrenia and other psychotic disorders, and other clinical presentations. Although all of these are diagnoses counselors should consider, the lifetime psychiatric comorbidity in clients with gender-related issues is high. Therefore, counselors should carefully consider co-occurring mental health problems during assessment and treatment planning.

Etiology and Treatment

Although pinpointing the specific cause of gender dysphoria is complex and difficult, research into the etiology of both gender incongruence and gender dysphoria has more recently focused on psychosocial, genetic, and biological components (APA, 2022a; Claahsen-van der Grinten et al., 2021). Gender development is thought to start at the time of conception, and the environment is a contributing factor that influences a child's gender development (Dragowski et al., 2011). Gender identity has genetic links and involves brain development (Boucher & Chinnah, 2020). For individuals experiencing gender incongruence, some parts of the brain develop patterns that are similar to the brain patterns consistent with those of their experienced gender (Uribe et al., 2020). Diamond (2013) conducted a study involving twins that suggested that genetics is more likely to play a role for gender incongruence than upbringing, and Claahsen-van der Grinten et al. (2021) noted the potential role of prenatal sex hormones and prenatal brain development. However, counselors must remember that gender nonconforming behaviors alone are not an indicator of gender dysphoria (APA, 2022a; Goodrich et al., 2017). The symptoms related to this diagnosis result from managing incongruence alone and not from an expected response to navigating a gender binary system that does not appreciate differing experiences of gender. In terms of gender dysphoria, more recent research has focused on biological differences in terms of atypical prenatal androgen exposure in utero (Foreman et al., 2019). Having an older age of onset and greater intensity of incongruence may also contribute to the development of gender dysphoria.

The NCTE (2016) indicated that over 92% of transgender people reported a history of engaging in counseling. Although there are currently no evidence-based treatments for gender dysphoria (Claahsen-van der Grinten et al., 2021), counselors need to understand that, for many people, gender is socially constructed (not about biological sex), and distress around incongruence is more a reaction to social expectations than one's desire to be another gender. Therefore, the focus of treatment is often on accepting the person and their experience and promoting a healthy identity in the face of discrimination or rejection. In contrast to other disorders in the *DSM*, the focus of treatment for gender dysphoria is not to change gendered behaviors. Rather, interventions should support clients in coping with experiences of incongruence and promote optimal functioning. Counselors should focus on interventions that target how these individuals internalize the effects of navigating a cisnormative environment (Lindley & Galupo, 2020) and the impact of stigma and discrimination, as well as any comorbid diagnosis.

Gender-affirming environments can have an impact on clients' experience of acceptance and self-acceptance. These environments may include gender-inclusive bathrooms, reading materials that encompass all experiences of gender identity, and an open and accepting spirit from the counselor. Counselors should respect clients' language, using their pronouns and chosen name on all materials and in sessions (Goodrich et al., 2017), as well as avoid gender binary language and assumptions on intake and other forms and materials

(A. A. Singh & Mingo, 2018). There is a growing body of work surrounding the treatment of transgender individuals experiencing mental health symptoms as a result of discrimination, stigma, and trauma. Cognitive behavioral therapies have also show promise in research. One such therapy is AFFIRM, an online affirmative CBT group therapy specifically for LGBTQ+ youth (Craig et al., 2021). SAIGE provides competencies (Burnes et al., 2010) and standards of care (Goodrich et al., 2017) for counselors working with transgender clients.

Children who experience gender incongruence may go on to develop gender dysphoria. Interventions for children should focus on helping to prevent the development of psychosocial problems that may carry into adolescence and adulthood (Balleur-van Rijn et al., 2012). In addition to realizing they are different from their peers, adolescents are also becoming more aware of the general public's reaction to them. Without proper treatment, this could lead to a negative self-concept. Counselors can look at how children see themselves and examine favorable aspects of children's self-concept (Balleur-van Rijn et al., 2012). This strength-based approach focuses on what is working rather than on how different the child is from others in their peer group. Other interventions may help clients explore and develop awareness of how gender differences affect their identities.

In terms of comprehensive intervention, working as a treatment team that includes medical and other health care professionals is recommended (Claahsen-van der Grinten et al., 2021). Gender-affirming care and gender-affirming treatment refer to interventions that support an individual to live their experienced gender. This may include gender-affirming medical care in addition to counseling and psychological support. There is evidence that early intervention in terms of gender-affirming hormone administration and puberty suppression may improve mental health for these individuals, but these studies are limited (Coleman et al., 2022). Gender-affirming surgery or gender-affirming reassignment surgery is increasing (R. J. Comer, 2022). Although not all clients will desire medical intervention, counselors may be working closely with medical professionals to help clients explore medical treatments available to them. SAIGE's standards of care state that counselors "Educate themselves on the process of transitioning, including all levels of action toward gender affirmation (e.g., social, hormonal, surgical, and non-surgical physical interventions)" (Goodrich et al., 2017, p. 206). These include surgical alterations of genital anatomy and hormonal treatments that alter body physiology. Studies further indicate low rates of adolescents detransitioning (1.9% and 3.5%; Brik et al., 2020; Wiepjes et al., 2018). The motivation behind this decision may include side effects from the medication, endorsing a nonbinary gender identity, and doubts about transitioning (Brik et al., 2020). Current studies regarding detransitioning are limited, and counselors are encouraged to create a gender-affirming environment in which clients are afforded open channels and opportunities for feedback about treatment (Goodrich et al., 2017).

Implications for Counselors

Not all individuals who experience incongruence with the sex assigned at birth and their expressed gender meet the criteria for gender dysphoria (APA, 2022a; Claahsen-van der Grinten et al., 2021; Davy & Toze, 2018). Therefore, it is essential that counselors do not generalize or pathologize individuals experiencing gender dysphoria. Counselors can work toward competent practice by learning language that is affirmative to clients and their developmental process; recognizing oppression; and creating informed, welcoming, and affirmative environments for transgender individuals and their loved ones (Goodrich et al., 2017; Hays & Erford, 2018). Counselors should be careful about making stereotypical assumptions or buying into parents' or family members' assumptions of clients' sex, gender, and gender identity. Psychoeducation for all parties is critical, as is strict adherence to the *ACA Code of Ethics* (ACA, 2014) relating to values, imposition, discrimination, and, above all else, promotion of the dignity and welfare of the client.

Because gender-affirming medical procedures often require some form of mental health treatment and/or letter from a mental health professional, counselors need to be prepared as this is one of the rationales for clients when they seek services. Counselors should discuss the expectations around this need early in therapy. If the counselor is unsure about how to proceed, supervision provided by someone who is competent in working with this population is key (A. A. Singh & Mingo, 2018). Furthermore, counselors should explore issues of privilege with clients who transition, including how gender shifts may impact their personal experience of power and privilege, such as the potential loss of male privilege (A. A. Singh & Mingo, 2018). Gender-affirming counseling includes understanding the range of gender diversity; knowing and implementing appropriate terminology; creating a safe environment, including appropriate intake, assessment, and interventions; and advocating and assisting clients with personal advocacy (Goodrich et al., 2017; A. A. Singh & Mingo, 2018).

Counselors need to note the role of social support and family systems when working with clients who experience gender dysphoria. This is even more necessary if the client with gender dysphoria is a child. Family sessions may help parents come to terms with letting their child dress as they want and be able to explore their bodies like most other children do during this time (Hein & Berger, 2012). Not only will this help the parents, but it will also help the child to see their parents taking a supportive role. Families are encouraged to support transgender members through affirming communication; support for engagement in preferred activities, mannerisms, and dress; and advocacy in social life (Coleman et al., 2022). Counselors can assist in this level of support by modeling these behaviors and engaging in psychoeducation processes, such as myth busting, with the family.

Counselors need to be aware of legislation that impact transgender clients, particularly transgender youth, in an ongoing way. In 2021, more than 140 bills were introduced in various states aimed at limiting the rights of transgender individuals, with 13 of the enacted bills targeting transgender youth specifically (Berg-Brousseau, 2022). In 2022, more than 137 bills targeting this population were introduced (Berg-Brousseau, 2022). And as of May 2023, a record-breaking over 520 anti-LGBTQ+ bills have been brought to state legislatures, many of which are an attempt to remove already existing protections (Peele, 2023). Some examples of the restrictions delineated in these bills include the restriction of access to gender-affirming care for minors, prevention of school personnel calling these individuals by their appropriate name or pronouns, requiring that these youth use the restroom consistent with their sex assigned at birth rather than the gender with which they identify, and restrictions requiring that these youth only play on sports teams consistent with their sex assigned at birth (Stark, 2022). In Texas, providing gender-affirming care for minors is considered child abuse, and other states such as Florida and Alabama have similar prohibitions (Stark, 2022).

Counselors must be aware of the mental health consequences of ongoing discrimination; 85% of transgender and nonbinary youth reported mental health impact resulting from the ongoing legislation (Berg-Brousseau, 2022). Not unexpectedly, transgender and nonbinary youth report depression, suicidality, self-harm, and eating disorders at much higher rates than their peers (Price-Feeney et al., 2020). Eighty-five percent of transgender youth who were impacted by a bathroom restriction reported increased depressive symptoms, and 60% reported an increase in suicidal ideation (Price-Feeney et al., 2021). Research indicates that transgender youth experience a decrease in depression and suicidality when they are treated with respect. Research by The Trevor Project (2021b) indicates that lower rates of suicide and depression occur for these youth when their pronouns and names are respected; when they are able to change birth certificates and driver's licenses; and when they have access to affirming spaces, including online, school, and home. Furthermore, gender-affirming hormone therapy often results in lower rates of depression and suicidality (A. E. Green et al., 2021).

These outcomes underscore the need for counselors to create safe and affirming spaces, assist families in creating these spaces, and engage in ongoing advocacy for these clients. Advocacy may include educating family members and other professionals who work with these clients about the deleterious impact of ongoing discrimination and the mental health benefits associated with respecting their needs (Stark, 2022). The SAIGE standards of care (Goodrich et al., 2017) compel counselors to understand the diversity associated with affectional orientation and the importance of advocacy. Counselors should consider the intersecting roles associated with culture when assessing, diagnosing, and creating effective treatment plans for these individuals. The continued monitoring of treatment effectiveness as well as ongoing engagement in professional development and obtaining new knowledge is crucial to appropriate, gender-affirming treatment. It is important for counselors to understand that gender dysphoria exists on a continuum. Although many counselors will not have the opportunity to work with clients who meet full diagnostic criteria for gender dysphoria, many will work with clients who experience gender role struggles and conflicts. Therefore, counselors need to clearly understand the needs of clients and remember that etiology and treatment are complex. As with any counseling-related issue, counselors should be open and willing to collaborate with other professionals as necessary. Counselors must reference the SAIGE standards of care (Goodrich et al., 2017), as well as WPATH recommendation (Coleman et al., 2022), when working with this population. As with other specialized practices in counseling, counselors must ensure they are adequately prepared and trained to help clients with these issues.

The *DSM-5-TR* includes alternative language when referencing those with "disorder of sex development," specifically using "difference" rather than "disorder." Differences of sex development include those individuals who are born with or develop varying sexual traits or reproductive anatomy that may not fit into what society considers "normal." Occurring in about 1.7% of the population, these individuals are also referred to as intersex people. They are represented by the I in LGBTQI+ (Intersex Campaign for Equality, 2015) and may or may not also identify as transgender (A. A. Singh & Mingo, 2018). Controversy surrounds diagnosis and medical treatment with this population. For example, the use of *disorder* indicates a problem to be fixed, but that is not universally embraced. APA (2022a) attempts to address this issue by using *differences*, a preferred term. Stemming from the ideology behind this language is the controversial use of surgical intervention during early childhood or infancy. Intersex surgery most often occurs before the individual is 2 years old, prohibiting input and/or consent from the individual. This practice can result in the intersex person experiencing gender incongruence, particularly if they are unaware of any or all facts related to the intervention. When working with this population, counselors are aware that these individuals also experience high rates of discrimination and stress (Simons et al., 2020; A. A. Singh & Mingo, 2018). They may struggle with gender identity development, bullying, and body problems (Simons et al., 2020). Mental health issues can develop from social cruelty, but, as with transgender individuals, being an intersex person does not mean having a disorder. Counselors use evidence-based treatments to address depression, anxiety, stress, and other symptoms resulting from maltreatment. Counselors may also treat symptoms related to gender identity development issues or gender dysphoria if those symptoms emerge.

Coding, Recording, and Specifiers

There is only one diagnostic code for gender dysphoria in children, F64.2, and gender dysphoria in adolescents and adults, F64.0. The diagnosis may include the specifier *with a disorder/difference of sex development* (e.g., a congenital adrenogenital disorder such as E25.0 congenital adrenal hyperplasia or E34.50 androgen insensitivity syndrome) if appropriate. This diagnosis is most likely made in a medical setting, and counselors should include the disorder of sex development specifier in addition to gender dysphoria. Other specified gender dysphoria is coded F64.8 and unspecified gender dysphoria is coded F64.9.

Counselors should also record the specifier *posttransition* when applicable. This specifier indicates that the individual has made the transition to living full-time in the experienced gender with or without legalization of gender change. For this specifier to be assigned, the individual must also have undergone at least one gender-affirming medical procedure or treatment regimen (APA, 2022a).

Case Example 1

Janice is a 4-year-old girl of White and Black American descent. She has an older brother and a younger sister and lives with her married, biological parents. Janice's parents describe her as bright, alert, and imaginative. She attends preschool and has many friends there. Although she has friends of both genders, her teacher said that she has more male friends and tends to play with them and participate in male-related activities.

When Janice was 3 years old, she asked her parents if she could start wearing boy underwear once she started using the toilet. As she got older, she wanted to wear her brother's clothes instead of her own clothes. She hardly plays with the toys she's been given and often fights to play with her brother's toys. Lately, she has been saying that she really is a boy. Janice's parents are starting to be concerned because she is identifying herself more as a boy as she gets older. They want to be supportive but are unsure of the next steps they should take.

Diagnostic Questions

1. Do Janice's presenting symptoms meet the criteria for gender dysphoria?
2. Based on the disorder identified in Question 1, which symptom(s) led you to select the diagnosis?
3. What would be the reason(s) a counselor may not diagnose Janice with gender dysphoria?
4. What rule-outs would you consider for Janice's case?
5. What other information may be needed to make an accurate clinical diagnosis?

Case Example 2

Tara, a 32-year-old White woman, sought counseling before an elective breast implant surgery. She stated that her parents and friends have urged her to speak with someone before the surgery because they feel she has a problem. Tara states that although she was born with male genitalia, she has always known she is a woman inside and wants the outside to reflect that. To this end, 4 years ago, she changed her name from Terrance to Tara even though her family strongly objected. Furthermore, her feelings and actions toward becoming fully female are a strong source of family tension since her childhood. She remembers her father walking in on her when she was 9 years old while she was putting on makeup. She was severely punished for this behavior. When she was 18, she began learning about the transgender community and made friends in some sanctuary spaces. Her parents and siblings again expressed concern, and for a while, her father refused to speak to her.

At age 32, Tara finally feels empowered to begin the transformation process. She states that this has caused so much friction within the family that her mother is depressed and calls her almost daily crying and begging her not to follow through. Tara agreed to talk to a counselor before the surgery because her mother is so upset, and she is reconsidering the surgery even though it has been a lifelong dream for her.

Diagnostic Questions

1. Do Tara's presenting symptoms meet the criteria for gender dysphoria?
2. What criteria would support giving this diagnosis?
3. What would be the reason(s) a counselor may not diagnose Tara with gender dysphoria?
4. What rule-outs must be considered?
5. What other information may be needed to make an accurate clinical diagnosis?

Questions for Consideration

1. What are the ethical issues associated with gender dysphoria as a diagnosis?
2. How is gender dysphoria different from mental health symptoms that result from various experiences of stigma and discrimination?
3. What can counselors do to address the symptoms of gender dysphoria?
4. How do we create gender-affirming spaces?

PART TWO

References

Abramowitz, J. S. (2018, Fall). The inhibitory learning approach to exposure and response prevention. *International OCD Foundation: OCD Newsletter, 32*(3), 10–12. https://iocdf.org/download/fall-2018-vol-32-num-3/

Abramowitz, J. S., Blakey, S. M., Reuman, L., & Buchholz, J. L. (2017). New directions in the cognitive-behavioral treatment of OCD: Theory, research, and practice. *Behavior Therapy, 49*(3), 311–322. https://doi.org/10.1016/j.beth.2017.09.002

Abramowitz, J. S., Wheaton, M. G., & Storch, E. A. (2008). The status of hoarding as a symptom of obsessive-compulsive disorder. *Behaviour Research and Therapy, 46*(9), 1026–1033. https://doi.org/10.1016/j.brat.2008.05.006

Aina, Y., & Susman, J. L. (2006). Understanding comorbidity with depression and anxiety disorders. *Journal of the American Osteopathic Association, 106*(5, Suppl. 2), S9–S14.

Akinhanmi, M. O., Biernacka, J. M., Strakowski, S. M., McElroy, S. L., Balls Berry, J. E., Merikangas, K. R., Assari, S., McInnis, M. G., Schulze, T. G., LeBoyer, M., Tamminga, C., Patten, C., & Frye, M. A. (2018). Racial disparities in bipolar disorder treatment and research: A call to action. *Bipolar Disorders, 20*(6), 506–514. https://doi.org/10.1111/bdi.12638

Akiskal, H. S. (2002). Classification, diagnosis and boundaries of bipolar disorders: A review. In M. Maj, H. S. Akiskal, J. J. López-Ibor, & N. Sartorius (Eds.), *Bipolar disorder* (pp. 33–54). Wiley.

Allen, B. C. (2016). A RADical idea: A call to eliminate "attachment disorder" and "attachment therapy" from the clinical lexicon. *Evidence-Based Practice in Child and Adolescent Mental Health, 1*(1), 60–71. https://doi.org/10.1080/23794925.2016.1172945

Alloy, L. B., Abramson, L. Y., Urosevic, S., Bender, R. E., & Wagner, C. A. (2009). Longitudinal predictors of bipolar spectrum disorders: A behavioral approach system (BAS) perspective. *Clinical Psychology: Science and Practice, 16*(2), 206–226. https://doi.org/10.1111/j.1468-2850.2009.01160.x

Altamura, A. C., Buoli, M., Caldiroli, A., Caron, L., Cumerlato Melter, C., Dobrea, C., Cigliobianco, M., & Zanelli Quarantini, F. (2015). Misdiagnosis, duration of untreated illness (DUI) and outcome in bipolar patients with psychotic symptoms: A naturalistic study. *Journal of Affective Disorder, 182,* 70–75. https://doi.org/10.1016/j.jad.2015.04.024

American Counseling Association. (2014). *ACA code of ethics.* https://www.counseling.org/resources/aca-code-of-ethics.pdf

American Heritage Dictionary. (n.d.). *Anxiety.* Retrieved January 25, 2023 https://www.ahdictionary.com

American Psychiatric Association. (1952). *Diagnostic and statistical manual of mental disorders.*
American Psychiatric Association. (1968). *Diagnostic and statistical manual of mental disorders* (2nd ed.).
American Psychiatric Association. (1980). *Diagnostic and statistical manual of mental disorders* (3rd ed.).
American Psychiatric Association. (1987). *Diagnostic and statistical manual of mental disorders* (3rd ed., rev.).
American Psychiatric Association. (1994). *Diagnostic and statistical manual of mental disorders* (4th ed.).
American Psychiatric Association. (2013a). *Diagnostic and statistical manual of mental disorders* (5th ed.). https://doi.org/10.1176/appi.books.9780890425596
American Psychiatric Association. (2013b). *Gender dysphoria.* https://www.psychiatry.org/file%20library/psychiatrists/practice/dsm/apa_dsm-5-gender-dysphoria.pdf
American Psychiatric Association. (2013c). *Highlights of changes from DSM-IV-TR to DSM-5.* https://www.psychiatry.org/File%20Library/Psychiatrists/Practice/DSM/APA_DSM_Changes_from_DSM-IV-TR_-to_DSM-5.pdf
American Psychiatric Association. (2013d). *Major depressive disorder and the "bereavement exclusion."* https://www.psychiatry.org/File%20Library/Psychiatrists/Practice/DSM/APA_*DSM*-5-Depression-Bereavement-Exclusion.pdf
American Psychiatric Association. (2022a). *Diagnostic and statistical manual of mental disorders* (5th ed., text rev.). https://doi.org/10.1176/appi.books.9780890425787
American Psychiatric Association. (2022b). *DSM-5-TR update: Supplement to the diagnostic and statistical manual of mental disorders, fifth edition, text revision.* https://www.psychiatry.org/getmedia/34c43e15-2618-4d2b-9f67-6bef5c40f75a/APA-DSM5TR-Update-September-2022.pdf
American Psychiatric Association. (2022c). *Major depressive disorder.* https://www.psychiatry.org/File%20Library/Psychiatrists/Practice/DSM/DSM-5-TR/APA-DSM5TR-MajorDepressiveDisorder.pdf
American Psychiatric Association. (2022d). *Persistent depressive disorder.* https://www.psychiatry.org/File%20Library/Psychiatrists/Practice/DSM/*DSM-5*-TR/APA-DSM5TR-PersistentDepressive.pdf
Angelakis, I., Gooding, P. A., & Panagioti, M. (2016). Suicidality in body dysmorphic disorder (BDD): A systematic review with meta-analysis. *Clinical Psychology Review, 49,* 55–66. https://doi.org/10.1016/j.cpr.2016.08.002
Anxiety and Depression Association of America. (2020). *Treatment & management.* https://adaa.org/understanding-anxiety/depression/treatment-management
Anxiety and Depression Association of America. (2022). *Anxiety disorders—Facts & statistics.* http://www.adaa.org/about-adaa/press-room/facts-statistics
Anxiety and Depression Association of America. (2023). *LGBTQ+ community.* https://adaa.org/find-help/by-demographics/lgbtq
Atwoli, L., Stein, D. J., Koenen, K. C., & McLaughlin, K. A. (2015). Epidemiology of posttraumatic stress disorder: Prevalence, correlates and consequences. *Current Opinion in Psychiatry, 28*(4), 307–311. https://doi.org/10.1097/YCO.0000000000000167
Ayers, C. R., Saxena, S., Golshan, S., & Wetherell, J. L. (2010). Age at onset and clinical features of late life compulsive hoarding. *International Journal of Geriatric Psychiatry, 25*(2), 142–149. https://doi.org/10.1002/gps.2310
Azoulay, M., Reuveni, I., Dan, R., Goelman, G., Segman, R., Kalla, C., Bonne, O., & Canetti, L. (2020). Childhood trauma and premenstrual symptoms: The role of emotion regulation. *Child Abuse & Neglect, 108,* Article 104637. https://doi.org/10.1016/j.chiabu.2020.104637
Bailey, R. K., Mokonogho, J., & Kumar, A. (2019). Racial and ethnic differences in depression: Current perspectives. *Neuropsychiatric Disease and Treatment, 15,* 603–609. https://doi.org/10.2147/NDT.S128584
Bains, N., & Abdijadid, S. (2023). *Major depressive disorder.* StatPearls. https://www.statpearls.com/articlelibrary/viewarticle/24655
Balleur-van Rijn, A., Steensma, T. D., Kreukels, B. P. C., & Cohen-Kettenis, P. T. (2012). Self-perception in a clinical sample of gender variant children. *Clinical Child Psychology and Psychiatry, 18*(3), 464–474. https://doi.org/10.1177/1359104512460621
Barzegar, H., Farahbakhsh, M., Azizi, H., Aliashrafi, S., Hossein, D., & Fakhari, A. (2021). A descriptive study of agoraphobic situations and correlates on panic disorder. *Middle East Current Psychiatry, 28,* Article 31. https://doi.org/10.1186/s43045-021-00110-y

Batelaan, N. M., Smit, F., De Graaf, R., Van Balkom, A. J. L. M., Vollebergh, W. A. M., & Beekman, A. T. F. (2010). Identifying target groups for the prevention of anxiety disorders in the general population. *Acta Psychiatrica Scandinavica, 122*(1), 56–65. https://doi.org/10.1111/j.1600-0447.2009.01488.x

Baxter, M. G., & Croxson, P. L. (2012). Facing the role of the amygdala in emotional information processing. *PNAS, 109*(52), 21180–21181. https://doi.org/10.1073/pnas.1219167110

Benjet, C., Bromet, E., Karam, E. G., Kessler, R. C., McLaughlin, K. A., Ruscio, A. M., & Koenen, K. C. (2016). The epidemiology of traumatic event exposure worldwide: Results from the World Mental Health Survey Consortium. *Psychological Medicine, 46*(2), 327–343. https://doi.org/10.1017/S0033291715001981

Berg-Brousseau, H. (2022, March 25). *ICYMI: Top lawmakers leading the fight against anti-LGBTQ+ bills in TX, AL, FL, KY, KS, and TN underscore urgency on the national crisis brewing in states, preview the path forward for LGBTQ+ people* [Press release]. Human Rights Campaign. https://www.hrc.org/press-releases/icymi-top-lawmakers-leading-the-fight-against-anti-lgbtq-bills-in-tx-al-fl-ky-ks-and-tn-underscore-urgency-on-the-national-crisis-brewing-in-states-preview-the-path-forward-for-lgbtq-people

Bicknell-Hentges, L., & Lynch, J. J. (2009). Everything counselors and supervisors need to know about treating trauma. *VISTAS Online.* https://www.counseling.org/resources/library/vistas/2009-V-Online/Bicknell-Hentges-Lynch.pdf

Bjornsson, A. S., Didie, E. R., Grant, J. E., Menard, W., Stalker, E., & Phillips, K. A. (2013). Age at onset and clinical correlates in body dysmorphic disorder. *Comprehensive Psychiatry, 54*(7), 893–903. https://doi.org/10.1016/j.comppsych.2013.03.019

Bjornsson, A. S., Didie, E. R., & Phillips, K. A. (2010). Body dysmorphic disorder. *Dialogues in Clinical Neuroscience, 12*(2), 221–232. https://doi.org/10.31887/dcns.2010.12.2/abjornsson

Blader, J. C., & Carlson, G. A. (2007). Increased rates of bipolar disorder diagnoses among U.S. child, adolescent, and adult inpatients, 1996–2004. *Biological Psychiatry, 62*(2), 107–114. https://doi.org/10.1016/j.biopsych.2006.11.006

Bloch, M. H., Bartley, C. A., Zipperer, L., Jakubovski, E., Landeros-Weisenberger, A., Pittenger, C., & Leckman, J. F. (2014). Meta-analysis: Hoarding symptoms associated with poor treatment outcome in obsessive-compulsive disorder. *Molecular Psychiatry, 19*(9), 1025–1030. https://doi.org/10.1038/mp.2014.50

Bloch, M. H., Landeros-Weisenberger, A., Kelmendi, B., Coric, V., Bracken, M. B., & Leckman, J. F. (2006). A systematic review: Antipsychotic augmentation with treatment refractory obsessive-compulsive disorder. *Molecular Psychiatry, 11*(7), 622–632. https://doi.org/10.1038/sj.mp.4001823

Bohne, A., Keuthen, N. J., Wilhelm, S., Deckersbach, T., & Jenike, M. A. (2002). Prevalence of symptoms of body dysmorphic disorder and its correlates: A cross-cultural comparison. *Psychosomatics, 43*(6), 486–490. https://doi.org/10.1176/appi.psy.43.6.486

Bolin, R. (1986). Disaster characteristics and psychosocial impacts. In B. Sowder & M. Lystad (Eds.), *Disasters and mental health: Selected contemporary perspectives* (pp. 3–28). National Institute of Mental Health.

Boucher, F. J. O., & Chinnah, T. I. (2020). Gender dysphoria: A review investigating the relationship between genetic influences and brain development. *Adolescent Health Medicine and Therapeutics, 5*(11), 89–99. https://doi.org/10.2147/AHMT.S259168.

Breen, L. J., & O'Connor, M. (2007). The fundamental paradox in the grief literature: A critical reflection. *Omega—Journal of Death and Dying, 55*(3), 199–218. https://doi.org/10.2190/om.55.3.c

Breh, D. C., & Seidler, G. H. (2007). Is peritraumatic dissociation a risk factor for PTSD? *Journal of Trauma & Dissociation, 8*(1), 53–69. https://doi.org/10.1300/j229v08n01_04

Brik, T., Vrouenraets, L. J. J. J., de Vries, M. C., & Hannema, S. E. (2020). Trajectories of adolescents treated with gonadotropin-releasing hormone analogues for gender dysphoria. *Archives of Sexual Behavior, 49*(7), 2611–2618. https://doi.org/10.1007/s10508-020-01660-8

Bruce, M., Young, D., Turnbull, S., Rooksby, M., Chadwick, G., Oates, C., Nelson, R. A., Young-Southward, G., Haig, C., & Minnis, H. (2019). Reactive attachment disorder in maltreated young children in foster care. *Attachment & Human Development, 21*(2), 152–169. https://doi.org/10.1080/14616734.2018.1499211

Bryant, R. A. (2007). Does dissociation further our understanding of PTSD? *Journal of Anxiety Disorder, 21*(2), 183–191. https://doi.org/10.1016/j.janxdis.2006.09.012

Bryant, R. A. (2013). Is pathological grief lasting more than 12 months grief or depression? *Current Opinion in Psychiatry, 26*(1), 41–46. https://doi.org/10.1097/yco.0b013e32835b2ca2
Bryant, R. A. (2022). Post-traumatic stress disorder vs traumatic brain injury. *Dialogues in Clinical Neuroscience, 13*(3), 251–262. https://doi.org/10.31887/DCNS.2011.13.2/rbryant
Bryant, R. A., Friedman, M. J., Spiegel, D., Ursano, R., & Strain, J. (2011). A review of acute stress disorder in *DSM-5*. *Depression and Anxiety, 28*(9), 802–817. https://doi.org/10.1002/da.20737
Bryant-Davis, T. (2019). The cultural context of trauma recovery: Considering the posttraumatic stress disorder practice guideline and intersectionality. *Psychotherapy, 56*(3), 400–408. https://doi.org/10.1037/pst0000241
Buchholz, J. L., & Abramowitz, J. S. (2020). The therapeutic alliance in exposure therapy for anxiety-related disorders: A critical review. *Journal of Anxiety Disorders, 70,* Article 102194. https://doi.org/10.1016/j.janxdis.2020.102194
Burnes, T. R., Singh, A. A., Harper, A. J., Harper, B., Maxon-Kann, W., Pickering, D. L., Moundas, S., Scofield, T. R., Roan, A., & Hosea, J. (2010). American Counseling Association competencies for counseling with transgender clients. *Journal of LGBT Issues in Counseling, 4*(3–4), 135–155. https://doi.org/10.1080/15538605.2010.524839
Burton, N. (2012, June 21). A short history of bipolar disorder. *Psychology Today.* http://www.psychologytoday.com/blog/hide-and-seek/201206/short-history-bipolar-disorder
Byrd-Bredbenner, C., Eck, K., & Quick, V. (2020). Psychometric properties of the Generalized Anxiety Disorder–7 and the Generalized Anxiety Disorder–Mini in United States university students. *Frontiers in Psychology, 11,* Article 550533. https://doi.org/10.3389/fpsyg.2020.550533
Calikusu, C., Kucukgoncu, S., Tecer, Ö., & Bestepe, E. (2012). Skin picking in Turkish students: Prevalence, characteristics, and gender differences. *Behavior Modification, 36*(1), 49–66. https://doi.org/10.1177/014544551142028
Cath, D. C., Nizar, K., Boomsma, D. I., & Mathews, C. A. (2017). Age-specific prevalence of hoarding and obsessive compulsive disorder: A population-based study. *American Journal of Geriatric Psychiatry, 25*(3), 245–255. https://doi.org/10.1016/j.jagp.2016.11.006
Centers for Disease Control and Prevention. (2010). Current depression among adults, 2006 and 2008. *Morbidity and Mortality Weekly Report, 59,* 1229–1235.
Centers for Disease Control and Prevention. (2022). *Depression is not a normal part of growing older.* https://www.cdc.gov/aging/depression/index.html
Chaffin, M., Hanson, R., Saunders, B. E., Nichols, T., Barnett, D., Zeanah, C., & Miller-Perrin, C. (2006). Report of the APSAC task force on attachment therapy, reactive attachment disorder, and attachment problems. *Child Maltreatment, 11*(1), 76–89. https://doi.org/10.1177/1077559505283699
Chamberlain, S. R., Menzies, L., Sahakian, B. J., & Fineberg, N. A. (2007). Lifting the veil on trichotillomania. *The American Journal of Psychiatry, 164*(4), 568–574. https://doi.org/10.1176/appi.ajp.164.4.568
Chatterton, M. L., Ke, X., Lewis, B. E., Rajagopalan, K., & Lazarus, A. (2008). Impact of bipolar disorder on the family: Utilization and cost of health care resources. *Pharmacy and Therapeutics, 33*(1), 15–34. http://www.ncbi.nlm.nih.gov/pmc/articles/PMC2730065/
Chia, K., Pasalich, D. S., Fassnacht, D. B., Ali, K., Kyrios, M., Maclean, B., & Grisham, J. R. (2021). Interpersonal attachment, early family environment, and trauma in hoarding: A systematic review. *Clinical Psychology Review, 90,* Article 102096. https://doi.org/10.1016/j.cpr.2021.102096
Chiang, K.-J., Tsai, J.-C., Liu, D., Lin, C.-H., Chiu, H.-L., & Chou, K.-R. (2017). Efficacy of cognitive-behavioral therapy in patients with bipolar disorder: A meta-analysis of randomized controlled trials. *PLOS ONE, 12*(5), Article e0176849. https://doi.org/10.1371/journal.pone.0176849
Chodzen, G., Hidalgo, M. A., Chen, D., & Garofalo, R. (2019). Minority stress factors associated with depression and anxiety among transgender and gender-nonconforming youth. *Journal of Adolescent Health, 64*(4), 467–471. https://doi.org/10.1016/j.jadohealth.2018.07.006
Christenson, G. A., & Mackenzie, T. B. (1995). Trichotillomania, body dysmorphic disorder, and obsessive-compulsive disorder. *The Journal of Clinical Psychiatry, 56*(5), 211–212.
Claahsen-van der Grinten, H., Verhaak, C., Steensma, T., Middelberg, T., & Roeffen, J., & Klink, D. (2021). Gender incongruence and gender dysphoria in childhood and adolescence—Current insights in diagnostics, management, and follow-up. *European Journal of Pediatrics, 180*(5), 1349–1357. https://doi.org/10.1007/s00431-020-03906-y

Clark, D., & Radomsky, A. S. (2014). Introduction: A global perspective on unwanted intrusive thoughts. *Journal of Obsessive-Compulsive and Related Disorders, 3*(3), 265–268. https://doi.org/10.1016/j.jocrd.2014.02.001

Cohen, J. A., Bukstein, O., Walter, H., Benson, R. S., Chrisman, A., Farchione, T. R., Hamilton, J., Keable, H., Kinlan, J., Schoettle, U., Siegal, M., & Stock, S., & Medicus, J. (2010). Practice parameter for the assessment and treatment of children and adolescents with posttraumatic stress disorder. *Journal of the American Academy of Child & Adolescent Psychiatry, 49*(4), 414–430. https://doi.org/10.1097/00004583-201004000-00021

Cohen, J. A., Mannarino, A. P., & Deblinger, E. (2006). *Treating trauma and traumatic grief in children and adolescents.* Guilford Press.

Coleman, E., Radix, A. E., Bouman, W.P., Brown, G. R., de Vries, A. L. C., Deutsch, M. B., Ettner, R., Fraser, L., Goodman, M., Green, J., Hancock, A. B., Johnson, T. W., Karasic, D. H., Knudson, G. A., Leibowitz, S. F., Meyer-Bahlburg, H. F. L., Monstrey, S. J., Motmans, J., Nahata, L., . . . Arcelus, J. (2022). Standards of care for the health of transgender and gender diverse people, Version 8. *International Journal of Transgender Health, 23*(S1), S1–S260. https://doi.org/10.1080/26895269.2022.2100644

Comer, J. S., Pincus, D. B., & Hoffman, S. G. (2012). Generalized anxiety disorder and the proposed associated symptoms criterion change for *DSM-5* in a treatment-seeking sample of anxious youth. *Depression and Anxiety, 29*(12), 994–1003. https://doi.org/10.1002/da.21999

Comer, R. J. (2022). *Abnormal psychology* (11th ed.). Worth.

Corey, G. (2022). *Theories and practice of counseling and psychotherapy* (10th ed.). Brooks/Cole.

Craig, S. L., Leung, V. W. Y., Pascoe, R., Pang, N., Iacono, G., Austin, A., & Dillon, F. (2021). AFFIRM online: Utilising an affirmative cognitive-behavioural digital intervention to improve mental health, access, and engagement among LGBTQA+ youth and young adults. *International Journal of Environmental Research and Public Health, 18*(4), Article 1541. https://doi.org/10.3390/ijerph18041541

Crooks, R. L., & Baur, K. (2013). *Our sexuality* (11th ed.). Cengage Learning.

Culver, J. L., Amow, B. A., & Ketter, T. A. (2007). Bipolar disorder: Improving diagnosis and optimizing integrated care. *Journal of Clinical Psychology, 63*(1), 73–92. https://doi.org/10.1002/jclp.20333

Cunningham, J., Yonkers, K. A., O'Brien, S., & Eriksson, E. (2009). Update on research and treatment of premenstrual dysphoric disorder. *Harvard Review of Psychiatry, 17*(2), 120–137. https://doi.org/10.1080/10673220902891836

Currier, J. M., Holland, J. P., & Neimeyer, R. A. (2007). The effectiveness of bereavement interventions with children: A meta-analytic review of controlled outcome research. Journal of Clinical Child and Adolescent Psychology, 36(2), 253–259. https://doi.org/10.1080/15374410701279669

Dailey, S. F., Parker, M. M., Emmanuel, A. D., & Campbell, A. (2022). Mental health and COVID-19: Symptom prevalence, sociodemographic associations, and implications for practice. *Journal of Mental Health Counseling, 44*(4), 343–361. https://doi.org/10.17744/mehc.44.4.05

Das, A. K., Olfson, M., Gameroff, M. J., Pilowsky, D. J., Blanco, C., Feder, A., & Weissman, M. M. (2005). Screening for bipolar disorder in a primary care practice. *JAMA, 293*(8), 956–963. https://doi.org/10.1001/jama.293.8.956

Davidson, C., O'Hare, A., Mactaggart, F., Green, J., Young, D., Gillberg, C., & Minnis, H. (2015). Social relationship difficulties in autism and reactive attachment disorder: Improving diagnostic validity through structured assessment. *Research in Developmental Disabilities, 40*, 63–72. https://doi.org/10.1016/j.ridd.2015.01.007

Davy, Z., & Toze, M. (2018). What is gender dysphoria? A critical systematic narrative review. *Transgender Health, 3*(1), 159–169. https://doi.org/10.1089/trgh.2018.0014

Daw, J. (2002, October). Is PMDD real? *Monitor on Psychology.* https://www.apa.org/monitor/oct02/pmdd

De La Cruz, L. F., Nordsletten, A. E., & Mataix-Cols, D. (2016). Ethnocultural aspects of hoarding disorder. *Current Psychiatry Reviews, 12*(2), 115–123. https://doi.org/10.2174/1573400512666160316004521

Den Braber, A., Ent, D. V., Blokland, G. A., van Grootheest, D. S., Cath, D. C., Veltman, D. J., de Ruiter, M. B., & Boomsma, D. I. (2008). An fMRI study in monozygotic twins discordant for obsessive-compulsive symptoms. *Biological Psychology, 79*(1), 91–102. https://doi.org/10.1016/j.biopsycho.2008.01.010

Diamond, M. (2013). Transsexuality among twins: Identity concordance, transition, rearing, and orientation. *International Journal of Transgenderism, 14*(1), 24–38. https://doi.org/10.1080/15532739.2013.750222

DiRocco, A., Liu, L., & Burrets, M. (2020). Enhancing dialectical behavior therapy for the treatment of bipolar disorder. *Psychiatric Quarterly, 91*(3), 629–654. https://doi.org/10.1007/s11126-020-09709-6

Djelantik, A. A. A. M. J., Smid, G. E., Mroz, A., Kleber, R. J., & Boelen, P. A. (2020). The prevalence of prolonged grief disorder in bereaved individuals following unnatural losses: Systematic review and meta regression analysis. *Journal of Affective Disorders, 265,* 146–156. https://doi.org/10.1016/j.jad.2020.01.034

Dragowski, E. A., Scharron-del Rio, M. R., & Sandigorsky, A. L. (2011). Childhood gender identity . . . disorder? Developmental, cultural, and diagnostic concerns. *Journal of Counseling & Development, 89*(3), 360–366. https://doi.org/10.1002/j.1556-6678.2011.tb00100.x

Dreger, A., Feder, E. K., & Tamar-Mattis, A. (2012). Prenatal dexamethasone for congenital adrenal hyperplasia: An ethics canary in the modern medical mine. *Journal of Bioethical Inquiry, 9*(3), 277–294. https://doi.org/10.1007/s11673-012-9384-9

Eisner, L., Eddie, D., Harley, R., Jacobo, M., Nierenberg, A. A., & Deckersbach, T. (2017). Dialectical behavior therapy group skills training for bipolar disorder. *Behavior Therapy, 48*(4), 557–566. https://doi.org/10.1016/j.beth.2016.12.006

Epstein, R. S., Fullerton, C. S., & Ursano, R. J. (1998). Posttraumatic stress disorder following an air disaster: A prospective study. *The American Journal of Psychiatry, 155*(7), 934–938. https://doi.org/10.1176/ajp.155.7.934

Escovar, E. L., Craske, M., Roy-Byrne, P., Stein, M. B., Sullivan, G., Sherbourne, C. D., Bystritsky, A., & Chavira, D. A. (2018). Cultural influences on mental health symptoms in a primary care sample of Latinx patients. *Journal of Anxiety Disorders, 55,* 39–47. https://doi.org/10.1016/j.janxdis.2018.03.005

Evans-Campbell, T., Lindhorst, T., Huang, B., & Walters, K. L. (2006). Interpersonal violence in the lives of urban American Indian and Alaska Native women: Implications for health, mental health, and help-seeking. *American Journal of Public Health, 96*(8), 1416–1422. https://doi.org/10.2105/ajph.2004.054213

Ezell, J. M., Salari, S., Rooker, C., & Chase, E. C. (2021). Intersectional trauma: COVID-19, the psychosocial contract, and America's racialized public health lineage. *Traumatology, 27*(1), 78–85. https://doi.org/10.1037/trm0000302

Fadus, M. C., Ginsburg, K. R., Sobowale, K., Halliday-Boykins, C. A., Bryant, B. E., Gray, K. M., & Squeglia, L. M. (2020). Unconscious bias and the diagnosis of disruptive behavior disorders and ADHD in African American and Hispanic youth. *Academic Psychiatry, 44*(1), 95–102. https://doi.org/10.1007/s40596-019-01127-6

Fanai, M., & Khan, M. A. (2023). *Acute stress disorder.* StatPearls. https://www.statpearls.com/point-of-care/29538

Farhat, L. C., Olfson, E., Nasir, M., Levine, J. L., Li, F., Miguel, E. C., & Bloch, M. H. (2020). Pharmacological and behavioral treatment for trichotillomania: An updated systematic review with meta-analysis. *Depression and Anxiety, 37*(8), 715–727. https://doi.org/10.1002/da.23028

Fava, G. A., Rafanelli, C., Tomba, E., Guidi, J., & Grandi, S. (2011). The sequential combination of cognitive behavioral treatment and well-being therapy in cyclothymic disorder. *Psychotherapy and Psychosomatics, 80*(3), 136–143. https://doi.org/10.1159/000321575

Fernández, A., Mendive, J. M., Salvador-Carulla, L., Rubio-Valera, M., Luciano, J. V., Pinto-Meza, A., Haro, J. M., Palao, D., Bellón, J. M., & Serrano-Blanco, A. (2012). Adjustment disorders in primary care: Prevalence, recognition and use of services. *British Journal of Psychiatry, 201*(2), 137–142. https://doi.org/10.1192/bjp.bp.111.096305

Ferrão, Y. A., Almeida, V. C., Bedin, N. R., Rosa, R. F. M., & Busnello, E. D. (2006). Impulsivity and compulsivity in patients with trichotillomania or skin picking compared with patients with obsessive-compulsive disorder. *Comprehensive Psychiatry, 47*(4), 282–288. https://doi.org/10.1016/j.comppsych.2005.11.005

Fineberg, N. A., Hollander, E., Pallanti, S., Walitza, S., Grünblatt, E., Dell'Osso, B., Albert, U., Geller, D. A., Brakoulias, V., Reddy, Y. J., Arumugham, S. S., Shavitt, R. G., Drummond, L. M., Grancini, B., De Carlo, V., Cinosi, E., Chamberlain, S. R., Ioannidis, K., Rodriguez, C. I., . . . Menchón, J. M. (2020). Clinical advances in obsessive-compulsive disorder: A position statement by the

International College of Obsessive-Compulsive Spectrum Disorders. *International Clinical Psychopharmacology, 35*(4), 173–193. https://doi.org/10.1097/yic.0000000000000314
Fineberg, N. A., Reghunandanan, S., Brown, A. M., & Pampaloni, I. (2013). Pharmacotherapy of obsessive-compulsive disorder: Evidence-based treatment and beyond. *Australian and New Zealand Journal of Psychiatry, 47*(2), 121–141. https://doi.org/10.1177/0004867412461958
First, M. (2010). Clinical utility in the revision of the *Diagnostic and statistical manual of mental disorder (DSM). Professional Psychology: Research and Practice, 41*(6), 465–473. https://doi.org/10.1037/a0021511
First, M., Pincus, H., Levine, J., Williams, J., Ustun, B., & Peele, R. (2004). Clinical utility as a criterion for revising psychiatric diagnoses. *The American Journal of Psychiatry, 161*(6), 946–954. https://doi.org/10.1176/appi.ajp.161.6.946
Fisher, A., Manicavasagar, V., Sharpe, L., Laidsaar-Powell, R., & Juraskova, I. (2018). A qualitative exploration of patient and family views and experiences of treatment decision-making in bipolar II disorder. *Journal of Mental Health, 27*(1), 66–79. https://doi.org/10.1080/09638237.2016.1276533
Flessner, C. A., Conelea, C. A., Woods, D. W., Franklin, M. E., Keuthen, N. J., & Cashin, S. E. (2008). Styles of pulling in trichotillomania: Exploring differences in symptom severity, phenomenology, and functional impact. *Behaviour Research and Therapy, 46*(3), 345–357. https://doi.org/10.1016/j.brat.2007.12.009
Flessner, C. A., & Woods, D. W. (2006). Phenomenological characteristics, social problems, and the economic impact associated with chronic skin picking. *Behavior Modification, 30*(6), 944–963. https://doi.org/10.1177/0145445506294083
Foa, E., Hembree, E. A., Rauch, S., & Rothbaum, B. O. (2019). *Prolonged exposure therapy for PTSD: Emotional processing of traumatic experiences—Therapist guide.* Oxford University Press.
Foreman, M., Hare, L., York, K., Balakrishnan, K., Sánchez, F. J., Harte, F., Erasmus, J., Vilain, E., & Harley, V. R. (2019). Genetic link between gender dysphoria and sex hormone signaling. *The Journal of Clinical Endocrinology & Metabolism, 104*(2), 390–396. https://doi.org/10.1210/jc.2018-01105
Frances, A. (2013). *Essentials of psychiatric diagnosis: Responding to the challenge of DSM-5.* Guilford Press.
Freeston, M. H., Rhéaume, J., Letarte, H., Dugas, M. J., & Ladouceur, R. (1994). Why do people worry? *Personality and Individual Differences, 17*(6), 791–802. https://doi.org/10.1016/0191-8869(94)90048-5
Friborg, O., Martinussen, M., Kaiser, S., Overgard, K. T., & Rosenvinge, J. H. (2013). Comorbidity of personality disorders in anxiety disorders: A meta-analysis of 30 years of research. *Journal of Affective Disorder, 145*(2), 143–155. https://doi.org/10.1016/j.jad.2012.07.004
Friedman, M. J., Resick, P. A., Bryant, R. A., Strain, J., Horowitz, M., & Spiegel, D. (2011). Classification of trauma and stressor-related disorders in *DSM-5. Depression and Anxiety, 28*(9), 737–749. https://doi.org/10.1002/da.20845
Frommberger, U., Angenendt, J., & Berger, M. (2014). Post-traumatic stress disorder—A diagnostic and therapeutic challenge. *Deutsches Ärzteblatt International, 111*(5), 59–65. https://doi.org/10.3238/arztebl.2014.0059
Frost, R. O., Steketee, G., & Tolin, D. F. (2011). Comorbidity in hoarding disorder. *Depression and Anxiety, 28*(10), 876–884. https://doi.org/10.1002/da.20861
Gage, N. M., & Baars, B. (2018). *Fundamentals of cognitive neuroscience: A beginner's guide.* Academic Press.
Gan, J., He, J., Fu, H., & Zhu, X. (2021). Association between obsession, compulsion, depression and insight in obsessive-compulsive disorder: a meta-analysis. *Nordic Journal of Psychiatry, 76*(7), 489–496. https://doi.org/10.1080/08039488.2021.2013532
Gershuny, B. S., Keuthen, N. J., Gentes, E. L., Russo, A. R., Emmott, E. C., Jameson, M., & Jenike, M. A. (2006). Current posttraumatic stress disorder and history of trauma in trichotillomania. *Journal of Clinical Psychology, 62*(12), 1521–1529. https://doi.org/10.1002/jclp.20303
Gibson, L. E. (2007). *Acute stress disorder.* U.S. Department of Veterans Affairs, National Center for PTSD. http://www.ptsd.va.gov/professional/pages/acute-stress-disorder.asp
Gilea, B. L., & O'Neill, R. M. (2015). *Disruptive mood dysregulation disorder.* American Counseling Association. https://www.counseling.org/docs/default-source/default-document-library/disruptive-mood-dysregulation-disorder.pdf

Gillan, C. M., Fineberg, N. A., & Robbins, T. W. (2017). A trans-diagnostic perspective on obsessive-compulsive disorder. *Psychological Medicine, 47*(9), 1528–1548. https://doi.org/doi:10.1017/S0033291716002786

Girdler, S. S., Leserman, J., Bunevicius, R., Klatzkin, R., Pedersen, C. A., & Light, K. C. (2007). Persistent alterations in biological profiles in women with abuse histories: Influence of premenstrual dysphoric disorder. *Health Psychology, 26*(2), 201–213. https://doi.org/10.1037/0278-6133.26.2.201

Gleason, M. M., Zamfirescu, A., Egger, H. L., Nelson, C. A., Fox, N. A., & Zeanah, C. H. (2011). Epidemiology of psychiatric disorders in very young children in a Romanian pediatric setting. *European Child & Adolescent Psychiatry, 20*(10), 527–535. https://doi.org/10.1007/s00787-011-0214-0

Gleser, G., Green, B., & Winget, C. (1981). *Prolonged psychosocial effects of disaster: A study of Buffalo Creek.* Academic Press.

Goetter, E., Frumkin, M. R., Palitz, S., Swee, B., Baker, A., Bui, E., & Simon, N. (2020). Barriers to mental health treatment among individuals with social anxiety disorder and generalized anxiety disorder. *Psychological Services, 17*(1), 5–12. https://doi.org/10.1037/ser0000254

Goodman, K. S. (2014). Reading: A psycholinguistic guessing game. In K. S. Goodman & Y. M. Goodman, *Making sense of learners making sense of written language: The selected works of Kenneth S. Goodman and Yetta M. Goodman* (pp. 103–112). Routledge.

Goodman, R. D., & West-Olatunji, C. (2008). Transgenerational trauma and resilience: Improving mental health counseling for survivors of Hurricane Katrina. *Journal of Mental Health Counseling, 30*(2), 121–136. https://doi.org/10.17744/mehc.30.2.q52260n242204r84

Goodrich, K. M., Farmer, L. B., Watson, J. C., Davis, R. J., Luke, M., Dispenza, F., Akers, W., & Griffith, C. (2017). Standards of care in assessment of lesbian, gay, bisexual, transgender, gender expansive, and queer/questioning (LGBTGEQ+) persons. *Journal of LGBT Issues in Counseling, 11*(4), 203–211. https://doi.org/10.1080/15538605.2017.1380548

Goodwin, R. D., Dierker, L. C., Wu, M., Galea, S., Hoven, C. W., & Weinberger, A. H. (2022). Trends in U.S. depression prevalence from 2015 to 2020: The widening treatment gap. *American Journal of Preventive Medicine, 63*(5), 726–733. https://doi.org/10.1016/j.amepre.2022.05.014

Gort, G. (1984). Pathological grief: Causes, recognition, and treatment. *Canadian Family Physician, 30,* 914–924.

Gottlieb, B., Beitel, L. K., Nadarajah, A., Palioura, M., & Trifiro, M. (2012). The androgen receptor gene mutations database (ARDB): 2012 update. *Human Mutation, 33*(5), 887–894. https://doi.org/10.1002/humu.22046

Grant, J. E., & Chamberlain, S. R. (2015). Trichotillomania and skin-picking disorder: Different kinds of OCD. *Focus, 13*(2), 184–189. https://doi.org/10.1176/appi.focus.130212

Grant, J. E., & Chamberlain, S. R. (2020). Prevalence of skin picking (excoriation) disorder. *Journal of Psychiatric Research, 130,* 57–60. https://doi.org/10.1016/j.jpsychires.2020.06.033

Grant, J. E., Dougherty, D. D., & Chamberlain, S. R. (2020). Prevalence, gender correlates, and comorbidity of trichotillomania. *Psychiatry Research-Neuroimaging, 288,* Article 112948. https://doi.org/10.1016/j.psychres.2020.112948

Grant, J. E., Mancebo, M. C., Pinto, A., Eisen, J. L., & Rasmussen, S. A. (2006). Impulse control disorders in adults with obsessive compulsive disorder. *Journal of Psychiatric Research, 40*(6), 494–501. https://doi.org/10.1016/j.jpsychires.2005.11.005

Green, A. E., DeChants, J. P., Price, M. N., & Davis, C. K. (2021). Association of gender-affirming hormone therapy with depression, thoughts of suicide, and attempted suicide among transgender and nonbinary youth. *Journal of Adolescent Health, 70*(4), 643–649. https://doi.org/10.1016/j.jadohealth.2021.10.036

Green, B. L. (1990). Defining trauma: Terminology and generic stressor dimensions. *Journal of Applied Social Psychology, 20*(20, Pt. 2), 1632–1642. https://doi.org/10.1111/j.1559-1816.1990.tb01498.x

Green, B. L., & Solomon, S. (1995). The mental impact of natural and technological disasters. In J. Freedy & S. Hobfoll (Eds.), *Traumatic stress: From theory to practice* (pp. 163–180). Plenum.

Greist, J. H., Jefferson, J. W., Kobak, K. A., Katzelnick, D. J., & Serlin, R. C. (1995). Efficacy and tolerability of serotonin transport inhibitors in obsessive-compulsive disorder: A meta-analysis. *Archives of General Psychiatry, 52*(1), 53–60. https://doi.org/10.1001/archpsyc.1995.03950130053006

Hankin, B. L. (2009). Etiology of bipolar disorder across the lifespan: Essential interplay with diagnosis, classification, and assessment. *Clinical Psychologist, 16*(2), 227–230. https://doi.org/10.1111/j.1468-2850.2009.01161.x

Hantsoo, L., & Epperson, C. N. (2015). Premenstrual dysphoric disorder: Epidemiology and treatment. *Current Psychiatry Reports, 17*(11), Article 87. https://doi.org/10.1007/s11920-015-0628-3

Hartl, T. L., Duffany, S. R., Allen, G. J., Steketee, G., & Frost, R. O. (2005). Relationships among compulsive hoarding, trauma, and attention-deficit/hyperactivity disorder. *Behaviour Research and Therapy, 43*(2), 269–276. https://doi.org/10.1016/j.brat.2004.02.002

Hatchett, G. T. (2022). Treatment planning strategies for youth with disruptive mood dysregulation disorder. *The Professional Counselor, 12*(1), 36–48. https://doi.org/10.15241/gth.12.1.36

Hayes, S. C., & Lillis, J. (2014). Acceptance and commitment therapy. In G. R. VandenBos, E. Meidenbauer, & J. Frank-McNeil (Eds.), *Psychotherapy theories and techniques: A reader* (pp. 3–8). American Psychological Association. https://doi.org/10.1037/14295-001

Hayes, S. C., Strosahl, K., & Wilson, K. G. (1999). *Acceptance and commitment therapy: An experiential approach to behavior change.* Guilford Press.

Hays, D., & Erford, B. T. (2018). *Developing multicultural counseling competence: A systems approach* (3rd ed.). Pearson Education.

Hein, L. C., & Berger, K. C. (2012). Gender dysphoria in children: Let's think this through. *Journal of Child and Adolescent Psychiatric Nursing, 25*(4), 237–240. https://doi.org/10.1111/jcap.12014

Hickey, D., Carr, A., Dooley, B., Guerin, S., Butler, E., & Fitzpatrick, L. (2005). Family and marital profiles of couples in which one partner has depression or anxiety. *Journal of Marital and Family Therapy, 31*(2), 171–182. https://doi.org/10.1111/j.1752-0606.2005.tb01554.x

Himle, J. A., Bybee, D., O'Donnell, L. J., Weaver, A., Vlnka, S., DeSena, D. T., & Rimer, J. M. (2018). Awareness enhancing and monitoring device plus habit reversal in the treatment of trichotillomania: An open feasibility trial. *Journal of Obsessive-Compulsive and Related Disorders, 16,* 14–20. https://doi.org/10.1016/j.jocrd.2017.10.007

Hinton, D. E., & Lewis-Fernández, R. (2010). Idioms of distress among trauma survivors: Subtypes and clinical utility. *Culture, Medicine, and Psychiatry, 34*(2), 209–218. https://doi.org/10.1007/s11013-010-9175-x

Hooper, M. W., Nápoles, A. M., & Pérez-Stable, E. J. (2020). COVID-19 and racial/ethnic disparities. *JAMA, 323*(24), 2466–2467. https://doi.org/10.1001/jama.2020.8598

Hyland, P., Shevlin, M., Fyvie, C., & Karatzias, T. (2018). Posttraumatic stress disorder and complex posttraumatic stress disorder in *DSM-5* and *ICD-11*: Clinical and behavioral correlates. *Journal of Traumatic Stress, 31*(2), 174–180. https://doi.org/10.1002/jts.22272

Ikoma, A., Ebata, T., Fukuda, R., Takase, Y., Taniguchi, N., Takemura, K., Vaglio, J., Poncet, M., & LeClercq, D. (2020). Prevalence of pruritus in the elderly with dementia: A multicenter survey of Japanese patients. *Acta Dermato Venereologica, 100*(14), Article 5822. https://doi.org/10.2340/00015555-3572

Intersex Campaign for Equality. (2015). *How common is intersex? An explanation of the stats.* https://www.intersexequality.com/how-common-is-intersex-in-humans/

Ivers, N. N., Johnson, D. A., & Rogers, J. L. (2021). The association between implicit racial bias and mindfulness in mental health practitioners. *Journal of Counseling & Development, 99*(1), 11–23. https://doi.org/10.1002/jcad.12350

Ivey, A. E., D'Andrea, M. J., & Ivey, M. B. (2012). *Counseling and psychotherapy: A multicultural perspective* (7th ed.). Sage.

Jacoby, R. J., & Abramowitz, J. S. (2016). Inhibitory learning approaches to exposure therapy: A critical review and translation to obsessive-compulsive disorder. *Clinical Psychology Review, 49,* 28–40. https://doi.org/10.1016/j.cpr.2016.07.001

Jafferany, M., & Osuagwu, F. C. (2018). Trichotillomania: Basic concepts. In K. França & M. Jafferany (Eds.), *Trichotillomania: Clinical characteristics, psychological interventions and emotional effects* (pp. 21–34). Nova Science.

Jafferany, M., & Patel, A. (2018). Therapeutic aspects of trichotillomania: A review of current treatment options. *The Primary Care Companion for CNS Disorders, 20*(6), Article 18nr02344. https://doi.org/10.4088/pcc.18nr02344

Jamison, K. R. (2000). Suicide and bipolar disorder. *Journal of Clinical Psychiatry, 61*(Suppl. 9), 47–51.

Jenkins, M. M., Youngstrom, E. A., Washburn, J. J., & Youngstrom, J. K. (2011). Evidence-based strategies improve assessment of pediatric bipolar disorder by community practitioners. *Professional Psychology: Research and Practice, 42*(2), 121–129. https://doi.org/10.1037/a0022506

Johansson, K., Sandman, P. O., & Karlsson, S. (2004). Picking behaviour in cognitively impaired residents in geriatric settings: Prevalence of the behaviour and characteristics of the residents. *Scandinavian Journal of Caring Sciences, 18*(1), 12–18. https://doi.org/10.1111/j.1471-6712.2004.00261.x

Kabat-Zinn, J. (2003). Mindfulness-based stress reduction (MBSR). *Constructivism in the Human Sciences, 8*(2), 73–83.

Karno, M., Golding, J. M., Sorenson, S. B., & Burnam, M. A. (1988). The epidemiology of obsessive-compulsive disorder in five US communities. *Archives of General Psychiatry, 45*(12), 1094–1099. https://doi.org/10.1001/archpsyc.1988.01800360042006

Kaur, K., Patel, V., Kumar, P., Vasavada, D., Nerli, L., & Tiwari, D. (2021). A prospective study of major depressive disorder among COVID 19 survivors at a tertiary care hospital. *Archives of Mental Health, 22*(1), 23–27. https://journals.lww.com/amhe/fulltext/2021/22010/a_prospective_study_of_major_depressive_disorder.5.aspx

Kehoe, E., & Egan, J. (2019). Interpersonal attachment insecurity and emotional attachment to possessions partly mediate the relationship between childhood trauma and hoarding symptoms in a non-clinical sample. *Journal of Obsessive-Compulsive and Related Disorders, 21,* 37–45. https://doi.org/10.1016/j.jocrd.2018.12.001

Kendler, K. S., Myers, J., & Zisook, S. (2008). Does bereavement-related depression differ from major depression associated with other stressful life events? *The American Journal of Psychiatry, 165*(11), 1449–1455. https://doi.org/10.1176/appi.ajp.2008.07111757

Kerns, K. E., Comer, J. S., Pincus, D. B., & Hofmann, S. G. (2013). Evaluation of the proposed social anxiety disorder specifier change for *DSM-5* in a treatment-seeking sample of anxious youth. *Depression and Anxiety, 30*(8), 709–715. https://doi.org/10.1002/da.22067

Kessler, R. C., Chiu, W. T., Demler, O., & Walters, E. E. (2005). Prevalence, severity, and comorbidity of 12-month *DSM-IV* disorders in the National Comorbidity Survey Replication. *Archives of General Psychiatry, 62*(6), 617–627. https://doi.org/10.1001/archpsyc.62.6.617

Kessler, R. C, Petukhova, M., Sampson, N. A., Zaslasvky, A., & Wittchen, H. U. (2012). Twelve-month and lifetime prevalence and lifetime morbid risk of anxiety and mood disorders in the United States. *International Journal of Methods in Psychiatric Research, 21*(3), 169–184. https://doi.org/10.1002/mpr.1359

Kessler, R. C., Sampson, N. A., Berglund, P., Gruber, M. J., Al-Hamzawi, A., Andrade, L., Bunting, B., Demyttenaere, K., Florescu, S., de Girolamo, G., Gureje, O., He, Y., Hu, C., Huang, Y., Karam, E., Kovess-Masfety, V., Lee, S., Levinson, D., Medina Mora, M. E., . . . Wilcox, M. A. (2015). Anxious and non-anxious major depressive disorder in the World Health Organization World Mental Health Surveys. *Epidemiology and Psychiatric Sciences, 24*(3), 210–226. https://doi.org/10.1017/S2045796015000189

Kessler, R. C., Sonnega, A., Bromet, E., Hughes, M., & Nelson, C. B. (1995). Post-traumatic stress disorder in the National Comorbidity Survey. *Archives of General Psychiatry, 52*(12), 1048–1060. https://doi.org/10.1001/archpsyc.1995.03950240066012

Ketter, T. A. (2010). Diagnostic features, prevalence, and impact of bipolar disorder. *The Journal of Clinical Psychiatry, 71*(6), Article e14. https://doi.org/10.4088/JCP.8125tx11c

Keuthen, N. J., O'Sullivan, R., Ricciardi, J. N., Shera, D., Savage, C. R., Borgmann, A. S., Jenike, M. A., & Baer, L. (1995). The Massachusetts General Hospital (MGH) Hairpulling Scale: 1. Development and factor analyses. *Psychotherapy and Psychosomatics, 64*(3–4), 141–145. https://doi.org/10.1159/000289003

Kira, I. A., Shuwiekh, H. A. M., Alhuwailah, A., Ashby, J. S., Sous Fahmy Sous, M., Baali, S. B. A., Azdaou, C., Oliemat, E. M., & Jamil, H. J. (2021). The effects of COVID-19 and collective identity trauma (intersectional discrimination) on social status and well-being. *Traumatology, 27*(1), 29–39. https://doi.org/10.1037/trm0000289

Ko, C.-H., Liu, T.-L., Wu, H.-C., Yeh, Y.-C., Tsai, W.-X., & Yen, J.-Y. (2021). Psychiatric comorbidities and emotional intelligence in internet gaming disorder, major depressive disorder, generalized anxiety disorder, and social anxiety disorder. *Psychiatry and Clinical Neurosciences, 75*(11), 352–354. https://doi.org/10.1111/pcn.13295

Ko, S. M. (1996). Obsessive compulsive disorder—A neuropsychiatric illness. *Singapore Medical Journal, 37*(2), 186–188.

Kong, D., Li, M., Wang, J., Davitt, J. K., & Dong, X. (2019). The relationship between depressive symptoms and health services utilization in U.S. Chinese older adults. *The Gerontologist, 59*(3), 447–455. https://doi.org/10.1093/geront/gny010

Koran, L. M., Abujaoude, E., Large, M. D., & Serpe, R. T. (2008). The prevalence of body dysmorphic disorder in the United States adult population. *CNS Spectrums, 13*(4), 316–322. https://doi.org/10.1017/s1092852900016436

Kraepelin, E. (1921). *Manic-depressive insanity and paranoia.* Ayer.

Kress, V., & Paylo, M. (2018). *Treating those with mental disorders. A comprehensive approach to case conceptualization and treatment.* Pearson.

Kulkarni, J., Leyden, O., Gavrilidis, E., Thew, C., & Thomas, E. H. X. (2022). The prevalence of early life trauma in premenstrual dysphoric disorder (PMDD). *Psychiatry Research, 308,* Article 114381. https://doi.org/10.1016/j.psychres.2021.114381

Landaas, E. T., Halmoy, A., Oedegaard, K. J., Fasmer, O. B., & Haavik, J. (2012). The impact of cyclothymic temperament in adult ADHD. *Journal of Affective Disorder, 142*(1–3), 241–247. https://doi.org/10.1016/j.jad.2012.04.034

Landau, D., Iervolino, A. C., Pertusa, A., Santo, S., Singh, S., & Mataix-Cols, D. (2011). Stressful life events and material deprivation in hoarding disorder. *Journal of Anxiety Disorders, 25*(2), 192–202. https://doi.org/10.1016/j.janxdis.2010.09.002

Latham, A. E., & Prigerson, H. G. (2004). Suicidality and bereavement: Complicated grief as psychiatric disorder presenting greatest risk for suicidality. *Suicide and Life Threatening Behavior, 34*(4), 350–362. https://doi.org/10.1521/suli.34.4.350.53737

Lee, H. J., Espil, F. M., Bauer, C. C., Siwiec, S. G., & Woods, D. W. (2018). Computerized response inhibition training for children with trichotillomania. *Psychiatry Research, 262,* 20–27. https://doi.org/10.1016/j.psychres.2017.12.070

Leibovici, V., Koran, L. M., Murad, S., Siam, I., Odlaug, B. L., Mandelkorn, U., Feldman-Weisz, V., & Keuthen, N. J. (2015). Excoriation (skin-picking) disorder in adults: a cross-cultural survey of Israeli Jewish and Arab samples. *Comprehensive Psychiatry, 58,* 102–107. https://doi.org/10.1016/j.comppsych.2014.12.008

Lewis-Fernández, R., Guarnaccia, P. J., Patel, S., Lizardi, D., & Diaz, N. (2005). Ataque de nervios: Anthropological, epidemiological, and clinical dimensions of a cultural syndrome. In A. M. Georgiopoulos & J. F. Rosenbaum (Eds.), *Perspectives in cross-cultural psychiatry* (pp. 63–85). Lippincott, Williams & Wilkins.

Liebowitz, M. R. (1987). Social phobia. In T. A. Ban, P. Pichot, & W. Poldinger (Eds.), *Modern problems of pharmacopsychiatry* (pp. 143–171). Karger. https://doi.org/10.1159/000414022

Lin, H., Katsovich, L., Ghebremichael, M., Findley, D. B., Grantz, H., Lombroso, P. J., King, R. A., Zhang, H., & Leckman, J. F. (2007). Psychosocial stress predicts future symptom severities in children and adolescents with Tourette syndrome and/or obsessive-compulsive disorder. *Journal of Child Psychology and Psychiatry, 48*(2), 157–166. https://doi.org/10.1111/j.1469-7610.2006.01687.x

Lindley, L., & Galupo, M. P. (2020). Gender dysphoria and minority stress: Support for inclusion of gender dysphoria as a proximal stressor. *Psychology of Sexual Orientation and Gender Diversity, 7*(3), 265–275. https://doi.org/10.1037/sgd0000439

Lochner, C., Roos, A., & Stein, D. J. (2017). Excoriation (skin-picking) disorder: A systematic review of treatment options. *Neuropsychiatric Disease and Treatment, 13,* 1867–1872. https://doi.org/10.2147/ndt.s121138

Lochner, C., Simeon, D., Niehaus, D. J., & Stein, D. J. (2002). Trichotillomania and skin-picking: A phenomenological comparison. *Depression and Anxiety, 15*(2), 83–86. https://doi.org/10.1002/da.10034

Lotzin, A., Krause, L., Acquarini, E., Ajduković, D., Ardino, V., Arnberg, F. K., Böttche, M., Bragesjö, M., Dragan, M., Figueiredo-Braga, M., Gelezelyte, O., Grajewski, P., Anastassiou-Hadjicharalambous, X., Javakhishvili, J. D., Kazlauskas, E., Lenferink, L. I. M., Lioupi, C., Lueger-Schuster, B., Tsiskarishvili, L., . . . Schäfer, I. (2021). Risk and protective factors, stressors, and symptoms of adjustment disorder during the COVID-19 pandemic—First results of the ESTSS COVID-19 pan-European ADJUST study. *European Journal of Psychotraumatology, 12*(1), Article 1964197. https://doi.org/10.1080/20008198.2021.1964197

Lundorff, M., Holmgren, H., Zachariae, R., Farver-Vestergaard, I., & O'Connor, M. K. (2017). Prevalence of prolonged grief disorder in adult bereavement: A systematic review and meta-analysis. *Journal of Affective Disorders, 212,* 138–149. https://doi.org/10.1016/j.jad.2017.01.030

Maciejewski, P. K., Zhang, B., Block, S. D., & Prigerson, H. G. (2007). An empirical examination of the stage theory of grief. *JAMA, 297*(7), 716–723. https://doi.org/10.1001/jama.297.7.716

Maercker, A., Forstmeier, S., Pielmaier, L., Spangenberg, L., Brähler, E., & Glaesmer, H. (2012). Adjustment disorders: Prevalence in a representative nationwide survey in Germany. *Social Psychiatry and Psychiatric Epidemiology, 47*(11), 1745–1752. https://doi.org/10.1007/s00127-012-0493-x

Malcolm, A., Pikoos, T. D., Castle, D. J., & Rossell, S. L. (2021). An update on gender differences in major symptom phenomenology among adults with body dysmorphic disorder. *Psychiatry Research, 295,* Article 113619. https://doi.org/10.1016/j.psychres.2020.113619

Mancebo, M. C., Garcia, A. M., Pinto, A., Freeman, J. B., Przeworski, A., Stout, R., & Rasmussen, S. A. (2008). Juvenile-onset OCD: Clinical features in children, adolescents and adults. *Acta Psychiatrica Scandinavica, 118*(2), 149–159. https://doi.org/10.1111/j.1600-0447.2008.01224.x

Manning, J. S. (2010). Tools to improve differential diagnosis of bipolar disorder in primary care. *Primary Care Companion to the Journal of Clinical Psychiatry, 12*(Suppl. 1), 17–22. https://doi.org/10.4088/PCC.9064su1c.03

Marnane, C., & Silove, D. (2013). *DSM-5* allows separation anxiety disorder to grow up. *Australian and New Zealand Journal of Psychiatry, 47*(1), 12–15. https://doi.org/10.1177/0004867412461285

Mataix-Cols, D., Pertusa, A., & Leckman, J. F. (2007). Issues for *DSM-V*: How should obsessive-compulsive and related disorders be classified? *The American Journal of Psychiatry, 164*(9), 1313–1314. https://doi.org/10.1176/appi.ajp.2007.07040568

McIntyre, R. S., Alda, M., Baldessarini, R. J., Bauer, M., Berk, M., Correll, C. U., Fagiolini, A., Fountoulakis, K., Frye, M. A., Grunze, H., Kessing, L. V., Miklowitz, D. J., Parker, G., Post, R. M., Swann, A. C., Suppes, T., Vieta, E., Young, A., & Maj, M. (2022). The clinical characterization of the adult patient with bipolar disorder aimed at personalization of management. *World Psychiatry, 21*(3), 364–387. https://doi.org/10.1002/wps.20997

McKnight-Eily, L. R., Okoro, C. A., Strine, T. W., Verlenden, J., Hollis, N. D., Njai, R., Mitchell, E. W., Board, A., Puddy, R., & Thomas, C. (2021). Racial and ethnic disparities in the prevalence of stress and worry, mental health conditions, and increased substance use among adults during the COVID-19 pandemic—United States, April and May 2020. *Morbidity and Mortality Weekly Report, 70*(5), 162–166. https://doi.org/10.15585/mmwr.mm7005a3

Meany-Walen, K. K., Bratton, S. C., & Kottman, T. (2014). Effects of Adlerian play therapy on reducing students' disruptive behaviors. *Journal of Counseling & Development, 92*(1), 47–56. https://doi.org/10.1002/j.1556-6676.2014.00129.x

Medeiros, G. C., Torres, A. R., Boisseau, C. L., Leppink, E. W., Eisen, J. L., Fontenelle, L. F., Rosário, M. C. D., Mancebo, M. C., Rasmussen, S. A., Ferrão, Y. A., & Grant, J. E. (2017). A cross-cultural clinical comparison between subjects with obsessive-compulsive disorder from the United States and Brazil. *Psychiatry Research, 254,* 104–111. https://doi.org/10.1016/j.psychres.2017.04.024

Melville, N. A. (2013, April 11). CBT beats adjunctive antipsychotic for refractory OCD. *Medscape Medical News.* http://www.medscape.com/viewarticle/782351

Merikangas, K. R., Akiskal, H. S., Angst, J., Greenberg, P. E., Hirschfeld, R. M., Petukhova, M., & Kessler, R. C. (2007). Lifetime and 12-months prevalence of bipolar spectrum disorder in the National Comorbidity Survey Replication. *Archives of General Psychiatry, 64*(5), 543–552. https://doi.org/10.1001/archpsyc.64.5.543

Mervis, C. B., & John, A. E. (2008). Vocabulary abilities of children with Williams syndrome: Strengths, weaknesses, and relation to visuospatial construction ability. *Journal of Speech, Language, and Hearing Research, 51*(4), 967–982. https://doi.org/10.1044/1092-4388(2008/071)

Meyer, I. H. (1995). Minority stress and mental health in gay men. *Journal of Health and Social Behavior, 36*(1), 38–56.

Milad, M. R., & Rauch, S. L. (2012). Obsessive-compulsive disorder: Beyond segregated cortico-striatal pathways. *Trends in Cognitive Sciences, 16*(1), 43–51. https://doi.org/10.1016/j.tics.2011.11.003

Miller, J. N., & Black, D. W. (2020). Bipolar disorder and suicide: A review. *Current Psychiatry Reports, 22*(2), Article 6. https://doi.org/10.1007/s11920-020-1130-0

Mimoun, E., Ben Ari, A., & Margalit, D. (2020). Psychological aspects of employment instability during the COVID-19 pandemic. *Psychological Trauma: Theory, Research, Practice, and Policy, 12*(Suppl. 1), S183–S185. https://doi.org/10.1037/tra0000769

Minnis, H., Macmillan, S., Pritchett, R., Young, D., Wallace, B., Butcher, J., Sim, F., Baynham, K., Davidson, C., & Gillberg, C. (2013). Prevalence of reactive attachment disorder in a deprived population. *British Journal of Psychiatry, 202*(5), 342–346. https://doi.org/10.1192/bjp.bp.112.114074

Misery, L., Chastaing, M., Touboul, S., Callot, V., Schollhammer, M., Young, P., & Dutray, S. (2012). Psychogenic skin excoriations: Diagnostic criteria, semiological analysis and psychiatric profiles. *Acta Dermato-Venereologica, 92*(4), 416–418. https://doi.org/10.2340/00015555-1320

Mohammadi, M. R., Badrfam, R., Khaleghi, A., Ahmadi, N., Hooshyari, Z., & Zandifar, A. (2021). Lifetime prevalence, predictors and comorbidities of tic disorders: A population-based survey of children and adolescents in Iran. *Child Psychiatry & Human Development, 53*(5), 1036–1046. https://doi.org/10.1007/s10578-021-01186-7

Mohr, C., & Schneider, S. (2013). Anxiety disorders. *European Child and Adolescent Psychiatry, 22*(Suppl. 1), S17–S22. https://doi.org/10.1007/s00787-012-0356-8

Moreno, C., Laje, G., Blanco, C., Jiang, H., Schmidt, A. B., & Olfson, M. (2007). National trends in the outpatient diagnosis and treatment of bipolar disorder in youth. *Archives of General Psychiatry, 64*(9), 1032–1039. https://doi.org/10.1001/archpsyc.64.9.1032

Morgan-Sowada, H., & Gamboni, C. (2021). Needing to be "perfect" to be loved: The intersection of body dysmorphic disorder, sexual identity, and gay culture in gay men. A qualitative study. *Sexual and Relationship Therapy,* 1–19. https://doi.org/10.1080/14681994.2021.1975672

Morris, S. P., Zickgraf, H. F., Dingfelder, H. E., & Franklin, M. E. (2013). Habit reversal training in trichotillomania: Guide for the clinician. *Expert Review of Neurotherapeutics, 13*(9), 1069–1077. https://doi.org/10.1586/14737175.2013.827477

Morrison, J. (2006). *DSM-IV made easy: The clinician's guide to diagnosis.* Guilford Press.

Mozdzierz, G. J., Peluso, P. R., & Lisiecki, J. (2011). Evidence-based psychological practices and therapist training: At the crossroads. *Journal of Humanistic Psychology, 51*(4), 439–464. https://doi.org/10.1177/0022167810386959

Mutabaruka, E., Sawadogo, M., Tarnagda, Z., Ouédraogo, L., Sangare, L., Ousmane, B., & Nsubuga, P. (2011). The West Africa Field Epidemiology and Laboratory Training Program, a strategy to improve disease surveillance and epidemic control in West Africa. *Pan African Medical Journal, 10*(Suppl. 1), 10.

Myers, J. E., & Harper, M. (2004). Evidence-based effective practices with older adults. *Journal of Counseling & Development, 82*(2), 207–218. https://doi.org/10.1002/j.1556-6678.2004.tb00304.x

Nakao, T., & Kanba, S. (2019). Pathophysiology and treatment of hoarding disorder. *Psychiatry and Clinical Neurosciences, 73*(7), 370–375. https://doi.org/10.1111/pcn.12853

National Center for Health Statistics. (2020). *Early release of selected estimates based on data from the 2019 National Health Interview Survey.* Centers for Disease Control and Prevention. https://www.cdc.gov/nchs/data/nhis/earlyrelease/EarlyRelease202009-508.pdf

National Center for Transgender Equality. (2016). *2015 U.S. transgender survey executive summary.* https://transequality.org/sites/default/files/docs/usts/USTS-Executive-Summary-Dec17.pdf

National Institute of Mental Health. (n.d.-a). *Any anxiety disorder.* https://www.nimh.nih.gov/health/statistics/any-anxiety-disorder

National Institute of Mental Health. (n.d.-b). *Bipolar disorder.* https://www.nimh.nih.gov/health/statistics/bipolar-disorder

National Institute of Mental Health. (n.d.-c). *Persistent depressive disorder (dysthymic disorder).* https://www.nimh.nih.gov/health/statistics/persistent-depressive-disorder-dysthymic-disorder

National Institute of Mental Health. (2021). *Depression.* https://www.nimh.nih.gov/health/publications/depression

National Institute of Mental Health. (2023a). *Coping with traumatic events.* https://www.nimh.nih.gov/health/topics/coping-with-traumatic-events

National Institute of Mental Health. (2023b). *Major depression.* https://www.nimh.nih.gov/health/statistics/major-depression

Neal-Barnett, A., Flessner, C., Franklin, M. E., Woods, D. W., Keuthen, N. J., & Stein, D. J. (2010). Ethnic differences in trichotillomania: Phenomenology, interference, impairment, and treatment efficacy. *Journal of Anxiety Disorders, 24*(6), 553–558. https://doi.org/10.1016/j.janxdis.2010.03.014

Nordsletten, A. E., Fernandez de la Cruz, L., Aluco, E., Alonso, P., López-Solà, C., Menchón, J. M., Nakao, T., Kuwano, M., Yamada, S., Fontenelle, L. F., Campos-Lima, A. L., & Mataix-Cols, D. (2018). A transcultural study of hoarding disorder: Insights from the United Kingdom, Spain, Japan, and Brazil. *Transcultural Psychiatry, 55*(2), 261–285. https://doi.org/10.1177/1363461518759203

Norris, F. H., & Elrod, C. C. (2006). Psychological consequences of disaster. In F. H. Norris, S. Galea, M. J. Friedman, & P. J. Watson (Eds.), *Methods for disaster mental health research* (pp. 20–44). Guilford Press.

Odlaug, B. L., & Grant, J. E. (2010). Pathologic skin picking. *American Journal of Drug and Alcohol Abuse, 36*(5), 296–303. https://doi.org/10.3109/00952991003747543

Office of Disease Prevention and Health Promotion. (n.d.). *Healthy People 2030: Social determinants of health.* https://health.gov/healthypeople/priority-areas/social-determinants-health

Ogle, C. M., Rubin, D. T., Berntsen, D., & Siegler, I. C. (2013). The frequency and impact of exposure to potentially traumatic events over the life course. *Clinical Psychological Science, 1*(4), 426–434. https://doi.org/10.1177/2167702613485076

Orsolini, L., Latini, R., Pompili, M., Serafini, G., Volpe, U., Vellante, F., Fornaro, M., Valchera, A., Tomasetti, C., Fraticelli, S., Alessandrini, M., La Rovere, R., Trotta, S., Martinotti, G., Di Giannantonio, M., & De Berardis, D. (2020). Understanding the complex of suicide in depression: From research to clinics. *Psychiatry Investigation, 17*(3), 207–221. https://doi.org/10.30773/pi.2019.0171

Østergaard, S. D., & Foldager, L. (2011). The association between physical illness and major depressive episode in general practice. *Acta Psychiatrica Scandinavica, 123*(4), 290–296. https://doi.org/10.1111/j.1600-0447.2010.01668.x

Pallanti, S., Grassi, G., Sarrecchia, E. D., Cantisani, A., & Pellegrini, M. (2011). Obsessive-compulsive disorder comorbidity: Clinical assessment and therapeutic implications. *Frontiers in Psychiatry, 2,* Article 70. https://doi.org/10.3389/fpsyt.2011.00070

Paris, J. (2009). The bipolar spectrum: A critical perspective. *Harvard Review of Psychiatry, 17*(3), 206–213. https://doi.org/10.1080/10673220902979888

Paris, J., Chenard-Poirier, M., & Biskin, R. S. (2013). Antisocial and borderline personality disorders revisited. *Comprehensive Psychiatry, 54*(4), 321–325. https://doi.org/10.1016/j.comppsych.2012.10.006

Pascual-Vera, B., Akin, B., Belloch, A., Bottesi, G., Clark, D. J., Doron, G., Fernández-Álvarez, H., Ghisi, M., Gómez, B. L., Inozu, M., Jiménez-Ros, A., Moulding, R., Ruiz, M., Shams, G., & Sica, C. (2019). The cross-cultural and transdiagnostic nature of unwanted mental intrusions. *International Journal of Clinical and Health Psychology, 19*(2), 85–96. https://doi.org/10.1016/j.ijchp.2019.02.005

Pearlstein, T., & Steiner, M. (2008). Premenstrual dysphoric disorder: Burden of illness and treatment update. *Journal of Psychiatry & Neuroscience, 33*(4), 291–301.

Peele, C. (2023). *Roundup of anti-LGBTQ+ legislation advancing in states across the country.* Human Rights Campaign. https://www.hrc.org/press-releases/roundup-of-anti-lgbtq-legislation-advancing-in-states-across-the-country

Perilla, J. L., Norris, F. H., & Lavizzo, E. A. (2002). Ethnicity, culture and disaster response: Identifying and explaining ethnic differences in PTSD six months after Hurricane Andrew. *Journal of Social and Clinical Psychology, 21*(2), 20–45. https://doi.org/10.1521/jscp.21.1.20.22404

Pertusa, A., Frost, R. O., Fullana, M. A., Samuels, J., Steketee, G., Tolin, D., & Mataix-Cols, D. (2010). Refining the diagnostic boundaries of compulsive hoarding: A critical review. *Clinical Psychology Review, 30*(4), 371–386. https://doi.org/10.1016/j.cpr.2010.01.007

Peterson, C. M., Matthews, A., Copps-Smith, E., & Conard, L. A. (2017). Suicidality, self-harm, and body dissatisfaction in transgender adolescents and emerging adults with gender dysphoria. *Suicide and Life-Threatening Behavior, 47*(4), 475–482. https://doi.org/10.1111/sltb.12289

Phillips, K. A. (2004). Psychosis in body dysmorphic disorder. *Journal of Psychiatric Research, 38*(1), 63–72. https://doi.org/10.1016/s0022-3956(03)00098-0

Phillips, K. A., Menard, W., & Fay, C. (2006). Gender similarities and differences in 200 individuals with body dysmorphic disorder. *Comprehensive Psychiatry, 47*(2), 77–87. https://doi.org/10.1016/j.comppsych.2005.07.002

Pillai, V. T., & Sündermann, O. (2020). Racial teasing and body dysmorphic disorder symptoms—A cross-sectional study of Asian ethnic groups in Singapore. *Asia Pacific Journal of Counselling and Psychotherapy, 11*(1), 47–59. https://doi.org/10.1080/21507686.2019.1708425
Pilver, C. E., Desai, R. D., Kasl, S., & Levy, B. R. (2011). Lifetime discrimination associated with greater likelihood of premenstrual dysphoric disorder. *Journal of Women's Health, 20*(6), 923–931. https://doi.org/10.1089/jwh.2010.2456
Pope, C. G., Pope, H. G., Menard, W., Fay, C., Olivardia, R., & Phillips, K. A. (2005). Clinical features of muscle dysmorphia among males with body dysmorphic disorder. *Body Image, 2*(4), 395–400. https://doi.org/10.1016/j.bodyim.2005.09.001
Postlethwaite, A., Kellett, S., & Mataix-Cols, D. (2019). Prevalence of hoarding disorder: A systematic review and meta-analysis. *Journal of Affective Disorders, 256,* 309–316. https://doi.org/10.1016/j.jad.2019.06.004
Price-Feeney, M., Green, A. E., & Dorison, S. H. (2020). Understanding the mental health of transgender and nonbinary youth. *Journal of Adolescent Health, 66*(6), 684–690. https://doi.org/10.1016/j.jadohealth.2019.11.314
Price-Feeney, M., Green, A. E., & Dorison, S. H. (2021). Impact of bathroom discrimination on mental health among transgender and nonbinary youth. *Journal of Adolescent Health, 68*(6), 1142–1147. https://doi.org/https://doi.org/10.1016/j.jadohealth.2020.11.001
Prigerson, H. G., Kakarala, S., Gang, J., & Maciejewski, P. K. (2021). History and status of prolonged grief disorder as a psychiatric diagnosis. *Annual Review of Clinical Psychology, 17*(1), 109–126. https://doi.org/10.1146/annurev-clinpsy-081219-093600
Prior, V., & Glaser, D. (2006). *Understanding attachment and attachment disorders: Theory, evidence and practice.* Jessica Kingsley.
Pritchett, R., Pritchett, J., Marshall, E. M., Davidson, C., & Minnis, H. (2013). Reactive attachment disorder in the general population: A hidden ESSENCE disorder. *The Scientific World Journal, 2013,* Article 818157. https://doi.org/10.1155/2013/818157
Reddy, Y. J., Sudhir, P. M., Manjula, M., Arumugham, S. S., & Narayanaswamy, J. C. (2021). Clinical practice guidelines for cognitive-behavioral therapies in anxiety disorders and obsessive-compulsive and related disorders. *Indian Journal of Psychiatry, 62*(Suppl. 2), S230–S250. https://doi.org/10.4103/psychiatry.indianjpsychiatry_773_19
Reghunandanan, S., Fineberg, N. A., & Stein, D. J. (2015). *Obsessive-compulsive and related disorders.* Oxford University Press.
Reid, W. H., & Wise, M. G. (1995). *DSM-IV training guide.* Brunner-Routledge.
Resick, P. A., Monson, C. M., & Chard, K. M. (2016). *Cognitive processing therapy for PTSD: A comprehensive manual.* Guilford Press.
Riggs, D. W., Ansara, G. Y., &Treharne, G. J. (2015). The mental health of transgender Australians. *Australian Psychologist, 50*(1), 32–39. https://doi.org/10.1111/ap.12088
Rothschild, B. (2017). *The body remembers: Vol. 2. Revolutionizing trauma treatment.* Norton.
Rubonis, A. V., & Bickman, L. (1991). Psychological impairment in the wake of disaster: The disaster-psychopathology relationship. *Psychological Bulletin, 109*(3), 384–399. https://doi.org/10.1037/0033-2909.109.3.384
Ruscio, A. M., Stein, D. J., Chiu, W. T., & Kessler, R. C. (2010). The epidemiology of obsessive-compulsive disorder in the National Comorbidity Survey Replication. *Molecular Psychiatry, 15*(1), 53–63. https://doi.org/10.1038/mp.2008.94
Sabaß, L., Buchenrieder, N., Rek, S. V., Nenov-Matt, T., Lange, J., Barton, B. B., Musil, R., Jobst, A., Padberg, F., & Reinhard, M. A. (2022). Attachment mediates the link between childhood maltreatment and loneliness in persistent depressive disorder. *Journal of Affective Disorders, 312,* 61–68. https://doi.org/10.1016/j.jad.2022.06.021
Sadiq, F. A., Slator, L., Skuse, D., Law, J., Gillberg, C., & Minnis, H. (2012). Social use of language in children with reactive attachment disorder and autism spectrum disorders. *European Child & Adolescent Psychiatry, 21*(5), 267–276. https://doi.org/10.1007/s00787-012-0259-8
Salmond, C. H., Meiser-Stedman, R., Glucksman, E., Thompson, P., Dalgleish, T., & Smith, P. (2011). The nature of trauma memories in acute stress disorder in children and adolescents. *Journal of Child Psychology and Psychiatry, 52*(5), 560–570. https://doi.org/10.1111/j.1469-7610.2010.02340.x

Samet, S., Fenton, M. C., Nunes, E., Greenstein, E., Aharonovich, E., & Hasin, D. (2012). Effects of independent and substance-induced major depressive disorder on remission and relapse of alcohol, cocaine and heroin dependence. *Addictions, 108*(1), 115–123. https://doi.org/10.1111/j.1360-0443.2012.04010.x

Samuels, J. F., Bienvenu, O. J., Grados, M. A., Cullen, B., Riddle, M. A., Liang, K. Y., Eaton, W. W., & Nestadt, G. (2008). Prevalence and correlates of hoarding behavior in a community-based sample. *Behaviour Research and Therapy, 46*(7), 836–844. https://doi.org/10.1016/j.brat.2008.04.004

Sauer, A. N. K., & Gill, C. S. (2020). Treating disruptive mood dysregulation disorder: An Adlerian and equine therapy integrated approach. *The Journal of Individual Psychology, 76*(4), 372–385. https://doi.org/10.1353/jip.2020.0036

Schechter, D. S., & Willheim, E. (2009). Disturbances of attachment and parental psychopathology in early childhood. *Child and Adolescent Psychiatric Clinics of North America, 18*(3), 665–686. https://doi.org/10.1016%2Fj.chc.2009.03.001

Schooler, D. (2007). Body image, ethnicity/race and gender. In J. J. Arnett (Ed.), *Encyclopedia of children, adolescents, and the media* (Vol. 1, pp. 116–117). Sage. https://doi.org/10.4135/9781412952606.n52

Schnurr, P. P. (n.d.). *Epidemiology and impact of PTSD.* U.S. Department of Veterans Affairs. https://www.ptsd.va.gov/professional/treat/essentials/epidemiology.asp

Schuck, K., Keijsers, G. P. J., & Rinck, M. (2011). The effects of brief cognitive-behaviour therapy for pathological skin picking: A randomized comparison to wait-list control. *Behaviour Research and Therapy, 49*(1), 11–17. https://doi.org/10.1016/j.brat.2010.09.005

Segal, Z. V., Teasdale, J. D., Williams, J. M., & Gemar, M. C. (2002). The Mindfulness-Based Cognitive Therapy Adherence Scale: Inter-rater reliability, adherence to protocol and treatment distinctiveness. *Clinical Psychology & Psychotherapy, 9*(2), 131–138. https://doi.org/10.1002/cpp.320

Shapiro, F. (2017). *Eye movement desensitization and reprocessing (EMDR) therapy: Basic principles, protocols, and procedures.* Guilford Press.

Shear, M. K., Simon, N., Wall, M., Zisook, S., Neimeyer, R., Duan, N., & Keshaviah, A. (2011). Complicated grief and related bereavement issues for *DSM-5. Depression and Anxiety, 28*(2), 103–117. https://doi.org/10.1002/da.20780

Shephard, E. A., Stern, E., van den Heuvel, O. A., Costa, D. P., Batistuzzo, M. C., Godoy, P. B. G., Lopes, A. A., Brunoni, A. R., Hoexter, M. Q., Shavitt, R. G., Reddy, Y. J., Lochner, C., Stein, D. J., Simpson, H. B., & Miguel, E. C. (2021). Toward a neurocircuit-based taxonomy to guide treatment of obsessive-compulsive disorder. *Molecular Psychiatry, 26*(9), 4583–4604. https://doi.org/10.1038/s41380-020-01007-8

Simons, J. D., Gonzalez, J. M., & Ramdas, M. (2020). Supporting intersex people: Effective academic and career counseling. *Journal of LGBT Issues in Counseling, 14*(3), 191–209. https://doi.org/10.1080/15538605.2020.1790465

Simpson, H., Foa, E., Liebowitz, M., Ledley, D., Huppert, J., Cahill, S., & Petkova, E. (2008). A randomized, controlled trial of cognitive-behavioral therapy for augmenting pharmacotherapy in obsessive-compulsive disorder. *The American Journal of Psychiatry, 165*(5), 621–630. https://doi.org/10.1176/appi.ajp.2007.07091440

Singh, A. A., & Mingo, T.M. (2018). Gender and sexism. In D. Hays & B. T. Erford (3rd ed.). *Developing multicultural counseling competence: A systems approach* (3rd ed.). Pearson Education.

Singh, A. R., & Veale, D. (2019). Understanding and treating body dysmorphic disorder. *Indian Journal of Psychiatry, 61*(Suppl 1), S131. https://doi.org/10.4103/psychiatry.IndianJPsychiatry_528_18

Skovgaard, A. M. (2010). Mental health problems and psychopathology in infancy and early childhood. An epidemiological study. *Danish Medical Bulletin, 57*(10), Article B4193.

Snorrason, I., Belleau, E. L., & Woods, D. W. (2012). How related are hair pulling disorder (trichotillomania) and skin picking disorder? A review of evidence for comorbidity, similarities and shared etiology. *Clinical Psychology Review, 32*(7), 618–629. https://doi.org/10.1016/j.cpr.2012.05.008

Solheim, C., Ballard, J., Fatiha, N., Dini, Z., Buchanan, G. J. R., & Song, S. (2022). Immigrant family financial and relationship stress from the COVID-19 pandemic. *Journal of Family and Economic Issues, 43*(2), 282–295. https://doi.org/10.1007/s10834-022-09819-2

Solomon, S. D., & Smith, E. S. (1994). Social support and perceived control as moderators of responses to dioxin and flood exposure. In R. J. Ursano, B. G. McCaughey, & C. S. Fullerton (Eds.), *Individual and community response to disaster: The structure of human chaos* (pp. 179–200). Cambridge University Press.

Sood, E. D., Mendez, J. L., & Kendall, P. C. (2012). Acculturation, religiosity, and ethnicity predict mothers' causal beliefs about separation anxiety disorder and preferences for help seeking. *Journal of Cross-Cultural Psychology, 43*(3), 393–409. https://doi.org/10.1177/0022022110389492

Sprock, J., & Fredendall, L. (2008). Comparison of prototypic cases of depressive personality. *Journal of Clinical Psychology, 64*(12), 1293–1317. https://doi.org/10.1002/jclp.20538

Stange J. P., Eisner, L. R., Hölzel, B. K., Peckham, A. D., Dougherty, D. D., Rauch, S. L., Nierenberg, A. A., Lazar, S., & Deckersbach, T. (2011). Mindfulness-based cognitive therapy for bipolar disorder: effects on cognitive functioning. *Journal of Psychiatric Practice, 17*(6), 410–419. https://doi.org/10.1097/01.pra.0000407964.34604.03

Stanley, M. A., Breckenridge, J. K., Snyder, A. G., & Novy, D. M. (1999). Clinician-rated measures of hair pulling: A preliminary psychometric evaluation. *Journal of Psychopathology and Behavioral Assessment, 21,* 157–170. https://doi.org/10.1023/A:1022160522908

Stark, C. (2022, July 29). Supporting transgender and gender-expansive youth. *Counseling Today.* https://ct.counseling.org/2022/07/supporting-transgender-and-gender-expansive-youth/

Stein, D. J., Chamberlain, S. R., & Fineberg, N. (2006). An ABC model of habit disorders: Hair-pulling, skin-picking, and other stereotypic conditions. *CNS Spectrums, 11*(11), 824–827. https://doi.org/10.1017/s1092852900014978

Stein, D. J., Costa, D. L. C., Lochner, C., Miguel, E. C., Reddy, Y. C. J., Shavitt, R. G., van den Heuvel, O. A., & Simpson, H. B. (2019). Obsessive-compulsive disorder. *Nature Reviews Disease Primers, 5,* Article 52. https://doi.org/10.1038/s41572-019-0102-3

Stein, D. J., Craske, M. G., Friedman, M. J., & Phillips, K. A. (2011). Meta-structure issues for the *DSM-5*: How do anxiety disorders, obsessive compulsive and related disorders, post-traumatic disorders, and dissociative disorders fit together? *Current Psychiatry Reports, 13*(4), 248–250. https://doi.org/10.1007/s11920-011-0207-1

Stein, D. J., Fineberg, N. A., Bienvenu, O. J., Denys, D., Lochner, C., Nestadt, G., Leckman, J. F., & Rauch, S. L., & Phillips, K. A. (2010). Should OCD be classified as an anxiety disorder in DSM-V? Depression and Anxiety, 27(6), 495–506. https://doi.org/10.1002/da.20699

Stein, D. J., Kogan, C. S., Atmaca, M. M., Fineberg, N. A., Fontenelle, L. F., Grant, J. A., Matsunaga, H., Reddy, Y. J., Simpson, H. B., Thomsen, P., van den Heuvel, O., Veale, D. J., Woods, D. W., & Reed, G. T. (2016). The classification of obsessive-compulsive and related disorders in the *ICD-11. Journal of Affective Disorders, 190*(Suppl. 1), 663–674. https://doi.org/10.1016/j.jad.2015.10.061

Steinkuller, A., & Rheineck, J. E. (2009). A review of evidence-based therapeutic interventions for bipolar disorder. *Journal of Mental Health Counseling, 31*(4), 338–350. https://doi.org/10.17744/mehc.31.4.97456k6027503j21

Substance Abuse and Mental Health Services Administration. (2014). *SAMHSA's concept of trauma and guidance for a trauma-informed approach* (HHS Publication No. [SMA] 14-4884). https://ncsacw.acf.hhs.gov/userfiles/files/SAMHSA_Trauma.pdf

Sundquist, J., Ohlsson, H., Sundquist, K., & Kendler, K. S. (2017). Common adult psychiatric disorders in Swedish primary care where most mental health patients are treated. *BMC Psychiatry, 17*(1), 235–244. https://doi.org/10.1186/s12888-017-1381-4

Swartz, H. A., Frank, E., Frankel, D. R., Novick, D., & Houck, P. (2009). Psychotherapy as monotherapy for the treatment of bipolar II depression: A proof of concept study. *Bipolar Disorder, 11*(1), 89–94. https://doi.org/10.1111/j.1399-5618.2008.00629.x

Swartz, H. A., Levenson, J. C., & Frank, E. (2012). Psychotherapy for bipolar II disorder: The role of interpersonal and social rhythm therapy. *Professional Psychology: Research and Practice, 43*(2), 145–153. https://doi.org/10.1037/a0027671

Takeshima, M., Otsubo, T., Funada, D., Murakami, M., Usami, T., Maeda, Y., Yamamoto, T., Matsumoto, T., Shimane, T., Aoki, Y., Otowa, T., Tani, M., Yamanaka, G., Sakai, Y., Murao, T., Inada, K., Yamada, H., Kikuchi, T., Sasaki, T., . . . Takaesu, Y. (2021). Does cognitive behavioral therapy for anxiety disorders assist with discontinuation of benzodiazepines among patients with anxiety disorders? A systematic review and meta-analysis. *Psychiatry and Clinical Neuroscience, 79*(4), 119–127. https://doi.org/10.1111/pcn.13195

Tanidir, C., Adaletli, H., Gunes, H., Kilicoglu, A. G., Mutlu, C., Bahali, M. K., Aytemiz, T., & Uneri, O. S. (2015). Impact of gender, age at onset, and lifetime tic disorders on the clinical presentation and comorbidity pattern of obsessive-compulsive disorder in children and adolescents. *Journal of Child and Adolescent Psychopharmacology, 25*(5), 425–431. http://doi.org/10.1089/cap.2014.0120

Tedeschi, R. G., & Calhoun, L. G. (1996). The Posttraumatic Growth Inventory: Measuring the positive legacy of trauma. *Journal of Traumatic Stress, 9*(3), 455–471. https://doi.org/10.1002/jts.2490090305

Teng, E. J., Woods, D. W., & Twohig, M. P. (2006). Habit reversal as a treatment for chronic skin picking. *Behavior Modification, 30*(4), 411–422. https://doi.org/10.1177/0145445504265707

Tenneij, N. H., Van Megen, H. J. G. M., Denys, D. A. J. P., & Westenberg, H. G. (2005). Behavior therapy augments response of patients with obsessive-compulsive disorder responding to drug treatment. *Journal of Clinical Psychiatry, 66*(9), 1169–1175. https://doi.org/10.4088/jcp.v66n0913

The Trevor Project (2019). *The Trevor Project research brief: Data on transgender youth.* https://www.thetrevorproject.org/wp-content/uploads/2021/08/The-Trevor-Project-Research-Brief-February-2019.pdf

The Trevor Project. (2021a). *Estimate of how often LGBTQ youth attempt suicide in the U.S.* https://www.thetrevorproject.org/research-briefs/estimate-of-how-often-lgbtq-youth-attempt-suicide-in-the-u-s/

The Trevor Project. (2021b). *2021 national survey on LGBTQ+ youth mental health.* www.thetrevorproject.org/survey-2021/?section=Introduction

Tolin, D. F., Franklin, M. E., Diefenbach, G. J., Anderson, E., & Meunier, S. A. (2007). Pediatric trichotillomania: Descriptive psychopathology and an open trial of cognitive behavioral therapy. *Cognitive Behaviour Therapy, 36*(3), 129–144. https://doi.org/10.1080/16506070701223230

Tolin, D. F., Maltby, N., Diefenbach, G. J., Hannan, S. E., & Worhunsky, P. (2004). Cognitive-behavioral therapy for medication nonresponders with obsessive-compulsive disorder: A wait-list-controlled open trial. *Journal of Clinical Psychiatry, 65*(7), 922–931. https://doi.org/10.4088/jcp.v65n0708

Tramontin, M., & Halpern, J. (2007). The psychological aftermath of terrorism: The 2001 World Trade Center attack. In E. K. Carll (Ed.), *Trauma psychology: Issues in violence, disaster, health, and illness* (pp. 1–31). Greenwood.

Tucker, B. V., Woods, D. W., Flessner, C. A., Franklin, S. A., & Franklin, M. E. (2011). The skin picking impact project: Phenomenology, interference, and treatment utilization of pathological skin picking in a population-based sample. *Journal of Anxiety Disorders, 25*(1), 88–95. https://doi.org/10.1016/j.janxdis.2010.08.007

Tundo, A., Salvati, L., Busto, G., Di Spigno, D., & Falcini, R. (2007). Addition of cognitive-behavioral therapy for nonresponders to medication for obsessive-compulsive disorder: A naturalistic study. *Journal of Clinical Psychiatry, 68*(10), 1553–1557. https://doi.org/10.4088/JCP.v68n1013

Uribe, C., Junque, C., Gómez-Gil, E., Abos, A., Mueller, S. C., & Guillamon, A. (2020). Brain network interactions in transgender individuals with gender incongruence. *Neuroimage, 211,* Article 116613. https://doi.org/10.1016/j.neuroimage.2020.116613

Ursano, R. J. (2004). Introduction. In R. J. Ursano, C. S. Fullerton, & A. E. Norwood (Eds.), *Bioterrorism: Psychological and public health interventions* [CD-ROM]. Cambridge University Press.

Ursano, R. J., McCaughey, B. G., & Fullerton, C. S. (1994). *Individual and community responses to trauma and disaster: The structure of human chaos.* Cambridge University Press.

Van de Put, W., & Eisenbruch, M. (2004). Internally displaced Cambodians: Healing trauma in communities. In L. Rasco & K. Miller (Eds.), *The mental health of refugees: Ecological approaches to healing and adaptation* (pp. 133–159). Taylor & Francis.

van den Heuvel, O. A., van Wingen, G., Soriano-Mas, C., Alonso, P., Chamberlain, S. R., Nakamae, T., Denys, D., Goudriaan, A. E., & Veltman, D. J. (2016). Brain circuitry of compulsivity. *European Neuropsychopharmacology, 26*(5), 810–827. https://doi.org/10.1016/j.euroneuro.2015.12.005

Van der Kolk, B. A., McFarlane, A. C., & Weisaeth, L. (1996). *Traumatic stress: The effects of overwhelming experience on mind, body, and society.* Guilford Press.

Van der Velden, P. G., Kleber, R. J., Christiaanse, B., Gersons, B. P., Marcelissen, F. G., Drogendijk, A. N., Grievink, L., Olff, M., & Meewisse, M. L. (2006). The independent predictive value of peritraumatic dissociation for postdisaster intrusions, avoidance reactions, and PTSD symptom severity: A 4-year prospective study. *Journal of Traumatic Stress, 19*(4), 493–506. https://doi.org/10.1002/jts.20140

Van Dijk, S., Jeffrey, J., & Katz, M. R. (2013). A randomized, controlled, pilot study of dialectical behavior therapy skills in a psychoeducational group for individuals with bipolar disorder. *Journal of Affective Disorders, 145*(3), 386–393. 10.1016/j.jad.2012.05.054

Van Grootheest, D. S., Cath, D. C., Beekman, A. T., & Boomsma, D. I. (2005). Twin studies on obsessive-compulsive disorder: A review. *Twin Research and Human Genetics, 8*(5), 450–458. https://doi.org/10.1375/183242705774310060

Van Meter, A. R., Moreira, A. L. R., & Youngstrom, E. (2019). Updated meta-analysis of epidemiologic studies of pediatric bipolar disorder. *The Journal of Clinical Psychiatry, 80*(3), Article 18r12180. https://doi.org/10.4088/JCP.18r12180

Van Meter, A. R., Youngstrom, E. A., Birmaher, B., Fristad, M. A., Horwitz, S. M., Frazier, T. W., Arnold, L. E., & Findling, R. L. (2017). Longitudinal course and characteristics of cyclothymic disorder in youth. *Journal of Affective Disorders, 215*, 314–322. https://doi.org/10.1016/j.jad.2017.03.019

Van Meter, A. R., Youngstrom, E. A., & Findling, R. L. (2012). Cyclothymic disorder: A critical review. *Clinical Psychology Review, 32*(4), 229–243. https://doi.org/10.1016/j.cpr.2012.02.001

Vázquez, G. H., Kapczinski, F., Magalhaes, P. V., Córdoba, R., Lopez Jaramillo, C., Rosa, A. R., Sanchez de Carmona M., Tohen, M., & Ibero-American Network on Bipolar Disorders Group. (2011). Stigma and functioning in patients with bipolar disorder. *Journal of Affective Disorders, 130*(1–3), 323–327. https://doi.org/10.1016/j.jad.2010.10.012

Villarroel, M. A. (2020). *Symptoms of depression among adults: United States, 2019* (NCHS Data Brief No. 379). National Center for Health Statistics. https://www.cdc.gov/nchs/data/databriefs/db379-H.pdf

Vontress, C. E., Woodland, C. E., & Epp, L (2007). Cultural dysthymia: An unrecognized disorder among African Americans? *Journal of Multicultural Counseling and Development, 35*(3), 135–141. https://doi.org/10.1002/j.2161-1912.2007.tb00055.x

Warren, B. J. (2007). Cultural aspects of bipolar disorder: Interpersonal meaning for clients and psychiatric nurses. *Journal of Psychosocial Nursing and Mental Health Services, 45*(7), 32–37. https://doi.org/10.3928/02793695-20070701-09

Watkins, N. K., Salafia, C., & Ohannessian, C. M. (2022). Family functioning and anxiety symptoms in adolescent: The moderating role of mindfulness. *Journal of Child and Family Studies, 31*(5), 1474–1488. https://doi.org/10.1007/s10826-021-02219-4

Watson, J., Whiting, P., & Brush, J. E. (2020). Interpreting a COVID-19 test result. *BMJ, 369*, Article m1808. https://doi.org/10.1136/bmj.m1808

Weinstock, L. M., Strong, D., Uebelacker, L. A., & Miller, I. W. (2009). Differential item functioning of *DSM-IV* depressive symptoms in individuals with a history of mania versus those without: An item response theory analysis. *Bipolar Disorder, 11*(3), 289–297. https://doi.org/10.1111/j.1399-5618.2009.00681.x

Wheaton, M. G., Berman, N. C., Fabricant, L. E., & Abramowitz, J. S. (2013). Differences in obsessive-compulsive symptoms and obsessive beliefs: A comparison between African Americans, Asian Americans, Latino Americans, and European Americans. *Cognitive Behaviour Therapy, 42*(1), 9–20. https://doi.org/10.1080/16506073.2012.701663

Widom, C., Czaja, S., & Paris, J. (2009). A prospective investigation of borderline personality disorder in abused and neglected children followed up into adulthood. *Journal of Personality Disorder, 23*(5), 433–446. https://doi.org/10.1521/pedi.2009.23.5.433

Wiepjes, C. M., Nota, N. M., de Blok, C. J., Klaver, M., de Vries, A. L., Wensing-Kruger, S. A., de Jongh, R. T., Bouman, M. B., Steensma, T. D., Cohen-Kettenis, P., & Gooren, L. J. (2018). The Amsterdam Cohort of Gender Dysphoria Study (1972–2015): Trends in prevalence, treatment, and regrets. *Journal of Sexual Medicine, 15*(4), 582–590. https://doi.org/10.1016/j.jsxm.2018.01.016

Wild, J., McKinnon, A., Wilkins, A., & Browne, H. (2022). Post-traumatic stress disorder and major depression among frontline healthcare staff working during the COVID-19 pandemic. *British Journal of Clinical Psychology, 61*(3), 859–866. https://doi.org/10.1111/bjc.12340

Williams, B. (2014). Animal hoarding—Recognition and possible interventions. *InPractice, 36*(4), 199–205. https://doi.org/10.1136/inp.g1974

Williams, J. M., Alatiq, Y., Crane, C., Barnhofer, T., Fennell, M. J., Duggan, D. S., Hepburn, S., & Goodwin, G. M. (2008). Mindfulness based cognitive therapy (MBCT) in bipolar disorder: Preliminary evaluation of immediate effects on between-episode functioning. *Journal of Affective Disorders, 107*(1–3), 275–279. https://doi.org/10.1016/j.jad.2007.08.022

Williams, M., & Halstead, M. (2019). Racial microaggressions as barriers to treatment in clinical care. *Directions in Psychiatry, 39*(4), 265–280.

Williams, M. T., Elstein, J. G., Buckner, E. V., Abelson, J. M., & Himle, J. A. (2012). Symptom dimensions in two samples of African Americans with obsessive-compulsive disorder. *Journal of Obsessive-Compulsive and Related Disorders, 1*(3), 145–152. https://doi.org/10.1016/j.jocrd.2012.03.004

Williams, M. T., Rouleau, T. M., La Torre, J. T., & Sharif, N. (2020). Cultural competency in the treatment of obsessive-compulsive disorder: Practitioner guidelines. *The Cognitive Behaviour Therapist, 13,* Article e48. https://doi.org/10.1017/s1754470x20000501

Williams-Washington, K. N., & Mills, C. P. (2018). African American historical trauma: Creating an inclusive measure. *Journal of Multicultural Counseling and Development, 46*(4), 246–263. https://doi.org/10.1002/jmcd.12113

Wolf, J., Padberg, F., Nenov-Matt, T., Amann, B. L., Barton, B. B., Tang, J., Glessner, G., Brakemeier, E.-L., Jobst, A., Musil, R., & Reinhard, M. A. (2022). Suicidal behaviors are associated with loneliness and decrease during inpatient CBASP treatment for persistent depressive disorder. *Journal of Psychiatric Research, 154,* 139–144. https://doi.org/10.1016/j.jpsychires.2022.07.059

Woods, D. W., Flessner, C. A., Franklin, M. E., Keuthen, N. J., Goodwin, R. D., Stein, D. J., & Walther, M. R. (2006). The Trichotillomania Impact Project (TIP): Exploring phenomenology, functional impairment, and treatment utilization. *Journal of Clinical Psychiatry, 67*(12), 1877–1888. https://doi.org/10.4088/jcp.v67n1207

Woods, D. W., & Houghton, D. P. (2014). Diagnosis, evaluation, and management of trichotillomania. *Psychiatric Clinics of North America, 37*(3), 301–317. https://doi.org/10.1016/j.psc.2014.05.005

Woolgar, F., Garfield, H., Dalgleish, T., & Meiser-Stedman, R. (2022). Systematic review and meta-analysis: Prevalence of posttraumatic stress disorder in trauma-exposed preschool-aged children. *Journal of the American Academy of Child & Adolescent Psychiatry, 61*(3), 366–377. https://doi.org/10.1016/j.jaac.2021.05.026

World Health Organization. (2007). *International statistical classification of diseases and related health problems, 10th revision.*

World Health Organization. (2019). *International statistical classification of diseases and related health problems, 10th revision* (Version 2019). https://icd.who.int/browse10/2019/en

World Health Organization (2021). *International statistical classification of diseases and related health problems, 11th revision.* https://icd.who.int/

World Health Organization. (2023). *Depressive disorder (depression).* https://www.who.int/news-room/fact-sheets/detail/depression

World Professional Association for Transgender Health. (2011). *Standards of care for the health of transexual, transgender, and gender nonconforming people* (7th version). https://www.wpath.org/media/cms/Documents/SOC%20v7/SOC%20V7_English.pdf

Wu, K. D., & Watson, D. (2005). Hoarding and its relation to obsessive-compulsive disorder. *Behaviour Research and Therapy, 43*(7), 897–921. https://doi.org/10.1016/j.brat.2004.06.013

Yancy, C. W. (2020). COVID-19 and African Americans. *JAMA, 323*(19), 1891. https://doi.org/10.1001/jama.2020.6548

Yehuda, R., & Lehrner, A. (2018). Intergenerational transmission of trauma effects: Putative role of epigenetic mechanisms. *World Psychiatry, 17*(3), 243–257. https://doi.org/10.1002/wps.20568

Zalaquett, C. P., & Stens, A. N (2006). Psychosocial treatments for major depression and dysthymia in older adults: A review of the research literature. *Journal of Counseling & Development, 84*(2), 192–201. https://doi.org/10.1002/j.1556-6678.2006.tb00395.x

Zeanah, C. H., & Gleason, M. M. (2010). *Reactive attachment disorder: A review for DSM-V.* American Psychiatric Association.

Zeanah, C. H., & Gleason, M. M. (2015). Annual research review: Attachment disorders in early childhood—Clinical presentation, causes, correlates, and treatment. *Journal of Child Psychology and Psychiatry, 56*(3), 207–222. https://doi.org/10.1111/jcpp.12347

Zhu, N., & Chang, L. (2019). Evolved but not fixed: A life history account of gender roles and gender inequality. *Frontiers in Psychology, 10,* Article 1709. https://doi.org/10.3389/fpsyg.2019.01709

Zordan, R., Bell, M. L., Price, M. A., Remedios, C., Lobb, E. A., Hall, C., & Hudson, P. J. (2019). Long-term prevalence and predictors of prolonged grief disorder amongst bereaved cancer caregivers: A cohort study. *Palliative & Supportive Care, 17*(5), 507–514. https://doi.org/10.1017/s1478951518001013

Part Three

Changes and Implications Involving Addictive, Impulse-Control, and Specific Behavior-Related Concerns

Introduction

The disorders covered in Part Three are divided into four chapters: Chapter 12, Substance-Related and Addictive Disorders; Chapter 13, Disruptive, Impulse-Control, and Conduct Disorders; Chapter 14, Personality Disorders; and Chapter 15, Specific Behavioral Disruptions. As with Part Two, Part Three includes diagnoses commonly seen by most counselors. However, the difference between this section and the previous section is that disorders in Part Three frequently manifest through more visible, external behavioral concerns (e.g., substance use or eccentric behavior) rather than less visible, internal experiences (e.g., depression or mania). The frequency with which counselors work with these concerns varies widely; therefore, we provide detailed information for those disorders that counselors are more likely to diagnose in practice, such as substance use or disruptive behavior disorders, and provide less detail for those disorders that counselors are less likely to diagnose, such as sleep disorders or sexual dysfunctions. Readers should assume diagnoses that do not include a "Major Changes From *DSM-5* to *DSM-5-TR*" section have had no significant changes. Likewise, instances in which differential diagnoses or cultural considerations are sparse or not included indicate a dearth of research on the topic.

Major changes in substance use disorders occurred in the transition from the *DSM-IV-TR* to the *DSM-5*. These included the collapsing of substance abuse and substance dependence into one category. Previous differentiation between abuse and dependence insinuated that abuse was less severe than dependence. The *DSM* authors changed this to reflect one overarching substance use disorders section with specifiers to indicate the extent of impairment. Gambling disorder was also moved here as part of the addictive disorders and process and remains in this section in the *DSM-5-TR*. When the *DSM-5* authors placed gambling disorder in this chapter, the change represented a significant shift in the way in which the mental health community conceptualized addictive disorders. This remains the case in the updated nosology. And, aside from overarching changes in the text sections relevant to all chapters, including recent research and literature and more nuanced attention to culture, sex-, and gender-related diagnostic issues in this category, there are no other major changes.

Chapter 13 includes disruptive, impulse-control, and conduct disorders. Although there are minimal changes from the *DSM-5* to the *DSM-5-TR* for these disorders, there was substantial reconceptualization and reorganization of these disorders from the *DSM-IV-TR* to the *DSM-5*. In the *DSM-5-TR*, counselors will find conduct disorder, oppositional defiant disorder, intermittent explosive disorder, kleptomania, and pyromania all included under the Disruptive, Impulse-Control, and Conduct Disorders chapter. In the *DSM-IV-TR*, these disorders were found under Impulse-Control Disorders Not Elsewhere Specified or Disorders Usually First Diagnosed in Infancy, Childhood, or Adolescence. The *DSM-5* was the first time all mental health disorders evidenced by disruptive behavior and impulse-control problems, including those that go against social norms (i.e., pyromania and kleptomania), had been clustered together. This remains the case in the *DSM-5-TR*, and aside from revised text and literature updates, there are no major changes from the *DSM-5* to the *DSM-5-TR* for this chapter.

Although there are minimal changes to the Personality Disorders chapter from the *DSM-5* to the *DSM-5-TR*, we have included an expanded discussion of each disorder in Chapter 14 and included a detailed description of the alternative model for diagnosing personality disorders found in Section III of the *DSM-5-TR*. Case examples are provided to help counselors practice using this alternative hybrid model of personality disorders proposed for the future.

Disorders found within Chapter 15, Specific Behavior Disruptions, include feeding and eating disorders, elimination disorders, sleep-wake disorders, sexual dysfunctions, and paraphilic disorders. Although these are separate disorders in the *DSM-5-TR*, they have been grouped together into one chapter because they all evidence similar patterns of behavioral disruption. There are no major changes for these disorders from the *DSM-5* to the *DSM-5-TR*.

Finally, as with other parts of this *Learning Companion*, readers will find a description of each disorder or group of disorders that includes essential features and major changes from the *DSM-5* to the *DSM-5-TR*, special considerations, and case examples to help counselors better apply diagnoses to work with clients. Note, unlike Part Two, we have not included information for specified or unspecified disorders for each disorder in this section, because the criteria for these diagnoses are similar to those found in Part One. For more detailed information regarding specified and unspecified diagnosis, see Chapter 5.

Chapter 12

Substance-Related and Addictive Disorders

> After my husband died, I drank more and more to numb the pain. It started out with a few glasses of wine a day, which then turned into a few bottles. I would wake up in the middle of the night and have a glass of wine. I would drink before work and during lunch. That was before I stopped going to work altogether. My family and friends wanted me to get help, but I didn't care. The only thing that dulled the pain was drinking.—Carise

Substance-related disorders include 10 classes of drugs (alcohol; caffeine; cannabis; hallucinogens; inhalants; opioids; sedatives, hypnotics, and anxiolytics; stimulants; tobacco; and other/unknown substances) that activate the brain's reward system (APA, 2022). Use of these substances often leads to impairments in multiple areas of functioning that indicate the presence of diagnosable disorders. There are three substance-related classifications: use, intoxication, and withdrawal (APA, 2022). Prevalence rates of substance use are extremely high, with 59.3 million individuals in the United States reporting use of illegal substances within the past year; this represents 8.9% of the total population over 12 years of age (SAMHSA, 2022). Additionally, according to the CDC (2022), a staggering 17.7 million people ages 12 and older were classified as heavy drinkers, and approximately 29 people die in alcohol-related accidents daily. Additionally, 22.7 million people ages 12 or older used nicotine products, with tobacco identified as the most frequent cause of death that is preventable (SAMHSA, 2022).

According to the American Society of Addiction Medicine (ASAM, 2019),

> Addiction is a treatable, chronic medical disease involving complex interactions among brain circuits, genetics, the environment, and an individual's life experiences. People with addiction use substances or engage in behaviors that become compulsive and often continue despite harmful consequences. Prevention efforts and treatment approaches for addiction are generally as successful as those for other chronic diseases. (paras. 1–2)

Addiction is ongoing and often cyclical, with many negative effects on psychological and physiological wellness. Addiction is present and problematic within and across social, cultural, and economic groups (ASAM, 2019; SAMHSA, 2022). The cost of addiction is enormous, with an annual overall price tag in the trillions for illegal substances, alcohol, and tobacco (Recovery Centers of America, 2022).

Because of the devastating impact on and high prevalence rates of individuals with diagnosable substance-related and addictive disorders, virtually all counselors—regardless of their professional settings—will work directly with this population or provide services for the family members and loved ones of individuals with these disorders. Substance-related and addictive disorders appear throughout the life span in people of all socio-economic levels, educational attainment, gender identity, culture, ethnicity, and religion (ASAM, 2019). It is critical that counselors possess a strong understanding of assessment for substance-related disorders.

The *DSM-5-TR* authors note the importance of using nonstigmatizing language when discussing substance use disorders. The National Institute for Drug Abuse (NIDA, 2021) provides helpful language guidelines and tips for terms to avoid when discussing addiction.

Major Changes From *DSM-5* to *DSM-5-TR*

The *DSM-5* restructured the prior classification of abuse and dependence to address substance use disorders as existing on a fluid, continuous spectrum (APA, 2013a, 2022; First et al., 2022), resulting in the current classification of substance use disorder. These classifications are structured the same way in the *DSM-5-TR* (APA, 2022).

Once clinicians note the presence of a substance use disorder, they may specify severity of usage using the ratings *mild*, *moderate*, and *severe*. Research supports an increasing spectrum of severity across addictions and addictive behaviors that occurs as a continuous variable that progresses over time (APA, 2022; First et al., 2022).

It is important to note that the diagnoses in this chapter are distinctive disorders. For example, caffeine-related disorders are separate from cannabis-related disorders. However, despite being distinctly separate diagnoses, all substance use disorders are based on the same core set of criteria. Substance use criteria are also separate from substance-specific intoxication and withdrawal criteria. For example, alcohol use disorder, alcohol intoxication, and alcohol withdrawal are all coded separately. The only exceptions are hallucinogen-related and inhalant-related disorders. The symptoms of withdrawal have not been sufficiently documented for these substances, so the withdrawal criterion has been eliminated. There is no change for these disorders from the *DSM-5* to the *DSM-5-TR*.

The only behavioral addiction included in this chapter is gambling disorder. This is due to an abundance of research that shows gambling activates the brain's reward system in ways that are consistent with substance use (APA, 2022; Limbrick-Oldfield et al., 2017). The symptoms of gambling disorder also hold similarities to substance use disorders, and gambling disorder possesses similar etiology in terms of presentation, biological underpinnings, and treatment.

The *DSM-5-TR* continues to list internet gaming disorder under the Conditions for Further Study chapter in Section III. Internet gaming disorder may well be added as an addictive disorder to subsequent iterations of the manual. Other types of "behavioral addictions" such as exercise, shopping, or social media addictions have not yet been shown to identify a diagnostic profile or similar developmental course. These may also be considered for inclusion in future editions of the manual (APA, 2022).

For additional specifiers in the chapter, *early remission* is still defined as at least 3 but not more than 12 months' absence of meeting diagnostic criteria for substance use disorders. *Sustained remission* is used for over 12 months below the diagnostic threshold. *On maintenance therapy* and *in a controlled environment* are additional specifiers clinicians should use as indicated (APA, 2022).

Substance-Related Disorders

The *DSM-5-TR* includes specific criteria sets for each substance and applicable disorders related to that substance (e.g., use, intoxication, withdrawal). All diagnostic labels include the name of the specific substance, such as cannabis use disorder, cannabis intoxication, and cannabis withdrawal. If an individual meets the criteria for multiple substance-related diagnoses, all diagnoses are listed. The manual is explicit in noting the likelihood of comorbidity of substance-related disorders (APA, 2022; SAMHSA, 2022).

Essential Features

According to APA (2022), "a substance use disorder is a cluster of cognitive, behavioral, and physiological symptoms indicating that the individual continues using the substance despite significant substance-related problems" (p. 544). In severe and long-term use, these changes may be observed through underlying changes in brain circuits (NIDA, 2022). The first four criteria for substance use disorders encompass impaired control, social impairment, risky use, and pharmacological criteria. Criteria 5 to 7 cover social, occupational, and interpersonal problems. Criteria 8 and 9 focus on risk taking related to use of the substance, and Criteria 10 and 11 are tolerance and withdrawal, respectively. Assuming an individual meets the general requirement for "clinically significant impairment or distress" related to pattern of use, just two specific criteria must be met to justify assignment of a clinical diagnosis.

Substance Intoxication and Withdrawal

Substance intoxication develops temporarily after ingestion of a substance. The subsequent psychological changes result from the physiological effects of the substance. Intoxication often includes alterations in attention, thinking, judgment, perception, interpersonal behavior, psychomotor behavior, and wakefulness. The diagnosis of substance intoxication is separate from substance use disorder, and the specific substance of intoxication is listed in the disorder. The *DSM-5-TR* includes criteria sets specific to intoxication for each substance category. *ICD-10-CM* coding will change based on the comorbidity of a substance use disorder. For example, there are different codes for alcohol intoxication with comorbid alcohol use disorder, mild (F10.129) than for alcohol intoxication with comorbid alcohol use disorder, moderate (F10.229) or alcohol intoxication without comorbid alcohol use disorder (F10.929).

Substance withdrawal includes physiological and psychological effects from stopping or reducing substance utilization after significant, prolonged use. Withdrawal can be distinctly unpleasant and trigger a cycle of renewed use to counterbalance the deleterious effects of the withdrawal. An individual can become intoxicated by, and have withdrawal from, more than one substance concomitantly. The *DSM-5-TR* includes criteria sets specific to withdrawal from each substance, with the exception of inhalant-related and hallucinogen-related disorders. Generally, withdrawal criteria are opposite what one would expect with substance intoxication for the substance. As with substance intoxication, the diagnosis of substance withdrawal can occur with or without the comorbid diagnosis of a substance use disorder (APA, 2022).

Coding, Recording, and Specifiers

There are separate diagnostic codes for all substance-related disorders (see list below). In making a diagnosis for a substance-related disorder, counselors must identify specifiers accurately. In addition to specification of substance use disorders as *mild*, *moderate*, or *severe* as discussed earlier, specifiers include *in early remission*, *in sustained remission*, *on maintenance therapy*, and *in a controlled environment*, with the last being an additional specifier for remission. Jails, locked hospital units, and therapeutic living settings are examples of controlled environments.

Counselors use the codes that apply to the specific substances with the name of the specific substance included, for example, alcohol use disorder, mild (F10.10). Other substance use disorder should be used if a substance does not fit into one of the enumerated classes. It should be noted that all codes derive from the *ICD-10-CM*.

Diagnostic Codes for Substance Use Disorders

Alcohol-Related Disorders

F10.10	Alcohol use disorder, mild
F10.20	Alcohol use disorder, moderate
F10.20	Alcohol use disorder, severe
F10.129	Alcohol intoxication with use disorder, mild
F10.229	Alcohol intoxication with use disorder, moderate or severe
F10.929	Alcohol intoxication without use disorder
F10.239	Alcohol withdrawal without perceptual disturbances
F10.232	Alcohol withdrawal with perceptual disturbances
F10.99	Unspecified alcohol-related disorders

Caffeine-Related Disorders

F15.929	Caffeine intoxication
F15.33	Caffeine withdrawal
F15.99	Unspecified caffeine-related disorder

Cannabis-Related Disorders

F12.10	Cannabis use disorder, mild
F12.20	Cannabis use disorder, moderate
F12.20	Cannabis use disorder, severe
F12.129	Cannabis intoxication without perceptual disturbance with use disorder, mild
F10.229	Cannabis intoxication without perceptual disturbance with use disorder, moderate or severe
F10.929	Cannabis intoxication without perceptual disturbance without use disorder
F12.122	Cannabis intoxication with perceptual disturbance with use disorder, mild
F10.222	Cannabis intoxication with perceptual disturbance with use disorder, moderate or severe
F10.922	Cannabis intoxication with perceptual disturbance without use disorder
F12.288	Cannabis withdrawal
F12.99	Unspecified cannabis-related disorders

Hallucinogen-Related Disorders

F16.10	Phencyclidine use disorder, mild
F16.20	Phencyclidine use disorder, moderate
F16.20	Phencyclidine use disorder, severe
F16.10	Other hallucinogen use disorder, mild
F16.20	Other hallucinogen use disorder, moderate
F16.20	Other hallucinogen use disorder, severe
F16.129	Phencyclidine intoxication with use disorder, mild
F16.229	Phencyclidine intoxication with use disorder, moderate or severe
F16.929	Phencyclidine intoxication without use disorder
F16.129	Other hallucinogen intoxication with use disorder, mild
F16.229	Other hallucinogen intoxication with use disorder, moderate or severe
F16.929	Other hallucinogen intoxication without use disorder
F16.983	Hallucinogen persisting perception disorder
F16.99	Unspecified phencyclidine-related disorder
F16.99	Unspecified hallucinogen-related disorder

Inhalant-Related Disorders

Specify the particular inhalant

F18.10	Inhalant use disorder, mild
F18.20	Inhalant use disorder, moderate
F18.20	Inhalant use disorder, severe
F18.129	Inhalant intoxication with use disorder, mild
F18.229	Inhalant intoxication with use disorder, moderate or severe
F18.929	Inhalant intoxication without use disorder
F18.99	Unspecified inhalant-related disorders

Opioid-Related Disorders

Specify if: on maintenance therapy or in a controlled environment

F11.10	Opioid use disorder, mild
F11.20	Opioid use disorder, moderate
F11.20	Opioid use disorder, severe
F11.129	Opioid intoxication without perceptual disturbance with use disorder, mild
F11.229	Opioid intoxication without perceptual disturbance with use disorder, moderate or severe
F11.929	Opioid intoxication without perceptual disturbance without use disorder
F11.122	Opioid intoxication with perceptual disturbance with use disorder, mild
F11.222	Opioid intoxication with perceptual disturbance with use disorder, moderate or severe
F11.922	Opioid intoxication with perceptual disturbance without use disorder
F11.23	Opioid withdrawal
F11.99	Unspecified opioid-related disorders

Sedative-, Hypnotic-, or Anxiolytic-Related Disorders

F13.10	Sedative, hypnotic, or anxiolytic use disorder, mild
F13.20	Sedative, hypnotic, or anxiolytic use disorder, moderate
F13.20	Sedative, hypnotic, or anxiolytic use disorder, severe
F13.129	Sedative, hypnotic, or anxiolytic intoxication with use disorder, mild
F13.229	Sedative, hypnotic, or anxiolytic intoxication with use disorder, moderate or severe
F13.929	Sedative, hypnotic, or anxiolytic intoxication without use disorder
F13.239	Sedative, hypnotic, or anxiolytic withdrawal without perceptual disturbance
F13.222	Sedative, hypnotic, or anxiolytic withdrawal with perceptual disturbance
F13.99	Unspecified sedative-, hypnotic-, or anxiolytic-related disorder

Stimulant-Related Disorders

F15.10	Amphetamine-type substance use disorder, mild
F15.20	Amphetamine-type substance use disorder, moderate
F15.20	Amphetamine-type substance use disorder, severe
F15.10	Cocaine use disorder, mild
F15.20	Cocaine use disorder, moderate
F15.20	Cocaine use disorder, severe
F15.10	Other or unspecified stimulant use disorder, mild
F15.20	Other or unspecified stimulant use disorder, moderate
F15.20	Other or unspecified stimulant use disorder, severe
F15.129	Amphetamine or other stimulant intoxication without perceptual disturbance with use disorder, mild
F15.229	Amphetamine or other stimulant intoxication without perceptual disturbance with use disorder, moderate or severe
F15.929	Amphetamine or other stimulant Intoxication without perceptual disturbance without use disorder
F14.129	Cocaine intoxication without perceptual disturbance with use disorder, mild
F14.229	Cocaine intoxication without perceptual disturbance with use disorder, moderate or severe
F14.929	Cocaine intoxication without perceptual disturbance without use disorder
F15.122	Amphetamine or other stimulant intoxication with perceptual disturbance with use disorder, mild
F15.222	Amphetamine or other stimulant intoxication with perceptual disturbance with use disorder, moderate or severe
F15.922	Amphetamine or other stimulant intoxication with perceptual disturbance without use disorder
F14.122	Cocaine intoxication with perceptual disturbance with use disorder, mild
F14.222	Cocaine intoxication with perceptual disturbance with use disorder, moderate or severe
F15.922	Cocaine intoxication with perceptual disturbance without use disorder
F15.23	Amphetamine or other substance withdrawal
F14.23	Cocaine withdrawal
F15.99	Unspecified amphetamine or other substance-related disorders

F14.99	Unspecified cocaine-related disorders

Tobacco-Related Disorders
Specify if: On maintenance therapy or In a controlled environment

Z72.0	Tobacco use disorder, mild
F17.200	Tobacco use disorder, moderate
F17.200	Tobacco use disorder, severe
F17.203	Tobacco withdrawal
F17.209	Unspecified tobacco-related disorder

Other (or Unknown) Substance-Related Disorders

F19.10	Other (or unknown) substance use disorder, mild
F19.20	Other (or unknown) substance use disorder, moderate
F19.20	Other (or unknown) substance use disorder, severe
F19.129	Other (or unknown) substance intoxication with use disorder, mild
F19.229	Other (or unknown) substance intoxication with use disorder, moderate or severe
F19.929	Other (or unknown) substance intoxication without use disorder
F19.239	Other (or unknown) substance
F19.99	Unspecified other (or unknown) substance-related disorder

Etiology and Treatment

Individuals diagnosed with substance-related and addictive disorders are at risk for myriad comorbid disorders (APA, 2022). These include depressive, anxiety, trauma and stressor-related, personality, and other substance-related disorders to name a few. Because of their high prevalence rates, these diagnoses are frequently the focus of clinical attention for counselors. Substance use, intoxication, and withdrawal often include multiple substances, thus emphasizing the need for comprehensive assessment. The 18–24 age group of has the highest prevalence for substance-related disorder, with substance intoxication typically first occurring during adolescence (APA, 2022).

Treatment for addictions should be multimodal and include assessment of the impact on self-efficacy, relationships, physical health, career, and overall psychosocial functioning. Treatments such as motivational interviewing, CBT, medication-assisted therapy, family therapy, and 12-step facilitation can benefit clients. Attention to trauma-informed care and knowledge of the risk factors from childhood trauma are important when working with this population (see CDC, 2023). Substance-related disorders possess psychobiological factors that include genetic predisposition, social and cultural contexts, and life events (APA, 2022, Kress & Paylo, 2018).

Implications for Counselors

Substance use severity is assessed on three levels, which lends to enhanced and tailored treatment options. The *mild* level of severity for substance use disorders (two to three criteria met) provides early intervention opportunities; individuals who present with *moderate* (four or five symptoms) or *severe* (six of more symptoms) substance use disorders may require more intensive treatments.

Initial substance use typically takes place during the mid-teens for most individuals, with early onset lending to higher clinical diagnoses (Alcover & Thompson, 2020). Considering the negative psychological, physiological, and environmental effects of substance-related disorders, counselors need to thoroughly assess and engage in treatment modalities early in the course of the disorder.

The symptom of craving is identified as persistent even into remission. Craving has been supported through epidemiological studies as a highly prominent and core feature of substance use disorders (NIDA, 2020). Presence of cues, negative moods, and stress reactions often lead to an increase in craving.

An important area for counselors to address in treatment is the lingering symptom of substance craving that can present a challenge for client relapse prevention. The desire and yearning for a specific substance or substances is a common symptom that can exist well beyond cessation of use (Kunas et al., 2022; NIDA, 2020). Instillation of adaptive coping mechanisms and substitution of positive behaviors can be important elements of treatment in working with residual craving. Motivational interviewing and mindfulness training have been shown to reduce craving by addressing awareness of the emotion and redirection of thoughts.

Specific Substance-Related Disorders Overview

The following sections provide brief descriptions and key elements of substance-related disorders outlined in the *DSM-5-TR*. The manual also contains a section for other (or unknown) substance-related disorders that encompasses substances that fall outside of the specific types enumerated below.

Alcohol-Related Disorders

There is a high prevalence of alcohol use disorder in the United States, with lifetime prevalence of approximately 36% of adult men and 22.9% of adult women (APA, 2022). The highest annual prevalence is among Native Americans and Alaska Natives (12.1%), and the lowest is among Asian Americans and Pacific Islanders (4.5%). Age of onset peaks in the late teens, and most individuals who will develop alcohol use disorder do so by their late 30s (APA, 2022; Panza et al., 2022).

Individuals from cultures in which alcohol availability and use are widespread are more prone to the development of the disorder. This is especially true if there are genetic predispositions to alcohol use disorder, as is the case in almost 50% of individuals who develop the disorder. Genetic factors can contribute to alcohol-related disorders and craving, which make some individuals particularly vulnerable to alcohol use disorder. From a physiological standpoint, individuals with bipolar disorder, schizophrenia, and general impulsivity concerns have a heightened risk for alcohol-related disorders (APA, 2022; Panza et al., 2022). There are separate codes for alcohol withdrawal and intoxication, which are likely diagnosed in medical settings.

Caffeine-Related Disorders

The *DSM-5-TR* does not identify caffeine use disorder as a diagnosable condition. Although some evidence supports the diagnosis of caffeine use disorder, there is not yet sufficient information supporting impairment resulting from a problematic pattern of caffeine use. The United States has a high number of caffeine users—more than 85% of adults and youth use caffeine regularly. Thus, caffeine use disorder is included in Section III of the manual as a condition for further study. The *DSM-5-TR* includes caffeine intoxication and withdrawal as diagnosable disorders (APA, 2022).

Caffeine withdrawal requires stopping caffeine use after prolonged daily consumption, with physical symptoms of headache, fatigue, dysphoric mood, difficulty concentrating, and possible flulike symptoms that cause clinically significant distress. This is similar to withdrawal criteria for substance-related disorders listed in this chapter. It is interesting to note that excessive caffeine use is often seen in individuals with mental health disorders such as eating disorders and other substance-related disorders (APA, 2022). The growing popularity of energy drinks with high caffeine content poses a concern, especially because young people tend to be frequent consumers of such beverages.

Cannabis-Related Disorders

Cannabis, or marijuana, is known to be the most frequently used drug, with a definitive link found between cannabis use and mood disorders (National Academies of Sciences, Engineering, & Medicine, 2017). Although it is illegal at the federal level, several states have legalized cannabis for medical and recreational use. Cannabis use is widespread in the United States, and the number of users is projected to increase over the next decade (CDC, 2022). Cannabis use (especially in large doses) is associated with temporary psychosis and schizophrenia (Volkow et al., 2016). Heavy use also increases rates of depression and social anxiety.

Cannabis withdrawal includes physical symptoms arising after cessation of heavy use, which is defined as daily or almost daily use for a minimum of several months (APA, 2022). Irritability, anger, aggression, nervousness, restlessness, and sleep disturbance are a few of the symptoms. Additionally, genetic factors can contribute to cannabis use and withdrawal, thus providing further rationale for their categorization in the manual (APA, 2022).

Hallucinogen-Related Disorders

Hallucinogens are a heterogeneous grouping of substances that can have the same type of alterations of cognition and perception in users. These substances are most often taken orally, although some are smoked or injected. These types of drugs (e.g., lysergic acid diethylamide [LSD]; 3,4-methylenedioxy-methamphetamine [MDMA or ecstasy]; psychedelic mushrooms) have a long half-life that can extend from hours to days. Hallucinogen use disorder has an annual prevalence rate of 0.1% in adults, with men more likely than women to engage in use (APA, 2022; SAMHSA, 2022). Hallucinogens can have long-term effects on brain functioning. In diagnosing hallucinogen use disorder, counselors should identify the specific substance (e.g., "ecstasy use disorder" rather than the more general "hallucinogen use disorder"). Because withdrawal from hallucinogens has not been clearly documented, the withdrawal criterion is absent for hallucinogen use disorder (APA, 2022).

Hallucinogens are sometimes used in religious practices (i.e., peyote in the Native American Church). Controlled use during religious observances is not to be considered a diagnosable condition. As with the diagnosis of any mental health disorder, cultural factors must be taken into account during assessment and treatment delivery (APA, 2022).

Inhalant-Related Disorders

Inhalants such as glues, paints, fuels, and other "volatile hydrocarbons" are all included in this diagnostic classification. A small percentage (0.4%) of adolescents between the ages of 12 and 17 meet the criteria for inhalant use disorder, although usage rates for young people may be as high as 10% (SAMHSA, 2022). This disorder is typically not seen in older children or adults (APA, 2022).

Because of a dearth of documented physiological and psychological effects related to cessation of use, inhalant withdrawal is not included in the *DSM-5-TR* (APA, 2022). Inhalant use is quite dangerous and can be fatal. One author of this *Learning Companion* had a friend who died of inhalant poisoning at 18 years of age. It is important for counselors to effectively identify inhalant-related disorders, especially counselors specializing in adolescent treatment. Counselors should be very concerned about reports of inhalant use. This problem afflicts children from all socioeconomic backgrounds and from families with both high and low levels of parental education.

Opioid-Related Disorders

Opioid use has multiple deleterious physical effects. Because opioids are frequently injected, there are many risks for infection and disease. Common opioids include morphine, oxycodone, and heroin (APA, 2022). Counselors must be aware of the risks of needle sharing, which puts opioid users at higher risk for HIV, hepatitis, and tuberculosis. There is a heightened suicide risk and high mortality rate for opioid users (up to 2% yearly). Jim Morrison, Janis Joplin, John Belushi, Chris Farley, River Phoenix, Heath Ledger, Tom Petty, and Prince were all famous people, to name just a few, who died from opioid overdoses.

Opioid use disorder typically develops in early adulthood and spans many years. Rates of opioid use are higher in males than females (APA, 2022). Problems first occur in adolescence and early adulthood. Opioid use disorder is seen across ethnicities; tolerance and withdrawal are commonly evident criteria. Babies born to mothers who have used opioids during their pregnancy can be born physiologically dependent (APA, 2022). The severity of negative health effects underscores the need for early and effective interventions for opioid users, including medication-assisted therapy (U.S. Food and Drug Administration, 2023).

Sedative-, Hypnotic-, or Anxiolytic-Related Disorders

This class of substances includes all prescription sleep medications and almost all anxiety medications. One great danger is the swift buildup of tolerance and withdrawal for these substances, often resulting in craving. Individuals in adolescence and early adulthood are at the highest risk for the disorder and often engage in concomitant use of other substances (APA, 2022).

If sedatives, hypnotics, or anxiolytics are prescribed for specific medical purposes and the medication is taken as prescribed, an individual would not meet diagnostic criteria for the use disorder. Sometimes, individuals who receive a prescription will build tolerance and seek out additional access from multiple physicians; thus, counselors should be careful to assess for patterns of use even for clients who report accessing substances through medical providers. Sedative-, hypnotic-, or anxiolytic-related disorders are often comorbid with alcohol and tobacco use disorders, personality disorders, depressive disorders, anxiety disorders, and bipolar disorders (APA, 2022).

Stimulant-Related Disorders

Substances included in this section include, but are not limited to, amphetamines, dextroamphetamines, methamphetamines, and cocaine. Stimulants can be taken orally, injected, or smoked and typically result in drastic changes in behavior and a concomitant feeling of subjective well-being. Violent and aggressive behavior occurs with stimulant use and can lead to interpersonal and legal difficulties. Withdrawal can cause significant depressive symptoms as well as medical conditions including cardiac difficulties, seizures, neurocognitive impairment, and respiratory problems. Stimulant-related disorders are likely to co-occur with other substance-related disorders and gambling disorder. It is notable that amphetamines are sometimes medically prescribed to treat ADHD, obesity, and narcolepsy (APA, 2022).

Tobacco-Related Disorders

Approximately one in five adolescents in the United States will use tobacco on a regular basis; most individuals will develop tobacco use disorder prior to the age of 21. Many tobacco users attempt to quit, with most making multiple attempts before successfully stopping usage (APA, 2022). Tobacco is linked to a plethora of physical health problems and accounts for approximately one in every five deaths in the United States. Tobacco smokers have a life-span projection that is about 10 years shorter than nonsmokers (CDC, 2022).

Tobacco intoxication is not included in the *DSM-5-TR*. Tobacco withdrawal was a new diagnosis in the *DSM-5* and remains unchanged in the *DSM-5-TR*. Tobacco withdrawal involves symptoms of irritability, anxiety, difficulty concentrating, increased appetite, restlessness, depressed mood, and insomnia. There is a significant comorbidity of individuals with tobacco use disorder to also meet criteria for other substance-related, anxiety, depressive, bipolar, and personality disorders (APA, 2022).

Tobacco use has declined in the United States in the past decades, in part from heightened awareness of the health risks and restrictions on smoking accessibility. However, people from lower socioeconomic backgrounds are more likely to begin smoking tobacco and less likely to quit successfully. Young people may be especially vulnerable to electronic cigarette usage, also known as vaping. According to the CDC (2021), adolescents, young adults, and pregnant women are at particular risk. There are enormous health benefits to tobacco cessation, with those able to quit tobacco use mitigating risk of death from related disease by 90% (APA, 2022; CDC, 2022).

Case Example

Maria is a 33-year-old Latina, heterosexual married mother of two young children. Previously employed as a bank manager, Maria has been working as a homemaker since the birth of her second child 2 years ago. Although a social drinker throughout her early adulthood, she began consuming alcohol on a daily basis about a year and a half ago. She started out drinking only wine but quickly progressed to vodka. For close to a year, Maria has been consuming in excess of seven drinks daily.

Maria hides her alcohol use from her family and friends. There have been times when she tried to quit drinking for several days, but those attempts were unsuccessful. Maria thinks about drinking more often than not and admits to driving multiple times under the effects of alcohol, although she denies any impairment or risk. She often starts drinking first thing in the morning several days of the week to get rid of hangover symptoms.

Maria feels stressed by her responsibilities parenting her two small children and maintaining the household. She also feels unfulfilled in her life and believes that she has wasted her career potential. As a devout Catholic, she also feels her drinking and lying are sinful. This makes her sad and leads to her drinking more to numb the pain.

Maria presents for counseling as a result of her husband confronting her about her drinking. She verbalizes that she loves her husband and family, which is why she sought help from counseling. She denies having a problem and states that she has "everything under control" and can "stop drinking anytime."

Diagnostic Questions

1. Do Maria's presenting symptoms meet the criteria for alcohol use disorder?
2. Based on your answer to Question 1, what severity specifier would you assign to Maria's diagnosis?
3. What would be the reason(s), if any, a counselor may not diagnose Maria with an alcohol use disorder?
4. Would Maria be more accurately diagnosed with a mood or personality disorder? If so, why? If not, why not?
5. What rule-outs would you consider for Maria's case?
6. What other information may be needed to make an accurate clinical diagnosis?

Gambling Disorder (F63.0)

> It was like my whole life revolved around being in the casino. I would spend all day there and then dream about it at night. It didn't matter how much money I lost because I just knew that the next time I pulled the slot, I would hit the jackpot. I quit caring about my relationships or the fact that I had been fired from another job.—Johi

Gambling disorder is the only nonsubstance-related disorder included in the Substance-Related and Addictive Disorders chapter of the *DSM-5-TR*. Its location in this section of the *DSM-5-TR* reflects similarities in neurocircuitry related to brain reward systems and behavior patterns. Gambling disorder criteria remain unchanged from the *DSM-5* to the *DSM-5-TR* (APA, 2022; NIDA 2022).

The behavior of gambling activates the brain reward system. It has been posited that most addictions involve the development of a delivery mechanism of some kind; that is, gambling addiction can involve addiction to poker or roulette, which provides the conduit for receiving rewards (APA 2022; Limbrick-Oldfield et al., 2017).

As noted in the *DSM-5-TR*, "gambling involves risking something of value in the hopes of obtaining something of greater value" (APA, 2022, p. 662). The earlier gambling behaviors begin, the more likely an individual is to develop the disorder. Cultural, environmental, and genetic factors can lead an individual to be at higher risk for the development of gambling disorder. Animal and human research supports a strong neurological basis of addiction, including twin studies that have uncovered a higher prevalence in identical versus fraternal twins (APA, 2013a; NIDA, 2022).

Cultural Considerations

Males are more likely to develop gambling disorder than females and tend to engage in different types of gambling (APA, 2022). Playing cards and betting on sports and horse racing are more prevalent gambling activities in males, whereas playing bingo and using slot machines are more common gambling activities for females. Gambling patterns often increase during times of stress or personal difficulty.

There is a higher prevalence of gambling disorder among Black Americans compared with other racial/ethnic groups. Native Americans have the highest prevalence rates of the disorder (APA, 2022). Gambling disorder can manifest throughout the life span with occurrences from adolescence through older adulthood (Limbrick-Oldfield et al., 2017).

Differential Diagnosis

Nondisordered gambling, manic episodes, personality disorders, and other medical conditions should all be considered as possible differential diagnoses. Examples of nondisordered gambling are professional and social gambling. Discipline and control with minimal and acceptable losses are key elements for professional and social gambling. Gambling issues can be seen in individuals with personality disorders (e.g., antisocial personality disorder, borderline personality disorder). If an individual with a diagnosable personality disorder meets the criteria for gambling disorder, both can be diagnosed (APA, 2022).

Certain medications can enhance urges to gamble (e.g., dopaminergic medications prescribed for Parkinson's disease). Additionally, it is important to rule out disordered gambling that occurs during the course of a manic episode. Manic episodes are often characterized by impaired impulse control, loss of judgment, and engagement in excessive pleasurable activity; for some, gambling may result (APA, 2022).

Coding, Recording, and Specifiers

There is only one diagnostic code for gambling disorder: F63.0. Specifiers for gambling disorder are *episodic*, which means symptoms meet diagnostic criteria with amelioration of symptoms for at least several months, and *persistent*, which means symptoms are continuous and ongoing over the course of several years or more. There are both *early remission* and *sustained remission* with durations of 3 months and 12 months, respectively. Levels of severity are *mild* (four to five criteria met), *moderate* (six to seven criteria met), and *severe* (eight to nine criteria met).

Implications for Counselors

The inclusion of gambling disorder as an addictive disorder in the *DSM-5* brought a reconceptualization for counselors working with clients who struggle with problematic gambling (APA, 2013a). Because of its convergent etiology with substance-related disorders, it is important for counselors to be aware of the sequelae of the diagnosis and its psychosocial impact. Clients with gambling disorder frequently face impairment in multiple facets of their lives and often have specific financial hardship because of their behaviors.

Counselors across settings should be aware of treatment needs, comorbidity, and differential diagnoses for these clients. Lifestyle modifications must often be made to alleviate temptation and negative peer influences. If there is a comorbid disorder, the special clinical needs of those clients should be taken into account. Addressing the impact on family members is an important part of treatment (NIDA, 2022).

The diagnosis of gambling disorder as a nonsubstance addiction holds the potential to assist people with access to treatment. Several treatment modalities have proved efficacious with this population of clients. These include mindfulness training, CBT, behavior modification, contingency management, and motivational interviewing, to name a few (Limbrick-Oldfield et al., 2017)

Although gambling disorder is the only nonsubstance-related disorder in the Substance-Related and Addictive Disorders chapter of the *DSM-5-TR*, Section III of the manual includes internet gaming disorder as a condition for further study. Currently, other potentially addictive behaviors, such as sex, work, shopping, and exercise addictions, are not included in the manual as codable disorders or conditions for further study (APA, 2022).

Counselors working across client populations and clinical settings need to be aware of the diagnostic criteria, functional impairments, and effective approaches for supporting clients with gambling disorder and internet gaming difficulties. Counselors not working directly with clients with behavioral addictions may still witness pervasive and negative impacts on loved ones across clinical settings. As with substance-related disorders, gambling disorder (and potentially internet gaming) holds wide-reaching negative consequences.

Case Example

> Akule is a single, Native American, 26-year-old male graduate student living in a metropolitan area. Akule has been a full-time student all of his adult life and has had to support himself through employment and student financial aid because his family does not have the means to provide financial support. Akule considers himself close to his parents and siblings, although over the last year, he has been avoiding contact with them because he has been "too busy."
>
> Akule originally started gambling during a vacation with a group of friends. Excited by initial winnings and the accolades of his peers, Akule began gambling

regularly upon his return home. At first, he was on a lucky streak and was able to pay some bills with his winnings. That soon changed, and he began losing. Over the course of the past year, Akule started gambling multiple days per week, often missing class because he stayed out late at the casino. He would grow irritable and anxious in the days following a string of losses; this began to affect his friendships and his relationship with his girlfriend, who tired of his being out late at night and his irritability. After catching him in a lie about how much money he lost gambling, she broke up with him.

After the breakup, at risk of being put on academic probation, and facing about $10,000 in debt, Akule seeks counseling services. Akule states that he is anxious and depressed but minimizes his gambling behavior and shrugging that it is "not really a problem."

Diagnostic Questions

1. Do Akule's presenting symptoms meet the criteria for gambling disorder?
2. Based on the disorder identified in Question 1, what severity specifier would you assign for Akule's diagnosis?
3. What would be the reason(s) a counselor may not diagnose Akule with a personality disorder?
4. Would Akule be more accurately diagnosed with bipolar disorder? If so, why? If not, why not?
5. What rule-outs would you consider for Akule's case?
6. What other information may be needed to make an accurate clinical diagnosis?

Questions for Consideration

1. How might the physiological nature of the substance-related disorders impact client treatment recommendations?
2. What are the diagnostic overlaps among substance use disorders and gambling disorder?
3. How can awareness of clinical comorbidities help with assessment and treatment planning for these clients?
4. What might represent a common treatment recommendation(s) for an individual diagnosed with a substance-related disorder?

Chapter 13

Disruptive, Impulse-Control, and Conduct Disorders

The Disruptive, Impulse-Control, and Conduct Disorders chapter of the *DSM-5-TR* includes problems of self-control and consolidates disorders related to emotional or behavioral dysregulation (APA, 2022). Included in this chapter are oppositional defiant disorder (ODD), intermittent explosive disorder (IED), conduct disorder (CD), pyromania, and kleptomania. Antisocial personality disorder (ASPD) is also listed in this chapter but is described in the Personality Disorders chapter.

Characteristics of disruptive, impulse-control, and conduct disorders are aggressive or self-destructive behavior, destruction of property, conflict with authority figures, disregard for personal or social norms, and persistent outbursts of anger disproportionate to the situation (APA, 2022). Whereas the urge to engage in behaviors that harm oneself or others is common to many mental health concerns (e.g., substance-related and addictive disorders), the behaviors listed in this diagnostic category include those that either violate the rights of others or diverge significantly from societal norms (APA, 2022; Coccaro, 2012).

Two disorders within this chapter, pyromania and kleptomania, are quite rare and characterized by tension and release behavior. Like obsessive-compulsive and related disorders, clients may feel a sense of affective arousal (i.e., tension) before engaging in the antisocial behavior of fire setting (pyromania) or theft (kleptomania). What differentiates these disorders from obsessive-compulsive related disorders is that individuals with impulse-control disorders are generally sensation-seeking, whereas individuals with obsessive-compulsive related disorders have risk-avoidant behavior such as constantly checking and rechecking locks, repetitive hand washing, or picking at hair and skin (see Chapter 9 for more information).

> ***Note:*** Nearly all children and adolescents engage in defiant, rule-breaking, and disobedient behavior at some point in their development. However, the regularity, pervasiveness, and impairment experienced by some exceed normative behavior for their age, gender, and culture (APA, 2022).

Although underlying causes vary greatly, all diagnoses in this chapter share the common characteristic of problems with emotional or behavioral regulation (APA, 2022). Moreover, all disorders in this chapter are marked by significant impairment. More common in males than females, the age of first onset of disruptive, impulse-control, and conduct disorders tends to be in childhood or adolescence (APA, 2022).

There is a developmental relationship between ODD, CD, and ASPD in that individuals diagnosed with ASPD often have a history of CD, and those diagnosed with CD often have a history of ODD (Azeredo et al., 2018; Eskander, 2020). However, this does not mean that most children with ODD eventually develop CD or that most with CD eventually develop ASPD. Although those with ODD are at risk for various mental health concerns, particularly depressive or anxiety disorders, they are not preordained to be diagnosed with CD (APA, 2022; Dugré & Potvin, 2022). We will attend to unique developmental pathways and considerations as we explore special considerations related to each major disorder covered in this chapter.

Changes From *DSM-5* to *DSM-5-TR*

There are no major changes in disruptive, impulse-control, and conduct disorders from the *DSM-5* to the *DSM-5-TR*. Rather, changes are concentrated in the text sections, including updated literature and more nuanced attention to culture-, sex-, and gender-related diagnostic issues in this category. This includes overt recognition of context in which disruptive behaviors may be normative or adaptive, as well as recognition of racialized diagnostic bias among practitioners and the potential for youth of color to engage in what appear to be oppositional or disruptive behaviors in response to racism or trauma.

Differential Diagnosis

It is quite common for individuals diagnosed with ODD or CD to also exhibit symptoms of ADHD (APA, 2022; Azeredo et al., 2018; Eskander, 2020; Gorman et al., 2015; Noordermeer et al., 2016; Pardini & Frick, 2013). ASPD, because of its close association with CD, is cross-listed in this chapter as well as the Personality Disorders chapter. Symptoms of disruptive, impulse-control, and conduct disorders have commonly been misdiagnosed as pediatric bipolar disorder. Given the addition of disruptive mood dysregulation disorder (DMDD) in the *DSM-5*, counselors are advised to consider carefully whether temper outbursts are related to an underlying mood concern such as DMDD or behavior disorders such as IED, ODD, and CD.

Disruptive behavior disorders are often comorbid with each other, with ADHD, ODD, and CD studied and reported together rather than separately. Counselors can differentiate disruptive, impulse-control, and conduct disorders from other disorders by attending to key features of each disorder. For example, IED is related to impaired ability to regulate emotions, ODD is focused on irritability and attitude toward others, and CD centers more on engagement in behavior that violates the rights of others. Whereas ADHD and substance use disorders involve difficulties with impulse management, this is not the primary feature of these disorders.

Researchers often focus on disruptive behaviors or disruptive behavior disorders as a cluster. However, these disorders are frequently comorbid with disorders found elsewhere in the *DSM-5-TR*. A systematic review of disorders experienced by adolescents in detention or correctional facilities (presumably for aggressive or rule-breaking behaviors) revealed that 62% of males and 59% of females met diagnostic criteria for CD (Beaudry et al., 2021). They also had elevated rates of major depressive disorder (10% males, 26% females), ADHD (17% males, 18% females), and PTSD (9% males, 18% females). Another study of youth in reform schools showed high rates of substance use disorders (i.e., 29%) and affective disorders (18%) alongside CD (Manninen, 2022). Likewise, IED and ODD are associated with depression and anxiety (APA, 2022). These studies highlight the importance of holistic assessment when working with individuals who present with disruptive behavior and impulse-control concerns. At a minimum, this assessment should consider the potential for the presence of ADHD, depression, anxiety, and substance use disorders.

A thorough differential diagnosis is essential given evidence of contextual factors, comorbidity, and ethnoracial disparities when diagnosing behavior problems. Youth who witness interpersonal partner violence at home have higher levels of externalizing behavior (Fong et al., 2019). Likewise, researchers have found increased prevalence of childhood sexual abuse for those diagnosed with CD (Maniglio, 2014). These findings clearly show a link between exposure to trauma and behavioral concerns. Yet, Black youth exposed to multiple adverse childhood experiences (CDC, 2023) were three times more likely than their White counterparts to receive disruptive behavior diagnoses (Thyberg & Lombardi, 2022), whereas White and Latinx youth were more likely to receive depression and anxiety diagnoses. Likewise, Black male youth in correctional settings were 32% less likely to receive psychiatric treatment than White male youth (Baglivio et al., 2017). Together, these data point to the likelihood that providers may perceive disruptive behaviors differently based on race, thus missing trauma and highly treatable mental health disorders, especially among youth of color (Beaudry et al., 2021).

Etiology and Treatment

Researchers have long worked to better understand the etiological development of disruptive, impulse-control, and conduct disorders. These include attention to genetic, neurological, and environmental factors associated with these disorders. Despite being grouped together diagnostically, separate pathways regarding the development of each disorder are found in the literature. Some researchers are beginning to identify separate pathways within individual disorders as well (e.g., Dugré & Potvin, 2022; Pardini & Frick, 2013). Understanding unique pathways may be key to uncovering approaches to prevention and intervention that are effective and customized to the needs of individual clients.

A systematic review of genetic and environmental risk factors in ADHD, CD, and ODD indicated greater genetic than environmental links, with CD and ODD sharing genetic influences around externalizing behaviors (Azeredo et al., 2018). Likewise, APA (2022) consistently highlights genetic or neurological contributions, specifically an overlap between neurobiological markers associated with irritability in ODD, depression, and anxiety. There also seem to be genetic links to aggression and family history observed in CD and IED. Children with ADHD appear to be predisposed to ODD and CD (Azeredo et al., 2018). However, a systematic review of neuroimaging related to ODD and CD revealed strong evidence of amygdala involvement for ODD and CD (Noordermeer et al., 2016), as well as abnormalities in executive functioning related to motivation and affect distinct from those observed in ADHD. These are consistent with APA-reported temperamental risk factors around undercontrol (CD) and emotion regulation (ODD).

Many researchers emphasized environmental origins for disruptive behavior disorders, often focusing on child-rearing practices with a particular emphasis on the impact of the mother. These findings are complex, sometimes mixed, and likely indicate an intersection of environmental, temperamental, and genetic influences. For example, mothers who smoked or used alcohol during pregnancy were approximately two times more likely to have children with conduct problems (Ruisch et al., 2018), and mothers with bipolar disorders were at greater risk of having children with ODD and CD (Ayano et al., 2021). Parental substance use disorders, crime history, and mental health are associated with both ODD and CD (Azeredo et al., 2018). Although these disorders may impact the caregiving environment, it is also possible that they indicate an underlying vulnerability for all involved.

Child-rearing practices and stability are of high interest in understanding the origins of conduct problems as seen in ODD and CD (APA, 2022), with the strength of findings varying across studies and disorders. In a systematic review article (Rowell & Neal-Barnett, 2022), parents' emotional availability and discipline approaches to their children appear to be linked to their own mental health status and exposure to adverse childhood experiences, leading them toward a permissive or authoritarian discipline that may not effectively address children's behavioral concerns. In another meta-analysis (Johnson et al., 2017), parents' emotional socialization behaviors had a small but significant impact on conduct problems, with stronger correlations for younger children and when socialization was negative.

Parental influences may play out differently for the development of and response to ODD and CD; again, findings are mixed and complex. In a nationally representative sample, Lindhiem et al. (2023) found that deficits in parents' knowledge of behavior management skills were strongly associated with their children's CD but not ODD, leading the researchers to conclude that ODD may be more about children's temperament and affect than behavior. However, Azeredo et al. (2018) found that the family environment has a stronger influence on ODD than on CD. Still others point to the uniqueness of risk factors based on development. Pardini and Frick (2013) found that individuals who are younger when CD emerges may have a stronger convergence of neurological and environmental factors compared with those who engage in disruptive behavior in adolescence only.

In a national sample of individuals with CD, Moore et al. (2017) worked to differentiate the experiences of those with life-course persistent CD from those with adolescent-limited CD. Compared with individuals with CD just in adolescence, those with life-course CD were 3.5 times more likely to have low childhood socioeconomic status and more than twice as likely to lack maternal closeness and have a history of harsh discipline (Moore et al., 2017). While some might argue for a causal link between early family environment and CD, others might wonder whether those with difficult temperaments and early behavior problems elicit a different parenting response, especially when their caregivers may be underresourced or addressing their own trauma and mental health needs.

Treatment for disruptive behavior disorders is complex given a variety of risk factors and contributing factors. Treatment is critical because those with ODD or CD are at over three times greater risk for substance use disorders compared with the general population (Groenman et al., 2017). Those with both ADHD and CD are 2.7 times less likely to complete high school, 3.5 times more likely to engage in criminal violence, and 3.3 times more likely to become pregnant before age 23. The latest evidence points to the need for interventions that address a variety of risk and contextual factors for both parent and child (Fong et al., 2019). Effective intervention may help disrupt the developmental trajectory from ODD to CD (Lindhiem et al., 2023).

Choice of intervention may be tied to an emerging understanding of unique developmental pathways in disruptive behavior disorders, especially given that standard protocols may focus too narrowly on problem behavior rather than what drives problem behavior (Weisz et al., 2019). Pardini and Frick (2013) identified developmental pathways to CD, including the age of onset, presence or absence of callous-unemotional traits, and presence or absence of anger regulation. These factors created unique subgroups of people with CD. More recently, Dugré and Potvin (2022) identified irritability, interpersonal callousness, hyperactivity/impulsivity, and depression/anxiety as emerging in unique ways across different presentations of CD; these subtypes predicted aggressive behavior and rule-breaking behavior differently. Together, the evidence points to the need for mental health professionals to individualize interventions based on what is driving behaviors. For example, caregiver warmth might protect against callous-unemotional traits (Pardini & Frink, 2013). On the other hand, youth with irritability and anger dysregulation may benefit from problem-solving and emotion-regulation interventions (Dugré & Potvin, 2022; Lindhiem et al., 2023).

Caveats regarding treatment selection aside, evidence-based treatments for disruptive behavior disorders fall into three primary categories: family-focused interventions, CBT, and medication. To date, the literature does not include differentiated interventions for ODD and CD (Lindhiem et al., 2023), nor does it include any evidence-based treatment for IED, pyromania, or kleptomania (Tahir et al., 2022). In a meta-analysis of counseling outcomes for youth with CD, Erford et al. (2017) reviewed 21 clinical trials and found an overall medium treatment effect. Approaches varied widely and included parent training, multisystemic therapy, individual, and group. Erford and colleagues also found similar effect sizes across studies, without differences in effectiveness based on approach or length of treatment. Weisz et al. (2019) found a very similar effect size for treatment of conduct problems over time; however, they noted concerns with the effect being unchanged or declining over time, perhaps due to systemic or contextual challenges that limit improvement or create challenges to maintaining gains once counseling concludes.

There are several evidence-based psychosocial or family-focused treatments for youth with disruptive behavior disorders, and findings regarding their effectiveness vary. Typically, parent training approaches include positive time between parent and child, modeling of behaviors, the introduction of rewards and consequences, and coping skills for dealing with difficult behavior. One systematic review of parenting programs showed that they can work in the short term and were cost-effective for parents with 3–12-year-old children, although parents may need booster sessions to maintain gains over time (Barlow & Coren, 2018). In a meta-analysis of psychosocial interventions for externalized behavior, Baumel et al. (2021) found small to moderate effects that were sustained over time. These interventions were more effective for younger children and tended to include parent-only interventions. However, some studies showed evidence that involving parents and children in individual settings was the most effective intervention.

Parent management training (PMT) and parent-child interactive therapy (PCIT) are popular approaches to working with disruptive behaviors. In PMT, parents learn strategies to address behavior problems while enhancing relationships. A meta-analysis by Helander et al. (2022) showed that PMT had moderate effects on children's disruptive behavior and social skills and large effects on parental skills; adding CBT did not improve results. PCIT is an individual parent-child program that provides focused education and coaching for parents of children ages 2 to 7 years. Meta-analytic results for PCIT were particularly promising with large effects on children's disruptive behavior, especially with younger children (Helander et al., 2022).

Individually focused interventions are available as well, with CBT being the most researched intervention. Through CBT, counselors help clients modify cognitive distortions fueling disruptive behavior. This approach helps children and adolescents develop problem-solving skills to improve inhibition, recognize problems and triggers for disruptive behavior, and pursue more effective alternatives. Riise et al.'s (2021) systematic review of CBT for CD and ODD showed large effect sizes with nearly half of participants reaching remission. Despite the focus on parental involvement in other literature, Riise et al. found that nearly 90% of parents received some form of treatment, but their engagement did not moderate youth's outcomes, nor did treatment format (e.g., individual, group, or combination) influence outcomes. Individuals who were younger, had more severe symptoms, and engaged in a larger number of sessions had the most positive outcomes. A randomized control trial called Tuning Youth Temper, a brief, six-session, school-based CBT intervention for elementary-age children, showed promising results for reducing conduct problems and symptoms of ODD without parental involvement (Riise et al., 2021). It may be that these youth-focused interventions or others such as dialectic behavior therapy

(Lindhiem et al., 2023) are most appropriate for those whose behaviors are fueled by irritability and emotion dysregulation.

There are limited psychopharmacological treatments for disruptive behavior disorders, although there is frequent off-label prescribing of antipsychotic medications for behavior problems (Hambly et al., 2016). Medication is most effective if ADHD is present; addressing ADHD first may create a window to work with emotion regulation and behavior (Gorman et al., 2015). Although there is some evidence that risperidone, quetiapine, haloperidol, valproate, and lithium may be helpful for aggressive behaviors associated with ODD or CD, they carry significant side effects, leading psychiatric professionals to largely recommend against them. A systematic review of psychopharmacology for impulse-control disorders such as IED, kleptomania, and pyromania showed that these interventions are largely understudied (Tahir et al., 2022). However, there is evidence of efficacy for oxcarbazepine and fluoxetine in the treatment of IED; naltrexone may be efficacious for treating kleptomania.

Implications for Counselors

Counselors across settings will work with clients who engage in behaviors considered deviant and problematic to others. Kleptomania and pyromania are rare. The prevalence of kleptomania in the general population is 0.3% to 0.6%; only 1.0% to 1.1% of the population engages in any fire-setting behavior, just one criterion for pyromania (APA, 2022). On the other hand, disruptive behavior disorders such as ODD and CD are quite common in the general population (Eskander, 2020). Unique challenges in working with individuals with disruptive behaviors include the dynamics of working with children and adolescents in general, the dynamics of working with offenders or nonvoluntary populations, family engagement, other assessment considerations, and interdisciplinary collaboration.

Few counselors will argue that the development of a strong therapeutic relationship is essential for counseling success. Counselors may struggle to develop relationships with adolescents in general, and this struggle may be compounded given that the very nature of disruptive behavior and impulse-control disorders means that individuals are most likely engaging in deviant behavior, have difficulty considering others' perspectives, and may not present to counseling voluntarily. Like many offender populations, youth with disruptive behavior disorders may be mandated into counseling because they have engaged in behavior that adults in their lives find problematic. These youth may have difficult or traumatic relationships with other adults; thus, it is only normal that they may have difficulty trusting and connecting with other adults. Counselors need to consider methods for developing nonjudgmental relationships that do not unintentionally condone defiant or oppositional behavior.

Abuse, neglect, and other unhealthy family dynamics are risk factors for disruptive behavior disorders. Counselors should consider carefully whether an individual's behavioral difficulties are the result of difficult or dangerous conditions within the home, school, or community. At the same time, counselors must not jump to conclusions, pathologize, or otherwise blame caregivers of children with disruptive behavior disorders for their children's difficulties. Certainly, family engagement can be difficult yet critical to counseling success, and it is the foundation of many evidence-based treatments, especially for younger clients. Counselors who work with family systems may deepen their understanding of the family system by screening parents for trauma and mental health concerns that may impact their parenting behaviors and emotional availability (Rowell & Neal-Barnett, 2022).

Developmental pathways between ADHD, ODD, CD, ASPD, and adult criminal behavior and evidence of striking comorbidity with other disorders make it important for counselors to have an accurate assessment of individuals with disruptive behavior disorders. Counselors should consider barriers to accurate assessment, including the likelihood of clients underreporting or denying deviant behaviors in manners consistent with those experienced by individuals with substance use disorders. Several behavior assessments are available to help with this process (see Erford et al., 2019). We urge counselors to look beyond difficult behaviors to consider possible underlying concerns related to trauma, learning, mood, and anxiety. This includes systematic screening and holistic assessment for those referred for disruptive behaviors, especially in correctional settings (Beaudry et al., 2021; Manninen, 2022). Counselors need to take special care and embrace cultural humility and antioppressive practice, especially when working with youth of color who are disproportionately diagnosed with disruptive behavior disorders despite exposure to trauma (Thyberg & Lombardi, 2022).

As noted previously, ADHD frequently occurs alongside disruptive behavior disorders, and disruptive behavior at school may also be a result of unrecognized learning difficulties or frustrations. Careful assessment prior to counseling can help counselors and families understand children's developmental, academic, and social needs; co-occurring mental health concerns; barriers to treatment; and preferences. Once disruptive behaviors are identified, counselors can select from a range of evidence-based treatments to work with youth and families.

Finally, counselors who work with individuals who present with disruptive, impulse-control, and conduct disorders should be prepared to collaborate with professionals in other disciplines. Individuals may present to counseling with a court mandate, with the hopes of reducing legal involvement, or when having substantial problems within school or community settings. Thus, counselors may find themselves members of interdisciplinary treatment teams or in positions to advocate for children within their systems.

The rest of this chapter outlines each disorder within the Disruptive, Impulse-Control, and Conduct Disorders chapter of the *DSM-5-TR*. As with other chapters in this text, coverage for each disorder includes highlights of essential features and special considerations for counselors. Readers should refer to the *DSM-5-TR* for a full understanding of diagnostic criteria and features; subtypes and specifiers (if applicable); prevalence; development and course; risk and prognostic factors; association with suicidal thoughts or behaviors; and culture-, sex-, and gender-related diagnostic issues.

Oppositional Defiant Disorder (F91.3)

> Everything is an argument, and not just with me. Michael fights with his teachers, his mom, and his siblings. For at least a year now, he has been angry, irritable, and restless. He refuses to follow any rules and seems to deliberately defy his mother and me. Honestly, it is his behavior toward our 8-year-old neighbor Max that worries me the most. Sometimes he just seems cruel, even malicious toward him.—Everett (Michael's dad)

Essential Features

Oppositional defiant disorder (ODD) is characterized by a repetitive pattern of defiant, disobedient, hostile, and negative behavior toward others (APA, 2022). This disorder consists of three categories of behavior: (a) anger and irritability, (b) quarrelsome and defiant behavior, and (c) vindictiveness. Within any of these three categories, at least four symptoms (see diagnostic Criterion A for ODD in the *DSM-5-TR*) must be present for at least 6 months and out of proportion to what might be expected developmentally and culturally.

Special Considerations

According to the *DSM-5-TR*, the prevalence of ODD within the general population is 3.3%; however, the prevalence has been estimated to be as high as 11.2% in males and 9.2% in females (Eskander, 2020). ODD symptoms may begin as early as the preschool years, and it is rare to see onset after early adolescence. Although many studies indicate ODD is more prevalent in boys, especially when diagnosed prior to adolescence, societal norms may simply influence the expression of oppositional behavior.

Youth diagnosed with ODD typically are unaware that their attitude and behavior are oppositional (APA, 2022). Behavior becomes a repetitive pattern, often leading the individual to have significant problems interacting with others. It is not surprising that ODD is more common in families in which childcare is disrupted and caregivers are harsh or inconsistent.

When diagnosing any type of disruptive behavior, counselors need to tread carefully because these diagnoses tend to describe a broad range of behavioral problems, many of which may be developmentally appropriate. Counselors should inquire with multiple parties about the youth's argumentative behavior characteristics of ODD. Counselors might start by asking whether the youth gets into power struggles with authority figures and by requesting information about settings and scenarios in which the behavior occurs. It is not uncommon for ODD to be exclusively present at home; when symptoms are present within more than one setting, counselors should consider the behavior to be more severe. Symptoms that occur in a specific setting or circumstance may be normal, developmental, or adaptive responses to difficult environments.

Counselors must be sure that behaviors used to make the ODD diagnosis are not expected for the client's developmental stage or normative for the client's gender or culture. For example, it is not unusual for children to display independence-seeking behavior that may be considered disruptive or argumentative (e.g., temper tantrums; APA, 2022). However, if a behavior is persistent, lasts at least 6 months, and is clearly disruptive toward others, counselors may need to consider a diagnosis of ODD. An occasional temper tantrum may not be problematic, especially in young children; however, ODD may be present when tantrums occur alongside many other symptoms and result in educational and social impairment (e.g., being asked to leave a playgroup, suspension from school). Finally, manifestations of the disorder have been found to be consistent across cultural backgrounds (APA, 2022). Still, counselors are advised to consider carefully whether what they perceive to be oppositional behaviors could be adaptive and even normative communication patterns within a client's sociocultural context, especially for those experiencing discrimination.

Differential Diagnosis

A diagnosis of ODD cannot be given if individuals meet criteria for DMDD (APA, 2022). If criteria for DMDD are met, it is assumed that the mood disorder accounts for the child's oppositional behavior and attitudes. Although ODD may be diagnosed alongside CD, ADHD, or IED, counselors should consider carefully whether symptoms meet criteria for all disorders. For example, minor rule-breaking behaviors associated with ODD may be more about pushing limits and irritating adults, whereas law-breaking behaviors associated with CD may result in significant injury to individuals or damage to property. As noted in the *DSM-5-TR*, anger in ODD tends to be generalized, whereas anger in IED is characterized by aggression toward others. Given that ADHD is commonly diagnosed alongside ODD, counselors should carefully consider comorbidity with ADHD and may consider providing a referral for neurological assessment to further explore executive functioning. Finally, it is important to note that children and adolescents may manifest mood concerns with irritability and agitation rather than sadness, and there are overlapping neurobiological markers of ODD, depression, and anxiety (APA, 2022). Thus, counselors should consider the possibility that what looks oppositional may well be depression or anxiety.

Coding, Recording, and Specifiers

There is only one diagnostic code for ODD: F91.3. Counselors must indicate the current severity of *mild*, *moderate*, or *severe*. There are no codes associated with these specifiers.

> ***Note:*** Severity ratings are limited to the number of settings in which symptoms manifest.

Intermittent Explosive Disorder (F63.81)

> I was 23 years old when my best friend from high school told me she was done with our friendship. She said my temper was out of control and she never knew when I was going to "fly off the handle." I thought she was being melodramatic, but 6 months later I had three separate charges for assault. I tried to explain to my lawyer how all of a sudden I just feel rage. Someone would piss me off and, bam, I would have to hit them or throw something.— Raquel

Essential Features

Intermittent explosive disorder (IED) is characterized by an inability to control response to a stressor or frustration. IED results in excessive, unplanned verbal or physical outbursts in individuals at least 6 years of age. According to the *DSM-5-TR*, less severe outbursts must occur at least twice weekly over a period of 3 months; individuals may also qualify for IED if they engage in at least three episodes that result in damage to property or injury to others over the period of a year (APA, 2022).

Special Considerations

Diagnostic criteria for IED have been poorly operationalized historically, although revised *DSM-5* criteria are likely to result in better identification of those with aggression, impulsivity, family risk, and neurobiological markers related to aggression (Coccaro, 2012). The *DSM-5-TR* reports a 1-year prevalence of 2.6% and a lifetime prevalence of 4.0% for IED. There are mixed findings regarding prevalence by sex and ethnoracial identity, although a cross-national study showed greater risk for those who were male, young, unemployed, divorced or separated, and had less education. History of trauma in youth (APA, 2022) and exposure to violence (APA, 2022; Scott et al., 2016) are associated with IED risk.

Researchers have worked to understand the emotional processing and attribution of those with IED. These findings can help counselors understand the disorder more fully and craft responsive interventions. For example, individuals with IED engage in more anger rumination and have greater difficulty identifying feelings compared with healthy volunteers and individuals with other mental health disorders (Fahlgren et al., 2019). It appears that individuals with IED have a harder time with emotions and spend more time focusing on them, misattributing anger, and struggling to perceive sadness (Patoilo et al., 2021). They may not be able to recognize lower levels of anger in ways that lead them to experience explosive episodes as if they came out of nowhere, yet they may also be quite empathic and hypersensitive to negative emotions. In this case, cognitive intervention techniques such as distraction, reappraisal, and mindfulness work may help to address emotion and cognition fueling explosive outbursts (Fahlgren et al., 2019).

A good question counselors can ask clients is, "Do you ever become hostile or destructive when you get angry?" Follow-up questions regarding the nature and frequency of anger episodes will help counselors assess for the possibility of IED-related aggression. There are several distinct subgroups with IED (Ciesinski et al., 2022) with variations in emotional dysregulation, empathy, reflective rumination, and sense of positive urgency. Counselors can use this information to understand more deeply the experiences that precipitated and followed explosive episodes.

Differential Diagnosis

IED includes recurrent behavioral outbursts or disruptions. IED is frequently assessed alongside alcohol use and depressive disorders, and 82% of those with IED have at least one other disorder (Scott et al., 2016). When assessing for IED, counselors would be wise to consider several other disorders in which behavioral outbursts are present. These may include ODD, CD, ADHD, DMDD, bipolar and related disorders, and personality disorders in which individuals have trouble with impulse control. It is also possible that one experiences aggressive outbursts only when under the influence of a substance; in this case, substance use disorder or substance intoxication may better account for symptoms. Although counselors should not diagnose IED if another disorder better explains the concern, the *DSM-5-TR* includes a notation that IED can be diagnosed alongside other disorders if "recurrent impulsive aggressive outbursts are in excess of those usually seen in these disorders and warrant independent clinical attention" (APA, 2022, p. 527).

Coding, Recording, and Specifiers

There is only one diagnostic code for IED: F63.81. There are no specifiers for this disorder.

Conduct Disorder (F91._)

> Jessica was arrested for destruction of property and stealing 4 weeks ago. She and some friends went into a convenience store after it had closed and bashed in the windows, destroyed all shelving, and took everything they could. This isn't the first time either. I found out later she did this at another convenience store and frequently shoplifts at Target and other large stores. Jessica has been charged only once for destruction of property, but she just blamed it on her friends. She doesn't seem to even care about what she is doing. She shows no remorse, even when she has seen her friends get into serious trouble. She just acts like she doesn't care. Honestly, I am afraid to ask her about anything else. I know there is more. For years she has been skipping school, getting into fights, stealing my car, and, although no one has directly accused her, I know she hurt our neighbor's rabbit which used to live in a shed in their backyard.—AJ (Jessica's father)

Essential Features

Conduct disorder (CD) is characterized by "a repetitive and persistent pattern of behavior in which the basic rights of others or major age-appropriate societal norms or rules are violated" (APA, 2022, p. 530). The *DSM-5-TR* operationalizes this as at least three symptoms over the course of 1 year; because CD is most common among youth, at least one symptom must be present in the most recent 6 months. Symptoms fall into four clusters involving aggression toward people and animals, destruction of property, deceitfulness or theft, and serious violations of rules. See Criterion A within the *DSM-5-TR* for specific examples of CD symptoms.

Special Considerations

APA (2022) identifies the 1-year prevalence of CD as 2% to 10% and lifetime prevalence at about 12.0% for males and 7.1% for females. This is consistent with meta-analytic data regarding the global prevalence of CD (Mohammadi et al., 2021). On average, boys show symptoms around 11 years of age, and girls show symptoms around 15 years of age (Mohammadi et al., 2021).

As discussed earlier, CD appears to be part of a developmental pathway from ODD to CD to ASPD. Although flawed in some ways, this hypothesis has been supported by numerous researchers. Some evidence suggests that earlier onset of CD is associated with less favorable outcomes compared with late-onset CD. The *early onset* and *with limited prosocial emotions* specifiers are in the *DSM-5* in attempts to capture behaviors associated with future antisocial outcomes. Some researchers are concerned about measurement error and lack of strong effect sizes in research, warning that using the specifier for clinical decision-making or prognostic purposes may be detrimental (Colins et al., 2020).

As discussed earlier, CD is linked to a variety of environmental and genetic factors, and there is emerging evidence of unique developmental pathways within CD (Dugré & Potvin, 2022; Pardini & Frick, 2013). Certainly, a child who engages in aggression toward people and animals from an early age and has a strong family history of violence very likely needs a different approach than an adolescent who is brought in by concerned parents because they steal items of nontrivial value, stay out overnight, and lie to obtain favors. Considering the presence or absence of irritability, callousness, hyperactivity/impulsivity, and depression/anxiety may help counselors customize a counseling approach (Dugré & Potvin, 2022).

When assessing for CD, counselors should inquire with multiple parties about the client's behavior; this is particularly important because individuals who have CD may lie or deceive others as part of their symptomatology or to avoid the consequences of their behavior. Counselors should start by asking whether the client gets into trouble at home, in school, at work, or in the community. Once general concerns are identified, counselors may talk with clients, parents, and school personnel to determine the likelihood that behavioral concerns meet the criteria for CD.

Differential Diagnosis

Individuals who have CD may have remarkably similar diagnoses as individuals who qualify for an ASPD diagnosis. Indeed, diagnosis of CD prior to age 15 is one criterion of ASPD. Fortunately, most of those who meet the criteria for CD will not go on to develop ASPD. When assessing CD in adults, counselors should consider ASPD as a primary differential diagnosis.

As noted previously, counselors will also need to consider ADHD and other behavioral disorders when diagnosing CD. In addition, symptoms may be related to DMDD, bipolar disorder, or coexisting substance use disorders.

Coding, Recording, and Specifiers

There is only one general diagnostic code for CD: F91._; the final digit within the code notes whether the client experienced *childhood-onset type* prior to age 10 years (F91.1), *adolescent-onset type* after age 10 years (F91.2), or *unspecified onset* (F91.9). Depending on the number and seriousness of specific symptoms, counselors must indicate whether the disorder is *mild*, *moderate*, or *severe*. There are no codes associated with these specifiers. Finally, the *DSM-5-TR* includes a *with limited prosocial emotions* specifier for those who have a poorer prognosis as indicated by two or more of the following symptoms across time and setting: lack of remorse or guilt, callous–lack of empathy, unconcerned about performance, and shallow or deficient affect (APA, 2022).

Pyromania (F63.1)

> Nothing gave me a high like setting fires did. It started off small but eventually, I needed to see something just burn and burn. I was sent to prison after the last fire, and that's where I was mandated to therapy.—Demitri

Essential Features

Pyromania, typified by recurrent, purposeful fire-setting behaviors, is characterized by fascination and pleasure from starting or watching fires (APA, 2022). Fire-setting behavior in general is fairly uncommon, although some people find pleasure in setting fires. Individuals with pyromania are distinct in that they often experience arousal or tension leading up to the event and gratification after the fire begins. The behavior is deliberate and purposeful, but without ill intention, such as in CD where the aim is to cause serious physical harm to people or property. Individuals diagnosed with pyromania will demonstrate fascination, curiosity, and attraction to everything related to fire (APA, 2022). However, this focus is not due to an underlying motivation such as covering up a crime, protesting an injustice, or a psychotic delusion or hallucination.

Special Considerations

Among the general adult population, the lifetime prevalence of fire setting is 1%; however, the prevalence of pyromania is unknown (APA, 2022). It is not unusual for children and adolescents to play with fire experimentally. Fire starting as an essential feature of pyromania in children is rare (APA, 2022). In cases where children or adolescents are not simply experimenting or motivated by boredom, counselors need to act. Pyromania can become chronic over the life span and is associated with addictive and impulse-control disorders.

Counselors need to be aware of the potentially dangerous, even life-threatening, nature of pyromania. If engaging clients in treatment, counselors should apply the *ACA Code of Ethics* (ACA, 2014), especially related to danger to others and the duty to warn. A pragmatic approach is best for screening for pyromania. Counselors should directly ask the client about fire-starting behavior and inquire how many times the client has engaged in this behavior. Fire-setting behavior is associated with a more extensive history of conduct problems, family adversity, and emotional dysregulation (Perks et al., 2019). Counselors who work with those engaging in fire setting should consider these experiences as well.

Because pyromania is so rare, there are no evidence-based treatments. Some have proposed psychotherapeutic options consistent with those for other disruptive and impulse-control disorders (Cermain & Lejoyeux, 2010; J. E. Grant et al., 2013). These may include CBT, outpatient programs, and behavioral therapy. For youth, psychoeducation has often proved useful, as has collaboration with fire prevention communities and mental health agencies. There is also evidence to support multimodal interventions, including family treatment, individual psychotherapy, psychoeducation, and behavioral interventions (Cermain & Lejoyeux, 2010).

Differential Diagnosis

According to the *DSM-5-TR*, true instances of pyromania are very rare. Counselors working with individuals who set fires should consider whether the behavior was purposeful or accidental. In the case of purposeful fire setting, counselors should note that fire setting may be a function of developmental experimentation, a political statement, or instrumental (e.g., to cover up a crime). Fire setting may also be associated with CD or ASPD, or it may occur in response to psychosis or neurocognitive concerns (APA, 2022).

Coding, Recording, and Specifiers

There is only one diagnostic code for pyromania: F63.1; there are no specifiers associated with this disorder.

Kleptomania (F63.2)

It started out small. When I was in school, I picked up my friends' pencils. As I got older, I wanted to take things more and more. I would take the entire rack of sunglasses out of a department store. I was really good until I got caught.—Sharon

Essential Features

Occurring three times as often in women as in men, kleptomania refers to continuous theft for pleasure rather than object obtainment or financial reasons (APA, 2022). Although the act of shoplifting is not uncommon, true kleptomania is rare. According to the *DSM-5-TR*, kleptomania affects just 0.3% to 0.6% of the population and just 4% to 24% of those who are arrested for shoplifting.

The etiology of this disorder is not known. Theorists posit a strong correlation between kleptomania and substance use disorders, arguing that they could be categorized together (APA, 2022; Cermain & Lejoyeux, 2010). Like pyromania, a sense of tension precedes the initiation of the act (APA, 2022). Unlike other acts of stealing in which there is a concrete or practical motivation for the act, the act itself is the reward in kleptomania.

Special Considerations

Because of the estimated 3:1 female-to-male ratio and lack of need associated with stealing, this disorder is often associated with White middle- to upper-class women, and almost no data exist on culture or cultural implications (Torales et al., 2020). The onset of kleptomania is typically in adolescence, and it can present with varying courses, including chronic, sporadic, and episodic (APA, 2022). Individuals with this disorder do not typically present for treatment and may be secretive about their behavior because of shame or guilt (Torales et al., 2020).

Individuals may present for counseling only after legal or disciplinary involvement. As with pyromania, counselors should take a pragmatic approach when screening for kleptomania and should directly ask about theft and inquire how many times the client has engaged in this behavior. There have been few studies on the effectiveness of various treatments with this population, and most theorists base their treatment approaches on what is known about treating other disruptive behavior or impulse-control disorders.

Differential Diagnosis

When working with individuals who are involved in shoplifting, counselors may consider more likely differential diagnoses such as ordinary theft, neurodevelopmental or neurocognitive impairments, CD, ASPD, and manic episodes (APA, 2022). Moreover, high comorbidity with many disorders, including substance use disorders, depressive disorders, and bipolar disorders, has been noted in the literature (APA, 2022; Torales et al., 2020).

Coding, Recording, and Specifiers

There is only one diagnostic code for kleptomania: F63.2. There are no specifiers associated with this disorder.

Questions for Consideration

1. How can counselors differentiate between developmentally or contextually expected troublesome behavior and clinically significant troublesome behavior?
2. How might the emerging brain science regarding pathways for disruptive behavior, depressive, and anxiety disorders inform development of more effective counseling approaches?
3. How can you ensure you are attending holistically and buffering against bias when working with youth of color who have a history of trauma and are engaging in disruptive behaviors?

Chapter 14

Personality Disorders

Personality disorders covered in this chapter can be found in both Sections II and III of the *DSM-5-TR*. We first discuss personality disorders found in Section II, which lists all current diagnostic criteria and codes being used by clinicians. Following this description, we explain the proposed model for diagnosing and conceptualizing personality disorders found in Section III of the *DSM-5-TR*, titled "Emerging Measures and Models." We explain the reasoning behind this newly proposed approach, describe various viewpoints regarding the new model, and list practice implications for counselors regarding these proposed changes. Counselors currently in practice should note this model has not been adopted into the general nomenclature system. Currently, this new approach only serves the purpose of stimulating future research endeavors and generating discussion about a dimensional versus hybrid (i.e., containing both categorical and dimensional criteria) approach to personality dysfunction. Readers will find this discussion useful because we anticipate that the diagnostic criteria for personality disorders will be replaced.

Apart from the addition of diagnostic information related to culture and other sweeping changes found in the latest text revision of the *DSM*, there have been only minor changes to personality disorders since the publication of the *DSM-IV-TR*. Therefore, we have chosen to cover these disorders in less detail, providing readers with a short description of each disorder that includes essential features, special and general cultural considerations, and common differential diagnoses. We wish to emphasize that counselors who currently understand personality disorder nomenclature as presented in the *DSM-IV-TR* only need to be concerned with very minor, mostly semantic, changes to this section of the *DSM-5-TR*.

Personality disorders permeate an individual's internal and external presentation, are typically rigid and uncompromising, have an onset prior to early adulthood, are chronic dysfunctions (as opposed to episodic), and are very slow to change (APA, 2022; Durand et al., 2018; Paris, 2015). The disorders discussed in this chapter fall within 10 distinct types: paranoid, schizoid, schizotypal, antisocial, borderline, histrionic, narcissistic, avoidant, dependent, and obsessive-compulsive. All these disorders share common biological etiology (i.e., inherited traits) and are grouped according to symptomatology. Cluster A disorders are characterized by odd, eccentric thinking or behavior; Cluster B by dramatic, overly emotional thinking or behaviors; and Cluster C by anxious, fearful, or obsessive thinking and behavior (APA, 2022).

> **Note:** There is no empirical evidence supporting the clustering system used by the APA in the *DSM-5-TR*. This system was maintained in the *DSM-5-TR* for the purpose of clinical utility and to be used in research and academic settings.

Disorders found within the Personality Disorders chapter of the *DSM-5-TR* are characterized by persistent maladaptive patterns of behavior, cognition, affect, and interpersonal functioning that deviate from one's cultural norms (APA, 2022). These traits have a significant negative impact on the client's life, limiting their ability to function in essential areas of functioning such as work, home, or school. Lifetime prevalence of Cluster A personality disorders is estimated at 4.5%, 2.8% for Cluster B, and 10.5% for Cluster C (APA, 2022). However, some claim this number is drastically inflated and merely a product of poorly constructed diagnostic criteria (Paris, 2015). The APA (2022) defines personality disorder as

> An enduring pattern of inner experience and behavior that deviates markedly from the expectations of the individual's culture, is pervasive and inflexible, has an onset in adolescence or early adulthood, is stable over time, and leads to distress or impairment. (p. 735)

This definition seems to have an inherent message that personality disorders are permanent and thus resistant to treatment (Paris, 2015). Individuals diagnosed with personality disorders are generally stereotyped as difficult, unlikable, and extremely challenging (Frances, 2013). Although we agree this population is challenging to treat, we side with Paris (2015), who challenged the claim that treatment for these disorders is ineffective. These disorders have been misunderstood primarily because of their complexity; differentiating between normal personality functioning and pathological personality functioning is a complicated task.

Critics of the *DSM-IV-TR* (and subsequently *DSM-5-TR*) nosology have claimed the current categorical diagnoses within this chapter are just as confusing as the definitions. Clinicians maintain there is significant overlap and comorbidity between the 10 personality disorder categories (Paris, 2015; Rosenbaum & Pollock, 2002). There is also considerable heterogeneity within diagnostic classifications, as evidenced by some diagnoses that require only five of 10 criteria (Paris, 2015). Finally, clinical utility has traditionally been difficult, as evidenced by overuse of the formerly referenced not otherwise specified personality disorder diagnosis (Pagan et al., 2005; Rosenbaum & Pollock, 2002).

Adding to this challenge is evidence that these disorders typically respond better to psychotherapeutic treatment than to psychotropic medication (Mercer et al., 2009; Olabi & Hall, 2010). Because research points to the therapeutic alliance as the primary predictor of positive client outcomes (Bachelor, 2013; Lambert & Barley, 2001), it is difficult for many within the mental health field to conceptualize that counseling is a more effective treatment modality. Aside from the therapeutic alliance, empirical evidence is limited as to the efficacy of different treatment approaches; thus, treatment decisions are typically arbitrary (Rosenbaum & Pollock, 2002).

These controversies fueled the *DSM-5* Personality and Personality Disorders Work Group to present a new model for diagnosing personality disorders. The final model, discussed in more detail toward the end of this chapter, proposes a hybrid categorical and dimensional approach. The original proposal, a strictly dimensional model, scored trait dimensions as a way to reduce ambiguous boundaries. Only measuring deviations from normal functioning or "amplifications of normal personality profiles" (Paris, 2015, p. 157), this model was rejected. A second model by the work group was proposed, but this model was also rejected because the approach minimized personality disorder categories and lacked empirical validation (Paris, 2015). As a result, only minor changes were made to the Personality Disorders chapter of the *DSM-5*, and a proposed model for diagnosing personality disorders remains within Section III of the *DSM-5-TR*. Before discussing this proposed model and future implications for counselors, we briefly review changes from *DSM-IV-TR* to *DSM-5-TR*.

Major Changes From *DSM-5* to *DSM-5-TR*

Personality disorders have been included in the *DSM* since its inception in 1952. Over the years, the disorders listed within the section have changed alongside the field's evolving understanding of personality disorders. Counselors who are relatively new to the *DSM* should understand the history of this diagnostic category and specifically that all disorders listed in this chapter have remained unchanged from the *DSM-IV-TR* to the *DSM-5-TR*, except for very minor text modifications (e.g., adding clarification for unspecified personality disorder; see APA, 2022, p. 734) and overarching changes made to different iterations of the manual. For example, the major change to personality disorders within the *DSM-5* (and carried over to the *DSM-5-TR*) resulted from the collapse of the multiaxial system into one axis such that these disorders were no longer listed separately under the second axis. As a result, personality disorders were no longer differentiated from other disorders as they had been in the past. APA (2013b) reported the former distinction was artificial and stated that there are no basic differences between Axis I and Axis II disorders (Ruocco, 2005). Furthermore, whereas a dimensional approach is applied to all other disorders in the manual, personality disorders have not been changed to match this philosophical shift and are still represented categorically.

More predominantly featured in the *DSM-5-TR* are changes to the cultural sections of each personality disorder. While small, these changes improve the understanding of cultural experiences and impact of culture as situational context for reactions and behaviors. Contextualization and elaboration afford clinicians a clearer understanding of the intersections of culture within the disorders. For example, antisocial personality disorder tends to be overdiagnosed among individuals who experience economic insecurity. Acculturation problems may look diagnostically similar to avoidant personality disorder but have very different etiological origins. Finally, a high level of productivity as well as a strong focus on work is a cultural trend within some cultures and could potentially be characteristic of obsessive-compulsive personality disorder. Including this information is the *DSM-5-TR* can help counselors avoid misdiagnosis and allow for better representation of cultural issues that are not pathological (Mulder, 2018).

The intent of an alternative set of diagnostic criteria for personality disorders, located in the back of the *DSM-5-TR*, was to address these and other concerns. However, the proposed model remains unapproved for use as a diagnostic tool. Notably, even though the proposed model may appear more complicated than the current model, clinicians who have tested its utility thus far have found it to be more practical, particularly for explaining diagnoses to individuals and their families (Oldham, 2015). Nonetheless, uncertainty remains as to whether the field should transition to the proposed model, and testing is ongoing.

Essential Features

Personality disorders are marked by a significant cultural deviation in the pattern of actions and internal focus and require that the individual experience problems in at least two of four areas (APA, 2022). These areas include a pattern of cognitive distortions as related to perceptions of self, others, and the external world; affective or emotional responses that can be intense, inappropriate, and vary widely in nature; intense difficulty with interpersonal interactions; and impulse-control impairment.

Special Considerations

The patterns associated with personality disorders exist in nearly all aspects of clients' lives and vary little in application to their life roles and relationships (Comer, 2017). The onset usually begins in adolescence or early adulthood and results in clinically significant distress and impairment in multiple areas of functioning (APA, 2022). Furthermore, as with other disorders, the symptoms of personality disorders cannot be attributed to any other disorder or the effects of medication or a medical condition (APA, 2022). It is important to note that the diagnosis must be given only when a stable, long-term pattern of these behaviors has been established. However, in terms of diagnosing, counselors will not typically be the primary mental health provider assigning a personality disorder diagnosis to a client.

Social and Cultural Considerations

Because personality disorders represent a persistent, marked change from the client's cultural patterns and norms, it is imperative that counselors understand the client's culture, cultural origin, and cultural expectations, including customs, habits, religion, and political views. Additionally, gender is an important consideration in diagnosing, and counselors should carefully watch for gender bias (Durand et al., 2018). Antisocial personality disorder is more prevalent in men than in women; however, borderline, histrionic, and dependent personality disorders tend to be diagnosed, perhaps overdiagnosed, more often in women than in men. Again, counselors are encouraged to diagnose in an ethical manner consistent with the *ACA Code of Ethics* (ACA, 2014).

Differential Diagnosis

Because personality disorders are lifelong pervasive disorders rather than brief changes in personality, counselors need to ensure that the symptoms observed are not related to a change in personality due to substance use, medications, or another medical condition. Counselors should also note the overlap in symptoms among the personality disorders as well as significant comorbidity within this diagnostic class (Durand et al., 2018). What makes differential diagnosis of personality disorders challenging is the prevalence of comorbidity with other diagnoses. It is not uncommon for individuals diagnosed with a personality disorder to also exhibit symptoms that meet the clinical threshold for major depressive disorder, substance use disorders, and eating disorders (Friborg et al., 2014; Høye et al., 2021; Schnell & Herpertz, 2018). Furthermore, a significant amount of literature has focused on the comorbidity between borderline personality disorder (BPD) and bipolar disorder. For example, following a meta-analysis of 42 articles examining this diagnostic pairing, Fornaro et al. (2016) found a prevalence of 18.5% of individuals with BPD also met the diagnostic criteria for bipolar disorder, and approximately 20% of individuals diagnosed with bipolar disorder have a comorbid diagnosis of BPD. Within each disorder, we discuss the distinctive elements of each disorder in detail to make differentiating these a bit easier.

Other common comorbid diagnoses that counselors may want to consider include panic disorders, social phobias, and/or schizophrenia spectrum or other psychotic disorders. Although comorbidity of personality disorders with schizophrenia and other psychotic disorders is relatively uncommon (APA, 2022), cases in which a client is unable to recognize social maladaptation (e.g., being persecuted by others) may be better classified as a delusion. For such clients, a schizophrenia spectrum or other psychotic disorder may be a more appropriate diagnosis.

Etiology and Treatment

The exact cause of personality disorders is not fully understood, but the etiological origin is thought to be a combination of genetic, environmental, and developmental factors (Reichborn-Kjennerud, 2010). Environmental factors that may contribute to the development of personality disorders include trauma, abuse, neglect, and other adverse experiences in childhood or adulthood. These experiences may disrupt the normal development of an individual's personality and lead to the development of maladaptive patterns of thinking, feeling, and behaving. Developmental factors may also contribute to the development of personality disorders. For example, if an individual does not have healthy and supportive relationships during their formative years, they may be more at risk for developing a personality disorder.

It is important to note that the etiology of personality disorders is complex and multifaceted; different individuals may develop the same disorder but present with vastly different psychosocial backgrounds. Researchers (e.g., Reichborn-Kjennerud, 2010) have suggested that personality disorders may have a genetic component, with some personality disorders having a higher genetic connection than others. For example, schizoid and schizotypal personality disorders have been reported to have a genetic component based on the prevalence of these disorders in families across multiple generations. However, the relative contribution of genetics in the development of personality disorders, as compared to other factors such as the environment and life experiences, is unclear.

Historically, psychotherapeutic treatment for personality disorders was believed to be ineffective (Bateman & Fonagy, 2000; Hadjipavlou & Ogrodniczuk, 2010), but more recent research has demonstrated that a combination of psychosocial therapies and psychopharmacology can be effective (Bateman et al., 2015). As with most disorder classifications, no one-size-fits-all approach exists. Specific treatment approaches depend on the individual's needs and diagnosis. As such, each disorder in this chapter includes at least one evidence-informed therapeutic approach. However, counselors should note that the evidence base for personality disorder treatments is predominantly focused on BPD, with the other nine personality disorders having only a marginal evidence base on which to draw recommendations (Budge et al., 2013).

Common individual treatment approaches for personality disorders include CBT, dialectical behavior therapy, and schema-focused therapy. Group therapy, including psychoeducation groups, skills-based groups, and support groups, can also be effective treatment for personality disorders, because such approaches allow individuals to practice the interpersonal skills that are the core of these disorders and learn from others experiencing similar challenges (Bo et al., 2017; Inchausti et al., 2022). Psychopharmacology can help stabilize clients and reduce symptoms (Bateman et al., 2015). For immediate concerns and crises, hospitalization leverages both psychopharmacology and psychotherapy.

Implications for Counselors

Because of the significant impact on daily life and function, timely recognition and diagnosis of personality disorders are imperative to establish and maintain secure and appropriate relationships with clients. It is important to note that personality disorder treatment is often a long-term process with periods of improvement and setbacks. Counselors working with individuals with personality disorders should work closely with the client's treatment team and should be patient and consistent in their efforts. As with many disorders, early recognition and diagnosis can lead to more effective treatment and better outcomes for the individual. For personality disorders specifically, proper diagnosis can help individuals understand their own behavior and motivations, which can in turn empower them and lead to greater levels of self-awareness (Harvey & Gumport, 2015). Leveraging a client's increased self-awareness, counselors can develop more specific and targeted treatment goals tailored to the individual's specific needs. Furthermore, counselors who have a basic understanding, familiarity with, and guide to effective treatments for clients presenting with symptoms common to personality disorders may be better prepared to work with clients who, by nature of their disorder, often lack awareness of unhealthy patterns of thinking, feeling, and behaving. This is especially critical because of the tendency of individuals diagnosed with personality disorders to engage in risky and/or self-destructive behaviors.

To help with understanding and identification of the personality disorders identified within this chapter of the *DSM-5-TR*, the following sections provide information regarding the essential features; special considerations; differential diagnosis; and coding, recording, and specifiers for each of 13 personality disorders. Readers should note this *Learning Companion* is not a stand-alone diagnostic resource; when diagnosing clients, counselors should also reference the *DSM-5-TR*. It is essential that the diagnostic criteria and features, subtypes and specifiers (if applicable), prevalence, course, and risk and prognostic factors for each disorder are clearly understood prior to diagnosis.

> ***Note:*** The *DSM-5-TR* includes a section on general personality disorder. This is not a diagnosis. Rather, this section provides general information regarding personality disorders, and it is assumed that individuals diagnosed with a personality disorder also meet the criteria listed.

Paranoid Personality Disorder (F60.0)

The defining characteristics of paranoid personality disorder include a mistrust and suspicion of other people and their motives, beginning in early adulthood and persisting across multiple aspects of the individual's life (APA, 2022; Durand et al., 2018). The mistrust must be manifested in at least four areas, including constant suspicion that others are planning to trick, harm, or exploit the individual; an inability to trust or believe in the loyalty of friends; and/or difficulty confiding in people because of fear that what is shared will be used against the individual. An individual with paranoid personality disorder may have a pervasive pattern of not forgiving others, perceive threats or insults in normal events or conversations, believe that others are engaging in assaults on their character and feel the need to attack in response, and chronically believe that their spouse or partner is unfaithful (APA, 2022).

Paranoid personality disorder may leave those affected feeling distrustful, isolated, and fearful. Diagnostic characteristics lead the client to perceive others' words and acts as specifically and purposefully harmful or unsafe (APA, 2022). Individuals with paranoia may also struggle to forgive others for real or perceived slights based on these assumptions regarding others' intentions and may create their own, often negative, version of events (APA, 2022). This may contribute to individuals lashing out in response to perceived attacks and betrayals.

Essential Features

It is important for counselors to ensure that the symptoms associated with paranoid personality disorder do not only occur during psychosis, a manic episode, or an episode of major depression with psychotic features and that the symptoms are not a result of another medical condition, medications, or substance use (APA, 2022). Individuals with this disorder will have relationship difficulties and often seem to be argumentative, hostile, aloof, or cold toward others. Difficulties with family and partner relationships are not uncommon, as individuals diagnosed with paranoid personality disorder are often extremely self-reliant, controlling, and suspicious. Furthermore, associated with diagnostic characteristics, seeking treatment is challenging, and when individuals diagnosed with paranoid personality disorder do seek treatment, engaging in a trusting relationship with a counselor is difficult (Durand et al., 2018).

Individuals with paranoid personality disorder may find that their social and occupational functioning is limited due to difficulty trusting others' intentions. Because of the paranoia, these individuals have immense fear of opening up to others. If any shared information is misused or perceived to be misused, individuals diagnosed with paranoid personality disorder may respond in a manner that is disproportionate to the situation. These behavioral patterns may result in social isolation, in turn significantly impairing occupational functioning.

Special Considerations

The prevalence of paranoid personality disorder in the general population has a median estimate of 3.2%; however, in forensic settings, the prevalence is estimated to be approximately 23% (APA, 2022). The onset for paranoid personality disorder happens between childhood and early adulthood, with childhood patterns typically consisting of initial behaviors of social anxiety, poor academic performance, difficulty with peer relations, and hypersensitivity. Adolescents and young adults diagnosed with paranoid personality disorder often have a history of maltreatment, abuse, externalization of symptoms, and bullying of peers. Paranoid personality disorder can be premorbid to other disorders, such as delusional disorder and schizophrenia (APA, 2022).

Cultural and Social Considerations

Paranoid personality disorder is diagnosed more frequently in men than in women (Durand et al., 2018), and it is estimated that about 4.4% of the general population has this disorder (APA, 2022). Symptoms of this disorder should not be confused with reactions related to the experience of disenfranchised or oppressed groups, such as minorities, immigrants, or refugees (Iacovino et al., 2014). These behaviors are not symptoms of paranoid personality disorder but rather symptoms of circumstances or experiences resulting from systemic oppression, racism, and/or discrimination. Counselors should pay special attention to such extraneous factors when navigating this diagnosis. Individuals with a family history of psychotic disorders or those who have unique experiences such being incarcerated are more susceptible to being diagnosed with paranoid personality disorder (Durand et al., 2018).

> ***Note:*** Throughout this chapter, readers will notice that most personality disorders occur more frequently in men than in women. However, gender bias in diagnosing personality disorders is not uncommon (Durand et al., 2018; Ford & Widiger, 1989). Although prevalence information regarding gender is important, counselors should carefully consider the client's diagnostic profile and watch for gender bias. Prevalence studies regarding gender have not established whether paranoid personality disorder is more common in men or in women (Freeman et al., 2011).

Differential Diagnosis

Paranoid personality disorder should not be confused with the symptoms of psychotic disorders such as schizophrenia. This diagnosis should only be given if the symptoms occur before psychotic symptoms and continue after psychosis abates. If this occurs, paranoid personality disorders should be listed with the word *premorbid* following the diagnosis. It is important to note that there is a strong comorbidity among personality disorders, and counselors must carefully screen to ensure that another personality disorder, such as schizotypal, is not warranted (APA, 2022; Durand et al., 2018).

Comorbidity

Comorbid disorders for paranoid personality disorder include schizotypal, schizoid, narcissistic, avoidant, and borderline. Due to the features of this disorder, individuals with this diagnosis are at an increased risk for substance use disorders, agoraphobia, obsessive-compulsive disorder (OCD), and major depressive disorder. Brief, extreme stress has the potential to induce temporary psychotic episodes lasting between minutes and hours.

Evidence-Based Treatment Option

A few therapeutic theories have empirical support for use in treating paranoid personality disorder, including cognitive analytic therapy (CAT), which focuses on reframing and examining relationship patterns. CAT allows those with paranoid personality disorder to reexamine and combat their pervasive feelings of distrust toward others (Kellett & Hardy, 2014). Dialectic behavioral therapy (DBT) was created with the intention of treating personality disorders and remains a leading treatment model for paranoid personality disorder (Linehan, 2014; Lynch, 2018). DBT's focus on helping clients accept themselves and minimize dangerous or damaging behaviors makes this treatment modality a good fit for high-risk clients. Another commonly recognized approach for paranoid personality disorder is transference-focused psychotherapy (TFP); although used mainly to treat BPD, TFP has been explored in other personality disorders, including recent studies showing evidence for usefulness in treating paranoid personality disorder (Maisel, 2020). TFP's focus on identifying client transference and looking at situations separate from oneself allows the client to consider intentions and motivations from a less polarized lens.

Coding, Recording, and Specifiers

The only diagnostic code for paranoid personality disorder is F60.0. There are no specifiers for this diagnosis.

Schizoid Personality Disorder (F60.1)

The defining characteristics of schizoid personality disorder are a lack of interest in social relationships, limited emotional expression, and a tendency toward introspection and solitary activities (APA, 2022; Durand et al., 2018). Individuals diagnosed with schizoid personality disorder may seem aloof, indifferent, or detached from others, and they may have difficulty expressing their feelings or experiencing pleasure from activities that are typically enjoyable. Some common traits associated with schizoid personality disorder include avoiding close relationships, indifference to or a lack of desire for social interaction, and a limited range of and/or difficulty expressing emotions and responding to social cues.

Essential Features

Individuals with schizoid personality disorder have little to no interest in relationships, even family relationships (APA, 2022; Durand et al., 2018). They may prefer to engage in activities by themselves, have few or no friends, rarely experience pleasure in activities, and may have little to no interest in sex or intimate relationships. They may have difficulty experiencing emotions or emotional reactions and appear cold or indifferent to others and to assessments of others, such as encouragement or criticism. The symptoms of this disorder should not occur exclusively during a psychotic episode such as those associated with schizophrenia, nor should they be better attributed to autism spectrum disorder (APA, 2022). Finally, the symptoms of this disorder must impair the individual's functioning significantly for a diagnosis to be made.

Appearing first in childhood, schizoid personality disorder often results in severe impairment in social, socioeconomic, and occupational functioning. Although it is estimated that 3.1% of the population has this disorder (APA, 2022), individuals with this disorder will not typically seek treatment (Durand et al., 2018; Martens, 2010). Furthermore, it can be argued that schizoid personality disorder receives the least attention of all the personality disorders, both clinically and empirically (Kosson et al., 2008).

Individuals with schizotypal personality disorder often present for treatment because of depression or anxiety, and more than half of the individuals diagnosed with this disorder have also experienced a major depressive episode (Comer, 2017). Individuals with schizotypal personality disorder are often unemployed or underemployed; have challenges living independently; and experience issues with working memory, attentiveness, inhibition, and abstract thought processing (McClure et al., 2013).

Special Considerations

Relatively uncommon in clinical settings, schizoid personality disorder has historically been reported as occurring more frequently in men than in women (APA, 2013a). However, the *DSM-5-TR* specifically clarifies that no sufficient evidence has emerged regarding gender prevalence for this disorder.

Cultural and Social Considerations

Cultural context is essential in the formation of peer relationships and social and behavioral characteristics. Therefore, counselors should carefully consider the client's cultural background when diagnosing schizoid personality disorder, because certain cultures emphasize defensive behaviors or detachment (Martens, 2010). Caldwell-Harris and Ayçiçegi (2006) researched autonomy and interdependence among individuals from individualist (i.e., Boston, Massachusetts) and collectivist (i.e., Istanbul, Turkey) cultures. The researchers found that individuals who expressed personality characteristics outside their normative cultural group were at risk of psychiatric symptoms that correlated with symptoms of schizoid personality disorder. Of course, having personal attributes that are inconsistent with the values of society is not associated with psychiatric symptoms. However, these results do illustrate that counselors must be very careful not only when diagnosing schizoid personality disorder but also when assessing clients for all types of personality dysfunction. Finally, special consideration should also be given to individuals who have changed cultures, such as immigrants, or who experience acculturation stress (Cobb et al., 2016).

Differential Diagnosis

When considering a diagnosis of schizoid personality disorder, counselors should be sure that the symptoms are not related to medications or another medical condition, such as those that affect the central nervous system (APA, 2022). Counselors should also evaluate clients for extraneous life factors that may affect their current condition, for example, whether symptoms and changes are due to drug-related conditions marked by substance use. If symptoms present in response to a specific stressor or generalized stress, very brief psychotic episodes may be experienced (APA, 2022); however, this disorder should not be diagnosed when the symptoms only occur as a part of psychosis. If there is psychosis, schizoid symptoms should precede this and continue after the episode has resolved to be diagnosed. If this does occur, the diagnosis should be written with the word *premorbid* at the end. It is easy to confuse symptoms of other personality disorders and autism spectrum disorder with schizoid personality disorder (APA, 2022).

Furthermore, while somewhat similar, schizotypal personality disorder can be differentiated from delusional disorder, schizophrenia, and bipolar and depressive disorders due to a lack of psychotic symptoms (APA, 2022). When schizotypal personality disorder is diagnosed in tandem with another personality disorder, the symptoms for schizotypal personality disorder must predate the psychotic symptoms of the new diagnosis. Additionally, individuals with schizotypal personality disorder can be distinguished by their preference for being alone and lack of paranoia, suspicion, and desire for social intimacy. When deciding whether an individual's symptoms qualify for schizotypal personality disorder or autism spectrum disorder, one should consider key indicators about autism, particularly hyperfixation and social communications and interactions, to inform the decision. These considerations are particularly important for lower severity cases, as low-impact schizotypal personality disorder and autism can present similarly. Careful screening over a period of time is crucial for an accurate diagnosis to be made.

Comorbidity

Comorbidity is not unusual; as described throughout this chapter, there is considerable overlap with other personality disorders (APA, 2022; Rosenbaum & Pollock, 2002). Individuals with schizotypal personality disorder often present for treatment because of depression or anxiety (Comer, 2017), and more than half of the individuals diagnosed with this disorder have also experienced a major depressive episode (Comer, 2017).

Evidence-Based Treatment Option

Whereas antipsychotic medication has been given in low doses with some success, CBT is frequently used to address unusual or inappropriate thoughts and behaviors (Comer, 2017). Schizoid personality disorder often presents in childhood or adolescence, along with a lack of social relationships, poor academic performance, and solitary habits (APA, 2022). Parpottas (2012) claimed that when this disorder is conceptualized from an attachment theory lens, CBT partnered with a psychodynamic perspective may be the best approach. Parpottas argued that the role of the counselor is crucial because individuals experiencing this disorder need a model for interpersonal relationships. Additionally, counselors should be aware that individuals with this disorder may experience brief psychotic episodes when under stress or duress (APA, 2022). Finally, compassion-focused therapy and metacognitive reflection and insight therapy have recently emerged as helping to alleviate symptoms of schizoid personality disorder (Cheli et al., 2023). Compassion-focused therapy helps individuals cope with the symptoms of schizotypal personality disorder by promoting feelings of safety and the ability to self-soothe in stressful situations. Metacognitive reflection and insight therapy may also be useful in treating psychosis and other related negative symptoms (Cheli et al., 2023).

Coding, Recording, and Specifiers

The only diagnostic code for schizoid personality disorder is F60.1. There is one specifier for this diagnosis, *premorbid*, which should be included in parentheses.

Schizotypal Personality Disorder (F21)

Schizotypal personality disorder is pervasive and includes bizarre ideation and social constriction or avoidance (APA, 2022; Paris, 2015). The symptoms of schizotypal personality disorder appear similar in many ways to schizophrenia. Some consider schizotypal personality disorder a milder, nonpsychotic form of schizophrenia; however, manifestations of this disorder do not typically include positive symptoms of hallucinations or delusions (Paris, 2015; Ripoll et al., 2013). Schizotypal personality disorder is characterized by discomfort with any type of close relationships, bizarre or distorted cognitions, and strange behaviors (Comer, 2017). This pattern of behaviors, which often begins during early adulthood, may include sensations of an external presence, odd physical awareness, magical thinking, or the belief that one's powers may control the behavior of others (APA, 2022; Comer, 2017; Paris, 2015). Individuals diagnosed with schizotypal personality disorder often think unrelated events pertain to them personally.

Essential Features

Individuals with schizotypal personality disorder exhibit paranoia, flat affect, and odd communication patterns such as loose associations, and they usually have an eccentric appearance (Comer, 2017; Ripoll et al., 2013). Although not formally considered as schizophrenia spectrum disorder, both these disorders are actually cross-listed in the *DSM-5*. The primary reason is because of symptom similarity and because clients diagnosed with schizotypal personality disorder have the same biological markers as clients with schizophrenia (Paris, 2015). However, because schizotypal personality disorder is not a precursor to schizophrenia, it has been retained in the Personality Disorders chapter of the *DSM-5*.

Individuals diagnosed with schizotypal personality disorder do not have many close friends and continue to be paranoid even when a close relationship does exist (APA, 2022; Comer, 2017). For example, these individuals tend to appear socially anxious even around family. If symptoms of this disorder only occur as part of depression, bipolar, or schizophrenia disorders, then it is not a true schizotypal personality disorder. If it is diagnosed before the onset of schizophrenia, the word *premorbid* should follow the diagnosis (APA, 2022). However, as stated previously, schizotypal personality disorder is not a precursor to schizophrenia (Paris, 2015).

Individuals with schizotypal personality disorder are able to identify their lack of social abilities and tend to be uncomfortable when trying to interact with others. Their misinterpretations of events often cast a negative lens on situations and may add to their suspicion and paranoia. Odd forms of speech, movement, and dress may indicate schizotypal personality disorder when presented in tandem with other more serious symptoms, including the belief that they have magical control over their life and situations around them.

Special Considerations

The prevalence of schizotypal personality disorder in the general population is inconsistent (APA, 2022). However, both the current and prior iterations of the *DSM* indicated this disorder occurred in approximately 3.9% of individuals in the general population (APA, 2013a, 2022). Individuals with schizotypal personality disorder often present for treatment because of depression or anxiety (Comer, 2017). Because they have difficulty with interpersonal relationships and have few friends, their feelings of intense loneliness are not uncommon. Individuals with schizotypal personality disorder are often unemployed or underemployed; have challenges living independently; and experience issues with working memory, attentiveness, inhibition, and abstract thought processing (McClure et al., 2013).

Social and Cultural Considerations

Beliefs or behaviors that appear bizarre or outside the norm should always be evaluated within the context of the individual's cultural and religious beliefs. Counselors must fully understand the impact of family, religion, and culture on behavior before making a diagnosis of schizotypal personality disorder. For example, speaking in tongues, belief in the afterlife, and phenomena such as voodoo are not considered schizotypal symptoms if these beliefs and behaviors are within the client's cultural context (Mulder, 2018). As with most Cluster A personality disorders, there is evidence that this disorder occurs more in men than in women (APA, 2022). Finally, individuals who have family members with a history of schizophrenia are more likely to be diagnosed with schizotypal personality disorder (Durand et al., 2018).

Differential Diagnosis

Schizotypal personality disorder should not be diagnosed if the symptoms can be better explained by use of substances or medications or by a medical condition (APA, 2022). If these are present, then a diagnosis of schizotypal personality disorder may not be appropriate. Although some individuals with schizotypal personality disorder experience brief moments of psychosis when under stress, this disorder should not be confused with delusional, psychotic, depressive, or bipolar disorders. Counselors should look for symptoms that are pervasive and begin before or continue after other types of episodes, such as mania and psychosis. In children, symptoms of a communication disorder or autism spectrum disorder may appear similar to schizotypal personality disorder (APA, 2022). When considering a diagnosis of autism or schizotypal personality disorder, it can be helpful to look at the individual level of social awareness and possible presence of communication disorders. When a lack of social awareness is evident, and symptoms associated with a communication disorder are under consideration, it is likely that the symptoms can be diagnosed as autism.

Comorbidity

Comorbidity is not unusual given considerable overlap with symptoms associated with other personality disorders, particularly schizoid, paranoid, and avoidant personality disorders (APA, 2022; Rosenbaum & Pollock, 2002). If an individual meets all criteria for multiple disorders, all can be diagnosed. However, counselors should note that psychotic symptoms are not present in individuals diagnosed with schizotypal personality disorder. Finally, more than half of the individuals diagnosed with this disorder have also experienced a major depressive episode (Comer, 2017). As with other personality disorders, a thorough assessment over a period of time is necessary to ensure an accurate diagnosis is made.

Evidence-Based Treatment Option

Although antipsychotic medication has been given in low doses with some success, CBT is frequently used to address unusual or inappropriate thoughts and behaviors (Comer, 2017). Recent literature has also identified two types of metacognitive-oriented psychotherapies as potentially successful in promoting positive outcomes for clients diagnosed with schizotypal personality disorder: metacognitive interpersonal therapy and metacognitive reflection and insight therapy. Metacognitive interpersonal therapy allows clients to examine what they value and create a new focus away from maladaptive coping mechanisms (Cheli et al., 2019). Metacognitive reflection and insight therapy helps clients become less affected by thought interference, distractibility, and hypersensitivity to interpersonal issues (Cheli et al., 2019).

Coding, Recording, and Specifiers

The only diagnostic code for schizotypal personality disorder is F21. There is one specifier for this diagnosis, *premorbid*, which should be included in parentheses.

Antisocial Personality Disorder (F60.2)

As the first disorder listed under Cluster B personality disorders in the *DSM-5-TR*, antisocial personality disorder is often referred to as "psychopathy," "sociopathy," or "dissocial" personality disorder (APA, 2022, p. 748). Antisocial personality disorder is characterized by a complete disregard for the feelings, rights, and concerns of others, often resulting in harm to self or others and/or incarceration (Comer, 2017). Individuals with this disorder will have at least three of the following symptoms: illegal behaviors, chronic lying, a lack of regard for personal or others' safety, aggressive behavior frequently leading to fights, a pattern of impulsivity and lack of forethought, problems working and/or meeting financial responsibilities, and chronic indifference to the feelings of others without regret or remorse (Durand et al., 2018; Frances, 2013). Individuals diagnosed with antisocial personality disorder often receive pleasure from their destructive behavior, such as feeling pleasure when deceiving others.

Antisocial personality disorder is typically associated with a long-term pattern of disregard for and violation of the rights of others, as well as manipulation and an inability to maintain long-term relationships (APA, 2022). Lack of empathy, rule breaking, and violent and impulsive behavior are also common. Antisocial personality disorder has been associated with a history of abuse and neglect during childhood.

Essential Features

Antisocial personality disorder is characterized by deceitfulness, manipulation, anger, irresponsibility, and reckless decision-making followed by hazardous behavior (APA, 2022). Two key characteristics for diagnosing antisocial personality disorder are deceit and manipulation (Paris, 2015). Those with antisocial personality disorder have a strong disregard for the rights of others, often violating boundaries and trust. Irresponsibility, lack of empathy, and the propensity to blame others are other common characteristics. Counselors often find that individuals with antisocial personality disorder are usually charming, self-assured, and manipulative, particularly in close personal or sexual relationships (Durand et al., 2018). When working with clients demonstrating symptoms associated with antisocial personality disorder, counselors have found it useful to gather information from additional sources, such as family members or friends, as symptoms associated with antisocial personality disorder often make it challenging to fully understand the nature of the client's presenting concerns.

Individuals diagnosed with antisocial personality disorder may find it incredibly difficult to maintain a job or stay out of trouble, because they often lack sufficient regard for laws or social norms, resulting in challenging consequences, including frequent unemployment and incarceration. Maintaining healthy social relationships is also often a challenge, predominantly due to a lack of respect toward others, and can understandably impact the development of a strong counselor-client alliance.

Special Considerations

Because of the high rates of criminal activity and incarceration associated with antisocial personality disorder, most of the research on this disorder is conducted on inmates, former inmates, or parolees (Frances, 2013). It is estimated that as many as 30% of those incarcerated have antisocial personality disorders (Comer, 2017). Because of this, and also because of the lack of remorse associated with this disorder, it is unlikely that counselors will see these individuals voluntarily; most counselors will work with these individuals as a result of court mandate. Furthermore, rates of alcohol and drug use can be very high in this population (Comer, 2017).

Although general population estimates for this disorder range from 0.6% to 3.6%, rates are consistently much higher in the male population than in the female population, perhaps as high as three to one (APA, 2022; Comer, 2017). Child abuse, erratic or neglectful parenting, and inconsistent discipline are common social factors that may contribute to the development of antisocial personality disorder (DeLisi et al., 2019). There is also evidence for a genetic predisposition toward antisocial personality disorder (Glenn et al., 2013). Antisocial tendencies usually begin to present around the age of 8, with over 80% of people who are diagnosed presenting some symptoms before the age of 11 (Anderson & Kelley, 2022; Mark et al., 2022). To be diagnosed with antisocial personality disorder, individuals must be at least 18 years old, and symptoms associated with conduct disorder must have started before the age of 15 and continued through adulthood. Although the diagnosis cannot be made prior to age 18, symptoms seem to decrease in later life, with criminal activity in particular decreasing after the age of 40 (Paris, 2015).

Cultural and Social Considerations

Socioeconomic vulnerability and racial identity are uniquely important factors to consider when making this diagnosis, as research has supported increased prevalence among individuals who have experienced poverty (Anderson & Kelley, 2022). This is often due to the sociocultural factors associated with poverty and discriminatory diagnostic practices that lead to overdiagnosis of young, poor persons of color being more likely to be diagnosed with a conduct disorder, which is often viewed as a precursor for an antisocial personality disorder diagnosis. Involvement in gangs should also be considered, as young members often form a protective antisocialism that can be confused with antisocial personality disorder.

Women diagnosed with antisocial personality disorder are more likely to have experienced various forms of childhood trauma and abuse (Schorr et al., 2020). However, antisocial personality disorder may present differently in women, resulting in underdiagnosis. Men with antisocial personality disorder often have a comorbid substance use disorder, whereas women more often present with antisocial personality disorder and somatization disorders (APA, 2022).

Differential Diagnosis

Behaviors must occur before 18 years of age and must be preceded by symptoms of conduct disorder occurring before age 15 (APA, 2022). Symptoms cannot be attributed to substance use, another medical condition, or medication use, nor can they occur solely during a psychotic or manic episode. Substance use disorder can be difficult to differentiate from antisocial personality disorder, but symptoms of antisocial personality disorder should begin in younger years, often preceding the substance use (APA, 2022). When these are co-occurring, they can be diagnosed simultaneously. If a differentiation is not able to be made, meaning the antisocial personality disorder presentation could be associated with substance use, a diagnosis of antisocial personality disorder cannot be made.

Symptoms of antisocial personality disorder must occur prior to or outside of a manic or psychotic episode for this diagnosis to be given. There may be overlap with the symptoms of other personality disorders, particularly other Cluster B personality disorders. Antisocial personality disorder can be differentiated by the lack of empathy, aggression, impulsivity, and manipulation of others purely for personal gains (Comer, 2017). However, if criteria are met for more than one disorder, counselors may diagnose all applicable disorders (APA, 2022). Additionally, when antisocial behaviors occur solely within the onset of schizophrenia or bipolar disorder, then they may not be diagnostic criteria for antisocial personality disorder. If multiple personality disorders are suspected, both antisocial personality disorder and multiple personality disorder may be diagnosed if all criteria are met for both disorders.

Finally, criminal behavior that is not associated with antisocial personality disorder criteria (i.e., theft for personal gain) may not be considered for diagnosis, and counselors must note the difference between committing a crime and having antisocial personality disorder. Criminal behavior is only one symptom of this disorder, and at least three other symptoms must be met, in addition to age requirements, to make this diagnosis.

Comorbidity

Conduct disorder with onset in childhood is nearly a universal occurrence (Paris, 2015), but counselors are strongly cautioned against assuming that a diagnosis of conduct disorder in childhood will lead to adult antisocial personality disorder. Other common comorbid disorders include dysphoria, anxiety disorder, mood disorders, substance use or process additions (e.g., gambling disorder), or somatic symptom disorders (APA, 2022).

Coding, Recording, and Specifiers

The only diagnostic code for antisocial personality disorder is F60.2. There are no specifiers for this diagnosis.

Evidence-Based Treatment Option

In general, counseling and therapeutic interventions for clients with antisocial personality disorder are extremely challenging, largely because these individuals do not see the need to change (Comer, 2017; Paris, 2015). Motivational interviewing or cognitive treatments have been used to increase awareness of behavioral impact. Counselors working with clients diagnosed with this disorder should note the challenges associated with a low or absent capacity for remorse, resulting in failure to see the impact or associated harm of their behavior for others. When planning treatment, a team-based approach with supervision and peer-to-peer coaching is recommended (Gibbon et al., 2020). Cognitive behavioral, solution-focused, person-centered, dialectical behavior, and client-centered psychotherapies have also been identified as treatment approaches suitable for addressing empathy and behavioral concerns (Van den Bosch et al., 2018). Finally, counselors need to be cognizant of the propensity for violence and suicide in this population and conduct risk and suicide assessments as needed (Frances, 2013).

Borderline Personality Disorder (F60.3)

First noted in the *DSM-III* (APA, 1980), individuals with borderline personality disorder (BPD) "lack a sense of self and engage in intense and unstable relationships" (Montes, 2013, p. 34). Represented by a pattern of unstable relationships, impulsive behavior, and emotional dysregulation (APA, 2022), individuals diagnosed with BPD are especially sensitive to social rejection and perceived abandonment and experience social expectations more negatively (Liebke et al., 2018). The extreme fear of abandonment often results in individuals pushing away those close to them, damaging relationships. The intense fear can also lead to difficulty maintaining jobs and achieving personal goals given the tendency toward self-sabotage as a coping mechanism. This pervasive pattern of instability begins in early adulthood and can be observed through the individual's functioning (Durand et al., 2018; Frances, 2013).

Essential Features

Individuals diagnosed with BPD may be impulsive in two, potentially self-damaging, areas, including gambling, sex, spending, or substance abuse. These individuals may frequently threaten and attempt suicide, make gestures indicating suicidal ideation, or engage in self-injurious behaviors such as cutting or burning (Comer, 2017; Durand et al., 2018; Videler et al., 2019). Mood instability is not uncommon and can be characterized by change of mood within only a few hours. Symptoms may also include chronic feelings of emptiness, inappropriate expressions of anger including extremely angry or sarcastic outbursts, and even physical aggression and fights. Furthermore, dissociation, depersonalization, and paranoid ideation can occur when the individual is under stress (Comer, 2017; Videler et al., 2019).

At least five out of nine symptoms must be present, and the symptoms can include chronic fear, real or imagined, of impending abandonment by loved ones, friends, or caregivers; intense relationships that vary between idealizing and disappointment in the other person; and unstable or unsure identity patterns, as evidenced by unexpected or sudden changes in career, sense of self, values, or sexual identity (APA, 2022). Individuals with BPD also exhibit issues relating to their self-concept, including self-esteem and identity diffusion, such that they may not have a sense of their authentic self. This creates a challenge when maintaining a distinct sense of self across time (Wright et al., 2022).

Higher levels of suicidality, violence, self-mutilation, and disability are seen in individuals diagnosed with BPD, particularly in comparison with other personality disorders (Comer, 2017; Frances, 2013; Gunderson et al., 2018). Estimates suggest that 75% of these individuals attempt suicide at least one time (Comer, 2017) and 8% to 10% complete suicides (APA, 2022; Frances, 2013). As a result, counselors must be vigilant to assess symptoms of this disorder and suicidality in these clients. Counseling these clients can be difficult and emotionally draining because of the lack of boundaries, constant fear of abandonment, and ever-changing emotions (Comer, 2017).

Individuals with BPD frequently present for outpatient services, with estimates at 10% to 20% of those seen in clinics (Biskin, 2013). Counselors need to be aware that there are severe consequences for an individual who has this disorder, including emotional, financial, and interpersonal consequences for the individual and family (Crowell et al., 2009). Therefore, it is important for counselors working with these clients to practice self-care, be alert to the signs of professional impairment, and engage in services only within the boundaries of their competence in accordance with the *ACA Code of Ethics* (ACA, 2014).

Special Considerations

The prevalence for BPD is 2.7% in the general population and 20% in the psychiatric patient population (APA, 2022). Those with an immediate family member diagnosed with BPD are five times more likely to have BPD themselves (Amad et al., 2014). The development of BPD is also associated with childhood abuse and neglect, and the severity of the disorder is associated with the severity of experienced abuse, with those in inpatient settings having experienced more abuse or neglect than those in outpatient settings (APA, 2022). Symptoms of BPD can appear as early as 12 years old. It is important to note that prior to adulthood, symptoms that could be typical teenage behavior can be confused with symptoms of this disorder.

Cultural and Social Considerations

In clinical samples, BPD is more common in women than in men (APA, 2022); however, the general population shows equal prevalence across genders. Counselors should also note that clinical samples, which report prevalence rates for females as high as 75%, are potentially skewed because of disparities in help seeking between women and men. Moreover, clinical characteristics based on men and women may be different, with women demonstrating more internalized behaviors than men (APA, 2022). Finally, while very limited information exists for BPD and sociocultural contexts, the patterns associated with this disorder have been noted in various cultures worldwide (APA, 2022). As repeatedly highlighted throughout this *Learning Companion*, cultural norms and values are extremely important to consider within the clients' presenting concerns. For individuals presenting with symptoms consistent with BPD, counselors should consider, for example, whether social demands, cultural views on authority, and acceptance of others are being erroneously associated with BPD characteristics.

Differential Diagnosis

A diagnosis of BPD should not be given if the symptoms occur because of another medical condition, substance use, or medication use. Furthermore, if the symptoms occur only during a manic or depressive episode, BPD, which has a pervasive pattern of lifelong symptoms, should not be given (APA, 2022). This disorder often runs concomitant with depressive, bipolar, and some other personality disorders. It is important to ensure that symptoms of this disorder either occur prior to or continue after symptoms of other disorders have subsided. Counselors should be especially cognizant of the high rate of misdiagnoses (i.e., depressive and bipolar disorders) and, as a result, incorrect treatment for individuals with BPD (Paris, 2015). Finally, there is significant overlap in the symptoms of this personality disorder and other personality disorders (APA, 2022). Counselors should remember that BPD is uniquely characterized by co-occurring feelings of emptiness, self-destructiveness, and unstable personal relationships.

Comorbidity

BPD often co-occurs with depression and bipolar disorder. Those with BPD have an increased risk of suicidality, largely due to intense bouts of fear and catastrophizing, and comorbidity with depression (APA, 2022). However, counselors should ensure multiple cross-sections of symptoms before making a diagnosis. BPD is differentiated from separation anxiety by the occurrence of impulsivity and interpersonal functioning. Other personality disorders may be diagnosed when sufficient criteria for each disorder are met. Personality change due to a medical condition must be distinguished from criteria for BPD. When BPD is diagnosed with substance use disorders, criteria for BPD must have been met before the beginning of substance use. Identity problems that occur during childhood do not inherently meet criteria for BPD; situational aspects should be considered, such as acute stressors that may elicit similar symptoms.

Coding, Recording, and Specifiers

The only diagnostic code for BPD is F60.3. There are no specifiers for this diagnosis.

Evidence-Based Treatment Option

Recovery is often difficult, because symptom presentation tends to be fairly stable and, unlike some other personality disorders, do not typically decrease as the client gets older (d'Huart et al., 2022). Many symptoms of BPD make it difficult for affected individuals to hold lasting relationships, which include the therapeutic alliance. However, treatment options for individuals with BPD have improved greatly in the past 2 decades. Based in the belief that internal factors (e.g., trouble with emotional regulation caused by neurotransmitter systems) and external factors (e.g., parental abandonment; physical or sexual abuse) combine to explain this disorder, the biosocial development model, developed originally by Marsha Linehan, is frequently used to understand the etiology of this disorder (Comer, 2017; Crowell et al., 2009). Furthermore, DBT, based on CBT and also developed by Linehan (2014), has been used with individuals with BPD and has documented success (Comer, 2017). Because DBT focuses on forming new, healthy behaviors to replace or combat old destructive ones, it can be helpful for alleviating common symptoms of BPD. DBT can also help those with BPD become more confident and secure in themselves, as well as learn how to handle emotional dysregulation (Wetterborg et al., 2020). Early intervention is emphasized in both the biosocial development model and DBT.

Histrionic Personality Disorder (F60.4)

As with all personality disorders, histrionic personality disorder, referred to as *hysterical personality* in some contexts, is pervasive, with lifelong patterns of deviant behavior. Individuals with this disorder will present as attention seeking and excessively emotional (Durand et al., 2018), and they may desperately seek attention through physical appearance, such as dressing in eye-catching colors; grandiose gestures and excessively impressionistic speech; and inappropriate seductive or sexual behaviors (Comer, 2017; Durand et al., 2018). They often act in a theatrical manner (*histrionic* means "theatrical in manner"), as if they are on stage and everyone is watching, and become extremely uncomfortable, even sad or upset, when they are not the center of attention (Comer, 2017; Durand et al., 2018). Their often shallowly expressed emotions shift rapidly, and they are highly suggestible and easily influenced by others.

Individuals with this disorder tend to see relationships as more intimate than they are, exchange long-term relationships for more exciting new ones, and seek excitement in romantic partners who may not treat them well (APA, 2022; Comer, 2017). Represented by an interpersonal style composed of excessive attention-seeking and unwarranted or disproportionate demonstrations of emotion (Cale & Lilienfeld, 2002; Perrotta, 2021), individuals with histrionic personality disorder are uncomfortable when not the center of attention and will go to great lengths and even demand to be the center of attention.

Essential Features

Individuals with histrionic personality disorder tend to embarrass and alienate their friends through their excessive behaviors, have difficulty maintaining long-term romantic relationships, and are more likely to seek treatment than individuals with other personality disorders (Comer, 2017). Although actual suicide risk is not known, these individuals may use suicidal ideation or gestures as part of attention-seeking or manipulative behaviors. Furthermore, counselors may find these clients require a lot of patience because they may act in a sexually seductive manner or become demanding or claim to experience change to gain attention or make the counselor happy (Comer, 2017; Durand et al., 2018).

Common characteristics of histrionic personality disorder include having large personas, presenting theatrically, talking "big," and making bold statements with little personal conviction (APA, 2022; Perrotta, 2021). Individuals with histrionic personality disorder often suffer from interpersonal impairment, meaning they may be incredibly trusting, pick up new beliefs quickly, and are easily influenced by others. Difficulty making and maintaining genuine connections with others is common. Behaviors may span from a "warmer dominance" (APA, 2022, p. 758), where individuals are more theatrical and attention seeking, to a "colder dominance" (p. 758), which presents as more controlling and aggressive. Individuals with histrionic personality disorder may also struggle with occupational functioning; for example, they are prone to behaviors such as taking on a big project but losing interest (Perrotta, 2021). The inability of most individuals diagnosed with histrionic personality disorder to form substantial, meaningful interpersonal relationships may also make it difficult for them to secure connections to advance in the workplace. Histrionic personality disorder has a prevalence of 0.9% to 1.8% in the general population (APA, 2022), beginning by early adulthood and remaining steady throughout the lifetime. Counselors should note the National Comorbidity Survey Replication, which was based on probability sampling, estimated the prevalence of this disorder as 0.0% (APA, 2022), causing some to question the validity of this disorder (Bakkevig & Karterud, 2010).

Special Considerations

Cultural and Social Considerations

When considering diagnosis, bear in mind the general expressiveness of the client's culture, as well as their behavior in relation to their age and gender. Histrionic personality disorder may be more prevalent in women than in men, but research on this has been equivocal (APA, 2022; Comer, 2017). Furthermore, culture must be considered when assessing for this disorder. The disorder may be more prevalent in cultures that are accepting of overt sexuality or overdramatization (Comer, 2017; Durand et al., 2018). Counselors should remember that symptoms must be pervasive and result in clinically significant functional impairment (APA, 2022).

Differential Diagnosis

Histrionic personality disorder should not be diagnosed when the symptoms can be attributed to substance use, medications, or another medical condition resulting in personality change (APA, 2022). Histrionic personality disorder can be distinguished by the exaggerated emotions and exaggerated intimacy in relationships, by the flamboyant dress and behavior to gain or keep attention, and willingness to be viewed as dependent or fragile to get attention (APA, 2022). Key differences such as motive are important to consider in these cases, as manipulation is a criterion for several disorders, but the defining factor for histrionic personality disorder is that the manipulation is motivated by gaining attention and acceptance as compared to practical or material gains (e.g., money, power; APA, 2022).

Comorbidity

There is considerable overlap with other personality disorders, such as narcissistic, borderline, and dependent personality disorders (Comer, 2017; Durand et al., 2018; Paris, 2015). Because of limited empirical evidence, comorbidity with other personality disorders, and a lack of clinical utility, histrionic personality disorder was proposed to be eliminated from the *DSM-5*. This proposal was rejected but certainly points to a shift counselors will likely see in the future regarding diagnostic classifications of personality. Aside from other personality disorders, histrionic personality disorder is often diagnosed alongside somatic symptom disorder, substance use disorder, functional neurological symptom disorder (conversation disorder), and major depressive disorder (APA, 2022).

Coding, Recording, and Specifiers

The only diagnostic code for histrionic personality disorder is F60.4. There are no specifiers for this diagnosis.

Evidence-Based Treatment Option

Treatment for histrionic personality disorder can help reduce symptoms and raise self-awareness. CBT and psychodynamic therapy have been used with individuals who have histrionic personality disorder to encourage insight, independence, and internal satisfaction, with some reported success. For example, clients diagnosed with this disorder tend to view the world in terms of black and white (Durand et al., 2018), and cognitive therapies can help individuals recognize this polarized thinking and take action to refute the clients' self-statements. Specifically, CAT has been shown to have some success in treating histrionic personality disorder (Kellett, 2007). CAT focuses on the client's relationship patterns, which can allow harmful patterns and practices to surface and become more apparent for the client. From there, counselors can aid those with histrionic personality disorder in identifying and practicing strategies to challenge thoughts and behaviors. Regardless of what theory or treatment approach is utilized, counselors must be up front with the client and address the reality that there will be an end to the sessions with the client, and they should do so transparently and continually. It is important to include skills and coping mechanisms that have been introduced throughout the course of therapy to help the client adjust to this aspect of treatment.

Narcissistic Personality Disorder (F60.81)

Initially introduced in the *DSM-III*, the key components of narcissistic personality disorder are grandiosity, a desperate need for acknowledgment and admiration by others, and a lack of empathy (Comer, 2017). Individuals with narcissistic personality disorder may also exhibit exaggerated self-importance, as evidenced by an expectation that others will acknowledge them as superior. They may spend time thinking about or reinforcing their belief in personal unlimited success, beauty, or love. Often requiring excessive praise and acknowledgment, these individuals may also hold the firm belief that they are special and their problems are unique to them. They may expect that others will do what they want or comply with their desires automatically, and they often exploit people to get what they want. They may be arrogant, jealous, or believe others are jealous of them, and they often lack empathy, assuming that others should be concerned only for their well-being (APA, 2022; Comer, 2017).

Essential Features

Narcissistic personality disorder is characterized by grandiosity, a desire for adoration, a sense of entitlement, arrogance, idealized fantasies, and an absence of empathy (APA, 2022). Narcissism originates from the Greek word *narkissos* or *Narcissus*, the latter being the name in Greek mythology of a man so vain he died while attempting to capture his own reflection (Comer, 2017). Individuals with narcissistic personality disorder are "obsessed with overblown notions of self-worth" (Montes, 2013, para. 10), so much so that they are unable to understand others' points of view or empathize with them. Because of their high self-esteem, they may also be vulnerable to narcissistic injury from criticism or lack of success, sometimes resulting in severe disappointment and depression (APA, 2022; Comer, 2017).

Individuals with narcissistic personality disorder can generally experience the disorder in one of two ways: either as a strong sense of grandiosity or as a feeling of incredible vulnerability and desperation for recognition (APA, 2022). The way individuals experience their symptoms is impacted by social factors, for example, whether they are promoted or demoted at work. Individuals with narcissistic personality disorder depend on external factors to validate their self-image, and when their real-life experiences challenge this self-image, it can result in a negative emotional and psychological decline, including feelings of anger, depression, frustration, or other adverse emotional reactions. They have a high desire to be seen, recognized, and admired, and they have no empathy for others when attempting to obtain recognition.

Special Considerations

Although estimates for prevalence for narcissistic personality disorder range from around 1% (Comer, 2017) to as high as 6.2%, the median prevalence of narcissistic personality disorder is 1.6% (APA, 2022). Interestingly, like histrionic personality disorder, the National Comorbidity Survey Replication also estimated the prevalence of this disorder as 0.0% (APA, 2022). Most studies indicate 50% to 75% of individuals with this disorder are men.

Researchers have indicated an increase in narcissistic traits, such as self-esteem and extraversion, within the United States (Twenge & Foster, 2010) as potentially contributing to high rates of prevalence and potentially over- or misdiagnosis. Stinson et al. (2008) conducted an epidemiological study on narcissistic personality disorder that revealed a 3.2% lifetime prevalence of this disorder in adults over 65 years of age. As age decreased, lifetime prevalence increased: 5.6% of people 45 to 64 years of age, 7.1% of those 30 to 44 years of age, and 9.4% of those 20 to 29 years of age. Many researchers claim the reason for this change could potentially be an increased focus on individualism in Western society (Chopik & Kitayama, 2018; Twenge, 2001; Twenge & Foster, 2010). Although future research needs to investigate the reason for this generational increase, Twenge and Foster (2010) posited that school programs that focus on increasing self-esteem (i.e., "I Am Special" programs) may be a contributing factor. Vater et al. (2018) and Twenge and Foster (2010) referred to this as the "narcissism epidemic."

Counselors also need to consider client development. While narcissistic traits may be present in adolescents, they are more developmentally driven and do not necessarily indicate the likelihood of future narcissistic personality disorder diagnosis (Di Giuseppe et al., 2020). Furthermore, narcissistic personality disorder onset is largely initiated by life events, such as aging, job loss, divorce, and challenging life experiences (APA, 2022). Functional impairment for those with narcissistic personality disorder can also vary; some individuals diagnosed with narcissistic personality disorder are able to achieve and maintain successful careers, whereas others decompensate when faced with challenges, criticism, and self-doubt. Finally, suicide attempts are more common and lethal for individuals with narcissistic personality disorder compared with those with other personality disorders, likely due to their high expectations and perfectionist tendencies invoking suicidality following instances of failure (APA, 2022).

Cultural and Social Considerations

Narcissistic traits are more common in individualistic sociocultural contexts. Because of this, such traits and associated behaviors may be socially acceptable in those contexts and may not need clinical attention. As such, counselors need to carefully consider social conditioning, cultural factors, or environmental contexts that may lead the clients to experience challenges and difficulties associated with narcissistic traits. Bianchi (2014) argued that narcissistic self-centeredness may act as a protective factor during economic prosperity by driving resource accumulation, risk-taking, competitiveness, networking, adaptability, and resilience, but these traits can have drawbacks and become less advantageous during economic downturns due to interpersonal difficulties and reduced cooperation. In women, trauma survivors, college students, and adolescents, researchers have pointed to the possibility of narcissistic traits serving as a defensive coping mechanism (Kramer et al., 2019; Venema & Pfattheicher, 2021).

Differential Diagnosis

As with many personality disorders, certain narcissistic traits overlap with other personality traits and disorders (APA, 2022). Counselors can distinguish narcissistic personality disorder from histrionic, antisocial, and borderline personality disorders based on the unique characteristic of grandiosity and a stable sense of self, which are the most distinguishing features of this disorder. If all criteria for multiple disorders are present, all may be diagnosed. A narcissistic personality disorder diagnosis should not be given when persistent substance use better accounts for the symptoms (APA, 2022). Narcissistic symptoms should also be differentiated from symptoms of drug use. In addition, care should be taken to distinguish manic and hypomanic episodes from the narcissistic trait of grandiosity. Grandiosity can be part of mania or hypomania, but symptoms of narcissistic personality disorder will be pervasive and lifelong. Also, those with narcissistic personality disorder need the admiring attention and expect the appreciation of others (APA, 2022).

Comorbidity

As with most personality disorders, there is considerable overlap with other personality disorders, such as histrionic, borderline, antisocial, and paranoid personality disorders (APA, 2022). In addition, individuals diagnosed with this disorder often present with depressive disorders, feeding and eating disorders, and substance use disorders.

Coding, Recording, and Specifiers

The only diagnostic code for narcissistic personality disorder is F60.81. There are no specifiers for this diagnosis.

Evidence-Based Treatment Options

Individuals with narcissistic personality symptoms have lower rates of help seeking and usually come to counseling for depression or another problem not related to the personality disorder. For counselors, individuals with narcissistic personality disorder can be particularly difficult to treat (Paris, 2015). These clients will not likely see the need to change, they may look down on the counselor as not intelligent enough to help, or they may attempt to manipulate the counselor. They will have difficulty receiving feedback, acknowledging any weaknesses, or caring about the consequences of their behaviors on others (Comer, 2017). Approaches most often used include CBT and psychodynamic therapy, but there is little research to support success for either of these.

Diamond and Meehan (2013) argued for the use of TFP (Diamond & Hersh, 2020), a therapeutic approach that integrates object relations theory with attachment theory, an evidence-based treatment for narcissistic personality disorder. Because narcissistic personality disorder is largely triggered by experiences, it can also be successfully treated using TFP. Because of the recovery rate, narcissistic traits can reduce in severity and can become manageable. TFP requires an acknowledgment of symptoms and their origin, as well as taking responsibility for actions and behaviors (Diamond & Hersh, 2020). It also requires continued focus and discovery of the client's symptoms throughout the course of treatment. By focusing on problematic interpersonal patterns and continually identifying symptoms, counselors can help the client reach a sense of awareness.

Avoidant Personality Disorder (F60.6)

The hallmark of avoidant personality disorder, the first disorder listed under Cluster C personality disorders in the *DSM-5-TR*, is persistent and overwhelming fear of being inadequate, negatively evaluated, and rejected (APA, 2022). These feelings result in extreme discomfort in social situations and restriction of interactions with others (Durand et al., 2018). Symptoms will be noticed in early adulthood and may include fear of criticism or rejection that results in avoidance of work or social activities, including interpersonal interactions, unwillingness to become involved in a relationship without guarantee of acceptance, and holding back in close or sexual relationships because of fear. Individuals with this disorder will experience chronic rumination of thoughts of social rejection and will not fully engage in new relationships because they feel inadequate. They see themselves as fundamentally socially inadequate, inferior, or undesirable and will be reluctant to take risks or try new things for fear of embarrassment (APA, 2022; Comer, 2017).

Essential Features

Avoidant personality disorder is characterized by feelings of inadequacy, hypersensitivity, and social inhibition (APA, 2022). Individuals diagnosed with avoidant personality disorder tend to avoid group activities, and any close relationships must first be deemed by the individual as trustworthy and safe. Individuals with this disorder have an intense fear of being criticized and belittled, have poor self-image, and tend to assume perceived criticism and judgment.

Social isolation is common among individuals diagnosed with avoidant personality disorder because of extreme shyness and fear of being judged or criticized. They may struggle to interact with others and make social connections. When they are in social settings, they may not talk at all in an effort not to be noticed. The social isolation faced by many with avoidant personality disorder may mean that they have little to no social support system when facing challenges, which can in turn put them at greater risk for general loss and hardship. Similarly, they may turn down social benefits, like promotions, when offered because of their intense fear of failure and judgment.

Special Considerations

Often referred to as shy or isolated, individuals with avoidant personality disorder are so fearful of criticism or rejection that at times they overly agree or praise others (APA, 2022; Durand et al., 2018; Frances, 2013). They frequently pass up social and work engagements or even promotions for fear of being perceived negatively. Some may develop a detailed inner fantasy world and have a strong imagination. Prevalence of avoidant personality disorder is around 2.1% for the general population, and this disorder seems to occur equally in men and women, with the disorder being marginally more prevalent in women than in men (APA, 2022). Avoidant behaviors can be seen as early as childhood, with extreme shyness, isolation, and fear of new situations (APA, 2022). However, great care should be taken when considering whether symptoms are developmentally appropriate behaviors, because many cases lessen in severity as the child gets older. Some individuals will develop symptoms during adolescence. Symptoms of this disorder tend to lessen as individuals age, with the prevalence in the older adult to elderly general population falling to 0.8% (APA, 2022).

The diagnosis of avoidant personality disorder is typically not appropriate for children because this is a personality disorder characterized by pervasive patterns of social inhibition, feelings of inadequacy, and hypersensitivity to negative evaluation, which persist over time and across various situations (APA, 2022). Personality disorders are typically diagnosed in late adolescence or adulthood when personality traits are more stable and enduring. As such, in children, similar symptoms may be present but are typically considered within the context of other mental health conditions or developmental stages. For children, alternative diagnoses such as social anxiety disorder or selective mutism may be more appropriate to capture their specific symptoms and experiences (Bogels et al., 2010).

Cultural and Social Considerations

Avoidant behaviors may appear after an individual has experienced a large social embarrassment or has migrated to a new area or new country. The behaviors can be identified within the context of avoidant personality disorder if the client is purposefully avoiding social interactions as a form of safety and self-preservation. The perception of avoiding or avoidance will vary in different cultures, so counselors need to consider the individual's culture and acculturation status when considering this diagnosis (Mulder, 2018). As with other personality disorders (e.g., schizoid personality disorder) in which the client is inhibited in social interactions, counselors should pay close attention to whether the client's normative culture is geared toward collectivism (Caldwell-Harris & Ayçiçegi, 2006). A collectivist culture may incite an extreme fear of being rejected by others and personal reticence in clients with this disorder, which might adversely affect the client's personal, occupational, or other important areas of functioning.

Differential Diagnosis

The symptoms of social anxiety disorder and avoidant personality disorder can be difficult to differentiate. Counselors need to keep in mind that with avoidant personality disorder, the individual actively avoids social relationships, whereas with social anxiety disorder, the individual avoids the social setting (Comer, 2017). Furthermore, personality disorders, by definition, are pervasive and lifelong. Counselors also may be confused with the overlap in the symptoms of many personality disorders. Avoidant personality disorder can be distinguished by the avoidance of rejection and humiliation and fear of being embarrassed or perceived as inadequate, as opposed to schizoid personality disorder in which the person is not interested in personal relationships (Durand et al., 2018).

Comorbidity

An avoidant personality disorder diagnosis should not be given when substance use, medication, or another medical condition can account for the personality change (APA, 2022). As with most personality disorders, there is considerable overlap with other personality disorders, particularly schizoid personality disorder (APA, 2022). Individuals diagnosed with this disorder often present with depressive disorders, feeding and eating disorders, and substance use disorders. As noted, there is a great deal of overlap between this disorder and social anxiety disorder. If both sets of criteria are met, both disorders would be diagnosed.

Coding, Recording, and Specifiers

The only diagnostic code for avoidant personality disorder is F60.6. There are no specifiers for this diagnosis.

Evidence-Based Treatment Option

When individuals exhibiting symptoms associated with avoidant personality disorder come in for counseling, they are often looking for acceptance, but they may soon begin avoiding counseling sessions as consistent with avoidance traits. Building trust is important for these individuals. Various treatments have been tried, including CBT, psychodynamic therapy, behavioral therapy, and group therapy, to reinforce skills built (Comer, 2017). Social skills training provided through CBT can help increase social activities and reduce symptoms for the individual (Chan et al., 2015). Metacognitive interpersonal therapy has also emerged as a therapeutic option and has demonstrated promise due to its focus on looking internally toward what the individual values and desires (Simonsen et al., 2022).

Dependent Personality Disorder (F60.7)

Individuals with dependent personality disorder experience a deep need to be taken care of and an overwhelming fear of being separated from the perceived caretaker (Durand et al., 2018). As a result, these individuals may become submissive, needy, and clingy in relationships (Comer, 2017). They struggle with daily decisions, require a lot of reassurance before making any decision, and may look to another to take responsibility for daily living decisions. Furthermore, these individuals will not express disagreements and will avoid initiating or completing projects or tasks independently largely because they lack self-confidence.

Essential Features

Dependent personality disorder is characterized by the need to be cared for by others, leading to submissive and "people pleasing" behavior (APA, 2022). Individuals diagnosed with dependent personality disorder often have lower levels of self-confidence, depend on others to make decisions, and are strongly opposed to situations in which personal responsibility is required. When faced with the loss of an important relationship, individuals diagnosed with dependent personality disorder work to immediately replace the role that individual played in their life.

Individuals with dependent personality disorder will tolerate extreme conditions, such as physical and sexual abuse, and may go great lengths to gain and keep the support of others, even engaging in activities that they do not enjoy or tolerate unreasonable demands made by others. They feel uncomfortable being on their own and, believing that they cannot take care of themselves, will quickly and indiscriminately find another relationship if a close or intimate relationship ends (APA, 2022). An important characteristic of dependent personality disorder is that the need to be taken care of surpasses what is developmentally appropriate. To ensure that they are cared for by others, individuals diagnosed with dependent personality disorder may be incredibly submissive and believe themselves to be totally or largely incapable of typical functioning. Dependence on a caregiver to help them navigate the world around them is common.

Special Considerations

The median prevalence of dependent personality disorder in the general population is 0.4% (APA, 2022). Extreme care should be taken when considering diagnosing a child, as the behavior may still be developmentally or situationally appropriate. Because individuals with dependent personality disorder have low self-confidence, they may struggle to get a job or hold positions of leadership or responsibility. Socially, they may become overly dependent on friends or others around them.

Cultural and Social Considerations

Almost dropped from the *DSM-5*, the diagnostic criteria of this disorder were seen by some mental health professionals as too narrowly geared toward sociocentric males and to pathologize behaviors that are outside this cultural norm (Boeree, 2006). It is noteworthy that although prevalence within the general population is extremely low, with studies indicating 0.4% to 0.6%, women are diagnosed with this disorder much more frequently than men (APA, 2022).

As with other disorders described in this chapter, the perception of dependence as pathological will vary in different cultures. Counselors need to consider the client's culture and acculturation status when considering a diagnosis of dependent personality disorder (Mulder, 2018). Some cultures place an emphasis on politeness and passivity, especially for certain age groups (Caldwell-Harris & Ayçiçegi, 2006). Therefore, it is particularly important to consider culture, gender, and age when considering a diagnosis and planning treatment. As such, to meet diagnostic criteria for dependent personality disorder, presentation of symptoms should far bypass what is considered a sociocultural norm for the client.

Differential Diagnosis

Dependent personality disorder should not be diagnosed if the personality change can be related to substance use, another medical condition, or medications. As with other personality disorders, there are overlaps in symptoms and diagnostic criteria. Counselors can differentiate dependent personality disorder from other personality disorders by the distinguishing characteristics of submissiveness, obedience, clingy behavior, and desire to maintain a relationship at any cost or replace a lost relationship very quickly (APA, 2022).

Comorbidity

A diagnosis of dependent personality disorder should not be given when substance use, medication, or another medical condition can account for the personality change (APA, 2022). As with most personality disorders, there is considerable overlap with other personality disorders, particularly borderline, avoidant, and histrionic personality disorders (APA, 2022). Individuals diagnosed with this disorder also often present with anxiety and adjustment disorders, chronic physical illness, and persistent separation anxiety disorder and substance use disorders. As noted, there is a great deal of overlap between this disorder and social anxiety disorder. If both sets of criteria are met, both disorders would be diagnosed.

Evidence-Based Treatment Option

One of the most commonly diagnosed personality disorders in mental health clinics (B. F. Grant et al., 2004; Newton-Howes et al., 2010), dependent personality disorder is difficult to treat because individuals with this disorder tend to put the responsibility for treatment and outcomes on the counselor (Comer, 2017). Because individuals with dependent personality disorder tend to be submissive and obedient, they may comply with therapy but have no true self-awareness. Furthermore, they may easily become dependent on the counselor (Durand et al., 2018).

Various therapeutic treatments have been tried, including psychodynamic, cognitive behavior, behavioral, and assertiveness training, with some success (Comer, 2017). CAT has been proposed as a promising treatment option. While CAT has not been associated with full recovery in clients, it has been associated with symptom improvement (Kellett & Lees, 2020). CAT focuses on relationship patterns, which may help clients identify maladaptive patterns in their own life and focus on ways to change them. Universally, when treating clients with dependent personality traits, counselors need to focus on developing the client's state of independence, such as nurturing problem-solving skills and confidence, and not contribute to the problem by allowing the client to become overly dependent on the counselor.

Coding, Recording, and Specifiers

The only diagnostic code for dependent personality disorder is F60.7. There are no specifiers for this diagnosis.

Obsessive-Compulsive Personality Disorder (F60.5)

Individuals with obsessive-compulsive personality disorder have an all-consuming preoccupation with rules and orderliness, getting "it" perfect, perseveration, and interpersonal and mental control (Durand et al., 2018; Paris, 2015). Beginning in early adulthood, compulsions prohibit these individuals from being flexible, productive, and open to new experiences. Individuals with this disorder are unable to see the "big picture," focusing so much on details that they exclude the actual goal of the activity. Decision-making can be arduous, time-consuming tasks because of rigid perfectionism. These individuals will have difficulty completing projects because they cannot meet their own high standards. Personal or leisure activities, including friendships, may go unattended because the individual is so focused on the work or the project. Furthermore, individuals with obsessive-compulsive personality disorder are often reluctant to delegate tasks because others may not live up to their standards. Ideas of right and wrong (i.e., ethics or morality) are inflexible, and others may characterize these individuals as stubborn or rigid (i.e., being stingy with time, money, or personal items; APA, 2022).

Essential Features

Obsessive-compulsive personality disorder is characterized by an intense preoccupation with perfectionism, control of self and others, and orderliness (APA, 2022). These symptoms are compounded by the fact that behaviors are exhibited without regard for others, flexibility, or efficiency. Individuals with obsessive-compulsive personality disorder may have extreme difficulties letting go of physical items and feel that they must control everything that happens around them and to them.

Stubbornness and inflexibility are key features of obsessive-compulsive personality disorder. Those with obsessive-compulsive personality disorder tend to work excessively and have difficulty relaxing, because they are often driven by a need to be involved with everything that is happening in their personal and occupational roles. While those with this disorder are generally financially stable, they are often perceived by others as "stingy" and tend to keep unneeded items due to the possibility of future use, which can lead to an overpossession of items. Tasks can take inordinate amounts of time because those with obsessive-compulsive personality disorder often believe that doing things another way is inexcusable, regardless of efficiency or quality. Social connections are difficult because of common characteristic such as being rigid (e.g., stiff) and overly formal. Individuals diagnosed with this disorder may struggle occupationally, particularly in jobs where change and adaptation are necessary.

Prevalence of obsessive-compulsive personality disorder in the general population is high in comparison with other personality disorders, with estimates ranging from 2.4% to 4.7% (APA, 2022). The National Epidemiological Survey on Alcohol and Related Conditions reported 7.9%, but critics cite this study as being inflated due to the clinical population used (Winsper et al., 2020). Equally represented in all studies is the finding that this disorder is equally prevalent in men and women (APA, 2022).

Special Considerations

Despite the name of the disorder, obsessive-compulsive personality disorder is entirely separate from OCD. Also, unlike OCD, there is very limited research and empirical validation for this disorder. Not surprisingly, this disorder was proposed for elimination from the *DSM-5*, so it is likely counselors will not see this disorder in future iterations of the *DSM*.

Cultural and Social Considerations

As with other personality disorders, cultural context must be considered. Some cultures place more value on work and work-related activities, and this should be considered before a diagnosis of obsessive-compulsive personality disorder is given. Past research has indicated a genetic predisposition for this disorder (McKeon & Murray, 1987; Stone, 1993), but most of this has been disregarded for a discussion of individuals who have specific personality traits, such as favoring structure and perfectionism, as more likely to be diagnosed with this disorder (Durand et al., 2018). A diagnosis of obsessive-compulsive personality disorder should not be assigned to individuals who exhibit behaviors that are reflective of habits or customs interpersonally associated with the client's cultural group, provided these are within boundaries of normative expression. As an example, some cultures may at times express rigid adherence to constrictive social environments, adhere to inflexible codes of conduct, or prioritize cultural standards such as meticulousness, moral diligence, and perfectionism that may seem reflective of obsessive-compulsive personality traits. In such cases, a diagnosis of obsessive-compulsive personality disorder cannot be made unless these are deemed by the client as outside of their cultural or religious identification. Finally, twice as many men are diagnosed with obsessive-compulsive personality disorder as women (APA, 2022).

Differential Diagnosis

Obsessive-compulsive personality disorder should not be diagnosed when long-term substance use, medications, or another medical condition could better account for the personality change (APA, 2022). As with other personality disorders, there is a considerable overlap in symptoms, especially with Cluster C personality disorders (e.g., avoidant, dependent, and obsessive-compulsive personality disorders). The key features that differentiate obsessive-compulsive personality disorder are the extreme perfectionism, inflexible rules, miserly spending habits, and self-criticism not typically found in other personality disorders (APA, 2022). Counselors are cautioned against confusing OCD with this disorder, which can be differentiated by a lack of obsessive thoughts and the associated compulsive behaviors associated with OCD (Durand et al., 2018). Although some symptoms are similar, clients with OCD present with true obsessions and compulsions. Furthermore, there is an overlap in symptoms with hoarding disorder. When distinguishing between these disorders, counselors need to remember that obsessive-compulsive personality disorder includes a pervasive pattern of lifelong rigidity that is not present with hoarding disorder (APA, 2022).

Comorbidity

A diagnosis of obsessive-compulsive personality disorder should not be given when substance use, medication, or another medical condition can account for the personality change (APA, 2022). As with most personality disorders, there is considerable overlap with other personality disorders, particularly borderline, avoidant, and histrionic personality disorders (APA, 2022). Individuals diagnosed with this disorder also often present with anxiety and adjustment disorders, chronic physical illness, and persistent separation anxiety disorder and substance use disorders. As noted, there is a great deal of overlap between this disorder and social anxiety disorder. If both sets of criteria are met, both disorders would be diagnosed.

Evidence-Based Treatment Option

Individuals with obsessive-compulsive personality disorder rarely seek treatment. Like individuals diagnosed with paranoid personality disorder and schizoid personality disorder, individuals with this disorder are often not aware that their obsessive traits are problematic and see no reason to change (Comer, 2017; Durand et al., 2018). If they do present for treatment, symptoms of depression or anxiety are often the client's primary reason for seeking counseling. As with many other personality disorders, psychodynamic therapy or CBT is often used to treat these individuals (Comer, 2017). Rational emotive behavior therapy may be appropriate to address the dichotomous thinking and perfectionism that tend to be pervasive in this personality disorder. CBT can be helpful for some individuals with obsessive-compulsive personality disorder (Bhukhari et al., 2018). Using CBT techniques, clients can become less rigid and better able to restructure their thought patterns around perfectionism and compulsive habits. A lessening of anxiety and depression symptoms has also been reported.

Coding, Recording, and Specifiers

The only diagnostic code for obsessive-compulsive personality disorder is F60.5. There are no specifiers for this diagnosis.

Personality Change Due to Another Medical Condition (F07.0)

Personality change due to another medical condition refers to symptoms that appear and are a result of a medical condition. These symptoms can cover any range within the personality disorders spectrum that are not diagnosable as a specific personality disorder due to the existence of another identified medical condition (APA, 2022). Symptom presentation must be distinctly different from an individual's disposition and personality prior to the medical condition. Symptoms must also result in significant functional and interpersonal impairment.

Essential Features

Akin to other personality disorder characteristics, individuals with personality change due to another medical condition lack insight into their personality changes, yet others around them note a marked difference (APA, 2022). Poor impulse control, rage, apathy, and suspicion that deviate from the client's typical functioning and presentation are common identifiers of this disorder. Because a broad spectrum of illnesses and medical conditions can result in a personality change, no particular condition is associated with causing personality changes.

Differential Diagnosis

Chronic medical conditions, major neurocognitive disorders, substance use disorders, and other mental disorders are all possible given the vague diagnostic criteria and sudden onset of personality change due to another medical condition (APA, 2022). Understanding an individual's history, and sometimes getting a second client history and report of symptoms from a relative or close friend, can bring counselors to the most accurate diagnosis.

Coding, Recording, and Specifiers

The only diagnostic code for personality change due to another medical condition is F07.0. Specify for *labile type, disinhibited type, aggressive type, apathetic type, paranoid type, other type, combined type,* or *unspecified type.*

Other Specified Personality Disorder (F60.89)

Other specified personality disorder is used when clients present symptoms that are characteristic of a personality disorder, including major social and occupational impairment, but do not meet full criteria for any one personality disorder (APA, 2022). This specific diagnosis is used when the clinician chooses to specify the reason that the client's symptoms do not qualify for any one personality disorder.

Coding, Recording, and Specifiers

The only diagnostic code for other specified personality disorder is F60.89. When recording, indicate "other specified personality disorder," followed by the rationale for why the client did not meet the full criteria for a specific personality disorder.

Unspecified Personality Disorder (F60.9)

Unspecified personality disorder is used when clients present symptoms that are characteristic of a personality disorder, including major social and occupational impairment, but do not meet full criteria for any one personality disorder (APA, 2022).

Coding, Recording, and Specifiers

The only diagnostic code for unspecified personality disorder is F60.9. There are no specifiers for this diagnosis.

Summary

We have outlined personality disorders within the *DSM-5-TR* that, because all alternative proposals were rejected, are nearly identical to the personality disorders found within the *DSM-IV-TR* and *DSM-5*. In the following section, we detail an alternative model for diagnosing personality disorders. Although this alternative model has not officially been integrated into the manual, it can be found in Section III, Emerging Measures and Models, of the *DSM-5-TR*. Proposed by APA for the purpose of providing empirical support for the proposed changes and increasing clinical utility through training and familiarization (Bornstein, 2011), this model has been questioned because of problems with clinical utility and a lack of empirical validation, especially in relation to eliminating four personality disorders from diagnostic nosology (Bornstein, 2011). However, we feel it is important to orientate counselors to this alternative model and to discuss the philosophy behind these modifications, varying perspectives of these changes, and implications for counseling professionals who diagnose and work with personality disorders.

Because of controversy surrounding the alternative model, it is our opinion that this proposed approach will change—maybe significantly—before publication in the diagnostic section of the next full iteration of the *DSM*. However, as we highlight in the final chapter of this *Learning Companion*, it is essential for counselors to become involved in future modifications to diagnostic nomenclature for mental health professionals. Without understanding the historical context, philosophy, and research (or lack thereof) behind changes to the *DSM*, counselors will be unable to make informed decisions and advocate for appropriate modifications to diagnostic nomenclature. Whether the topic be the *ICD* or the *DSM*, counselors need to have a clear, informed voice in every one of these discussions.

Alternative Model for Diagnosing Personality Disorders

In 1999, APA began working with the NIMH, the WHO's Division of Mental Health, and the World Psychiatric Association on a research agenda for the *DSM-5*. One of the identified priorities in this research agenda was personality and relational disorders (see Kupfer et al., 2002, for the full *DSM-5* research agenda). In 2007, the DSM-5 Task Force named Andrew E. Skodol as chair and John M. Oldham as cochair of the Personality and Personality Disorders Work Group. The primary aims of this work group were to move away from categorical assessment, eliminate personality disorder comorbidity, reduce within-disorder heterogeneity, and increase clinical utility. Skodol and Bender (2009) stated,

> The limitations of *DSM* categorical conceptualizations of personality disorders are well known: excessive co-occurrence among disorders, extreme heterogeneity among patients receiving the same diagnosis, arbitrary diagnostic thresholds for the boundaries between pathological and "normal" personality functioning, and inadequate coverage of personality psychopathology such that the diagnosis of personality disorder not otherwise specified. (p. 388)

The work group spent nearly 6 years developing (and redeveloping) an alternative model for diagnosing personality disorders (Skodol & Bender, 2009). During this time, an extensive review of the personality and personality disorders literature was conducted by work group members and advisers (APA, 2022; Bornstein, 2011; Mulder, 2018). Findings revealed that paranoid, schizoid, and histrionic personality disorders lacked significant clinical utility and that only three disorders—antisocial, borderline, and schizotypal—had empirical evidence of validity and clinical utility (Skodol & Bender, 2009). There was also considerable overlap or comorbidity for all 10 personality disorders (Bornstein, 2011). Other issues discussed by the work group included philosophical challenges to the current categorical system, not only for personality disorders but for all disorders in the *DSM* (Demjaha et al., 2009; First, 2010; Kraemer, 2007; Paris, 2015). Overuse of personality disorder not otherwise specified (the precursor to other specified personality disorder and unspecified personality disorder) led researchers Pagan et al. (2005) to state,

> The manner in which the *DSM* classifies [personality disorders] is not optimal. Some variation of a hierarchical model or a dimensional model of personality pathology may be more useful for documenting and conceptualizing the problems and characteristics of personality pathology. (p. 688)

The "Personality Disorders" section of the *DSM* was thought to be a prime candidate for dimensional assessment due to the inherent complexity and variability of personality. This was based on the premise that personality dysfunction was mostly a range of trait variation, with normal personality functioning on one end and abnormal personality functioning on the other. Paris (2015) explained,

> A dimensional approach sees personality disorders as dysfunctional amplifications of normal personality profiles. It assumes that there is no fundamental difference between normal and abnormal personality, but a continuum between trait variation and [personality disorders] that can be seen in both community and clinical populations. (p. 157)

A purely dimensional model, a radical change from the current diagnostic structure, was rejected by a majority of the work group and met with significant political opposition (Paris, 2015; Mulder, 2018). After years of deliberation, during which two work group members resigned, an alternative approach was created that introduced a hybrid dimensional-categorical model. This model both assesses symptoms and characterizes five broad areas of personality dysfunction. As opposed to 10 separate diagnostic criteria, this proposed model identifies five personality types with a specific pattern of impairments and traits. In the end, however, this alternative model was rejected by the APA Board of Trustees "to preserve continuity with current clinical practice, while also introducing a new approach that aims to address numerous shortcomings of the current approach to personality disorders" (APA, 2022, p. 881).

The reasons for rejection can be summarized into two basic concepts: lack of clinical utility and lack of empirical evidence. The model was difficult for clinicians to use, requiring training most mental health professionals did not possess (Paris, 2015). Additionally, deemed inappropriate for clinical use by the *DSM-5* Scientific Advisory Committee, the model significantly lacked empirical validity. Therefore, instead of this new model being included in Section II of the *DSM-5-TR* under diagnostic criteria, readers can find the Alternative *DSM-5* Model for Personality Disorders chapter in Section III, Emerging Measures and Models, on pages 881–901.

The Proposed Model

The alternative model proposes diagnosis of personality disorders as a three-step process. First, counselors must assess elements of personality functioning toward *self* (specifically evaluating identity and self-direction) and *interpersonal functioning* (specifically evaluating empathy and intimacy; APA, 2022). Second, counselors must assess 25 pathological personality traits, grouped into five broad areas: negative affectivity, detachment, antagonism, disinhibition, and psychoticism. Finally, using the information gathered from assessment of personality functioning (Step 1) and pathological personality traits (Step 2), counselors will identify one of six specific personality disorders: antisocial, avoidant, borderline, narcissistic, obsessive-compulsive, or schizotypal personality disorder. For individuals who do not fit into one of these six specific personality disorders, a personality disorder–trait specified (PD-TS) diagnosis may be selected. Although many would consider Step 2, assessing pathological personality traits using a pathological trait taxonomy, a categorical diagnosis, Step 3 is the "categorical" part of the alternative model because counselors will select a specific personality disorder. These six specific personality disorders and PD-TS contain diagnostic criteria relevant to the level of personality functioning and pathological personality traits inherent to the typical features of the specific disorder. Personality functioning (Step 1) can be measured by the Level of Personality Functioning Scale, found on pages 895–898 of the *DSM-5-TR*. Likewise, the five personality disorder trait domains and 25 facets can be found on pages 899–901 of the *DSM-5-TR*.

Counselors will also need to ensure that patterns in personality functioning are pervasive, meaning they occur in multiple contexts, and are stable over time (d'Huart et al., 2022). APA (2022) emphasized that personality disorders are chronic conditions, beginning almost universally in adolescence. Of course, counselors should not be polarized in their thinking about personality functioning. These dysfunctions are repeated patterns that do not change, but there is some variability in presentation even within the same individual. APA (2022) stated,

> Impairments across personality functioning and pathological personality traits are *relatively* pervasive across a range of personal and social contexts. . . . The term *relatively* reflects the fact that all except the most extremely pathological personalities show some degree of adaptability. The pattern in personality disorders is maladaptive and relatively inflexible, which leads to disabilities in social, occupational, or other important pursuits, as individuals are unable to modify their thinking or behavior, even in the face of evidence that their current approach is not working. (p. 882)

Finally, as with most disorders in the *DSM-5-TR*, symptoms may not be better explained by another mental disorder, use of a substance, or existence of another medical condition or be due to the individual's developmental stage (APA, 2022).

Level of Personality Functioning

The first element of personality functioning, *self*, is made up of two factors: identity and self-direction (APA, 2022). *Identity* is the ability to experience oneself as a unique individual with clear boundaries. Stability of self-esteem and the ability to emotionally regulate oneself are essential. Clients who would have difficulty in this area are those who are overly dependent on others, have low self-esteem, are overtly egocentric, or vacillate between emotional extremes. *Self-direction* is related to motivation, one's ability to pursue meaningful short- and long-term goals, possession of a standard in which one bases one's behaviors (i.e., a moral compass), and the ability for interpersonal reflection (i.e., being able to assess oneself both accurately and productively). Clients who would have difficulty in this area of personality functioning would have extremely high, potentially unrealistic, or unstable goals; fail to conform to ethical behavior; have legal problems; or have an inflated sense of morality (APA, 2022).

Interpersonal functioning, the second element of personality functioning, is also made up of two factors: empathy and intimacy (APA, 2022). *Empathy* is the ability to appreciate the experience of others, to accept others' views, and to acknowledge that one's behavior can adversely affect others. Clients who would have difficulty in this area of personality functioning are those who lack concern for others or are deceitful, egocentric, or manipulative. *Intimacy* is related to one's ability to form a genuine relationship with another human being. Having a desire for closeness and deep and enduring relationships in one's life is characteristic of someone who possesses intimacy. Clients who would have difficulty in this area of personality functioning are those who fear closeness with others; worry that they will be embarrassed or mocked by others; or tend to control, deceive, or coerce others as opposed to having genuine relationships.

> To quantify all the elements, counselors will use the Level of Personality Functioning Scale (see pages 895–898 of the *DSM-5-TR*). This scale uses a Likert-type scale consisting of four choices, ranging from 0 (*little to no impairment*) to 3 (*severe impairment*). APA (2022) justifies this dimensional scale by claiming that personality, although fluid and unique to each person, generally allows for appropriate patterns of familial, social, and occupational functioning. Although personality is complex, APA claims that most individuals' personality allows for meaningful relationships; appropriate levels of intimacy; a respect for boundaries and social norms, including laws and moral guidelines; and a care for the well-being of others. Conversely, APA also claims that maladaptive personality functioning contributes to personality pathology that inhibits not only personal relationships but also one's ability to conform to societal standards, perform accurate self-appraisal, and experience empathy for others. APA (2022) stated,

> Like most human tendencies, personality functioning is distributed on a continuum. Central to functioning and adaptation are individuals' characteristic ways of thinking about and understanding themselves and their interactions with others. An optimally functioning individual has a complex, fully elaborated, and well-integrated psychological world that includes a mostly positive, volitional, and adaptive self-concept. . . . At the opposite end of the continuum, an individual with severe personality pathology has an impoverished, disorganized, and/or conflicted psychological world that includes a weak, unclear, and maladaptive self-concept; a propensity to negative, deregulated emotions; and a deficient capacity for adaptive interpersonal functioning and social behavior. (p. 891)

This fluid conceptualization of personality is what counselors use to indicate whether a client has *little to no impairment*, *some impairment*, *moderate impairment*, or *severe impairment* in terms of self (identity and self-direction) and interpersonal (empathy and intimacy) functioning.

Pathological Personality Traits

Stated previously, the *DSM-5-TR* uses a pathological trait taxonomy that consists of five domains: negative affectivity, detachment, antagonism, disinhibition, and psychoticism. Within these domains are 25 facets (see below). These domains and facets are based on the trait-based five-factor model (FFM) of general personality functioning, a widely accepted model used extensively in studies of personality functioning (Samuel & Widiger, 2008; Widiger, 2005; for more information on the FFM, see Digman, 1990). Numerous studies and meta-analytic reviews have concluded that most personality disorders have a meaningful profile of traits that can be linked to these five domains. These traits, or facets, represent different characteristics of the domain. Defined by APA (2022) as "a tendency to feel, perceive, behave, and think in relatively consistent ways across time and across situations" (p. 892), a personality trait is considered more fluid than a personality function (i.e., identity, self-direction, empathy, or intimacy). For example, individuals with high levels of emotional lability may be able to perform at work without high levels of emotionality. However, they would have a pattern of instability with emotional regulation despite being able to choose situations, such as work, in which they were able to regulate their emotional nature more easily. The alternative model for personality disorders asserts that these 25 personality traits, and subsequentially the five domains, apply to all individuals and that all individuals are "located on the spectrum of trait dimensions . . . personality traits apply to everyone in different degrees rather than being present versus absent" (APA, 2022, p. 892). See the table titled "Definitions of *DSM-5* Personality Disorder Trait Domains and Facets," on pages 899–901 in the *DSM-5-TR* for a detailed description of the personality trait model. The following is a summary of the five domains and associated pathological traits:

Negative affectivity: Emotional lability, anxiousness, separation insecurity, submissiveness, hostility, perseveration, and restricted affectivity (lack of*)

Detachment: Withdrawal, intimacy avoidance, anhedonia, depressivity, restricted affectivity, and suspiciousness

Antagonism: Manipulativeness, deceitfulness, grandiosity, attention seeking, callousness, and hostility

Disinhibition: Irresponsibility, impulsivity, distractibility, risk taking, and rigid perfectionism (lack of*)

Psychoticism: Unusual beliefs and experiences, eccentricity, and cognitive and perceptual dysregulation

(The asterisk indicates that low levels as well as high levels are part of the facet definition. For example, a lack of restricted affectivity indicates low levels of negative affectivity, and a lack of rigid perfectionism indicates low levels of disinhibition.)

Specific Personality Disorders

Section III of the *DSM-5-TR* retained six personality types: BPD, obsessive-compulsive personality disorder, avoidant personality disorder, schizotypal personality disorder, antisocial personality disorder, and narcissistic personality disorder (APA, 2022). Four personality disorders (i.e., paranoid, schizoid, histrionic, and dependent) were eliminated because of low clinical utility, inadequate evidence for validity, and high levels of comorbidity with other personality disorders (Bornstein, 2011). Narcissistic personality disorder was originally proposed for elimination, but it was retained because of pushback from clinicians as well as evidence of diagnostic validity, albeit limited, and evidence that incidences of narcissistic personality disorder have increased at unprecedented rates in the last few decades (Montes, 2013; Twenge & Foster, 2010).

The criteria for each personality disorder in the alternative model are diagnostically defined by levels of impairment in personality functioning and typical pathological personality traits. Because of considerable variability and overlap in personality disorders, counselors may also indicate other trait and level of personality functioning specifiers (either domains or facets) that are outside of the diagnostic criteria or considered useful for treatment (APA, 2022). This allows counselors to highlight additional features, for example, extreme negative affectivity traits such as depression, so these can be focused on during treatment. There are no other specifiers for these disorders, with the exception of a *psychopathy* specifier for antisocial personality disorder, which is used when there is a lack of fear and a general "bold interpersonal style" (APA, 2022, p. 885) that the individual uses as a screen for manipulative or fraudulent behavior.

Although not included in the specific criteria, these disorders may not be diagnosed if symptoms can be better explained by another mental disorder or are due to the use of a substance, due to existence of another medical condition, or are related to the individual's developmental stage (APA, 2022). Because this model is not currently used within a clinical setting, there is no recording guidance or associated codes for these disorders.

Personality Disorder–Trait Specified

In the event that an individual does not meet the criteria for one of the six proposed personality disorders, but the counselor does note severity of impairment in personality functioning and problematic personality trait(s), the counselor can diagnose a client with PD-TS (APA, 2013b, 2022). As with other disorders proposed in the alternative model, PD-TS includes an assessment of personality functioning and identification of specific personality traits related to personality pathology. Although in some ways this disorder closely represents personality disorder not otherwise specified, readers should note that PD-TS is much more precise regarding the extent of the personality pathology. Counselors can list, as specifiers, level of personality functioning (indicative of impairment) and the individual's unique pathological personality traits. APA (2022) claims diagnoses that were eliminated in the alternative model (i.e., paranoid, schizoid, histrionic, and dependent personality disorders) are represented by this diagnosis.

We remind counselors that good clinical judgment is critical in determining whether a diagnosis of PD-TS can be justified. To do so, counselors should carefully assess an individual's level of distress, as evidenced by extent of time the person has experienced personality dysfunction, level of difficulty experienced by the person, and the influence of these problems on social and occupational adjustment (Pagan et al., 2005).

There are two diagnostic criteria for PD-TS (A and B; APA, 2022). Criterion A requires moderate or greater impairment in level of personality functioning (i.e., identity, self-direction, empathy, and intimacy). Criterion B requires the individual meet the description for one or more of the five personality trait domains (i.e., negative affectivity, detachment, antagonism, disinhibition, or psychoticism) or express any of the specific trait facets within one or more of the above-listed pathological personality trait domains. Essentially, this means that (a) individuals must receive a score of 2 (moderate impairment) or higher on the Levels of Personality Functioning Scale (see pages 895–898 in the *DSM-5-TR*) in two of the four levels of personality functioning, and (b) individuals must meet the descriptive definition found within the pathological trait taxonomy (see pages 899–901 in the *DSM-5-TR*) for either one or more personality disorder trait domain or one or more specific facets within the domains.

Specifiers for PD-TS depend on the specific personality impairments related to Criterion B that an individual is experiencing (APA, 2022). Counselors would indicate the specific pathological personality trait domain(s) or specific trait facet(s) within the domains. The combination of these pathological personality traits will be unique for each client. For example, an individual who presents with negative affectivity, detachment, and impulsivity would be diagnosed with PD-TS with all of these included as specifiers. There are no subtypes for PD-TS because variations in this disorder are indicated by recording specifiers.

Using the Alternative *DSM-5* Model

To facilitate understanding of the proposed model, we provide readers with a case example and a brief description of diagnosis using the alternative model. We also provide two additional case examples at the end of this chapter to assist counselors in further understanding and applying the proposed model.

> Maurice, a 42-year-old African American, heterosexual, single man, is mandated to treatment because he violated probation. The violation involved stealing his sister's car and credit cards. Maurice explains that many women, including his sister, find him charming but he has no current girlfriend or any significant history of long-term relationships. His case file indicates he has had extensive legal problems dating back to early adolescence. These include petty theft, drug possession and distribution, numerous assault charges, and two incidences of domestic violence. Although he denies most charges, when asked about pushing his ex-girlfriend down the stairs 10 years ago, he reports, "She deserved it; she didn't pick up the phone when I called. I just showed her who was boss." Records indicate that Maurice has a long history of manipulation, risky behavior, impulsivity, and problems with anger management. He has never been able to keep a job or manage his financial responsibilities, but he is able to point to his criminal behavior as the reason for his inability to keep employment.

If using the alternative model for personality disorder, the first thing a counselor would do is assess Maurice's level of personality functioning using the Level of Personality Functioning Scale found within the *DSM-5-TR*. The counselor finds that Maurice scores a 3 (*severe impairment*) in the areas of empathy and intimacy and a 2 (*moderate impairment*) for identity and self-direction. The counselor gives the justification of severe impairment for empathy because Maurice lacks any concern for others, including his sister from whom he stole and his ex-girlfriend whom he physically abused. In terms of intimacy, Maurice scores a 3 (*severe impairment*) because he has never been able to maintain an interpersonal relationship and his primary means of interaction with others is based on deceit and manipulation. A score of 2 (*moderate impairment*) is given for identity because although Maurice's self-identity depends on others showing him respect, he does not have the weak sense of autonomy or emptiness required for severe impairment. He also scores a 2 (*moderate impairment*) on self-direction because he has some limited insight into his inability to maintain employment.

The next step a counselor would take using the alternative model would be to identify personality disorder trait domains and facets. Referencing the "Definitions of *DSM-5* Personality Disorder Trait Domains and Facets" table found in the *DSM-5-TR* (APA, 2022, pp. 899–901), a counselor could see the following traits applied to Maurice's case:

manipulativeness, callousness, deceitfulness, risk taking, impulsivity, and irresponsibility. These traits are part of the antagonism and disinhibition domains and relate specifically to the typical features of antisocial personality disorder found in the *DSM-5* alternative model for diagnosing personality disorders. The counselor would also consider the specifier *psychopathy* because Maurice indicates a lack of anxiety or fear and has a façade of being charming to others. Maurice's diagnosis, therefore, would be antisocial personality disorder, severe impairment (empathy and intimacy), with antagonism, disinhibition, and psychopathy.

> ***Note:*** Because information regarding diagnostic recording using the *DSM-5* alternative model for personality disorders is limited, it is the role of the counselor to determine what specifiers to list (or not list). Counselors may include additional personality features that may be present. Furthermore, although levels of personality functions are required for diagnosis, the actual level of functioning can be included as a specifier if the counselor feels it is appropriate to do so.

Case Example

Yosuko is a 43-year-old Japanese American, heterosexual, single woman who lives with her parents. Yosuko works at home as a medical records data-entry clerk and is seeking treatment because her parents are being strongly advised by their physician and Yosuko's older brother to move to an assisted living community. Yosuko strongly disagrees with her brother and is angry at her parents for considering the move, but she reports she is afraid of disagreeing with her family. She alternates between resentment and a "what-about-me" attitude. When asked about her family's health and why her parents' physician would suggest they leave their home, she reports she doesn't really know because her mother is usually the one who takes care of any medical issues regarding the family.

Yosuko's family has seen her turn down multiple job opportunities and even promotions at her current place of employment. She has worked for the same company for 15 years and is viewed as dependable and unassuming. When asked about turning down promotions, Yosuko states she doesn't want the responsibility of having to go into the office every day and supervise others. She says her mother refused to drive her to work every day, so she doesn't see how she could get there on her own. She has one very close friend, a neighbor, whom she has known since childhood. She goes to visit her friend regularly and feels lost if she doesn't see her friend every day. She states the hardest thing she has ever gone through in life was when her friend got married and considered moving to an adjacent neighborhood. Yosuko says her parents thinking of leaving her feels similar. She states, "I can't believe they would consider leaving me, I cannot live alone—they know that. I don't see why I can't move with them."

Diagnostic Questions

1. Using the current *DSM-5-TR* diagnostic criteria found in Section II, do Yosuko's presenting symptoms meet the criteria for a personality disorder? If so, which one?
2. Using the alternative model proposed for diagnosing personality disorders found in Section III of the *DSM-5-TR*, assess Yosuko's specific level of impairment in personality functioning using the Level of Personality Functioning Scale.
3. Using the alternative model proposed for diagnosing personality disorders found in

Section III of the *DSM-5*, assess Yosuko's pathological personality traits using the pathological trait taxonomy found on pages 899–901 of the *DSM-5-TR*.

4. Based on the information gathered in Questions 2 and 3, what personality disorder diagnosis would you assign Yosuko?
5. What specifiers or, if relevant, pathological personality trait combinations would you assign?

Case Example

Born in El Salvador but raised in the United States, Alexis is a 27-year-old bisexual woman who entered therapy because she has a tendency to get involved in relationships with incompatible and disappointing partners. As Alexis talks about these relationships, the counselor begins to recognize a pattern: Alexis tends to idolize her partners early in the relationship; she then sets unattainable standards for them (e.g., finishing law school or getting a promotion) and is routinely disappointed when these "goals" are not met. She also seems to have considerable problems with boundaries, having lived for a very short time with at least three different partners over the course of 4 years and thinking that calling her partners multiple times a day is appropriate.

When asked about her childhood, Alexis reports people would often call her "intense." She reports having significant problems when her parents divorced and her father remarried. She states her parents still think she is overdramatic, easily upset, sullen, and angry. Her treatment history records are extensive, indicating extreme mood lability and aggressive tendencies toward her parents, siblings, and friends at school. She was suspended from school numerous times for yelling at teachers but was never expelled. According to her own report, she was terrified when she got suspended and, each time, begged the principal and her parents to let her go back to school. Alexis has a history of two suicide attempts and significant scars from cutting herself. She has been on numerous medications but reports, "None of them seem to do anything, but they are a pain in the ass to take so I just take them when I feel like it." She has no history of legal or physical health problems. She admits to using alcohol but does not meet the criteria for a substance use disorder.

Diagnostic Questions

1. Using the current diagnostic criteria found in Section II of the *DSM-5-TR*, do Alexis's presenting symptoms meet the criteria for a personality disorder? If so, which one?
2. Using the alternative model proposed for diagnosing personality disorders found in Section III of the *DSM-5-TR*, assess Alexis's specific level of impairment in personality functioning using the Level of Personality Functioning Scale in the *DSM-5-TR*.
3. Using the alternative model proposed for diagnosing personality disorders found in Section III of the *DSM-5-TR*, assess Alexis's pathological personality traits using the pathological trait taxonomy found on pages 899–901 of the *DSM-5-TR*.
4. Based on the information gathered in Questions 2 and 3, what personality disorder diagnosis would you assign Alexis?
5. What specifiers or, if relevant, pathological personality trait combinations would you assign?
6. What other information would you like to know about Alexis in order to make a more accurate assessment of her presenting problem(s)?

Conclusion

Regardless of model used, careful assessment of the client can reveal a long history of personality dysfunction. Before making a diagnosis, counselors need to assess whether the dysfunction is stable over time, is experienced in multiple contexts, is not better accounted for by another mental health diagnosis, and is not due to the effect of another substance or another medication condition. The dysfunction needs to always involve problems in behavior and emotional and thinking patterns, and personality patterns need to have started early in the client's life. Counselors should ask about patterns in the client's life that relate to personality concerns and be sure to interview family members, friends, teachers, colleagues, and other health professionals to better understand the client's life history.

Questions for Consideration

1. What unique counseling skills and dispositions could you bring to an interdisciplinary treatment team serving people with personality disorders?
2. How do counselors provide comprehensive care and guard against bias when working with clients diagnosed with borderline personality disorder?
3. What strategies might you use to differentiate between personality disorders grouped under Cluster B and bipolar disorder?

Chapter 15

Specific Behavioral Disruptions

The disorders covered in this chapter are divided into five sections: feeding and eating disorders, elimination disorders, sleep-wake disorders, sexual dysfunctions, and paraphilic disorders. These disorders have been grouped together because they all evidence similar patterns of behavioral disruption (APA, 2022).

Feeding and Eating Disorders

Feeding Disorders: Essential Features

Feeding disorders in infants and young children are complex and include pica, rumination disorder, and avoidant/restrictive food intake disorder. Like eating disorders, feeding disorders are often characterized by some type of avoiding or restricting food intake; however, feeding disorders typically manifest in early childhood rather than adolescence (APA, 2022; Hilbert, 2020). Feeding disorders and short-term feeding issues may present similarly at first. Thus, counselors should pay close attention to diagnostic criteria so they may more accurately differentiate between developmentally appropriate behavior (e.g., a child being a "picky eater") and disordered eating (e.g., a child steering clear of events that entail eating or nutritional deficiency as a result of eating behavior).

Eating Disorders: Essential Features

Similar to feeding disorders in infants and young children, eating disorders in adolescents and adults are complex in nature and have a significant daily impact for those who experience them. An eating disorder is an illness that negatively affects an individual's diet. This can range from eating small amounts of food or nothing at all to eating extremely large amounts of food (NIMH, 2023). Eating disorders can be detrimental to one's physical health, emotional well-being, and interpersonal relationships. Some counselors may struggle to comprehend how eating disorders develop. Given that they can present in a number of ways across age, race, and ethnicity, eating disorders can pose challenges for any mental health professional (Hilbert, 2020). Eating disorders covered in this chapter include anorexia nervosa, bulimia nervosa, and binge-eating disorder (APA, 2020).

Almost 20 million women and 10 million men have suffered from some kind of eating disorder in their lives (Deloitte Access Economics, 2020). As high as these figures are, many individuals who have eating disorders or are at risk for them do not seek treatment. Over 10,000 deaths annually occur from the effects of an eating disorder (Deloitte Access Economics, 2020).

Prevalence rates for eating disorders vary considerably. Over a 12-month period, the prevalence rate of anorexia nervosa is approximately 0.4% among the general U.S. population, whereas the prevalence of bulimia nervosa is 1.0% to 1.5% (APA, 2022). The 12-month prevalence of binge-eating disorder is 1.6% among adult females and 0.8% among adult males in the United States (APA, 2022).

Adolescence is the period of greatest risk for developing an eating disorder (Hilbert, 2020). However, concerns about body shape, image, and weight that underlie eating disorder processes may begin much younger; 40% to 60% of elementary school girls (ages 6–12) expressed concern about weight or becoming fat (Smolak, 2011). Eating disorders can develop in individuals during the college years and into adulthood (Schwitzer, 2012; Wade & O'Shea, 2015).

Although many feeding and eating disorders have similar psychological and behavioral features, with the exception of pica, only one diagnosis can be given. Diagnostic criteria for the disorders are mutually exclusive, meaning it is not possible to have both binge-eating disorder and bulimia. This ensures differentiation of each disorder and helps counselors target treatment planning and outcome management to unique characteristics of the disorders (APA, 2022).

Note: Disorders in this section will sometimes resemble substance use disorders (APA, 2022). For example, symptoms such as craving and compulsive usage are typical to both diagnostic categories. This is because eating and substance use disorders involve the same neural systems that control self-regulation and reward. More research is needed regarding commonalities between development and treatment of eating disorders and substance abuse; however, cognitive behavioral interventions appear to be effective in the treatment of both eating and substance use disorders.

Changes From *DSM-5* to *DSM-5-TR*

There are no major changes for these disorders from the *DSM-5* to the *DSM-5-TR*. APA (2013a) rendered *DSM-5* changes in diagnostic criteria that provided a more representative look at clients' behaviors and symptoms as they deal with these conditions throughout the life span. It is important to know that individuals or their caregivers who seek treatment for pica, rumination disorder, or avoidant/restrictive food intake disorder are more likely to present to a medical facility as opposed to a mental health clinic (Berg & Peterson, 2013).

Differential Diagnosis

Feeding and eating disorders can present in many ways. Counselors should understand whether the behavior and accompanying symptoms can be better explained by another medical or psychiatric condition. For all eating disorders, it is important to look at the following variables: weight status, fear of weight gain, dietary restriction, overevaluation of shape and weight, body image disturbance, presence and frequency of binge eating, and presence and frequency of compensatory behaviors (Berg & Peterson, 2013). Although popular culture links anorexia nervosa to restricted eating and bulimia nervosa to binge-purge behavior, both disorders include mention of restriction and compensatory behaviors. Careful assessment regarding disorder processes, underlying thought patterns, and impairments will help counselors identify the eating disorder that best fits the client's experience.

Many individuals who have an eating disorder also have additional mental health concerns. These may include depression, anxiety, substance use disorders, and personality disorders (Bryant-Waugh, 2019; Eisenberg et al., 2011). In addition, changes in appetite and eating are characteristic of depressive and anxiety disorders, and screening for mood disorders should also be a part of any screening process for eating disorders (Fichter et al., 2015).

Etiology for Feeding Disorders

Feeding difficulties are fairly common among infants and children, but not all difficulties will manifest into feeding disorders (Dahlgren et al., 2017). However, it is important to make note of such difficulties and treat them to prevent them from turning into a disorder. Feeding disorders often have different medical and developmental etiologies that call for various interventions (Hilbert, 2020).

It may be difficult to notice if a child has a feeding disorder because the child may still gain weight and not have any medical conditions while symptoms and behaviors of the disorder occur. These children are often seen in different settings and by both medical and mental health professionals. Because there is an overlap of physical and psychological problems, professionals may struggle to determine cause and effect of feeding disorders (Hilbert, 2020).

As with treatment of other childhood concerns, feeding disorders need to be addressed from a variety of contexts. More detailed assessments may give better insight to the origin of these problems alongside other emotional and behavioral symptoms (Flichter et al., 2015).

Etiology for Eating Disorders

Disordered eating can be caused by genetic, biological, behavioral, psychological, and social factors (NIMH, 2023). Often, etiology of eating disorders is seen as black-and-white in that there are either biological or cultural influences that cause these disorders without taking into account possible links between other factors (Hilbert, 2020). Although some researchers emphasize cultural considerations within eating disorders, it is difficult to determine how much of a role one's culture plays in the development. There is not one specific factor that causes eating disorders, and multiple causal factors may influence each other to differing degrees. These interactions between the different factors, for example, genetic factors interacting with social-cultural influences such as media images, may work in shaping the onset and maintenance of eating disorders (Smolak & Chun-Kennedy, 2013). It is important to look at eating disorders holistically.

Core features of eating disorders include body image disturbance, control in eating, and exhibition of behaviors to control weight (APA, 2022). The body image disturbance can lead to internalizing the thin ideal and can lead one to put greater value on being thin. An individual may then control food consumption by restricting calories. However, if the thin ideal is internalized by someone who is at risk for bulimia nervosa or binge-eating disorder, the individual may lose control over the amount of food consumed.

Treatment of Feeding and Eating Disorders

Complex etiologies of feeding and eating disorders can make their treatment difficult and multifaceted. Treatment varies based on the disorder as well as the individual presentation of the client but should include attention to physical, behavioral, and emotional health. The disorders are also treated at different levels of care, ranging from outpatient to inpatient and residential (Berg et al., 2012), depending on the level of severity at time of presentation.

Different approaches look at the importance of the therapeutic relationship in the treatment of eating disorders. Oftentimes, clients need to feel a sense of security before beginning the therapeutic process. Eating disorders generally isolate a client because many of the behaviors are secretive. Typically, this is due to denial or difficulty understanding the need for treatment. Counselors treating clients with eating disorders need to work to develop a therapeutic alliance and help clients and families understand why treatment may be appropriate (Kress & Paylo, 2018).

DBT has been used to treat various eating disorders. DBT is often an effective treatment for individuals who have tried other methods but have been unsuccessful. Using DBT may work with individuals who are ambivalent to change as well as those who present as rigid and perfectionistic. This type of therapy helps individuals see that they can act on their own behalf (Federici et al., 2012). In addition to DBT, CBT and interpersonal psychotherapy may be effective for the treatment of eating disorders (Kress & Paylo, 2018). Eating and feeding disorders may primarily be treated in medical settings with counselors working as part of an interdisciplinary treatment team.

Implications for Counselors

Given the high prevalence rates of eating and feeding disorders, it is likely that counselors will encounter clients with eating disorders and disordered eating (APA, 2022; Deloitte Access Economics, 2020; Masheb et al., 2021). Counselors should be particularly concerned with mortality rates of eating disorders: 4% for anorexia nervosa, 3.9% for bulimia nervosa, and 5.2% for eating disorder not otherwise specified (Crow et al., 2009). Because eating disorders are complex in etiology, medical consequences, and treatment, counselors will likely collaborate with physicians, dietitians, psychiatrists, and other medical professionals as needed to provide the best possible treatment (Berg & Peterson, 2013). There is no one cause of eating disorders, and they must be looked at from a variety of perspectives, including understanding social and cultural influences that may have facilitated the rise of body image disturbance and eating disorders over the years (APA. 2022; Masheb et al., 2021).

Proper assessment is necessary for accurate identification of individuals with eating disorders and selection of effective treatment plans (APA, 2022; Kress & Paylo, 2018). Individuals who are at a normal weight or have not experienced major weight changes may still experience eating disorders or be at risk for developing an eating disorder. Therefore, it is important for counselors to screen for eating disorders even among individuals who appear to be at a normal weight. Asking general questions about various behaviors in terms of self-care can help counselors get a better idea of whether an individual might be at risk for an eating disorder (Berg & Peterson, 2013).

Counselors should be aware that individuals with eating disorders are more likely to have other co-occurring symptoms. These individuals are at increased risk for suicide and self-injury. Counselors need to be aware of these risks and should take extra time to conduct a thorough suicide risk assessment (Joiner et al., 2022). Individuals with anorexia nervosa and bulimia nervosa often deal with low self-esteem, low self-concept, depression, and anxiety (APA, 2022).

Adolescents and adults may experience eating disorders in different ways, including the internalization of maternal messages and communication to be thin, social and peer group comparisons, and birth order issues. It is important for counselors to take these into consideration when evaluating their clients and developing treatment plans (Joiner et al., 2022). Because eating disorders are complex and often involve medical issues, it is also important that counselors refer clients with suspected eating disorders for medical evaluation and develop working relationships with medical providers (APA, 2022).

The following sections outline each disorder within the Feeding and Eating Disorders chapter of the *DSM-5-TR*. Although a summary and special considerations for counselors are provided for each disorder, counselors should reference the *DSM-5-TR* directly when considering a diagnosis. It is essential that counselors understand diagnostic criteria and features, subtypes and specifiers (if applicable), prevalence, course, and risk and prognostic factors for each disorder prior to diagnosis.

SPECIFIC FEEDING DISORDERS

Pica (F98.3 Children; F50.8 Adults)

Essential Features

Pica is a feeding disorder that is characterized by the repetitive eating of nonnutritive, nonfood substances including dirt, paper, and paint (APA, 2022). Pica is a common diagnosis in individuals with intellectual disabilities (Bryant-Waugh, 2019). Understanding pica can be complex because there is not a single etiology for the disorder. There are no significant changes to the diagnostic criteria for pica in the *DSM-5-TR*.

An essential feature of pica is eating nonnutritive, nonfood substances for a period of at least 1 month (APA, 2022). These consumed substances do not aid in the development of the individual. The minimum age for diagnosis is recommended to be 2 years so the developmentally normal practice of mouthing objects is excluded. It is important to recognize that the consumption of nonfood substances is also not part of a cultural or social practice. If pica is present in conjunction with another mental disorder or medical condition, counselors should only diagnose pica if it requires additional clinical attention (APA, 2022).

Special Considerations

The prevalence of pica is not clear, although it does seem to occur at a higher rate in individuals with intellectual disability and increases with the severity of the condition (APA, 2022). Because of its self-injurious nature, pica has been known to lead to death in individuals with developmental disabilities. Although pica can be diagnosed in otherwise normally developing children, adults who are diagnosed with it typically have an intellectual disability or other mental disorder (APA, 2022).

Although feeding disorders are typically seen in medical settings, therapeutic approaches such as CBT have been found effective for treating pica. Typically used in conjunction with parental involvement, strategies such as self-monitoring, behavioral experiments, and cognitive restructuring have yielded successful treatment outcomes (Bryant-Waugh, 2019). In milder cases of pica, behavioral interventions such as positive reinforcement and overcorrection have reduced symptoms (Kress & Paylo, 2019).

Pathological pica behavior can be seen across cultural, regional, and socioeconomic boundaries. The prevalence of pica varies widely across diverse social and clinical contexts (Hartmann et al., 2012). There are some populations for which eating dirt or other nonnutritive substances has spiritual, cultural, or other social value. If the behavior of eating such substances is due to one of these practices, a diagnosis of pica would not be applicable (APA, 2022). Counselors will want to refer for medical evaluation when clients present with symptoms of pica.

Differential Diagnosis

Common differential diagnoses for pica include anorexia nervosa, factitious disorder, and nonsuicidal self-injurious behaviors in personality disorders (APA, 2022). Pica may also be a symptom in individuals who have a developmental disability or other pervasive developmental disorders (Bryant-Waugh, 2019).

Coding, Recording, and Specifiers

The diagnostic code for pica is F98.3 for children and F50.8 for adults. If, after the full criteria have been met for the disorder, the diagnostic criteria have not been met for a sustained period of time, a person can be considered *in remission* (APA, 2022). Although the *DSM-5-TR* does not indicate a specific duration for this specifier, counselors can assume that an individual must consistently not ingest any nonnutritive, nonfood substance for at least 1 month.

Rumination Disorder (F98.21)

Essential Features

Rumination disorder is a feeding disorder that involves repetitive regurgitation of swallowed or partially digested food. The individual may then rechew, reswallow, or spit out the food. Although the disorder is typically found in children, it occurs across age ranges and can develop in healthy adolescents (Schroedl et al., 2013). Rumination disorder occurs most often in infants within the first or second year of life. However, it has been known to develop at a later age in individuals with intellectual disabilities.

One of the essential features of rumination disorder is the repeated regurgitation of food. This regurgitation must occur over a period of at least 1 month. The regurgitation occurs frequently, often daily, and at least several times per week. The symptoms should not occur during any other episodes of a different feeding or eating disorder. Symptoms may occur during another mental disorder; however, for a rumination disorder diagnosis, these symptoms should be a main aspect of the presenting issue (APA, 2022).

Special Considerations

The prevalence for rumination disorder is unclear; however, this disorder is more common among individuals with intellectual disabilities (APA, 2022). Research does not indicate one specific medical or mental health–based treatment approach to treating rumination disorder. Different behavioral techniques may help lessen symptoms. One treatment method that seems to be effective in infants with rumination disorder is intense nurturing. In older individuals, counselors have found cognitive techniques beneficial in improving self-control. Although interventions do not totally disrupt the behavior, they do offer individuals an improved quality of life and enhanced functioning (Schroedl et al., 2013).

Because rumination disorder is rare, it is difficult to assess cultural considerations. However, research shows that the disorder dates back as early as the 17th century and cuts across social classes (Parry-Jones, 1994). As the world became more industrialized in later centuries, the disorder occurred less and tended to be typically present in settings where there was not enough social and environmental stimulation (Parry-Jones, 1994).

Differential Diagnosis

Common differential diagnoses for rumination disorder include gastrointestinal conditions, anorexia nervosa, and bulimia nervosa (APA, 2022). Medical assessment plays an integral role in accurate diagnosis.

Coding, Recording, and Specifiers

There is only one diagnostic code for rumination disorder: F98.21. It should be specified if the disorder is *in remission*. It is in remission if, after the full criteria are met, the diagnostic criteria have not been met for a sustained period of time (APA, 2022). As with pica, the *DSM-5-TR* does not clarify duration for this specifier. Counselors should ensure that an individual must consistently not regurgitate or rechew food for at least 1 month.

Avoidant/Restrictive Food Intake Disorder (F50.8)

Essential Features

Avoidant/restrictive food intake disorder is a feeding condition that typically occurs in middle childhood. As the name implies, this disorder occurs when a child evades or severely limits their intake of food. Parents may not notice avoidant or restrictive food processes if children do not have visible weight loss or growth impairment (Bryant-Waugh, 2019). Moreover, atypical eating behaviors and disturbances are common in young children (Equit et al., 2012), and differentiating between developmentally appropriate behavior and disordered eating behavior is challenging for parents, guardians, or caretakers. One difference between atypical eating behaviors and avoidant/restrictive food intake disorder is that individuals with the disorder are likely to have little interest in eating (Equit et al., 2012).

Core symptoms of restrictive eating and food refusal are avoidance of certain foods, unwillingness to try new foods and only eating certain foods, and consumption of smaller than normal amounts of food as well as the complete refusal of food (Equit et al., 2012).

An essential feature of avoidant/restrictive food intake disorder is avoiding or restricting food intake that leads to persistent failure to meet necessary nutritional needs. The eating disturbance does not occur during the course of anorexia nervosa or bulimia nervosa. There is no disturbance of one's body weight or shape (APA, 2022). The food restriction can be related to a lack of interest in food or eating, avoidance of food for sensory reasons, and avoidance because of feared consequences of eating (Bryant-Waugh, 2019).

Special Considerations

Although this disorder is typically more common in children than adults, there could be a delay between the onset and when it actually presents (APA, 2022). This disorder can sometimes be confused with other feeding or eating disorders; however, individuals with avoidant/restrictive food intake disorder do not express concern with weight or body shape.

Although feeding disorders are typically seen in medical settings, therapeutic approaches such as CBT have been found effective for treating avoidant/restrictive food intake disorder. Typically used in conjunction with parental involvement, strategies such as self-monitoring, behavioral experiments, and cognitive restructuring have yielded successful treatment outcomes (Bryant-Waugh, 2019).

In terms of cultural considerations, it is necessary to make sure that the food disturbance is not part of a culturally approved ritual such as fasting, which is common in many world religions (APA, 2022). If it is part of a culturally approved ritual, it would not be considered avoidant/restrictive food intake disorder.

Differential Diagnosis

Common differential diagnoses for avoidant/restrictive food intake disorder are medical conditions including but not limited to gastrointestinal disease and food allergies, specific neurological or congenital disorders, reactive attachment disorder, autism spectrum disorder, specific phobias or anxiety disorders, anorexia nervosa, OCD, MDD, schizophrenia spectrum disorder, and factitious disorder (APA, 2022). Moving this disorder to the Feeding and Eating Disorders chapter allows it to be looked at across age ranges. Additionally, this disorder has a range of symptoms and presentations, which can make it difficult to diagnosis (Bryant-Waugh, 2019). Selective and restrictive eating behaviors may be associated with anxiety and oppositional symptoms. Equit et al. (2012) found that children who exhibited these restrictive and selective eating behaviors were likely to externalize oppositional symptoms and internalize anxiety symptoms.

Coding, Recording, and Specifiers

There is only one diagnostic code for avoidant/restrictive food intake disorder: F50.8. It should be specified if the disorder is *in remission*. It is in remission if, after the full criteria were met, the diagnostic criteria have not been met for a sustained period of time (APA, 2022). Similar to other disorders in this section, the *DSM-5-TR* does not clarify a specific duration for the *in remission* specifier. Because of the diagnostic criteria for this disorder, counselors can assume that individuals in remission are free of symptoms and have restored all related adverse health effects, such as weight loss and nutritional deficiencies; no longer require enteral feeding or oral nutritional supplements; and have marked improvements in psychosocial functioning.

SPECIFIC EATING DISORDERS

Anorexia Nervosa (F50.0_)

Essential Features

People with anorexia nervosa often view themselves as being overweight, even if they are visibly underweight. They weigh themselves repetitively and often obsess over what they eat and how much they weigh (Joiner at al., 2022; NIMH, 2023). Common symptoms of anorexia nervosa include extreme thinness, an unwillingness to maintain a healthy body weight, restricted eating, and disordered body image (NIMH, 2023; Uri et al., 2021).

Essential features of anorexia nervosa include energy intake restriction, significantly low weight, and an intense fear of becoming fat. In addition, individuals experience a disturbance in their perceived body weight or shape (APA, 2022). Predictors of anorexia nervosa include history of eating disorder, family information, sexual problems, and co-occurring disorders. Counselors should note that an increased risk is present for clients who have biological relatives who have been diagnosed with anorexia, particularly the binge-eating/purging type (APA, 2022). Other genetic risk factors include biological relatives with a history of bipolar or depressive disorders. Children who display anxiety or obsessive-compulsive behavior also have a higher risk of developing anorexia nervosa. Finally, environments in which thinness is valued, including occupations or vocational activities such as modeling or sports, are associated with higher rates of anorexia nervosa (Hilbert, 2020).

Counselors should not underestimate the seriousness of anorexia nervosa. This disorder has one of the highest mortality rates among all psychiatric disorders (APA, 2022). Although rates may vary based on how the death is reported (e.g., heart failure, malnutrition), there is a 4% mortality rate for anorexia nervosa (Crow et al., 2009).

Changes from *DSM-5* to *DSM-5-TR*

There are no major changes from the *DSM-5* to the *DSM-5-TR*. The current calculation of body mass index (BMI) and the requirement that an individual be at "significantly low weight . . . defined as a weight that is less than minimally normal or, for children and adolescents, less than minimally expected" (APA, 2022, p. 382) remain in the updated manual. Individuals who deny having an intense fear of gaining weight will still meet the criterion if they engage in behaviors such as fasting or excessive exercising to prevent or avoid weight gain.

Special Considerations

The prevalence rate for women with anorexia nervosa ranges from 0.4% to 0.9% (APA, 2022). Less is known about prevalence for men with anorexia nervosa, although the rate for lifetime prevalence has been reported at 0.3% (Masheb et al., 2021).

Counselors who work with clients who have eating disorders need to be fully aware of risk factors, including previous treatment for an eating disorder, and consult with others when necessary. Individuals who have been treated for, and have recovered from, anorexia nervosa may still display some eating disorder symptoms such as drive for thinness; however, the symptoms are not as strong following recovery (Kaye et al., 2000). Additionally, these individuals are often fixated on their weight. An important therapeutic goal might be to focus more on a healthy weight range because weight often fluctuates.

According to the NIMH (2023), there are three components in treating anorexia nervosa: (a) restoring the individual to a healthy weight, (b) treating the psychological issues related to the eating disorder, and (c) reducing or eliminating behaviors or thoughts that lead to the eating issue and preventing relapse. CBT is often used in treating clients with anorexia nervosa. Brown et al. (2013) found the CBT approach more effective if the counselor focused on eating and weight gain issues instead of depending on the therapeutic alliance to bring about change.

Family-based treatments may be beneficial when treating adolescents, although more research is needed to determine the full effect. Counselors may face some barriers when working with families, including the time commitment needed from families, parental consistency, and lack of attention to co-occurring symptoms. Additionally, barriers such as not having family meals together can negatively affect treatment. This can stall treatment because the individual with anorexia nervosa needs to be able to work on changing behaviors in real-life situations outside of the counselor's office (Couturier et al., 2013).

Anorexia nervosa occurs across diverse populations but is typically seen more in postindustrialized, high-income countries. One study looking at a military population showed higher rates of anorexia nervosa and bulimia nervosa among women (Masheb et al., 2021). It is important to take into consideration weight concerns across different cultures and regions (APA, 2022). There is evidence that subcultural norms among peer groups can influence attitudes and behaviors about eating (Linville et al., 2011). The prevalence of eating disorders in the United States is higher among White Americans (APA, 2022).

The category of other specified feeding or eating disorder represents current symptom presentation that does not meet the full criteria for the enumerated disorders. Listed in this area are atypical anorexia nervosa, bulimia nervosa (low frequency and/or limited duration), binge-eating disorder (low frequency and/or limited duration), purging disorder, and night eating syndrome (see pp. 396–397 in the *DSM-5-TR*). Atypical anorexia can be particularly easy to miss because individuals can be at normal weight. Counselors should remain knowledgeable about all possible feeding/eating disorders and include specialists as indicated (APA, 2022).

Differential Diagnosis

Common differential diagnoses for anorexia nervosa are medical conditions, MDD, schizophrenia, substance use disorders, social anxiety disorder, OCD, body dysmorphic disorder, bulimia nervosa, and avoidant/restrictive food intake disorder (APA, 2022). Individuals with anorexia nervosa have reported higher functional impairment and lower BMI scores than individuals without eating disorders (Dahlgren et al., 2017).

Coding, Recording, and Specifiers

The *ICD-10-CM* code depends on the subtype, whether it is the *restricting type* (F50.01) or *binge-eating/purging type* (F50.02). In the restricting type, the individual has not engaged in recurrent episodes of binge eating or purging over the last 3 months. Additionally, the presentation in this subtype typically involves weight loss through dieting, fasting, or excessive exercise. In the binge-eating/purging type, the individual has engaged in repetitive episodes of binge eating or purging over the last 3 months (APA, 2022).

Counselors should specify if the disorder is *in full remission* or *in partial remission*. The disorder is in partial remission if, after full criteria were previously met, low body weight has not been met for a sustained period of time, and there is still an intense fear of gaining weight or disturbance in self-perception of weight or shape. The disorder is in full remission if no criteria have been met for a sustained period of time (APA, 2022). The *DSM-5* is unclear about duration needed for remission, but counselors can assume that all physical and medical health concerns, such as low body weight, fear of becoming fat, restriction of food intake, and disturbances in self-perception related to weight, must be reconciled.

Finally, the severity level of the disorder should also be specified. Attained by measuring one's current BMI, these levels are as follows: *mild* (BMI $\geq$ 17 kg/m^2), *moderate* (BMI = 16–16.99 kg/m^2), *severe* (BMI = 15–15.99 kg/m^2), and *extreme* (BMI < 15 kg/m^2; APA, 2022). For children and adolescents, counselors should use the appropriate BMI percentile. This can be calculated by a physician; a BMI percentile calculator for children and adolescents can be found on the CDC website (www.cdc.gov).

Case Example

Taisha is a 36-year-old who identifies as a African American heterosexual woman. She has a successful job in advertising. Taisha has always been worried about her weight. When she was in college, she was worried about getting fat. She exercised a lot and restricted her calories on a regular basis. She was also a picky eater, so she would usually only eat the same things. She said that she exercised a lot because she had always been active as a kid and through high school and played sports. She said that not playing sports in college led her to worry more about gaining weight (or at least the dreaded "freshman 15").

These issues plagued her well into her 20s. When she started graduate school a year after finishing her undergraduate program, she used eating as a way to control some aspects of her life. She was so busy with classes, studying, and being a teaching assistant that she felt like what she ate was the only thing she could control.

Taisha's behaviors have picked up again now that she works nearly 80 hours per week. She said that exercising regularly helps relieve the stress associated with her job. She also said that sometimes she will work out twice a day when she is really stressed and will go to the gym before work and often after pulling a late night at work. She does not eat regularly, and when she does, the portions are very small. She said that watching what she eats is a way to make sure that she does not gain any extra weight.

Diagnostic Questions

1. Do Taisha's presenting symptoms meet the criteria for anorexia nervosa?
2. Based on the disorder identified in Question 1, which symptom(s) led you to select the diagnosis?
3. What would be the reason(s) a counselor may not diagnose Taisha with anorexia nervosa?
4. Would Taisha be more accurately diagnosed with bulimia nervosa? Why or why not?
5. What rule-outs would you consider for Taisha's case?
6. What other information may be needed to make an accurate clinical diagnosis?

Bulimia Nervosa (F50.2)

Essential Features

There are three essential features of bulimia nervosa: recurrent episodes of binge eating, repetitive compensatory behaviors, and self-evaluation that is influenced by body shape and weight. For a diagnosis to be made, binge eating and engaging in compensatory behaviors must occur at least once a week for 3 months (APA, 2022). Binge eating is often triggered by negative affect. Binge-eating episodes may also be set off when there are interpersonal stressors involved along with dietary restraint. After experiencing an episode of binge eating, the individual will engage in an inappropriate compensatory behavior such as purging or excessive exercising (APA, 2022; Hilbert, 2020; Sensi et al., 2022).

Individuals with bulimia nervosa engage in frequent and recurrent episodes of binge eating and then feel a lack of control following those episodes (NIMH, 2023). This lack of control often causes one to engage in behaviors to compensate for binge eating. These behaviors can include vomiting, excessive exercise, and use of laxatives (APA, 2022). Although some studies have shown a lack of relationship between meal frequency and binge eating, restraint theory models propose that the dietary restrictions will often lead to purging behaviors (Masheb et al., 2021). These behaviors, coupled with feelings of lack of control, can make this a cyclical process. Physical symptoms of bulimia nervosa include but are not limited to inflamed and sore throat, swollen salivary glands, worn tooth enamel, and severe dehydration (APA, 2002; NIMH, 2023). A study by Fichter and Quadflieg (2016) showed that mortality rate for bulimia nervosa was significantly lower than anorexia nervosa, although health problems remain a concern.

Special Considerations

The prevalence of bulimia nervosa is 1.0% to 1.5% over a 12-month period (APA, 2022). Individuals with bulimia nervosa are usually at a healthy or normal weight, so it can be difficult to look at someone and determine whether the individual has the disorder (NIMH, 2023). Between 25% to 30% of individuals presenting to treatment centers with bulimia nervosa have had a prior history of anorexia nervosa. Rates of bulimia may increase as adolescents move through young adulthood (Hilbert, 2020; Linville et al., 2011).

CBT is often used when treating clients with bulimia nervosa (NIMH, 2023). Kaye et al. (2000) found that CBT was effective for at least 60% to 70% of individuals with bulimia nervosa and led to remission of binge eating and purging in 30% to 50% of cases. In addition, Kaye et al. pointed out that CBT helps improve some symptoms including body dissatisfaction and perfectionism. CBT for bulimia nervosa can help individuals establish regular meal and snack patterns, breaking chronic restrained eating that has been shown to lead to cycles of binge eating and purging (Masheb et al., 2021). Interpersonal psychotherapy and DBT have also been shown to be effective interventions for clients with bulimia nervosa (Kress & Paylo, 2018).

Differential Diagnosis

Common differential diagnoses for bulimia nervosa are anorexia nervosa, binge-eating/purging type, binge-eating disorder, Kleine-Levin syndrome, MDD with atypical features, and borderline personality (APA, 2022). Individuals with bulimia nervosa noted significantly higher levels of functional impairment, suicidality, and emotional distress than those without bulimia nervosa (Stice et al., 2013).

> ***Note:*** Kleine-Levin syndrome, although rare, is a neurological disorder that causes significant problems with cognitive and behavioral functioning (Arnulf et al., 2005). One of these disturbances includes bulimic-like cravings for food, or compulsive hyperphagia, which may result in self-induced vomiting. Counselors can differentiate between Kleine-Levin syndrome and bulimia nervosa because individuals diagnosed with Kleine-Levin syndrome do not alternate between periods of self-induced vomiting and voluntary fasting.

Coding, Recording, and Specifiers

There is only one diagnostic code for bulimia nervosa: F50.2. It should be specified if the disorder is *in partial remission* or *in full remission*. Partial remission is indicated if some criteria have been met for a sustained period of time after the full criteria had been previously met. Likewise, full remission is indicated if no criteria have been met for a sustained period of time (APA, 2022). Finally, counselors should indicate the current level of severity. Severity is based on the frequency of compensatory behaviors engaged in per week. The levels of severity are *mild* (an average of one to three episodes of inappropriate compensatory behavior per week), *moderate* (an average of four to seven episodes of inappropriate compensatory behavior per week), *severe* (an average of eight to 13 episodes of inappropriate compensatory behavior per week), and *extreme* (an average of 14 or more episodes of inappropriate compensatory behavior per week; APA, 2022).

Case Example

> Nisha is a 21-year-old Indian American female who is in her junior year of college. She is currently seeing a counselor at the college counseling center. She told her counselor that she has had concerns about her weight during adolescence and into her young adult life. Nisha has her sights set on being a professionally trained dancer. She was taught early on to restrict her weight. Looking back, she thinks that her training led to a preoccupation with her weight and body image. She recalls her instructors constantly telling her she was not thin enough even though she dieted continuously. Her friends began to notice her thinness. Nisha has not really been able to get rid of the feeling that she is too fat even though she weighs 110 pounds and is 5 feet 10 inches tall. Nisha has said that she sometimes gets so hungry after dieting for several days at a time that she would lose control of her eating and eat large amounts of cookies, ice cream, and doughnuts, after which she would feel awful about what she just ate and how she broke her diet. She would then force herself to throw up what she had eaten. She disclosed to her counselor that she has repeated this cycle once a week for quite a few years.

Diagnostic Questions

1. Do Nisha's presenting symptoms meet the criteria for bulimia nervosa?
2. Based on the disorder identified in Question 1, which symptom(s) led you to select the diagnosis?
3. What would be the reason(s) a counselor may not diagnose Nisha with bulimia nervosa?
4. Would Nisha be more accurately diagnosed with binge-eating disorder? Why or why not?
5. What rule-outs would you consider for Nisha's case?
6. What other information may be needed to make an accurate clinical diagnosis?

Binge-Eating Disorder (F50.8)

Essential Features

Binge eating involves consuming a large amount of food in a certain period of time. Individuals diagnosed with binge-eating disorder lose control over their ability to control food intake. However, unlike bulimia nervosa, the individual with binge-eating disorder does not engage in any compensatory behaviors, such as taking laxatives, purging, or engaging in excessive exercise (APA, 2022). Past binges may lead to feelings of guilt and shame, which may in turn lead to more binges (NIMH, 2023). Most people who have binge-eating disorder are overweight or obese, but this is not always the case. Obese individuals with binge-eating disorder experience more psychological and medical problems than obese individuals who do not engage in binge eating (Barnes et al., 2011).

An essential feature of binge-eating disorder is recurrent episodes of excessive eating in a short period of time. These episodes must occur, on average, at least once per week for 3 months. A binge-eating episode is defined as "eating, in a discrete period of time, an amount of food that is definitely larger than most people would eat in a similar period of time under similar circumstances" (APA, 2022, pp. 350–351). Counselors should also consider the context of where the eating occurs when determining if the amount of food is excessive. Individuals who are of normal weight, overweight, or obese can be diagnosed with binge-eating disorder.

Special Considerations

The 12-month prevalence of binge-eating disorder in the United States is 1.6% among adult women and 0.8% among adult men (APA, 2022). There is higher prevalence of the disorder for those who are in treatment for weight loss compared with the general population (APA, 2022). When evaluating clients who have been diagnosed with binge-eating disorder, counselors should examine at least two specific examples of their binge-eating behaviors. This will provide information about the food eaten as well as the context in which it was consumed (Berg & Peterson, 2013). Binge eating is somewhat of an abstract concept, so it might be difficult for an individual to be able to conceptualize the amount of food consumed. This could lead to one minimizing how much food is eaten or to deny if a large amount of food has been eaten.

Treatment for binge-eating disorder is similar to treatment for bulimia nervosa. CBT has been shown to be an effective treatment (NIMH, 2023). Because individuals with binge-eating disorder tend to eat a similar number of meals but consume a higher frequency of snacks than individuals without binge-eating disorder, CBT techniques can help individuals reduce overeating and atypical behaviors by reducing cognitions associated with their current eating behaviors (Masheb et al., 2021).

Prevalence rates of binge-eating disorder in ethnic or racial minority females are similar to the rates for White females. It should also be noted that binge-eating disorder is seen mostly in industrialized countries (APA, 2022).

Differential Diagnosis

Common differential diagnoses for binge-eating disorder are bulimia nervosa, obesity, bipolar and depressive disorders, and borderline personality disorders. One of the distinguishing differences between binge-eating disorder and bulimia nervosa is that the compensatory behaviors (i.e., purging, excessive exercising) seen in bulimia nervosa are not present in binge-eating disorder (APA, 2022).

When bipolar or depressive disorders are also present, it is important to look for full criteria for both disorders if one is to make a diagnosis of both disorders. Binge eating is part of the impulsive behavior criterion for borderline personality disorder. If full criteria for both disorders are met, a diagnosis for both disorders should be made (APA, 2022). Individuals who binge eat may also be more likely to display higher depressive or negative affect, which may, in turn, lead to greater levels of binge eating.

Coding, Recording, and Specifiers

There is only one diagnostic code for binge-eating disorder: F50.8. It should be specified if the disorder is *in partial remission* or *in full remission*. The disorder should be specified as partial remission if binge eating occurs at an average frequency of less than one episode per week for a sustained period of time after the full criteria had been previously met. Full remission should be specified if none of the criteria have been met for a sustained period of time after the full criteria had been previously met (APA, 2022). Finally, counselors should also indicate the current level of severity. The levels of severity are *mild* (one to three binge-eating episodes per week), *moderate* (four to seven binge-eating episodes per week), *severe* (eight to 13 binge-eating episodes per week), and *extreme* (14 binge-eating episodes per week; APA, 2022).

Case Example

> Mikeal is a 35-year-old, 6-feet, 280-pound man who presented to the clinic to discuss problems with his eating habits over the years. He was an athlete in high school and college; frequent athletic practices allowed him to eat whatever he wanted and not see any changes in his weight. Many of his friends have commented on his large appetite. He could eat two pizzas, a bag of popcorn, a gallon of ice cream, and a two-liter soda during a movie. After graduation, Mikeal still ate these large amounts of food. He began to notice that eating these large amounts of food without any physical activity caused him to gain weight. He started to feel unhappy about his appearance, which then led him to feel unhappy about other parts of his life. When he felt unhappy, he turned to food to comfort him.
>
> Over the past few months, Mikeal began to notice some changes in his eating habits. He started to experience a lack of control with his eating. He stated that now he often feels like he cannot stop eating, whereas before he would choose to eat larger amounts of food but was able to stop eating. Mikeal has started to feel ashamed about his eating as well as the fact that he has gained more weight recently. His family, originally from Latvia, has noticed these binges and has encouraged him to try and control his eating. Mikeal tried dieting and would eat only salads and healthy sandwiches while at work. However, he found himself eating large amounts of food by himself whenever he got home from work at night. He states he feels ashamed and doesn't know what to do.

Diagnostic Questions

1. Do Mikeal's presenting symptoms meet the criteria for binge-eating disorder?
2. Based on the disorder identified in Question 1, which symptom(s) led you to select the diagnosis?
3. What would be the reason(s) a counselor may not diagnose Mikeal with binge-eating disorder?
4. Would Mikeal be more accurately diagnosed with bulimia nervosa? Why or why not?
5. What rule-outs would you consider for Mikeal's case?
6. What other information may be needed to make an accurate clinical diagnosis?

ELIMINATION DISORDERS

Elimination disorders involve repeated voluntary or involuntary voiding of urine (enuresis) or passing of feces (encopresis) at inappropriate times (APA, 2022; Comer, 2017). The disorders are diagnosed after an age when it is assumed an individual should be able to control these functions. In general, prevalence of the disorder decreases with age; only about 1% of children experience symptoms by age 13 (Comer, 2017).

Differential Diagnoses

Differential diagnoses for elimination disorders center primarily around medical conditions and medication side effects (APA, 2022). It is important to ensure that symptoms are not related to medical problems, medications, or normal development. A thorough assessment of background and medical history is essential and beyond the scope of counseling practice; counselors should refer individuals for a medical examination prior to diagnosing the disorder.

Etiology and Treatment

There are multiple theories as to the etiology of elimination disorders; the research in this area does not clearly endorse one explanation over others (Comer, 2017; Shapira & Dahlen, 2010). Theories regarding enuresis include biological reasons, such as reduced bladder capacity related to developmental delays or inability to produce the normal amount of antidiuretic hormones. Enuresis may run along familial lines because children whose fathers reported nighttime issues of bedwetting are 10 times as likely to experience nocturnal bedwetting (APA, 2022). Additional theories include anxious response to conflict or problematic family situations, abuse (Comer, 2017), and slow or inappropriate toilet training (APA, 2022; Comer, 2017). The most common theory for etiology of involuntary encopresis seems to be biological, specifically that it relates to intestinal functioning and repeated constipation (Comer, 2017). Whereas environment may also be a factor in involuntary encopresis, voluntary encopresis, which is much less common, may be related to another mental disorder, such as ODD (APA, 2022).

Elimination disorders will resolve with age for most individuals, but treatments can assist in accelerating this process. Behavioral therapy is often effective in treating nocturnal enuresis. Specific examples of this include the urine alarm treatment and dry-bed training (Comer, 2017). Other therapies include retention control training, stream interruption exercises, overlearning, and cleanliness training (Shepard et al., 2017). A variety of medications can be prescribed to assist in decreasing these symptoms, and alternative therapies such as hypnotherapy and acupuncture have been suggested (Shapira & Dahlen, 2010). Whereas behavioral therapy may be more effective in the long term than certain types of medications, combination therapies using both may be most effective for enuresis and encopresis. For encopresis, the use of behavioral therapies along with addressing constipation has been shown effective. Constipation can be addressed through medication but also through diet, increasing fiber and water, and cutting out foods such as cheese. Other treatments may include biofeedback and mineral oils (Comer, 2017; Shepard et al., 2017). Making recommendations regarding nutrition or medications is outside the scope of counseling practice; counselors should always collaborate with medical professionals when navigating these decisions.

Implications for Counselors

Because shame, family problems, social withdrawal, and embarrassment are associated with elimination disorders (APA, 2022; Comer, 2017), counselors should take care to offer safe and accepting environments in which children can begin to express emotions related to these disorders, which may include behavioral or emotional problems (Hilbert, 2020). Children experiencing elimination disorders can have low self-esteem and fear of rejection by caregivers or peers. In addition to encouraging positive coping, counselors need to focus on therapies that are shown to be effective with children. Furthermore, counselors can address family systems as appropriate and give information on additional evidence-based treatments such as behavioral therapies and referrals for medication assessment (Kress & Paylo, 2018).

Enuresis (F98.0)

Essential Features

Enuresis is characterized by repeatedly urinating at inappropriate times, either voluntarily or involuntarily. Often referred to as "wetting" or "bed-wetting," this disorder is diagnosed after the age of 5, or when it becomes clear that the individual is developmentally at the level where they should be able to control this bodily function. Enuresis affects a surprisingly large number of children. Comer (2017) reported that between 13% and 33% of children have had an experience with bed-wetting, and one in 10 children will meet criteria for enuresis at some point. Voluntary and daytime inappropriate urination occurs at a lower rate (APA, 2022).

Individuals who experience enuresis either voluntarily or involuntarily urinate repeatedly and inappropriately in bed or in their clothing. The individual must be at least 5 years of age, and the episodes must occur at least twice a week for 3 consecutive months. This cannot be related to a medical condition, substance, or medication side effects and must be impairing or clinically significant (APA, 2022).

Special Considerations

Although enuresis has a high prevalence, there continues to be a stigma around these symptoms. Children who have this disorder often experience teasing, restricted social interactions, decreased self-confidence, and embarrassment related to the family secret (Kress & Paylo, 2018). Counselors should be careful to address the emotional impact of this disorder on the individual and family system. Boys tend to experience nocturnal enuresis more frequently than do girls, whereas girls struggle more with diurnal enuresis than boys. For both, the symptoms diminish greatly with age, with less than 1% of those over 18 years of age continuing to have symptoms (APA, 2022). Most data suggest that the rate of enuresis does not change with ethnicity or geographic area.

Differential Diagnosis

Differential diagnoses for enuresis typically involve medical conditions or influence of a medication that induces incontinence (APA, 2022). Counselors should inquire about physical conditions or medications that clients may be taking that could affect urination during the day or night. ODD criteria should also be considered as a differential diagnosis.

Coding, Recording, and Specifiers

There is only one code for enuresis: F98.0. APA (2022) allows for three different specifiers: *nocturnal only* (at night), *diurnal only* (waking hours), or a combination of *nocturnal and diurnal*.

Case Example

> Allison is a 6-year-old Caucasian girl who wets the bed almost every night. Her mother is very frustrated, stating that this did not occur with the older siblings whom she potty trained the same way. Allison's father is much more compassionate, reporting that he had the same issues as a child and understands how difficult this must be for Allison. Her parents have brought her to counseling because she cries all morning after the accidents, and they have trouble getting her to go to school. Furthermore, Allison tells you that she had a friend stay over at her house and she wet the bed that night. The friend found out and told other students, who now tease her.
>
> Allison and her parents deny any history of physical or sexual abuse. She is not on medications but hasn't been to a medical doctor in 2 years. She has never been to counseling before and performs very well in school. However, her grades are beginning to suffer because of chronic tardiness. She has begun refusing to talk to her classmates.

Diagnostic Questions

1. Do Allison's presenting symptoms meet the criteria for an elimination disorder? If so, which one?
2. Would be the reason(s) a counselor would not diagnose Allison with an elimination disorder?
3. Would she be accurately diagnosed with enuresis?
4. What rule-outs would you consider?
5. What other information may be needed to make an accurate clinical diagnosis?

Encopresis (F98.1)

Essential Features

There have been no major changes to the criteria for encopresis in the *DSM-5-TR*. Encopresis occurs less frequently than enuresis, occurs mainly in males, and has been associated with low socioeconomic status (APA, 2022; Comer, 2017).

Encopresis refers to defecating at inappropriate times, either voluntarily or involuntarily. This will occur at least once a month for 3 months or longer. The diagnosis can only be made after the child is 4 years of age and cannot be given if the symptoms can be explained by a medical condition, substance use, or medications (APA, 2022).

Special Considerations

Encopresis occurs most often in males and is largely due to constipation and intestinal tract issues. For some individuals, the experience of this disorder can be quite painful and shaming. These individuals may experience fear of engaging in normal childhood experiences, social problems, and anxiety or depression (Christophersen & Friman, 2010). These individuals may also experience ongoing urinary tract infections (APA, 2022). As with enuresis, encopresis does not appear to be associated with ethnicity but is more prevalent in low-income groups.

Differential Diagnosis

Differential diagnoses for encopresis would typically involve medical conditions or the influence of a medication that may induce involuntary defecation (APA, 2022). Counselors should always inquire about physical conditions or medications that clients may be taking.

Coding, Recording, and Specifiers

There is only one code for encopresis: F98.1. Counselors can specify *with constipation and overflow incontinence* or *without constipation and overflow incontinence*. With constipation and overflow incontinence is typically involuntary in nature, and the related feces may not hold shape. Without constipation and overflow incontinence occurs when incontinence is not present, does not occur frequently, and is often associated with intentional defecation (APA, 2022).

SLEEP-WAKE DISORDERS

Sleeping difficulties can have a profound impact on quality of life and can result in major negative effects to everyday functioning, including mental and physical well-being, productivity, and safety (Szentkirályi et al., 2009). The National Highway Traffic Safety Administration (n.d.) estimates that in 2021, there were 684 fatalities in the United States due to drivers who fall asleep or are drowsy behind the wheel. Sleep-wake disorders can take both emotional and financial tolls in people's lives.

Changes From *DSM-5* to *DSM-5-TR*

There have been no major changes to sleep-wake disorders in the *DSM-5-TR*. Sleep-wake disorders underwent changes in the *DSM-5* to enhance the clinical utility, validity, and reliability of the diagnoses. These changes are also in alignment with the findings of sleep disorder medicine.

Most counselors will not be diagnosing sleep-wake disorders, so we cover essential features and special considerations we feel counselors may need to know when working with clients diagnosed with these conditions. We encourage counselors who are working with clients experiencing sleep disorders to consult with medical professionals and sleep specialists and to seek training in the areas of sleep dysfunction, because this is not an area commonly addressed in counselor training.

Insomnia Disorder (G47.00)

> What is really frustrating is when I am lying there and really want to fall asleep so my body is already tired but I can't shut my mind off enough to fall asleep. When I wake up in the night, time seems really weird, and I keep hoping it's earlier in the night so there's a chance I can get sleep. Then I wake up in the morning like that, and I am still really tired because I haven't really slept anyway so I can't function at work, even with tons of coffee.—Christa

Essential Features

Insomnia disorder affects about one third of adults (APA, 2022), and women present about two times more than men with this disorder. Individuals with insomnia disorder experience great difficulty falling asleep and maintaining sleep, as well as early-morning awakening with inability to return to sleep. These symptoms create significant clinical distress in these individuals' lives and must occur at least 3 nights per week for at least 3 months (APA, 2022).

Special Considerations

Clients will often come to counseling because of problems with their sleep. Oftentimes, they have been having sleep difficulties for months or even years, and it has been negatively affecting their work or personal life. Counselors will frequently hear clients complain of going to bed at a certain time and lying awake for several hours, sometimes until the early morning, before finally drifting off to sleep. In contrast, some clients might have no difficulties falling asleep at night but wake up 1 to 3 hours before their alarm clock goes off and be unable to fall back asleep.

Insomnia contributes to poor physical and emotional health (Kalmbach et al., 2018). In diagnosing and treating insomnia disorder, counselors need to explore other contributing factors to the sleep disturbances, including poor sleep hygiene, use of psychostimulants, and psychosocial stressors such as job loss, divorce, or financial problems. Counselors should consider referral to a sleep disorder specialist for comprehensive assessment. Additionally, this disorder is highly comorbid with anxiety disorders, MDD, and other sleep-related disorders (APA, 2022). Therefore, counselors should pinpoint why the sleep difficulties are occurring in order to find the best treatment. There is one diagnostic code for insomnia disorder: G47.00. See the *DSM-5-TR* for specifiers.

Hypersomnolence Disorder (G47.10) and Narcolepsy (G47.4 _ _)

> Sometimes I sleep as much as 14 hours a day. I know I shouldn't be tired but I still am. I feel as though I could never stop sleeping. My coworkers look at me suspiciously and suggest I should see a doctor. I know they think I'm taking drugs but I'm not.—Philip

Essential Features

Although counselors will most likely not be diagnosing hypersomnolence disorder or narcolepsy, it is important for them to know the symptoms of these disorders. Clients displaying these symptoms should be referred to a medical professional for further evaluation. Hypersomnolence disorder is characterized by excessive sleepiness despite having a full night's sleep with difficulty being fully awake throughout the day. Narcolepsy is a neurological disorder that has maintained its name in the *DSM-5-TR*. It is characterized by periods of uncontrollable need to sleep, lapsing into sleep, or napping occurring in the same day. Hypersomnolence disorder affects about 4% to 6% of the population, whereas narcolepsy is much more rare, affecting 0.02% to 0.04% of the population (APA, 2022).

Clients with these two disorders will often complain of feeling overly tired, even after getting a full night's sleep. Individuals with hypersomnolence disorder may often complain of feeling so tired that they need to nap throughout the day. Another common symptom is that individuals may fall asleep the night before and wake up in the late afternoon the next day, often sleeping through important responsibilities such as work or school. Clients with narcolepsy will frequently complain of an irrepressible need to sleep that comes out of nowhere throughout the day. Some individuals experience this need to sleep while driving and will need to pull over and nap before continuing to drive. These individuals will most likely already be diagnosed with narcolepsy by their medical doctor before coming in to see a counselor.

Special Considerations

Hypersomnolence disorder is comorbid with mood disorders, specifically depressive disorders or episodes (APA, 2022). Other causes for this disorder can include an inability to cope with stress or the need to fill a void by sleeping (Morrison, 2006). It is important for counselors to treat the depressive symptoms and explore other reasons why clients are experiencing these clinically distressing sleep disturbances. Counselors need to explore the reason for the sleep disorder and may need to refer a client to a medical doctor for medication.

Narcolepsy is strongly hereditary (Morrison, 2006), and the onset is typically in childhood or adolescence (APA, 2022). Counselors should complete a family history assessment if clients are experiencing symptoms related to narcolepsy and have not yet been diagnosed by a medical doctor. Narcolepsy may co-occur with other disorders such as bipolar disorder, depressive disorders, and anxiety disorders. There is one diagnostic code for hypersomnolence disorder: G47.10. Diagnostic coding for narcolepsy depends on medical conditions such as cataplexy, hypocretin deficiencies, or Type 2 diabetes. Please see the *DSM-5-TR* for recording criteria.

Breathing-Related Sleep Disorders

Essential Features

In the *DSM-5-TR*, breathing-related sleep disorders are divided into three distinct disorders: obstructive sleep apnea hypopnea, central sleep apnea, and sleep-related hypoventilation. Obstructive sleep apnea hypopnea is characterized by sleeping disturbances such as snoring, gasping, breathing pauses during sleep, or daytime sleepiness or fatigue despite sufficient sleep the night before. Central sleep apnea is characterized by apneas (temporary suspension of breathing) and hypopneas (abnormally shallow and slow breathing) during sleep caused by inconsistency in respiratory effort. Sleep-related hypoventilation is characterized by decreased respiration associated with elevated CO_2 levels (APA, 2022). Physicians normally give a polysomnograph to individuals experiencing any of these symptoms to verify any breathing-related sleep disorders diagnosis. Although breathing-related sleep disorders can only be formally diagnosed by medical doctors with a polysomnograph, it is important for counselors to recognize the symptoms of these disorders, because clients who display symptoms of a breathing-related sleep disorder and are not diagnosed with one should be referred to a medical doctor for further evaluation.

Clients suffering from breathing-related sleep disorders often have partners who complain about their snoring or who report that they temporarily stop breathing or have shallow breathing while sleeping. Counselors may hear clients themselves complain of fatigue, morning headaches, impotence, restlessness at night, irritability, cognitive deficiencies, sweating, sleep talking, or sleep terrors associated with these disorders (Morrison, 2006). If clients are displaying these symptoms and have not previously been diagnosed with a breathing-related sleep disorder, counselors should refer them for a medical evaluation as soon as possible.

Special Considerations

Obstructive sleep apnea hypopnea is the most common breathing-related sleep disorder. It is even more common in older adults, affecting more than 20% of these individuals. If an older client complains about sleep disturbances or daytime sleepiness, they should be referred to a medical doctor for an evaluation, because breathing-related sleep disorders are potentially lethal (Kalmbach et al., 2018; Morrison, 2006). Also, as with other sleep-wake disorders, obstructive sleep apnea hypopnea is strongly hereditary (APA, 2022), and counselors should complete a full family history during the intake process. Counselors should note that obesity is often a predisposing factor to developing sleep-related hypoventilation. Unlike obstructive sleep apnea hypopnea, which counselors are likely to see, both central sleep apnea and sleep-related hypoventilation are rare disorders, and the unique prevalence is unknown (APA, 2022). Counselors will most likely not see these disorders present in their clients. It is important, however, to recognize the implications of these disorders and how their symptoms manifest in clients.

Parasomnias

> I could feel my heart pounding and I was sweating. It was always dark and I would run as fast as I could but I never got away. The monster was always right behind me in the shadows. I would wake up with my bed covers wrapped around my legs. I had been running in my sleep again.—Sue

Essential Features

Parasomnias are characterized by abnormal occurrences during sleep. The parasomnias section of the *DSM-5-TR* comprises three separate disorders; non–rapid eye movement (NREM) sleep arousal disorders, nightmare disorder, and REM sleep behavior disorder (APA, 2022).

NREM sleep arousal disorders are characterized by episodes of incomplete awakening from sleep accompanied by either sleepwalking or sleep terrors (abrupt and panicked arousal from sleep; APA, 2022). Individuals with NREM sleep arousal disorders usually have no recollection of the dream or the episode of sleepwalking or sleep terror. Sleepwalking carries a very high lifetime prevalence of 29.2% in adults, but not all adults who sleepwalk have NREM sleep arousal disorders (APA, 2022). Episodes of sleep terrors are less common in adults and much more common in children, with a prevalence of up to 36.9% (APA, 2022).

Nightmare disorder is characterized by extended and dysphoric dreams that the individual can remember vividly. These dreams can be quite frightening and usually involve the individual feeling a threat to their safety or security. Nightmares often occur after a traumatic event, forcing the individual to relive the trauma. In adults, there is a 6% prevalence of nightmares occurring at least once per month, whereas frequent nightmares are less common, ranging from 1% to 2% (APA, 2022). Counselors should note that nightmare disorder should not be diagnosed if an individual only has one nightmare, because nightmares are common among the general population. The reoccurrence and duration of the nightmares must be considered before counselors diagnose nightmare disorder.

Lastly, REM sleep behavior disorder is characterized by repeated episodes of arousal from REM sleep. This often occurs with loud vocalization or violent motor behaviors such as kicking, punching, hitting, or jumping out of bed. These behaviors often reflect the individual's dream and can be quite disturbing to their partner. This disorder is rare, occurring in approximately 0.38% to 0.5% of the general population (APA, 2022).

Special Considerations

Parasomnias can be very disturbing to both the individual and the partner sharing a bed. Individuals coming for counseling might not remember sleepwalking or having sleep terrors, but their partners can certainly testify to these nighttime disturbances. NREM sleep arousal disorders have been associated with serious bodily harm to self and others and have been associated with homicide, automobile accidents, and destruction of property (Fleetham & Flemming, 2014). It is important for counselors to make detailed notes of episodes of sleepwalking in case the individual's records are subpoenaed by court.

Parasomnias have been found to be strongly comorbid with other disorders. Sleepwalking has been associated with major depressive episodes and OCD. Nightmare disorder is frequently comorbid with PTSD, insomnia, schizophrenia, mood disorders, anxiety disorders, adjustment disorders, and personality disorders. REM sleep behavior disorder is also present in approximately 30% of individuals diagnosed with narcolepsy (APA, 2022). It is important for counselors to distinguish whether the parasomnia is occurring due to another psychiatric disorder or if it is a separate diagnosis.

Circadian Rhythm Sleep-Wake Disorders

Circadian rhythm sleep-wake disorders are characterized by the relative absence of a circadian pattern in an individual's sleep-wake cycle (Zee & Vitiello, 2009). The subtypes of circadian rhythm sleep-wake disorders include *delayed sleep phase type*, *advanced sleep phase type*, *irregular sleep-wake type*, *non-24-hour sleep-wake type*, and *shift work type.*

Essential Features

Delayed sleep phase type is characterized by delayed sleep onset and awakening without being able to fall asleep and awaken when desired. This type of disorder has a prevalence of 7% in adolescents. Advanced sleep phase type is characterized by advanced sleep onset and awakening times without the ability to remain awake or asleep when desired. This type of disorder has a prevalence of 1% in middle-aged adults. Irregular sleep-wake type is characterized by a disorganized sleep-wake pattern that is variable throughout a 24-hour period. Prevalence of this type is unknown. Non-24-hour sleep-wake type is characterized by sleep-wake cycles not synchronized to the 24-hour environment, consisting of a consistent daily drift of sleep onset and wake times. This type of disorder is very common in individuals who are blind, with prevalence rates of 50%. Lastly, shift work type is characterized by insomnia during major sleep times or sleepiness during major awake times related to an unconventional shift work schedule. This type of disorder is prevalent in 5% to 10% of individuals who work overnight (APA, 2022).

Special Considerations

Counselors should be aware of comorbidity with some types of circadian rhythm sleep-wake disorders. Delayed sleep phase type is strongly comorbid with depression, personality disorders, somatic symptom disorder, or illness anxiety disorder. Irregular sleep-wake type is comorbid with neurodegenerative and neurodevelopmental disorders such as major neurocognitive disorder, intellectual developmental disorder, and traumatic brain injuries. Non-24-hour sleep-wake type is comorbid with blindness, and shift work type is comorbid with substance use disorders and depression.

Treatment interventions for circadian rhythm sleep-wake disorders can include prescribed sleep scheduling, circadian phase shifting, hypnosis, and stimulant medications. Counselors can plan with clients to ensure that they are getting plenty of sunlight during the day to reset their body's natural circadian rhythm and make sure they have a set time to sleep and wake up each day. Taking melatonin in the afternoon or evening can promote a regular sleep cycle (Kress & Paylo, 2018). Counselors should inform clients that they should always check with a medical professional before taking melatonin or any other sleep aid.

Restless Legs Syndrome (G25.81)

> My experience has been that it usually happens when I'm just about to fall asleep and my leg starts twitching so it wakes me up. I try to relax so the twitching stops but as soon as I relax the twitching starts again and it's uncontrollable.—Arno

Restless legs syndrome is a neurological sleep disorder characterized by an irresistible urge to move the legs or arms, which is relieved by movement. This disorder is associated with uncomfortable sensations in the limbs, usually worsening in the evening and at night. The prevalence of this disorder varies widely, with a range of 2% to 7% (APA, 2022). Depressive and anxiety disorders are often comorbid with restless legs syndrome.

Substance/Medication-Induced Sleep Disorder

The key feature of substance/medication-induced sleep disorder is a clinically significant sleep disturbance that is attributable to the effects of a substance (APA, 2022). There are four specifier types for this disorder: *insomnia type*, *daytime sleepiness type*, *parasomnia type*, and *mixed type*. Specify if *with onset during intoxication* or *with onset during discontinuation/withdrawal*. Females are affected more than males by a 2:1 ratio.

SEXUAL DYSFUNCTIONS

Sexual functioning is an essential part of well-being. Disturbances in sexual desire or problems with physiological functions that characterize sexual responses are included in the Sexual Dysfunctions chapter of the *DSM-5-TR*. Sexual disturbances, such as delayed ejaculation or erectile disorder, cause marked distress and interpersonal difficulties in those who experience them (APA, 2022; Crooks et al., 2020).

These dysfunctions interfere with one's desire to achieve and maintain healthy sexual functioning and can be related to significant distress, including depressive symptoms and lower reported quality of life (Crooks et al., 2020). Problems related to sexual disturbances can also be compounded by feelings of shame from individuals who experience them. Seeking help for sexual problems is often difficult, so clients do not typically present for counseling until the problem causes hardship in their social or interpersonal relationships (Crooks et al., 2020; Hyde & DeLamater, 2013).

Masters and Johnson (1966) outlined a four-stage model of the human sexual response cycle: excitement, plateau, orgasm, and resolution. As a result of their model, societal norms surrounding sexuality and medical developments have made significant headway in rethinking how the mental health and medical communities define healthy sexuality. For example, medical advances in addressing erectile dysfunction have aided men in achieving an erection with the use of psychosexual therapies, pharmacological treatments, or both. Although these advances are quite significant for men who are diagnosed with sexual dysfunctions, there is still a considerable amount of research that needs to be conducted regarding female dysfunction. There is also a dearth of research on the understanding of sexual dysfunctions and their treatment within different cultures (Irfan et al., 2020; Moreau et al., 2016).

Special Considerations

For assessment purposes, it is important for counselors to refer clients with sexual problems and dysfunctions to a medical professional for examination. Additionally, counselors need to address both psychological and biological factors that may contribute to the dysfunction and always be aware that these issues are difficult for people to talk about and are often misunderstood, especially between partners (Crooks et al., 2022; Hyde & DeLamater, 2013).

Sexual dysfunctions can also be a major contributor to co-occurring mental health disorders such as MDD or a substance use disorder. Counselors should consider co-occurring conditions in assessment and treatment planning. Finally, counselors must also never fail to take into consideration the clients' cultural worldview and norms within their society about sexual functioning (APA, 2022).

The Sexual Dysfunctions chapter in the *DSM-5-TR* includes delayed ejaculation, erectile disorder, female orgasmic disorder, female sexual interest/arousal disorder, genito-pelvic pain/penetration disorder, male hypoactive sexual desire disorder, premature (early) ejaculation, and substance/medication-induced sexual dysfunction (APA, 2022). As with most diagnoses in the *DSM-5-TR*, other specified and unspecified sexual dysfunctions are also listed. Counselors should note these disorders do not occur in isolation; if an individual meets the criteria for several diagnoses, all relevant sexual dysfunctions should be diagnosed (APA, 2022).

Changes From *DSM-5* to *DSM-5-TR*

The Sexual Dysfunctions chapter, dedicated solely to disturbances in sexual desire or problems related to physiological sexual functioning, was a new chapter in the *DSM-5*. There are no major changes in the *DSM-5-TR*.

Coding, Recording, and Specifiers for All Sexual Dysfunctions

There is only one diagnostic code for each disorder within the Sexual Dysfunctions chapter of the *DSM-5-TR*:

- Delayed ejaculation, F52.32
- Erectile disorder, F52.21
- Female orgasmic disorder, F52.31
- Female sexual interest/arousal disorder, F52.22
- Genito-pelvic pain/penetration disorder, F52.6
- Male hypoactive sexual desire disorder, F52.0
- Premature (early) ejaculation, F52.4

The same subtype indicators are used for each disorder to designate the onset of the difficulty, the level of severity, and whether the disorder occurs in all instances or only in some situations. These indicators include whether delayed ejaculation has been *lifelong* or *acquired*. The *acquired* specifier indicates whether the problem began after the client had established normal sexual function. Also indicated for each sexual dysfunction disorder are specifiers of *generalized*, meaning they are not situational, and *situational*, which indicates dysfunction with specific stimulations or partners. Counselors will also need to indicate current severity of *mild*, *moderate*, or *severe*, which is indicated by the evidence of distress experienced by the client.

The coding for substance/medication-induced sexual dysfunction is noted for the specific substance/medication (see page 504 of the *DSM-5-TR*). The coding includes the specific substance/medication in the diagnosis and is also accompanied by specifiers in relation to *with onset during intoxication, with onset during withdrawal,* or *with onset after medication use.* Counselors will also need to indicate current severity of *mild, moderate,* or *severe,* which is indicated by the evidence of distress experienced by the client.

The following sections outline each disorder within the Sexual Dysfunctions chapter of the *DSM-5-TR.* Readers should note this is not a stand-alone resource for diagnosis. Although a summary and special considerations for counselors are provided for each disorder, when diagnosing clients, counselors need to reference the *DSM-5-TR.* It is essential that the diagnostic criteria and features, subtypes and specifiers, prevalence, course, risk, and prognostic factors for each disorder are clearly understood prior to diagnosis.

Delayed Ejaculation (F52.32)

> My partner eventually got frustrated and left me. At first, he enjoyed that I could go long periods of time without ejaculating, but eventually he would want to discontinue and I didn't. He would stop enjoying himself long before I could finish. We were both frustrated.—Thomas

Essential Features

Delayed ejaculation is the marked delay in or inability to achieve ejaculation, either during intercourse or with manual stimulation (APA, 2022). During delayed ejaculation, a male is able to attain sexual stimulation and has the desire to ejaculate but is unable to do so. Although the *DSM-5-TR* does not stipulate what length of time is adequate in achieving ejaculation, the delay must not be purposeful or a result of any other physical or psychological problems or be a result of substance/medication use (APA, 2022). Also referred to as "retarded ejaculation," "inhibited ejaculation," or "anejaculation," the emotional impact of this disorder is severe because it typically results in a lack of sexual fulfillment for both the man and his partner.

Problems with delayed ejaculation can range from significant delay in ejaculation or a complete inability to ejaculate. Some men with delayed ejaculation report being able to ejaculate during masturbation but not through intercourse. Delayed ejaculation is a self-report diagnosis, and symptoms must be present for a minimum of approximately 6 months (APA, 2022). Because the *DSM-5-TR* does not stipulate a length of time when ejaculation should occur, the clinical impression should be made as to the significant distress of the man or his partner. After prolonged stimulation, the man may feel frustrated as he fails to reach orgasm, or his partner may feel pain from continued intercourse. In such cases, a diagnosis of delayed ejaculation is appropriate.

Special Considerations

Delayed ejaculation is usually reported in early sexual experiences and continues over the course of a man's life span. Although delayed ejaculation varies across countries and cultures, Asian populations have presented with more complaints than men in Europe, Australia, or the United States (APA, 2022). If a man has never ejaculated through any form of stimulation including wet dreams, masturbation, or intercourse, counselors should always consult with a medical professional to determine if there is a physical cause. The most common causes for delayed ejaculation are psychological and could include life stressors (e.g., stress at work), lack of attraction for partner, atypical sexual or masturbation patterns, traumatic events, substance use or medications, or neurological damage (Corona et al., 2013). In terms of differential diagnoses, medications, medical illness, injury, and emotional or mental stressors can interfere with ejaculation and should be considered by counselors. In some cases, situational experiences, such as the choice of partner, can contribute to delays or an inability to ejaculate (Corona et al., 2013).

Erectile Disorder (F52.21)

> It's been so embarrassing that I just quit trying to date at all. I told my friends that I'm done with women, but honestly, I've tried to have sex different times and just can't keep an erection, even during oral sex. Then I get anxious and it gets worse. I miss the days when I felt like a real man.—Josh

Essential Features

Erectile disorder (ED) is the repeated inability to develop or maintain an erection during sexual stimulation or activity (APA, 2022). The inability to achieve or maintain an erection must occur at least 75% of the time over the course of at least 6 months. As with delayed ejaculation, ED may persist throughout one's lifetime or develop within one's lifetime, hence the specifiers *lifelong* or *acquired.* ED can also be situational, only occurring in certain situations or with certain partners. ED is often extremely disturbing to men and may cause low self-esteem, low self-confidence, a decreased sense of masculinity, and depressed affect (APA, 2022).

Special Considerations

The prevalence of ED in the general population is strongly correlated to age (APA, 2022). The *DSM-5-TR* highlights that 20% of men fear erectile problems and 8% experience some erectile problems with their first sexual experience. Similar to most sexual dysfunctions, ED can interfere with fertility and further compound individual and interpersonal distress (APA, 2022). Cultural factors are unknown and have been found to vary across countries. Because ED is a self-report diagnosis, counselors should also consider erectile expectations within the client's cultural background.

Differential Diagnosis

Special consideration should be made as to the man's expectations of what sexual functioning means to him and his partner for a diagnosis of ED. MDD and ED are closely associated (Crooks et al., 2020). Secondary causes of ED can stem from the use of alcohol, substances, and medications that can cause decreases in erectile function. If the cause is due to a medical condition, the individual would not receive a mental health diagnosis (APA, 2022).

Female Orgasmic Disorder (F52.31)

> I wouldn't say I've never had an orgasm, but it's been so long that I couldn't tell when the last time was. My boyfriend takes it personally. He gets his feelings hurt, especially when I try to pretend. I think he will leave me soon.—Carole

Essential Features

Female orgasmic disorder represents difficulty in experiencing orgasm or markedly reduced intensity of orgasmic sensations on almost all or all (approximately 75% to 100%) occasions of sexual activity (APA, 2022). The symptoms need to be present for a minimum of 6 months. The *DSM-5* does not operationally define marked delay in orgasm. The *DSM-5-TR* does report that there are measurable physiological changes that occur during female orgasm, including changes in hormones, pelvic floor musculature, and brain activation; however, it is unclear to what degree this affects a woman's overall satisfaction with sexual activity (APA, 2022).

Special Considerations

The prevalence of female orgasmic disorder in women varies from 10% to 42% depending on multiple factor such as age, culture, duration, and severity of symptoms. Studies have shown that these numbers did not account for distress; only a proportion of women experiencing female orgasmic disorder also reported distress (APA, 2022). Young women may not feel as comfortable with their own bodies; worry about pregnancy or relationship problems can also be contributing factors. When a woman presents with pronounced strain over her inability to achieve an orgasm, factors such as anxiety, relationship dynamics, and knowledge of her own bodily responses need to be taken into account (APA, 2022). In any case, counselors should refer clients presenting with symptoms of female orgasmic disorder for medical evaluation.

The importance of orgasm to a woman and its impact on overall sexual satisfaction vary widely by culture (Crooks et al., 2020). The *DSM-5-TR* notes there may be marked sociocultural and generational differences in women's orgasmic ability. Inability to reach orgasm ranges from 17.7% (in Northern Europe) to 42.2% (in Southeast Asia; APA, 2022).

Differential Diagnosis

If symptoms of sexual dysfunction result from interpersonal factors such as partner violence, distress in personal relationships, or other significant stressors, the diagnosis of female orgasmic disorder would not be made (APA, 2022). The lack of sexual interest or pleasure is also a diagnostic criterion for some depressive disorders, such as MDD. Depressive disorders can also contribute to a woman's inability to experience orgasm. However, if the cause of dysfunction is due to another mental health disorder or a medical condition, the woman would not receive the diagnosis. Finally, the use of alcohol, substances, and medications can diminish a woman's overall sexual desire and response (Crooks et al., 2020).

Female Sexual Interest/Arousal Disorder (F52.22)

> I've wanted to date but I just don't have much interest in sex. I don't even think about it for the most part. Companionship would be great, but men usually want to be with someone who gets into sex, and I haven't had sexual feelings in years even though I've made out with attractive men. I just don't care about it.—Contra

Essential Features

Female sexual interest/arousal disorder is defined as the marked absence or decrease in sexual activity or sexual/erotic thoughts and fantasies for a minimum of 6 months. The lack of or significantly reduced sexual interest/arousal must be followed by at least three of six criteria, including lack of interest in sex, little or no thoughts or fantasies involving sex, lack of receptivity to sex or no sexual activity at all, no enjoyment of sex or most sexual encounters, limited or nonexistent response to sexual cues, and limited or no response or sensations during almost all sexual encounters (APA, 2022).

Special Considerations

The prevalence of female sexual interest/arousal disorder, as defined by the *DSM-5-TR*, is unknown and varies with factors such as cultural background, duration of symptoms, relationship history, past traumatic experiences, and presence of distress (APA, 2022). According to the *DSM-5-TR*, there is marked variation in prevalence rates across cultures. East Asian women may have lower sexual desire than Euro-Canadian women. Counselors should always take the woman's cultural influences and background into account (APA, 2022).

Differential Diagnosis

MDD is marked by the lack of sexual interest or pleasure and may contribute to a woman's sexual desire; if this is the case, then a diagnosis of female sexual interest/arousal disorder would not be made. The use of alcohol, substances, and medications can diminish a woman's overall sexual functioning and response. If the cause is due to a medical condition, the woman would not receive a mental diagnosis. The *DSM-5-TR* highlights contributing interpersonal factors such as partner violence, distress in personal relationships, and other significant stressors; if any of these are present, the diagnosis of female orgasmic disorder would not be made (APA, 2022). This holds true for individuals who identify as asexual; a diagnosis of female sexual interest/arousal disorder would not be made.

Genito-Pelvic Pain/Penetration Disorder (F52.6)

> I just don't ever want to feel that way again. It hurt so badly. I don't care if I never have sex again or how my boyfriend feels about it. I'm just too scared.—Hilde

Essential Features

Genito-pelvic pain/penetration disorder is the presence of pain with vaginal penetration during intercourse, and the symptoms must persist for a minimum of approximately 6 months. Genital pain during sexual activity typically causes significant distress in the woman, which might be accompanied by tensing or tightening of the pelvic floor muscles during attempted vaginal penetration or marked fear of attempted vaginal penetration. Genito-pelvic pain/penetration disorder can be described as a shooting pain, burning, cutting, or throbbing with or attempted penetration during intercourse.

Special Considerations

The prevalence of genito-pelvic pain/penetration disorder is unknown. The *DSM-5-TR* reports that approximately 15% of women in North America report recurrent pain during intercourse (APA, 2022). The *DSM-5-TR* notes that, in the past, cultural considerations were related to inadequate sexual education and religious orthodoxy; however, limited research does not support this assumption.

Differential Diagnosis

Inadequate sexual stimulation should be considered as a possible explanation for genito-pelvic pain upon penetration. Counselors should note that a diagnosis cannot be given if symptoms are due to another medical condition. If a medical condition is present, it might contribute to the genito-pelvic pain/penetration disorder; treating the medical condition might relieve the genito-pelvic pain/penetration symptoms.

Male Hypoactive Sexual Desire Disorder (F52.0)

> It's very upsetting at times that I no longer have those thoughts or desires. I can't even remember the last time I really wanted to have sex. I don't even have fantasies. It's not that I can't get aroused, but my wife knows that I'm not into it anymore. She seems hurt.—Connor

Essential Features

Male hypoactive sexual desire disorder is defined by two criteria: (a) persistently or recurrently deficient (or absent) sexual/erotic thoughts or fantasies and desire for sexual activity, and (b) the symptoms must cause distress in the person (APA, 2022). In making an assessment of male hypoactive sexual desire disorder, counselors need to consider interpersonal factors. Although this disorder is primarily identified in older men, an overall interpersonal assessment should be completed (Crooks et al., 2020). Symptoms of male hypoactive sexual desire disorder need to be present for a minimum of approximately 6 months.

Special Considerations

The prevalence rates for men with hypoactive sexual desire disorder are reported in the *DSM-5-TR* and vary depending on the country of origin and method of assessment. The *DSM-5-TR* notes that approximately 6% of younger men (ages 18 to 24 years) and 41% of old men (ages 66 to 74 years) have problems with sexual desire (APA, 2022).

The *DSM-5-TR* notes that there is marked variability in prevalence rates of low desire across cultures, ranging from 12.5% in Northern European men to 28% in Southeast Asian men ages 40 to 80 years. Interpersonal conflicts with personal belief systems and culture may contribute to a man's inhibition of sexual desires (APA, 2022).

Differential Diagnoses

MDD is marked by the lack of sexual interest or pleasure and may contribute to a man's sexual desire; if this is the case, then the male hypoactive sexual desire disorder diagnosis would not be made. The use of alcohol, substances, and medications can diminish a man's overall sexual abilities. If the cause is due to a medical condition, the individual would not receive a diagnosis. The *DSM-5-TR* points out that if the cause is due to interpersonal factors, such as severe relationship distress or other significant stressors, the diagnosis of hypoactive sexual desire disorder would not be made. The same is true for individuals who identify as asexual.

Premature (Early) Ejaculation (F52.4)

> This is really hard for me to talk about, especially since I am only 21, but I feel like I don't know what else to do. As soon as I start having sex, I finish, sometimes in as little as 15 seconds. It has always been this way. I don't know why I even try.—James

Essential Features

Persistent or recurrent premature (early) ejaculation disorder is characterized by a pattern of ejaculation within approximately 1 minute of penetration. Premature (early) ejaculation must occur during partnered sexual intercourse, not during masturbation or sexual activities that do not include penetration, and must occur before the individual wishes to ejaculate. These symptoms represent the marked lack of control that occurs prior to or shortly after penetration. The symptoms need to be present for a minimum of 6 months. Although controversial, the time length was adopted to align with the International Society of Sexual Medicine, which requires that unwanted ejaculation occur within 1 minute (Binik et al., 2010). It is important to note that premature ejaculation is applicable to nonvaginal sexual activity (APA, 2022).

Special Considerations

According to the *DSM-5-TR*, the prevalence of premature (early) ejaculation varies widely depending on the definition used. Internationally, more than 20% to 30% of men ages 18 to 70 years report concern about how quickly they ejaculate upon penetration. The *DSM-5-TR* notes that with the 1-minute criterion, only 1% to 3% of men would be considered with thc diagnosis. It is important for counselors to rule out medical or substance-induced causes and to use self-report on the symptoms, taking into account personal history of sexual experiences. If substance or medication is the cause of premature (early) ejaculation, then substance/medication-induced sexual dysfunction should be diagnosed (APA, 2022).

Substance/Medication-Induced Sexual Dysfunction

Essential Features

Substance/medication-induced sexual dysfunction refers to the significant disturbance in sexual function as a result of substance use or medication. The *DSM-5-TR* stipulates that two criteria must be met: (a) The symptoms occur during or soon after the substance intoxication or withdrawal or after exposure to medication, and (b) the involved substance/medication is capable of producing the symptoms. Sexual dysfunctions can occur in association with intoxication with the following classes of substances: alcohol; opioid; sedative, hypnotic, or anxiolytic; stimulants (including cocaine); and other (or unknown) substances. Medication can cause sexual dysfunction, which includes but is not limited to antidepressants, antipsychotics, and hormonal contraceptives (APA, 2022).

Special Considerations

Although antidepressants are widely used to treat a number of disorders, one of the most common side effects of antidepressants is difficulty with orgasm or ejaculation (Corona et al., 2013; Hyde & DeLamater, 2013). Because of possible underreporting, prevalence rates for substance/medication-induced sexual dysfunction are unclear. The *DSM-5-TR* reports the data on prevalence rates vary depending on the agent; approximately 25% to 80% of individuals taking monoamine oxidase inhibitors, tricyclic antidepressants, serotonergic antidepressants, and combined serotonergic-adrenergic antidepressants report sexual side effects. There may be some cultural implications as to how a culture views taking medications for sexual functioning.

Differential Diagnosis

Sexual functioning can also be related to mental health problems such as depressive, bipolar, anxiety, and psychotic disorders. A thorough medical and clinical assessment should take place before a diagnosis of substance/medication-induced sexual dysfunction is given by a medical professional.

PARAPHILIC DISORDERS

Paraphilic disorders consist of eight disorders characterized by abnormal or unnatural sexual tendencies that cause significant impairment to the person or cause harm to others (APA, 2022). Theorists posit the existence of at least 547 categories of paraphilia, but the term itself originated from the Greek words *para* meaning "beside" and *philia* meaning "love" (Beech & Harkins, 2012). Common paraphilic activities revolve around themes of objects or animals, self- or partner humiliation or suffering, and nonconsenting persons. Although exact etiology is unknown, paraphilias may be biomedical in nature (Beech & Harkins, 2012; Crooks et al., 2020).

Rates of paraphilia within the general population are unknown. Individuals who exhibit symptoms of paraphilic disorders do not always consider their behavior or sexual tendencies to be problematic. Moreover, paraphilic behaviors typically do not come to the attention of counselors unless the behavior has caused conflict with sexual partners or the individual has been charged with an illegal act. Judging from the large commercial market for paraphilic pornography and paraphernalia, as well as the abundance of websites and online chat rooms devoted to such material, prevalence within the community is believed to be far higher than that indicated by statistics from clinical facilities (Crooks et al., 2020; Krueger et al., 2017).

In the *DSM-5-TR*, paraphilic disorders are organized into distinct categories, including those that are activity specific and those that are target specific. Activity-specific disorders loosely reflect courtship, for example, voyeuristic disorder, exhibitionistic disorder, and frotteuristic disorder (APA, 2022). Also within the activity-specific category are two disorders involving physical pain that APA (2022) refers to as *algolagnic disorders*: sexual masochism disorder and sexual sadism disorder. The second category, target-specific disorders, includes pedophilic disorder, fetishistic disorder, and transvestic disorder. Whereas behaviors associated with some of these disorders are clearly illegal (i.e., voyeuristic disorder, exhibitionistic disorder, pedophilic disorder, and frotteuristic disorder), a gray area exists for others. In the context of mutual consent between adults, behaviors involved in sexual masochism disorder and sexual sadism disorder are not illegal (Beech & Harkins, 2012).

Most individuals with atypical sexual preferences do not have a mental disorder. An individual with a paraphilia does not necessarily have a paraphilic disorder (APA, 2022). Counselors should take care to avoid pathologizing sexual interests that do not cause any harm, distress, or impairment to self or others.

Differential Diagnoses

Differentiating paraphilias from other disorders is not difficult because this group has distinctive features. However, within the paraphilic disorders grouping, differentiation can be complicated by the tendency for individuals to experience multiple, sometimes related, paraphilias (Comer, 2017). For example, an individual who has transvestic disorder may also have an underwear fetish. Carefully assessing and understanding the individual's symptoms, severity, and consequences can facilitate an appropriate diagnosis (APA, 2022). Finally, it is critical that counselors differentiate between a diagnosable mental disorder and sexual behavior that is outside of societal norms but does not present clinically significant distress or impairment.

Etiology and Treatment

Although most etiological explanations for paraphilic disorders have a limited research base (Comer, 2017), theorists typically propose ideas consistent with theoretical belief systems. For instance, psychodynamic theorists, such as Freud, may believe that deviance arises as a result of problems with childhood development; behaviorists would posit that it is the result of conditioning. Moreover, many contend that paraphilic disorders have both biological and developmental components (Garcia & Thibaut, 2011).

Treatment options are often based on constructs surrounding etiology. Options include medication, psychotherapy, and a combination of medication and psychotherapy. Psychological treatments are long-standing and can include behavioral techniques, CBT, aversion therapies such as ammonia aversion and olfactory aversion therapy, masturbatory reconditioning, directed masturbation, and verbal satiation (Beech & Harkins, 2012). Multiple options for biologically based treatments have been more recently developed than psychotherapeutic treatments. These are based on reducing sexual arousal level and should only be considered after a full medical examination. These can include antidepressants, such as selective serotonin reuptake inhibitors, and hormones, such as estrogen, steroidal antiandrogens, and gonadotrophin-releasing hormones (Garcia & Thibaut, 2011). Many of these have negative side effects, and ethical considerations are paramount (Krueger et al., 2017).

Implications for Counselors

The most common paraphilic disorders counselors will come across are also the most common sexual offenses, and more often than not, clients are in treatment because of involvement of the legal system (Comer, 2017). These include pedophilic disorder (sexual activity with children), exhibitionistic disorder (genital self-exposure to strangers), voyeuristic disorder (watching strangers who are naked, undressing, or having sex), and frotteuristic disorder (touching an unconsenting person). Counselors should note that almost all individuals with these four most common paraphilic disorders are male (APA, 2022). The most common psychotherapy modalities include cognitive behavioral or behavioral approaches. Because of the potential for harm to others, counselors have a responsibility to know and adhere to the state laws regarding mandated reporting and the *ACA Code of Ethics* (ACA, 2014) when working with these clients. Specialized training is necessary for counselors to institute the best standard of care in clinical work with this population.

Counselors need to understand that psychosocial impairment is common among individuals diagnosed with paraphilias. Individuals diagnosed with paraphilic disorders also have higher rates of exposure to medical risks such as sexually transmitted infections (Comer, 2017). While being careful not to pathologize individuals diagnosed with these disorders, counselors should always inquire about medical history and whether the client has had a recent physical exam (Crooks et al., 2020).

The following sections include descriptions, essential features, differential diagnoses, and case examples for training. In an effort to not stigmatize individuals diagnosed with paraphilias, we have chosen not to include fictitious client testimonials.

Pedophilic Disorder (F65.4)

Essential Features

Pedophilic disorder is the most common type of paraphilia, occurring in an estimated 3% to 5% of men (APA, 2022). Characterized by sexual attraction to children, individuals diagnosed with pedophilic disorder prefer to engage in sexual encounters with children as opposed to adults (Nolen-Hoeksema, 2006). Counselors will most likely come across individuals who have been mandated to treatment after engaging in oral sex with a child or touching a child's genitals, as most individuals diagnosed with this disorder do engage in penetration. One important distinction includes whether the individual is exclusively sexually attracted to children, because most individuals diagnosed with pedophilic disorder prefer to have sexual encounters with children. More prevalent in males than females, pedophilic behaviors normally begin during adolescence, and behaviors are escalatory in nature.

Criteria for pedophilic disorder include recurrent intense sexual desires, fantasies, or behaviors involving sexual activity with an individual age 13 or under. The person must experience these symptoms for at least 6 months, be at least 16 years of age, and be at least 5 years older than the child. Perhaps the most important criterion for counselors to consider when diagnosing an individual with pedophilic disorder is that the sexual desires, fantasies, or behaviors must cause clinically significant distress or impairment in work, social, or personal functioning or the person has acted on these desires (APA, 2022).

Special Considerations

As mandated, and in accordance with the *ACA Code of Ethics* (ACA, 2014), counselors should take the criterion of acting on those desires into serious consideration. If a client is currently acting on pedophilic behaviors or state that they will act on them, counselors must report these actions to the proper authorities. Unless counselors believe doing so may cause further harm to a child, this should involve a conversation with the client regarding the mandated report this will entail. Another important consideration for counselors is the age requirement for this disorder. For example, if a 15-year-old is in a sexual relationship with a 12-year-old, they would not fit criteria for pedophilic disorder. It is essential that counselors educate themselves on state laws regarding sexual relationships between children and adolescents.

Beech and Harkins (2012) reviewed the literature on evidence-based treatment for those who have been diagnosed with pedophilic disorder. They reported some success with treatments involving CBT or behavioral therapy combined with medication. Studies involving sexual crimes against children generally indicate that individuals who received treatment reoffended at much lower rates (Beech & Harkins, 2012).

Many counselors, especially novice counselors, vocalize how difficult it would be for them to work with sex offenders, often stating they would most likely want to refer to other professionals. It is important to remember, however, that most individuals diagnosed with pedophilic disorder have experienced neglect and extreme punishment as children (Comer, 2017). As counselors, we must adhere to the *ACA Code of Ethics* (ACA, 2014), which stresses the significance of competence and the professional responsibility we have to our clients (see Section C of the *ACA Code of Ethics*).

Differential Diagnosis

The differential diagnosis for pedophilic disorder includes ASPD, because individuals with this disorder may be more likely to engage in illegal activities. They may be more willing to approach a minor or engage in activities that could injure others. The impact of alcohol and substance use should be considered as individuals under the influence may be more likely to approach someone who is underage or to engage in related activities. Finally, counselors should consider OCD before giving this diagnosis (APA, 2022).

Coding, Recording, and Specifiers

There is only one diagnostic code for pedophilic disorder: F65.4. The specifier given for individuals who are attracted only to children is *exclusive type*, and *nonexclusive type* is applied to those who are not attracted only to children. Counselors can use specifiers to identify whether the individual is *sexually attracted to males*, *sexually attracted to females*, or *sexually attracted to both*. In addition, one can specify whether the behavior is *limited to incest* (APA, 2022).

Case Example

> Donald, a 45-year-old White man, was mandated to treatment after being released from prison for a sex offense conviction. Donald reports that his earliest memory includes sexual play with his older female babysitter. As an adult, Donald found himself sexually aroused by the bodies of young girls. Despite this attraction, Donald married at age 24 and had three children (all boys) with his wife, who was his age. Throughout his marriage, Donald began secretly collecting pornographic magazines featuring children. When his sexual tension became too high, Donald would masturbate and think about the pictures in his magazines. By age 30, Donald and his wife began having marital problems, and Donald took up photography. He would invite neighborhood children, specifically 8- to 9-year-old girls, to his house and persuaded them to pose for him either partially or fully naked. Donald found satisfaction in taking these pictures and never touched any of the children. His wife found the pictures in his laptop one

day and called the police. Donald was arrested; his wife filed for divorce while he was incarcerated. During his intake, Donald stated that he didn't think that taking pictures of children while they were naked could cause them any harm. He also stated, "I'm not proud of it, but it was something that I couldn't resist."

Diagnostic Questions

1. Do Donald's presenting symptoms meet the criteria for a paraphilic disorder? If so, which disorder?
2. Based on the disorder identified in Question 1, which symptom(s) led you to select that diagnosis?
3. What rule-outs would you consider for Donald's case?
4. What other information may be needed to make an accurate clinical diagnosis?

Exhibitionistic Disorder (F65.2)

Essential Features

Exhibitionistic disorder is one of the most common paraphilic disorders. As many as one in three women report having an experience in which a man exposed himself (Comer, 2017). Counselors will most likely come across males with this disorder who expose themselves to females of any age, including children. Individuals with exhibitionistic disorder usually begin exposing themselves to strangers before the age of 18, do not try to contact the person they expose themselves to, and typically do not pose a danger to their targeted victim. The urge to expose self to others often comes in waves, occurring most often when the person is stressed or has free time (Comer, 2017; Morrison, 2006).

Exposing oneself can be quite different for each individual. Men may expose their penis while it is erect or flaccid. Some men could masturbate while exposing themselves, craving a reaction from their victims, whereas others may quickly expose themselves and run away. Although individuals with this disorder may fantasize about having intercourse with those they expose themselves to, they seldom act on these fantasies. Many individuals with exhibitionistic disorder lead relatively normal lives, have successful intimate and sexual relationships (Morrison, 2006), and are unlikely to seek treatment unless they experience legal issues.

To be diagnosed with exhibitionistic disorder, individuals must have recurrent and intense sexual desires, fantasies, or behaviors regarding genital self-exposure to unsuspecting strangers for at least 6 months. This must either cause significant distress or impairment in the individual's life or result in exposure to someone who has not or cannot consent. Examples of distress or impairment can include loss of work, relationship problems, lack of sleep, or legal ramifications due to desires, fantasies, or engagement in exhibitionistic behaviors (APA, 2022).

Special Considerations

Individuals diagnosed with exhibitionistic disorder may also engage in other paraphilic behaviors such as pedophilic, frotteuristic, or voyeuristic behaviors (APA, 2022; Crooks et al., 2020; Morrison, 2006). It would be prudent for counselors to look for these types of behaviors when working with clients diagnosed with exhibitionistic disorder. Moreover, as with pedophilic disorder, exhibitionistic behaviors are illegal if acted upon. Reporting sexual fantasies about exhibitionistic behavior has been strongly related to the likelihood of engaging in such behaviors (Långström & Seto, 2006). It is important for counselors to discuss limits of confidentiality should clients report they will cause harm by exposing their genitals to others.

Beech and Harkins (2012) identified CBT, behavioral therapy, and empathy training as primary treatment modalities for exhibitionistic disorder. They posited that because there is no physical contact, individuals who engage in this behavior may be less likely to empathize with the people to whom they have exposed themselves. The most common behavioral treatments include covert sensitization, ammonia aversion, and minimal arousal conditioning.

Differential Diagnosis

As with other paraphilias, counselors should explore the impact of substance use before making a diagnosis. If the behavior is related only to substance abuse, that diagnosis may be more accurate. Furthermore, conduct disorder and ASPD should be explored as alternative or coexisting diagnoses (APA, 2022).

Coding, Recording, and Specifiers

There is only one diagnostic code for exhibitionistic disorder: F65.2. Specifiers include *sexually aroused by exposing genitals to prepubertal children*, *sexually aroused by exposing genitals to physically mature individuals*, and *sexually aroused by exposing genitals to prepubertal children and physically mature individuals.* Counselors can identify *in a controlled environment* and *in full remission* as specifiers where appropriate (APA, 2022).

Voyeuristic Disorder (F65.3)

Essential Features

Voyeuristic disorder is characterized as sexual arousal from watching unsuspecting strangers engage in private activities. Also known as "peeping toms," a term from 17th-century England, these individuals are almost always men (Comer, 2017); prevalence rates may be as high as 12% in the male population (APA, 2022). Many individuals with this disorder masturbate while watching unsuspecting victims. They almost never take steps to have any contact, sexual or not, with victims. Similar to those with exhibitionistic disorder, individuals diagnosed with a voyeuristic disorder lead relatively normal lives with intimate relationships and take great precautions to avoid being caught in their paraphilic activities (Morrison, 2006).

A diagnosis of voyeuristic disorder requires two criteria after the age of 18. First, the individual must exhibit at least 6 months of recurrent and intense sexual desires, fantasies, or behaviors regarding the act of watching unsuspecting individuals who are naked, disrobing, or having sex. Second, the individual must have engaged in the behavior or the tendencies must cause significant distress or impairment in the individual's life (APA, 2022).

Special Considerations

As with pedophilic and exhibitionistic behaviors, voyeuristic activities are illegal if acted upon. It is important for counselors to distinguish between individuals who are aroused by watching pornography and individuals who are aroused by lurking around windows or dressing rooms, utilizing hidden cameras, and the like. The latter is illegal and must be looked at more closely by counselors when clients report that they will engage in illegal behaviors that put others at risk for harm.

As with other paraphilic disorders, counselors must adhere to state laws as well as the *ACA Code of Ethics* (ACA, 2014) regarding confidentiality. Individuals who report voyeuristic behaviors are more likely to report current mental disorders. Exhibitionistic and voyeuristic behaviors have been related to psychological problems, substance use, and sexual risk taking or novelty seeking (Crooks et al., 2020; Långström & Seto, 2006). Counselors should take note of comorbidity with other paraphilic disorders as well as other mental disorders in the *DSM-5-TR*. Behavioral therapies and CBT are commonly used approaches to treating this disorder (Beech & Harkins, 2012).

Differential Diagnosis

Substance abuse, conduct disorder, and ASPD may have overlapping symptoms with voyeuristic disorder. However, the symptoms of voyeuristic disorder will persist for at least 6 months and are related to intense sexual arousal. Conduct and antisocial symptoms will be related to a pattern of rule-breaking behaviors; a single episode while intoxicated tends to be related to substance use disorders (APA, 2022).

Coding, Recording, and Specifiers

There is only one diagnostic code for voyeuristic disorder: F65.3. As with other paraphilias, specifiers can be given to indicate certain conditions, such as *in a controlled environment* and *in full remission* (APA, 2022).

Frotteuristic Disorder (F65.81)

Essential Features

Frotteuristic disorder is the last of the four most common paraphilic disorders counselors will come across in their practice. It is also the final paraphilic disorder for which action or engagement can lead to serious legal ramifications. Frotteuristic disorder is defined as at least 6 months of repeated and intense sexual desires, fantasies, or behaviors involving touching and rubbing a nonconsenting person. As with other paraphilic disorders, the desires or behaviors must cause significant distress or impairment in the individual's life or they must have acted on such desires (APA, 2022).

The prevalence of frotteuristic disorder is unknown. However, frotteuristic acts occur in up to 30% of the male population (APA, 2022). Males are most likely to be diagnosed with frotteuristic disorder, most often approaching females while sometimes fantasizing about being in a relationship with that person (Comer, 2017; Crooks et al, 2020). Unlike exhibitionistic and voyeuristic tendencies, individuals with frotteuristic disorder act out their fantasies and violate the rights of others by touching or rubbing nonconsenting victims. Frotteuristic acts frequently occur in public places such as subways or crowded sidewalks and may involve rubbing genitals against or fondling another person.

Special Considerations

Frotteuristic offenses tend to go underreported, and research in this area is lacking. What is known is that individuals with frotteuristic disorder often begin exhibiting behaviors during adolescence and may have a history of other sexually deviant behaviors such as rape, exhibitionism, pedophilia, sexual sadism, and voyeurism. Individuals with frotteuristic disorder often experience anxiety, shame, negative self-image, and other emotional concerns related to their diagnosis (Comer, 2017). Although researchers do not typically address frotteurism separately from other paraphilias, counselors should note that solution-focused therapy might be an effective way to treat this disorder (Guterman et al., 2011).

Differential Diagnosis

As with other paraphilic disorders, conduct disorder and ASPD should be considered. If the behaviors are partly related to a pattern of norm-breaking behaviors, frotteuristic disorder may not apply. Isolated episodes that occur with the use of alcohol or other substances will not be part of frotteurism (APA, 2022).

Coding, Recording, and Specifiers

There is only one diagnostic code for frotteuristic disorder: F65.81. Specifiers for this disorder include *in a controlled environment* and *in full remission* (APA, 2022).

Sexual Masochism Disorder (F65.5) and Sexual Sadism Disorder (F65.52)

Essential Features

Whereas sexual masochism is characterized by gaining sexual pleasure from receiving pain or suffering, sexual sadism, named such after the infamous Marquis de Sade, is characterized by gaining sexual pleasure from inflicting pain or humiliation (Comer, 2017). These two disorders have much in common and have a high rate of comorbidity with each other (up to 30%); thus, we discuss them together. Unlike the previous four most common paraphilic disorders, sexual masochism and sexual sadism disorders do not usually lead to sexual offenses or legal ramifications. In fact, intimate partners who engage in masochistic and sadistic behaviors are highly consenting and will often have safety words to indicate a time to stop the behaviors (APA, 2022; Crooks et al, 2020).

Both sexual masochistic and sadistic tendencies begin in childhood and are typically chronic. Individuals participate in masochistic and sadistic behaviors in numerous ways, including beating, choking, bondage, blindfolding, spanking, pricking, shocking, hitting, cutting, asphyxiation, or humiliation. Individuals with these disorders commonly require an increase in the severity of these methods to produce the same degree of sexual satisfaction (Crooks et al., 2020).

Criteria for sexual masochistic disorder and sexual sadism disorder are quite similar. Sexual masochistic disorder requires at least 6 months of fantasies, behaviors, and desires focused on being made to suffer, humiliated, bound, or beaten (APA, 2022). The sexual urges are persistent and intense in nature and sometimes involve the individual being forced into sex against their will (Comer, 2017). In some ways, sexual sadism disorder is the exact opposite. This disorder requires at least 6 months of repeated, intense sexual urges, fantasies, or behaviors in which pain is inflicted by the individual on someone else (APA, 2022). Both disorders require significant distress or impairment in the individual's functioning. Note that unlike the previous four common paraphilic disorders, an individual cannot be diagnosed for merely participating or engaging in the behaviors with a consenting adult; they must experience clinically significant distress or impairment because of their masochistic or sadistic tendencies (APA, 2022).

Special Considerations

There are numerous aspects to consider with these two disorders. As with the previously mentioned paraphilic disorders, sexual masochism disorder is predominantly seen in men (APA, 2022). As with other disorders, treatment tends to focus on behavioral therapy, aversion therapies, and CBT, but research into efficacy is very limited (Beech & Harkins, 2012). Furthermore, some individuals act out sexual sadism with nonconsenting partners. Although there have been cases in which murderers and rapists have been diagnosed with this disorder (Comer, 2017), fewer than 10% of offenders who rape can be diagnosed with sexual sadism disorder (Frances & Wollert, 2012). It is of utmost importance that counselors working with this population ensure that the well-being of both partners is protected.

Lastly, the risks of sexual sadistic and masochistic methods should be examined. Methods such as asphyxiation can lead to serious health-related concerns. Also, engagement in asphyxiation leads to a few accidental deaths per million people each year. Counselors can take a psychoeducational role and educate themselves and clients on how to safely engage in these somewhat atypical sexual practices to reduce the risk of health-related concerns and accidental death.

Differential Diagnosis

For both sexual masochistic and sexual sadistic disorders, it is important to differentiate between nonimpairing sexual behaviors and a disorder, which requires clinical levels of distress or impairment. When giving the diagnosis, counselors should determine if the urge or behavior is based on giving or receiving pain. Furthermore, counselors should consider substance use, hypersexuality, or antisocial personality symptoms with these disorders. In addition to being potentially different diagnoses, they are often comorbid with sexual masochistic and sexual sadistic disorders (APA, 2022).

Coding, Recording, and Specifiers

There is only one diagnostic code for sexual masochistic disorder: F65.51. Sexual masochistic disorder has a unique specifier of *with asphyxiophilia*. Sexual sadistic disorder is coded as F65.52 and has no unique specifiers. Both disorders have specifiers of *in a controlled environment* and *in full remission* (APA, 2022).

Fetishistic Disorder (F65.0)

Essential Features

The *DSM-5-TR* identifies the criteria for fetishistic disorder as intense, repeated sexual fantasies, urges, or behaviors related to the use of an inanimate object or body parts that are not genitals. The object cannot be part of items used or related to cross-dressing or be used solely for genital stimulation. The fantasies, urges, or behaviors must last for at least 6 months, and the individual must experience impairment or clinically significant distress (APA, 2022).

Fetishistic disorder, a common paraphilia, is marked by sexual arousal over inanimate objects or nongenital body parts, such as feet, often rejecting all other stimuli (Comer, 2017). Objects vary widely and can include anything from the common fetish of underwear or shoes to less typical objects such as cars or balloons. This disorder is far more common in men than in women, and the fetishes typically first present in adolescence. The desire to collect the object can result in acts such as stealing women's worn clothing (APA, 2022; Comer, 2017).

Special Considerations

There are differing theories as to the etiology of fetishistic disorder, but the exact cause has yet to be determined. Treatments based on different theories have met with some success, particularly CBT and behavioral therapies. Behaviorists posit that conditioning is responsible for fetish behavior. As a result, treatments such as aversion therapy, masturbatory satiation, and orgasmic reorientation have been used (Comer, 2017). Beech and Harkins (2012) reported evidence that these treatments have met with some success. Furthermore, evidence supports the use of CBT and a combined treatment of directive guidance and behavioral modification for reducing symptoms (Beech & Harkins, 2012). When working with individuals diagnosed with fetishistic disorder, counselors need to clearly identify and follow the client's goals. Goals may differ among clients, with some interested in symptom reduction or termination and others desiring relationship improvement or avoidance of legal issues (Beech & Harkins, 2012).

Differential Diagnosis

When differentiating fetishistic disorder from transvestic disorder, counselors should consider the role of the fetish object. If it is an article of clothing or other object used only during cross-dressing, then transvestic disorder is more applicable. Sexual masochistic disorder can be diagnosed along with fetishistic disorder, but if the fetish object is related only to being harmed or coerced, fetishism should not be diagnosed (APA, 2022). Furthermore, counselors are reminded that having a fetish does not necessarily indicate a disorder. There must be a clinically significant level of distress or impairment for a diagnosis to be given; care and concern should be taken not to stigmatize or shame the individual (Comer, 2017).

Coding, Recording, and Specifiers

There is only one diagnostic code for fetishistic disorder: F65.0. Specifiers for this disorder are related to the type of fetish and include *body parts(s)*, *nonliving object(s)*, or *other*, as well as *in a controlled environment* and *in full remission* (APA, 2022).

Transvestic Disorder (F65.1)

Essential Features

Typically beginning in prepubescence and often referred to as "cross-dressing," about 3.2% of the U.S. population reports experiencing at least one episode of transvestic behavior. Transvestic disorder is primarily a male disorder, occurring in an estimated 2.8% of the male population (Långström & Zucker, 2005). Symptoms range from wearing a single item of other-gender clothing underneath the individual's clothing to fully dressing as a member of the opposite gender (Comer, 2017). For individuals in heterosexual relationships, this can cause distress and conflict within the relationship.

The defining characteristics of transvestic disorder include intense sexual arousal resulting from dressing, or fantasies and urges surrounding dressing, in clothing typically associated with the opposite gender (Comer, 2017). This behavior must be recurrent for at least 6 months and result in impairment in functioning or clinically significant distress or both (APA, 2022).

> ***Note:*** Cross-dressing does not indicate a diagnosis of transvestic disorder. To qualify for this diagnosis, the individual must experience sexual arousal and excitement almost every time they engage in this behavior. The behavior will cause distress or impairment in functioning, often as related to relationships with significant others.

Special Considerations

Transvestic disorder typically has an onset for boys prior to adolescence and can be episodic over the lifetime. The etiology of the disorder is uncertain; some theorists point to operant conditioning in childhood (Comer, 2017). Furthermore, because individuals present for treatment infrequently, there is little reported in terms of evidence-based treatments. A few studies indicate effectiveness in medication therapy; however, they involve case studies with limited generalizability (Garcia & Thibaut, 2011). Counselors should be aware of clients' goals and their own personal biases when working with this population. Complete elimination of the behaviors may not be the client's goal. Instead, the goal may be symptom management, reduction of behaviors, or relationship improvement.

Counselors should also be aware of the potential for comorbidity with other disorders, such as fetishism and sexual masochism (APA, 2022). There are also indicators that individuals with transvestic disorder may experience pleasure from exposing themselves to others, watching others have intercourse, or using pain as part of sexual arousal (Långström & Zucker, 2005). Careful screening is crucial here, as is awareness of the *ACA Code of Ethics* (ACA, 2014) and potential for harm to others.

Differential Diagnosis

Differentiating transvestic disorder from fetishistic disorder can be challenging. Whereas those who experience fetishism will focus on an object or body part, an individual with transvestic disorder will have sexual arousal related to the experience of dressing as the opposite gender or imagining themself as a member of the opposite gender. Transvestic disorder can be mistaken for gender dysphoria. However, the differentiating factor between the two disorders is that individuals experiencing gender dysphoria report lack of congruence between physical and emotional gender, whereas those with transvestic disorder experience sexual arousal when cross-dressing. Furthermore, those with gender dysphoria have a desire to change genders, whereas those with transvestic disorder typically do not. These disorders can co-occur, and both should be diagnosed when there is evidence for both (APA, 2022).

Coding, Recording, and Specifiers

There is only one diagnostic code for transvestic disorder: F65.1. Transvestic disorder specifiers include *with fetishism*, indicating that the individual is aroused by materials, fabrics, or clothing; and *with autogynephilia*, indicating that the individual is aroused by fantasies or pictures of themselves with these items (APA, 2022). Counselors can specify if acts occur *in a controlled environment* or are *in full remission*.

Questions for Consideration

1. How might receiving a diagnosis outlined in this chapter impact the client and family?
2. What environmental conditions might predispose an individual to developing a sleep disorder?
3. How might an integrated treatment team be important for treating sexual dysfunction(s)?
4. What could represent an effective initial treatment recommendation(s) for an individual diagnosed with a feeding or eating disorder?

Part Three

References

Alcover, K. C., & Thompson, C. C. (2020). Patterns of mean age at drug use initiation among adolescents and emerging adults, 2004–2017. *JAMA Pediatrics, 174*(7), 725–727. https://doi.org/10.1001/jamapediatrics.2019.6235

Amad, A., Ramoz, N., Thomas, P., Jardri, R., & Gorwood, P. (2014). Genetics of borderline personality disorder: Systematic review and proposal of an integrative model. *Neuroscience & Biobehavioral Reviews, 40,* 6–19. https://doi.org/10.1016/j.neubiorev.2014.01.003

American Counseling Association. (2014). *ACA code of ethics.* https://www.counseling.org/resources/aca-code-of-ethics.pdf

American Psychiatric Association. (1980). *Diagnostic and statistical manual of mental disorders* (3rd ed.).

American Psychiatric Association. (2013a). *Diagnostic and statistical manual of mental disorders* (5th ed.). https://doi.org/10.1176/appi.books.9780890425596

American Psychiatric Association. (2013b). *Personality disorders.* https://www.psychiatry.org/File%20Library/Psychiatrists/Practice/DSM/APA_*DSM-5*-Personality-Disorder.pdf

American Psychiatric Association. (2022). *Diagnostic and statistical manual of mental disorders* (5th ed., text rev.). https://doi.org/10.1176/appi.books.9780890425787

American Society of Addiction Medicine. (2019). *Definition of addiction.* https://www.asam.org/quality-care/definition-of-addiction

Anderson, J. L., & Kelley, S. E. (2022). Antisocial personality disorder and psychopathy: The AMPD in review. *Personality Disorders: Theory, Research, and Treatment, 13*(4), 397–401. https://doi.org/10.1037/per0000525

Arnulf, I., Zeitzer, J. M., File, J., Farber, N., & Mignot, E. (2005). Kleine-Levin syndrome: A systematic review of 186 cases in the literature. *Brain, 128*(Pt. 12), 2763–2776. https://doi.org/10.1093/brain/awh620

Ayano, G., Betts, K., Maravilla, J. C., & Alati, R. (2021). A systematic review and meta-analysis of the risk of disruptive behavioral disorders in the offspring of parents with severe psychiatric disorders. *Child Psychiatry & Human Development, 52*(1), 77–95. https://doi.org/10.1007/s10578-020-00989-4

Azeredo, A., Moreira, D., & Barbosa, F. (2018). ADHD, CD, and ODD: Systematic review of genetic and environmental risk factors. *Research in Developmental Disabilities, 82,* 10–19. https://doi.org/10.1016/j.ridd.2017.12.010

Bachelor, A. (2013). Clients' and therapists' views of the therapeutic alliance: Similarities, differences and relationship to therapy outcome. *Clinical Psychology & Psychotherapy, 20*(2), 118–135. https://doi.org/10.1002/cpp.792

Baglivio, M., Wolff, K., Piquero, A., Greenwald, M., & Epps, N. (2017). Racial/ethnic disproportionality in psychiatric diagnoses and treatment in a sample of serious juvenile offenders. *Journal of Youth & Adolescence, 46*(7), 1424–1451. https://doi.org/10.1007/s10964-016-0573-4

Bakkevig, J. F., & Karterud, S. (2010). Is the *Diagnostic and statistical manual of mental disorders, fourth edition,* histrionic personality disorder category a valid construct? *Comprehensive Psychiatry, 51*(5), 462–470. https://doi.org/10.1016/j.comppsych.2009.11.009

Barlow, J., & Coren, E. (2018). The effectiveness of parenting programs: A review of Campbell reviews. *Research on Social Work Practice, 28*(1), 99–102. https://doi.org/10.1177/1049731517725184

Barnes, R. D., Masheb, R. B., White, M. A., & Grilo, C. M. (2011). Comparison of methods for identifying and assessing obese patients with binge eating disorder in primary care settings. *International Journal of Eating Disorders, 44*(2), 157–163. https://doi.org/10.1002/eat.20802

Bateman, A., & Fonagy, P. (2000). Effectiveness of psychotherapeutic treatment of personality disorder. *British Journal of Psychiatry, 177*(2), 138–143. https://doi.org/10.1192/bjp.177.2.138

Bateman, A., Gunderson, J. G., & Mulder, R. T. (2015). Treatment of personality disorder. *The Lancet, 385*(9969), 735–743. https://doi.org/10.1016/s0140-6736(14)61394-5

Baumel, A., Mathur, N., Pawar, A., & Muench, F. (2021). Psychosocial interventions for children with externalized behavior problems: An updated meta-analysis of moderator effects. *Journal of Child & Family Studies, 30*(1), 65–86. https://doi.org/10.1007/s10826-020-01863-6

Beaudry, G., Yu, R., Långström, N., & Fazel, S. (2021). An updated systematic review and meta-regression analysis: Mental disorders among adolescents in juvenile detention and correctional facilities. *Journal of the American Academy of Child & Adolescent Psychiatry, 60*(1), 46–60. https://doi.org/10.1016/j.jaac.2020.01.015

Beech, A. R., & Harkins, L. (2012). *DSM-IV-TR* paraphilia: Descriptions, demographics and treatment interventions. *Aggression and Violent Behavior, 17*(6), 527–539. https://doi.org/10.1016/j.avb.2012.07.008

Berg, K. C., & Peterson, C. B. (2013). Assessment and diagnosis of eating disorders. In L. H. Choate (Ed.), *Eating disorders and obesity: A counselor's guide to prevention and treatment* (pp. 91–117). American Counseling Association.

Berg, K. C., Peterson, C. B., & Frazier, P. (2012). Assessment and diagnosis of eating disorders: A guide for professional counselors. *Journal of Counseling & Development, 90*(3), 262–269. https://doi.org/10.1002/j.1556-6676.2012.00033.x

Bhukhari, S. R., Saba, F., & Fatima, S. I. (2018). The efficacy of cognitive behavior therapy for obsessive compulsive personality disorder. *Pakistan Journal of Clinical Psychology, 17*(1), 29–38.

Bianchi, E. C. (2014). Entering adulthood in a recession tempers later narcissism. *Psychological Science, 25*(7), 1429–1437. https://doi.org/10.1177/0956797614532818

Binik, Y. M., Brotto, L. A., Graham, C. A., & Segraves, R. T. (2010). Response of the *DSM-V* sexual dysfunctions subworkgroups to commentaries published in *DSM. International Society for Sexual Medicine, 7*(7), 2382–2387. https://doi.org/10.1111/j.1743-6109.2010.01899.x

Biskin, R. (2013). Treatment of borderline personality disorder in youth. *Journal of the Canadian Academy of Child and Adolescent Psychiatry, 22*(3), 230–234.

Bo, S., Sharp, C., Beck, E., Pedersen, J. H., Gondan, M., & Simonsen, E. (2017). First empirical evaluation of outcomes for mentalization-based group therapy for adolescents with BPD. *Personality Disorders: Theory, Research, and Treatment, 8*(4), 396–401. https://doi.org/10.1037/per0000210

Boeree, G. C. (2006). *Personality disorders.* http://webspace.ship.edu/cgboer/persdisorders.html

Bogels, S. M., Alden, L., Beidel, D. C., Clark, L. A., Pine, D. S., Stein, M. B., & Voncken, M. (2010). Do early maladaptive schemas mediate the relationship between childhood experiences and avoidant personality disorder features? A preliminary investigation in a non-clinical sample. *Cognitive Therapy and Research, 34*(4), 343–358. https://doi.org/10.1007/s10608-009-9250-1

Bornstein, R. F. (2011). Reconceptualizing personality pathology in *DSM-5*: Limitations in evidence for eliminating dependent personality disorder and other *DSM-IV* syndromes. *Journal of Personality Disorders, 25*(2), 235–247. https://doi.org/10.1521/pedi.2011.25.2.235

Brown, A., Mountford, V., & Waller, G. (2013). Therapeutic alliance and weight gain during cognitive behavioural therapy for anorexia nervosa. *Behaviour Research and Therapy, 51*(4–5), 216–220. https://doi.org/10.1016/j.brat.2013.01.008

Bryant-Waugh, R. (2019). Avoidant/restrictive food intake disorder. *Child and Adolescent Psychiatric Clinics of North America, 28(*4), 557–565. https://doi.org/10.1016/j.chc.2019.05.004

Budge, S. L., Moore, J. W., Del Re, A., Wampold, B. E., Baardseth, T. P., & Nienhuis, J. (2013). The effectiveness of evidence-based treatments for personality disorders when comparing treatment-as-usual and bona fide treatments. *Clinical Psychology Review, 33*(8), 1057–1066. https://doi.org/10.1016/j.cpr.2013.08.003

Caldwell-Harris, C. L., & Ayçiçegi, A. (2006). When personality and culture clash: The psychological distress of allocentrics in an individualist culture and idiocentrics in a collectivist culture. *Transcultural Psychiatry, 43*(3), 331–361. https://doi.org/10.1177/1363461506066982

Cale, E. M., & Lilienfeld, S. O. (2002). Histrionic personality disorder and antisocial personality disorder: Sex-differentiated manifestations of psychopathy? *Journal of Personality Disorders, 16*(1), 52–72. https://doi.org/10.1521/pedi.16.1.52.22557

Centers for Disease Control and Prevention. (2021). *Electronic cigarettes.* https://www.cdc.gov/tobacco/basic_information/e-cigarettes/index.htm

Centers for Disease Control and Prevention. (2022). *Marijuana and public health: Data and statistics.* http://cdc.gov/marijuana/data-statistics.htm

Centers for Disease Control and Prevention. (2023). *Adverse childhood experiences (ACEs).* https://www.cdc.gov/violenceprevention/aces/index.html

Cermain, G., & Lejoyeux, M. (2010). Pyromania: Clinical aspects. In E. Aboujaoude & L. M. Koran (Eds.), *Impulse control disorders* (pp. 255–268). Cambridge University Press.

Chan, C. C., Bach, P. A., & Bedwell, J. S. (2015). An integrative approach using third-generation cognitive-behavioral therapies for avoidant personality disorder. *Clinical Case Studies, 14*(6), 466–481. https://doi.org/10.1177/1534650115575788

Cheli, S., Chiarello, F., & Cavalletti, V. (2023). A psychotherapy oriented by compassion and metacognition for schizoid personality disorder: A two cases series. *Journal of Contemporary Psychotherapy, 53*(4), 61–70. https://doi.org/10.1007/s10879-022-09566-3

Cheli, S., Lysaker, P. H., & Dimaggio, G. (2019). Metacognitively oriented psychotherapy for schizotypal personality disorder: A two-case series. *Personality and Mental Health, 13*(3), 155–167. https://doi.org/10.1002/pmh.1447

Chopik, W. J., & Kitayama, S. (2018). Personality change across the life span: Insights from a cross-cultural, longitudinal study. *Journal of Personality, 86*(3), 508–521. https://doi.org/10.1111/jopy.12332

Christophersen, E. R., & Friman, P. C. (2010). *Encopresis and enuresis.* Hogrefe.

Ciesinski, N. K., Drabick, D. A. G., & McCloskey, M. S. (2022). A latent class analysis of intermittent explosive disorder symptoms. *Journal of Affective Disorders, 302,* 367–375. https://doi.org/10.1016/j.jad.2022.01.099

Cobb, C. L., Xie, D., Meca, A., & Schwartz, S.J. (2016). Acculturation, discrimination, and depression among unauthorized Latino/as in the United States. *Cultural Diversity and Ethnic Minority Psychology, 23*(2), 258–268. https://doi.org/10.1037/cdp0000118

Coccaro, E. F. (2012). Intermittent explosive disorder as a disorder of impulse aggression for *DSM-5. American Journal of Psychiatry, 169*(6), 577–588. https://doi.org/10.1176/appi.ajp.2012.11081259

Colins, O. F., Van Damme, L., Hendriks, A. M., & Georgiou, G. (2020). The *DSM-5* with limited prosocial emotions specifier for conduct disorder: A systematic literature review. *Journal of Psychopathology and Behavioral Assessment, 42*(2), 248–258. https://doi.org/10.1007/s10862-020-09799-3

Comer, R. J. (2017). *Abnormal psychology* (10th ed.). Worth.

Corona, G., Rastrelli, G., Ricca, V., Jannini, E. A., Vignozzi, L., Monami, M., Sforza, A., Forti, G., Mannucci, E., & Maggi, M. (2013). Risk factors associated with primary and secondary reduced libido in male patients with sexual dysfunction. *Journal of Sexual Medicine, 10*(4), 1074–1089. https://doi.org/10.1111/jsm.12043

Couturier, J., Kimber, M., Jack, S., Niccols, A., Van Blyderreen, S., & McVey, G. (2013). Understanding the uptake of family-based treatment for adolescents with anorexia nervosa: Therapist perspectives. *International Journal of Eating Disorders, 46*(2), 177–188. https://doi.org/10.1002/eat.22049
Crooks, R., Baur, K., & Widman, L. (2020). *Our sexuality* (14th ed.). Cengage Learning,
Crow, S. J., Peterson, C. B., Swanson, S. A., Raymond, N. C., Specker, S., Eckert, E. D., & Mitchell, J. E. (2009). Increased mortality in bulimia nervosa and other eating disorders. *American Journal of Psychiatry, 166*(12), 1342–1346. https://doi.org/10.1176/appi.ajp.2009.09020247
Crowell, S. E., Beauchaine, T. P., & Linehan, M. M. (2009). A biosocial developmental model of borderline personality: Elaborating and extending Linehan's theory. *Psychological Bulletin, 135*(3), 495–510. https://doi.org/10.1037/a0015616
Dahlgren, C. L., Wisting, L., & Rø, Ø. (2017). Feeding and eating disorders in the *DSM-5* era: Systematic review of prevalence rates in non-clinical male and female samples. *Journal of Eating Disorders, 5*(1), Article 56. https://doi.org/10.1186/s40337-017-0186-7
DeLisi, M., Drury, A. J., & Elbert, M. J. (2019). The etiology of antisocial personality disorder: The differential roles of adverse childhood experiences and childhood psychopathology. *Comprehensive Psychiatry, 92,* 1–6. https://doi.org/10.1016/j.comppsych.2019.04.001
Deloitte Access Economics. (2020). *The social and economic cost of eating disorders in the United States: A report for the Strategic Training Initiative for the Prevention of Eating Disorders and the Academy for Eating Disorders.* https://www.hsph.harvard.edu/striped/report-economic-costs-of-eating-disorders/
Demjaha, A., Morgan, K., Morgan, C., Landau, S., Dean, K., Reichenberg, A., Sham, P. C., Fearon, P., Hutchinson, G., Jones, P. B., Murray, R. M., & Dazzan, P. (2009). Combining dimensional and categorical representation of psychosis: The way forward for *DSM-V* and *ICD-11*? *Psychological Medicine, 39*(12), 1943–1955. https://doi.org/10.1017/s0033291709990651
D'Huart, D., Steppan, M., Seker, S., Bürgin, D., Boonmann, C., Birkhölzer, M., Jenkel, N., Fegert, J. M., Schmid, M., & Schmeck, K. (2022). Prevalence and 10-year stability of personality disorders from adolescence to young adulthood in a high-risk sample. *Frontiers in Psychiatry, 13,* Article 840678. https://doi.org/10.3389/fpsyt.2022.840678
Di Giuseppe, M., Perry, J. R. B., Conversano, C., Gelo, O. C. G., & Gennaro, A. (2020). Defense mechanisms, gender, and adaptiveness in emerging personality disorders in adolescent outpatients. *Journal of Nervous and Mental Disease, 208*(12), 933–941. https://doi.org/10.1097/nmd.0000000000001230
Diamond, D., & Hersh, R. G. (2020). Transference-focused psychotherapy for narcissistic personality disorder: An object relations approach. *Journal of Personality Disorders, 34*(Suppl.), 159–176. https://doi.org/10.1521/pedi.2020.34.supp.159
Diamond, D., & Meehan, K. B. (2013). Attachment and object relations in patients with narcissistic personality disorder: Implications for therapeutic process and outcome. *Journal of Clinical Psychology, 69*(1), 1148–1159. https://doi.org/10.1002/jclp.22042
Digman, J. M. (1990). Personality structure: Emergence of the five-factor model. *Annual Review of Psychology, 41*(1), 417–440. https://doi.org/10.1146/annurev.ps.41.020190.002221
Dugré, J. R., & Potvin, S. (2022). Multiple developmental pathways underlying conduct problems: A multitrajectory framework. *Development and Psychopathology, 34*(3), 1115–1124. https://doi.org/10.1017/S0954579420001650
Durand, V. M., Barlow, D. H., & Hofmann, S. G. (2018). *Essentials of abnormal psychology* (8th ed.). Cengage Learning.
Eisenberg, D., Nicklett, E. J., Roeder, K., & Kirz, N. (2011). Eating disorder symptoms among college students: Prevalence, persistence, correlates, and treatment-seeking. *Journal of American College Health, 59*(8), 700–707. https://doi.org/10.1080/07448481.2010.546461
Equit, M., Palmke, M., Becker, N., Moritz, A., & Becker, S. (2012). Eating problems in young children: A population-based study. *Acta Paediatrica, 102*(2), 149–155. https://doi.org/10.1111/apa.12078
Erford, B. T., Bardhoshi, G., Haecker, P., Shingari, B., Schleichter, J., & Atalay, Z. (2019). Selecting assessment instruments for problem behavior outcome research with youth. *Measurement and Evaluation in Counseling and Development, 52*(1), 52–68. https://doi.org/10.1080/07481756.2017.1358063

Erford, B. T., Bardhoshi, G., Ross, M., Gunther, C., & Duncan, K. (2017). Meta-analysis of counseling outcomes for youth with conduct disorders. *Journal of Counseling & Development, 95*(1), 35–44. https://doi.org/10.1002/jcad.12115

Eskander, N. (2020). The psychosocial outcome of conduct and oppositional defiant disorder in children with attention deficit hyperactivity disorder. *Cureus, 12*(8), Article e9521. https://doi.org/10.7759/cureus.9521

Fahlgren, M. K., Puhalla, A. A., Sorgi, K. M., & McCloskey, M. S. (2019). Emotion processing in intermittent explosive disorder. *Psychiatry Research, 273,* 544–550. https://doi.org/10.1016/j.psychres.2019.01.046

Federici, A., Wisniewski, L., & Ben-Porath, D. (2012). Description of an intensive dialectical behavior therapy program for multidiagnostic clients with eating disorders. *Journal of Counseling & Development, 90*(3), 330–338. https://doi.org/10.1002/j.1556-6676.2012.00041.x

Fichter, M., & Quadflieg, N. (2016). Mortality in eating disorders—Results of a large prospective clinical longitudinal study. *International Journal of Eating Disorders, 49*(4), 391–401. https://doi.org/10.1002/eat.22501

Fichter, M. M., Quadflieg, N., Gierk, B., Voderholzer, U., & Heuser, J. (2015). The Munich Eating and Feeding Disorder Questionnaire (Munich ED-Quest) *DSM-5/ICD*-10: Validity, reliability, sensitivity to change and norms. *European Eating Disorders Review, 23*(3), 229–240. https://doi.org/10.1002/erv.2348

First, M. B. (2010). Clinical utility in the revision of the *Diagnostic and statistical manual of mental disorders* (*DSM*). *Professional Psychology: Research and Practice, 41*(6), 465–473. https://doi.org/10.1037/a0021511

First, M. B., Yousif, L. H., Clarke, D. E., Wang, P. S., Gogtay, N., & Appelbaum, P. S. (2022). *DSM-5-TR*: Overview of what's new and what's changed. *World Psychiatry, 21*(2), 218–219. https://doi.org/10.1002/wps.20989

Fleetham, J. A., & Fleming, J. A. (2014). Parasomnias. *Canadian Medical Association Journal, 186*(8), E273–E280. https://doi.org/10.1503/cmaj.120808

Fong, V. C., Hawes, D., & Allen, J. L. (2019). A systematic review of risk and protective factors for externalizing problems in children exposed to intimate partner violence. *Trauma, Violence, & Abuse, 20*(2), 149–167. https://doi.org/10.1177/1524838017692383

Ford, M., & Widiger, T. A. (1989). Sex bias in the diagnosis of histrionic and antisocial personality disorders. *Journal of Consulting and Clinical Psychology, 57*(2), 301–305. https://doi.org/10.1037/0022-006x.57.2.301

Fornaro, M., Orsolini, L., Marini, S., De Berardis, D., Perna, G., Valchera, A., Ganança, L., Solmi, M., Veronese, N., & Stubbs, B. (2016). The prevalence and predictors of bipolar and borderline personality disorders comorbidity: Systematic review and meta-analysis. *Journal of Affective Disorders, 195,* 105–118. https://doi.org/10.1016/j.jad.2016.01.040

Frances, A. (2013). *Essentials of psychiatric diagnosis: Responding to the challenge of DSM-5.* Guilford Press.

Frances, A., & Wollert, R. (2012). Sexual sadism: Avoiding its misuse in sexually violent predator evaluations. *Journal of the American Academy of Psychiatry and the Law, 40*(3), 409–416.

Freeman, D., McManus, S., Brugha, T., Meltzer, H. Y., Jenkins, R., & Bebbington, P. (2011). Concomitants of paranoia in the general population. *Psychological Medicine, 41*(5), 923–936. https://doi.org/10.1017/s0033291710001546

Friborg, O., Martinussen, M., Kaiser, S., Øvergård, K. T., Martinsen, E. W., Schmierer, P., & Rosenvinge, J. H. (2014). Personality disorders in eating disorder not otherwise specified and binge eating disorder: A meta-analysis of comorbidity studies. *The Journal of Nervous and Mental Disease, 202*(2), 119–125. https://doi.org/10.1097/nmd.0000000000000080

Garcia, F. D., & Thibaut, F. (2011). Current concepts in the pharmacotherapy of paraphilias. *Drugs, 71*(6), 771–790. https://doi.org/10.2165/11585490-000000000-00000

Gibbon, S., Duggan, C., Stoffers, J., Huband, N., Völlm, B., Ferriter, M., & Lieb, K. (2010). Psychological interventions for antisocial personality disorder. *Cochrane Database of Systematic Reviews.* https://doi.org/10.1002/14651858.cd007668.pub2

Glenn, A. L., Johnson, A. K., & Raine, A. (2013). Antisocial personality disorder: A current review. *Current Psychiatry Reports, 15*(12), 427–432. https://doi.org/10.1007/s11920-013-0427-7

Gorman, D. A., Gardner, D. M., Murphy, A. L., Feldman, M., Bélanger, S. A., Steele, M. M., Boylan, K., Cochrane-Brink, K., Goldade, R., Soper, P. R., Ustina, J., & Pringsheim, T. (2015). Canadian guidelines on pharmacotherapy for disruptive and aggressive behaviour in children and adolescents with attention-deficit hyperactivity disorder, oppositional defiant disorder, or conduct disorder. *The Canadian Journal of Psychiatry, 60*(2), 62–76. https://doi.org/10.1177/070674371506000204

Grant, B. F., Hasin, D. S., Stinson, F. S., Dawson, D. A., Chou, S. P., Ruan, W., & Pickering, R. P. (2004). Prevalence, correlates, and disability of personality disorders in the United States: Results from the National Epidemiologic Survey on Alcohol and Related Conditions. *The Journal of Clinical Psychiatry, 65*(7), 948–958. https://doi.org/10.4088/JCP.v65n0711

Grant, J. E., Schreiber, L. R., & Odlaug, B. L. (2013). Phenomenology and treatment of behavioural addictions. *Canadian Journal of Psychiatry, 58*(5), 252–259. https://doi.org/10.4088/JCP.v65n0711

Groenman, A. P., Janssen, T. W. P., & Oosterlaan, J. (2017). Childhood psychiatric disorders as risk factor for subsequent substance abuse: A meta-analysis. *Journal of the American Academy of Child & Adolescent Psychiatry, 56*(7), 556–569. https://doi.org/10.1016/j.jaac.2017.05.004

Gunderson, J. G., Herpertz, S. C., Skodol, A. E., Torgersen, S., & Zanarini, M. C. (2018). Borderline personality disorder. *Nature Reviews Disease Primers, 4*(1), Article 18029. https://doi.org/10.1038/nrdp.2018.29

Guterman, J. T., Martin, C. V., & Rudes, J. (2011). A solution-focused approach to frotteurism. *Journal of Systemic Therapies, 30*(1), 59–72. https://doi.org/10.1521/jsyt.2011.30.1.59

Hadjipavlou, G., & Ogrodniczuk, J. S. (2010). Promising psychotherapies for personality disorders. *The Canadian Journal of Psychiatry, 55*(4), 202–210. https://doi.org/10.1177/070674371005500403

Hambly, J. L., Khan, S., McDermott, B., Bor, W., & Haywood, A. (2016). Pharmacotherapy of conduct disorder: Challenges, options and future directions. *Journal of Psychopharmacology, 30*(10), 967–975. https://doi.org/10.1177/0269881116658985

Hartmann, A. S., Becker, A. E., Hampton, C., & Bryant-Waugh, R. (2012). Pica and rumination disorder in DSM-5. *Psychiatric Annals, 42*(11), 426–430.

Harvey, A. G., & Gumport, N. B. (2015). Evidence-based psychological treatments for mental disorders: Modifiable barriers to access and possible solutions. *Behaviour Research and Therapy, 68,* 1–12. https://doi.org/10.1016/j.brat.2015.02.004

Helander, M., Asperholm, M., Wetterborg, D., Öst, L.-G., Hellner, C., Herlitz, A., & Enebrink, P. (2022). The efficacy of parent management training with or without involving the child in the treatment among children with clinical levels of disruptive behavior: A meta-analysis. *Child Psychiatry & Human Development.* Advance online publication. https://doi.org/10.1007/s10578-022-01367-y

Hilbert, A. (2020). Childhood eating and feeding disturbances. *Nutrients, 12*(4), Article 972. https://doi.org/10.3390/nu12040972

Høye, A., Jacobsen, B. K., Bramness, J. G., Nesvåg, R., Reichborn-Kjennerud, T., & Heiberg, I. (2021). Total and cause-specific mortality in patients with personality disorders: The association between comorbid severe mental illness and substance use disorders. *Social Psychiatry and Psychiatric Epidemiology, 56*(10), 1809–1819. https://doi.org/10.1007/s00127-021-02055-3

Hyde, J. S., & DeLamater, J. D. (2013). *Understanding human sexuality* (12th ed.). McGraw-Hill.

Iacovino, J. M., Jackson, J. J., & Oltmanns, T. F. (2014). The relative impact of socioeconomic status and childhood trauma on Black-White differences in paranoid personality disorder symptoms. *Journal of Abnormal Psychology, 123*(1), 225–230. https://doi.org/10.1037/a0035258

Inchausti, F., Velázquez-Basterra, G., Fonseca-Pedrero, E., MacBeth, A., Popolo, R., & Dimaggio, G. (2022). Metacognitive interpersonal group therapy for adolescents with avoidant personality disorder: The case of Sofia. *Journal of Clinical Psychology, 78*(8), 1579–1589. https://doi.org/10.1002/jclp.23356

Irfan, M., Hussain, N. H. N., Noor, N. M., Mohamed, M., Sidi, H., & Ismail, S. B. (2020). Epidemiology of male sexual dysfunction in Asian and European regions: A systematic review. *American Journal of Men's Health, 14*(4), Article 1557988320937200. https://doi.org/10.1177/1557988320937200

Johnson, A. M., Hawes, D. J., Eisenberg, N., Kohlhoff, J., & Dudeney, J. (2017). Emotion socialization and child conduct problems: A comprehensive review and meta-analysis. *Clinical Psychology Review, 54,* 65–80. https://doi.org/10.1016/j.cpr.2017.04.001

Joiner, T. E., Robison, M., McClanahan, S., Riddle, M., Manwaring, J., Rienecke, R. D., & Blalock, D. V. (2022). Eating disorder behaviors as predictors of suicidal ideation among people with an eating disorder. *International Journal of Eating Disorders, 55*(10), 1352–1360. https://doi.org/10.1002/eat.23770

Kalmbach, D. A., Anderson, J. H., & Drake, C. L. (2018). The impact of stress on sleep: Pathogenic sleep reactivity as a vulnerability to insomnia and circadian disorders. *Journal of Sleep Research, 27*(6), Article e12710. https://doi.org/10.1111/jsr.12710

Kaye, W. H., Klump, K. L., Frank, G. K. W., & Strober, M. (2000). Anorexia and bulimia nervosa. *Annual Review of Medicine, 51,* 299–313. https://doi.org/10.1146/annurev.med.51.1.299

Kellett, S. (2007). A time series evaluation of the treatment of histrionic personality disorder with cognitive analytic therapy. *Psychology and Psychotherapy, 80*(3), 389–405. https://doi.org/10.1348/147608306X161421

Kellett, S., & Hardy, G. E. (2014). Treatment of paranoid personality disorder with cognitive analytic therapy: A mixed methods single case experimental design. *Clinical Psychology & Psychotherapy, 21*(5), 452–464. https://doi.org/10.1002/cpp.1845

Kellett, S., & Lees, S. (2020). Quasi-experimental N = 1 evaluation of the effectiveness of cognitive analytic therapy for dependent personality disorder. *Journal of Psychotherapy Integration, 30*(3), 458–475. https://doi.org/10.1037/int0000170

Kosson, D. S., Blackburn, R., Byrnes, K. A., Park, S., Logan, C., & Donnelly, J. (2008). Assessing interpersonal aspects of schizoid personality disorder: Preliminary validation studies. *Journal of Personality Assessment, 90*(2), 185–196. https://doi.org/10.1080/00223890701845427

Kraemer, H. C. (2007). *DSM* categories and dimensions in clinical and research contexts. *International Journal of Methods in Psychiatric Research, 16*(S1), S8–S15. https://doi.org/10.1002/mpr.211

Kramer, M. J., Wilborn, D. D., Spencer, C., Stevenson, B. L., & Dvorak, R. D. (2019). Protective behavioral strategies moderate the association between narcissistic traits and alcohol pathology in college student drinkers. *Substance Use & Misuse, 54*(5), 863-867. https://doi.org/10.1080/10826084.2018.1547909

Kress, V., & Paylo, M. (2018). *Treating those with mental disorders. A comprehensive approach to case conceptualization and treatment.* Pearson.

Krueger, R. B., Reed, G. M., First, M. B., Marais, A., Kismödi, E., & Briken, P. (2017). Proposals for paraphilic disorders in the *International Classification of Diseases and Related Health Problems, Eleventh Revision (ICD-11). Archives of Sexual Behavior, 46*(5), 1529–1545. https://doi.org/10.1007/s10508-017-0944-2

Kunas, S. L., Stuke, H., Plank, I. S., Laing, E. M., Bermpohl, F., & Ströhle, A. (2022). Neurofunctional alterations of cognitive down-regulation of craving in quitting motivated smokers. *Psychology of Addictive Behaviors, 36*(8), 1012–1022. https://doi.org/10.1037/adb0000820

Kupfer, D. J., First, M. B., & Regier, D. A. (2002). *A research agenda for DSM-V.* American Psychiatric Association.

Lambert, M. J., & Barley, D. E. (2001). Research summary on the therapeutic relationship and psychotherapy outcome. *Psychotherapy, 38*(4), 357–361. https://doi.org/10.1037/0033-3204.38.4.357

Långström, N., & Seto, M. C. (2006). Exhibitionistic and voyeuristic behavior in a Swedish national population survey. *Archives of Sexual Behavior, 35,* 427–435. https://doi.org/10.1007/s10508-006-9042-6

Liebke, L., Koppe, G., Bungert, M., Thome, J., Hauschild, S., Defiebre, N., Izurieta Hidalgo, N. A., Schmahl, C., Bohus, M., & Lis, S. (2018). Difficulties with being socially accepted: An experimental study in borderline personality disorder. *Journal of Abnormal Psychology, 127*(7), 670–682. https://doi.org/10.1037/abn0000373

Limbrick-Oldfield, E. H., Mick, I., Cocks, R., McGonigle, J., Sharman, S., Goldstone, A., Stokes, P., Waldman, A. D., Erritzoe, D., Bowden-Jones, H., Nutt, D. J., Lingford-Hughes, A., & Clark, L. (2017). Neural substrates of cue reactivity and craving in gambling disorder. *Translational Psychiatry, 7*(1), Article e992. https://doi.org/10.1038/tp.2016.256

Lindhiem, O., Burke, J. D., Feldman, J. A., Kolko, D. J., & Pilkonis, P. A. (2023). Deficits in parent knowledge of behavior management skills is strongly associated with CD symptoms but not ODD symptoms. *Journal of Psychopathology and Behavioral Assessment, 45*(1), 18–26. https://doi.org/10.1007/s10862-022-09989-1

Linehan, M. (2014). *DBT? Skills training manual.* Guilford Press.

Linville, D., Stice, E., Gau, J., & O'Neil, M. (2011). Predictive effects of mother and peer influences on increases in adolescent eating disorder risk factors and symptoms: A 3-year longitudinal study. *International Journal of Eating Disorders, 44*(8), 745–751. https://doi.org/10.1002/eat.20907

Lynch, T. R. (2018). *Radically open dialectical behavior therapy: Theory and practice for treating disorders of overcontrol.* New Harbinger.

Maisel, D. (2020). *Paranoid personality disorder: A theoretical treatment using integrated components from dialectical behavior therapy and transference focused psychotherapy* [Unpublished doctoral dissertation]. Chicago School of Professional Psychology.

Maniglio, R. (2014). Prevalence of sexual abuse among children with conduct disorder: A systematic review. *Clinical Child & Family Psychology Review, 17*(3), 268–282. https://doi.org/10.1007/s10567-013-0161-z

Manninen, M. (2022). Lifetime psychiatric diagnoses among adolescents with severe conduct problems—A register-based follow-up study. *Child Abuse & Neglect, 131,* Article 105765. https://doi.org/10.1016/j.chiabu.2022.105765

Mark, D., Roy, S., Walsh, H., & Neumann, C. S. (2022). Antisocial personality disorder. In S. K. Huprich (Ed.), *Personality disorders and pathology: Integrating clinical assessment and practice in the DSM-5 and ICD-11 era* (pp. 391–411). American Psychological Association. https://doi.org/10.1037/0000310-018

Martens, W. H. J. (2010). Schizoid personality disorder linked to unbearable and inescapable loneliness. *European Journal of Psychiatry, 24*(1), 38–45. https://doi.org/10.4321/s0213-61632010000100005

Masheb, R. M., Ramsey, C. M., Marsh, A. G., Decker, S. E., Maguen, S., Brandt, C., & Haskell, S. G. (2021). *DSM-5* eating disorder prevalence, gender differences, and mental health associations in United States military veterans. *International Journal of Eating Disorders, 54*(7), 1171–1180. https://doi.org/10.1002/eat.23501

Masters, W. H., & Johnson, V. E. (1966). *Human sexual response.* Bantam Books.

McClure, M. M., Harvey, P. D., Bowie, C. R., Iacoviello, B. M., & Siever, L. J. (2013). Functional outcomes, functional capacity, and cognitive impairment in schizotypal personality disorder. *Schizophrenia Research, 144*(1–3), 146–150. https://doi.org/10.1016/j.schres.2012.12.012

McKeon, P. O., & Murray, R. M. (1987). Familial aspects of obsessive-compulsive neurosis. *British Journal of Psychiatry, 151*(4), 528–534. https://doi.org/10.1192/bjp.151.4.528

Mercer, D., Douglass, A. B., & Links, P. S. (2009). Meta-analyses of mood stabilizers, antidepressants and antipsychotics in the treatment of borderline personality disorder: Effectiveness for depression and anger symptoms. *Journal of Personality Disorders, 23*(2), 156–174. https://doi.org/10.1521/pedi.2009.23.2.156

Mohammadi, M.-R., Salmanian, M., & Keshavarzi, Z. (2021). The global prevalence of conduct disorder: A systematic review and meta-analysis. *Iranian Journal of Psychiatry, 16*(2), 205–225.

Montes, S. (2013, November 1). Facing a rising tide of personality disorders. *Counseling Today.* https://ct.counseling.org/2013/11/facing-a-rising-tide-of-personality-disorders/

Moore, A. A., Silberg, J. L., Roberson-Nay, R., & Mezuk, B. (2017). Life course persistent and adolescence limited conduct disorder in a nationally representative US sample: Prevalence, predictors, and outcomes. *Social Psychiatry and Psychiatric Epidemiology, 52*(4), 435–443. https://doi.org/10.1007/s00127-017-1337-5

Moreau, C., Kågesten, A., & Blum, R. (2016). Sexual dysfunction among youth: An overlooked sexual health concern. *BMC Public Health, 16*(1), Article 1170. https://doi.org/10.1186/s12889-016-3835-x

Morrison, J. (2006). *DSM-IV made easy: The clinician's guide to diagnosis.* Guilford Press.

Mulder, R. T. (2018). Cultural aspects of personality disorder. In W. J. Livesley & R. Larstone (Eds.), *Handbook of personality disorders: Theory, research and treatment* (pp. 88–100). Guilford Press.

National Academies of Sciences, Engineering, and Medicine. (2017). *The health effects of cannabis and cannabinoids: The current state of evidence and recommendations for research.* National Academies Press. https://doi.org/10.17226/24625

National Highway Traffic Safety Administration. (n.d.). *Drowsy driving.* https:www.nhtsa.gov/risky-driving/drowsy-driving

National Institute of Mental Health. (2023). *Eating disorders.* https://www.nimh.nih.gov/health/topics/eating-disorders

National Institute on Drug Abuse. (2020). *Common comorbidities with substance use disorders research report.* https://www.ncbi.nlm.nih.gov/books/NBK571451/

National Institute on Drug Abuse. (2021). *Words matter—Terms to use and avoid when talking about addiction.* https://nida.nih.gov/nidamed-medical-health-professionals/health-professions-education/words-matter-terms-to-use-avoid-when-talking-about-addiction

National Institute on Drug Abuse. (2022). *Drugs and the brain.* https://nida.nih.gov/publications/drugs-brains-behavior-science-addiction/drugs-brain

Newton-Howes, G., Tyrer, P., Anagnostakis, K., Cooper, S., Bowden-Jones, O., & Weaver, T. (2010). The prevalence of personality disorder, its comorbidity with mental state disorders, and its clinical significance in community mental health teams. *Social Psychiatry and Psychiatric Epidemiology, 45*(4), 453–460. https://doi.org/10.1007/s00127-009-0084-7

Nolen-Hoeksema, S. (2006). The etiology of gender differences in depression. In C. M. Mazure & G. P. Keita (Eds.), *Understanding depression in women: Applying empirical research to practice and policy* (pp. 9–43). American Psychological Association.

Noordermeer, S. D. S., Luman, M., & Oosterlaan, J. (2016). A systematic review and meta-analysis of neuroimaging in oppositional defiant disorder (ODD) and conduct disorder (CD) taking attention-deficit hyperactivity disorder (ADHD) into account. *Neuropsychology Review, 26*(1), 44–72. https://doi.org/10.1007/s11065-015-9315-8

Olabi, B., & Hall, J. (2010). Review: Borderline personality disorder: Current drug treatments and future prospects. *Therapeutic Advances in Chronic Disease, 1*(2), 59–66. https://doi.org/0.1177/2040622310368455

Oldham, J. M. (2015). The alternative *DSM-5* model for personality disorders. *World Psychiatry, 14*(2), 234–236. https://doi.org/10.1002/wps.20232

Pagan, J. L., Oltmanns, T. F., Whitmore, M. J., & Turkheimer, E. (2005). Personality disorder not otherwise specified: Searching for an empirically based diagnostic threshold. *Journal of Personality Disorders, 19*(6), 674–689. https://doi.org/10.1521/pedi.2005.19.6.674

Panza, K. E., Kline, A. C., Na, P. J., Potenza, M. N., Norman, S. B., & Pietrzak, R. H. (2022). Epidemiology of *DSM-5* alcohol use disorder in U.S. military veterans: Results from the National Health and Resilience in Veterans Study. *Drug and Alcohol Dependence, 231*, Article 109240. https://doi.org/10.1016/j.drugalcdep.2021.109240

Pardini, D., & Frick, P. J. (2013). Multiple developmental pathways to conduct disorder: Current conceptualizations and clinical implications. *Journal of Canadian Child and Adolescent Psychiatry, 22*(1), 20–25.

Paris, J. (2015). *The intelligent clinician's guide to the DSM-5* (2nd ed.). Oxford University Press.

Parpottas, P. (2012). A critique on the use of standard psychopathological classifications in understanding human distress: The example of 'schizoid personality disorder.' *Counselling Psychology Review, 27*(1), 44–52. https://doi.org/10.53841/bpscpr.2011.27.1.44

Parry-Jones, B. (1994). Mercyism or rumination disorder: A historical investigation and current assessment. *British Journal of Psychiatry, 165*(3), 303–314. https://doi.org/10.1192/bjp.165.3.303

Patoilo, M. S., Berman, M. E., & Coccaro, E. F. (2021). Emotion attribution in intermittent explosive disorder. *Comprehensive Psychiatry, 106*, Article 152229. https://doi.org/10.1016/j.comppsych.2021.152229

Perks, D. L. C., Watt, B. D., Fritzon, K., & Doley, R. M. (2019). Juvenile firesetters as multiple problem youth with particular interests in fire: A meta-analysis. *Aggression and Violent Behavior, 47*, 189–203. https://doi.org/10.1016/j.avb.2019.04.003

Perrotta, G. (2021). Histrionic personality disorder: Definition, clinical profiles, differential diagnosis and therapeutic framework. *Archives of Community Medicine and Public Health, 7*(1), 1–5. https://doi.org/10.17352/2455-5479.000123

Recovery Centers of America. (2022). *Economic cost of substance abuse disorder in the United States, 2019.* https://recoverycentersofamerica.com/resource/economic-cost-of-substance-abuse-disorder-in-united-states-2019/

Reichborn-Kjennerud, T. (2010). The genetic epidemiology of personality disorders. *Dialogues in Clinical Neuroscience, 12*(1), 103–114. https://doi.org/10.31887/dcns.2010.12.1/trkjennerud

Riise, E. N., Wergeland, G. J. H., Njardvik, U., & Öst, L.-G. (2021). Cognitive behavior therapy for externalizing disorders in children and adolescents in routine clinical care: A systematic review and meta-analysis. *Clinical Psychology Review, 83*, Article 101954. https://doi.org/10.1016/j.cpr.2020.101954

Ripoll, L. H., Zaki, J., Perez-Rodriguez, M. M., Snyder, R., Strike, K. S., Boussi, A. R., Bartz, J. A., Ochsner, K. N., Siever, L. J., & New, A. S. (2013). Empathic accuracy and cognition in schizotypal personality disorder. *Psychiatry Research-Neuroimaging, 210*(1), 232–241. https://doi.org/10.1016/j.psychres.2013.05.025

Rosenbaum, J. F., & Pollock, R. (2002). *DSM-V*—Plans and perspectives. *Medscape Psychiatry.* http://www.medscape.org/viewarticle/436403

Rowell, T., & Neal-Barnett, A. (2022). A systematic review of the effect of parental adverse childhood experiences on parenting and child psychopathology. *Journal of Child & Adolescent Trauma, 15*(1), 167–180. https://doi.org/10.1007/s40653-021-00400-x

Ruisch, I. H., Dietrich, A., Glennon, J. C., Buitelaar, J. K., & Hoekstra, P. J. (2018). Maternal substance use during pregnancy and offspring conduct problems: A meta-analysis. *Neuroscience & Biobehavioral Reviews, 84,* 325–336. https://doi.org/10.1016/j.neubiorev.2017.08.014

Ruocco, A. C. (2005). Reevaluating the distinction between Axis I and Axis II disorders: The case of borderline personality disorder. *Journal of Clinical Psychology, 61*(12), 1509–1523. https://doi.org/10.1002/jclp.20205

Samuel, D. B., & Widiger, T. A. (2008). A meta-analytic review of the relationships between the five-factor model and *DSM-IV-TR* personality disorders: A facet level analysis. *Clinical Psychology Review, 28*(8), 1326–1342. https://doi.org/10.1016/j.cpr.2008.07.002

Schnell, K., & Herpertz, S. C. (2018). Emotion regulation and social cognition as functional targets of mechanism-based psychotherapy in major depression with comorbid personality pathology. *Journal of Personality Disorders, 32*(Suppl.), 12–35. https://doi.org/10.1521/pedi.2018.32.supp.12

Schorr, M. T., Tietbohl-Santos, B., De Oliveira, L. N., Terra, L., De Borba Telles, L. E., & Hauck, S. (2020). Association between different types of childhood trauma and parental bonding with antisocial traits in adulthood: A systematic review. *Child Abuse & Neglect, 107,* Article 104621. https://doi.org/10.1016/j.chiabu.2020.104621

Schroedl, R. L., Alioto, A., & DiLorenzo, C. (2013). Behavioral treatment for adolescent rumination syndrome: A case report. *Clinical Practice in Pediatric Psychology, 1*(1), 89–93. https://doi.org/10.1037/cpp0000010

Schwitzer, A. M. (2012). Diagnosing, conceptualizing, and treating eating disorders not otherwise specified: A comprehensive practice model. *Journal of Counseling & Development, 90*(3), 281–289. https://doi.org/10.1002/j.1556-6676.2012.00036.x

Scott, K. M., Lim, C. C. W., Hwang, I., Adamowski, T., Al-Hamzawi, A., Bromet, E., Bunting, B., Ferrand, M. P., Florescu, S., Gureje, O., Hinkov, H., Hu, C., Karam, E., Lee, S., Posada-Villa, J., Stein, D., Tachimori, H., Viana, M. C., Xavier, M., & Kessler, R. C. (2016). The cross-national epidemiology of *DSM-IV* intermittent explosive disorder. *Psychological Medicine, 46*(15), 3161–3172. https://doi.org/10.1017/S0033291716001859

Sensi, C., Ricca, V., Gravestock, S., & Bertelli, M. O. (2022). Feeding, eating and weight disorders. In M. O. Bertelli, D. Shoumitro, K. Munir, A. Hassiotis, & L. Salvador-Carulla (Eds.), *Textbook of psychiatry for intellectual disability and autism spectrum disorder* (pp. 655–684). Springer. https://doi.org/10.1007/978-3-319-95720-3_25

Shapira, B. E., & Dahlen, P. (2010). Therapeutic treatment protocol for enuresis using an enuresis alarm. *Journal of Counseling & Development, 88*(2), 246–252. https://doi.org/10.1002/j.1556-6678.2010.tb00017.x

Shepard, J. A., Poler, J. E., & Grabman, J. H. (2017). Evidence-based psychosocial treatments for pediatric elimination disorders. *Journal of Clinical Child & Adolescent Psychology, 46*(6), 767–797. https://doi.org/10.1080/15374416.2016.1247356

Simonsen, S., Popolo, R., Juul, S., Frandsen, F. W., Sorensen, P., & Dimaggio, G. (2022). Treating avoidant personality disorder with combined individual metacognitive interpersonal therapy and group mentalization-based treatment: A pilot study. *The Journal of Nervous and Mental Disease, 210*(3), 163–171. https://doi.org/10.1097/NMD.0000000000001432

Skodol, A. E., & Bender, D. S. (2009). The future of personality disorders in *DSM-V*? *American Journal of Psychiatry, 166*(4), 388–391. https://doi.org/10.1176/appi.ajp.2009.09010090

Smolak, L. (2011). Body image development in childhood. In T. Cash & L. Smolak (Eds.), *Body image: A handbook of science, practice, and prevention* (2nd ed., pp. 67–75). Guilford Press.

Smolak, L., & Chun-Kennedy, C. (2013). Sociocultural influences on the development of eating disorders and obesity. In L. H. Choate (Ed.), *Eating disorders and obesity: A counselor's guide to prevention and treatment* (pp. 3–20). American Counseling Association.

Stice, E., Marti, C. N., & Rohde, P. (2013). Prevalence, incidence, impairment, and course of the proposed *DSM-5* eating disorder diagnoses in an 8-year prospective community study of young women. *Journal of Abnormal Psychology, 122*(2), 445–457. https://doi.org/10.1037/a0030679

Stinson, F. S., Dawson, D. V., Goldstein, R. B., Chou, S. P., Huang, B., Smith, S. L., Ruan, W. J., Pulay, A. J., Saha, T. D., Pickering, R. P., & Grant, B. F. (2008). Prevalence, correlates, disability, and comorbidity of *DSM-IV* narcissistic personality disorder. *The Journal of Clinical Psychiatry, 69*(7), 1033–1045. https://doi.org/10.4088/jcp.v69n0701

Stone, M. H. (1993). *Abnormalities of personality: Within and beyond the realm of treatment.* Norton.

Substance Abuse and Mental Health Services Administration. (2022). *Key substance use and mental health indicators in the United States: Results from the 2021 National Survey on Drug Use and Health* (HHS Publication No. PEP22-07-01-005, NSDUH Series H-57). https://www.samhsa.gov/data/sites/default/files/reports/rpt39443/2021NSDUHFFRRev010323.pdf

Szentkirályi, A., Madarász, C. Z., & Novák, M. (2009). Sleep disorders: Impact on daytime functioning and quality of life. *Expert Review of Pharmacoeconomics & Outcomes Research, 9*(1), 49–64. https://doi.org/10.1586/14737167.9.1.49

Tahir, T., Wong, M. M., Maaz, M., Naufal, R., Tahir, R., & Naidoo, Y. (2022). Pharmacotherapy of impulse control disorders: A systematic review. *Psychiatry Research, 311,* Article 114499. https://doi.org/10.1016/j.psychres.2022.114499

Thyberg, C. T., & Lombardi, B. M. (2022). Examining racial differences in internalizing and externalizing diagnoses for children exposed to adverse childhood experiences. *Clinical Social Work Journal, 50*(3), 286–296. https://doi.org/10.1007/s10615-022-00842-2

Torales, J., González, I., Castaldelli-Maia, J. M., & Ventriglio, A. (2020). Kleptomania as a neglected disorder in psychiatry. *International Review of Psychiatry, 32*(5–6), 451–454. https://doi.org/10.1080/09540261.2020.1756635

Twenge, J. M. (2001). Birth cohort changes in extraversion: A cross-temporal meta-analysis, 1966–1993. *Personality and Individual Differences, 30*(5), 735–748. https://doi.org/10.1016/s0191-8869(00)00066-0

Twenge, J. M., & Foster, J. D. (2010). Birth cohort increases in narcissistic personality traits among American college students, 1982–2009. *Social Psychological and Personality Science, 1*(1), 99–106. https://doi.org/10.1177/1948550609355719

Uri, R. C., Wu, Y., Baker, J. H., & Munn-Chernoff, M. A. (2021). Eating disorder symptoms in Asian American college students. *Eating Behaviors, 40,* Article 101458. https://doi.org/10.1016/j.eatbeh.2020.101458

U.S. Food and Drug Administration. (2023). *Information about medication-assisted treatment (MAT).* https://www.fda.gov/drugs/information-drug-class/information-about-medication-assisted-treatment-mat

Van Den Bosch, L., Rijckmans, M., Decoene, S., & Chapman, A. (2018). Treatment of antisocial personality disorder: Development of a practice focused framework. *International Journal of Law and Psychiatry, 58,* 72–78. https://doi.org/10.1016/j.ijlp.2018.03.002

Vater, A., Moritz, S., & Roepke, S. (2018). Does a narcissism epidemic exist in modern Western societies? Comparing narcissism and self-esteem in East and West Germany. *PLOS ONE, 13*(1), Article e0188287. https://doi.org/10.1371/journal.pone.0188287

Venema, T. A., & Pfattheicher, S. (2021). Perceived susceptibility to COVID-19 infection and narcissistic traits. *Personality and Individual Differences, 175,* Article 110696. https://doi.org/10.1016/j.paid.2021.110696

Videler, A. C., Hutsebaut, J., Schulkens, J. E. M., Sobczak, S., & Van Alphen, S. P. J. (2019). A life span perspective on borderline personality disorder. *Current Psychiatry Reports, 21*(7), Article 51. https://doi.org/10.1007/s11920-019-1040-1

Volkow, N. D., Swanson, J. M., Evins, A. E., DeLisi, L. E., Meier, M. H., Gonzalez, R. S., Bloomfield, M. A. P., Curran, H. V., & Baler, R. (2016). Effects of cannabis use on human behavior, including cognition, motivation, and psychosis: A review. *JAMA Psychiatry, 73*(3), 292–297. https://doi.org/10.1001/jamapsychiatry.2015.3278

Wade, T. D., & O'Shea, A. E. (2015). *DSM-5* unspecified feeding and eating disorders in adolescents: What do they look like and are they clinically significant? *International Journal of Eating Disorders, 48*(4), 367–374. https://doi.org/10.1002/eat.22303

Weisz, J. R., Kuppens, S., Ng, M. Y., Vaughn-Coaxum, R. A., Ugueto, A. M., Eckshtain, D., & Corteselli, K. A. (2019). Are psychotherapies for young people growing stronger? Tracking trends over time for youth anxiety, depression, attention-deficit/hyperactivity disorder, and conduct problems. *Perspectives on Psychological Science, 14*(2), 216–237. https://doi.org/10.1177/1745691618805436

Wetterborg, D., Dehlbom, P., Långström, N., Andersson, G., Fruzzetti, A. E., & Enebrink, P. (2020). Dialectical behavior therapy for men with borderline personality disorder and antisocial behavior: A clinical trial. *Journal of Personality Disorders, 34*(1), 22–39. https://doi.org/10.1521/pedi_2018_32_379

Widiger, T. A. (2005). Five factor model of personality disorder: Integrating science and practice. Journal of Research in Personality, 39(1), 67–83. https://doi.org/10.1016/j.jrp.2004.09.010

Winsper, C., Bilgin, A., Thompson, A., Marwaha, S., Chanen, A. M., Singh, S. P., Wang, A., & Furtado, V. (2020). The prevalence of personality disorders in the community: A global systematic review and meta-analysis. British Journal of Psychiatry, 216(2), 69–78. https://doi.org/10.1192/bjp.2019.166

Wright, L., Lari, L., Iazzetta, S., Saettoni, M., & Gragnani, A. (2022). Differential diagnosis of borderline personality disorder and bipolar disorder: Self-concept, identity and self-esteem. Clinical Psychology & Psychotherapy, 29(1), 26–61. https://doi.org/10.1002/cpp.2591

Zee, P. C., & Vitiello, M. V. (2009). Circadian rhythm sleep disorder: Irregular sleep wake rhythm type. Sleep Clinic, 4(2), 213–218. https://doi.org/10.1016/j.jsmc.2009.01.009

Part Four

Changes and Implications Involving Diagnoses Commonly Made by Other Professionals

Introduction

Part Four covers disorders that are commonly diagnosed by other professionals, including primary care physicians, psychiatrists, and psychologists with specialized training in neuropsychological or neurodevelopmental functioning. We have divided this section into four chapters: Chapter 16, Neurodevelopmental and Neurocognitive Disorders; Chapter 17, Schizophrenia Spectrum and Other Psychotic Disorders; Chapter 18, Dissociative Disorders; and Chapter 19, Somatic Symptom and Related Disorders. Differing from the two previous sections, this part of the *Learning Companion* includes diagnoses that are seen but less commonly diagnosed in a counseling setting. Although counselors certainly work with these concerns, some of these disorders are diagnosed using highly specialized assessments or require an extensive medical examination by a physician or other qualified medical professional.

Changes to Chapter 16, Neurodevelopmental and Neurocognitive Disorders, include the enumeration of *intellectual developmental disorder (intellectual disability)* that aligns with the *ICD-11* and U.S. law. *Intellectual disability* remains acceptable for clinical use. Public Law 111–256, Rosa's Law, is a 2010 federal statute that legally replaces the term *mental retardation* with *intellectual disability*. Regardless of nomenclature, limitations in pervasive intellectual functioning qualify as intellectual developmental disorder (intellectual disability). Current diagnoses are rendered by level of functioning as opposed to a specific standardized IQ (APA, 2022a).

There are minimal changes from the *DSM-5* to the *DSM-5-TR* for disorders in Chapter 17, Schizophrenia Spectrum and Other Psychotic Disorders. Criterion 4 in Other Specified Schizophrenia Spectrum and Other Psychotic Disorder was updated in the *DSM-5-TR* to replace references to delusional symptoms in a partner and to "delusional symptoms in context of relationship with an individual with prominent delusions" (APA, 2022a, p. 138). Section III of the *DSM-5-TR* continues to propose attenuated psychosis syndrome as a condition for further study. Criterion A has been updated to remove language about "relatively intact reality testing." It now names specific, attenuated positive symptoms.

For Chapter 18, Dissociative Disorders, there are no major changes from the *DSM-5* to the *DSM-5-TR*. Rather, changes are concentrated in the text sections, including updated literature and more nuanced attention to culture-, sex-, and gender-related diagnostic issues in this category.

There are no major changes to Chapter 19, Somatic Symptom and Related Disorders from the *DSM-5* to the *DSM-5-TR*. The only modification is with functional neurological symptom disorder, which now lists conversion disorder parenthetically—functional neurological symptom disorder (conversion disorder). This was done to align with the international health community and to facilitate the use of neutral terminology.

As with other parts of this *Learning Companion*, readers will find a description of each disorder or group of disorders, including essential features and changes from the *DSM-5* to the *DSM-5-TR*. Where applicable, special considerations, cultural considerations, and case examples are given to assist counselors in understanding diagnoses and working with clients.

Chapter 16

Neurodevelopmental and Neurocognitive Disorders

The neurodevelopmental and neurocognitive disorders discussed in this chapter share the commonality of probable biological etiology. Neurodevelopmental disorders tend to appear in the beginning phases of the life span, whereas neurocognitive disorders are most prevalent toward the end of the life span. The neurodevelopmental disorders in the *DSM-5-TR* include intellectual developmental disorders, communication disorders, autism spectrum disorder (ASD), ADHD, specific learning disorder, and motor disorders. The neurocognitive disorders encompass delirium and major and mild neurocognitive disorders with multiple etiological subtypes (APA, 2022a; Francés et al., 2022; Mikami et al., 2019; Nikolich & Hyman, 2015). These classifications of disorders require specialized diagnostic assessment and are not typically diagnosed by professional counselors. Referral for specialized assessment is indicated for all disorders in this chapter.

NEURODEVELOPMENTAL DISORDERS

> It's my son. I'm a health care professional and kept saying that I knew there was something wrong; on many levels he wasn't developing as he should. It was actually a relief to get the diagnosis. It made me look forward to working with a treatment team to help us. Family counseling was a great benefit too.—Raj

Neurodevelopmental disorders are a cluster of disorders that typically display during early childhood, are assumed to have a neurological basis, and encompass difficulty in multiple areas of functioning, including delays in achieving expected milestones. This grouping of syndromes shares the symptomatology of behavioral deficits and excesses. Neurodevelopmental disorders have varying prevalence rates, with ADHD occurring in up to 7.2% of the world population and ASD extant in between 1% and 2% of individuals (APA, 2022a; Dalsgaard et al., 2020; Francés et al., 2022). Neurodevelopmental disorders are frequently diagnosed in medical and educational settings, although counselors often provide valuable services for diagnosed individuals and their families. Onset during childhood makes these disorders even more relevant to counselors working across multiple agency and school settings.

Recent advances in science show differences in brain development in children and adults with neurodevelopmental disorders (Francés et al., 2022). Because individuals with neurodevelopmental disorders have pervasive impairment in personal, social, occupational, and academic areas, it is important for counselors to understand the nosology of the disorders. The implicit genetic and neurological factors render early identification, effective treatment delivery, and access to support services critical (APA, 2022a).

Major Changes From *DSM-5* to *DSM-5-TR*

The predominant change from the *DSM-5* to the *DSM-5-TR* is the enumeration of *intellectual developmental disorder (intellectual disability)*, which aligns with the *ICD-11* and U.S. law. The term *intellectual disability* remains acceptable for clinical use. Public Law 111–256, known as Rosa's Law, is a 2010 federal statute that legally replaces *mental retardation* with *intellectual disability*. Regardless of nomenclature, limitations in pervasive intellectual functioning qualify as intellectual developmental disorder (intellectual disability). Current diagnoses are rendered by level of functioning as opposed to a specific standardized IQ (APA, 2022a).

Readers should note there are coding changes to the neurocognitive disorders; APA (2022b) published a neurocognitive disorders supplement in October 2022 that may be helpful for clinicians working with these disorders. There are also other specified and unspecified disorders associated with each of these categories. We have included a section on other specified and unspecified disorders in the *DSM-5-TR* in Chapter 5, Practice Implications for Counselors, which explains how counselors go about selecting, recording, and coding these diagnoses.

Implications for Counselors

Counselors working across settings should be comfortable with the nomenclature for neurodevelopmental disorders. By definition, symptoms of neurodevelopmental disorders begin in childhood and affect functioning in home and school settings (APA, 2022a). This underscores the importance of assessment and clinical intervention for clients and their families.

It is imperative for counselors to have strong knowledge of diagnostic criteria and differential diagnoses for neurodevelopmental disorders; this is especially relevant because of the benefits for early diagnosis of ASD, the frequency of ADHD diagnoses, and the impact of each of the developmental disorders. Several important areas for counselors to focus on are identification of signs and symptoms indicative of need for assessment referral, provision of appropriate clinical treatment services, referral and treatment team case planning, and facilitation of client and family education (Bourgeron, 2015; Dalsgaard et al., 2020; Peters & Matson, 2020).

Neurodevelopmental disorders can persist throughout youth and into adulthood, sometimes requiring long-term support strategies (APA, 2022a). Clinical interventions and adjunctive support should be emphasized for children, youth, and adults. It is advantageous for counselors to use a spectrum approach depending on each client's level of ability; clinical interventions can then be tailored to specific client needs. The diagnosis is retained, even if the criteria are not currently met, to reflect successful behavioral interventions or environmental changes; this allows for continued treatment services for clients (Aito et al., 2020).

Intellectual Developmental Disorders

This category of disorders encompasses deficits in cognitive functioning, typically characterized by limitations in adaptive behaviors such as activities of daily living (e.g., self-management skills such as hygiene, feeding, and organizing life tasks); social skills, including social judgment and interpersonal communication skills; and conceptualization skills such as language, reading, writing, and memory (APA, 2022a). This is also more consistent with the manual's developmental emphasis on neurobiological etiology.

Intellectual Developmental Disorder (Intellectual Disability) (F7_)

Essential Features

Intellectual developmental disorder (intellectual disability) refers to deficits in cognitive ability in which expected levels of functioning are not met (e.g., age-appropriate activities of daily living). The parenthetical *intellectual disability* is still acceptable as noted in the *DSM-5-TR*. For this diagnosis to be given, intelligence and adaptive functioning both need to be assessed. The level of adaptive functioning determines severity of the disorder. This diagnosis is only used for individuals old enough to complete standardized assessments measuring intellectual ability; although these ability tests are important, they are not sufficient to render the diagnosis. There is a 1% prevalence rate of the disorder in the general U.S. population with some worldwide variation (APA, 2022a).

Differential Diagnosis

If an individual is diagnosed with intellectual developmental disorder (intellectual disability), there is a three-to-four-times heightened probability of a co-occurring disorder(s). Common co-occurring disorders for this diagnosis are major and mild neurocognitive disorders, communication disorders, specific learning disorder, and ASD (APA, 2022a).

Coding, Recording, and Specifiers

The *ICD-10-CM* codes for intellectual developmental disorder (intellectual disability) are linked with the severity specifiers: 317 (F70) *mild*, 31**8.0** (F71) *moderate*, 31**8.1** (F72) *severe*, and 31**8.2** (F73) *profound*. Severity levels are assigned based on functioning, not intellectual ability, with the assessment of conceptual, social, and practical domains. Readers can refer to Table 1: Severity Levels for Intellectual Developmental Disorder (Intellectual Disability) on pages 39–41 of the *DSM-5-TR* for specific information related to the assessment of each specifier (APA, 2022a).

Global Developmental Delay (F88)

According to the *DSM-5-TR*, global developmental delay consists of a child's failure to meet milestones across multiple areas of functioning, specifically in children younger than 5 years of age. This diagnosis should be given when a child cannot be fully assessed or participate in standardized testing because of age. Global developmental delay is a temporary diagnosis and requires further specialized assessment; this diagnosis is often viewed as a precursor for intellectual developmental disorder (intellectual disability).

Communication Disorders

Communication disorders include language disorder (previously expressive and mixed receptive-expressive language disorder), speech sound disorder (previously phonological disorder), childhood onset fluency disorder (previously stuttering), and social (pragmatic) communication disorder. This category of disorders encompasses deficits in language, speech, and communication through verbal and nonverbal behaviors. As with all diagnoses, cultural contexts must be taken into account (APA, 2022a).

Language Disorder (F80.9)

Essential Features

Language disorder possesses the core feature of deficits in language acquisition and use that are seen in verbal and written communication. This includes the use of sign language and must be "substantially and quantifiable below that expected for age" (APA, 2022a, p. 48). In the *DSM-5-TR*, language disorder is coded as F80.9. There are no specifiers for this disorder.

Differential Diagnosis

The counselor should be aware of normal variations in language, hearing, or sensory impairment. Other differential diagnoses are intellectual developmental disorder (intellectual disability), neurological disorders, and language regression (which could be an indicator of ASD). There is often a family history of language disorder; by the age of 4 years, it becomes a stable diagnosis that typically extends into adulthood (APA, 2022a).

Speech Sound Disorder (F80.0)

Essential Features

The hallmark of speech sound disorder is marked difficulty with the articulation of individual sounds (phonemes). Deficits in knowledge of phonemes and coordination of sound-inducing movements occur. In children without speech sound disorder, speech should be understandable by 3 years of age (APA, 2022a). In the *DSM-5-TR*, speech sound disorder is coded as F80.0. There are no specifiers for this disorder.

Differential Diagnosis

Differential diagnoses for speech sound disorder represent normal variations in speech, hearing or other sensory impairment, structural deficits (e.g., cleft palate), dysarthria (when there is a motor disorder affecting speech), and selective mutism (APA, 2022a).

Childhood-Onset Fluency Disorder (Stuttering) (F80.81)

Essential Features

Childhood-onset fluency disorder replaced the term *stuttering* to more accurately reflect the etiology of the disorder and eliminate negative connotations associated with the latter terminology. Key features represent difficulties with normal fluency and timing of speech that is inappropriate for developmental age. Anxiety can worsen the difficulty, and individuals with this disorder sometimes avoid situations that involve public speaking.

Childhood-onset fluency disorder (stuttering) is extant by 6 years of age for 80% to 90% of diagnosed individuals. Prognosis is good, with 65% to 85% recovering from the dysfluency (APA, 2022a). In the *DSM-5-TR*, childhood-onset fluency disorder (stuttering) is coded as F80.81. There are no specifiers for this disorder.

Differential Diagnosis

Counselors should be aware of sensory deficits (e.g., hearing), normal speech difficulties, medication side effects, adult-onset dysfluency (not a *DSM-5-TR* disorder), or Tourette's disorder as differential diagnoses (APA, 2022a). Referral to a speech-language specialist is recommended.

Social (Pragmatic) Communication Disorder (F80.82)

Essential Features

The core features of social (pragmatic) communication disorder are deficits in social uses of language and communication that can result from lack of effective communication, social participation, or development of social relationships. Language impairment is the most common feature. This diagnosis is rarely given in children younger than 4 years of age because they are in the natural process of language acquisition and utilization (APA, 2022a). In the *DSM-5-TR*, social (pragmatic) communication disorder is coded as F80.82. There are no specifiers for this disorder.

Differential Diagnosis

Social (pragmatic) communication disorder was new in the *DSM-5*, and it is an important differential diagnosis for ASD. Social (pragmatic) communication disorder focuses on verbal and nonverbal social deficiencies in communication and represents an important differential category for ASD. The key difference between social (pragmatic) communication disorder and ASD is the mandatory absence of repeated restrictive behaviors, interests, and activities in diagnosing the former (APA, 2022a).

Common differential diagnoses are social anxiety disorder (social phobia), ADHD, intellectual developmental disorder (intellectual disability), and global developmental delay (APA, 2022a). As previously discussed, the diagnosis of social (pragmatic) communication disorder is intended to encompass individuals with deficiencies in social communication but without restricted repetitive behaviors, interests, and activities extant with ASD.

Autism Spectrum Disorder (F84.0)

> I knew from early on that my child was different. My sister's baby was close to the same age and interacted with family and friends quite differently than my child. They smiled and laughed and played while my child didn't. It made me very sad, and I didn't know what to do. Our pediatrician was the first person to mention the word *autism* to me; it was a scary time for us. Now, though, my child is getting help, and my husband and I are in counseling too. We are learning to appreciate the little things and love our little one so much. We've learned being on the autism spectrum doesn't define someone.—Chris

The only change to the diagnosis of autism spectrum disorder (ASD) in the *DSM-5-TR* is with clarification for Criterion A. Specifically, the phrase "as manifested by the following" was revised to read "as manifested by all of the following" to improve its clarity. The revision was made to maintain a high diagnostic threshold by requiring "all of the following" and not "any of the following" criteria, as could be mistakenly implied by the previous wording.

Prevalence rates for ASD are reported at one in 80, with the diagnosis by a specialist imperative for access to services (CDC, 2022; Francés at al., 2022). Because ASD is a lifelong disorder, most individuals living with the diagnosis are adults (APA, 2022a; Peters & Matson, 2020).

Essential Features

ASD includes (a) deficits in social communication and social interaction across different settings and (b) restricted repetitive behaviors, interests, and activities. Specifically, three criteria address shortcomings in social communication and interaction: deficits in social-emotional reciprocity; nonverbal communication in social interactions; and developing, maintaining, and understanding relationships. All three must be met currently or historically. Two of the following four restrictive behavior criteria must also be met: overly dependent on routines, highly sensitive to changes in their environments, intensely focused on particular items, and sensory input sensitivity (APA, 2022a). There is no age requirement of symptom detection by 3 years of age; although symptoms may be extant, concerns may have gone undetected until the child started school and was faced with increased social demands (Mikami et al., 2019).

Special Considerations

Clinicians should keep in mind that the previous diagnosis of Asperger's disorder was encompassed under the ASD diagnosis with the publication of the *DSM-5* and remains so in the *DSM-5-TR*. There may be adult clients (previously diagnosed with Asperger's) and family members who could benefit from psychoeducation in this regard (APA, 2022a).

Differential Diagnosis

According to APA (2022a), common differential diagnoses for ASD are Rett syndrome, selective mutism, language disorders, social (pragmatic) communication disorder, intellectual developmental disorder (intellectual disability) without ASD, stereotypic movement disorder, ADHD, and schizophrenia. Social (pragmatic) communication disorder might be a valid and appropriate diagnosis for some individuals because it allows for social difficulties in absence of the restricted repetitive behaviors. Comorbidities are common, with ADHD and intellectual developmental disorder (intellectual disability) most prevalent (Dalsgaard et al., 2020).

Coding, Recording, and Specifiers

There are no subtypes for ASD. The assigned specifiers are *with or without accompanying intellectual impairment*; *with or without accompanying language impairment*; *associated with a known medical or genetic condition or environmental factor*; *associated with another neurodevelopmental, mental, or behavioral disorder*; or *with catatonia*. Severity levels are Level 1 (*mild*), requiring support; Level 2 (*moderate*), requiring substantial support; and Level 3 (*severe*), requiring very substantial support (see p. 58 of the *DSM-5-TR*).

Case Example

> Adam is a 5-year-old, African American kindergartner and is the only child of loving, busy career parents who adopted Adam from foster care during infancy. Little is known about his birth parents or their background.
>
> Since Adam was about 18 months old, his parents, Cindy and Samantha, noticed that he acted differently than the other children in his playgroup. Adam did not interact with the other children and rarely responded to play with smiles

or laughter. As he got older, it was clear that Adam preferred to play by himself. Because he was rarely upset or caused trouble, Cindy and Samantha didn't worry too much about his preference for solitude until Adam started kindergarten.

Adam's teacher noticed these behaviors and also observed that he would engage in multiple rituals, including rocking back and forth (stimming), untying and tying his shoes, and coloring only with a blue crayon. Adam's teacher referred him to the school counselor, who recommended that Adam receive follow-up testing for a possible neurodevelopmental disorder.

Diagnostic Questions

1. Do Adam's presenting symptoms meet the criteria for ASD?
2. Based on an affirmative answer to Question 1, what specifier(s) would you assign for Adam's diagnosis? What level of severity?
3. What would be the reason(s) a counselor may not diagnose Adam with intellectual disability (intellectual developmental disorder)?
4. Would Adam be more accurately diagnosed with ADHD? If so, why? If not, why not?
5. What rule-outs would you consider for Adam's case?
6. What other information may be needed to make an accurate clinical diagnosis?

Attention-Deficit/Hyperactivity Disorder (F90._)

> Zach was so precocious as a little boy; he lit up the room and entertained everyone. It wasn't until he started school and his teacher contacted us about her concerns that we realized something was wrong. It's true that Zach can't sit still or focus. Now we are being told he needs medication, and we don't want that. Counseling seems to be our best choice to try and help him.—Tom (Zach's dad)

Attention-deficit/hyperactivity disorder (ADHD) is the most common neurodevelopmental disorder in childhood. According to APA (2022a), 5% of children and 2.5% of adults are diagnosed with ADHD. The CDC (2022) lists childhood ADHD prevalence as 9.8%.

Along with the high prevalence rates, there has been heightened awareness of differential diagnoses and identification of comorbidities for individuals with ADHD (Dalsgaard et al., 2020).

Essential Features

ADHD has 18 symptoms divided between the domains of inattention and hyperactivity/impulsivity. The main feature of ADHD is ongoing inattention and hyperactivity/impulsivity that are disruptive across many areas of functioning. Symptoms of ADHD must occur before age 12 (APA, 2022a). ADHD continues to be diagnosable in adults. The concomitant diagnosis of ADHD and ASD is allowed. The same 18 symptoms are used within the domains of inattention and hyperactivity/impulsivity (APA, 2022a).

DSM-5-TR enhancements to the criteria include specific examples for diagnosis across the life span and requirement of cross-situational evidence. In adults, five symptoms are required for the diagnosis instead of six; this chronological expansion of ADHD opens up treatment options for diagnosed adults (Aito et al., 2020). For ADHD and learning disorders, counselors should achieve a level of comfort with the diagnostic changes and coding. Research-informed practice allows counselors to advocate for clients and implement targeted interventions in their clinical settings. Individuals with ADHD respond well to structured treatment approaches, including behavioral therapy and CBT (Mikami et al., 2019).

Differential Diagnosis

Language, motor, and social developmental delays are often comorbid with ADHD. Learning disorders also have frequent co-occurrence, with some reports of comorbidity as high as 50% (APA, 2022a; Dalsgaard et al., 2020). There are multiple additional differential diagnoses: ODD, IED, other neurodevelopmental disorders, specific learning disorder, intellectual disability (intellectual developmental disorder), ASD, RAD, anxiety disorders, depressive disorders, bipolar disorder, DMDD, substance use disorders, personality disorders, psychotic disorders, medication-induced symptoms of ADHD, and neurocognitive disorders (APA, 2022a). For counselors, clear understanding of the criteria for ADHD is imperative because of high prevalence rates and pervasive familial, social, and educational impact.

Coding, Recording, and Specifiers

The coding for ADHD is based on presentation type: F90.2 *combined presentation* if inattention and hyperactivity/impulsivity are met for the past 6 months, F90.0 *predominantly inattentive presentation*, and F90.1 *predominantly hyperactive/impulsive presentation*. The specifier *in partial remission* is used if the criteria have been previously met and there is ongoing impairment in social, academic, or occupational functioning. Severity specifiers of *mild*, *moderate*, and *severe* reflect number of symptoms and level of impairment (APA, 2022a).

Case Example

> Lee is a single, 21-year-old, Asian American college student living with his parents and younger siblings. Although he would like to move out on his own, he has not been able to maintain a job while also keeping his grades high enough to avoid academic probation.
>
> Lee's parents often treat him like a child, and this upsets him. They tell him they will treat him like an adult when he acts like one. Sometimes his friends get angry with him, and he has never really had a girlfriend.
>
> Since Lee was in elementary school, he has struggled with his schoolwork. He is disorganized and has trouble attending to details. Others have constantly told Lee that he is distracted too easily and is extremely forgetful. He is often frustrated with himself but can't seem to change his behaviors.
>
> Lee used to get in trouble at school for talking too much and fidgeting. He still has problems listening and sitting quietly. Lee seeks counseling services at his college counseling center for help with his academic struggles. After speaking with his counselor during the intake session, he realizes that counseling may benefit him in his personal relationships as well.

Diagnostic Questions

1. Do Lee's presenting symptoms meet the criteria for ADHD?
2. Based on your answer to Question 1, what presentation and severity specifiers would you assign for Lee's diagnosis?
3. What would be the reason(s) a counselor may not diagnose Lee with ADHD?
4. Would Lee be more accurately diagnosed with ODD? If so, why? If not, why not?
5. What rule-outs would you consider for Lee's case?
6. What other information may be needed to make an accurate clinical diagnosis?

Specific Learning Disorder (F81._)

Essential Features

Specific learning disorder includes reading disorder, mathematics disorder, disorder of written expression, and learning disorder not otherwise specified. Coded specifiers are included for each type. APA (2022a) emphasizes that specific learning disorders are highly comorbid with each other (see also Dalsgaard et al., 2020).

Specific learning disorder has biological etiology and underlying cognitive deficits and challenges. It is two to three times more common in males than females. Problems with reading, mathematics, and writing frequently co-occur. In the *DSM-5-TR*, the learning disorders of impairment in reading, in written expression, and in mathematics are coded as one disorder and identified with specifiers (APA, 2022a).

Differential Diagnosis

Differential diagnoses for all three subtypes of specific learning disorder are intellectual developmental disorder (intellectual disability), neurocognitive disorders, normal ability differences, and neurological or sensory disorders. It is important for counselors to make appropriate assessment referrals if a client displays symptoms of specific learning disorder (APA, 2022a).

Coding, Recording, and Specifiers

In the *DSM-5-TR*, the diagnostic code for specific learning disorder *with impairment in reading* is F81.0, *with impairment in written expression* is F81.81, and *with impairment in mathematics* is F81.2. There are three severity specifiers: *mild*, *moderate*, and *severe*. *Mild* represents some deficits in one or two academic domains with limited need for support; *moderate* shows significant difficulty in learning skills in at least one domain with a need for substantial support; and *severe* includes extreme difficulties in learning skills affecting multiple areas existing even with substantial support across school and home environments (APA, 2022a).

Motor Disorders

Motor disorders listed in this chapter include developmental coordination disorder, stereotypic movement disorder, and tic disorders. The tic criteria (Tourette's disorder, persistent [chronic] motor or vocal tic disorder, and provisional tic disorder) have been standardized since the publication of the *DSM-5*. All the motor disorders must cause impairment or distress and interfere with activities of daily living (APA, 2022a). Motor disorders are rarely diagnosed in counseling settings; however, accurate discernment of the diagnoses remains important. Counselors should be aware of the criteria and provide assessment referral as indicated.

Developmental Coordination Disorder (F82)

Essential Features

Developmental coordination disorder represents marked deficits in coordinated motor skills that affect daily activities across settings. Symptoms must have onset in early childhood and must not be better explained by intellectual developmental disorder (intellectual disability) or attributable to a neurological condition. There is a 5% to 6% prevalence rate in children between the ages of 5 and 11 years, with boys more likely than girls to be diagnosed with the disorder (APA, 2022a). The *DSM-5-TR* code for developmental coordination disorder is F82. There are no specifiers for this disorder.

Differential Diagnosis

Differential diagnoses for developmental coordination disorder are impairments due to another medical condition, intellectual developmental disorder (intellectual disability), ADHD, ASD, and joint hypermobility syndrome. ADHD is the most frequent co-occurring disorder, with a 50% comorbidity rate (APA, 2022a).

Stereotypic Movement Disorder (F98.4)

Essential Features

Stereotypic movement disorder consists of repetitive and purposeless motor behavior that appears to be internally driven. These behaviors are often done in a rhythmic way, and the individual may or may not respond to efforts to inhibit them. The movements must interfere with functioning; frequency varies greatly and often changes according to context (e.g., the specific setting or mood). Self-injurious behaviors can occur and can include incidents of head banging, face slapping, self-biting, and eye poking (APA, 2022a).

Differential Diagnosis

Differential diagnoses for stereotypic movement disorder are ASD, obsessive-compulsive and related disorders, tic disorders, and other neurological or medical conditions. Additionally, body-focused repetitive behavior disorder, listed in the Obsessive-Compulsive and Related Disorders chapter, should be ruled out, and normative childhood behavior should be considered (APA, 2022a).

Coding, Recording, and Specifiers

The *DSM-5-TR* code for stereotypic movement disorder is F98.4. Specifiers are *with self-injurious behavior*; *without self-injurious behavior*; and *associated with a known medical or genetic condition, neurodevelopmental disorder, or environmental factor*. Use additional coding to identify a medical condition or other neurodevelopmental disorder. Specify also if *mild* (symptoms easily suppressed), *moderate* (symptoms require explicit protective measures), or *severe* (symptoms need continuous monitoring; APA, 2022a).

Tic Disorders (F95._)

Essential Features

A tic is a "sudden, rapid, recurrent, nonrhythmic motor movement or vocalization" (APA, 2022a, p. 93). There are three tic disorder classifications: (a) Tourette's disorder, which possesses both multiple motor and one or more vocal tics; (b) persistent (chronic) motor or vocal tic disorder, which excludes both motor and vocal (must be one or the other); and (c) provisional tic disorder, in which single or multiple motor and/or vocal tics are present for less than 1 year. Onset for all three classifications must be younger than 18 years of age (APA, 2022a).

Differential Diagnosis

Differential diagnoses for tic disorders are abnormal movements due to other medical conditions, stereotypic movement disorder, substance-induced and paroxysmal dyskinesias, myonoclus (quick and insuppressible with the lack of a prior urges), and obsessive-compulsive and related disorders (APA, 2022a).

Coding, Recording, and Specifiers

The *DSM-5-TR* codes for tic disorders are Tourette's disorder F95.2, persistent (chronic) motor or vocal tic disorder F95., and provisional tic disorder F95.0. The specifier *with motor tics only* or *with vocal tics only* is required for (chronic) motor or vocal tic disorder (APA, 2022a).

NEUROCOGNITIVE DISORDERS

> I noticed it gradually in mom's behaviors. At first, I would have to repeat myself more and more. The forgetfulness started in earnest shortly after that, and mom had trouble remembering many things. Then she appeared to have forgotten how to take care of herself. Now, she sometimes doesn't even recognize friends or family.—Nora

Neurocognitive disorders represent mental health disturbances with underlying physical pathology that can sometimes be genetically determined. This differentiates them from other classifications in the *DSM-5-TR*. The term *neurocognitive* stems from the *DSM-5* Neurocognitive Disorders Work Group's use of *cognitive*, which has a broad meaning encompassing all information processing, with *neuro* emphasizing brain functioning. Neurocognitive disorders are prevalent, with a staggering 67 million individuals in the United States who will meet the criteria for a major neurocognitive disorder by 2030. Individuals with dementia will top 115 million worldwide by the year 2050 (McDonald, 2017).

Although health professionals and laypersons often think of older adults in relation to neurocognitive dysfunction (e.g., Alzheimer's), it is important to remember that these disorders also affect younger individuals. For example, in 2021, traumatic brain injuries resulted in over 214,000 inpatient hospitalizations and approximately 190 deaths daily in the United States (CDC, 2023). Neurocognitive disorders are not limited to memory or cognition problems but also affect complex cognitive processes, language, motor functioning, and social cognition. Early diagnosis and intervention are key. Recent research clearly shows that underlying pathology of these disorders can be seen before symptoms occur (APA, 2022a; Sousa et al., 2020).

Major Changes From *DSM-5* to *DSM-5-TR*

There are minimal changes from the *DSM-5* to the *DSM-5-TR*, with minor text revision and coding updates highlighted in the *DSM-5-TR* neurocognitive disorders supplement. There are six identified neurocognitive domains—cognitive attention, executive function, learning and memory, language, perceptual-motor, and social cognition—for which APA (2022a) provides definitions, examples for major and mild neurocognitive disorder, and corresponding assessments. Thorough comprehension of these domains is imperative for understanding essential features and diagnostic criteria within this section. Please refer to the *DSM-5-TR* for specific definitions and to the neurocognitive disorders supplement (APA, 2022b) for coding updates from the initial March 2022 publication.

Mild neurocognitive disorder, first appearing in the *DMS-5,* identifies individuals early in the etiology of the disease. The diagnosis of mild neurocognitive disorder is important from a nosological perspective to assist with early identification of neurocognitive dysfunction (McDonald, 2017).

Etiology and Treatment

Neurocognitive disorders can manifest throughout the life span and may be seen in cognitive functioning concerns resulting from traumatic brain injury or HIV infection. By definition, there must be an acquired decline from previous levels of functioning (APA, 2022a; Sousa et al., 2020). The decline must be clinically determined and must include assessment batteries for primary domains of complex attention, executive ability, learning and memory, language, perceptual-motor ability, and social cognition. Information can be obtained from the client, from a significant other, or by clinical observation. For neurocognitive disorders, the underlying pathology is often known, which aids in identification of specific etiology. This provides for efficacious treatment development, including health interventions, medication management, and counseling services (McDonald, 2017).

Implications for Counselors

Neurocognitive disorders represent diagnoses made in medical settings with counselors often working as part of a treatment team for affected individuals and their families. For mild neurocognitive disorders, clients experience initial difficulties performing activities of daily living that can be assuaged by behavioral techniques and supportive counseling. Education and adjustment time can help individuals and their families, providing a critical window whereby a course of action can be set, support services identified, and future plans mapped out.

With this classification system, there is a strong opportunity for counselors to help clients throughout the progression of the disease. We encourage counselors who work with clients living with major and mild neurocognitive disorders to consult with medical professionals, neuropsychologists, and etiological specialists in addition to seeking specialized training, because neurocognitive disorders are not commonly addressed in counselor education. Counselors will likely provide services to loved ones and caretakers of individuals diagnosed with a neurocognitive disorder and need to possess a full understanding of the clients' experiences to provide optimal support.

We urge counselors to thoroughly review the Neurocognitive Disorders chapter in the *DSM-5-TR*. Table 1: Neurocognitive Domains (pp. 669–671 of the *DSM-5-TR*) may be particularly useful for counselors because it highlights symptoms for each of the cognitive domains and gives examples of specific assessments. For example, in the cognitive domain of complex attention, a symptom of mild neurocognitive disorder would be longer time needed to complete tasks with accompanying errors in routine activities; the assessment example would be checking sustained, selective, and divided attention (APA, 2022a).

Delirium

Essential Features

Delirium represents a disturbance in attention or awareness with concomitant decline in cognitive functioning inclusive of a "reduced ability to direct, focus, sustain, and shift attention" (APA, 2022a, p. 672). This is accompanied by decreased awareness of the external environment. The decline cannot be better explained by another neurocognitive disorder (either already existing or developing). It is typical for an individual with delirium to have difficulty responding appropriately to questions or orienting to their environment.

The decline in functioning happens quickly (within days and sometimes hours) and fluctuates, which is critical in distinguishing delirium from major and mild neurocognitive disorders. There must be evidence that the delirium results from the physiological consequences of a medical condition, substance intoxication or withdrawal, medication usage, or exposure to a toxin. There must also be a change in at least one other area of cognitive functioning such as memory or language (APA, 2022a).

Special Considerations

Prevalence rates for delirium are age dependent, with occurrences of up to 14% in adults older than 85 years (APA, 2022a). For the overall population, the prevalence rate is 1% to 2%. Early identification and treatment for delirium is critical because it shortens the duration of the disorder and improves prognosis. There are both environmental (e.g., low levels of activity; drug and alcohol use) and physiological (e.g., major and mild neurocognitive disorders, illness, age; APA, 2022a) risk factors.

Differential Diagnosis

Common differential diagnoses for delirium are psychotic disorders, bipolar and depressive disorders with psychotic features, acute stress disorder, malingering, factitious disorder, and major and mild neurocognitive disorders. Although delirium is diagnosed in a medical setting, with a majority of cases occurring in hospital or nursing care, counselors should be aware of conditions that can commonly be mistaken for delirium so appropriate treatment interventions can be sought (APA, 2022a). It is important to note that the presence of delirium almost always indicates the need for immediate medical attention; counselors should assist clients in managing this urgency.

Coding, Recording, and Specifiers

All *ICD-10-CM* codes are both substance and specifier specific: *with use disorder, mild*; *with use disorder, moderate or severe*; and *without use disorder*. For example, substance intoxication delirium with inhalant use disorder, mild is F18.121; substance intoxication delirium, moderate (or severe) is F18.221; and substance intoxication delirium without inhalant use disorder is F18.921.

There is also *medication-induced delirium* with the *ICD-10-CM* code depending on the type of medication. With *delirium due to another medical condition*, the name of the condition should be included, for example, F05 delirium due to hepatic encephalopathy. And with *delirium due to multiple etiologies*, separate codes should be used for each etiology. Due to the medical nature of these diagnoses, they are frequently rendered in medical settings.

Clinicians should specify if the diagnosis is *acute* (lasting a few hours or days) or *persistent* (lasting weeks or months) as well as if *hyperactive*, *hypoactive*, or *mixed level of activity*. Even though diagnosis of delirium is not made in counseling settings, we encourage counselors working with this population to review the specifiers and recording procedures listed on pages 672–723 of the *DSM-5-TR*.

Major Neurocognitive Disorder

Essential Features

Impairment in only one of the identified cognitive domains (complex attention, executive ability, learning and memory, language, perceptual-motor ability, and social cognition) is required for a diagnosis of major neurocognitive disorder, with an emphasis on deterioration from baseline functioning (Stokin et al., 2015). For appropriate diagnosis, the decline must be significant. The contributing information is based on two factors: (a) worry from the individual, a "knowledgeable informant," or a clinician and (b) neurological testing or quantitative assessment. The decline in functioning must interfere with activities in daily living, not occur during a delirium, and not be explained by another mental disorder (APA, 2022a).

Special Considerations

Assessment testing must be done before a diagnosis of major neurocognitive disorder is made, and as with all *DSM-5-TR* diagnoses, age, culture, occupation, and gender are important issues to address during assessment (APA, 2022a). Providing an integrated and culturally responsive treatment team benefits the client and caregivers.

Mild Neurocognitive Disorder

Essential Features

Research supports a spectrum approach to neurocognitive disorders. There must be evidence of "modest" cognitive decline in at least one of the six previously enumerated cognitive domains. This is in contrast to "substantial" cognitive decline for major neurocognitive disorder (APA, 2022a). The information must be based on worry from the individual, a "knowledgeable informant," or a clinician as well as neurological testing/quantitative assessment. The decline in functioning must interfere with activities of daily living, not occur during a delirium, and not be better explained by another mental disorder (APA, 2022a).

Special Considerations

Supportive counseling services can help individuals and their families enhance coping mechanisms and plan for the future. Researchers hope to identify biomarkers that can follow the etiological spectrum from normal functioning to mild neurocognitive disorder to major neurocognitive disorder (Sousa et al., 2020). The establishment of mild neurocognitive disorder could spur research initiatives to better assist with identification and early intervention for individuals before they experience significant decline in functioning.

Major and Mild Neurocognitive Disorders

Differential Diagnosis

Differential diagnoses for major and mild neurocognitive disorders are normal cognition, delirium, MDD, specific learning disorder, and other neurodevelopmental disorders (APA, 2022a). Thorough assessment of an individual's previous cognitive functioning will help with effective differential diagnoses because establishment of baseline performance is necessary in assessing major and mild neurocognitive disorders.

Coding, Recording, and Specifiers

For major and mild neurocognitive disorders, specification of an etiological subtype is required. All criteria must be met for major and mild neurocognitive disorders and not be better explained by cerebrovascular disease; another neurodegenerative disease; the effects of a substance; or another mental, neurological, or systemic disorder. Because of the complexity of recording procedures for neurocognitive disorders, we list the *DSM-5-TR* coding of the etiological subtypes in Table 16.1.

Table 16.1
Comparison of Multiaxial Versus Nonaxial Systems

DSM-III *and* DSM-IV *Multiaxial System*	DSM-5 *Nonaxial System*
Axis I: Clinical disorders and other conditions that are the focus of treatment *Axis II:* Personality disorders and intellectual disability (i.e., mental retardation) *Axis III:* General medical conditions	Combined attention to clinical disorders, including personality disorders and intellectual disability (i.e., mental retardation); other conditions that are the focus of treatment; and medical conditions continue to be listed as a part of the diagnosis.
Axis IV: Psychosocial and environmental stressors	Special notations for psychosocial and contextual factors are now listed by using V codes or *ICD-10-CM* Z codes. An expanded list of V codes has been provided in the *DSM-5*. In rare cases where psychosocial and contextual factors are not listed, counselors can include the specific factor as it is related to the client's diagnosis.
Axis V: Global Assessment of Functioning (GAF)	Special notations for disability are listed by using V codes or *ICD-10-CM* Z codes. The World Health Organization Disability Assessment Schedule 2.0 (WHODAS 2.0) has been included in Section III and is listed on APA's website (www.psychiatry.org) within the online assessment measures section.

Case Example

Robbie is an 81-year-old retired, married man who has enjoyed robust physical and mental health throughout his life. Robbie served in the military and took pride in his service. Shortly after his 80th birthday, Robbie's wife began to notice changes in his memory and behaviors. At first, it was little things, such as where he had left his glasses. Then he started to forget names of his veteran friends. One day, while his wife was out, he almost burned the kitchen down heating up leftovers.

As the year progressed, Robbie would get angry if his wife mentioned talking to his physician about his forgetfulness and irritability. The final straw came when he pushed her during a fight, which he had never done in their 55 years of marriage. She took the initiative to contact his physician, who requested he come in for an appointment and referred him for neurological testing. In deference to his wife's urgings, Robbie agreed to attend a counseling session with her even though he insisted nothing was wrong and maintained that she was overreacting.

Diagnostic Questions

1. Do Robbie's presenting symptoms meet the criteria for a major or mild neurocognitive disorder?
2. Based on an affirmative answer to Question 1, would you select major or mild neurocognitive disorder? What are the reasons for your selection?
3. What would be the reason(s) a counselor may not diagnose Robbie with a neurocognitive disorder?
4. Would Robbie more accurately be diagnosed with delirium? If so, why? If not, why not?
5. What rule-outs would you consider for Robbie's case?
6. What other information may be needed to make an accurate clinical diagnosis?

Questions for Consideration

1. How might the diagnosis of a neurodevelopmental or neurocognitive disorder impact the client and family?
2. What would a strong treatment team look like for these individuals and their families?
3. How can gathering comprehensive biopsychosocial information assist with differential diagnosis?
4. What might be important adjunctive recommendations for clients and their families?

Chapter 17

Schizophrenia Spectrum and Other Psychotic Disorders

> They don't sound like voices at first. One day, maybe I hear someone call my name. Another day, I can hear whispers but I don't know what they are saying. Sometimes it's just sounds. I want it to stop but it won't. It won't let me sleep. The beer helps me sleep.—Ray

Schizophrenia spectrum and other psychotic disorders are "defined by abnormalities in one or more of the following five domains: delusions, hallucinations, disorganized thinking (speech), grossly disorganized or abnormal motor behavior (including catatonia), and negative symptoms" (APA, 2022a, p. 101). This chapter includes overviews of delusional disorder, brief psychotic disorder, schizophreniform disorder, schizophrenia, schizoaffective disorder, substance/medication-induced psychotic disorder, psychotic disorder due to another medical condition, and catatonia. The *DSM-5-TR* also includes cross-referencing of schizotypal personality disorder (see Chapter 14 of this *Learning Companion* for more information regarding personality disorders).

Psychotic disorders involve a constellation of positive, negative, and related cognitive symptoms. Whereas positive symptoms involve thoughts or behaviors one would not expect, negative symptoms involve absence of expected experiences (NIMH, 2021). Core positive symptoms include delusions, hallucinations, and thought or movement disorders in which a person loses touch with reality. Delusions are fixed beliefs that are not grounded in reality and for which individuals cannot be convinced otherwise. Hallucinations are sensory experiences in which a person sees (visual hallucinations), hears (auditory hallucinations), smells (olfactory hallucinations), tastes (gustatory hallucinations), or feels (tactile or somatic hallucinations) something for which there is no physical stimulus. Auditory hallucinations are most common, tactile hallucinations are often linked to substance withdrawal or intoxication, and olfactory and gustatory hallucinations may indicate a medical problem. Disorganized thinking, also known as thought disorder, involves disruptions in the flow of thoughts in such a way that makes communication difficult (APA, 2022a; NIMH, 2021). Disorganized or abnormal motor behavior, also known as movement disorder, involves agitation, repeated motions, or inability to move or respond to stimuli (i.e., catatonia).

Negative symptoms include a lack of pleasure, motivation, engagement in activities of daily living, or emotional experiences (NIMH, 2021). Finally, cognitive symptoms involve difficulty with executive functioning, attention, or memory. Refer to the *DSM-5-TR* for a more thorough discussion of key symptoms and terminology associated with them.

Psychotic symptoms and experiences occur across a wide range of medical and mental health concerns; however, psychotic disorders are relatively uncommon. According to APA (2022a), prevalence rates for disorders reviewed in this chapter range from 0.2% to 0.7%. As we discuss throughout the chapter, individuals who meet the criteria for psychotic disorders are diverse and have different experiences. Studies of individuals experiencing their first-episode psychosis highlight the wide variety of experiences with psychotic disorders. In recent years, meta-analyses indicated that 32% to 38% of those with first-episode psychosis go on to complete recovery (Catalan et al., 2021; Huxley et al., 2021), and 54% had remission of symptoms (Huxley et al., 2021). For more than 50% of individuals, a psychotic disorder diagnosis presents a lifelong challenge requiring consistent care to maintain some level of functioning (Gaebel, 2011). A sizable minority, especially those with later age of onset and higher levels of functioning at onset, may remain quite functional in their ability to manage symptoms over time.

Counselors in clinical and school settings may encounter clients and family members of people who are experiencing psychotic disorders. Counselors are responsible for recognizing signs of new onset of psychosis; collaborating with interdisciplinary treatment teams; and supporting loved ones in providing environments to enhance dignity, wellness, and functioning.

Major Changes From *DSM-5* to *DSM-5-TR*

There are minimal changes to disorders in this section in the *DSM-5-TR*. Criterion 4 in Other Specified Schizophrenia Spectrum and Other Psychotic Disorder was updated to replace references to delusional symptoms in a partner and to "delusional symptoms in context of relationship with an individual with prominent delusions" (APA, 2022a, p. 138). Section III of the *DSM-5-TR* continues to propose attenuated psychosis syndrome as a condition for further study. Criterion A was updated to remove language about "relatively intact reality testing." It now names specific, attenuated positive symptoms.

Although not located in this specific chapter of the *DSM-5-TR*, counselors may wish to note that the update includes new methods for handling situations in which an individual experiences both a psychotic disorder *and* a depressive or manic episode not expected with the psychotic disorder. See Chapters 6 and 7 of this text for a synopsis of these changes.

Differential Diagnosis

Positive symptoms of psychosis do not automatically indicate the presence of a psychotic disorder. Rather, psychotic symptoms may be a regular part of substance intoxication or withdrawal, medical conditions, and other mental health disorders. Precipitating factors, history, and the constellation of other symptoms will determine whether a client who has psychotic symptoms meets the criteria for a schizophrenia spectrum or other psychotic disorder.

Because medical conditions and substance use can lead to the onset or worsening of psychosis, counselors should refer all clients who report new onset of psychotic symptoms for a thorough medical evaluation (Barrio Minton & Prosek, 2019). This evaluation is critical for informing accurate diagnosis and, in turn, appropriate treatment. A client who has psychotic symptoms in response to a prescription medication (as may happen in response to commonly prescribed steroids) will have very different medical needs compared with a client who hallucinates while withdrawing from alcohol. Both clients will have different needs from someone who experiences a long, slow deterioration in functioning before developing paranoid delusions. Later in the chapter, we mention specific medical conditions and substances that may trigger psychotic symptoms.

Severe depressive disorders, bipolar disorders, and PTSD frequently involve elements of psychosis that may include or resemble delusions and hallucinations. The Clinician-Rated Dimensions of Psychosis Symptom Severity (CRDPSS) in the *DSM-5-TR* includes attention to depressive and manic symptoms as a reminder of the importance of assessing for preexisting or co-occurring mood concerns that inform diagnosis and require attention. Depression and negative symptoms have much in common, especially as both include a lack of interest or pleasure in everyday living and may result in poor self-care. Negative symptoms and cognitive deficits in schizophrenia spectrum disorders may mirror social impairment associated with autism spectrum disorder and decline associated with neurocognitive disorders. Dissociation common with acute stress disorder and PTSD may also appear as part of thought or speech disorders within the schizophrenia spectrum. Similarly, beliefs associated with some obsessive-compulsive and related disorders and somatic symptom disorders often take on delusional qualities, and individuals who are experiencing psychotic symptoms may find themselves quite anxious and agitated because of their hallucinations and delusions. Differential diagnosis must include the order in which symptoms developed and the core experiences of each.

Individuals with schizophrenia spectrum disorders experience an array of coexisting health and mental health concerns. APA (2022a) reports high comorbidity with substance-related and anxiety disorders. Systematic analyses show high rates of suicide behaviors across the schizophrenia spectrum (Álvarez et al., 2022): schizophrenia (20%), schizoaffective disorder (47%), delusional disorder (11%), and first-episode psychosis (13%). Another research synthesis showed that over one quarter of those with first-episode psychosis experienced suicidal thoughts, one in five attempted suicide, and up to 4% died by suicide (Sicotte et al., 2021). These risks can compound when considering levels of functioning, depression, adjustment, and cannabis use (Sánchez-Gutiérrez et al., 2022). Likewise, APA (2022a) estimates suicide risk for schizophrenia and schizoaffective disorders at 5% to 6%. When combined with the functional consequences of schizophrenia and decreased engagement in health-related activities (APA, 2022a; Rubin & Trawver, 2011), people with schizophrenia and other psychotic disorders have lower life expectancies and quality of life.

Counselors who work with individuals experiencing psychosis must remain alert to the likelihood of these concerns. At the same time, it is important to keep hopeful, strength-based perspectives. Just as experiencing a psychotic episode does not need to mean lifetime impairment, early intervention in psychosis is associated with decreased risk and more positive outcomes (Sicotte et al., 2021). Resilience also influences experiences in meaningful ways (Yeo et al., 2022). As is addressed next, there is strong evidence that pharmacological, psychosocial, and holistic interventions are effective at enhancing the quality of life for people with psychotic disorders.

Etiology and Treatment

Researchers are still working to determine specific causes of psychotic disorders. As mentioned previously, substance use and medical conditions may cause brain changes that lead to psychotic symptoms. Research indicates strong genetic and physiological components of schizophrenia (NIMH, 2021). Individuals with first-degree relatives who have schizophrenia are at much greater risk for developing the disorder, and neuroscience research has revealed that people with schizophrenia have different brain structure, function, and neurotransmitter activity compared with those without (APA, 2022a; Cattarinussi et al.,

2022; NIMH, 2021; Weng et al., 2022). There may also be risk related to substance use, with youth who use cannabis, even at low frequency, at increased risk of early onset schizophrenia (Godin & Shehata, 2022).

Counselors who work with those experiencing psychotic disorders usually do so in one of two primary locations: (a) crisis stabilization hospitals in which individuals present with new onset of psychotic symptoms or crisis in relation to symptoms and (b) community mental health centers in which clients engage in long-term treatment to manage symptoms and promote functioning (Barrio Minton & Prosek, 2019). In both cases, counselors will serve on multidisciplinary teams consisting of psychiatrists, nurses, social workers, case managers, and/or rehabilitation specialists. Counselors' roles will vary by setting and are likely to include elements of case management, psychosocial services, and family and caregiver support.

Three pillars of treatment of the schizophrenia spectrum include medications for symptom relief and relapse management, psychosocial interventions to support coping and prevent relapse, and rehabilitation to ensure the highest possible degree of social and occupational functioning (Rössler, 2011). McDonagh et al. (2017) conducted a rigorous synthesis of treatment research that served as a foundation for APA's "Practice Guideline for the Treatment of Patients With Schizophrenia" (Keepers et al., 2020). Although specific to schizophrenia, the principles are often applied across disorders in the schizophrenia spectrum. During the acute phase, providers will focus on minimizing harm and reducing the most striking of symptoms, often through medication management (Pillar 1) and basic supportive care. In the months following the acute phase, medication will continue, and focus will include the introduction of psychosocial interventions to reduce stress and educate clients and caregivers regarding elements of the illness (Pillar 2). Once the client is stabilized, clinicians may continue medication and psychoeducation; however, they will turn attention to preventing relapse through psychosocial treatments that include education, skills training, CBT, family intervention, supported employment, and assertive community treatment (Pillar 3).

Psychopharmacotherapy for clients with psychotic disorders often focuses on treatment of positive symptoms such as hallucinations, delusions, and disorganized speech and behavior. This trial-and-error process tends to involve the use of antipsychotics such as olanzapine, aripiprazole, risperidone, quetiapine, and ziprasidone; haloperidol is also effective but with a higher side effect profile (McDonagh et al., 2017). Psychiatrists may also integrate other classes of medications, such as antidepressants, anxiolytics, lithium, and antiepileptic drugs. Medications may be oral or in the form of long-acting injectables. Although not without drawbacks, injectables have been found in meta-analyses to improve medication adherence and social functioning while reducing symptoms, rehospitalizations, emergency department visits, and medical costs (Okoli et al., 2022).

Clients may find treatment regimens confusing and overwhelming, especially given that cognitive deficits are common within psychotic disorders. In addition, side effects may be uncomfortable and lead to problems with medication adherence. Fortunately, strong therapeutic relationships are associated with more positive attitudes and adherence to medication recommendations (McCabe et al., 2012). Counselors may find themselves helping educate clients and families regarding medication management and facilitating communication between clients and psychiatrists. In addition, they may be encouraged by findings that there are several effective interventions to boost adherence to medications (Cahaya et al., 2022). These include motivational interviewing, technology-assisted communication, and collaborative care.

There are numerous evidence-based psychosocial interventions for schizophrenia spectrum disorders. The following list features interventions that improved specific client outcomes compared to treatment as usual:

> assertive community care (core illness symptoms, function), cognitive behavioral therapy (core illness symptoms, function, quality of life), cognitive remediation (core illness symptoms), family interventions (core illness symptoms, function, relapse), illness self-management (core illness symptoms), psychoeducation (core illness symptoms, function, relapse), social skills training (core illness symptoms, function), and supported employment (core illness symptoms, employment). (McDonagh et al., 2017, "Key Messages" section)

Integrative CBT reduces positive symptoms and sustains gains for treatment-resistant schizophrenia (Ryan et al., 2022). Effective approaches highlight the medium impact of medication and psychosocial interventions, the small impact of CBT, and the very large impact of transcranial direct stimulation (Phelan & Sigala, 2022). Clients with recent-onset psychosis have also indicated satisfaction with mindfulness-based interventions, acceptance and commitment therapy, and compassion-based interventions (Li et al., 2021). Counselors who often work with these populations can use continuing education to develop skills in these evidence-based interventions.

Rehabilitation resources are essential in the treatment and long-term management of schizophrenia spectrum disorders (Rössler, 2011). Evidence-based rehabilitation resources include assertive community treatment (ACT) and focused programs such as supported employment and supportive housing (McDonagh et al., 2017; Rössler, 2011). ACT is an intensive, multidisciplinary approach focused on providing services that allow individuals with severe and persistent mental illness to function outside of institutional settings. Services are tailored to the individual and their family. SAMHSA (2008) provides an ACT evidence-based practice kit in which counselors can learn more about best practices for ACT.

There is limited professional counseling literature regarding working with clients experiencing psychosis, and the resources in this chapter are mostly from psychiatry and social work. There is a growing body of evidence that a holistic, strength-oriented perspective works even amid severe illness. Resilience appears to be particularly important.

> Higher level of resilience was associated with lower severity of specific symptomatology including positive, negative, depressive symptoms, suicidal ideation, cognitive deficits, and better insight. Moreover, higher resilience was significantly associated with different aspects of illness course (such as shorter duration of untreated psychosis, longer duration of illness, improved symptom remission and recovery), internal factors (such as lower stigma, better self-esteem), and psychosocial functioning (better overall, real-life, social and interpersonal functioning, better quality of life). Resilience also acts as a mediator in pathways leading to depression, functioning, and quality of life within schizophrenia spectrum conditions. (Yeo et al., 2022, p. 1)

Likewise, coping strategies can have both positive and negative impacts on the outcomes of first-episode psychosis (Riera-López de Aguileta et al., 2020). Both resilience and coping are naturally part of counseling focus and interventions.

Holistic interventions are also associated with enhancing the quality of life for people with schizophrenia and related disorders. Isaacs et al. (2022) conducted a systematic review of "personal recovery facilitators" in schizophrenia using the CHIME framework, which stands for connectedness, hope and optimism, identity, meaning and purpose, and empowerment. These facilitators are often individual and adjunctive to standard approaches. Well connected to wellness frameworks, yoga and music therapy increased hope and optimism, and creative outlets like narrative photovoice and art making also proved promising. People with schizophrenia who engaged in aerobic exercise had meaningful improvements in cognition, attention, working memory, and verbal learning; gains were greatest in groups, when supervised by experts, and when exercise was 90 minutes per week for 12 or more weeks (Shimada et al., 2022).

In short, treatment for schizophrenia spectrum and other psychotic disorders will include a personalized combination of medication, structured psychosocial interventions, and rehabilitation supports. Resilience, coping, and holistic support can also increase functioning and well-being for people with psychosis.

Implications for Counselors

It is highly unlikely that counselors will provide lead diagnostic services when working with clients who have psychotic disorders. However, counselors may encounter clients with psychotic disorders in front-line service settings, such as mental health crisis and emergency services. They may also provide longer term care as part of their work with community mental health and hospital settings. Both situations provide unique challenges and opportunities.

When clients present with active psychotic symptoms, counselors should attend closely to facilitating therapeutic communication while linking clients to levels of care and professionals who can respond to acute-phase symptoms. Positive therapeutic relationships impact the outcome of treatments for early psychosis (Goldsmith et al., 2015). Counselors may struggle to facilitate therapeutic communication when the very nature of psychotic symptoms means clients may be out of touch with reality, struggle to communicate in meaningful ways, be distrustful of counselors and others in their lives, and appear uninterested in social relationships. Even when symptoms are not grounded in reality, hallucinations and delusions are very real to clients, and they may feel confused, agitated, or even terrorized (Walsh, 2011). For these reasons, Walsh (2011) recommended mental health professionals engage in five therapeutic communication strategies: (a) remembering the relationship may provide a link between the client with an essential sense of safety in their world, (b) exploring and anchoring thoughts and feelings rather than arguing about reality, (c) processing distress, (d) slowly and gently providing alternative explanations of experiences, and (e) introducing possibilities within the social world.

Counselors may use relationship skills to help clients understand the need for future treatment and link to necessary services. During the acute phase, these services are likely to involve hospitalization, in which clients can begin to stabilize on medication and make connections needed to support their long-term recovery and management. The hospitalization process can be frightening to those who have not yet navigated the process or who have had negative experiences in the past. Indeed, one half of individuals with first-episode psychosis develop PTSD symptoms, and one third meet the full criteria for PTSD related to their psychotic episodes (Pinho et al., 2021). Pinho et al. (2021) attributed this to "coercive intervention such as involuntary hospitalization, seclusion, restraint or being forced to take medication, as well as being around sick or anxious patients" (p. S454). Counselors can facilitate transitions through compassionate reflection and discussion with clients and family members regarding what to expect and what comfort measures they may take.

When providing services in longer term settings, counselors will best serve clients if they develop a strong understanding of schizophrenia spectrum disorders, evidence-based treatments, and interdisciplinary perspectives. Counselors should remain alert to the risk of suicidal thoughts and behaviors in clients, integrating ongoing attention to these throughout the recovery process. They may also attend to clients' fear of relapse, as such fears are related to depression, suicidal ideation, and negative self-esteem (Zukowska et al., 2022). Counselors' unique training and perspectives equip them to contribute to treatment teams in meaningful ways, especially given the body of research supporting resilience and holistic interventions. For example, counselors' focus on strengths and resilience, understanding of family systems and human development, and general facilitation skills may be unique among treatment team members. Counselors are uniquely situated to support caregivers and address caregiver burden in ways that benefit clients and their families (Karambelas et al., 2022). It is precisely this orientation and the creativity that often comes with it that makes counselors well suited for advocating for clients and maximizing well-being.

In the remainder of the chapter, we outline major disorders within the Schizophrenia Spectrum and Other Psychotic Disorders chapter of the *DSM-5-TR*. We include a summary of the essential features of each disorder and note special considerations such as disorder characteristics, treatment considerations, and coding procedures. In each case, readers should refer to the *DSM-5-TR* for a full explication of diagnostic criteria.

Delusional Disorder (F22)

Essential Features

Delusional disorder is characterized by a period of 1 month or more during which someone experiences at least one delusion (APA, 2022a). Other criteria rule out schizophrenia; co-occurring mood episodes; or onset caused by substances, medications, or medical conditions. People with delusional disorder do not experience functional impairment or exhibit bizarre behaviors when not experiencing delusions. The nature of delusions can range from experiences that may occur in daily life (e.g., belief that one has a special relationship with another) to those that are completely implausible (e.g., belief that one's thoughts are being stolen by an outside entity). The *DSM-5-TR* includes subtypes to categorize specific content of delusions.

Special Considerations

Delusional disorder is estimated to have a lifetime prevalence of just 0.2% (APA, 2022a). There is little research regarding characteristics of people with this disorder. Counselors may struggle to detect delusional disorder because functional consequences may be quite low. By definition, individuals who have delusions do not identify them as such. Delusions may appear plausible to others as well, especially when the person with the delusion is the primary source of information. For example, counselors may not question reports of events consistent with delusional disorder (e.g., affairs as in *jealous type*, workplace harassment or discrimination as in *persecutory type*).

Counselors should take care to assess whether delusional content is better accounted for by another disorder. For example, an individual who has delusional-level beliefs associated with OCD or body dysmorphic disorder should receive a more specific diagnosis (APA, 2022a). Similarly, delusions are often present in other psychotic, depressive, and bipolar disorders. Counselors must assess fully to make sure one of these more common diagnoses does not better account for the delusion. The presence of negative symptoms or other longer term impairments may mean schizophrenia is a more appropriate diagnosis (APA, 2022a).

There is just one code for delusional disorder: F22; however, the *DSM-5-TR* includes several specifiers. Subtypes focused on the nature of the delusion include *erotomanic type*, *grandiose type*, *jealous type*, *persecutory type*, *somatic type*, *mixed type*, and *unspecified type*. People who experience delusions that could not possibly happen should receive a *with bizarre content* specifier. Counselors may choose from a variety of course specifiers indicating whether an individual is experiencing *first episode* or *multiple episodes* and whether that episode is currently in *acute episode*, *partial remission*, *full remission*, or *continuous*. Clinicians rate severity using the CRDPSS (APA, 2022a).

Brief Psychotic Disorder (F23)

Essential Features

Brief psychotic disorder is characterized by 1 day to 1 month in which one or more positive psychotic symptoms (e.g., delusions, hallucinations, disorganized speech, and/or disorganized behavior) are present. Symptoms must involve a full remission and return to functioning (APA, 2022a). When symptoms continue beyond 1 month, counselors should consider schizophreniform disorder instead.

Special Considerations

Little is known about the lifetime prevalence of brief psychotic disorder; however, the disorder accounts for about 2% to 7% of first-onset psychosis cases (APA, 2022a). Sudden onset of psychotic symptoms is often associated with substance/medication intoxication, substance/medication withdrawal, and medical conditions. For these reasons, counselors should refer clients who appear to meet the criteria for this disorder for medical evaluation. Counselors who work with clients who have personality disorders or who may have something to gain from appearing to have mental illness should be alert to the possibility that sudden-onset psychotic symptoms could be intentionally produced or a transient response to stressors (APA, 2022a).

Brief psychotic disorder has just one diagnostic code: F23. Specifiers include *with marked stressor(s)*, *without marked stressor(s)*, and *with postpartum onset*. Clinicians should note and dual-code if *with catatonia*. Severity is assessed through the CRDPSS (APA, 2022a).

Schizophreniform Disorder (F20.81)

Essential Features

Schizophreniform disorder is a stepping stone between brief psychotic disorder and schizophrenia. Essential features include 1 to 6 months in which an individual experiences two or more psychotic symptoms, including hallucinations, delusions, disorganized speech, disorganized or catatonic behavior, or negative symptoms. At least one positive symptom must be present to qualify for the diagnosis. When symptoms are present for 6 months or more, counselors must consider schizophrenia as an alternative diagnosis (APA, 2022a).

Special Considerations

As with other schizophrenia spectrum disorders, relatively little is known about the prevalence and characteristics of schizophreniform disorder. APA (2022a) notes that those affected are similar to people with schizophrenia. Approximately two thirds of those with schizophreniform disorder go on to meet the full criteria for schizophrenia or schizoaffective disorder. One third of those diagnosed with schizophreniform disorder recover within 6 months.

Treatment considerations for schizophreniform disorder are like those for schizophrenia, although there is an emerging body of literature regarding first-episode psychosis. Early intervention appears to be critical. For example, results of a random control trial of integrated treatment with individuals with first-onset psychosis indicated that 95% of participants had remission of symptoms compared with just 59% of those in a medication-only treatment group (Valencia et al., 2012). Counselors can use findings to inspire hope that diagnosis on the schizophrenia spectrum does not automatically imply negative outcomes.

Certainly, schizophreniform disorder even includes a specifier to denote the presence of *good prognostic features*, such as rapid onset of symptoms, confusion at the height of symptoms, good functioning at onset, and absence of negative symptoms (APA, 2022a). In contrast, those who have slow deterioration in functioning and negative symptoms are more likely to go on to develop schizophrenia.

The *DSM-5-TR* includes just one code for schizophreniform disorder: F20.81. Counselors must specify whether the syndrome is *with good prognostic features* or *without good prognostic features*. A *with catatonia* specifier is available for dual coding, and severity is rated on the CRDPSS (APA, 2022a). When a diagnosis is made in the initial 6 months and outcome is not known, counselors should note the diagnosis as *provisional* (APA, 2022a).

Schizophrenia (F20.9)

Essential Features

Schizophrenia stands at the heart of this chapter and is characterized by at least 1 month of two or more of the following symptoms: delusions, hallucinations, disorganized speech, grossly disorganized or catatonic behavior, or negative symptoms. As with schizophreniform disorder, delusions, hallucinations, and/or disorganized speech must be present. In addition, individuals must have deterioration in functioning such that the total duration is at least 6 months. Exclusionary criteria include concurrent depressive or manic episodes, physiological effects of a substance, coexisting medical considerations, and preexisting neurodevelopmental disorders.

Special Considerations

Schizophrenia affects about 0.3% to 0.8% of people around the world (APA, 2022a). In most cases, people begin showing signs of schizophrenia by late adolescence or early adulthood. Men display signs earlier than women. Onset of symptoms in childhood and early adolescence is associated with longer term and more negative impacts (Pagsberg, 2013). In contrast, those who experience later onset and higher premorbid development have more positive prognoses (Rubin & Trawver, 2011). Both early and late onset are rare. Although prevalence of schizophrenia appears to be stable across cultures, symptoms may manifest in culturally specific ways, perhaps contributing to over- or underdiagnosis (APA, 2022a).

Many individuals who have schizophrenia will experience a degree of lifelong disability related to the condition (Gaebel, 2011). This may be due to neurocognitive problems that remain even when there are no active positive symptoms. Horan et al. (2011) advised clinicians to be alert to four key areas in need of attention: (a) real-world functioning in work, independent living, and social domains; (b) well-being and satisfaction with life; (c) ability to engage successfully in treatment; and (d) functional capacity in social situations. When functioning in these areas is enhanced, clients with schizophrenia will have a higher quality of life and a lower need for daily support. In all cases, family support, education, and engagement are critical when working to manage the impacts of schizophrenia (Rössler, 2011).

The *DSM-5-TR* includes just one code for schizophrenia: F20.9. Counselors may use a variety of course specifiers: *first episode, currently in acute episode*; *first episode, currently in partial remission*; *first episode, currently in full remission*; *multiple episodes, currently in acute episode*; *multiple episodes, currently in partial remission*; *multiple episodes, currently in full remission*; *continuous*; and *unspecified*. A *with catatonia* specifier is available for dual coding, and severity may be rated on the CRDPSS (APA, 2022a).

Schizoaffective Disorder (F25._)

Essential Features

Schizoaffective disorder is characterized by concurrent, overlapping psychosis (i.e., Criterion A of schizophrenia) and mood episodes (i.e., major depressive and/or manic). More precise *DSM-5-TR* criteria require the presence of positive symptoms for 2 or more weeks in absence of a mood episode as well as the presence of a mood episode for a majority of the illness. When clients experience only depressive episodes with psychosis, the disorder is the *depressive type*. Clients who experience manic episodes alone or in combination with depressive episodes have the *bipolar type* (APA, 2022a).

Special Considerations

APA (2022a) estimates lifetime prevalence of just 0.3% for schizoaffective disorder, and the characteristics of individuals with the disorder are assumed to be like those associated with schizophrenia. Schizoaffective disorder is a historically unstable and unreliable diagnosis, and scholars have argued whether schizoaffective disorder is one distinct disorder or better conceptualized by overlapping schizophrenia and mood disorders. Clinicians may struggle to come to a diagnostic agreement (Santelmann et al., 2016a) and need to update diagnoses as new information about symptoms and patterns emerge (Santelmann et al., 2016b).

Treatment strategies for schizoaffective disorder are like those for schizophrenia and mood disorders. In addition to using the three pillars of treatment for schizophrenia discussed earlier, treatment may include additional medication to target depressive or manic episodes. Counselors and treatment teams may tailor strategies to match the most pressing or apparent symptoms at any given time. They should also stay alert to suicide risk as about one half of those with schizoaffective disorder have at least one suicide attempt, the highest risk of all psychotic disorders (Álvarez et al., 2022).

The *DSM-5-TR* includes two codes for schizoaffective disorder: F25.0 for *bipolar type* and F25.1 for *depressive type*. Course and catatonia specifiers are identical to those used for schizophrenia. Severity may be rated on the CRDPSS (APA, 2022a).

Substance/Medication-Induced Psychotic Disorder

Essential Features

Substance/medication-induced psychotic disorder is diagnosed when individuals have delusions and/or hallucinations with evidence that the symptoms are caused by intoxication, withdrawal, or exposure to a medication or substance. Psychotic disorders may be induced by alcohol; cannabis; phencyclidine; other hallucinogens; inhalants; sedatives, hypnotics, or anxiolytics; amphetamines (or other stimulants); cocaine; or other (or unknown) substances (APA, 2013).

Special Considerations

A clinician qualified to assess both the physiological impacts of a substance and psychological after-effects must render the diagnosis of substance/medication-induced psychotic disorder. Treatment may include medical attention to manage the effects of the substance, attention to coexisting substance use disorders, and management of psychotic symptoms. The disorder includes specifiers to note *with onset during intoxication* and *with onset during withdrawal.* Clinicians insert the name of the specific substance into the name of the disorder (e.g., alcohol-induced psychotic disorder). *ICD-10-CM* codes are specific to substances and indicate the presence of mild or moderate/severe substance use disorders. Again, severity should be noted using the CRDPSS (APA, 2022a).

Psychotic Disorder Due to Another Medical Condition

Essential Features

Psychotic disorder due to another medical condition is diagnosed when an individual has delusions and/or hallucinations and there is evidence that the symptoms are caused by a medical condition. The *DSM-5-TR* includes lists of neurological conditions, endocrine conditions, metabolic conditions, fluid or electrolyte imbalances, hepatic or renal diseases, and autoimmune disorders that may cause psychotic symptoms.

Special Considerations

As with substance/medication-induced disorders, diagnoses must be made by a medical professional who is qualified to confirm the presence of the medical condition and the likelihood that the condition caused the psychosis. Treatment attends to the underlying medical condition causing the disorder and management of resulting psychotic symptoms. The name of the medical condition is inserted in the name of the disorder (e.g., psychotic disorder due to hyperthyroidism). Disorders characterized by *with delusions* are coded as F06.2, and those characterized by *with hallucinations* are coded as F06.0 (APA, 2022a).

Catatonia (F06.1)

Essential Features

Catatonia is not a distinct diagnosis; however, it is associated with a variety of neurodevelopmental, psychotic, bipolar, and mood disorders (APA, 2022a) and medical conditions. Catatonia involves psychomotor problems such as immobility, decreased engagement, or excessive motor behaviors. To meet criteria for this condition, one must have three or more symptoms of the following: stupor, catalepsy, waxy flexibility, mutism, negativism, posturing, mannerism, stereotypy, agitation, grimacing, echolalia, or echopraxia. Refer to the *DSM-5-TR* for definitions of each symptom.

Special Considerations

Catatonia is a specifier alongside other disorders. It is always coded as F06.1. Clinicians note it as catatonia associated with another mental disorder, catatonic disorder due to another medical condition, or unspecified catatonia (APA, 2022a).

Case Example

> Cheryl is a 28-year-old mother of two young children who is separated from her partner and lives alone with the support of a housing voucher. She was referred to the county mental health center for multidisciplinary services as a condition of her release from a behavioral health hospital. The case manager initiating the referral indicated that this was Cheryl's first hospitalization; the stay was precipitated by her presentation to the county hospital emergency room with a bag of pennies and a request that the staff fill her teeth with the pennies to

block the FBI from stealing her thoughts. At admission, a drug screen showed evidence of cannabis and alcohol in her system. The case manager indicated that the children were living with their father because of Cheryl's inability to care for them. She was being discharged to home after stabilizing on several atypical antipsychotic medications.

In the interview, you note Cheryl to be unusually slim with an unkempt appearance. Although generally cooperative, Cheryl seems to have difficulty engaging in the interview. She makes little eye contact, speaks in monotone, and rarely says more than a few words at a time. At several points during the interview, Cheryl appears to space out, occasionally shaking her head as if to refocus her attention. She responds to your inquiry regarding hallucinations with a shrug and a comment that the "drugs make everything fuzzy." When you ask about the situation that precipitated the hospital stay, Cheryl simply says that "the truth will come to be." She admitted that she occasionally uses alcohol or marijuana when feeling agitated or tense.

Although details are limited, you gather that Cheryl has not had any treatment for prior mental health concerns. In high school, she had several friends, and her grades were mostly As and Bs. She graduated from high school, discovered she was pregnant, and married her high school boyfriend. She worked for several years in the retail sector. Her supervisor terminated her employment 2 years ago because she "made others uncomfortable." About that time, her family asked her to get help, presumably for depression. Although Cheryl denied being sad or down, her family members apparently noted her lack of connections with others, lack of motivation, and progressive deterioration of self-care. Cheryl appeared unaffected that her husband left with the children approximately 6 months ago, shrugging and saying, "He knew what he needed to do."

Diagnostic Questions

1. Do Cheryl's presenting symptoms appear to meet the criteria for a schizophrenia spectrum disorder? If so, which disorder?
2. Based on your answer to Question 1, which symptom(s) led you to select that diagnosis?
3. What would be the reason(s), if any, a counselor may not diagnose Cheryl with that disorder?
4. Would Cheryl be more accurately diagnosed with a mood disorder? If so, why? If not, why not?
5. What rule-outs would you consider for Cheryl's case?
6. What other information may be needed to make an accurate clinical diagnosis?

Questions for Consideration

1. What unique counseling skills and dispositions could you bring to an interdisciplinary treatment team serving people with schizophrenia spectrum disorders?
2. How might you balance hope and optimism with possibility for lifelong distress when working with someone who is experiencing their first episode of psychosis?
3. What strategies might you use to differentiate between schizophrenia spectrum disorders and other disorders with psychotic features?

Chapter 18

Dissociative Disorders

> Our child came to us through the foster care system. When they found her, she could not speak, walk, or play. Over the past year, she's learned to do all those things. She does really well most days, but sometimes the smallest things can undo her. We were driving home from a visit with the case manager who helped get her out of that horrid place, and she just checked out. She was staring right at me, but it was like she wasn't even there. Later, she asked me how we got home. She didn't even remember being in the car.—Juan

Dissociation involves a "disconnection or lack of connection between things usually associated with each other" (International Society for the Study of Trauma and Dissociation [ISSTD], n.d.-b) and is a normal part of many life experiences. Everyday dissociation is quite common. For example, some people get so focused on a book, video game, or film that they lose track of time and surroundings. Some others may go on a drive and later realize they do not remember parts of the drive. Others may temporarily find themselves between sleep and wakefulness, feeling as if they are out of their body or in another reality. Many people experience dissociation after a traumatic incident as the brain works to protect itself; however, most will not go on to develop dissociative disorders.

Dissociative disorders "are characterized by a disruption of and/or discontinuity in the normal integration of consciousness, memory, identity, emotion, perception, body representation, motor control, and behavior" (APA, 2022a, p. 329). The ISSTD (n.d.-b) defined five types of dissociation addressed in *DSM-5-TR*: depersonalization, derealization, amnesia, identity confusion, and identity alteration. According to the ISSTD (n.d.-b), depersonalization is a "sense of being detached from, or 'not in' one's body," whereas derealization is a "sense of the world not being real." Amnesia involves a loss of ability to access stored information one would be expected to remember. Identity confusion involves an uncharacteristic change in one's sense of self. Identity alteration "is the sense of being markedly different from another part of oneself . . . subtler forms of identity alteration can be observed when a person uses different voice tones, range of language, or facial expressions" (ISSTD, n.d.-b).

Although disassociation is central to dissociative disorders, dissociation commonly occurs across a broad range of mental disorders, most commonly, PTSD, BPD, and conversion disorder (Lyssenko et al., 2018). There is also clear evidence of dissociative experiences in substance-related and addictive disorders, feeding and eating disorders, anxiety disorders, obsessive-compulsive disorders, and depression. When dissociation is present in the context of other mental disorders, especially PTSD and BPD, it is often associated with greater severity and risk (Al-Shamali et al., 2022; Atchley & Bedford, 2021; Scalabrini et al., 2017).

Prevalence of this class of disorders is high and estimated at 2% to 10% of the general population (ISSTD, n.d.-b). In a meta-analysis regarding the prevalence of dissociative disorders among college populations, Kate et al. (2020) found that 17% of college students reported dissociative experiences, and 11.4% of students met criteria for a dissociative disorder. The presence and legitimacy of dissociative disorders have long been controversial, with myths and misunderstandings contributing to stigma, limiting understanding of dissociative disorders, and stymying the development of effective treatment approaches (Brand et al., 2014, 2016; Lynn et al., 2019). This history increases the likelihood that dissociative disorders are simply missed in counseling settings.

Unfortunately, individuals who experience dissociative disorders are among the most vulnerable and high-risk clients. This population experiences near-universal trauma, high rates of comorbid disorders, and risk of nonsuicidal self-injury and suicidal behavior (Kate et al., 2020; Lyssenko et al., 2018; Rafiq et al., 2018; Scalabrini et al., 2017). This chapter includes a discussion of essential features and special considerations for dissociative identity disorder (DID), dissociative amnesia, and depersonalization/derealization disorder. As with other chapters, the *DSM-5-TR* includes other specified dissociative disorder and unspecified dissociative disorder.

Major Changes From *DSM-5* to *DSM-5-TR*

There are no major changes from the *DSM-5* to the *DSM-5-TR*. Rather, changes are concentrated in the text sections, including updated literature and more nuanced attention to culture-, sex-, and gender-related diagnostic issues in this category.

Differential Diagnosis

Like many other mental health symptoms, dissociative symptoms may be part of other disorders, caused by medical conditions, or triggered by substance use. Neurological conditions leading to symptoms that mimic dissociative disorders may include seizures, traumatic brain injuries, and neurocognitive disorders. Dissociation can also occur in substance-related disorders as part of intoxication or withdrawal (APA, 2022a). Counselors who work with clients experiencing dissociative symptoms should refer them for a complete medical evaluation and psychiatric consultation and consider whether a diagnosis is within their scope of ethical practice in accordance with the ACA *Code of Ethics* (ACA, 2014).

Trauma is almost always at the root of dissociative disorders, so counselors should carefully consider whether a diagnosis of PTSD or acute stress disorder may better account for dissociative experiences. This requires careful assessment to determine whether dissociation occurs only in relation to a traumatic event (e.g., amnesia for trauma, flashbacks, instruction, avoidance) or more generally. Given the strong evidence of a dissociative component of PTSD (Atchley & Bedford, 2021), individuals who experience depersonalization and/or derealization in the context of that disorder should be diagnosed using that specifier for PTSD.

ISSTD (2011) recommended special attention to bipolar, affective, psychotic, seizure, and borderline personality disorders when engaging in differential diagnosis. Mood changes may be indicative of identity alteration rather than fluctuations associated with bipolar disorders. Panic attacks have a dissociative quality to them, thus indicating anxiety disorders as potential differential diagnoses. Individuals with dissociative disorders may describe out-of-body experiences, have beliefs regarding possession, or hear different voices that lead one to suspect a psychotic disorder or psychotic features of depression rather than dissociation. Dissociation during times of stress, instability of identity, and history of interpersonal trauma are characteristic of BPD. Indeed, meta-analyses revealed that those with BPD scored high on measures of dissociation (Lyssenko et al., 2018) and that 17% of those with depersonalization/derealization disorder also have BPD; the presence of dissociation is related to higher severity of BPD (Al-Shamali et al., 2022). Finally, dissociation may be misidentified as behavioral problems (e.g., temper tantrums in ODD, inattention in ADHD) among children (ISSTD, n.d.-a).

Dissociative disorders are comorbid with multiple mental disorders addressed above (APA, 2022a). Counselors should be particularly alert to self-injurious and suicidal behavior, especially given that 70% of those with DID have a history of the latter. Similarly, individuals who experience dissociation also tend to report somatic concerns, thus implicating somatic symptom disorders as differential or comorbid diagnoses (ISSTD, 2011).

Etiology and Treatment

The ISSTD (n.d.-b) characterized dissociation as having both environmental and biological components. In nearly all cases, dissociative disorders may be linked to experiences of traumatic events, especially early in life. Precipitating experiences leading to dissociation in children and adolescents may include physical, sexual, or emotional abuse; chronic neglect; witnessing violence; loss of loved ones or disruption in caregiving; physical injury, medical conditions, or medical procedures; and accidents or disasters (ISSTD, n.d.-a). Neurobiological research supports theories that early experiences of trauma and neglect affect brain development in ways that may lead to dissociative disorders (Brand et al., 2012). Brain studies on individuals with dissociative disorders also provide evidence of divergent brain structure and function (APA, 2022a; Brand et al., 2012; Lotfinia et al., 2020).

There are two primary schools of thought on the etiology of dissociative disorders (Lynn et al., 2019). Those who adhere to the *trauma model* posit that dissociative experiences are a direct result of traumatic experiences. Those who adhere to the *sociocognitive model* or *fantasy model* believe that individuals experiencing dissociative disorders are suggestible, fantasy-prone, and influenced by media. Meta-analysis and critical review of the evidence regarding dissociative disorders point to strong support for the trauma model (Brand et al., 2016; Kate et al., 2020) and a lack of support for the fantasy model (Brand et al., 2016). APA (2022a) noted a striking 90% prevalence of childhood abuse and neglect among individuals with DID. Developmental models of DID posit that

> DID does not arise from a previously mature, unified mind or "core personality" that becomes shattered or fractured. Rather, DID results from a failure of normal developmental integration caused by overwhelming experiences and disturbed caregiver-child interactions (including neglect and the failure to respond) during critical early developmental periods. This, in turn, leads some traumatized children to develop relatively discrete, personified behavioral states that ultimately evolve into the DID alternate identities. (ISSTD, 2011, p. 123)

There is no scientific evidence to support models that proposed clinicians created DID among highly suggestible clients (Brand et al., 2016; ISSTD, 2011). In contrast, there is evidence that severity and frequency of trauma are related to dissociative amnesia (APA, 2022a). Likewise, depersonalization/derealization disorder is linked to experiences of emotional abuse or interpersonal conflicts, with 25% to 35% of those experiencing abuse meeting criteria for the disorder (Yang et al., 2023).

Unfortunately, severe dissociative disorders in adults may be among the most difficult, time-intensive, and costly to treat (Brand, 2012; ISSTD, 2011). Dissociation in youth appears to be more amenable to treatment than dissociation in adulthood, requiring less time and resulting in more positive outcomes (International Society for the Study of Dissociation [ISSD}, 2004). Research regarding evidence-based treatments for dissociative disorders is rare, and there is a lack of controlled treatment trials (Brand, 2012; Brand et al., 2012). Still, there is evidence that trauma-focused psychotherapy for DID works when it targets dissociative symptoms (Brand et al., 2014); likewise, dissociative-type PTSD requires a specific targeting of dissociation (Atchley & Bedford, 2021). There is no evidence to suggest that current standards of treatment for DID are harmful. Limited research suggests that attention to complex traumas and dissociation may lead to treatment effects ranging from moderate to large across a variety of symptoms such as depression, dissociation, anxiety, somatic symptoms, and substance use. There are mixed findings regarding the degree to which medications are effective for treating dissociative symptoms. Counselors working with these clients benefit from additional training and interdisciplinary support.

The primary goal of treatment for DID is the achievement of integrated functioning (ISSTD, 2011). The ISSTD (2011) advocated for a staged approach to treatment with a focus on "1. Establishing safety, stabilization, and symptom reduction; 2. Confronting, working through, and integrating traumatic memories; and 3. Identify integration and rehabilitation" (p. 135). If the client does not present a danger to self, most treatment is conducted on an individual outpatient basis, one to three times weekly, over an extended duration. The ISSTD (n.d.-b) characterized most treatments as psychodynamic with the incorporation of approaches such as CBT, DBT, hypnosis, and eye-movement desensitization and reprocessing. Most individuals will also receive psychotropic medication focused on specific distressing symptoms. Readers interested in learning more should review the "Guidelines for Treating Dissociative Identity Disorder in Adults" (ISSTD, 2011), "Guidelines for the Evaluation and Treatment of Dissociative Symptoms in Children and Adolescents" (ISSD, 2004), and *ISTSS Expert Consensus Treatment Guidelines for Complex PTSD in Adults* (Bisson et al., 2019).

Implications for Counselors

Scholars of dissociative disorders warn that they are among the most overlooked disorders in clinical practice. Counselors may not consider dissociative disorders because of their own lack of awareness, beliefs, and potential biases. Counselors should consider whether they endorse six common myths that get in the way of effective attention to DID:

> (1) belief that DID is a fad, (2) belief that DID is primarily diagnosed in North America by DID experts who overdiagnose the disorder, (3) belief that DID is rare, (4) belief that DID is an iatrogenic, rather than trauma-based, disorder, (5) belief that DID is the same entity as borderline personality disorder, and (6) belief that DID treatment is harmful to patients. (Brand et al., 2016, p. 257)

Likewise, counselors must be careful not to stigmatize normal experiences that may present as dissociation. Experiences related to dissociation may occur during the normal course of other neurological conditions (APA, 2022a), and individuals across cultures may experience dissociation related to highly distressing conflicts or stressors. APA (2022a) advises careful consideration for diagnoses based on possession states because such experiences are often a normal part of spiritual practice. Similarly, experiences of depersonalization/derealization may be common in the general population and are often the goal of meditative practices (APA, 2022a).

It is also possible that dissociative disorders are missed in practice because clients are not aware of the dissociation or minimize the importance of dissociative experiences. Yet, a meta-analysis using evidence-based tools for detecting dissociation found that 11% of college students met criteria for a dissociative disorder (Kate et al., 2020). In a review of research regarding depersonalization/derealization disorder, Yang et al. (2023) found that up to 2% of the general population, 5% to 20% of outpatient clients, and 18% to 42% of inpatient clients met criteria for the disorder. Counselors work in settings where dissociative experiences and dissociative disorders are likely to be present; therefore, they are responsible for opening doors to conversation and assessment.

Experts recommend systematic assessment of trauma (Rafiq et al., 2018) and dissociation (ISSTD, 2011; Lyssenko et al., 2018; Scalabrini et al., 2017) across clinical populations. Counselors may find validated assessment and screening tools helpful for detecting dissociative experiences in practice (Brand et al., 2012). Structured interviews appear to be particularly effective at identifying dissociative disorders accurately (Mychailyszyn et al., 2021). The ISSTD (n.d.-a, n.d.-b) provides several screening and assessment tools for consideration. Counselors who work with youth may wish to consult ISSTD (n.d.-a; see also ISSD, 2004) for practical recommendations regarding the assessment of dissociative symptoms in children and adolescents.

Opportunities to attend to dissociative experiences are likely to arise during discussions of experiences of trauma or abuse and during screenings conducted in everyday counseling practice. Counselors should be alert to signs of dissociation when initially discussing a client's history of trauma or abuse, when a client provides details related to trauma or abuse, or when a client experiences changes that may serve as triggers to previous experiences. It is important to recognize the protective function of dissociation for many and to refrain from pressing for details if a client appears vulnerable or overwhelmed by the experience.

If counselors find themselves working with populations who have a high risk of dissociative disorders, it is critical that they take proactive steps to ensure competency consistent with their ethical obligations (ACA, 2014). This includes attending to expert recommendations regarding standards of practice (e.g., Brand et al., 2012; ISSTD, 2011) and engaging in continuing education through well-recognized programs such as those offered by ISSTD. Although there are very few counseling-specific resources regarding working with people who have dissociative disorders, one study reminds us of the importance of keeping true to core counseling foundations. Jacobson et al. (2015) interviewed survivors of DID regarding their perspectives on counseling. Clients reported pacing, secure structure, universality within a group, grounding resources, coping resources, and the therapeutic relationship as essential to their success. Clients also reported that they found counselors who appropriately shared insights, remained client centered, modeled, and attended to the relationship to be helpful. At the same time, clients found counselors ineffective when they overfocused on techniques, did not establish safety, confronted inappropriately, or lacked plans. Although some responses were consistent with specialty approaches to dissociative disorders, the heart of their responses reminds us of the importance of the counseling relationship.

Dissociative Identity Disorder (F44.81)

Essential Features

Dissociative identity disorder (DID) was previously known as multiple personality disorder. This disorder is accompanied by usual gaps in everyday recall. Experiences may be recurrent, may be observed, must cause distress or impairment, must not be culturally accepted, and may not be substance induced or due to medical conditions. DID specifically involves

> Disruption of identity characterized by two or more distinct personality states, which may be described in some cultures as an experience of possession. The disruption in identity involves marked discontinuity in sense of self and sense of agency, accompanied by related alterations in affect, behavior, consciousness, memory, perception, cognition, and/or sensory-motor functioning. (APA, 2022a, p. 330)

Special Considerations

Estimates of DID prevalence vary widely. The *DSM-5-TR* reports a 12-month prevalence of DID at 1.5%, yet meta-analysis of college students indicated a prevalence of 3.7% (Kate et al., 2020). These numbers will be higher in clinical samples. Men and women appear to experience DID in approximately equal numbers but may vary in their presentation (APA, 2022a). It is important to note that DID is likely to be much less dramatic and pronounced than one might believe based on popular cultural representations. There is just one code for DID: F44.81. There are no specifiers associated with this disorder.

Dissociative Amnesia (F44.0)

Essential Features

Dissociative amnesia is characterized by "an inability to recall important autobiographical information, usually of a traumatic or stressful nature, that is inconsistent with ordinary forgetting" (APA, 2022a, p. 337). The amnesia may be localized (focused on a specific period of time), selective (involving loss of memory for some aspects of a period of time), generalized (complete loss of information), systematized (focused on a category of information), or continuous (focused on the loss of new information; Spiegel et al., 2011). As with other disorders, the amnesia must cause impairment or distress and may not be substance or medically induced.

Special Considerations

APA (2022a) estimates a 12-month prevalence of 1.8% among the general population; however, there is evidence of prevalence as high as 7.3% among international samples (Spiegel et al., 2011). Now included in the diagnosis of dissociative amnesia, dissociative fugue is believed to be very rare, occurring in 0% to 0.2% of the population (ISSTD, n.d.-b). When coding only dissociative amnesia, counselors should use F44.0. When coding dissociative amnesia *with dissociative fugue*, counselors should use F44.1.

Depersonalization/Derealization Disorder (F48.1)

Essential Features

Depersonalization/derealization disorder is characterized by the presence of depersonalization and/or derealization with intact reality testing and resulting distress or impairment; the experience cannot be substance induced or medically caused or due to another mental disorder (APA, 2022a). In general, depersonalization, or the feeling of being outside oneself, involves five elements: numbing, unreality of self, unreality of other, temporal disintegration, and perceptional alterations (Spiegel et al., 2011). Derealization is characterized by feeling as if the world is unreal.

Special Considerations

Individuals in the general population may experience aspects of depersonalization or derealization on a regular basis, with half of all U.S. adults reporting experience of depersonalization or derealization at least once in their lifetime (APA, 2022a). The ISSTD (n.d.-b) reported that some researchers believe depersonalization/derealization disorder follows depression and anxiety as the most common mental disorders. However, a systematic review indicates a prevalence of 0% to 1.9% in the general population and exponentially higher risk among those in mental health treatment, with young people and those in inpatient settings particularly at risk (Yang et al., 2023). There is just one code for depersonalization/derealization disorder: F48.1. The disorder has no specifiers.

Case Example

Delila is a 35-year-old married woman who lives with her husband Alex. They have been married for nearly 15 years. Delila works full-time in the accounting office of a medium-sized company where she is well liked and appreciated for her selfless support of others. Delila reports no contact with her family of origin, disappointed acceptance regarding her inability to have children, and regular engagement in the community. Delila is accompanied to counseling by Alex, who insisted they see a counselor to explore the possibility that she may be experiencing bipolar disorder. Dressed in neatly pressed khakis and a button-up shirt, Delila listens with respect and slight amusement as Alex reports a growing sense of discomfort regarding several recent changes in Delila.

Initially, Alex noted spending sprees during which Delila acquired a wardrobe that was uncharacteristically expensive and revealing. Unconcerned about finances, Alex attributed the changes to Delila's desire to "keep things alive" in their marriage. He became confused and then suspicious when Delila began denying using the credit card and refused to wear the clothes, acting as if she had never seen them before or as if Alex purchased them for her. Delila maintained her innocence yet shrugged off the concern, noting that she had become so busy she must have forgotten a trip to the mall.

Alex noted other times Delila "just wasn't herself." Alex relayed several incidents in which Delila picked fights, sometimes snapping at him and other times mocking him. Hours later, she would deny having the conversation or act as if nothing had happened. Alex wasn't alone in his observations. Delila was recently sent home from work after several altercations with coworkers that led her boss to express concerns about her ability to handle stress. Alex was shocked to come home and find her heavily intoxicated in the middle of the day because she is normally a very light drinker. Delila appeared to be as dismayed as Alex, claiming that she would never drink during the day and must have been drugged by a coworker.

Diagnostic Questions

1. Do Delila's presenting symptoms appear to meet the criteria for a dissociative disorder? If so, which disorder?
2. Based on your answer to Question 1, which symptom(s) led you to select that diagnosis?
3. What would be the reason(s), if any, a counselor may not diagnose Delila with that disorder?
4. What other diagnoses might you consider for Delila? Why?
5. What rule-outs would you consider for Delila's case?
6. What other information may be needed to make an accurate clinical diagnosis?

Questions for Consideration

1. Counselors tend to miss dissociative disorders in practice. What additional training or strategies might you utilize to sensitize yourself to these disorders?
2. How might you differentiate between relatively typical experiences of dissociation and dissociative disorders?

Chapter 19

Somatic Symptom and Related Disorders

> I am sick and tired of being sick and tired. I have to struggle to get through the day. The doctors tell me it's all in my head. If I get agitated during an appointment, they use that as more evidence that I'm nuts. Of course I'm upset a lot—I am in pain all the time, and nobody will do anything about it. I just don't know what to do anymore.—Ayana

The somatic symptom and related disorders, previously known as somatoform disorders, were first classified together in the *DSM-5*. They are characterized by the presence of physical or somatic complaints; problematic thoughts, feelings, and behaviors in relation to the complaints; and resulting distress and impairment. Individuals who experience these disorders almost always present for medical care to address their very real physical experiences and distress. As many as one third to one half of medical complaints cannot be explained despite strong evidence of symptoms. Individuals living with a somatic symptom disorder can face lack of understanding and judgment from others. This then lends to additional relational stressors that can exacerbate presenting symptoms. There is need for research on the prevalence of this grouping of disorders and additional support mechanisms for individuals dealing with the sequelae of somatic symptoms (APA, 2022a; Aydogmus, 2020; Dimsdale et al., 2013).

Given the focus on finding medical explanations for symptoms, individuals with distress regarding somatic concerns may only turn to professional counselors at the urging of multiple physicians and after unsuccessful attempts to identify the source of their ailments. Substantial comorbidity among depressive disorders, anxiety disorders, and somatic concerns means that counselors may find themselves working with clients who experience physical distress alongside other mental health diagnoses (APA, 2022a; Haller et al., 2015; Quinn, 2020).

Major Changes From *DSM-5* to *DSM-5-TR*

There are no major changes to the Somatic Symptom and Related Disorders chapter from the *DSM-5* to the *DSM-5-TR*. The only modification is with functional neurological symptom disorder, which now lists conversion disorder parenthetically—functional neurological symptom disorder (conversion disorder). This was done to align with the international health community and to facilitate the use of neutral terminology, with functional neurological symptom disorder representing the preferred term.

Somatic symptom disorder and illness anxiety disorder were new diagnoses in the *DSM-5*. They replaced somatization disorder, hypochondriasis, pain disorder, and undifferentiated somatoform disorder. Hypochondriasis as a term is no longer officially used in diagnostic classification (APA, 2013; Dimsdale et al., 2013).

Clients who have concerns regarding the meaning of physical symptoms or experiences are now diagnosed with somatic symptom disorder (if somatic symptoms are present) or illness anxiety disorder (if no somatic symptoms are present). Clients with pain concerns may be diagnosed with somatic symptom disorder or psychological factors affecting other medical conditions.

Differential Diagnosis

Because the signs of somatic symptom and related disorders are medical, initial diagnostic focus must be on medical examination to determine the specific nature of the concern. *DSM-5-TR* criteria allow for the presence of diagnosable health concerns alongside distressing reactions to the concerns. Thus, primary differential diagnosis includes determination regarding (a) which medical conditions are present and (b) whether one's response to the medical concerns are in excess of what would be considered normal. For individuals who are experiencing concerns related to significant medical diagnosis, an adjustment disorder diagnosis may be more appropriate (APA, 2022a; Edwards et al., 2021). If one's reaction to medical concerns or symptoms is simply a culturally expected response to a situation, assignment of a Z code may be indicated.

There is substantial overlap as well as comorbidity among depressive disorders, anxiety disorders, and somatic symptom disorders. Research has also addressed the link with neurocognitive disorders and chronic pain (Edwards et al., 2021; Sammartino-Arbor et al., 2022). There is strong evidence of a cultural component to expressing anxious or depressive distress somatically. Thus, counselors should consider anxiety and depressive disorders as differential and comorbid diagnoses. Somatic and anxiety symptoms can also be common among individuals with substance use concerns. Finally, given evidence that somatic symptoms are a frequent response to trauma, counselors should consider the possibility of trauma- and stressor-related disorders as differential diagnoses (APA, 2022a; Boone, 2021).

Etiology and Treatment

Initially, somatic symptom and related disorders were viewed as psychodynamic responses to stressors in which an individual converted psychological concerns into physical symptoms as a way of coping or expressing distress. Today, there are various models and explanations regarding etiology of somatic symptom and related disorders. The *DSM-5-TR* identifies genetic and biological vulnerability, early traumatic experiences, learning, and cultural/social norms as likely underlying factors. Still, as So (2008) observed, "Ethnographic fieldwork has long indicated the presence of a specific type of culturally mediated illness where an individual suffering from psychological issues expresses distress in the form of physical symptoms and somatic complaints, with no known organic cause" (p. 168). Some posit that somatic symptom and related disorders are more likely to develop in individuals who do not have strong insight and those who fear psychiatric stigmatization. Treatment involves stress management, support, and reduction in symptoms.

Because somatic symptom and related disorders are considered quite rare, there is a relatively small body of literature regarding treatment considerations. Sharma and Manjula, (2013) stated,

> The basic premise of any psychological intervention in disorders with somatic symptoms is that somatization is a universal phenomenon and is a direct consequence of common psychological disorders such as anxiety or depression resulting in autonomic arousal symptoms or somatic complaints; it may be an idiom for help-seeking for severe social adversities such as poverty, domestic violence, stigma, associated with mental illness. (p. 117)

Treatment of somatic symptom disorder in primary care settings may include psychiatric consultation and psychopharmaceutical intervention, reattribution therapy, problem-solving, psychoeducation, and CBT (Sharma & Manjula, 2013). Among all these treatments, CBT has been found to be most effective for somatic concerns. Similarly, treatment for illness anxiety disorder includes psychoeducation, CBT, and medication (Schnabel et al., 2022; Seitz et al., 2022). Psychoeducation may be appropriate for responding to mild concerns and includes a focus on coping strategies, role of stress in bodily sensations, and relaxation training rather than attempts to convince clients their symptoms are not real or provide reassurance regarding medical concerns. Couples and family counseling can enhance communication and engender support for affected clients.

Implications for Counselors

As with all aspects of counseling, a strong therapeutic relationship is essential when working with individuals who have somatic symptom and related disorders, especially given the stigma and lack of understanding they may face from overworked health care providers (APA, 2022a; Kline et al., 2022; Kress & Paylo, 2018). Because clients may be distressed about their symptoms, may be sensitive, and, in some situations, may feel misunderstood, they may be quick to discontinue counseling if they sense they are not being taken seriously (Sharma & Manjula, 2013). Counselors can provide and model empathy through understanding symptoms as a form of emotional communication.

Counselors can best serve this population of clients by ensuring they receive appropriate medical evaluation and support, remaining alert to potential harms of this diagnosis in terms of access to services, and recognizing that clients who have medically unexplained symptoms can and do develop other medical concerns (APA, 2022a; Frances & Chapman, 2013). Professional counselors will need to take care when determining what types and levels of expression regarding health concerns are "excessive" and "maladaptive" enough to warrant diagnosis. It is critical for counselors to keep multicultural and diversity elements at the forefront to avoid possible diagnostic bias based on gender and ethnoracial identity (Kline et al., 2022).

DSM-5-TR criteria emphasize neurological examination and deemphasize the assumption that one will readily recognize psychological factors leading to concerns upon initial presentation (APA, 2022a). Referral for a medical assessment (if the client is not already under medical supervision) is critical for appropriate diagnosis and treatment.

In working with clients experiencing somatic symptoms, counselors must remember that, regardless of the medical foundations of concerns, distress and impairment are real. A client-centered, supportive approach can be beneficial (APA, 2022; Kress & Paylo, 2018). These may include cognitive, emotional, physical, behavioral, medical, and social experiences (Sharma & Manjula, 2013). For example, somatization is linked to problems such as missed time from work, health care utilization, hypervigilance in detecting and expressing symptoms, and dissatisfaction with treatment (Sharma & Manjula, 2013). Accurate screening, early identification, and targeted clinical trials can be imperative to ameliorate symptoms and defray societal costs (Rief et al., 2017; Toussaint et al., 2020). The most beneficial approach for individuals with a somatic symptom disorder may be to frame services as focused on helping to cope with stress related to their medical problems. CBT and psychoeducation can be of benefit on multiple levels (Newby et al., 2018).

Somatic concerns may be universal phenomena, and there is evidence that symptom experiences vary by culture. Furthermore, symptoms may be culturally normal and expected responses (Brown & Lewis-Fernández, 2011). Somatization is quite stigmatized in Western cultures that focus on mind-body duality; however, a degree of somatization experiences are quite common in cultures in which mind-body holism is accepted and expected.

Counselors must be careful not to stigmatize culturally specific ways of expressing distress or judge difficulties differentiating feelings from bodily sensations as somehow less developed or less valid. This is particularly important given higher rates of concerns among vulnerable populations (Kline et al., 2022), including those with lower socioeconomic status, lower education, poor working conditions, and more exposure to violence. Additional research is needed on cross-cultural factors as there is scant current knowledge in this area. Family counseling can enhance relationships and assist with symptom monitoring and support (APA, 2022a).

Somatic Symptom Disorder (F45.1)

Essential Features

Somatic symptom disorder is characterized by the presence of distressing or disruptive somatic symptoms for 6 or more months and strong preoccupation with these symptoms (APA, 2022a). These can be considered excessive based on the proportion of time spent thinking about the concern, level of anxiety surrounding the concern, or degree of time and energy devoted to the concern. Criteria include a focus on positive symptoms in which a client experiences distressing or disruptive somatic symptoms alongside "excessive thoughts, feelings, or behaviors related to the somatic symptoms" (APA, 2022a, p. 349).

Clients who have somatic concerns with or without co-occurring medical conditions may be diagnosed with somatic symptom disorder if they have both unexplained somatic symptoms and maladaptive responses to those symptoms (APA, 2022a; Dimsdale et al., 2013). Many individuals with previous diagnoses of hypochondriasis and pain disorder will be diagnosed with somatic symptom disorder. Health care professionals may make this diagnosis for cases in which somatic symptoms are not medically explained.

Special Considerations

Individuals with a somatic symptom disorder may also have an additional medical diagnosis. Women are more likely to be diagnosed than men, and the disorder is more common and persistent in individuals who have lower socioeconomic status, lower educational attainment, and more pronounced experiences of stressors (APA, 2022a).

Coding

There is just one code for somatic symptom disorder: F45.1. The *DSM-5-TR* includes the specifiers *with predominant pain* and *persistent* (for use with severe symptoms, marked impairment, and long duration). Counselors characterize severity as *mild*, *moderate*, or *severe* depending on degree of concern related to the excessive thoughts, feelings, and behaviors (APA, 2022a).

Illness Anxiety Disorder (F45.21)

Essential Features

Illness anxiety disorder is characterized by a 6-month period in which individuals are preoccupied "with having or acquiring a serious illness" (APA, 2022a, p. 357) although somatic symptoms are absent or very mild. Individuals with illness anxiety disorder have high levels of anxiety about their health and engage in excessive or maladaptive health-related behaviors. Those with this disorder are more distressed about the potential of a diagnosis than experiencing the symptoms.

Special Considerations

Individuals with illness anxiety disorder can be vigilant and readily worried about their health. This is often accompanied by anxiety that results in distress and maladaptive functioning (APA, 2022a). It is not unusual for those with illness anxiety disorder to consult multiple health care providers, although a smaller percentage avoid medical attention for their illness anxiety. Differential diagnosis includes medical conditions, phobia of disease exposure, somatic symptoms associated with depressive and anxiety disorders, body dysmorphic disorder, and delusional disorder. The *DSM-5-TR* also includes the following differential diagnoses: adjustment disorders, somatic symptom disorder, and OCD (APA, 2022a).

One third to one half of individuals meeting the criteria for illness anxiety disorder have transient symptoms. These clients are less likely to have psychological comorbidities. Anxiety disorders, OCD, and depressive disorders are comorbid with this disorder, with the majority of those diagnosed with illness anxiety disorder evidencing at least one *DSM-5-TR* comorbidity (APA, 2022a).

Coding

There is just one code for illness anxiety disorder: F45.21. Health care professionals may use specifiers to note whether an individual has *care-seeking type* or *care-avoidant type*. Diagnosis of illness anxiety disorder is often done in health care settings and can include physical and psychological assessment.

Functional Neurological Symptom Disorder (Conversion Disorder)(F44._)

Essential Features

Functional neurological symptom disorder, also known as conversion disorder, is characterized by symptoms suggesting problems with voluntary motor or sensory function (e.g., paralysis, problems swallowing, speech problems, seizures) in which there is no neurological evidence for the condition. The problem cannot be explained by another concern and must lead to impairment, distress, or medical evaluation (APA, 2022a).

The terminology has been updated in the *DSM-5-TR* with functional neurological symptom disorder being the primary identifier to promote neutrality and harmonize with the international community. Conversion disorder is presented parenthetically and still considered acceptable for use.

Special Considerations

The *DSM-5-TR* criteria maintain the requirement that symptoms be proceeded by a psychological stressor because stressors may not be evident to or reported by clients. Focus on medical examination and clinical assessment becomes all the more important when making this diagnosis (APA, 2022a; Kline et al., 2022).

The prevalence of functional neurological symptom disorder (conversion disorder) is unknown; however, it appears to account for approximately 5% of neurology clinic referrals (APA, 2022a). Brown and Lewis-Fernández (2011) noted that prevalence among men and women varies culturally; however, functional neurological symptom disorder (conversion disorder) is consistently more common among women and those with lower socioeconomic status.

Functional neurological symptom disorder (conversion disorder) is often comorbid with dissociative, depressive, and anxiety disorders. Although there is some evidence in North America that suggests this disorder is of short duration, a body of literature shows longer effects in other cultural contexts (Brown & Lewis-Fernández, 2011).

Coding

The *ICD-10-CM* code for functional neurological symptom disorder (F44._) will vary based on subtype: *with weakness or paralysis, with abnormal movement, with swallowing symptoms, with speech symptom, with attacks or seizures, with anesthesia or sensory loss, with special sensory symptom*, or *with mixed symptoms.* Counselors may specify whether a client is experiencing an *acute episode* (less than 6 months) or a *persistent episode* (longer than 6 months) and whether the concern is *with psychological stressor (specify stressor)* or *without psychological stressor* (APA, 2022a).

Psychological Factors Affecting Other Medical Conditions (F54)

Essential Features

This diagnosis is used when individuals have a medical condition for which psychological or behavioral factors exacerbate symptoms, interfere with treatment, or compound risks. APA (2022a) stipulates that the psychological factors cannot be another diagnosable mental disorder. Examples provided in the *DSM-5-TR* include asthma made worse by anxiety, manipulation of insulin for weight loss, or denial of treatment for chest pain.

Special Considerations

APA (2022a) notes that prevalence for this diagnosis is unknown. Psychological factors must be differentiated from cultural differences in help seeking and may occur throughout the life span. Research in this area is needed to assist counselors and integrative health care teams in minimizing impairment and improving client outcomes.

Coding

There is one code for this disorder: F54. Clinicians may use impact on health to rate the disorder as *mild, moderate, severe*, or *extreme.*

Factitious Disorder (F68.10)

Essential Features

Factitious disorder is characterized by falsification of an illness in the absence of external rewards and other mental disorders explaining the behavior (APA, 2022a). Factitious disorder may be diagnosed for individuals who present themselves as ill (factitious disorder imposed on self) as well as individuals who represent another as ill (factitious disorder imposed on another) such as dependents in their care.

Special Considerations

Prevalence of factitious disorder is unknown, although it may present in about 1% of individuals in hospital settings. Differential diagnoses include somatoform disorder, illness anxiety disorder, adjustment disorder, and mental disorder due to another medical condition (APA, 2022a). Legal charges may ensue for factitious disorder imposed on another.

Coding

There is just one diagnostic code for factitious disorder: F68.10. Clinicians can specify the diagnosis as *single episode* or *recurrent episode.* In cases in which the disorder is imposed on another, the perpetrator receives the diagnosis of factitious disorder, and the victim may be assigned a diagnostic code pertaining to the abuse. As with other diagnoses in the chapter, factitious disorder is likely identified in a health care setting and should always include collaboration with health care professionals.

Case Example

Marcos is a single, 34-year-old Latinx man who holds a college degree. He presented to counseling for "support and stress management" at the suggestion of his physician. Over the past year, Marcos has experienced a number of medical concerns, especially headaches and light-headedness. He sought assistance from a physician who, upon noting normal blood chemistries and metabolic functioning, prescribed migraine control medication and advised him to be careful about not going too long between meals. When the medication did not bring relief, the physician ordered a complete diagnostic workup including more extensive blood work, an MRI (magnetic resonance imaging), and a CT (computed tomography). All tests were within normal limits; however, Marcos became convinced he had an undiagnosed brain tumor or aneurism. As his work performance decreased because of the effects of the symptoms and worry regarding their implications, Marcos began spending hours each night researching his symptoms and discussing them with others. Convinced his physician did not understand his concerns, he sought a second opinion. At his insistence, the second physician referred him to a neurologist for further evaluation. The neurologist reviewed test results, completed several additional procedures, and did not detect any concerns.

Over the next few months, Marcos developed additional concerns including gastrointestinal upset, shortness of breath, and sleep disturbance. He missed more work, withdrew from family and friends, and stopped going to the gym out of concern that the exertion may not be in his best interest. At this time, his blood pressure became elevated, heightening his concern regarding the possibility of a severe underlying disorder. Referral to a gastroenterologist led to an endoscopy that was normal with the exception of slight esophageal irritation, which the specialist recommended treating with over-the-counter heartburn medication.

In the meantime, Marcos's employer became increasingly frustrated with his lack of reliable attendance and frequent distraction at work. She warned Marcos that she would need to take disciplinary action if the behaviors continued without supporting documentation from his physician. Distraught at the potential loss of health insurance, Marcos visited his physician to explore his options. During a particularly difficult visit, his physician expressed doubts that they would ever find the "root of the concern" and advised Marcos to attend counseling to learn how to manage his symptoms and distress related to them. Although offended at the suggestion that it was "all in his head," Marcos made the call. After all, he said, the symptoms were distressing and he was realizing he might just have to deal with a lifelong illness.

Diagnostic Questions

1. Do Marcos's presenting symptoms appear to meet the criteria for a somatic concern or related disorder? If so, which disorder?
2. Based on your answer to Question 1, which symptom(s) led you to select that diagnosis?
3. What would be the reason(s), if any, a counselor may not diagnose Marcos with that disorder?
4. Would Marcos be more accurately diagnosed with an anxiety disorder? If so, why? If not, why not?
5. What rule-outs would you consider for Marcos's case?
6. What other information may be needed to make an accurate clinical diagnosis?

Questions for Consideration

1. How might the diagnosis of a somatic symptom disorder be challenging for medical professionals?
2. What role can counselors hold in relation to clinical treatment for someone diagnosed with a somatic symptom disorder?
3. How should comorbid diagnoses be addressed in working with this client population?
4. What might be a common treatment recommendation(s) for an individual diagnosed with a somatic symptom disorder?

PART FOUR

References

Aito, M., Hirota, T., Sakamoto, Y., Adachi, M., Takahashi, M., Osato-Kaneda, A., Kim, Y. S., Leventhal, B., Shui, A., Kato, S., & Nakamura, K. (2020). Prevalence and cumulative incidence of autism spectrum disorders and the patterns of co-occurring neurodevelopmental disorders in a total population sample of 5-year-old children. *Molecular Autism, 11*(1), Article 35. https://doi.org/10.1186/s13229-020-00342-5

Al-Shamali, H. F., Winkler, O., Talarico, F., Greenshaw, A. J., Forner, C., Zhang, Y., Vermetten, E., & Burback, L. (2022). A systematic scoping review of dissociation in borderline personality disorder and implications for research and clinical practice: Exploring the fog. *Australian & New Zealand Journal of Psychiatry, 56*(10), 1252–1264. https://doi.org/10.1177/00048674221077029

Álvarez, A., Guàrdia, A., González-Rodríguez, A., Betriu, M., Palao, D., Monreal, J. A., Soria, V., & Labad, J. (2022). A systematic review and meta-analysis of suicidality in psychotic disorders: Stratified analyses by psychotic subtypes, clinical setting and geographical region. *Neuroscience & Biobehavioral Reviews, 143,* Article 104964. https://doi.org/10.1016/j.neubiorev.2022.104964

American Counseling Association. (2014). *ACA code of ethics.* https://www.counseling.org/resources/aca-code-of-ethics.pdf

American Psychiatric Association. (2013). *Diagnostic and statistical manual of mental disorders* (5th ed.). https://doi.org/10.1176/appi.books.9780890425596

American Psychiatric Association. (2022a). *Diagnostic and statistical manual of mental disorders* (5th ed., text revision). https://doi.org/10.1176/appi.books.9780890425787

American Psychiatric Association. (2022b). *DSM-5-TR neurocognitive disorders supplement: Updated excerpts for delirium codes major and mild neurocognitive disorders.* https://psychiatryonline.org/pb-assets/dsm/update/*DSM*-5-TR_Neurocognitive-Disorders-Supplement_2022_APA_Publishing.pdf

Atchley, R., & Bedford, C. (2021). Dissociative symptoms in posttraumatic stress disorder: A systematic review. *Journal of Trauma & Dissociation, 22*(1), 69–88. https://doi.org/10.1080/15299732.2020.1760410

Aydogmus, M. E. (2020). Social stigma towards people with medically unexplained symptoms: The somatic symptom disorder. *Psychiatric Quarterly, 91*(2), 349–361. https://doi.org/10.1007/s11126-019-09704-6

Barrio Minton, C. A., & Prosek, E. (2019). Schizophrenia spectrum and other psychotic disorders. In V. E. Kress & M. Paylo (Eds.), *Treating those with mental disorders: A comprehensive approach to case conceptualization and treatment* (2nd ed., pp. 328–353). Pearson.

Bisson, J. I., Berliner, L., Cloitre, M., Forbes, D., Jensen, T. K., Lewis, C., Monson, C. M., Olff, M., Pilling, S., Riggs, D. S., Roberts, N. P., & Shapiro, F. (2019). The International Society for Traumatic Stress Studies new guidelines for the prevention and treatment of PTSD: Methodology and development process. *Journal of Traumatic Stress, 32*(4), 475–483. https://doi.org/10.1002/jts.22421

Boone, K. B. (2017). *Neuropsychological evaluation of somatoform and other functional somatic conditions: Assessment primer*. Taylor & Francis.

Bourgeron, T. (2015). What do we know about early onset neurodevelopmental disorders? In K. Nikolich & S. E. Hyman (Eds.), *Translational neuroscience: Toward new therapies*. MIT Press. https://www.ncbi.nlm.nih.gov/books/NBK569702/

Brand, B. L. (2012). What we know and what we need to learn about the treatment of dissociative disorders. *Journal of Trauma & Dissociation, 13*(4), 387–396. https://doi.org/10.1080/15299732.2012.672550

Brand, B. L., Lanius, R., Vermetten, E., Loewenstein, R. J., & Spiegel, D. (2012). Where are we going? An update on assessment, treatment, and neurobiological research in dissociative disorders as we move toward the *DSM-5*. *Journal of Trauma & Dissociation, 13*(1), 9–31. https://doi.org/10.1080/15299732.2011.620687

Brand, B. L., Loewenstein, R. J., & Spiegel, D. (2014). Dispelling myths about dissociative identity disorder treatment: An empirically based approach. *Psychiatry: Interpersonal & Biological Processes, 77*(2), 169–189. https://doi.org/10.1521/psyc.2014.77.2.169

Brand, B. L., Sar, V., Stavropoulos, P., Krüger, C., Korzekwa, M., Martínez-Taboas, A., & Middleton, W. (2016). Separating fact from fiction: An empirical examination of six myths about dissociative identity disorder. *Harvard Review of Psychiatry, 24*(4), 257–270. https://doi.org/10.1097/HRP.0000000000000100

Brown, R. J., & Lewis-Fernández, R. (2011). Culture and conversion disorder: Implications for *DSM-5*. *Psychiatry, 74*(3), 187–206. https://doi.org/10.1521/psyc.2011.74.3.187

Cahaya, N., Kristina, S. A., Widayanti, A. W., & Green, J. (2022). Interventions to improve medication adherence in people with schizophrenia: A systematic review. *Patient Preference & Adherence, 16,* 2431–2449. https://doi.org/10.2147/PPA.S378951

Catalan, A., Richter, A., Salazar de Pablo, G., Vaquerizo-Serrano, J., Mancebo, G., Pedruzo, B., Aymerich, C., Solmi, M., González-Torres, M. Á., Gil, P., McGuire, P., & Fusar-Poli, P. (2021). Proportion and predictors of remission and recovery in first-episode psychosis: Systematic review and meta-analysis. *European Psychiatry, 64*(1), 1–9. https://doi.org/10.1192/j.eurpsy.2021.2246

Cattarinussi, G., Kubera, K. M., Hirjak, D., Wolf, R. C., & Sambataro, F. (2022). Neural correlates of the risk for schizophrenia and bipolar disorder: A meta-analysis of structural and functional neuroimaging studies. *Biological Psychiatry, 92*(5), 375–384. https://doi.org/10.1016/j.biopsych.2022.02.960

Centers for Disease Control and Prevention. (2022). *Data and statistics about ADHD.* https://www.cdc.gov/ncbddd/adhd/data.html

Centers for Disease Control and Prevention. (2023). *National Center for Health Statistics: Mortality data on CDC WONDER*. https://wonder.cdc.gov/mcd.html

Dalsgaard, S., Thorsteinsson, E., Trabjerg, B. B., Schullehner, J., Plana-Ripoll, O., & Brikell, I. (2020). Incidence rates and cumulative incidences of the full spectrum of diagnosed mental disorders in childhood and adolescence. *JAMA Psychiatry, 77*(2), 155–164. https://doi.org/10.1001/jamapsychiatry.2019.3523

Dimsdale, J. E., Creed, F., Escobar, J., Sharpe, M., Wulsin, L., Barsky, A., Lee, S., Irwin, M. R., & Levenson, J. (2013). Somatic symptom disorder: An important change in *DSM*. *Journal of Psychosomatic Research, 75*(3), 223–228. https://doi.org/10.1016/j.jpsychores.2013.06.033

Edwards, K. R., McMurtry, C. M., Dick, B., Lewinson, R., Dhariwal, A., & Katz, J. (2021). Somatic symptom disorder, conversion disorder, and chronic pain: Pediatric clinician perspectives. *Clinical Practice in Pediatric Psychology, 9*(4), 394–404. https://doi.org/10.1037/cpp0000377

Frances, A., & Chapman, S. (2013). *DSM-5* somatic symptom disorder mislabels medical illness as mental disorder. *Australian & New Zealand Journal of Psychiatry, 47*(5), 483–489. https://doi.org/10.1177/0004867413484525

Francés, L., Quintero, J., Fernández, A., Ruiz, A., Caules, J., Fillon, G., Hervás, A., & Soler, C. V. (2022). Current state of knowledge on the prevalence of neurodevelopmental disorders in childhood according to the *DSM-5*: A systematic review in accordance with the PRISMA criteria. *Child and Adolescent Psychiatry and Mental Health, 16*(1), Article 27. https://doi.org/10.1186/s13034-022-00462-1

Gaebel, W. (2011). *Schizophrenia: Current science and clinical practice.* Wiley-Blackwell.

Godin, S. L., & Shehata, S. (2022). Adolescent cannabis use and later development of schizophrenia: An updated systematic review of longitudinal studies. *Journal of Clinical Psychology, 78*(7), 1331–1340. https://doi.org/10.1002/jclp.23312

Goldsmith, L. P., Lewis, S. W., Dunn, G., & Bentall, R. P. (2015). Psychological treatments for early psychosis can be beneficial or harmful, depending on the therapeutic alliance: An instrumental variable analysis. *Psychological Medicine, 45*(11), 2365–2373. https://doi.org/10.1017/S003329171500032X

Haller, H., Cramer, H., Lauche, R., & Dobos, G. (2015). Somatoform disorders and medically unexplained symptoms in primary care. *Deutsche Arztebl International, 112*(16), 279–287. https://doi.org/10.3238/arztebl.2015.0279

Horan, W. P., Harvey, P., Kern, R. S., & Green, M. F. (2011). Neurocognition, social cognition and functional outcome in schizophrenia. In W. Gaebel (Ed.), *Schizophrenia: Current science and clinical practice* (pp. 68–107). Wiley-Blackwell.

Huxley, P., Krayer, A., Poole, R., Prendergast, L., Aryal, S., & Warner, R. (2021). Schizophrenia outcomes in the 21st century: A systematic review. *Brain & Behavior, 11*(6), 1–12. https://doi.org/10.1002/brb3.2172

International Society for the Study of Dissociation. (2004). Guidelines for the evaluation and treatment of dissociative symptoms in children and adolescents. *Journal of Trauma & Dissociation, 5*(3), 119–150. https://doi.org/10.1300/J229v05n03_09

International Society for the Study of Trauma and Dissociation. (n.d.-a). *Child & adolescent FAQs.* https://www.isst-d.org/resources/child-adolescent-faqs/

International Society for the Study of Trauma and Dissociation. (n.d.-b). *Dissociation FAQs.* https://www.isst-d.org/resources/dissociation-faqs/

International Society for the Study of Trauma and Dissociation. (2011). Guidelines for treating dissociative identity disorder in adults, third revision. *Journal of Trauma & Dissociation, 12*(3), 115–187. https://doi.org/10.1080/15299732.2011.537247

Isaacs, A. N., Brooks, H., Lawn, S., Mohammadi, L., Vicary, E., & Sutton, K. (2022). Effectiveness of personal recovery facilitators in adults with schizophrenia and other psychoses: A systematic review of reviews and narrative synthesis. *Schizophrenia Research, 246,* 132–147. https://doi.org/10.1016/j.schres.2022.06.018

Jacobson, L., Fox, J., Bell, H., Zeligman, M., & Graham, J. (2015). Survivors with dissociative identity disorder: Perspectives on the counseling process. *Journal of Mental Health Counseling, 37*(4), 308–322. https://doi.org/10.17744/mehc.37.4.03

Karambelas, G. J., Filia, K., Byrne, L. K., Allott, K. A., Jayasinghe, A., & Cotton, S. M. (2022). A systematic review comparing caregiver burden and psychological functioning in caregivers of individuals with schizophrenia spectrum disorders and bipolar disorders. *BMC Psychiatry, 22*(1), 1–24. https://doi.org/10.1186/s12888-022-04069-w

Kate, M.-A., Hopwood, T., & Jamieson, G. (2020). The prevalence of dissociative disorders and dissociative experiences in college populations: A meta-analysis of 98 studies. *Journal of Trauma & Dissociation, 21*(1), 16–61. https://doi.org/10.1080/15299732.2019.1647915

Keepers, G. A., Fochtmann, L. J., Anzia, J. M., Benjamin, S., Lyness, J. M., Mojtabai, R., Servis, M., Walaszek, A., Buckley, P., Lenzenweger, M. F., Young, A. S., Degenhardt, A., & Hong, S.-H. (2020). The American Psychiatric Association practice guideline for the treatment of patients with schizophrenia. *The American Journal of Psychiatry, 177*(9), 868–872. https://doi.org/10.1176/appi.ajp.2020.177901

Kline, C. L., Shamshair, S., Kullgren, K. A., Leber, S. M., & Malas, N. (2022). A review of the impact of sociodemographic factors on the assessment and management of pediatric somatic symptom and related disorders. *Journal of the Academy of Consultation-Liaison Psychiatry, 61*(1), 58–64. https://doi.org/10.1016/j.jaclp.2022.10.266

Kress, V., & Paylo, M. (2018). *Treating those with mental disorders*. Pearson.

Li, Y., Coster, S., Norman, I., Chien, W. T., Qin, J., Tse, M. L., & Bressington, D. (2021). Feasibility, acceptability, and preliminary effectiveness of mindfulness-based interventions for people with recent-onset psychosis: A systematic review. *Early Intervention in Psychiatry, 15*(1), 3–15. https://doi.org/10.1111/eip.12929

Lotfinia, S., Soorgi, Z., Mertens, Y., & Daniels, J. (2020). Structural and functional brain alterations in psychiatric patients with dissociative experiences: A systematic review of magnetic resonance imaging studies. *Journal of Psychiatric Research, 128,* 5–15. https://doi.org/10.1016/j.jpsychires.2020.05.006

Lynn, S. J., Maxwell, R., Merckelbach, H., Lilienfeld, S. O., van Heugten-van der Kloet, D., & Miskovic, V. (2019). Dissociation and its disorders: Competing models, future directions, and a way forward. *Clinical Psychology Review, 73,* Article 101755. https://doi.org/10.1016/j.cpr.2019.101755

Lyssenko, L., Schmahl, C., Bockhacker, L., Vonderlin, R., Bohus, M., & Kleindienst, N. (2018). Dissociation in psychiatric disorders: A meta-analysis of studies using the Dissociative Experiences Scale. *American Journal of Psychiatry, 175*(1), 37–46. https://doi.org/10.1176/appi.ajp.2017.17010025

McDonagh, M. S., Dana, T., Selph, S., Devine, E. B., Cantor, A., Bougatsos, C., Blazina, I., Grusing, S., Fu, R., Kopelovich, S. L., Monroe-DeVita, M., & Haupt, D. W. (2017). *Treatment for adults with schizophrenia: A systematic review* (AHRQ Publication No. 17(18)-EHC031-EF). Agency for Healthcare Research and Quality. https://doi.org/10.23970/AHRQEPCCER198

McDonald, W. M. (2017). Overview of neurocognitive disorders. *Focus, 15*(1), 4–12. https://doi.org/10.1176/appi.focus.20160030.

Mikami, A. Y., Miller, M., & Lerner, M. D. (2019). Social functioning in youth with attention-deficit/hyperactivity disorder and autism spectrum: Transdiagnostic commonalities and differences. *Clinical Psychology Review, 68,* 54–70. https://doi.org/10.1016/j.cpr.2018.12.005

Mychailyszyn, M. P., Brand, B. L., Webermann, A. R., Şar, V., & Draijer, N. (2021). Differentiating dissociative from non-dissociative disorders: A meta-analysis of the structured clinical interview for *DSM* dissociative disorders (SCID-D). *Journal of Trauma & Dissociation, 22*(1), 19–34. https://doi.org/10.1080/15299732.2020.1760169

National Institute of Mental Health. (2021). *Schizophrenia* (NIH Publication No 21-MH-8082). https://www.nimh.nih.gov/health/publications/schizophrenia

Newby, J. M., Smith, J., Uppal, S., Mason, E., Mahoney, A. E. J., & Andrews, G. (2018). Internet-based cognitive behavioral therapy versus psychoeducation control for illness anxiety disorder and somatic symptom disorder: A randomized controlled trial. *Journal of Consulting and Clinical Psychology, 86*(1), 89–98. https://doi.org/10.1037/ccp0000248

Nikolich, K., & Hyman S. E. (Eds.). (2015). *Translational neuroscience: Toward new therapies.* MIT Press.

Okoli, C. T. C., Kappi, A., Wang, T., Makowski, A., & Cooley, A. T. (2022). The effect of long-acting injectable antipsychotic medications compared with oral antipsychotic medications among people with schizophrenia: A systematic review and meta-analysis. *International Journal of Mental Health Nursing, 31*(3), 469–535. https://doi.org/10.1111/inm.12964

Pagsberg, A. K. (2013). Schizophrenia spectrum and other psychotic disorders. *European Child & Adolescent Psychiatry, 22*(Suppl. 1), 3–9. https://doi.org/10.1007/s00787-012-0354-x

Peters, J. W., & Matson, J. L. (2020). Comparing rates of diagnosis using *DSM-IV-TR* versus *DSM-5* criteria for autism spectrum disorder. *Journal of Autism and Developmental Disorders, 50*(6), 1898–1906. https://doi.org/10.1007/s10803-019-03941-1

Phelan, S., & Sigala, N. (2022). The effect of treatment on insight in psychotic disorders—A systematic review and meta-analysis. *Schizophrenia Research, 244,* 126–133. https://doi.org/10.1016/j.schres.2022.05.023

Pinho, M., Martins, D., & Carvalho, S. (2021). Post-traumatic stress disorder after first-episode psychosis [Special issue: Abstracts of the 29th European Congress of Psychiatry]. *European Psychiatry, 64*(S1), S454. https://doi.org/10.1192/j.eurpsy.2021.1212

Quinn, K. M. (2020). *Somatic symptom disorder and personality: Associations and implications for treatment* (Publication No. 28027026) [Doctoral dissertation, Indiana University of Pennsylvania]. ProQuest Dissertations and Theses Global.

Rafiq, S., Campodonico, C., & Varese, F. (2018). The relationship between childhood adversities and dissociation in severe mental illness: A meta-analytic review. *Acta Psychiatrica Scandinavica, 138*(6), 509–525. https://doi.org/10.1111/acps.12969

Rief, W., Burton, C., Frostholm, L., Henningsen, P., Kleinstäuber, M., Kop, W. J., Löwe, B., Martin, A., Malt, U., Rosmalen, J., Schröder, A., Shedden-Mora, M., Toussaint, A., & van der Feltz-Cornelis, C. (2017). Core outcome domains for clinical trials on somatic symptom disorder, bodily distress disorder, and functional somatic syndromes: European Network on Somatic Symptom Disorders recommendations. *Psychosomatic Medicine, 79*(9), 1008–1015. https://doi.org/10.1097/PSY.0000000000000502

Riera-López de Aguileta, I., Vila-Badia, R., Usall, J., Butjosa, A., & Ochoa, S. (2020). Coping strategies in first-episode psychosis: A systematic review. *Early Intervention in Psychiatry, 14*(3), 252–262. https://doi.org/10.1111/eip.12847

Rosa's Law, Pub. L. No. 111–256 (2010). https://www.govinfo.gov/app/details/PLAW-111publ256

Rössler, W. (2011). Management, rehabilitation, stigma. In W. Gaebel (Ed.), *Schizophrenia: Current science and clinical practice* (pp. 217–246). Wiley-Blackwell.

Rubin, A., & Trawver, K. (2011). Overview and clinical implications of schizophrenia. In A. S. Rubin, D. W. Springer, & K. Trawver (Eds.), *Psychosocial treatment of schizophrenia: Clinician's guide to evidence-based practice* (pp. 1–22). Wiley-Blackwell.

Ryan, M., Sattenspiel, D., Chianese, A., & Rice, H. (2022). Cognitive behavioral therapy for symptom management in treatment-resistant schizophrenia. *The American Journal of Nursing, 122*(8), 24–33. https://doi.org/10.1097/01.NAJ.0000854488.48801.59

Sammartino-Arbour, A., Dufour, A., Frenette, V., Forget, M., Bruneau, M., Ducharme, S., Camicioli, R., Nguyen, Q. D., & Desmarais, P. (2022). The association between somatic symptom disorders and neurocognitive disorders: A systematic review. *The American Journal of Geriatric Psychiatry, 31*(1), 33–43. https://doi.org/10.1016/j.jagp.2022.07.007

Sánchez-Gutiérrez, T., Barbeito, S., Gómez-Juncal, R., Rodríguez-Ortega, E., Becerra-García, J. A., & Calvo, A. (2022). Neuropsychological functioning and suicidal behaviours in patients with first-episode psychosis: A systematic review. *Acta Psychiatrica Scandinavica, 146*(6), 515–528. https://doi.org/10.1111/acps.13501

Santelmann, H., Franklin, J., Bußhoff, J., & Baethge, C. (2016a). Diagnostic shift in patients diagnosed with schizoaffective disorder: A systematic review and meta-analysis of rediagnosis studies. *Bipolar Disorders, 18*(3), 233–246. https://doi.org/10.1111/bdi.12388

Santelmann, H., Franklin, J., Bußhoff, J., & Baethge, C. (2016b). Interrater reliability of schizoaffective disorder compared with schizophrenia, bipolar disorder, and unipolar depression—A systematic review and meta-analysis. *Schizophrenia Research, 176*(2–3), 357–363. https://doi.org/10.1016/j.schres.2016.07.012

Scalabrini, A., Cavicchioli, M., Fossati, A., & Maffei, C. (2017). The extent of dissociation in borderline personality disorder: A meta-analytic review. *Journal of Trauma & Dissociation, 18*(4), 522–543. https://doi.org/10.1080/15299732.2016.1240738

Schnabel, K., Petzke, T. M., & Witthöft, M. (2022). The emotion regulation process in somatic symptom disorders and related conditions—A systematic narrative review. *Clinical Psychology Review, 97*, Article 102196. https://doi.org/10.1016/j.cpr.2022.102196

Seitz, K. I., Ehler, N., Schmitz, M., Schmitz, S. E., Dziobek, I., Herpertz, S. C., & Bertsch, K. (2022). Affective and cognitive theory of mind in posttraumatic stress, major depressive, and somatic symptom disorders: Association with childhood trauma. *British Journal of Clinical Psychology, 61*(3), 680–700. https://doi.org/10.1111/bjc.12357

Sharma, M., P., & Manjula, M. (2013). Behavioural and psychological management of somatic symptom disorders: An overview. *International Review of Psychiatry, 25*(1), 116–124. https://doi.org/10.3109/09540261.2012.746649

Shimada, T., Ito, S., Makabe, A., Yamanushi, A., Takenaka, A., Kawano, K., & Kobayashi, M. (2022). Aerobic exercise and cognitive functioning in schizophrenia: An updated systematic review and meta-analysis. *Psychiatry Research, 314*, Article 114656. https://doi.org/10.1016/j.psychres.2022.114656

Sicotte, R., Iyer, S. N., Kiepura, B., & Abdel-Baki, A. (2021). A systematic review of longitudinal studies of suicidal thoughts and behaviors in first-episode psychosis: Course and associated factors. *Social Psychiatry & Psychiatric Epidemiology, 56*(12), 2117–2154. https://doi.org/10.1007/s00127-021-02153-2

So, J. K. (2008). Somatization as cultural idiom of distress: Rethinking mind and body in a multicultural society. *Counseling Psychology Quarterly, 21*(2), 167–174. https://doi.org/10.1080/09515070802066854

Sousa, S., Teixeira, L., & Paúl, C. (2020). Assessment of major neurocognitive disorders in primary health care: Predictors of individual risk factors. *Frontiers in Psychology, 11,* Article 1413. https://doi.org/10.3389/fpsyg.2020.01413

Spiegel, D., Loewenstein, R., Lewis- Fernández, R., Sar, V., Simeon, D., Vermetten, E., & Dell, P. F. (2011). Dissociative disorders in *DSM-5*. *Depression and Anxiety, 28*(9), 824–852. https://doi.org/10.1002/da.20874

Stokin, G. B., Krell-Roesch, J., Petersen, R. C., & Geda, Y. E. (2015). Mild neurocognitive disorder: An old wine in a new bottle. *Harvard Review Psychiatry, 23*(5), 368–376. https://doi.org/10.1097/HRP.0000000000000084

Substance Abuse and Mental Health Services Administration. (2008). *Assertive community treatment (ACT): Evidence-based practices (EBP) kit* (Publication No. SMA 08-4344).

Toussaint, A., Hüsing, P., Kohlmann, S., & Löwe, B. (2020). Detecting *DSM-5* somatic symptom disorder: Criterion validity of the Patient Health Questionnaire–15 (PHQ-15) and the Somatic Symptom Scale–8 (SSS-8) in combination with the Somatic Symptom Disorder–B Criteria Scale (SSD-12). *Psychological Medicine, 50*(2), 324–333. https://doi.org/10.1017/S003329171900014X

Valencia, M., Juarez, F., & Ortega, H. (2012). Integrated treatment to achieve functional recovery in first-episode psychosis. *Schizophrenia Research and Treatment, 2012,* Article 962371. https://doi.org/10.1155/2012/962371

Walsh, J. (2011). Therapeutic communication with psychotic clients. *Clinical Social Work Journal, 39*(1), 1–8. https://doi.org/10.1007/s10615-010-0287-0

Weng, Y., Lin, J., Ahorsu, D. K., & Tsang, H. W. H. (2022). Neuropathways of theory of mind in schizophrenia: A systematic review and meta-analysis. *Neuroscience & Biobehavioral Reviews, 137,* Article 104625. https://doi.org/10.1016/j.neubiorev.2022.104625

Yang, J., Millman, L. S. M., David, A. S., & Hunter, E. C. M. (2023). The prevalence of depersonalization-derealization disorder: A systematic review. *Journal of Trauma & Dissociation, 24*(1), 8–41. https://doi.org/10.1080/15299732.2022.2079796

Yeo, J. J., Chew, Q. H., & Sim, K. (2022). Resilience and its inter-relationship with symptomatology, illness course, psychosocial functioning, and mediational roles in schizophrenia: A systematic review. *Asia-Pacific Psychiatry, 14*(2), Article e12486. https://doi.org/10.1111/appy.12486

Zukowska, Z., Allan, S., Eisner, E., Ling, L., & Gumley, A. (2022). Fear of relapse in schizophrenia: A mixed-methods systematic review. *Social Psychiatry and Psychiatric Epidemiology, 57*(7), 1305–1318. https://doi.org/10.1007/s00127-022-02220-2

INDEX

References to tables are indicated by "t" following the page numbers

E

F

www.ingramcontent.com/pod-product-compliance
Ingram Content Group UK Ltd.
Pitfield, Milton Keynes, MK11 3LW, UK
UKHW051928100926
8556IPUK00022B/1446

9 781556 200267